TORONTO'S POOR

"*Toronto's Poor* shows us the importance of knowing and understanding our history because history can repeat itself. Whether it is in the nineteenth or twenty-first century, poor people's experience of cold and hunger, crummy shelter conditions, inadequate housing, and vulnerability to dying early are caused by bitter and punitive social policies. What is most exciting about this book is the mostly untold story of poor people's resistance, activism, and fight-back struggles that have and will continue to win huge victories alleviating poverty."

    —Cathy Crowe, Street Nurse

"Palmer and Héroux show that Toronto has been an exemplary Canadian city: its poverty has been inclusive, although not perfectly equal-opportunity. It has embraced male and female, young and old, city and suburban, immigrant and native born, and not excluding First Nations. This is Toronto's history from the bottom up, and with attitude. Long overdue."

    —Richard Harris, School of Geography and Earth Sciences,
      McMaster University

"*Toronto's Poor* is a trove of well-chronicled moments in the enduring history of oppression and dispossession of the lives lost in the cogs of "progress." It isn't just that poverty and marginalization have been the framework for centuries of economic scapegoating, it's that we begin to see the energy behind the travesty of disregarding the poor."

    —Victor Willis, Parkdale Activity-Recreation Centre (PARC)

"*Toronto's Poor* tells an important and under-told side of this city's history, where the civic narrative has often focused on waves of growth and prosperity, ignoring a continuum of dispossession and struggle here since before the city's founding. In an era of precarious employment and when poverty is even more hidden than ever in the suburbs and apartment towers, *Toronto's Poor* provides some context for current conditions."

—**Shawn Micallef**, editor at *Spacing, Toronto Star* columnist, author of *Stroll: Psychogeographic Walking Tours of Toronto* and *Frontier City: Toronto on the Verge of Greatness*

"An extremely well-documented history of how Toronto's destitute, homeless, and unemployed were scapegoated and typecast as undeserving of social support, and how they and others resisted and fought back against great odds. This is a history of capitalism, crisis, and class as played out in Canada's largest city over two centuries. It brings into the picture the dispossessed and the struggle for progressive social change, which historical research too often ignores. An excellent account for all who care about the struggle for social justice."

—**J. David Hulchanski**, professor of housing and community development, University of Toronto

TORONTO'S POOR

A REBELLIOUS HISTORY

BRYAN D. PALMER
GAÉTAN HÉROUX

BETWEEN THE LINES · Toronto

Toronto's Poor

© 2016 Bryan D. Palmer and Gaétan Héroux

First published in 2016 by
Between the Lines
401 Richmond Street West
Studio 277
Toronto, Ontario M5V 3A8
Canada
1-800-718-7201
www.btlbooks.com

Library and Archives Canada Cataloguing in Publication

Palmer, Bryan D., 1951-, author
        Toronto's poor : a rebellious history / Bryan D. Palmer and Gaétan Héroux; foreword by Frances Fox Piven.

Includes bibliographical references and index.
Issued in print and electronic formats.
ISBN 978-1-77113-281-7 (paperback).—ISBN 978-1-77113-282-4 (epub).—ISBN 978-1-77113-283-1 (pdf)

1. Poor—Ontario—Toronto—History. 2. Poverty—Ontario—Toronto—History. 3. Toronto (Ont.)—Social conditions. I. Héroux, Gaétan, author II. Title.

HV4050.T6P34 2016   305.5'6909713541   C2016-904718-0
                                             C2016-904719-9

Text and cover design by
David Vereschagin/Quadrat Communications
Front cover, top photo: York University Libraries, Clara Thomas Archives & Special Collections, *Toronto Telegram* fonds, ASC19077, *Evening Telegram* Staff. For details see p. 122. Front cover, bottom photo: OCAP Archives. For details see p. 363.

This book has been published with the help of a grant from the Federation for the Humanities and Social Sciences, through the Awards to Scholarly Publications Program, using funds provided by the Social Sciences and Humanities Research Council of Canada.

We acknowledge for their financial support of our publishing activities the Government of Canada through the Canada Book Fund, the Canada Council for the Arts, which last year invested $153 million to bring the arts to Canadians throughout the country, and the Government of Ontario through the Ontario Arts Council, the Ontario Book Publishers Tax Credit program, and the Ontario Media Development Corporation.

Printed in Canada

Third printing April 2019

For Catherine & Joan

Contents

Foreword
Frances Fox Piven

This remarkable book is an account of the political struggles of the poor in the city of Toronto over the last 150 years. The politics of the poor only rarely get this kind of scholarly attention. Social scientists who study the evolution of social policies focus instead on elites and reformers, on political parties and unions, or on inherited institutional constraints, while the efforts of the poor themselves as they try to shape the world they must inhabit are ordinarily ignored. Bryan Palmer and Gaétan Héroux break with that social science tradition and instead follow a path that connects them with the work of the social historians, especially the British historians of the past half century—mentors like E. P. Thompson, George Rudé, and Eric Hobsbawm—who placed the poor front and centre in their narratives of the past.

I think the historical moment demands that approach. We need to pay attention to the self-activity of the people at the bottom of our societies if only because the legions of the left-behind are growing, not only in the desperate regions of the southern hemisphere but also in the countries that were once the pioneers of redistributive welfare state policies.[1] Moreover, there are signs everywhere that the poor are in fact in motion, rising to protest their circumstances, even in the most affluent nations of the world.

So one reason this book is important is that we do not know much about political action by the people we call poor, and still less about their actual influence on public policy. In the pages that follow we learn a history that is rarely reported, and the careful and detailed narrative is valuable for that reason alone. The narrative also helps us understand something of why the politics of the poor remains in the shadows. An aroused poor only rarely find respected and powerful allies and, indeed, even when the poor are spurred to become defiant they rarely name themselves as poor. The very term indicates a socially humiliated stratum, and defiance leads people to seek a prouder identity. The poor become the Indignados, or they name themselves "Black" as in Black Lives Matter, or Palestinian or Zapatistas or Mothers. Note that in the 1960s, it was the United States government's "war on poverty" that responded to the riotous inner-city poor that deployed the language of poverty and not the rioters themselves.

Another reason this book is important is that the authors have a clear and illuminating understanding that the hardship and humiliations imposed on the poor mesh with the deteriorating life circumstances of the mass of working people. Note the parallel trends: as poverty and extreme poverty grow, so do the life conditions of the working people (who are not officially poor) become more insecure under the aggressive form of capitalism we call neoliberalism. Earnings are stagnant or shrinking, the terms of employment have become insecure or "precarious," and the trade unions that once fought for higher wages and improved the terms of work are weakened.

Palmer and Héroux see clearly that these trends are related, that the penury and insult that our policies impose on the people we call poor also enfeeble working people. This crucial relationship emerges clearly from the history of poor relief policies that branded (sometimes literally) the poor, displayed them for public ridicule in the marketplace, starved them in the poorhouse, all to shore up the dictum of "less eligibility," meaning that no one who depended on public charity should be as well off as even the lowest paid worker. "Less eligibility" is not merely a historical relic. Palmer and Héroux show how recently it was that the Toronto poor were made to toil at "breaking the stone" in return for their meagre fare. And in the United States, also a settler country and a child of the British Empire, a decades-long campaign against the programs that presumably encourage the "dependency" of the poor continues, with the result that assistance programs have been slashed and the number of households in extreme poverty is rising. Those households now include close to three million children.[2]

"Less eligibility," in other words, is not only a material arrangement pegging relief payments to wages, and it does not only affect the poor. It is an arrangement that distributes social acceptability and disgrace along with survival resources, and it distributes social acceptability in ways that inevitably affect not only those who are disgraced but also those who struggle to preserve whatever dignity is afforded them by wage work. Consider for example the U.S. campaign to slash cash assistance to poor families that resulted in 1996 in the elimination of a six-decades-old program called Aid to Families of Dependent Children. The campaign was fuelled by the argument that assistance to the poor sapped them of the drive for economic

xii

TORONTO'S POOR

self-reliance through wage work. The solution was to make assistance hard to get and harder to keep. And those who were assisted were subject to strict surveillance and rituals of humiliation. The welfare rolls plummeted and when the smoke had cleared the proportion of poor children who received cash assistance had fallen from 68 percent to 26 percent. In the process, New York City recipients were made to don orange Day-Glo vests while they cleaned the parks and roads, there to be observed by all those who were struggling to stay afloat on shrinking wages and lengthening hours.

This history of the Toronto poor helps us to see how people resist these policies. To be sure, they do not triumph, at least not yet. But their resistance against great odds reveals their extraordinary capacities and gives us hope that there will be a future.

Acknowledgements

This book has been sustained and nurtured in a variety of ways over the course of a number of years. Our thanks are many.

Gaétan Héroux gratefully acknowledges receipt of a John Bousfield Grant through the University of Toronto's Department of Geography. He also thanks the Toronto Jane Jacobs Walk, which provided him with an important venue to present the history of Downtown East Toronto in a popular format, enabling him to organize and better understand the research material he was working on. Bryan D. Palmer benefitted enormously from the support of the Canada Research Chairs program, administered through Trent University, where the Canadian Studies Department has provided a congenial research environment for more than a decade.

Portions of Part II appeared previously in our jointly-published essays, "Marching under Flags Black and Red: Toronto's Dispossessed and the Age of Industry," in Leon Fink, Joseph McCartin, and Joan Sangster, eds., *Workers in Hard Times: A Long View of Economic Crises* (Urbana: University of Illinois Press, 2014), 19–44 and "'Cracking the Stone': The Long History of Capitalist Crisis and Toronto's Dispossessed, 1830–1930," *Labour/Le Travail* 69 (Spring 2012): 9–62. We thank the editors of these volumes for permission to reproduce segments of essays that originally appeared in their pages.

Research of the kind that this book is built on depends on archives, libraries, special collections repositories, and the men and women who do so much to gather, preserve, and provide access to needed documents. We thank the knowledgeable and helpful staff of the Baldwin Room at the Toronto Reference Library, the City of Toronto Archives, the Ontario Archives, the Thomas Fisher Rare Book and Special Collections Library at the University of Toronto, and the Clara Thomas Archives and Special Collections at York University.

So many individuals have provided us with help and encouragement over the years that in naming only a few of those whose contributions were invaluable we risk passing over many others to whom we are grateful. Nonetheless, Gaétan Héroux thanks Stefanie Gould and Rachel Huot for encouraging him in his research and helping him to prepare grant proposals. He is indebted to all of those individuals who took the time to read and provide important criticism of the early, unpublished transcripts of his study of the history of Downtown East Toronto. He thanks as well the anti-poverty activists in Montreal with whom he worked over the years and who enhanced his understanding of poor people's struggles, in particular Richard St. Pierre and Alexandre Popovic. Bryan Palmer thanks especially two young scholars, David Thompson and Jonathan Greene, who generously made their unpublished dissertations on poor people's struggles available. His colleague in Canadian Studies at Trent University, Jim Struthers, not only read the entire manuscript with a critical and supportive eye, but also has contributed immensely to our understanding of the limits of the welfare state with his rigorous scholarship. Finally, we are indebted to Danielle Koyama, A. J. Withers, Beric German, and John Clarke who read Part V of the book and offered important and frank criticism of our treatment of OCAP and other developments associated with the recent history of Toronto's poor people's struggles.

We gratefully acknowledge the work of the many individuals in OCAP who have been involved in developing the organization's website and its archives, both of which proved invaluable in the writing of this book. Many individuals also provided photographs of OCAP demonstrations and activities over the last twenty-five years. In particular, we wish to thank Don Johnson, Graeme Bacque, and John Bonnar. Also noteworthy, in terms of other photographic material utilized in this study, are the abundance of illustrative riches present in the *Toronto Telegram* fonds of York University's Clara Thomas Archives and Special Collections, where we found Julia Holland especially helpful. We thank Stephen Gardiner of Trent University's Geography Department for designing the book's maps.

Gaétan Héroux has learned much from the many people living on social assistance in Toronto and who have organized selflessly over the years, building a poor people's movement in Toronto. Listing all of their names is impossible, but he wants to acknowledge in particular Ken Nebone, Steve Lane, Don Weitz, Brian DuBourdieu, and Marque Brill. In his work in various social service agencies and anti-poverty activism, Héroux met and interacted with thousands of poor people. Many have subsequently died, but their lives and stories remain very much with him and serve as a foundation on which he has conducted research and worked on this book.

Bryan Palmer's original contact with OCAP came through discussions with the late Norman Feltes. After Norman's death, his regard for OCAP deepened with a growing sense of the organization's militancy, appreciation of the practical contributions OCAP made in bettering the lives of Toronto's poor, and a profound respect for those like John Clarke and Peter Rosenthal, who worked with the anti-poverty organization in different capacities. He was also later influenced by his contact with a brilliant student in Trent's Canadian Studies Department, Sue Collis, whose OCAP activism preceded her development as a promising scholar.

Bryan Palmer owes a special debt to two historians, Sean Purdy and Marcello Badaró Mattos, who arranged a 2014 visit to Brazil and provided accommodations in Rio de Janeiro and Sao Paulo, where an important segment of the writing involved in this book took place.

For Gaétan Héroux, this book would have been impossible without the encouragement of his parents, Anna Gibson and Osias Héroux, both of whom have passed away since he began researching the history of Toronto's poor. Growing up in poverty with his parents, his three sisters Ginette, Jocelyne, Michelle, and his brother Alain, fundamentally shaped his understanding of what it means to be poor, developing his sense of class consciousness.

Toronto's Poor is dedicated to our partners Catherine Cumberland and Joan Sangster. We end with statements of our respective appreciations.

Gaétan Héroux: My work with OCAP and the writing of this book could not have happened without Catherine, my partner for more than forty years. Despite the stress that I have caused her through the many years of activism, the many arrests, periods of unemployment, and long hours spent at meetings, our relationship has survived and remains the most important part of my life.

Bryan D. Palmer: Joan Sangster's contribution to this book is not measured in statements corrected, sentences improved, or struggles reinterpreted. She does all of that, to be sure. But more importantly, this book is part hers because she understands my outrage and my refusals, my insistence that fundamental social transformation is indeed necessary. Without that understanding, so rare and so important in keeping alienation partially at bay, I cannot imagine writing books like this or indeed doing so many other things that occupy our time. The world we live in often seems to have ground to a bad halt, but Joan, after twenty years, still manages to make it go merrily round for me.

PART 1

Introduction

The Long History of Toronto's Poor:
Conceptualizing the Dispossessed

It is January 2015, and temperatures are plummeting, approaching -20 degrees Centigrade. Homeless men are dying on the streets of Toronto. Over the course of four days, three deaths are reported in the news, almost all of the accounts shrouded in the anonymity that covers the destitute in cold comforts. The first body was discovered on the morning of 5 January in a Davenport Road-Lansdowne Avenue shipping yard, where a regular at a local Drop-In Centre had been living in a derelict truck. A second homeless man was found less than twenty-four hours later in a Toronto Transit Commission shelter near Yonge-Dundas Square. Clad in only a T-shirt and blue jeans, he exhibited no vital signs and had apparently succumbed to hypothermia and cardiac arrest. He was pronounced dead on arrival at the hospital a short time later. A third victim of homelessness, aged sixty-one, died in his sleep at a Peter Street shelter on 8 January.[1]

Less than a week later, a fourth man came to a sorry end in an industrial area in the McGowan Road-Nugent Avenue vicinity. Acts of kindness culminated in the death of Grant "Gunner" Faulkner, who perished in a fire after another homeless man loaned Gunner his small makeshift hut for the night, as well as a propane heater to ward off the frigid temperatures. Apparently the device was turned up too high, and cardboard was placed over its top, probably to maximize the retention of heat next to the sleeping Faulkner. A conflagration then engulfed the shed and incinerated the homeless man who, in his late forties, was unemployed as a result of losing his job in an automotive systems factory in Cambridge. *Globe and Mail* columnist Marcus Gee pointed out that Faulkner, who was battling alcohol abuse at the time of his death, was a stark reminder that living on the streets was not just a problem associated with Toronto's downtown core. Studies conducted in 2006 and 2013 had shown that of the hundreds of people down-and-out in Toronto, upward of 30 percent of the dispossessed could be found in districts such as North

York, Scarborough, and Etobicoke. Yet of the forty-eight shelters run by the city, community organizations, and various agencies, only eight were then located in Toronto's blue-collar suburbs.[2]

As homeless men were dying in January 2015, mainstream political commentators were calling attention to the obvious. Konrad Yakabuski questioned the "smart growth" policies animating urban decision-making in places like Toronto. Drawing on a Demographia International Housing Affordability Survey, Yakabuski pointed out that a median-priced home in Toronto cost 6.5 times the city's mid-range household income, a rise of 65 percent over the course of a decade. With a multiple above 5.1, the Demographia data indicated that Toronto housing was in the "severely unaffordable" category, the city's accommodation costs surpassing those of New York. Even allowing for Demographia's political agenda, which undoubtedly looked to curtail restrictive legislation on land use and bypass eco-friendly initiatives to contain urban sprawl, housing in Toronto was clearly priced beyond the reach of many inhabitants. This situation was paralleled by a language of official politics that, in Jeffrey Simpson's words, collapsed public discussions of policy into the expansive container of "a terminological muddle" labelled "the middle class." What was of interest to this socioeconomic chimera, the widely appealed to middle class, structured the rhetorical and programmatic appeals of Conservatives, Liberals, and New Democrats alike. The poor, Simpson argued, "have disappeared in Canadian politics," as no Party leader was "prepared to ask citizens to think about the less fortunate, as if to do so would invite voters in the elastic middle class to think they might lose something in the process." Simpson's conclusion, coming from a voice of the liberal centre, was that a failure "to think about the poor, let alone talk about them, impoverishes politics—it spins the discourse around what's in it for me, rather than what's in it for all of us."[3]

We are not of the liberal mainstream. What follows brings the long history of Toronto's poor very much to the forefront. Readers of this book will be introduced to how the destitute, the homeless and the unemployed were socially constructed and characterized, often as "undeserving" of social assistance. They will also be shown how these same people fought against their subordination and the often worsening conditions of their lives. The dispossessed of Toronto's old urban core are examined, but so too are suburban homelessness and the struggles of out-of-work residents in these municipalities to raise relief rates and keep their homes amid efforts to evict them during the prolonged crisis of joblessness in the 1930s. Sadly, what is happening to the poorest of Toronto's poor today is anything but new. There is a history of the dispossessed reaching back to at least the 1830s and carrying forward to our current moment that is continuous and troubling. The plight of the poor that emerges out of this past is too often reduced to scapegoating and type-casting. Those who find themselves without waged work, without homes, and without sufficient wherewithal to provide adequately for themselves and their families have been criminalized and assailed as shirkers, unfairly labelled the architects of their own misery.[4]

These dispossessed are also routinely lost in the shuffle of responsibility among municipalities and provincial and federal governments, bodies that have long jockeyed to "pass the buck" of which level of government should pay how much for what kind of funding allocation. As we write this introduction, Ontario is leading a charge on behalf of the provinces against Ottawa, trying to negotiate a change in the management of $2 billion in annual transfer payments that relate to job training, funds paid out of Employment Insurance (EI) premiums. Meanwhile, the percentage of out-of-work Canadians who qualify for such unemployment support under the EI program has been steadily in decline for a number of years. It now dips below the 40 percent mark. This means that the majority of the 1.3 million Canadians who were jobless in 2014 would not have been eligible for traditional unemployment insurance benefits or for the programs of upgrading skills and retooling that are now built into EI's practices.[5] None of this is new. The story of the levels of the state fighting over the costs of provisioning for the poor, rather than combining to act on behalf of the disadvantaged themselves, is indeed an old tale. As this book shows, cities, provinces, and federal authorities have expended considerable energy dodging the bullets of joblessness and destitution as they are repeatedly fired from the weapon of capitalist crises, an armament aimed at the collective head of the waged *and* the wageless.

This study of Toronto's poor and out-of-work, which we refer to as the wage-less, the jobless, the unemployed, and, ultimately, the dispossessed, has its origins in an understandable, but somewhat unusual, collaboration. As an anti-poverty activist affiliated with the Ontario Coalition Against Poverty (OCAP), one of the authors, Gaétan Héroux, was involved with protests and confrontations with politicians and police over the course of the 1990s and early years of this century. He was told, time and time again, that poor people's mobilizations demanding adequate housing, diet, clothing, and basic necessities, were anything but the norm. OCAP, its critics and supporters alike often intimated, was pursuing a course of militant action with no precedent in Toronto's past. Yet when Héroux began to explore the history of those in Toronto who found themselves jobless and dependent on aid dispensed by institutions like the House of Industry in the nineteenth century or the relief administrations of Toronto's downtown wards or its working-class suburban municipalities in the 1930s, he discovered an obscured and little written about history of radical and relentless struggle. The more he dug into the primary sources of original newspaper coverage of poor people's campaigns, the more he saw continuities and parallels with his own OCAP experience. If anything, some of the actions of the out-of-work, especially during the Great Depression mobilizations of the Toronto unemployed, outstripped OCAP's endeavours in terms of audacity and angry confrontation.

The other author, Bryan D. Palmer, a historian of labour and the left, was drawn to OCAP in the 1990s and beyond precisely because of its militancy. As is the case with most historians of the working class, the bulk of Palmer's writing and research has addressed workers who were employed in waged occupations, who formed unions, and who participated in political parties of the left. For the most part, his published work has not been about the wageless, but addresses, instead, the waged. In this, his subject of research and writing has followed paths common to most working-class historians and labour studies practitioners. Nonetheless, as an advocate of militant working-class action, and as a researcher increasingly drawn to the history of the revolutionary left, Palmer was attracted to OCAP. The anti-poverty group led militant mobilizations of the poor at a time when revolutionary organizations were in disarray and mainstream trade unionism was in retreat, in danger of losing sight of its origins in class struggle and combative resistance.[6]

We thus first met, as activist and engaged labour historian, in the OCAP-organized mobilizations of the 1990s and 2000s. There was no talk of writing books. Our conversations turned on wrongs and rights; on injustices and how to overcome them; on rallies, and protests, and what happened at them and why.[7] There was, of course, always something of the activist in the labour historian, and a little of the labour historian in the activist. But we did not envision merging our roles, becoming collaborators in a project of the kind that ultimately resulted in this book. Nonetheless, amid police riots at the Ontario Legislature and legal battles that saw John Clarke, Héroux, and others put on trial for their activism, there was common agreement that if the dispossessed were ever to gain ground they had to be prepared to "fight to win." When, more than a decade later, various developments led us to discuss the possibility of co-authoring a wide-ranging study of the out-of-work and the kinds of mobilizations they sustained, a solid basis of common positions and co-operative thinking had long been in place.

Fundamental to the inquiry we envisioned was appreciation of three important conceptual premises: 1) the role of capitalism, as a system ordered by crises, in establishing the material conditions of deprivation, destitution, and dispossession that forced so many people into acts of resistance;[8] 2) the necessity to see the working class whole, not just as those employed in particular occupations, but as all of those people who have been dispossessed of fundamental control over their lives; and 3) the importance of grappling with the reciprocities of resistance, in which the role of conscious radical and revolutionary leadership is addressed without suppressing the agency and initiative of the dispossessed themselves.[9]

Precisely because these analytic fundamentals both animate the collaboration that orchestrates this study and underlie every page of our joint venture, they merit further comment. Moreover, if this book is to be more than a mere description of past happenings, as we hope it will be, it is vitally important to make explicit just how our approach is meant to inform future activism and broaden interpretive understandings in ways that have practical consequences. It is our purpose in this study to play some small role in insuring that the high price of dispossession does not continue to be paid in lives drained of hope or lost to deplorable conditions. Indeed, we provide this account of the past as a contribution toward the creation of a future in which abolition of the dispossessed is finally realized. What follows in this introductory section, then, introduces conceptual appreciations of capitalism, crisis, and class in ways that are meant to both explain the past and inform present struggles. We are not believers in the Biblical maxim that "the poor shall always be with you."

Capitalism, Crisis, and Class: Why *Have* the Poor Always Been with Us?

In the arm-twisting between the expropriated and the elite that reaches from the 1830s to the present lie important and suggestive insights into how capitalism functions as a socioeconomic political order, setting the stage on which calamities unfold and ideologies and cultural certitudes consolidate. In this process, class is, of course, made structurally, as a relationship to capitalism and its mills, factories, mines, construction lots, commercial outlets and other such sites of employment. But it is also forged in the crucible of struggle and resistance. As we will contend below, capitalist crises figure centrally in such a history of class confrontation, and the depressions, recessions, and panics that constitute the material reality of a crisis-ridden economic order routinely threaten and disrupt the employment security of working-class men and women, whose fundamental relationship to the means of production, and the wage that this generates, is one premised in expropriation. The Marxist economist Ernest Mandel identified seventeen global capitalist cycles over the course of the century-and-a-half reaching from 1816 to 1958, indicative of the recurring sequence of boom/prosperity, overproduction/crisis, slump/depression. If a working man had been fortunate enough to reach the age of seventy in 1921, as Alexander Keyssar points out in his study of unemployment in Massachusetts, he would have "lived through six downturns in the economy." In Canada, between 1873 and 1978, there were twenty-three recessions/depressions in which total production declined for at least six months. And Murray E. G. Smith has suggested that Canada since the 1970s has experienced routine decadal downturns.[10] The bad times, for workers, are as much a part of everyday life as the so-called good times. And in bad times, people lose their jobs, their homes, and their sense of self-worth. The very expropriation that leaves labour without ownership of the means of production too often leaves many without work at all.

Part of our purpose in writing this history of Toronto's dispossessed is to suggest that the out-of-work are as much a part of the working class as those engaged in wage labour; that the struggles to organize unions, resist wage cuts, and rally men and women to the banner of class struggle are organically linked to reciprocal campaigns of the jobless to secure work or to wrestle from authority minimal standards of existence. As James C. Scott has recognized, these struggles of the dispossessed are integral to the inseparable relations of class *and* state formation. "Gypsies, vagrants, homeless people, itinerants, runaway slaves, and serfs have always been a thorn in the side of states. Efforts to permanently settle these mobile people ... seemed to be a perennial state project—perennial, in part, because it so seldom succeeded."[11]

This book, then, contributes to an expansive understanding of class that resists attempts to reduce class to any simplistic understanding of this narrow group of paid workers or that particular stratum of *employees*. This perspective demands, moreover, that attempts to create a sense of new class formations rooted in precariousness will inevitably founder on the shoals of the hard reality that waged employment, seemingly secure in certain economic sectors, is in fact historically precarious and unstable. All workers, we argue, confront dispossession and walk the thin line separating employment and unemployment in ways that highlight possible job loss and potential dispossession. Whatever the seeming bounty of its ostensible high remuneration, union protections, and entitlements, wage employment is premised on the reality of dispossession, which can, at any time, given the possibility of capitalism lurching into crisis, be extended to the ultimate socioeconomic precipitation into wagelessness. The working class has no security that capitalism is bound to acknowledge, let alone preserve. Waged work in those

economic sectors associated in North America with the Fordist regime of accumulation, too easily and unthinkingly assumed to be layered in stability in the 1940s
and 1950s, has withered on the fragile vine of capitalist crises in the post-1973 years
of austerity and massive industrial job loss.[12]

We aim to demonstrate just how the emergence of a working class in one
of North America's leading cities, Toronto, was always structured by capitalism's
capacity, not just to create waged work, but to manufacture, as well, wagelessness.
In this dialectic of creation/destruction, capitalism foments crises to further its
insatiable accumulative appetite, which must be fed by profit, the rate of which
tends to fall as productive enterprise atrophies over time and the limitations of
markets are reached.[13] The amassing of wealth, which accrues from value extracted
from workers' productivity, necessitates new rounds of technological invention
and managerial reorganization of the labour process to enhance profit and lessen
reliance on waged workers. This process, in turn, leads to more and more workers
being employed in less and less secure and permanent ways, leaving labour more
partial and casual and, in periods of acute distress, subjecting workers to crises of
unemployment. This tension at the heart of class formation has been present, as
we discuss below, from the beginnings of capital's colonization of Upper Canada in
the decades before Confederation. It is a recurring theme in the everyday lives of
Canadians today. In both the social conflict of the Great Depression that erupted
in Toronto, and in protests of the poor and the organized labour movement across
Ontario in the 1980s, 1990s, and into the first years of the twenty-first century, there
were signs as well of how a militant labour revolt, on the part of both the waged and
the wageless, was brewing.[14]

Class has always been made as a relationship to the means of production,
to be sure, but this does not mean that it is *only* a productive relation. Cataclysmic
change within relations of production brought to the fore the inevitable and multi-
plying crises of capitalism. In the 1873 Afterword to the second German edition of
Capital: A Critical Analysis of Capitalist Production, Marx declared that,

> The contradictions inherent in the movement of capitalist society impress
> themselves upon the practical bourgeois most strikingly in the changes of
> the periodic cycle, through which modern industry runs, and whose crown-
> ing point is the universal crisis. That crisis is once again approaching,
> although as yet but in its preliminary stage; and by the universality of its
> theatre and the intensity of its action it will drum dialectics even into the
> heads of mushroom upstarts.

8

Capitalist progress was thus premised on capitalist destruction. "The growing incompatibility between the productive development of society and its hitherto existing relations of production expresses itself in bitter contradictions, crises, spasms," Marx wrote in the *Grundrisse,* concluding that, "The violent destruction of capital not by relations external to it, but rather as a condition of its self-preservation, is the most striking form in which advice is given it to be gone and give room to a higher state of social production." Socialism, Marx and Engels reasoned, was necessary if humankind was ever to transcend the destructive logic of the profit system, which was "too narrow to comprise the wealth" that it created: "And how does the bourgeoisie get over these crises? On the one hand, by enforced destruction of a mass of productive forces; on the other, by the conquest of new markets, and by the more thorough exploitation of the old ones. That is to say, by paving the way for more extensive and more destructive crises, and by diminishing the means whereby crises are prevented."

Class formation, about which Marx wrote relatively little, was never separable from this understanding of *capitalism as crisis.* Earlier epochs had seen society fragmented into "various orders, a manifold gradation of social rank [composed of] patricians, knights, plebeians, slaves ... feudal lords, vassals, guild-masters, journeymen, apprentices, serfs." Capitalism, in contrast, "simplified the class antagonisms." Under the revolutionizing drive of the bourgeoisie, civil society was split into "two great hostile camps, into two great classes directly facing each other: Bourgeoisie and Proletariat." This was, for Marx and Engels, the fundamental sociopolitical fact of the human relations of capitalism. As much as the working classes, pluralized in the mainstream language of the epoch, were fragmented by identities of nationality, religion, morality, and status, Marx and Engels insisted that the proletarians, recruited from all previous classes of the population, were finally brought together in inevitable association because of what they lacked: property. An original expropriation, generalized (sometimes over generations) to dispossession, defined the mass of humanity as inherently opposed to the propertied and powerful minority, and the isolations of labouring life would eventually give way "to revolutionary combination." Capitalism and the bourgeoisie had produced their "own gravediggers." This was fundamental to what Marx and Engels insisted was a process, spawned in all that was once solid melting into air, of men and women at last being "compelled to face with sober senses," their "real conditions of life."[15]

Such real conditions of life can perhaps be boiled down to one essential social fact: capitalism's irrevocable dependency on the continual creation and ongoing expansion of humanity's dispossessed. As Marx noted in an 1849 pamphlet,

Wage-Labour and Capital, that had its origins in a series of lectures delivered to the German Workingmen's Club of Brussels, the war for economic supremacy that characterized capitalism's ongoing development was "won less by recruiting than discharging the army of workers. The generals (the capitalists) vie with one another as to who can discharge the greatest number of industrial soldiers."[16]

"THOU SHALT NOT KILL!"

Dispossession: The Nursery of Class Struggle

In hindsight, and with a historical appreciation of the *longue durée* of class formation, it is clear that Marx and Engels wrote at a specific juncture, preceded by the dissolution of feudal relations and followed by the consolidation of increasingly structured capitalist social relations, of which differentiated labour markets were an integral part. To be sure, Marxist analysis of class relations necessarily addresses value, extraction of surplus, and regimes of accumulation, but the prior (and always historically ongoing[17]) process on which all of this is premised is necessarily expropriation and, in the long term, the continuity of dispossession. Marx declares, in his discussion of simple reproduction and the relations of seigneurs and serfs, "If one fine morning the lord appropriates to himself the land, the cattle, the seed, in a word, the means of production of this peasant, the latter will thenceforth be obliged to sell his labour power." In Chapter 25 of *Capital,* on "the general law of capitalist accumulation," Marx criticized (but drew on) Sir Fredric Morton Eden's book *The State of the Poor: Or, an History of the Labouring Classes of England* (1797). Against Eden's view that those emerging capitalists who commanded the produce of industry owed their exemption from labour "to civilization and order," Marx argued that

> the reproduction of a mass of labour-power, which must incessantly re-incorporate itself with capital for that capital's self-expansion; which cannot get free from capital, and whose enslavement to capital is only concealed by the variety of individual capitalists to whom it sells itself, this reproduction of labour-power forms, in fact, an essential of the reproduction of capital itself. Accumulation of capital is, therefore, increase of the proletariat.

Marx quoted the eighteenth-century satirist, philosopher, and political economist Bernard de Mandeville, who noted, "It would be easier, where property is well secured, to live without money than without the poor; for who would do the work?" Dispossession, then, is the basis of all proletarianization, which orders accumulation.[18]

This process was always disorderly: the old jostled with the new, layers of labour were structured into seemingly contradictory locales, with their designations running from the aristocratic (the black-coated worker) to the derogatory (the dangerous classes, the residuum).[19] And complicating this chaotic making and remaking of class experience was the potent disruption of capitalism's persistent underside: crisis. This ensured that class, once consolidated, was also always precarious.

Michael Denning, for instance, has recently suggested the necessity of radically reconceptualizing life under capitalism in ways that "decentre wage labour" and replace a "fetishism of the wage" and the "employment contract" with attention to "dispossession and expropriation." Marx, after all, did not invent the term "proletarian," but adapted it from its common usage in antiquity, when, within the Roman Empire, the word designated the uncertain social stratum, divorced from property and without regular access to wages, reproduced recklessly. J. C. L. Simonde de Sismondi drew on this understanding in an 1819 work of political economy that chronicled the "threat to public order" posed by a "miserable and suffering population," dependent as it was on public charity. "Those who had no property," Sismondi wrote, "were called to have children: *ad prolem generandum.*" Max Weber commented similarly: "As early as the sixteenth century the proletarianising of the rural population created such an army of unemployed that England had to deal with the problem of poor relief." Three centuries later, across the Atlantic, transient common labourers were being described in a discourse seemingly impervious to change: "a dangerous class, inadequately fed, clothed, and housed, they threaten the health of the community." Historically, then, it can be argued that "unemployment precedes employment, and the informal economy precedes the formal ... 'proletarian' is not a synonym for 'wage labourer' but for dispossession, expropriation, and radical dependence on the market." As Denning insists with a bluntness that is both insightful and myopic, "You don't need a job to be a proletarian ... wageless life, not wage labour, is the starting point for understanding the free market."[20]

For all that Denning stresses the fundamental importance of wagelessness, all the more so within a context of capitalism *as crisis*, his dichotomization of wageless life and waged labour substitutes subjective experience, as important as that may be, for objective assessment of how, under capitalism, dispossession, whatever its gradations, structures commonality as much as it accents division and differentiation. Denning thus nearsightedly clarifies the importance of dispossession while obscuring the extent to which this important foundational and ongoing reality of proletarianization is meaningless outside of the existence of the (often distant) wage as both an enduring if universally unpleasant end and a decisive means of survival within an economic order governed by the cash nexus. This reality frames the class resistance that invariably punctuates the social relations of capitalist political economy.

Capitalist Crises: Class Conflict from Above and Below

Toronto's mobilizations of the wageless, as we will show, followed the contours of capitalist crises. Economic dislocations haunted the pre-Confederation period, with recessionary downturns in the 1830s and 1840s and a major depression of 1853–57 realigning the relations of production and exchange. Closing out the last decades of the century were the economic crises of 1873–77 and 1893–96. The business cycle dipped dramatically in panics that punctuated the pre–First World War years, and if the 1920s was stamped by oscillations in the rhythms of material life, the 1930s were associated with unambiguous collapse, marking an entire decade as the Great Depression.

Thereafter, for the better part of three decades, the establishment of the welfare state and governing authorities' embrace of Keynesianism masked an always somewhat unstable economic order. The seeming calm of the 1945–75 period was broken less by protests of the out-of-work, although these did occur, than by youth revolt, antiwar mobilizations, and uprisings of radical nationalists in Quebec, wildcatting workers, women, and Aboriginal peoples—all associated with the tumultuous 1960s and the transition of a politics of disaffection into the 1970s.[21] But with the fiscal crisis of Western capitalist states unfolding in the mid-1970s, the periodic crises of capitalism went into accelerated overdrive. Toronto, like Canada and much of the advanced capitalist world, experienced the debilitating impact of twinned stagnation/inflation over the course of the mid- to late 1970s and early 1980s, unleashing the hounds of state repression. War was declared against the organized working class; employers sought concessions in collective bargaining, while the state looked to legislation to curb the supposed wage-push that was declared responsible for rising prices and currency devaluation. Then, under the gathering storm clouds of a neoliberalism kick-started by the coming to power of the New Right—Reagan and Thatcher—a concerted assault on all counters to the unfettered dominance of the "invisible hand" of the marketplace targeted the power of the unions and the entitlements of the poor simultaneously. By the 1990s, metropolitan centres like Toronto were increasingly rocked by global economic crises that stalked the years 1990–2008 incessantly. Financial and currency markets were left reeling, stock markets riding wildly to new highs that were then countered with dramatic lows. This paved the way to the subprime mortgage meltdown of 2007–8.[22]

The response of Toronto's poor and out-of-work was not always decisive, but it was persistently present. Unfolding weakly in the nineteenth century, albeit often in reciprocal relation to the better known and more adequately charted resistance of the waged working class, the force and conviction of the wageless strengthened throughout the depressions of the 1850s, 1870s and 1890s, and was bolstered by the working-class mobilization of the 1880s known as the Great Upheaval and associated with the Knights of Labor.[23] By the opening decades of the twentieth century, with the leadership of the waged working class consolidated in conservative trade unionism,[24] the struggles of the out-of-work began to be led by the revolutionary left. In the 1930s, as capitalist crisis registered in ways more dramatic than ever before, the leadership of the unemployed was not quite a monopoly of the left, but the decisive role of Communists in the agitations of the out-of-work was increasingly obvious. That influence was broken with the Cold War. As anticommunism permeated the unions in the late 1940s and 1950s, this reactionary turn drove many on the revolutionary left into retreat. It severed, in some ways, future struggles of the unemployed from the organic connection to radicalism that had developed out of the first left-led mobilizations of the jobless in the 1870s, 1880s, and 1890s, and that deepened with the developments of the pre– and post–First World War years, the 1920s, and the 1930s.[25]

Put on relative hold by the limited welfare state that was, in part, a response to the militant protests of 1930s Canada, and channelled into state-orchestrated inquiries and funding initiatives for youth, anti-poverty protest in the years 1945–75 was simmering but less than scorching. A relatively effective welfare state lid clamped down on much of the potential rebellion, containing somewhat the discontents of the dispossessed.[26] But stopgap measures and the limited programs of the "Just Society" could not be sustained over the long haul, especially as capitalism lurched from crisis to crisis after 1975. Capital, realizing that it was now locked in a war with the dispossessed, barred its teeth and dug in its heels; the state snapped to coercive attention. Class struggle's capacity to wrestle meaningful concessions and appropriate a part of the surplus extracted from the hide of exploited labour weakened dramatically as the terms of trade in the war between capital and labour, always mediated by the state, shifted. The routine tempo of class struggle, registering in advances that saw the percentage of the non-agricultural workforce organized in unions climb to 35–40 percent in Canada and the United States, slowed to a climacteric. Union density plummeted, dropping to below 11 percent in the United States and falling to around 27 percent in Canada, where highly organized public sector workers such as teachers and government clerks skewed the statistics. Among Canadian private sector workers the percentage of the workforce organized in unions declined to less than 14 percent. The confidence of working-class combatants waned as the advantage was seized by capital which, in the post-1975 years, utilized deepening and ongoing crises to discipline not only labour, but all dissident forces, drawing on the myriad powers of the state and unleashing an ideological assault of unprecedented vigour.[27]

Signs of strain were evident by the early 1980s, especially in British Columbia. A Solidarity movement brought the grievances of organized labour as well as the poor and a wide array of social movements together in a massive six-month campaign of resistance that, were it not for a tepid trade union officialdom, threatened to erupt in a province-wide general strike.[28] By the 1990s, with economic instability intensifying and the ideological climate no longer one of appeasement, but of attack and cutbacks to all manner of social programs and entitlements, the ranks of the wageless grew, the insecurities of the waged multiplied, and even an NDP government that came to power in Ontario with Bob Rae at its head in 1990 could not step down from the "restraint" bandwagon. It came under forceful attack from the very trade unions that social democracy had long considered its political friends.[29] With the subsequent rise to power of the Mike Harris Conservatives, with their "Common Sense Revolution," composed of dismantling the public sector, waging war on the unions, and adhering to nineteenth-century notions of "labour tests" (now called "work fare"), there was no corner in which the poor, the out-of-work, and the homeless might find refuge. Toronto became a site of the return and revenge of the dispossessed, organized as a fighting contingent by a militant band of committed activists known as the Ontario Coalition Against Poverty.

Toronto: A Locale within the Global

What happened in Toronto locally was unfolding internationally. In the global South, where rates of unionization were less the measure of proletarian well-being than the absolute immiseration of the dispossessed, the International Monetary Fund and other powerful agencies of deregulatory expropriation enforced programs of "de-peasantization." These initiatives quickened the flow of surplus rural labour to urban slums. The formal economy of waged employment was contracting at the same time as populations of the poor were expanding.[30] Processes such as this drove the engine of dispossession to the point that one billion of the world's people existed in dire poverty, surviving on less than $1.25 daily, while a further two billion found themselves classified in the ranks of the moderately poor, where sustenance could be calculated as costing $2.50 a day. Informal economies, black markets, and a Dickensian underworld of employments were now central to capitalist globalization.[31]

As John Bellamy Foster, Robert W. McChesney, and R. Jamil Jonna have suggested in the pages of *Monthly Review*, Marx's way of seeing class can now be appreciated for being ahead of its time. For Marx anticipated how modern imperialism and the relentless march of capital accumulation on a world scale would result in the quantitative expansion and qualitative transformation of the global reserve army of labour. The International Labor Organization (ILO) has recently estimated that this sector is now larger than the approximately 1.4 billion workers who are totally dependent on wage labor. An astronomical 1.7 billion workers can currently be classified as "vulnerably employed." A significant component of this rising reserve is undoubtedly wageless, members of marginal domestic economies eking out material being through unpaid labours, scavenging, and other illicit endeavours of the kind associated with life in the favelas, barrios, and shanty towns of the developing world. This sector knows little of the securities of the wage, which is usually unavailable or is accessed only intermittently, in sporadic, but always finite, clusterings of paid employment. For precarious workers such as these, subsistence rests as much on the trappings of petty entrepreneurialism of the self-exploiting penny capitalist kind as it does on classical waged employment. Mike Davis insists that what he calls the "global informal working class," a socioeconomic stratum that he sees "overlapping with but non-identical to the slum population," now surpasses one billion in number, its ranks expanding in an unprecedented frenzy of class formation. What all of this suggests is that in any analytic grappling with the historical record of workers and ongoing, accelerating capitalist crises, it is mandatory to see proletarianization whole. As Denning's excursion into wagelessness and Davis's slummification of the planet suggest, it is imperative not to centre our studies of labour in the logic of capital's determinations, in which the working class can be validated only to the extent that it is *waged*.[32]

As the 1970s gave way to the 1980s, a developing ideological hegemony reinforced and deepened material trends.[33] The implosion of the Soviet Union and the profound crisis sweeping through the locales of "actually existing socialism" from China to Cuba either culminated in or threatened capitalist restoration. A generalized demoralization of the revolutionary left and its organizations that had been ongoing in the capitalist West for decades meant that capital and the state faced an opposition as weak and incoherent as at any point since at least the 1880s. All of this left global capitalism crisis-ridden, the logic of its own contradictions intensifying, but not *in crisis*, in the sense that alternatives and challenges were seemingly in retreat. Relatively secure, global capital consolidated a political economy that crowned a triumphant post–Cold War American empire.[34]

The hegemony of neoliberal thought and its incomplete, but nonetheless significant, penetration of the consciousness of workers and their institutions combined with the declining capacity of labour to resist not only direct attacks but also devastating and destructive incursions on areas long held to be bastions of class distinction. This has heightened the sense that class is being remade in ways that undermine the possibilities of working-class strength. Proletarianization is accelerating, but in ways that often obfuscate understandings of collective class experience. Expropriation in the developing world marches forward in seven-league boots, while the uneven and combined nature of capitalist development elsewhere culminates in social relations of production in which precariousness is an increasingly common component of class formation in the modern world.[35] In Portugal and Spain, the marginally, casually, and insecurely employed are an expanding and increasingly significant percentage of the working class (upward of 40 percent), exhibiting organizational initiatives (such as the formation of the *Precári@s Inflexíveis* Movement) that reflect this reality.[36]

Expectations of job security have been eroded as a new principle of lean marketplaces; the young are bombarded with axioms that have taken root in the consciousness surrounding work and its possibilities. The message is unambiguously one of destabilization: jobs are not permanent, and labour, like life itself, is not structured around entitlements. Just how much all of this is truly new remains open for discussion, but the *perception* that the machinery of class has been broken apart into distinct components, with crucial new elements ostensibly added to the debris, is widespread. Class coherence has thus been dealt a series of harsh blows, and the dispossessed, many of whom are young people, have been force-fed an ideological diet fattening the individuated labour market. Acquisitive individualism in the capitalist West is the logical antidote to the collectivism of class, while in the developing world the Fanonesque "wretched of the earth" express the solidarities of the dispossessed in acts of desperation. Mike Davis concludes his discussion of the world's urban poor with a poignant summary of what he calls "a sinister and unceasing duet":

> Night after night, hornetlike helicopter gunships stalk enigmatic enemies in the narrow streets of slum districts, pouring hellfire into shanties or fleeting cars. Every morning the slums reply with suicide bombers and eloquent explosions. If the empire can deploy Orwellian technologies of repression, its outcasts have the gods of chaos on their side.[37]

In this climate, the overdetermining commonality of dispossession, in all of its diversity, is seemingly less significant in social relations than the layered gradations of difference, which chip away at the solidarities and consciousness of class, leaving in its place belief that the waged and the wageless are *distinct* socioeconomic entities, rather than two sides of the same class coin.[38]

One consequence of contemporary capitalist crisis is that proletarianization on a global scale is thus seemingly undermining and eroding the fully waged working class of the advanced capitalist nations, concentrated in the North, and expanding and destabilizing the waged and partially waged working class of the South. Figures released by the United Nations in the late 1990s indicate that 78 percent of all manufacturing employees in the world are now toiling outside of the relatively high-wage industrial economies that had dominated capitalist production prior to 1970.[39] The poor, we are left to think, are necessarily always with us.

Class Struggle in Our Times: Bringing the Dispossessed into the Picture

As a deep structure of being, then, dispossession is fundamental and throughout history has been a continuous thread that ties together exploitation, oppression, *and* resistance. Marx noted this in *Capital,* writing that capitalist enrichment was premised on "the condemnation of one part of the working class to enforced idleness by the over-work of the other part," accelerating "the production of the reserve army on a scale corresponding with the advance of social accumulation." Every proletarian can thus be categorized, not so much according to their waged work, but to the possible forms of surplus population, which Marx labelled "the floating, the latent, and the stagnant." This is why the accumulation of capital is also the accumulation of labour, but the Malthusian multiplication of the proletariat does not necessarily mean the working class will, in its entirety, be waged. "The lowest sediment of the relative surplus-population," Marx wrote,

> finally dwells in the sphere of pauperism ... the quantity of paupers increases with every crisis.... Pauperism is the hospital of the active labour-army and the dead weight of the industrial reserve army. Its production is included in that of the relative surplus population, its necessity in theirs; along the surplus population, pauperism forms a condition of capitalist production, and of the capitalist development of wealth. It enters into the *faux frais* of capitalist production.

As Marx noted in *Capital,* then, an *"absolute general law of capitalist accumulation"* was that "the more extensive ... the lazarus-layers of the working class, and the industrial reserve army, the greater is official pauperism." Once labouring people grasp this "secret," that capital accumulation proceeds on the basis that they work more, produce more, and create more wealth, only to find their lives "more precarious," they will discover the necessity of "regular co-operation between employed and unemployed in order to destroy or weaken the ruinous effects of this natural law of capitalistic production on their class." Such combinations of the waged and the wageless disturb the harmonious and revered laws of bourgeois order, giving rise to capital's cries of foul "infringement of the 'eternal' and ... 'sacred' law of supply and demand."[40]

For all that Marx and Engels could write in the pejorative language of the Victorian era about what would later be called "the underclass,"[41] they were also not unaware of how the "residuum" was reciprocally related to the stalwart proletarians on whom they based their hope for socialism. In later writings, Marx drew explicitly on Thomas More, for instance, whose *Utopia* was a source utilized in the writing of *Capital,* and who had represented the dispossessed as "dryen to this extreme necessitie, firste to steale, then to dye."[42] Engels' *The Condition of the Working-Class in England in 1844* had much of moralistic condemnation in it, especially with respect to immigrant Irish labour, but this did not mean that he saw the most downtrodden sectors of the proletariat as irredeemably separated out from the working class. Indeed, in an 1892 preface to his Manchester study, Engels recorded with considerable optimism the extent to which socialism's advance in England had registered even in a former bastion of the dispossessed—London's lumpenproletarianized East End. "That immense haunt of misery is no longer the stagnant pool that it was six years ago," Engels wrote, "It has shaken off its torpid despair, has returned to life, and has become the home of what is called the 'New Unionism'; that is to say the organisation of the great mass of 'unskilled' workers."[43]

Marx understood well, as Denning notes, that

> Political economy ... does not recognize the unemployed worker, the work-
> ingman, insofar as he happens to be outside this labour relationship. The
> rascal, swindler, beggar, the unemployed, the starving, wretched and crim-
> inal workingman—these are *figures* who do not exist *for political economy*
> but only for other eyes, those of the doctor, the judge, the grave-digger, and
> bum-bailiff, etc.; such figures are spectres outside its domain.[44]

Marx, of course, also had considerable empathy for what was *done to* the dispossessed, as is more than evident in his condemnation of the "barbarity in the treatment of the paupers" and his recognition of the "growing horror in which the working people hold the slavery of the workhouse," which he dubbed a "place of punishment for misery."[45]

In his 1842–43 *Rheinische Zeitung* articles on the debates in Germany over the law on the theft of wood, moreover, there is ample suggestion that Marx appreciated the ways in which capitalism's socioeconomic trajectory tended in the direction of wider criminalization of behaviours of the poor that were themselves critical to the survival of the dispossessed. Separated first from nature, the dispossessed then found themselves expropriated from the institutionalized protections of civil society. State formation, in Marx's view, proceeded on this basis: ruling class power and institutions subservient to such authority's ends made the law into a vehicle driving forward the expanding nature of dispossession, turning the apparatus of governance into a mailed fist of privileged interests. Concluding that, "Just as it is not fitting for the rich to lay claim to alms distributed in the street, so also in regard to these *alms of nature*" (the fallen woods of the forest), Marx insisted on the need for a universal set of "customary rights of the poor."[46] Needless to say, nothing of the sort materialized in the cauldron of capitalist class formation, and Marx concluded that the state had been turned into a servant of property. As Peter Linebaugh suggested in the mid-1970s, Marx's writings on the theft of wood provide a jumping off point for a discussion of class formation that necessitates analysis of the meaning of Marxist understandings of the controversial category the lumpenproletariat, a term that can only be interrogated when "the principle of historical specification" and "the concept of class struggle" are central to analysis.[47]

Class Politics and Dispossession: The Left and the Wageless

Study of the dispossessed, then, must begin with an understanding that working-class life is not defined by either the wage or wagelessness, but is in actuality bounded by both. It is on this plane of connectedness that class struggle is waged. Dispossession, however, is not in and of itself a guarantee of behaviours that will advance humanity, just as being a wage worker is no guarantee of militant embrace of class struggle and the need for social transformation. It is in uniting the dispossessed in struggles that can realize a new social order, one premised not on expropriation and ongoing dispossession, but on the collective production for the use and benefit of all, that constitutes the only possibility for meaningful progress.

This brings to the fore the importance of a leadership that can harness the discontents of dispossession to the vehicle of class struggle. Without such a leadership, the possibility of the descent of the dispossessed into the depths of a political compromise with reaction and worse is certainly a possibility, as those who have organized poor people's campaigns and unemployed struggles know all too well.[48] The history which we sketch below suggests, strongly so, that left-wing leaderships in the mobilizations of the out-of-work have been critical to the development of class struggle in general and the kinds of resistance fomented by the wageless in particular. In Toronto's past, the demands and activities of the dispossessed reached their most radical and socially conscious only when resistance was understood to be part of a larger working-class initiative, usually one that had been crafted consciously within reciprocal relations involving all segments of labour, orchestrated by left-wing activists. It is this coming together of the left and the dispossessed that can effectively harness the rage and resistance of the jobless, using the power of the waged and the wageless to effectively chart paths to progressive social change out of the morass of crisis that is capitalism's destructive legacy.

Building such an orientation is no easy task. As trade unions atrophy, both in terms of their capacity to organize labour and with respect to their willingness to put forward a politics of class that extends past the constrictions of business unionism, which focuses narrowly on specific class jurisdictions of occupational and waged employments, working-class solidarity is undermined as a critical component of social change. The revolutionary left, never weaker over the course of the last century than it is now, is a tragically understated presence in contemporary struggles, and has been usurped, as a critical political voice, by identity-driven social movements that reproduce the fragmentations inherent in capitalism's tendency to divide the better to conquer. Never, perhaps, in the history of the modern world, have progressive attachments to race, ethnicity, gender, and sexual orientation been stronger, yet rarely has the political possibility of transformative change seemed more of a chimera. Uniting the dispossessed can change this situation, bringing together the waged and the wageless of all progressive identities in defence of a humanity threatened with ongoing dispossession. For what hope is there for all men, women, and children, if dispossession retains its vise-like grip on human potential, thwarting the realization of the demands and dreams of the multitudes, whatever their particular identities?

A politics of class that speaks directly to the betterment of humanity through insistence that the expropriated are as one in their ultimate needs has never been more necessary. Such a politics recognizes new realities, but it also builds on old understandings: that an injury to one is an injury to all, and that the reciprocal powers (however subjectively different) of the employed and the out of-work must be organized and utilized to speak to the debilitating consequences of dispossession as well as the much more commonly struggled over areas of productions and payments. Once it is grasped that all proletarians suffer dispossession, and all of those suffering dispossession are proletarians, the possibilities of mounting an effective class struggle politics in our times expand. For the ultimate meaning of class lies in realizing its potential to change the world, making class being, rooted in dispossession and forged in the increasingly agitated cauldron of capitalist crises, the basis for a transformative politics.

In the discussion that follows we march, often with brisk strides, over a past in which the poor have always been with us, but in which it can not be said that they have always accepted their lot meekly and mildly. Resistance is the tangled thread of militant continuity that we have chosen to unravel in the pages that follow. It connects the decades of discord that make up the long history of Toronto's dispossessed, detailed below and ordered in four chronological, but sometimes overlapping, sections.

It must be noted at the outset that these components of our book may seem unbalanced. The two parts of our rebellious history of Toronto's poor that are longer and more detailed are, predictably, focussed on periods when the resistance of the poor and out-of-work surged to the forefront. During the prolonged and intense economic crisis of the Great Depression, left-led protest movements of the unemployed and relief recipients were highly visible and undeniably militant. These mobilizations outstripped in organizational acumen, public presence, and notoriety anything of a comparable nature that had happened in the century leading up to 1930. As the welfare state consolidated, the gloom of economic downturn lifting with the advent of the Second World War and the relative postwar prosperity that carried through into the 1970s, the resistance of the poor, while never eliminated, took a backseat to other developments. With the ongoing crises of the post-1973 years, however, poor people's campaigns again resurfaced, and our section on the years from the 1980s to the present is correspondingly much longer and more detailed. These substantial parts of the book are differentiated internally, as are the shorter sections, with specific chapter-like subsections, the major divisions being demarcated by bolded sub-section titles.

Part II explores the nineteenth- and early twentieth-century origins of Toronto's dispossessed, outlining how age-old understandings of the deserving and undeserving poor lay at the foundation of attempts to address the presence and increasing visibility of the out-of-work and down-and-out in one of the nation's leading urban centres. An institution like the House of Industry became something of a weather vane, indicating which ways the winds of convention and social construction of the dispossessed were blowing. In this stormy climate of class relations, the jobless were increasingly subject to "labour tests," in which "cracking the stone" was somehow proof of the deservedness of the dispossessed to receive aid. Resistance and protest against this disciplinary regime emerged, of course, and marched, in the century reaching up to the Great Depression, under flags black and red.

During the 1930s, in an unprecedented capitalist crisis of unemployment, it was the red flag which often rallied the poor and the out-of-work to rebellious protests. As we detail in Part III, Toronto's dispossessed did so in many ways. As single unemployed men and women they trekked to Queen's Park or Ottawa to voice their discontents. Dependent on public relief, the destitute might take officials of the inadequate administration of welfare hostage, just as they could block evictions that threatened the poor with homelessness. Some of the discontented, working on public employments for small compensations that kept food on the table and lodged their families, transferred the tactic of the strike into demands that their support not be cut back or that it be expanded to the point that it actually covered something approximating the necessities of life. This history of Toronto's unemployed movement in the "dirty thirties" is an illuminating core section of this study, indicative of what might be accomplished with the left-led organization of the out-of-work.

In Part IV, we attempt to fill a noticeable gap in the post–Second World War history of poor people's organization, exploring how an incomplete and inadequate welfare state emerged in Canada in the years leading from the 1940s into the 1960s. That same limited welfare state, while heralded as a great advance for the poor, nonetheless generated considerable opposition from below. Recessionary downturns elicited protests in the 1950s and 1960s radicalism nurtured important oppositional challenges. Ultimately, however, it was the repeated attack from above that was more disruptive. Capital and the state responded to the periodic crises of capitalist downturns that stretch from the mid-1970s to the present with an austerity program measured out in a thousand cutbacks. That assault on hard-fought-for entitlements, seemingly secured in the aftermath of the Great Depression, has set the stage for a new chapter in the long history of Toronto's rebellious poor.

We explore the dimensions of recent resistance among Toronto's homeless, unemployed, and destitute in Part V, where examination of OCAP's mobilizations of the 1990s and 2000s necessarily figures prominently. This brings our study of the dispossessed into the contemporary era. Capitalist crises now unfold with a rapidity and volatility that, while different than the prolonged, concentrated decade of singular crisis in the 1930s, have proven decidedly debilitating over the course of more than a quarter century of hard and hardening times.

PART II

"Cracking the Stone"

The Origins of Toronto's Dispossessed, 1830–1928

In Canada, the making of the working class as an act of dispossession reaches far back into a colonial history, with the first, decisive act of expropriation being that of Indigenous peoples. Colonizing agents—among them armies of Empire, marauding traders, religious orders, and the harbingers of future state formation—displaced various "Indian" bands, whose marginalization paved the way for the creation of a colonial settler society, replete with its racialized understandings of place and station, class divisions, and inequalities. As a Mississauga chief told an English traveller in 1820, describing a half century of indigenous-settler relations: "You came as wind blown across the great lake. The wind wafted you to our shores. We [received] you—we planted you—we nursed you. We protected you till you became a mighty tree that spread thro our Hunting Land. With its branches you now lash us."[1] This historical context is not easily assimilated to the formalized labour markets, state initiatives, and class mobilizations of later periods.

Nonetheless, the history of this original and ongoing dispossession of Indigenous peoples is, in our way of thinking, linked to later processes of dispossession that some have identified as less about place/land and more about time/value. Peter Kulchyski summarizes this position well when he argues that "what distinguishes anti-colonial struggles from the classic Marxist accounts of the working class is that oppression for the colonized is registered in the spatial dimension—as dispossession—whereas for workers oppression is measured as exploitation, as the theft of time."[2]

We understand this kind of interpretive bifurcation. But we also see the issue at stake somewhat differently. The long history of dispossession, which in Canada commences with the first expropriation of Indigenous peoples, continues in ways that routinely and repeatedly divorce non-Aboriginal settlers/producers from varied and complex means of production, all of which relate to the human capacity to exercise control and determination over material life. These components of production include land, of course, but they also encompass technologies, extractive resources, skills, knowledge, and a wide range of other factors, including developing infrastructures of a consolidating market economy. We appreciate the brutalizing and foundational nature of the colonizing dispossession of Indigenous peoples from the land. Indeed, it must be appreciated as the initial expropriation on which the future continuous and differentiated processes of establishing and sustaining the fundamental preconditions of capitalist accumulation rested. The severing of masses of people from the "ownership" conditions that allowed them to determine critically important components of their existence began with the displacement of Aboriginal peoples from their places of habitation, territories of sustenance, and customary political economies. An overt, original act of violence and displacement has historically given way to a multitude of disruptive undertakings, many of which are now routinely masked as the normal "relations" of social interactions regularized as the legitimate progeny of property, profit, and power.

It is thus an important purpose of this book, as outlined in the preceding introduction, to break down the notion that what is involved in the formation of the working class is simply the theft of value from those who labour, an expropriation of what Marx designated surplus and Kulchyski calls time. The exploitation of labour, as Marx quite rightly stressed, is crucial to capitalist accumulation, but the preconditions of this capitalist capacity to appropriate surplus value constitute nothing less than the historically complex processes—cumulative, far-reaching, and continuing—that divorce all producers from the capacity to control their productive lives.[3] In class terms, those who have been dispossessed include not only those working for wages but those who have also, to varying degrees, been locked out of the wage labour market. The unemployed may not be exploited, in the strictly economic sense of the term, which designates the production of surplus, but their dispossession is fundamental to capitalist power and the capacity to discipline and disorient the working class as a whole. Those workers who find themselves jobless, then, may not produce surplus value, but they are no less proletarian for that.

This understanding of dispossession thus structures our story. Accenting dispossession introduces a critical untidiness to historical analysis: it blurs lines of distinction that are seen as somehow natural and inevitable: urban/rural; waged employment/public charity; paternalism/freedom; petition/conflict. Those experiencing dispossession in the earliest stages of Canadian capitalist development did so in varied ways that yielded nothing approximating a collective, working-class solidarity. Not a few Native peoples, many of them known as Métis, the consequence of intermarriage among fur traders, colonist-settlers, and original First Nations inhabitants of the land, were integrated into the developing wage-labour society. But the bulk of the emerging Canadian working class experienced its dispossession as something other than that lived through by Indigenous peoples. As native-born landed producers, immigrant newcomers[4] (many of whom were Irish fleeing famine and landlordism in the Old World), or British mechanics, their "settler" separation from the land, their subordination to contractors and militias ruthless in enforcing the roughest of labouring environments on the early public works of canal and railroad construction, or their sense of artisan, apprenticed skills being debased, conditioned no community of common class interests. Nonetheless, these distinct streams of proletarianization were tributaries destined to feed a common process, one in which dependency on the wage was always rendered precarious by the harsh and recurring realities of being out of work.

Land and Labour in Old Ontario

Toronto's beginnings also lay in Native people's dispossession, a history that has been obscured if not obliterated in denials that now erase indigeneity from the landscape of Canada's leading metropolitan centre.[5] Yet there is no denying the original presence of First Nations. As J. M. S. Careless has pointed out, white colonizing settlement in the area now occupied by the city of Toronto did not really begin until the late eighteenth century. By the 1790s indigenous-settler tensions over the ostensible, but misunderstood, "sale" of traditional Aboriginal lands were more than evident. Prompted by fur trade developments and the petitions for land by prominent Montreal figures, many of them leading members of the North West Company, the British Governor-in-Chief of Quebec City, Lord Dorchester, plunked down £1,700 sterling in cash and trade goods and convinced the Mississauga to part with their "Indian land rights" to a then largely forested tract of what would later arguably become the most expensive slice of real estate in Canada. Known as the Toronto Purchase, this title encompassed a fourteen-mile stretch of lakefront from present-day Scarborough in the east past the Humber River to what now constitutes Etobicoke in the west, stretching inland to the north for twenty-eight miles. As Careless concludes, understatedly, the transaction was "a bargain basement deal."[6]

On the Upper Canadian frontier, in which Old Toronto, or Muddy York, was a metropolitan outpost destined for post-Confederation provincial dominance, the revolution in social relations that would follow in the wake of capitalist industrialization explored by Gregory S. Kealey may well seem obscure.[7] Toronto in 1834 had a population of a mere nine thousand. Its productive apparatus, dominated by the often paternalistic master-journeymen reciprocities of the artisan manufactory and the ostensible *noblesse oblige* of the Tory oligarchy, hardly crystallized unambiguous class antagonisms. It was still possible for a hermit-squatter such as the American Revolutionary War expatriate Joseph Tyler to carve accommodations out of the Don River's embankments, growing maize and tobacco, "manufacturing" pitch and tar, navigating the water course in his forty-foot-long hand-crafted canoe. But a part of Tyler's income came from transporting barrels of beer from Helliwell's brewery on the Don River to York's taverns, a sign of the changing nature of production and the commercialization of emerging socioeconomic relations.[8] As Albert Schrauwers has recently shown, the 1830s was a turning point in Toronto's evolution. The bitter fruits of dispossession were increasingly visible in the transition from a landed order in which the authority of the gentlemanly elite held sway to a more socially revolutionized and commodified market economy. The agricultural, commercial, financial, and industrial components of Toronto's economy were becoming subordinated to capitalist disciplines.[9]

Although a crisis on the land did not, in general, precipitate mass rural migration to the towns or less concentrated farming settlements in the west until the 1840s and 1850s, Upper Canadian landed relations were anything but tranquil.[10] The aristocratically-inclined capitalists that Shauwers identifies with the traditional Family Compact held much of the best land, either working it through hired hands or holding it in speculation, and the church and state with which this elite was intimately connected each took one-seventh of the province's acreage. Free land grants, originally designed to attract settlers, were turned back in 1826, replaced by sale through public auctions that were exploited by large land companies, unscrupulous colonizing agents, and nascent banking institutions, all of which were, again, never far removed from the influence and interests of powerful circles of Compact alignments. Assisted emigration efforts were curtailed, and prospective landowners now had to pay for their passages and purchase their lots on credit. Small freeholders, who had gained a foothold before and during the 1820s, found the going rather rough in later decades, especially in the midst of recurring economic downturns that invariably squeezed them off their meagre and modestly productive estates. As John Clarke has shown, the economics of land concentration between 1825 and 1834 left more and more holdings in the hands of a powerful minority, well served by their capacities to manipulate the credit market. A contemporary wrote in 1835, "The system of selling land on credit, and contracting debt at stores, hath proved ruinous of later years to settlers without capital, who have no other means of extricating themselves than selling their properties." Dispossession weighed heavily on those forced to depend on the uncertainties of the wage labour market. "Disappointment preys" on their spirit, concluded this pessimist. Even large families could not ensure their prosperity, and prior to 1840 only 2 to 5 percent of all rural producers in Upper Canada had over one hundred acres in cultivation. A distinct minority, to be sure, could afford to hire labour for the initial land clearance, but demand for such proletarians exceeded supply. Few new arrivals in Canada, except the most destitute (who often found their way into canal building and the casual labour afforded in the towns), were willing to work for wages, according to the complaints of those who seemed to be in the know. Lord Goderich, the colonial secretary, explained in 1831 the dilemma faced by patrician, polite society: "Without some division of labour, without a class of persons willing to work for wages, how can society be prevented from falling into a state of almost primitive rudeness, and how are the comforts and refinements of civilized life to be procured."[11]

By the mid-1830s, land policy, speculative endeavours and hoarding, and the penetration of the market and its solvent of social differentiation in town and country were lending considerable force to Goderich's insistence that "there should be in every society a class of labourers as well as a class of Capitalists or Landowners." This presaged Edward Gibbon Wakefield's later enunciation, in 1833, of a theory of "systematic colonization," which Marx integrated into his discussion of capitalist primitive accumulation.[12]

In the rural areas of the Home District, within which Toronto was located, some 10,172 out of 14,994 labouring-age males (68 percent) were landless by mid-century, and wage rates had plummeted across the Canadian colonial landscape.[13] Among the rough Irish canallers, these same years saw unprecedented destitution, casting thousands of labourers into concentrated shantytowns on the banks of rural public works projects.

The dispossession of this transatlantic proletarian contingent—two hundred and thirty thousand Irish migrated to British North America in the 1840s, fleeing famine in the old country—translated into a rural reserve army of labour, numbers of which inevitably found their way to Ontario's cities, Toronto pre-eminent among them. It was with reference to these poor and peripatetic Irish immigrants, routinely displaced from their waged work on canal sites in the 1830s and 1840s, that Upper Canadian newspapers first commented on the social distress associated with what they called "the vast accumulation of unemployed labourers," a contingent described as "in the last stages of starvation." When a House of Industry was ultimately established in Toronto in 1837, its purpose to provide relief to the "industrious" deserving poor, removing beggars from public thoroughfares, and instilling in the indigent "principles and habits of industry and moral virtue," two-thirds of those seeking aid from the new institution were Irish.[14]

Toronto inevitably confronted the fallout from this process of dispossession. Over the course of the winter of 1836–37 an economic crisis exacerbated the growing problem: commerce stagnated; houses stood empty for want of rent; the Bank of Upper Canada pressured its debtors to settle accounts, including an ironworks that was forced to close, its eighty employees thrown out of work; a Mechanics' Association was formed to lobby for the protection of the interests of tradesmen; and printers and tailors struck their masters. William Lyon Mackenzie, a newspaper editor and proprietor whose notoriety as a relentless critic of the aristocratic governing Tories and outspoken leader of the Reform element was well known, railed that his typographers should spend their evenings "studying the true principles of economy which govern the rule of wages." Meanwhile, the flood of pauper emigrants passing through Toronto, estimated in the 1830s to be in the tens of thousands annually, continued, with fears of recent cholera epidemics associated with the immigrant ships fresh in the minds of many. Newspapers carried letters from respectable citizens describing "pauperism" and "vagrancy" as "a great and growing evil." The poor who "now suffered to wander and beg in the streets," were said to bring on "themselves and offspring temporal distress and eternal ruin."[15]

A wageless, diseased population, increasingly visible on city streets and challenging the ruling order's sense of public propriety and paternal responsibility necessitated a response. This was especially the case if firebrands like William Lyon Mackenzie were not to make ideological capital out of their constant harangues that social development and harmonious relations were threatened by a pernicious oligarchy, which was daily fomenting a "universal agitation." Mackenzie's obnoxious claim that "privilege and equal rights" and "law sanctioned, law fenced in privilege" were at loggerheads in Upper Canada in 1837, forcing a terrible contest, was but one measure of dispossession's distressing consequences.[16]

Toronto's House of Industry

At the centre of this history of dispossession was the 1830s creation of a set of carceral institutions which, as Albert Schrauwers has argued, criminalized the poor.[17] Pivotal in this development, which extended beyond the Kingston Penitentiary and local and debtors' gaols, was Toronto's House of Industry. The push to create Toronto's first poorhouse came from the city elite toward the end of 1836, a large public meeting being convened to ascertain if there were not better "ways and means of relieving the poor."[18] A letter to the Mayor of Toronto, written by a clerk of the Bank of Canada who attended the December 26, 1836, discussion, stressed the pressing need to eliminate from public view all indications of material human distress and to do so in the most economical manner possible. Such aims were judged "essential to the comfort and happiness of the community at large." At the same time Toronto's Sheriff, William Botsford Jarvis, initiated proceedings that outlawed begging on city streets.[19] The first discussions around the creation of a poorhouse in Toronto were thus directly related to the perceived need to control and regulate the actions of the dispossessed.

An 1837 statute, authorizing Houses of Industry to be erected across Upper Canada, emerged out of these 1836 concerns. It conveyed well the mindset of embattled, even archconservative, paternalists, but there was enough of the patrician in the Reform leadership to draw some of its leading figures to the class purpose of the modified workhouse proposals associated with the entrenched, conservative elite.[20] This Tory-introduced legislation produced little immediately, for no Houses of Industry were established outside of Toronto until the late 1840s. Nonetheless, the criminalization and institutionalization of the wageless reflected both the growing unease among the patrician and propertied and their panicked recourse to discipline the unruly:

> That the persons who shall be liable to be sent into, employed and governed in the said House, to be erected in pursuance of this Act, are all Poor and Indigent Persons, who are incapable of supporting themselves; all persons able of body to work and without any means of maintaining themselves, who refuse or neglect so to do; all persons living a lewd dissolute vagrant life, or exercising no ordinary calling, or lawful business, sufficient to gain or procure an honest living; all such as spend their time and property in Public Houses, to the neglect of lawful calling.
> ... That all and every person committed to such House, if fit and able, shall be kept diligently employed in labour, during his or her continuance there; and in case the person so committed or continued shall be idle and not perform such reasonable task or labour as shall be assigned, or shall be stubborn, disobedient or disorderly, he, she or they, shall be punished according to the Rules and Regulations made or be made, for ruling, governing and punishing persons there committed.[21]

"The chief objects" of Toronto's House of Industry, wrote one commentator supporting its creation in 1836, were "the total abolition of street begging, the putting down of wandering vagrants, and securing an asylum at the least possible expense for the industrious and distressed poor."[22]

Toronto's Poor House, as it was colloquially known, fittingly took over an old, abandoned building that had previously served as York's Court House. At first, the House was used primarily by widows, deserted women, and their children, with few male inmates receiving so-called indoor relief. Outdoor relief, or the dispensing of food and fuel to needy families, constituted most of the House of Industry's work in providing for the poor. The first annual report of the House of Industry indicated that 46 persons received indoor relief, while the corresponding figure for recipients of outdoor relief was 857.[23]

In 1848 the House of Industry acquired a substantial new building. This expansion was not unrelated to waves of Irish immigration. The year before over thirty-eight thousand Irish emigrants had passed through Toronto, often arriving by boat from Quebec City or Montreal. While most of the newcomers undoubtedly moved on to seek employment in and around Hamilton and the Niagara District, many stayed. They taxed the young city's capacity to materially support a growing population of the dispossessed. Larratt Smith, a young Englishman, described the inundation of Toronto by the emigrant Irish poor, doing so in a way that made it entirely clear how waged employment and wagelessness were mere steps apart on the road of everyday life in early Canada:

> They arrive here to the extent of about 300 to 600 by any steamer. The sick are immediately sent to the hospital which has been given up to them entirely and the healthy are fed and allowed to occupy the Immigrant Sheds for 24 *hours;* at the expiration of this time, they are obliged to keep moving, their rations are stopped and if they are found begging are imprisoned at once. Means of conveyance are provided by the Corporation to take them off at once to the country, and they are accordingly carried off "willy-nilly" some 16 or 20 miles, North, South, East & West, and quickly put down, leaving *the country* to support them by giving employment.... John Gamble advertised for 50 for the Vaughan plank road, and hardly were the placards out, than the Corporation bundled 500 out and set them down.... It is a great pity we have not some railroads going on, if only to give employment to these thousands of destitute Irish swarming among us. The hospitals

contain over 600 and besides the sick and convalescent, we have hundreds of widows and orphans to provide for.

Sheriff W. B. Jarvis complained to Mayor Boulton that Irish immigrants could be seen "lying under the shelter of fences and trees, not only on the outskirts, but within the very heart of town—human beings begging for food, having disease and famine depicted in their countenances and without a shelter to cover them."[24]

By the early 1850s, the House of Industry refuge began taking in small numbers of homeless men, on average three a night, providing "an asylum to the indigent poor." According to antiquarian histories, "many a homeless waif" received "a night's lodging, with supper and breakfast, to invigorate him for the coming day's search for work," which was to be undertaken after male "lodgers" chopped some wood for the institution. These innovations and expanded assistance were implemented as temporary expedients, judged necessary as "the surest means of doing away with street begging." It was understood that the "casual homeless" would have one night of shelter and then be on their way. From 1837 to 1854, Toronto's refuge accommodated 2620 indigents, but its outdoor relief remained especially important.[25]

Toronto's House of Industry thus blended aspects of an older voluntaristic poor relief with the new institutionalism, implementing the criminalization of poverty at the same time as it accented the benefits an ameliorated workhouse system could bestow on the poor. To be sure, the House of Industry that emerged in Toronto was never simply a product of the 1837 Upper Canadian statue that stipulated that magistrates could establish carceral workhouses after receiving recommendations from three successive grand juries and, indeed, it was funded by voluntary subscriptions and offered outside relief to those in need but not living within its walls. As Richard B. Splane suggested decades ago, the Toronto House was in its beginnings both a house of refuge and a house of correction, a hybrid that could appeal to conservatives and liberals alike.[26]

James Buchanan's *Project for the Formation of a Depot in Upper Canada with a View to Relieve the Whole Pauper Population of England* (1834) envisioned a Foucauldian institution of inspection, monitoring, and training in religion, work discipline, and, for children, the rudiments of an education. This kind of response might be associated with high Toryism, congruent with its author's claimed "hatred of Democracy," but Buchanan had kinship connections with the leading family of moderate Reform, the Baldwins. Indeed, Dr. William Baldwin was to take up management of the Toronto House of Industry when it was established in March 1837. Thus the House of Industry proved a meeting ground of Tory and Reform on the eve

of the Rebellion of 1837, foreshadowing the extent to which the political antagonists of this era might well share a common unease as the threatening portents of
the dispossessed were increasingly obvious.[27] Toronto's wageless would exist in the
shadow of the House of Industry for decades.

In the Era of Confederation: Capitalist State Formation and the Poor

The Reform insurrection of 1837, however anti-climactic, dealt a series of
death blows to the *ancien regime*. In the subsequent era of state formation, culminating in Confederation in 1867, new senses of governance, public responsibility,
and political culture consolidated in the 1840s.[28] Mechanics and tradesmen petitioned legislatures in ways that would have been unimaginable in decades past,
while local government was fundamentally reconfigured.[29] Toronto's 1846 Act of
Incorporation was amended, widening the possible reach of control and coercion
that could be deployed against the wageless by providing for the establishment of
an industrial farm to complement the existing House of Industry, which drew, from
1839 onwards, not only on private donations but on annual provincial grants. Over
the course of the 1850s a spate of municipal legislation addressed the growing need
to attend to the destitute and the workless; by 1866 the Municipal Institutions Act
mandated that all townships in the province of Ontario with a population of over
twenty thousand provision houses of industry or refuge. Between 1840 and 1860,
moreover, Toronto's House of Industry competed with eight other local private
charitable institutions receiving government grants for the relief of the poor.[30] One
crucial piece of legislation that followed on the heels of Confederation was the 1867
Prison and Asylum Inspection Act. It defined provincial responsibilities for social
welfare. Criminalization, incarceration, and relief of the indigent were not just associated as part of a common response to proletarianization but were now bureau-
cratically congealed in a statute that assigned responsibility for these spheres of
"correctional intervention" to a single inspector, John Woodward Langmuir.[31]

Small wonder that the oscillating reciprocities of waged and wageless life
instilled in those undergoing proletarianization a recurrent sense of grievance. As
a carpenter declared in 1852: "He asks that it be fair, that for five months in the year
able and willing mechanics, are compelled to accept the alternative of walking the
streets or working for wages which do not afford ample remuneration for the labour
performed." Finally, "after submitting to all this, with apparent resignation—after
enriching their employers by the sweat of their brow, on terms which barely keep
the thread of life from snapping—they are told with barefaced effrontery that they
were employed in charity."[32] Seasonal labour markets, with their harsh material

ritual of winter's idleness and paternalistic alms, were by mid-century being challenged by the dispossessed.

Economic crisis was the necessity that proved the mother of this new inventive stage in the developing responses to joblessness, emanating not only from capital and the state but the proletarianized as well. The massive social dislocation occasioned by the arrival of tens of thousands of ill and impoverished famine Irish immigrants in the post-1847 years was one part of this process, helping to swell Toronto's population to forty-five thousand by 1860–61. At that point, Toronto contained more people who were by birth Irish than those who were born in England, and the 12,441 Irish-born trailed only the 19,202 Canadian-born, many of whom likely had Irish parentage.[33] So, too, with the emergence of the railroad and the advancing stages of industrial-capitalist production in urban centres were class differentiation, organization, and conflict becoming more visible. Among skilled workers, mechanization threatened entrenched craftsmen with the debasement of their trade and the possibility that they would be forced out of work as cheaper labour, including women, could be hired to take their places. Toronto's tailors led the struggle against machine erosion of craft skills in 1852, reviving a moribund society that had been established earlier in the 1840s. Dictating a new price list to their bosses at one of the merchant tailor firms, Hutchinson & Walker, the company responded to the upstart tailors by introducing the first sewing machine into a Canada West manufactory, bringing a woman operative with the device from New York City. The "knights of the needle" responded with a strike, and on the capitulation of their employer celebrated their victory on King Street. Parading about the town, they ridiculed the detested machine and symbolically buried it, hoisting it high in the air, carrying it on their shoulders after "the fashion of a corpse on its way to the burial grounds." The woman seamstress returned to the United States.[34]

This kind of defensive posture would not, ultimately, stem the tide of technological change. But the number of strikes in Canada soared in the 1850s, when seventy-three such work stoppages represented fully 55 percent of all labour-capital conflicts taking place in the entire 1815–59 period. No other decade saw more than thirty strikes, and newspapers and the public worried about the beginnings of "an insurrection of labour."[35] For the workless, however, it was the commercial collapse of 1857 that registered discontent most decisively, bringing discussion of unemployment more and more to the forefront.[36]

The cruel impact of the economic downturn occasioned perhaps the first mass protests of the obviously organized unemployed in the Canadian colonies. Upward of three thousand Quebec City out-of-work labourers, many of them shipwrights and other workers employed in the building of vessels, convened St. Roch protest meetings, marched through the streets of Lower Town, and demanded work, not alms. Recognizing that their wageless plight was "the effect of 'the crisis' upon the shipbuilding interest," the demonstrations of the workless, however moderate and often contradictory (rejecting alms they could also plead for bread and charitable relief from sources of government or private citizens), generated a mixed response on the part of the powerful. Newspapers could side with the demands of the workless, urging the colonial government to provide significant relief for the labouring poor, but as protests continued reporting took on a more critical tone, with headlines such as "More Mob Demonstrations."[37]

The crash of 1857 had a devastating effect on Toronto. Nineteenth-century commentators recorded the extent of the crisis, conveying how wagelessness was now associated with incorrigibility and criminality:

> Old established houses smashed like glass bottles, and mercantile credit erelong reached a state of collapse. Manufactures of all kinds were smitten by paralysis, and our streets swarmed with discharged operatives who could find no employment. Railway enterprise was at an end, and those lines already constructed were involved in embarrassments from which there seemed no possibility of extrication.... So depressed was trade, and so scarce was money during this direful year, that hundreds of persons in our city who had theretofore enjoyed all the ordinary comforts of life, for the first time felt the sharp pinch of poverty. There was much suffering and want among the labouring classes, with a corresponding amount of drunkenness, vice, and crime. There is good reason to believe that several persons died from starvation. For the first time in Toronto's history the streets swarmed with mendicants.

Newspapers from the local *Toronto Colonist* to the distant *New York Herald* noted the profusion of beggars, the former claiming that "the sturdy applicant for alms" was now ubiquitous: "They dodge you round corners, they follow you into shops, they are found at the church steps, they are at the door of the theatre, they infest the entrance to every bank, they crouch in the lobby of the post office, they assail you in every street, knock at your private residence, walk into your place of business." Asserting that "begging has assumed the dignity of a craft," the *Colonist* complained, "Whole families sally forth, and have their appointed rounds; children are taught to dissemble, to tell a lying tale of misery and woe, and to beg or steal as occasion offers." A correspondent for the *Herald* was more succinct, expressing his surprise at the profusion of beggars: "You cannot go into the streets without annoyance from them," he groused.[38]

Not surprisingly, Police Register records indicate that in 1857 alone, one in nine Toronto residents was arrested and brought before the police magistrate. Areas of the Don River Valley were emerging, by the 1850s, as Jennifer L. Bonnell shows in her recently published environmental history, as something of an urban frontier underworld, a repository for "urban discards," for sewage and industrial wastes, on the one hand, and, on the other, for the human "refuse" of the new commercial age's crisis-driven, alienating political economy. The prisoners of the Don Jail and the inmates of the adjacent House of Refuge were but the most visible of a growing population of Toronto transients and vagrants, many of whom frequented the wooded hillsides and river flats of the Don Valley as a way of establishing distance between themselves and the Toronto police. The Brooks Bush Gang, a collection of marginalized men and women who joined work in the dishonourable trades of the city with the street barters, coerced extortions, and the licentiousness of this developing community of the dispossessed gained notoriety in the 1850s and 1860s. The Gang was, among other things, the criminalized expression of the social turmoil paralleling the uncertain beginnings of a market in labour, in which the late 1850s was scarred by one of developing capitalism's periodic crises. Jesse Edgar Middleton's 1923 multi-volume official history of Toronto declared cryptically, "Much disorder was caused by railway construction laborers between 1852 and 1860."[39]

Over the course of the 1850s, the House of Industry reported that the number of people seeking relief doubled, and the municipality upped its grant to the refuge by 100 percent. Relief and regulation of the poor were also expanding. Immigration agents attended to the newly arrived, providing bread, temporary shelter, passage money, and information relevant to settlement and employment. A House of Providence soon outstripped the Toronto House of Industry in terms of those it sheltered, with the annual collective days stay of the poor in the former totalling 45,722 compared to 27,863 for the latter in 1872. But the House of Industry also expanded its operations, opening a soup kitchen for the poor in the late 1850s. An Orphans' Home, Boys and Girls Homes, and a Female Aid Society supplemented the charitable role of the House of Industry by the 1860s. But Toronto's Poor House still received the largest provincial grant of any such institution in Ontario, its annual subsidy of $2900 amounting to 10.5 cents for each inmate's daily stay. With small towns and villages in Toronto's hinterland urging their poor to seek relief at the

House of Industry, the Poor House served an increasingly mobile population of the poor, some of whom came not only from across Ontario but also from Europe and the United States. Bishop Strachan suggested, in 1857, that Toronto, with its "central position has become a sort of reservoir, and a place of refuge to the indigent from all parts of the Province." It was in this context that Toronto's House of Industry first introduced, in the early 1860s, a work test, implementing a woodcutting regime. "By these means," the Board boasted, it was pleased to report, "it has materially lessened the number of applicants for relief made by the lazy and the drunken."

There was growing discontent among the small and concentrated bureaucratized, managerial officialdom that monitored the funding and activities of houses of industry and providence. Langmuir, for instance, disapproved of Toronto's refuge even being called a "House of Industry." No industry, he claimed, took place within its walls, the suggestion being that the poor should indeed be made to labour for their bed and breakfast. Such institutions were "Poor-houses and nothing but that." Langmuir also suggested that absolute reliance on provincial funding was misplaced, since he believed it was well established that "every Municipality shall take care of its own poor." He further regretted that a generalized permissiveness undermined the good an institutionalized response to poverty and wagelessness might accomplish, bemoaning the lack of more compulsory measures. A common refrain echoing throughout reports of the trustees of the House of Industry in the 1850s and 1860s was the necessity of disciplining the public to accept the institutionalization of poor relief within the domain of publicly supported responsible agencies. This meant curtailing private charitable acts as well as limiting the role of an overarching state. Thus local maintenance was combined with the centralized authority of bodies like the House of Industry. "The managers cannot too strongly urge upon their patrons and the public in general the necessity of refusing to give to those vagrants who may apply to them in the streets or at the private residences of the charitable," wrote Toronto's trustees of the House of Industry in 1861, continuing on, "As this institution is established for the express purpose of assisting the destitute and the deserving poor in our midst, it is desired that all such applicants be sent to the House, where they would, upon being ascertained that they were deserving, receive a donation of coal, bread, and soup." Largely responsible for the Ontario Charity Aid Act of 1874, Langmuir elaborated a political economy of poor relief rooted in the belief that "unless we desire to see local Poor Houses *mainly* supported by Government but *entirely* controlled by municipalities or private boards, the principle that further Government aid to such establishments should depend upon the amount they obtain from the general public, cannot be yielded."[40]

In the aftermath of the destabilizing consequences of the 1840s and 1850s, especially the crisis unleashed with the commercial crash of 1857, state formation in Canada culminated in what Langmuir would later describe as "one of the most complete charitable and correctional systems on the continent." This was part and parcel of what Michael B. Katz, Michael J. Doucet, and Mark J. Stern have called "the social organization of early industrial capitalism."[41] The long recessionary downturn of 1873–96, punctuated by acute crises in the 1870s and 1890s, however, pressured this system to its break point. The wageless proliferated. They began to challenge seriously both the increasingly oppressive conditions imposed on them by economic depression and the demands for compulsion that were inevitably at work in a relief order that could not accommodate the expanding numbers of indigent families and out-of-work labourers. New kinds of resistance emerged.

The Underside of the Great Upheaval, 1873–1896

The years 1873–96 witnessed the culmination of Toronto's nineteenth-century industrial-capitalist revolution. In tandem, it experienced the unmistakable growth of workers' organizations, political mobilizations, and protests, including strikes, fully 122 of a national total of 425 fought over the course of the 1880s being waged in Toronto. Labour newspapers like the *Ontario Workman* and the *Palladium of Labor* anchored themselves in Toronto, just as the Nine-Hour League and the Canadian Labour Union in the 1870s and the Knights of Labor and the Trades and Labor Congress of Canada played significant roles in the now bustling manufacturing metropolis, which boasted a population approaching two hundred thousand by the end of the nineteenth century. This was the unmistakable expression of a working-class presence that, however much it was accommodated to the logic of capitalist class relations and the disciplines of the wage, did indeed challenge the hegemony of both employers and their often servile state.[42]

Since waged life was never entirely separable from wageless life, the articulation of proletarian interests through organizations of labour, demands for improved conditions in workplaces, and the

The salaried, the judiciary, and the Church on the back of the poor working class.

Grip, January 19, 1878, J. W. Bengough.

SITTING ON THE POOR MAN !
OR, THE INJUSTICE OF EXEMPTION.

withdrawal of waged services, it follows that further expressions of working-class protest would also surface, not at the point of production, but against the coercions of non-production. In this latter struggle, the entrenched ideologies of British Poor Law discourse figured forcefully. The "undeserving poor" were to be subject to the laws of "less eligibility," stipulating that relief would only be made available to those among the wageless who *would* work for their aid, which could only be dispensed in ways that made it even less attractive than what could be secured by the worst-paid unskilled labour. Toronto's *Globe* made all of this abundantly clear in an 1877 manifesto-like declaration on the wageless:

> We do not advocate a system which could leave them to starve, but we do say that if they are ever to be taught economical and saving habits, they must understand that the public have no idea of making them entirely comfortable in the midst of their improvidence and dissipation. If they wish to secure that they must work for it and save and plan. Such comfort is not to be had by loafing around the tavern door, or fleeing to charity at every pinch.

Three years earlier, the 1873 depression as its backdrop, the same newspaper denounced any "poor law as a legislative machine for the manufacture of pauperism. It is true mercy to say that it would be better that a few individuals should die of starvation than a pauper class should be raised up with thousands devoted to crime and the victims of misery."[43]

Over the course of the long downturn of the late nineteenth century, evidence of the precariousness of working-class life was unambiguous; the stereotype of improvidence and dissipation as *defining* elements of wagelessness was revealed as a caricature. Crisis-induced contractions in the labour market compounded seasonal lay-offs, technology-ordered dilutions of skill and erosions of secure work, and what seemed an almost endlessly arbitrary series of dips in the business cycle. As the winter of 1873 approached, the poet laureate of Montreal's poor, Joe Beef's Canteen-owner Charles McKiernan, penned an ode to the hard times in his patented doggerel verse:

> I must tell you that Kingston is dead. Quebec is
> Dying and out of Montreal, Ottawa and Toronto hundreds are flying
> In the country parts unless you can
> Parlez-vous. There is nothing for you to do

> And in John's office it is all the cry
> No Union printers for work need apply
> And if the landlord his rent you cannot
> Pay your sewing machine he will take
> Away.

McKiernan could only conclude: "So in the fall God help the/Poor of Montreal."[44]

A floating mass of workless males generated intensified panic as the depression of 1873 deepened before finally abating at the end of the decade. Masses of migrant labourers, ostensibly travelling to secure illusive waged employment, became the scourge of small towns and large cities alike. Welcomed with the lock-up and public derision in the press, tramps were criminalized and vilified, socially constructed as thieves and denigrated as "pests," "voracious monsters," "outrageously impertinent," an "irrepressible stampede" deserving of "a well-aimed dose of buckshot rubbed in well with salt-petre" and other forms of vigilante, lynch law. In Lindsay, Ontario, roughly ninety miles from Toronto and studied by Richard Anderson, the local newspaper (the *Canadian Post)* carried over one hundred news items relating to tramps in the years 1874–78. Their tone was almost universally derogatory, and tramps were in general depicted as an outcast stratum rarely interested in finding employment, poor because they were "work-shy and degenerate." Many, riding the rails, were en route to Toronto, where institutions like the House of Providence became "so overcrowded that many deserving poor and destitute had to be denied admittance." The *Globe,* commenting on the situation in 1875, bemoaned "the great destitution from men being out of employment," adding that applications to houses of refuge often had to be refused "as much from want of room as other necessities." Annual reports of Toronto's House of Industry in 1877 and 1878 detailed the extraordinary relief bill, attributing it to "the extreme commercial depression that has existed for some time past," warning of the need to avoid "direct encouragement of pauperism." In the same years, Toronto's gaols reported sheltering over twelve hundred "waifs" annually, and the Board of the House of Industry suggested that the distribution of relief might usefully be placed under "the supervision of the police."[45]

If the 1880s saw the economy struggle out of its 1870s doldrums, the recovery was anything but robust, and the migratory jobless continued to unsettle respectable society, as established in a study by James Pitsula. "Felix" wrote to the Knights of Labor newspaper, the *Palladium of Labor,* detailing how "hundreds of blacksmiths, machinists, and other mechanics … are today—through no fault of theirs—part and parcel of the great army of tramps." Toronto's mainstream newspapers, however, competed against one another to see who could push denunciations of the "loafing aristocracy" to new extremes, calling for the expulsion of tramps from the city, judicious use of the lash against those for whom work was "their aversion," and advocated a vigilant police monitoring of peripatetic vagrants given to "murders, burglaries, incendiaries, and highway robberies." To colour the discussion with a religious hue, a writer to the *Canadian Presbyterian* took aim at "the exacting demands" and impertinent dissatisfactions of those "vicious" improvident people who posed a burden on all responsible citizens. Hostile to any suggestion that the voluntarism of charity be replaced by legal obligation, this correspondent declared, "It will be a sad day for Canada when this course is adopted, for all experience goes to show that nothing is more efficient as a pauper-maker than legal provision for the support of the poor." A little "hard labour," suggested the *Globe,* would do this "dissipated" and "shiftless" element good since the Poor House had become increasingly lax in enforcing earlier expectations that those seeking accommodations for the night would chop wood for their food and lodging.

THE "DEPRESSION COMMITTEE" SIMPLIFIED.

The Depression of the 1870s.

Grip, April 29, 1876, J. W. Bengough.

Conditions in the cramped House worsened, with complaints of its "sickening smell" being made by municipal officials inspecting the premises; the *Globe* described the ward in which the overnight poor slept, often on the bare floor because beds could not be kept clean, as like "a carload of hogs in transit." The homeless were said to be packed into the wayfarer's lodge "apartments," thirty or forty strong, "as thickly packed as herring in a barrel." Toronto's Associated Charities pressed new forms of "labour tests" in 1881–85 as a prerequisite for relief, requiring tramps to break stone. Many found stone-breaking too onerous; they left the yard rather than undergo the rigours of the "labour test." At the House of Industry, the Associated Charities crusade to force the refuge to adopt similar unwaged work requirements proved futile, even though the House had in the past required manual labour from all of those who availed themselves of indoor relief. Instead the poorhouse concentrated on establishing an expanded wayfarer's lodge in 1884–85, where large numbers of indigent men could be put up for the night in a casual ward, their bodies soaked in a hot bath, their heads doused in vermin-killing liquid solution, and their clothes fumigated, "cleansed and classified" in the vernacular of poor relief officialdom, which was not above padding the expense claims of meagre breakfasts consisting of tea and six ounces of bread. But the growing number of habitual tramps furnished with temporary board and lodging by the House of Industry in the mid-1880s necessitated adoption of a modified "labour test," if only to deter the shiftless and physically weak from staying in the expanded casual ward of the refuge too long. Making inmates saw a quarter-cord of wood, a job that took the able-bodied and reasonably dexterous approximately three hours before they were allowed to lunch on a watery bowl of soup and a hunk of bread (managers insisted that it was not their responsibility to provide the workless with "sumptuous fare"), had its effect, as Pitsula shows. Those checking into the wayfarer's lodge declined from totals of 730 in 1886 to 548 in 1889. The worsening economic climate of the depressed 1890s saw an expanded need for the House of Industry's relief, however, and the casual ward was opened for the summer as well as winter months. The numbers of casuals staying at the House thus soared, climbing to highs of 1700 in 1891 and 1500 in 1895 and 1897, rarely falling below 1200. The average contingent sleeping at the House per night never dipped below 60 between 1890 and 1897, when a high of 100 was reached (a comparable figure for 1880–85 had been roughly 26). In 1891, 832 casuals stayed in the wayfarer's lodge of Toronto's House of Industry for two or three nights, while 415 lodged in the poor house for more than three days; 24 hardcore recidivists spent more than 100 nights in the refuge.[46]

The economies of this crisis of wagelessness drove the ideology and practice of poor relief in more disciplinary directions. Reverend Arthur H. Baldwin, the rector of Toronto's All Saints Church and one of the House of Industry's most outspoken trustees, gave evidence at the Toronto sessions of the Royal Commission on Prisons and the Reformatory System in November 1890. Baldwin provided notice that Toronto's premier institution of poor relief was not interested in continuing "the loafing system that is now going on," stressing that a more rigorous "work test" than that of cutting wood was needed if the encouragement of pauperism was to be avoided. "It seems a great pity," he pontificated, "that these people should be allowed to go in and dwell [in the casual ward] and do nothing but cut a little wood, as we insist upon their doing." Baldwin's words were no doubt valued by John W. Langmuir, who presided over the prison and reformatory system inquiry, and was long a sceptic of the coddling ways of Houses of Industry. Langmuir drew on no less of an authority than Queen Victoria to argue that,

To-day vagrancy is perhaps as great a nuisance in Ontario as in any state of the Union. Many of the lazy and worthless amongst our own people have adopted it as a profession. Under the system of assisted passages many have been brought to Canada from Europe who never intended to make a living by honest labour.

Toronto, especially in the winter, with its sheltered social assistance, had become the "chief... quarters of the army of tramps that infest this Province," wrote Langmuir in his report, noting that experience had taught the jobless that they could get by in summer by "doing small jobs, by begging, or by pilfering," and as colder weather set in they had merely to follow the well-worn tracks to Toronto's offerings. Baldwin testified in the same vein:

> These men are like bees, they go out through the country in the summer time and they are as great a curse to the Canadian farmer then as they are to us in the winter time. It is idleness that they are looking for and not work. They pretend to be in search of work and when a farmer gives them anything to do they leave him in a lurch and go away at an awkward time. We have 100 people who come to us winter after winter, and then in the summer time they go out and feed on the Canadian farmers. I think that something ought to be done to put an end to this state of things.[47]

A new labour regime was clearly in the offing.

Toronto's three main houses of refuge (the House of Industry, the House of Providence, and the Home for Incurables) expended over $63,000 on the jobless in 1893 alone. Only one-third of this amount had been secured through government grants, the remainder coming from private contributions. During the depression of the early 1890s, the number of families receiving outdoor relief from the House of Industry almost doubled, with many relying on this social assistance for prolonged periods. The 1893–94 Annual Report of the House of Industry indicated that 2,343 families comprising 10,685 persons

The charity season.
Grip, January 1, 1881.

THE CHARITY SEASON.
ON AN ERRAND OF "GENEROSITY!"

received outdoor relief, with more than half of these domestic units drawing sustenance for periods ranging from one to four years.[48]

Families relying on outdoor relief were one thing, but with the crisis of the 1890s swelling the numbers of vagrants appearing at the House of Industry's expanded casual lodge, looking for shelter, the imposition of work requirements for those "out of work" became an ideological as well as a material imperative. "Since the House of Industry has enlarged its capacity for taking in vagrants," testified Toronto's Chief of Police, Lieutenant-Colonel H. J. Grasett, before a Royal Commission in 1890, "we send them there ... otherwise they might be frozen to death." Amid the belt-tightening necessitated by the downturn, the disciplining of an invigorated "labour test" had decided attractions for those overseeing relief. Enforcing a more taxing expectation of the work ethic, exertion had the advantage of weeding out the undeserving poor, whose refusal of manual labour marked them as slothful and relegated them to fend for themselves in the economy of the waged, confirming that the unavailability of paid employment was less important than the failure of certain individuals to rise to its legitimate demands. So far had this thinking proceeded in the early 1890s that Toronto's House of Industry trustees were of a mind that the workless be criminalized, rehabilitated by being sent to a penal work colony:

> Hitherto we have brought the tramp up to a certain stage in recovering industrious inclinations, but we have allowed him to slip through our hands before those inclinations have been formed in habits of industry. What the Board now aims at is the establishment of a labour colony, to which all able-bodied chronic mendicants should be committed with interminate sentences.

Such an orientation also had material ramifications. Those among the out-of-work whose character defects prohibited them from labouring for their relief also lessened the rising material expenditure—the *non-wage bill*—of the charitable counter-offensive, which always had as one of its fundamental purposes obfuscating conscious appreciation of capitalism *as* crisis. As "work tests" became more stringent at Toronto's House of Industry over the course of the 1890s, "numbers refused relief on this account and doubtless many others refrained from making applications, hearing that the management resolved to apply the test without exception to all able to work."[49]

The shifting labour requirements expected of casuals lodging with Toronto's House of Industry were perhaps most clearly revealed in the change from wood-cutting to the more onerous stone-breaking. "Until the vagrant is offered some alternative that even he will recognize as more unpleasant and disagreeable than work," claimed the Board of the House of Industry in 1891–92, "the tramp trouble will never be cured." Cutting wood wasn't cutting it: relatively few refused this "labour test." Between 1891 and 1895, according to Pitsula's calculations from the *Annual Reports of the House of Industry,* 29,652 requests of the indigent to cut wood were complied with, while a bare 432 refusals were registered. In 1896, when the stone-breaking regime was implemented, the situation altered dramatically: only 792 completed the task of stone-breaking, compared to 1202 who refused to undertake the "labour test." As indicated by the vagrancy convictions of John Curry and Thomas Wilson in January 1896, those who refused stone-breaking assignments were soon subject to confinement. Magistrate Denison sentenced this duo, who said they preferred jail to the new "labour test," to a three-month term in the refuge of their choice. One month later, upping the ante, City Alderman Jolliffe introduced a motion making it mandatory for all able-bodied applicants for relief in Toronto applying for outdoor assistance to break a yard of stone in return for their coal subsidy, doubling the amount of work required to receive winter fuel. "The stonepile," as Pitsula concludes, had become "an emblem for the work ethic."

Those who demonstrated insufficient commitment to the regime of labour discipline were to be criminalized. When Reverend Baldwin was asked at the hearings into prisons and reformatory systems in Ontario in 1890 whether or not it would be a good idea to turn the House of Industry into a correctional facility, he replied authoritatively: "I think it would be a great advantage to the city." Indeed, Baldwin already suggested many among the workless could well be using gaols as refuges of first, rather than last, resort, because "these people ... find the gaol ten times more comfortable than our [House of Industry] quarters." The good Reverend made it absolutely clear that the primary concern was not necessarily the relief of the poor and the homeless but, rather, their elimination from Toronto, something that would not be accomplished if the indigent were pampered: "I do not see how we can get rid of them if we continue to give them charity. To keep them in comfortable quarters and to allow them to live in idleness is not a way to get rid of them." In 1889, of the roughly 12,500 people committed to Ontario's gaols, fully 2,165 were there on the grounds of vagrancy. The gaols, according to another authority, were "used for the reception of the aged and the infirm who are committed as vagrants," and during the depression of 1893–94, with Toronto besieged by tramps, police stations reported that "night after night these casuals were received" at their cells.[50]

A war against the tramps was clearly being waged in the name of morality and the disciplining power of relief. The *Toronto Evening Star* fired on the poor in an editorial volley:

> "If ye work not, neither shall ye eat", has, as dictum the sanction of the Holy Writ. Nothing can be more demoralizing than giving alms to men who are quite able to work, but very unwilling. At the instance of Ald. Jolliffe, the management of the House of Industry, one of the most costly and important of the Toronto charities, obtained from the City Council a large quantity of stone, with the intention of having it broken by the "casuals", who resort thither for out-door or indoor relief. The complaint of these people generally is that they can find no work to do, and are, therefore, forced to beg. The truth, as tested experiment is that very few of them are willing to work, while all are willing to depend on charity for their living. The discouraging result of the labor test in the House of Industry, so far from causing abandonment of the experiment, ought to impress on the City Council the absolute and urgent necessity of making a more general application of it. . . . While we have nothing but words of praise for the many excellent men and women who do so much to relieve distress, we have no toleration for that good natured, shiftlessness which prompts soft-hearted and soft-headed people to add to the demoralization of those who are already paupers in spirit. The best tonic for them is a strong daily dose of hard, manual labor, with a threat of starvation on the one hand, and the inducement of decent living on the other.[51]

Such thinking was echoed in many quarters, the *Globe* prefacing an 1890s discussion of unemployment with the comment that some of the out-of-work led lives of dissipation. "A predisposition to idleness is the birthright of not a few," it editorialized knowingly. Thomas Conant voiced all-too-common prejudices in his *Upper Canada Sketches*, asking bluntly "whether the hard-working and the thrifty ought to be taxed to provide for the lazy and the thriftless. Or again, is it wise to foster the growth of a class of persons whose filth and foul diseases are the result of laziness and their own vices." As the *All Saints Church Parish Magazine* declared authoritatively in 1895, this problem had to be tackled forthrightly. A simple solution beckoned: the labour test. "We should at the outset aim to separate the worthy from the unworthy poor," insisted the religious organ. "Probably the work test is the best means of sifting out the lazy imposters."[52]

WANTED---PROTECTION!!

Factories closing, the worker/unemployed bludgeoned, the state an idle spectator.

Grip, February 26, 1876, J. W. Bengough.

Protesting "Labour Tests"

The war against the dispossessed was not waged one-sidedly. Not only was stone-breaking unpopular, but the refusal to comply with the more stringent "labour test" occasioned organized protests by the poor. The rush of refusals in 1896 could not have happened without discussions and deliberations on the part of the wageless. Consequences of their recalcitrance were quite severe. For the single unemployed men, 65–75 percent of whom came from outside Toronto,[53] this tramps' refusal to break stone left them homeless, without visible means of support and sustenance. Family men seeking outdoor relief in the form of food and fuel put themselves, their wives, and children at risk with their refusals. And yet not only did they bolt from stone-breaking, but some of the indigent gathered outside of city hall to protest against Jolliffe's motion. An unidentified spokesman, described as "loud speaking" and "a strong hulk fellow," spoke for his out-of-work counterparts: "And they calls that charity, do they? Got to crack a heap o' stones for what yer get. Ain't no charity in that es' I can see."[54]

"Cracking the stone" was not only representative of the disciplining powers of relief dispensation. It also proved, in Toronto's 1890s, a limit on what the dispossessed would endure. Tramps continued to refuse to break stone into the winter of 1897, and there remained those who required outdoor relief who simply would not comply with the House of Industry's demanded "labour test," digging in their heels and insisting that they would rather steal than undergo the degradation of the ordeal.[55]

The rebellion of stone-breaking refusal in the 1890s was, to be sure, a minor event, but it signalled a shift in the activities of the workless, which took a more organized and collective turn in the depression of 1873–77 and its immediate aftermath. With industrialists acknowledging that "fifty percent of the manufacturing population of the country are out of work," and fledgling newspapers of the organized working class addressing unemployment and its evils, it was but a short step to deputations of the jobless marching in demand of some redress.[56]

In Montreal, two thousand unemployed demonstrated and paraded in December 1875, their protests taking on the character, according to historian David Thompson, of a bread riot. Demanding "Work or Bread," the unruly crowds also threatened "Blood." The *Montreal Star* asked, "Is it a Revolution?" A few years later, in 1878, Jean-Philip Mathieu has shown how riotous crowds congregated at Quebec City public work sites, their boisterous demands threatening constituted authority: "we want work, we want bread, if we can't have work and bread, we want blood." A newspaper warned that such disturbances proved

> that, unconsciously, we have been harbouring in our usually peaceful community a set of foreign revolutionary and Communistic characters who have tainted the lower orders of society with their dangerous principles, and, availing themselves of an exceptional period of commercial depression and consequent distress among the poor, have so worked upon rash and thoughtless minds as to foster, and, so to say, establish a discontented and turbulent spirit, which only needs the occasion to manifest itself in new and repeated excesses.[57]

Ottawa, as Debi Wells has shown in an unpublished thesis, became a centre of a late 1870s agitation, which began in April 1877 and reached into 1880. The capital was a natural enough location for this developing mobilization of the wageless given parliament's proximity and the possibility of federal politicians voting funds for expanded public works.[58] Over the course of the winter of 1879–80, Ottawa newspapers bristled with accounts of petitions, marches, torchlit processions, and other gatherings of hundreds of "unemployed workingmen." Editorials chastened those who were described as looking "needy and seemed determined to get work or fight," claiming that the government could not be expected to provide for them and that Canada was not a land of "State Socialism."[59]

To be sure, the unemployed protests of 1873–80 were seldom unambiguous stands of unity expressing a solidarity of the waged and the wageless. Much of the respectable labour discourse of dissent in these years still clung to an ideology of the deserving versus undeserving poor. Too much was conceded to the antiquated and class-compromised assumptions of earlier Poor Law perspectives. And in this era, labour racism was never far from the resentments against mainstream politicians who, while glorying in the nation-building exploits of the Canadian Pacific Railroad, seemed to care little for the plight of the workingman. The unemployed of 1880 protested the fairness of suggesting that mechanics in Canada's capital "leave the city" of Ottawa when they had contributed so much to "building it up." They buttressed this legitimate argument with angry statements far less salutary: "It was nonsense to ask residents of the city to go away west and live with Indians and half-breeds, and to work upon the railway in British Columbia, competing with Chinese cheap labour."[60]

Throughout the 1870s and 1880s many a voice was raised against the flooding of Canada with pauper immigrants, and the ways in which this divided the waged and the wageless, the native-born Canadian and the newly arrived, even the local resident and the outsider, were extensive. Thus Toronto's Board of the House of Industry insisted, amid the "tramp crisis" of the depression of the 1870s, that if "induced to emigrate," the newly arrived poor "should be provided employment in the country, they should not be allowed to hang about our cities, as a nucleus and encouragement to a pauper population." A decade later the *Globe* surveyed the casual ward of the House of Industry at 9:30 p.m., acknowledging that the conditions in which the transient single men congregated were anything but appealing, "all lying as best they could on the hard boards" of the floors. But who were these men, asked the newspaper?

> To look at them one would say that they are all able to work. Are they willing? In many cases, it is doubtful if they are.... The large proportion of these persons are dissipated, shiftless, and it is to be feared vicious.... How many of these shiftless and apparently utterly broken wrecks belonged to Toronto? Too many, but not nearly all. What is to be done with them? ... They are generally young and strong ... ought they not be forced to earn their living? In any case there seems little use in spending thousands of dollars every year in order to bring out immigrants in many cases merely to swell up the crowd of those weary, tattered, displaced locals. Numbers of these fellows crowd into Toronto and other cities in the winter, and then

in the summer betake themselves to walks in the country, frightening lone
women in solitary farm houses, and laying blackmail in the shape ... of
cash wherever they go.

Such rants assailed the undeserving poor, typecast them as lay-about immigrants
and dangerous sexual predators, and struck the parochial chord of "local" interests
that posed a perennial divide between the urban and the rural, the national and the
international. All of this undoubtedly worked to keep the dispossessed divided, for
such a pedagogy of parochial "protectionism" could not help but structure something of the consciousness of the poor, be they waged or wageless, born in Canada
or newly arrived in the country.[61]

Nonetheless, the trajectory of labouring experience in the 1880s was *toward*
a more inclusive sense of the collectivity of class experience, the common interests
of skilled and unskilled, and, as a consequence, the importance of addressing not
only the struggles of the waged but also the plight of the wageless. This demanded,
as the Knights of Labor promoted with its understanding of "one big union" of all
workers, organization.[62]

Labour reform intellectuals of the 1880s, such as Toronto's Phillips
Thompson, were acutely aware of the ongoing nature of capitalist crisis, of the economic system's insatiable appetite for accumulation, and of how that acquisitive
individualism could only be fed on the contributions of labour and the despoliation
of the working class:

> The wheels of industry and commerce revolve at high pressure, and short-
> sighted politicians and publicists are loud in their congratulations on the
> prosperity of the country, ignoring entirely the fact that all this crowding
> on of sail and expenditure of surplus productive energy is simply prepar-
> ing the way for the inevitable return of hard times. The inflation period is
> generally of short duration. Present demands are soon supplied, and goods
> again begin to accumulate in the factories and warehouses. The competi-
> tion between producers is no longer as to which shall turn out goods most
> rapidly and in greatest volume, but which shall sell the cheapest. Produc-
> tion slackens, wages fall, employés are discharged. Enforced economy
> diminishes the purchasing power and causes further stringency and greater
> distress among workers, and so the vicious circle is completed. Those who,
> reluctantly in some cases and willingly in others, crowded two days work
> into one, now think themselves fortunate to obtain one day's work in two.

TORONTO'S POOR

"Capitalism has created a monster which threatens to destroy the classes, if not the system, that gave it life," Thompson wrote. "The number of men and women who cannot get work on any terms implies a far larger class whose pay has become a mere pittance." Thompson's *The Politics of Labor* (1886) sought to break down the separations of the skilled and unskilled, and eradicate, to some degree, the barriers to working-class solidarity erected by gendered and racialized prejudice, not to mention craft exclusion. Against the constant appeals of capitalist competition, Thompson posed the possibilities of true working-class co-operation. "Where is the advantage of cheapness of production to the army of the unemployed and half-employed, or to those whose labor has been so cheapened by competition that their purchasing power is correspondingly lessened?" he asked, the question itself an acknowledgement of how proletarians necessarily shared the fruits, bitter and sweet, of always confronting the possibility of being waged and being wageless. The half-employed, the cheapeningly employed, and the unemployed—for Thompson this was the army that would march against capital. This was, arguably, the beginning of a union of the dispossessed.[63]

As this union struggled, against all odds, to realize itself in the 1880s, evidence of how the lives of the waged and the wageless shaded into one another surfaced in many quarters. Toronto workers surveyed by the Bureau of Industries at the end of the decade averaged only forty-four weeks of employment a year—if they happened to find work six days a week. This was in the best of times. For many workers, as Sager and Baskerville have pointed out, being out of work for a goodly part of every year was the norm. By the end of the century, at least one out of five urban Canadian workers was wageless at some point in the year regardless of whether the times were lean or fat. Testimony before the Royal Commission on the Relations of Labor and Capital in the late 1880s, from both employers and workers, made it abundantly clear that few industrial establishments, building projects, and transportation endeavours paid workers for more than eight to ten months of any given year. The Toronto House of Industry accommodated tramps, to be sure, but to the extent that the migratory wageless who depended on its shelter and subsistence fare can be classified occupationally, skilled workers were not far behind unskilled labourers in lining up for relief. Toronto printers claimed that thirty percent of their number were without work in the 1890s. "I am not alone in my trouble," declared one Toronto unemployed father of six in 1891, "There are two hundred members of the union to which I belong in the same position as myself." If the organization of the wageless was not dramatic in this period, it had nonetheless surfaced and made particular kinds of statements.[64]

At one of the 1880 Ottawa demonstrations of the unemployed, a black flag was unfurled by protest leader Finlay Ross, who also suggested hanging the prime minister in effigy. As a fitting symbol, the black flag, claimed by French revolutionary anarchist Louise Michel to be the banner of both striking proletarians and all those suffering want and hunger, signified for the angry workers who marched under it the possibility of death. This was the wages of the war on the dispossessed. But if those out of work understood that their own death by starvation might well be imminent, they shook their defiant fists in the face of authority and vowed "death to the government" that they claimed was responsible for their destitution. Carrying such a provocative symbol, insisted some who urged the presentation of a more cautious public face, might well lead to the jobless being "clubbed by the Police and shot down like dogs."[65]

Toronto's nine-teenth-century house of industry, Elm Street & Eliza-beth Street.

In February 1891, a Toronto procession protest of the wageless also carried a black flag, this one emblazoned with the words "Work or Bread." The mid-week march convened on St. Andrew's Square after an "innocent-looking paragraph" in an evening newspaper summoned the out-of-work to rally at 9:30 a.m. Accounts of the size of the demonstration varied, from reports of 1,000 to estimates stating that an original gathering of 500 started on a march to city hall and as it made its way "through the principal business streets the crowd swelled until it numbered 3,000." According to one account, "Mechanics were there in plenty who have not worked for months and see but little prospect of doing so." One of the unemployed declared: "There are many others hungry, but they could not trample same under their feet and walk with us." Some of the out-of-work, who were described as "of middle age, while a good number were well bent with years," were reluctant to admit that they had appealed to the public purse for the first time in their lives. Something of a late nineteenth-century "media event" in Toronto, the "Black Flag demonstration" elicited much comment in local newspapers and discussion of it even appeared in the pages of the *New York Times*. Liberal newspapers like Toronto's *Globe* editorialized on "The Unemployed," seeing the cause of their misery in the failings of Conservative economic policy. The country's leading Tory spokesman, Sir John A. Macdonald, castigated the complaining workingmen. Protest marches proceeded, in his view, under "a grievous misapprehension ... suffering from hallucination." The *Globe* pointed out that Toronto's real estate bubble had burst, that there were no jobs in the construction trades with speculative development grinding to a halt, and that buildings were sitting unoccupied. Other trades, such as iron moulding, were supposedly victims of the protective tariff that restricted markets for Canadian-made goods, forcing Toronto's foundries to cut back on production, driving tradesmen to the United States to look for work. According to one iron moulder, fully 157 of his 300 co-workers had gone on the proverbial tramp, seeking employment south of the border. Partisanship aside, even the *Globe* concluded that capitalism's regime of accumulation had an underside of impoverishment and dispossession: "The National Policy and such a land boom as our city has lately experienced mean wealth to a few and to the many a procession under the black flag."

In the *Labor Advocate*, this understanding of unemployment was posed even more unambiguously: "the increase of wealth and of poverty bear the relations of cause and effect and the reason why so many are starving is because others have superfluous wealth, which they have not earned." C. Wesley wrote to the *Advocate* about "the spectacle that was witnessed in our so-called pious city of Toronto of the unemployed with the black flag marching through the streets asking for bread or work." He was irate that in a city with so many churches people "went on praying while the poor unfortunates went on starving." A day of reckoning was coming. "So long, sir, as we tolerate high-priced canting clergymen, monopolist combines, trusts, or so-called intelligent men that applaud any clap-trap that is written in the press or spoken on the public platform," argued Wesley, the "bitter cry that went forth in France years ago" would inevitably come to Canada. Under the black flag in Toronto walked the ghost of the Paris Commune.

The jobless crowd that marched in Toronto's February 1891 protest was indeed agitated and angry, animated by class resentments. One of its leaders, James Lawlor, struck a note of demand rather than an appeal for alms: "What we want is the immortal loaf; we do not want charity; but when it comes to this we must show aristocracy and monopolies what distress exists in this city." The assembled crowd grew progressively more vocal and aggressive as Mayor Clarke, a veteran of the 1872 Toronto printers' strike whom many among the unemployed likely regarded as a fellow workingman, lapsed into the usual platitudes. At first, Clarke seemed sympathetic and promised that the City would look into finding wages for the wageless. But soon Toronto's chief official was telling the protesters that there were no more public works projects that could be funded. Clarke's remarks, delivered from the steps of city hall, drew forceful heckling and a heated exchange with J. Britton, one of the organizers of the march. Britton warned the Mayor "that if there is no work during the next two days there may be violence." Clarke's admonition to remain peaceful elicited a strong response. "Necessity knows no law," came the forceful reply. The assembled jobless were insistent that the need was for immediate work to feed "dependant famil[ies]." Departing city hall, the crowd made its way up Jarvis Street, "one of the principal residential thoroughfares of the city, to show the wealthy citizens ... how many were starving in the midst of plenty." The workmen promised to "march through [the] city for three days and demand work," and another smaller demonstration took place the next day, although it did not produce the "increased numbers" predicted. Fears of trouble dissipated as the City Council coughed up $15,000 for public relief work.

To be sure, the 1891 demonstration did not bridge all of the significant gaps separating those who felt themselves deserving because of their longstanding waged status and those who, as habitués of the House of Industry, might often be perceived as more acclimatized to their wagelessness. One reflection of this was discontent that family men were not being privileged over the single unemployed in the granting of work on some City sewer construction jobs. Such a "breadwinner" argument pitted the "casuals" and tramps of the House of Industry against the out-of-work building tradesmen, moulders and stove mounters, transportation workers, printers, and others who made up the bulk of the February 1891 protesters.[66]

Three years later, during the final winter of an economic downturn that had scarred the social landscape of Toronto for much of the early 1890s, a February–March 1894 uprising of the unemployed revealed, once again, that while protests of the dispossessed were now commonplace, forging a fighting unity proved a fragile and often fleeting endeavour. More than one thousand men were without work in the winter of 1894. So bad was the situation that Lady Aberdeen's National Council of Women lobbied Toronto to set up a temporary employment bureau. Four hundred mechanics promptly enrolled. Yet all the local relief officer could manage to scrounge up in the way of work was a solitary job cleaning out a cellar.[67]

The unemployed protests began in February 1894 as "respectable" and "orderly" appeals for "Work and Not Charity." A mass meeting drawing on a wide range of Toronto's skilled and unskilled labourers convened at St. Andrew's Hall on the Friday morning of February 16, 1894, the 250 out-of-work men determining to march to city hall. On arrival, they seated themselves in the gallery of Council Chambers, and W. T. Atwood, speaking on behalf of the assembled jobless, appealed to Mayor Kennedy: "We are here to ask you as Mayor of Toronto that work be provided to us at once. Some of us are on the verge of starvation, and cannot scrape together a loaf of bread. We want work tomorrow and our pay tomorrow night, so we can get Sunday dinner." Unsatisfied with the "stone-breaking system," which allowed married men the meagre earnings of $1.75 in any given seven-day cycle, the unemployed wanted any new labour requirements to be arranged so that relief would constitute the equivalent of a full two days of work weekly. Other speakers claimed that past practices under the labour-friendly regime of Mayor Howland in the 1880s provided the out-of-work with three days of labour a week during winter. Mayor Kennedy expressed his sympathy, but offered the delegation little in the way of commitments, only promising that there would be an abundance of waged work "in the spring." As the crowd groaned its displeasure, bombastic aldermen climbed on the protest bandwagon, suggesting that $100,000 be earmarked for public works projects and arguing that debentures be floated to bankroll the costs of wages for the unemployed. The mayor, meanwhile, was trying to climb down from the podium, calling an end to the proceedings on the grounds that it was noon and time to eat. A leader of the protest, temperance labour radical Isaac Mills, punctuated this proposal with a rejoinder: "I see we have to live on hope. This meeting is adjourned because it is dinner time. Is it dinner time with all of you? There are thousands of men in Toronto to-day who will have no dinner." Disappointed and dissatisfied, the unemployed dispersed, vowing to meet again that evening at St. Andrew's Hall.[68]

At the meeting that night, the leading figures in the movement exhibited the uneven consciousness of an uncertain movement. They were predictably unappeased by the Toronto Board of Works attempt to placate the protesters with a decision that afternoon to appropriate $5000 for public works. As Atwood, chairing the meeting, declared, this would barely cover two days of relief for the more than one thousand men in need of work and wages. Others speaking from the podium and floor of St. Andrew's Hall, such as Thomas Webb and W. Ward, advocated a mixed bag of enhanced public works, restriction of "cheap foreign labour," and the formation of unions or associations to protect the interests of the jobless. Many in the meeting wanted to appeal to church ministers and the financial elite of the city, and a motion was passed asking the clergy and the rich to "devise a scheme that will relieve the unemployed." This drew responses bordering on the sarcastic from two of the leaders of the mobilization, Atwood and James Boyle. "Toronto was a city of churches," Atwood recognized, but he added the punchline that in his opinion, "hungry people had no use for Christianity." Boyle was more biting, suggesting that "the mission workers ought to give some of their collections to the heathen at home." With calls for unionization punctuated with attacks on alien workers and appeals to the so-called morally and socially superior, the 1894 mobilization of the out-of-work clearly lacked a firm sense of cohesive direction.[69]

A week later the unemployed were growing more restless and resentful of civic authority's inaction. Six to seven hundred surrounded city hall on February 27, 1894, packing into the gallery of the City Council Chambers and overflowing into surrounding vestibules. Designated spokesmen and leaders of the unemployed crowd had difficulty keeping order. Fred Atwood harangued Mayor Kennedy, insisting "We want work at once—not a useless fake like snow cleaning, but productive work." He listed a range of possible public works projects—clearing dead trees out of parks, construction work on the courthouse, subway labour, and digging a tunnel across the bay—but Toronto's chief official stalled and prevaricated, dismissing the possibilities posed. "Boisterous and disorderly," the protest drove the mayor into seclusion behind closed doors, which he refused to open. "We'll smash in the doors and throw the City Hall in the bay," screamed someone in the crowd as cries of "Give us work and money" erupted. Unable to support the stomping throng, city hall began to creak and crack and, with plaster falling from ceilings and walls, a huge beam broke through the flooring. An engineer appeared to warn those causing the uproar that the building had to be cleared. "Let her rip," yelled one malcontent, "It won't be any worse than starving." Chants of "Money, work, or jail," and "tear it down" spoke of the determined resentment of the destitute. Only silver-tongued Alderman Lamb, who had played to the crowd at the previous city hall gathering, managed eventually to divert the hundreds of angry unemployed workers back to St. Andrew's Hall where he "talked them into a good humour."[70]

Now meeting regularly, the 1894 winter mobilization of the jobless had a distinct leadership. It straddled the fence of militant action and struggled to suppress the influence of radicals on the margins of the movement, on the one hand, and keep the agitation on course as fast-talking development hucksters moved in on captive, jobless audiences to offer breathtaking private/public works schemes, on the other.

As three hundred gathered at St. Lawrence Hall at the end of February, established figurehead James Booth declared forcefully from the chair that he had no intention of allowing the meeting to be "perverted from its objects by tricksters, canal schemers, or single tax advocates as it had been last night." This pre-emptive strike was in part aimed at the glib promoter and future mayor Ernest Albert Macdonald, dubbed by two Toronto historians "the mercurial Baron of Chester" because of his noisy building up of the area around Danforth and Broadview. Macdonald had packed the previous meeting of the out-of-work with his vocal hand-raisers so that he could pitch a $345 million private capital venture that he promised would prove a boon to the unemployed. The wild-eyed proposal, which Toronto historian J. E. Middleton marvels managed to have some traction at city hall and within the municipality's engineering department, involved constructing a canal/aqueduct from Georgian Bay via Lake Simcoe to Toronto, bringing clean water and energy to Ontario's metropolis.

Phillips Thompson, the radical Knights of Labor journalist of the 1880s, now embraced socialist politics. He rose to counter Macdonald's scheme by calling for an end to the "competitive commercial system." But Isaac Mills "warned the crowd against going over to anarchism or socialism." With capital infiltrating the movement of the jobless from one side, the *Evening Star* explained that radical collectivism was pressuring it from the other, Mills' remarks probably being "prompted by the fact that socialistic literature was distributed to the men yesterday." All in all, the relatively mainstream leadership of the out-of-work agitation had its hands full.

Calling for order and decorum, Mills noted that if it were to make headway, the unemployed protest would need the support and sympathies of the public. But as Chairman Booth reported, the clergy whose endorsement and aid had been solicited produced a resolution that insulted the out-of-work by suggesting that they were "largely made up of bums and loafers who wouldn't work." When Booth read the statement of the ministers, it was "loudly denounced."

Only Alderman Lamb showed up at one forum that was supposed to provide the wageless with an opportunity to discuss their worsening conditions with elected officials. Determined to form a union that would raise the wage rate above fifteen cents an hour, the more far-seeing of the unemployed could envision only a higher hourly pay that might open up the possibility of laying aside a personal fund that could carry them as individuals and families through the winter months of enforced idleness. A stopgap measure at best, this "solution" took the collectivist road to an end of acquisitive individualism, but its promise never translated into practical organizational advances. Not surprisingly, the struggling unemployed movement of the winter of 1894 came to an end shortly thereafter, a mid-March winter storm stifling a scheduled protest march. The band that was supposed to lead the rally's march never showed up, and the parade failed to follow through to its proclaimed destination. Under the unfurled banner of two Union Jacks rather than the black flag, the 1894 jobless protest dead-ended back at city hall, where the police now stood watch over a more guarded civic officialdom.[71]

This denouement notwithstanding, the February–March 1894 mobilization established that the unemployed were indeed prepared to fight against the conditions of joblessness. Toronto's dissident destitute were joined in protest by others in similar circumstances in Montreal, Halifax, Victoria, and Quebec City, as David Thompson shows in his thoroughly researched recent unpublished study. Even an irate *Saturday Night*, despite its representation of the Toronto unemployed agitators as operating "in the guise of highwaymen, and with the voice and manner of Anarchists," acknowledged that the out-of-work had created "a superbly organized commotion." There were signs, as well, of women's involvement in the public refusal to simply accept the unavailability of work. In the midst of the agitation, a "motley" crew of "women who had 'seen better days' and women who had not," crashed Eaton's to take advantage of handouts to the poor, an unruly display of resentment. In a rare occurrence of a woman addressing a rally of the jobless, a Mrs. Kellogg offered comment at a March assembly of protesting workers that labouring men were not inclined to sit silently as their wives and children went hungry or suffered the cold of winter without adequate clothing or fuel. Moreover, she also called attention to the domestic servants and laundresses "walking about the streets" of Toronto, "striving in vain to get some work to do, and suffering the pangs of hunger."[72]

But the protests also suggested a clash of orientations that now ran through the nascent and fragile out-of-work movement. Two old colleagues *and* combatants from within the Toronto workers' movement reveal something of the differences of approach that emerged out of jobless demonstrations in this period and the debates they put before the public. Long-time Grit working-class leader, Alfred Jury, a tailor and labour reformer whose activism reached back to the 1870s and the founding of the Canadian Labour Union and extended throughout the 1880s in all manner of Knights of Labor campaigns, urged "moderation" amid talk of anarchism and socialism among the unemployed of 1894. He thought that what was needed was "constant instead of spasmodic study of economics through the medium of trades unions." More radical, but also prone to caution against precipitous and imprudent acts of confrontation, the bohemian "brainworker" Phillips Thompson articulated a socialist analysis of unemployment. He moved a motion at one winter 1894 rally suggesting that "industrial co-operation under which opportunities will be equal, and the workers will receive all they produce," was the only approach that would end capitalist crisis and the ways in which it periodically drove labour into wagelessness. David Thompson suggests that for all of their differences, Jury and Thompson were, unlike Montreal's more avowedly revolutionary William Darlington, united somewhat in their advocacy of restraint. Darlington, a left-wing voice within the Knights of Labor who gravitated to the DeLeonite Socialist Labor Party, commented during the 1894 uprising of the unemployed in Montreal that "an organization of 500 Anarchists" could be mobilized to buttress the protests of the poor. Noting that workingmen could not be expected to starve quietly, Darlington warned authorities that if the jobless used "dynamite or guns the labor leaders [could] not be held responsible."[73]

When, in mid-October 1896, Toronto's unemployed again briefly reared their collective head in protest there would be similar rhetorical bravado. As hundreds of unemployed workers signed petitions demanding that the municipality assume the indebtedness of the wageless for their private utility bills and that relief work be distributed equally among the poor, a fiery radical, William Dunlop, called on the jobless to assemble and march under "the socialist flag." Demanding relief, a delegation advocating for the jobless disrupted City Council and clashed with Mayor Fleming, a real estate developer who managed to secure the support of the unemployed, whose cause he embraced with populist promise. However, when a lawyer and agitator, D. H. Watt, addressed civic authorities, declaring bombastically that the unemployed had access to rifles, "which always bring the people their rights," Fleming was aghast. The "people's mayor" denounced this display of "anarchism," protesting the "transgression upon the rules of propriety." Watt responded with coolness: "Let you be the men of peace … and let the mantle of rebel fall on me." Other professionals espoused a more moderate, "business enterprise" solution. In March 1897, noted Toronto feminist Dr. Emily H. Stowe wrote to the *Globe*, endorsing the labour exchange system as an option for those "crowded to the wall by the capitalistic wage system." She urged the unemployed to deposit the "products of [their] labour" at a recently established Queen Street East establishment of exchange, where a "certificate of deposit" would entitle workers to redeem their banked productions for other needed goods of comparable value. This promised, in Stowe's view, an opportunity for the beleaguered working class to extricate itself from "business stagnation," "money panics," "unhealthy speculations," "blocking of markets," "over-production and under-consumption," "idleness," and "crime from poverty." Stowe's "evolutionary method" never quite managed to overcome the problems of the unemployed, but it spoke to the ways that the eclectic radicalism of the period was forced to grapple with joblessness and the dilemmas posed by the presence of the dispossessed. Her panacea-like solution jostled with more overtly oppositional voices emanating directly from Toronto's jobless protests of the 1890s. But the unemployed did not speak a unified language of resistance. Meetings endorsed civic encouragement of "private capital in the employment of idle labor," while minority critics called for opposition to all "private capital," preferring instead "direct socialism."[74]

The 1890s mobilizations of Toronto's unemployed thus proclaimed the unwillingness of the jobless to simply accept their worsening lot in a crisis-ridden capitalist disorder. But they also exposed Achilles Heels of weakness. Contrasting leaderships and sensibilities, from anarchism and socialism on the radical and revolutionary left to the moderate trade union and reform mainstream, with its willingness to counter the scapegoating of the out-of-work through denunciation of the foreign-born and faith in the clergy and the pillars of polite society, revealed a movement very much in search of its strategic direction. Nonetheless, a new page had been turned in the late nineteenth century as workers began to address the experience of dispossession as one in which the discontents of waged and wageless life congealed. This hinted at the decisive role that a left politics would play in future mobilizations of what had now come to be commonly referred to as "the unemployed."[75]

The Black Flag Remembered; The Tramp Reviled

The black flag that flew at demonstrations of the wageless in the late nineteenth century proclaimed the presence of the left among the unemployed. Memories of this haunted Toronto's community of relief professionals for some time. In 1908 Superintendent Arthur Laughlen of Toronto's House of Industry explained how it had come to pass that the "labour test" of breaking stone, so exemplary in its disciplining capacities, had been charitably reduced from two yards to half a yard, which still constituted a crate weighing over six hundred pounds:

Black Flag procession in Jarvis Street, Toronto, February 1891.

Toronto *Globe*, February 21, 1891.

> Our work test is a splendid thing and tends to keep down the number of applicants for help to a minimum. Well, you see, we were the victims of considerable imposition during the depression about 14 years ago, when the unemployed were carrying the black flag.... We then decided to establish a stone-yard, and before we would give relief each able-bodied man had to break two yards of stone. This innovation was pronounced a success, and the applications for relief began to fall off at a rapid rate, until we had very few families to talk of. We found, however, that two yards of stone was too much for a man to break, and at

my suggestion the Board reduced it to one yard. It was afterwards reduced to half, and today they only have to break a quarter of a yard.

"The labour test" of "cracking the stone," it turns out, would be remembered in Toronto by the relief officialdom as being born under the black flag. Many must have associated this standard with the confrontation of proletarian anarcho-communists and the police on Chicago's Haymarket Square in 1886, an event that precipitated the first Red Scare in North American history.[76]

To be sure, the left would fly other flags, including those of "deepest red" that were associated with the arrival of socialism and Communism in the years 1890–1925. Indeed, not long after the unemployed of Toronto marched under the black flag, there were, as we have seen, those who urged the jobless to fall in under socialism's crimson banner. Nonetheless, the ranks of early twentieth-century revolutionaries were often divided, and for some in this often fissiparous and differentiated left, antagonism to the wageless as little more than capitalism's refuse would surface in denunciations of the poor as parasites. John Rivers, a writer in the socialist newspaper the *Western Clarion*, lumped hoboes, transients, the unemployed and the poor with others "at the bottom of the social pit" who were "unable to help themselves or assist others." The best thing for a socialist to do was to "ignore them." In Lindsay, Ontario, echoes of the earlier 1870s tramp panic could be heard in a Socialist Party of Canada publication, *Gems of Socialism* (1916), which declared confidently that, "The tramp and the millionaire are brothers under the skin. They both live without labor, or rather, live on the labor of others." As Ian McKay suggests, this was but the most jaundiced side of a more inclusive left response to the jobless. "Revolts of the unemployed" erupted across Canada in the opening decades of the twentieth century, fuelled as often as not by the crisis nature of capitalism. With the revolutionary left's involvement in and support of these uprisings, a more expansive understanding of the complex reciprocity that joined the waged and the wageless under capitalism emerged.[77]

Capitalist Consolidation and the Left-Led Unemployed Movement in Pre–First World War Toronto

Toronto helped nurture the Canadian socialist left in the 1880s and 1890s, becoming a haven for bohemian radicalism and dissident thought. It was a centre of the Canadian Socialist League, the first indigenous and popularly based socialist organization in the country, founded in 1899. The long capitalist crisis of 1873–96 had convinced many Toronto radicals, nascent socialists, and developing Marxists that chronic unemployment, among other afflictions plaguing the working class, could only be resolved by a root and branch alteration of the entire capitalist system. Many such critics were Christian socialists, and they found themselves locking horns with more conservative, churched voices in the eclectic Social Problems Conferences that often addressed issues of poverty in the 1890s. As early as 1889 such radical types had clashed in the Toronto Labour Council with one of Canada's leading liberal public intellectuals, Goldwin Smith. Smith had a penchant for denouncing William Morris, John Ruskin, the British Fabians, and other radical "poverty destroyers" at the same time as he played a pivotal role in sustaining the project of municipal relief through his material support for Toronto's Associated Charities and his later contributions to the salary of the city's relief officer in the 1893–94 crisis. This kind of approach contrasted with that of a broad left which, as it coalesced, articulated increasingly radical views on how capitalism, recurring economic crises, mechanization of industry, and concentration of wealth and ownership of the productive forces were widening the domain of wagelessness. Thus Colin McKay, in an 1897 letter to the *Montreal Herald* titled "Socialism Round the Corner: A Correspondent Replies to Prof. Goldwin Smith Regarding the Labor Problem and Its Solution," challenged Smith's view that resolving the unemployment crisis was simply a matter of providing work for the workless. Rather, McKay insisted, the problem of the wageless could only be addressed by resolving the problem of the waged, what he referred to as "the labour question." Calling for a "radical change in our social and economic system," McKay pushed for an end to the profit system as an answer to all of capitalism's "social ills." Against Smith's liberal call for a rational administration of public relief works that would give the poor a hand up out of the despairing pit of joblessness, McKay proposed that "the people ... take over the means of production and distribution, and operate them in the interest of all. The way out of our present social lunatic asylum is into socialism." By the opening decade of the twentieth century, this revolutionary perspective was gaining ground in Toronto. Local branches of the Socialist Party of Canada (SPC) and the immigrant-dominated Social Democratic Party of Canada (SDPC) consolidated an important presence among the jobless, often spearheading protests and sustaining organizational initiatives.[78]

During this period from 1900 to 1925, Toronto was transformed. The largest manufacturing centre in Ontario, the heartland of Canada's regionalized industrial-capitalist development, the city grew by leaps and bounds. Fed by a massive influx of immigrants from the British Isles, the United States, the "white Dominions" of Australia, New Zealand, South Africa, other parts of Canada such as Newfoundland,

and non-English speaking Europe, Toronto's population soared, increasing 75 percent between 1901 and 1911, when it surpassed 375,000. Annexation gobbled up new physical territory, which was needed for developing industries and working-class suburbs. Capital invested in manufacturing increased by 618 percent between 1900 and 1921, while the gross value of production, indexed at 100 in 1900, climbed to 148 in 1905, 255 in 1910, and 847 in 1919. Changes in the lives of working-class people living in Toronto abounded. White-collar jobs expanded, necessitated by the offices, financial institutions, and service sector employment needed to facilitate the accelerating pace of growth. Work opportunities for women, who now had employment alternatives to domestic service and sweated work in the garment trades, grew significantly. But for all the change experienced by Toronto's expanding working class, the continuity in capitalism as crisis was perhaps most decisive. Boom years were never long enough. Bust inevitably followed. Panics and acute depressions occurred in 1907–8, 1911–15, and again in the postwar climate of 1919–21. Wagelessness, even if it was limited to discrete periods, afflicted the vast majority of the waged, only a distinct minority of the working class escaping its clutches.[79]

The left perspective on capitalism, crisis, and unemployment may not have resonated that well in Toronto's boom years of expansion that followed on the heels of the final ending of the long, late nineteenth-century economic malaise. Samuel Gompers, patriarch of the conservative craft unions affiliated with the American Federation of Labor (AFL), received a rousing ovation from Toronto organized labour at an open-air rally in May 1900. His Hamilton organizer, John Flett, was quite successful in expanding the number of chartered locals of international unions in Canada, condemned by some employers as an "invasion." Claims were made that the Trades and Labor Congress of Canada had grown from a membership of eight thousand in 1900 to one hundred thousand in 1914, and much of this affiliation would have been in Gompers' international craft unions. These bodies, numbering only sixteen in Toronto in the 1880s, totalled 106 in 1902. No other city came even close to rivalling this AFL presence. When the voice of the unemployed was heard early in the century, it often spoke in the idiom of the rights of the skilled to be protected from competition in the labour market. In December of 1903, for instance, a "meeting of the unemployed of the city of Toronto," undoubtedly spurred to action by the prospect of winter's oncoming layoffs, adopted a resolution deploring the misrepresentation of industrial conditions in Canada and the resulting "encouragement of indiscriminate immigration." Convened by the mainstream labour movement, the protest was led by a thirty-year-old socialist, James "Jimmy" Simpson, about to become a fixture in Toronto municipal politics holding down positions on the Toronto School Board and the Toronto Board of Control, as well as taking up a brief stint as mayor in the 1930s. Simpson and the jobless marched to city hall and registered their discontent with the false representation of employment conditions being presented to British workmen by bodies like the Salvation Army.[80]

By 1907–8, however, with the economy slowed to a snail's pace and the ranks of the out-of-work reaching crisis proportions, Toronto was forced to open a Civic Bureau to register the names of those in need of work in January 1908. Three thousand promptly signed up, those three hundred fortunate enough to secure work at snow removal receiving $2.00 daily for a maximum three-day stint. The next December, winter again threatening, another Free Employment Bureau was opened, and within three months 5,500 jobless workers had registered. Few received relief, municipal cash for public works being in short supply. Working-class suburbs on the outskirts of Toronto, where labourers had purchased small plots and thrown up shacks, were said to be suffering for want of employment, and as the usual means of offering relief to city residents was not available, the *Globe* started a subscription campaign to alleviate the distress of "this class." City of Toronto disbursements for the House of Industry's usual outdoor relief jumped from an average of around $10,000 annually in 1904–7 to over $26,000 in the depressed years 1908–9. The carrot of relief, however, was never far distant from the stick, which included the awful conditions prevailing in the House of Industry, the rigours of the "labour test," and the threat of legal confinement if the poor refused to abide by the disciplinary rules. At the height of the 1908 economic crisis, 240 so-called tramps were being sheltered in Toronto's House of Industry, with fully ninety of them forced to sleep on concrete floors for want of beds. Those who refused to "crack the stone" for such accommodations faced the increased possibility of criminal charges and incarceration. Vagrancy arrests, never above 975 in any two-year period between 1901 and 1906, ballooned to over 800 annually in 1908–10. In this climate, when the wageless were driven to destitution and marked out for a variety of coercions, the left critique of capitalist crisis undoubtedly registered more forcefully with Toronto's dispossessed.[81]

Organized protests reflected this. Commencing in January 1908, the out-of-work rallied at Toronto's labour bureau, city hall, and the Salvation Army headquarters, pleading for waged or relief employment and denouncing the unfair enticing of British immigrants to Canada when there was no meaningful paid labour to be found. "Fancy coming over 3,000 miles to shovel snow from the sidewalk," remarked one disillusioned and bitter new arrival from England. March 1908 saw one thousand unemployed converge on Toronto's city hall, demanding work. Addressed by

James Lindala, a recent Finnish SPC mayoral candidate, the crowd was destined to be disappointed. Rebuffed by the mayor, who stated clearly that temporary employment would never be provided solely as a means of relief, the jobless retreated. A few days later they rallied at Queen's Park, hoping for a warmer reception from Premier James Whitney. But their demands for "work not charity" were deflected by the head of the Ontario government, who advised them there was employment to be had outside "the congested cities" and that the entire province was suffering the same conditions as Toronto and had an equal right to ask for material support. Meanwhile, the number of families on relief provided by the House of Industry more than tripled over the course of 1907–8.[82]

Nine months later the unemployed were back in force, a contingent of socialists at their head. The Toronto January 1909 wageless rebellion was led by well-known SPC soap-boxers and agitators Charles Lestor, Ernest Drury, and Wilfrid Gribble. More militant than their 1908 predecessors, one thousand unemployed surrounded city hall and spilled over into an adjacent street, blocking the road. Drury had barely begun to address the crowd when the police intervened, forcing the unemployed protest to reassemble in Bayside Park, a kilometre distant from the seat of municipal government. Ankle-deep in mud, the out-of-work listened to a parade of revolutionaries whose speeches scaled the heights of political denunciation of capitalism as well as addressing more immediate prosaic demands. There was talk of the forcible seizure of property to provide for the poor. But there was also interest in building a sustained movement of the jobless. Whatever the subject, the politics of class grievance animated every word. Gribble told the assembled that "It goes hard with me to have to stand here in three or four inches of mud when we want to hold a meeting. You men built these great buildings ... you built these railways, you built the big halls in this city, but when you want to meet you can't have one of them." A petition was soon placed with the City's Board of Control, demanding a hall at which the unemployed could come together in an orderly fashion.[83]

Five days later, the wageless again convened at city hall, their mood described as "dangerous." Albert Hill climbed atop a wagon to address the large throng, which had once again poured into the streets, prompting the police to disperse the gathering. He pointed out, as had Gribble earlier, that while the "big guns and important people" received warm welcomes at the municipal seat of power, the unemployed could not find a place to meet. Making their way to Bayside Park, the body promptly appointed a committee of twelve to return to city hall and demand access to St. Andrew's Hall as a public venue where the out-of-work could assemble. Five hundred demonstrators trailed the delegation and, on arrival at city hall, swarmed the front and side entrances, seeking out the top-floor meeting rooms of the Board of Control. Told to depart by the police, the unemployed offered no resistance but determined to return.[84]

As several hundred of the unemployed milled about city hall the next day, their movements watched closely by the police, Drury led a delegation into city hall, where the Board of Control was addressed. It was beseeched to let out St. Andrew's Hall for regular meetings of the unemployed, who needed a space to publicly discuss how best to urge on civic officials the necessity of providing the jobless with work. The delegation was treated to gratuitous insult. Mayor Oliver remarked that Drury had led "every unemployed deputation" that had crossed his threshold over the course of the last year-and-a-half. As Drury detailed the great suffering experienced by the wageless, the mayor told him that the House of Industry was always available to the destitute. One among the delegation heckled this Olympian advice, referring to the beds in the refuge as "bug traps." Controller Geary demanded to know how many of the small delegation were socialists. Three of the contingent acknowledged that they were indeed advocates of a radical overhaul of capitalist institutions. This unleashed a flurry of concern on the part of Board of Control members that St. Andrew's Hall would be used to "preach a doctrine of discontent." No doubt sensing that the municipal authorities cared less about the plight of the poor than they did about policing the politics of the wageless, Drury and his comrades withdrew. Accompanied by thirty watchful police, a large crowd of the unemployed made its way back to the now traditional gathering place, Bayside Park.[85]

Over the next few days, the nascent unemployed movement enlisted the support of sympathetic reverends, preeminent among them Dr. G. S. Eby of the College Street People's Church, aka the Church of the Revolution. The travails of the outdoor relief system were now being complained about by religious figures, such as Reverend Dean of the Methodist Church, who questioned the long delays experienced by destitute families applying for emergency aid from the House of Industry. The parsimonious actions of the City Council, which, under the pressure of unemployed agitation, had doled out a few thousand dollars for the poor, came under attack. The Associated Relief Charities, with 3,500 names on its registration rolls, was obviously unable to grapple with the dimensions of the crisis of joblessness. As David Thompson has noted, if the centralized Toronto charity agency were to provide relief work for three days a week at a mere $2.00 daily, the drain on the civic purse would have been $21,000 every seven days. Investigations to determine the deservedness of applications for relief were thus stepped up, but they were taking three and four days, leaving families without coal or bread during the coldest period of the winter. This, in turn, elicited criticisms from a Toronto alderman, J. J. Graham, who protested: "People should not be left to starve and freeze while their needs are being investigated." Meanwhile, an organized group of eighty-five refused the "labour test" at the poor house two days running. Protesting the extreme cold that the poor were required to endure in undertaking the mandatory outdoor work, this direct action left the single unemployed "casuals" homeless in the frigid temperatures of January. Phillips Thompson, Toronto's correspondent to the *Labour Gazette,* reported that the House of Industry was administering monthly outdoor relief to 2,152 families as well as to 552 "casuals" who had received 4,338 nights of lodging and 12,582 meals. Thompson tellingly noted, "Of those applying for relief, 280 had refused to break stone."[86]

Having wrested from Board of Control the right to meet at St. Andrew's Hall, over one thousand unemployed gathered there on January 21, 1909, to hear a rousing social gospel address from the Reverend Dr. Eby. "The day has come when men are tired of talking of hell and heaven," Eby thundered. "There are multitudes of people in the churches whom want to bring heaven to earth." Drury proved more provocative in his speech. Urging the wageless to refuse both the symbolism and the substance of the discipline of "cracking the stone," he railed against the quality of the House of Industry's provisions: "I advise you men to go there," he told the wageless, "not with the intention of breaking stone but of stealing a loaf of bread. I wouldn't give a pig the provisions I got there."[87]

Out of this initial St. Andrew's Hall meeting came an extraordinary set of recommendations, quite unlike anything before articulated by those seeking relief. Given what we know of the practices of the House of Industry, the list of six demands generated out of the unemployed mobilization of January 1909 stood as an unambiguous indictment of decades of Toronto's treatment of the dispossessed, governed as it was by routines of "labour tests" and procedures of "cleansing and classifying." They also united the interests of the "casual" single unemployed men who stayed overnight in the House of Industry, recipients of indoor relief, and those families who drew on the outdoor dispensations of the Poor House. The wageless, whatever their station, wanted the abolition of the civic relief department; the establishment of "running baths" for workmen; daily fare composed of more than eleven-cent-a-day servings of adulterated soup and stale bread; provision of adequate and warmer clothing in winter; investigation of the bread depots so that there was monitoring of their activities and assurances that distressed families would not suffer; and, finally, and most strikingly, taking control of the distribution of charity out of the hands of the Associated Charities of Toronto and vesting it in the committee of the unemployed. As David Thompson has recently shown, the jobless protest spawned an SPC-led organization, known as the Unemployed Association, which met as a body presided over by a chair and secretary, the key posts occupied, respectively, by Ernest Drury and Wilfrid Gribble. Phillips Thompson dated the founding of the new organization of the out-of-work to January 15, 1909, noting a membership of fifteen hundred, although the association had almost certainly been active earlier, in 1908. The president of the Association was future *Cotton's Weekly* editor and SPC founding member A. W. Mance. Not yet ready to demand the abolition of "cracking the stone," the socialist-led wageless had, in 1908–9, nonetheless mobilized their ranks, broadened their struggle, solidified organizationally, and crystallized a fundamental challenge to their dispossession.[88]

This rebellion of the dispossessed generated a predictable opposition, one that undoubtedly helped to stifle the stirrings of the unemployed. Mayor Oliver made threatening noises that trouble-makers would be deported, drawing from the poisoned well of racist, chauvinistic thought that routinely targeted immigrants as the cause of the difficulties experienced by the unemployed. There was talk of rescinding the right of the out-of-work to meet at St. Andrew's Hall. A letter to the editor of the *Toronto Star* bemoaned the "Brutal Treatment of the Unemployed," hinting at the way in which resistance to "cracking the stone" had unleashed an ideological counterassault of property and propriety:

> Though this city claims to be so very religious, you have a savage way of treating poor fellows that have nowhere to go. The statement that some of the men refused to work has appeared in the whole Canadian press from the Atlantic to the Pacific. But nobody ever asked why such a large percentage of men refused to work. No, they are simply put down as lazy. Now, when a man goes to a place like the House of Industry, it is plain that he is half starved already. There he gets bread and some warm water called tea, at night, and in the morning. Most likely he will not get a bed the first three nights, but will sleep on a floor, with hardly any room to turn. When he gets up in the morning, after what little sleep he had been able to get, he is required to break a lot of stones. The quantity of stones to be broken will take a man used to it three hours, but a man not used to that kind of work will take from four to six hours. Six hours hard work for a bit of dry bread and a rest on the floor. And we sing "Britons Never Shall be Slaves." Let the people of Toronto reflect a little on the conditions in this city and cease casting slurs upon those who are for the time being in bad circumstances.

The letter, signed simply "Out of Work," was a reflection of what the dispossessed were up against in their daily struggle to survive, as well as in their organized effort to resist. And if the stick of repression did not silence the unemployed, civic officials tried the carrot of enticement, unsuccessfully attempting to bribe the leaders of the jobless movement with promises of employment. With rumours spreading that the Unemployment Association was about to rally its forces to block the downtown intersection of Yonge and Queen, the police were summoned, only to have the protest pop up outside the civic labour bureau.[89]

The resilience and principled stands exhibited by the SPC-led unemployed agitation of 1909 pressured Toronto's civic authorities to expend more on public relief than ever before, $20,000 more than the previous year, according to David Thompson. Thompson attributes this material bumping of the collective rates to the intervention of the revolutionary left, concluding, "SPC activists had won relief increases, albeit with an intensification in liberal coercive repertoires." In its increased surveillance—3,115 relief investigations accompanied the rising expenditure on relief in 1908–9—the City of Toronto signalled its commitment to policing the poor. Its reinvigorated "labour test," as recognized by the letter-writer, "Out of Work," continued nineteenth-century traditions of providing only for those identifiable as deserving among the destitute. Reporting to the socialist newspaper the *Western Clarion* from his position "Amongst the Unemployed in Toronto," Alex Lyon provided a conclusion to the agitation of the out-of-work he had been involved with: "The City Council is beginning to realize that the workers are awakening from their long sleep and that the Socialists who are amongst the unemployed will stir the spirit of revolution in the workers until the red flag is flying triumphantly." There was to be more rock cracking, and further repression, before the revolution, however.[90]

A year later, in February 1910, seven members of the non-stone-breaking brotherhood refused the House of Industry "labour test" and found themselves before Magistrate Ellis, charged with vagrancy. Amid growing speculative animosity to the workless flooding into Toronto from parts unknown, turning the city into an "Eldorado of the tramp fraternity," the men became scapegoats in an age-old ideological assault on the "undeserving poor." The Superintendent of the House of Industry, who chastised the group refusing to "crack the stone" as merely "playing with the whole thing [labour test]" and having the temerity to feign indifference to "even go in the yard to look at the pile of stone," saw in this workless crew proof that many "casuals" seeking lodging at his institution "spend their money in outside towns and then come back to Toronto in droves and expect to be kept." The

Magistrate, obviously unimpressed with the lot before him, decided to teach those indigents who opted for recalcitrance a lesson: he sentenced them to jail terms of from thirty days to three months, promising them "a chance to do real work."

Meanwhile, the House of Industry, pleading insolvency, doubled the quantity of stone it required from all "casuals" receiving bread, water, and a place to lay their heads. According to civic officials, it cost Toronto eighteen cents a night to provide shelter to a single unemployed man, but the remuneration for one box of stone broken brought the city only ten cents. Therefore, the "labour test" had to be upped to two boxes of stone, which would, at twenty cents, recover the costs of sheltering and feeding homeless men at the House of Industry. Such boxes, more properly designated crates, were significant in their size, and in 1909 the Toronto correspondent to the *Labour Gazette*, Phillips Thompson, reported that one month's relief labour at the House of Industry yielded 48 toise of broken stone, hundreds of cubic metres.[91]

The criminalization of the dispossessed proceeding apace, the crisis of worklessness deepened in 1911–12 and plummeted even further as a severe depression gripped 1913–15. By this latter date, the federal government estimated the ranks of the unemployed had swelled to one hundred thousand nationally, with Toronto

Breaking stone for the House of Industry, circa 1900.

City of Toronto Archives, Series 810, File 2.

TORONTO'S POOR

claiming fifteen thousand out of work in January of 1914 and twenty thousand unemployed over the course of October 1914 to May 1915. Toronto's relief system sagged under the pressures of more and more applications for aid, with Superintendent Laughlen complaining that he "had never before seen anything like it." In the winter of 1914–15 more than five thousand families, representing in excess of twenty-five thousand people, were applying for relief to the beleaguered House of Industry. Long queues of men, "two and three deep, lined up outside the … building waiting for shelter for the night."[92]

The usual recourse to a series of start-up/close down Civic Employment Bureaus did little to ease the situation. Maladministered and overwhelmed by applications, such *ad hoc* agencies competed with corrupt private employment enterprises and managed, for the most part, only to secure temporary work, in limited amounts, for the growing army of the unemployed.

Throughout the crisis, which generated what Ian McKay has designated a "Canadian unemployed revolt," often led by the Industrial Workers of the World in the west and the Social Democratic Party of Canada in Ontario, reactionary calls for "able-bodied vagrants" to be "made to work for their living until they have acquired the habit of self-support" continued to be heard. Across Canada almost five thousand of the foreign-born were deported during the 1913–15 economic downturn, the single most important "cause" of their enforced state removal being that they had become "a public charge." Not all of the dispossessed could be dispensed with by government decree, however, necessitating a wider ideological attack. Ontario's Commission on Unemployment signalled the kind of mainstream scapegoating that was commonplace, Toronto being typecast as a magnet for miscreants:

> The vagrant thrives on Soup Kitchens, Houses of Industry, Salvation Army Shelters and similar institutions maintained for the purpose of rendering temporary assistance to a worthier class. The experience of Toronto in this respect is conclusive.… Men are coming into Toronto from the mining camps and smaller places, spending their money in drink, and complaining of not being able to get work. A lot of them don't want it and wouldn't take it if they had a chance. This class of men augment the already too numerous criminal class.[93]

In September 1914, six hundred delegates to the Toronto District Trades and Labour Council gathered in an effort to compile information on the unemployment crisis. They set up a committee system with captains appointed for each ward, tasked to assemble complete statistical returns on the dimensions of joblessness in the city. A labour movement funded Trades Industrial Toy Association was established to give work to unemployed mechanics in the manufacture of children's playthings. Joseph T. Marks, his *Industrial Banner* something of a beachhead of Toronto trade union labourite radicalism, spearheaded a "Provincial Publicity Campaign on Unemployment" but his efforts apparently led to little.[94]

As the crisis deepened, the activism of the left-led unemployed began to address sectors of the dispossessed long marginalized: ethnic minorities and women. A deputation assailed Toronto city hall in January 1915, charging civic officials with discriminatory practices in their dispensation of relief among the municipality's thirty-five thousand Jews. Louis Gorofsky spoke on behalf of the city's two thousand unemployed Jews, claiming they were the object of prejudice because they were not "ear-marked 'British born'." The situation for working women was particularly dire, and the Women's Patriotic League was urging "girls, whether office clerks or factory hands, or in whatever position held previously, to accept what can be secured for them to tide themselves over this period." With a single advertisement for a stenographer eliciting five hundred applications and, for the first time in living memory, the demand for domestic servants exceeding the supply, many women were driven to accept "situations in the country, glad to be able to rely thereby upon board and lodging at least." A 1912-established Women's Day Toilers Motherhood Protective Union sought to alleviate the worsening lot of such women, especially single mothers. It leased a sixteen-room house, ran a union laundry and public luncheon, and housed women in need of accommodations, drawing the praise of the *Industrial Banner*.[95]

Contemporary claims were made that the unemployment crisis of 1913–15 was the most severe in the history of the Dominion of Canada, with routine reports in the *Labour Gazette* detailing the worsening conditions in Toronto. The out-of-work thus faced an uphill battle.[96] The crisis, which decimated the trade unions, whose numbers in Ontario dropped 25 percent, and strained the disciplinary order of relief to the breakpoint, left the waged and the wageless in the same sinking boat of capitalist crisis.[97]

Many refused the labour discipline of "cracking the stone," expressing the preference that they be jailed rather than subjected to the "labour test." When William Brothers, an elderly homeless man, was brought before Magistrate Denison on vagrancy charges in December 1912 and admonished to go to the House of Industry, he replied with conviction that, "I'd lay down on the street and die before I'd go to the House of Industry or any such place. The jail's the place for me."

The Magistrate accommodated, sentencing Brothers to four months. In February 1915 "casuals" spending nights in the wayfarer's lodge ward of the House of Industry were again refusing to break stone for their keep. George Bust and Nick Melasel were charged with vagrancy for their insubordinate behaviour. Courtroom dialogue reveals a defiance bred in the realization of the unemployed that the inequalities of the class system produced counterposed interests in the midst of capitalist crisis, a sensibility that was being promoted among the wageless by socialist soap-boxers and organizers.

> Constable McBurney stated in prosecution, that Bust had been getting his meals free at the House of Industry and had refused to work for them—that is crack stone.
> "That's correct," said Bust with defiant air.
> "Oh, I see, you are one of those who has come to the conclusion that somebody has to support you," said Squire Ellis.
> "Oh yes," said Bust, who had a sullen expression on his face.
> "Did you refuse to crack stone for your meals?"
> "Yes, and there's lots like me."
> "And do you sleep at the police stations?"
> "Yes, with a hundred others," replied Bust.
> "Have you hunted for work?"
> "I certainly have."
> "Yet you refused to work for your food?" continued the Squire.
> "That's one way of looking at it—your way," said Bust.

Stands of combativeness before constituted authority had a way of being repaid in kind. "Well, I think you need looking after," concluded his Worship Squire Ellis, "it'll be $20 and costs or 90 days."[98]

Other shelters, too, faced similar resistance to the "labour test." The Fred Victor Mission, established by evangelical Methodists in 1886, and housing upward of 80–150 homeless men a night in the years before the First World War, always placed considerable emphasis on the salutary experience of work, making its residents labour for their relief, be it in the form of lodging or meals. It promoted its purpose under the slogan "We Make Them Work: It

St. Andrew's Hall, Richmond Street West, meeting place of unemployed, 1909.

City of Toronto Archives, fonds 1244, item 299/Lost Toronto Website.

is our rule to only give assistance to those who in some way earn it." Early super-intendents, such as the Reverend Shore, were not known for their progressive views of the dispossessed. Shore thought "nine-tenths" of those who attended Thursday night services, having to sit through a sermon before sitting down to supper, were "professional paupers" and "fakirs." The Reverend J. D. Fitzpatrick wrote of the Mission's clients: "What awful specimens of humanity. They are, speaking generally, the off-scourings of society—tramps, criminals, outcasts, wrecks—living pictures of the awfulness of sin." Small wonder that the unemployed organized a protest at the Fred Victor Mission, rebelling against what they considered "unfair practices." For its part, the Methodist Mission was of the view that the agitation was the work of socialists. Such socialists viewed the world quite differently than did the evangelicals of Fred Victor Mission, seeing in homeless, workless men not human expressions of the "awfulness of sin," but the carnage of "modern machine methods of production" which robbed workers of "their skill." This, wrote Toronto agitator and SDPC member D. Armstrong, was "the real cause of unemployment."[99]

The Left and the Toronto Jobless before the Great Depression, 1915–1925

The First World War ended the 1911–15 capitalist crisis. Wartime production eased wagelessness. This happened, for the most part, in the aftermath of wartime enlistment, be it coerced or voluntary. The pressures put on the relief order both by the sheer numbers of unemployed requiring assistance and the increasing and challenging activism of resistance to "cracking the stone," often orchestrated by left agitators, lessened. One measure of this is revealed in the statistics of the poor's utilization of police jail cells as lodging. In 1915, Toronto reports indicated that over 10,500 people had been sheltered at various police stations across the city. One year later, in 1916, with the war drive and its recruitment campaigns in full swing, less than 375 had availed themselves of police station "lodgings." The Canadian Patriotic Fund, privately financed and administered, provided the families of unemployed men who enlisted with what was widely, if somewhat inaccurately, promoted as a "reasonable standard of comfort," and tens of thousands of single men joined the armed forces to extricate themselves from wagelessness. Roughly 600,000 served in the Canadian Expeditionary Force, with 250,000 joining between June 1915 and May 1916. Sixty thousand families benefited from the Patriotic Fund's largesse, which totalled almost $40 million in 1914–19. The unemployed had been vanquished, as it were, as capitalism found something of a resolution to its economic and political crises in the breakout of hostilities in Europe. Defiant resistance was difficult to mount in these circumstances, especially as inducements to patriotic duty were everywhere and often overrode understandings of the class solidarities of the waged and the unwaged. In a January 1915 fund-raising entertainment at Massey Hall, organized by the Toronto District Labour Council on behalf of the out-of-work, the message of the necessity of fighting against wagelessness was drowned out in dutiful renditions of "The Death of Nelson" and "We'll Never Let the Old Flag Down," the evening being capped off by a recitation of "The Empire Flag," the address delivered by a speaker wrapped in the Union Jack.[100] No black flags flew at this unemployed rally.

War ended. Capitalist crisis continued. But war had mobilized the state to harness the productive enterprise and energy of the nation, refining a new apparatus of the regulatory state, and in doing so it had galvanized initiatives in monitoring and addressing unemployment. By war's end, amid the winding down of specialized industrial pursuits and the return of jobless veterans, it was feared that unemployment would swell to 250,000 in 1918 alone. Labour, having tasted the possibilities of full employment during wartime, providing waged and wageless to the battlefront lines, both domestically and in the European theatre, was in a combative mood. Tensions were exacerbated by a growing left-wing presence in the unions and among the unorganized and unwaged working class, where talk of the Revolution in Soviet Russia and ideas of production for use rather than profit were common. Coalition government leader Sir Robert Borden was warned by one high-ranking advisor in 1918: "People are not ... in a normal condition. There is less respect for law and authority than we probably have ever had in the country. If ... Canada faces acute conditions of unemployment without any adequate programme to meet the situation, no one can foresee just what might happen."

Setting up the Employment Service of Canada, a national network of labour exchanges funded and run by the joint efforts of the provincial and federal governments, was one component of the state response. So, too, was a wartime anti-loafing law that added new, coercive teeth to the state's ability to socially construct and restrictively contain the "vagrant" dispossessed. PC 815 made it a crime for an adult male not to be "regularly engaged in some useful occupation," punishable by a $100 fine or six months incarceration. Unemployment insurance systems were studied and drew a surprisingly strong consensus of favourable opinion among government officials, mainstream trade union leaders, and progressive employers. But the political will to implement such a system evaporated in the Red Scare climate of 1919. Clamping down on working-class militancy, suppressing a 1919 General Strike wave, deporting "alien" radicals, and using state trials of socialist agitators to establish decisively that the red flag, Soviets, and workers' control of production would not become part of the Canadian way of life trumped a forceful state program that would address unemployment in new and decisive ways.[101]

Toronto had contributed more recruits to the war effort than any other city. It would see the return of more soldiers, all of them looking for work, as well. No city, however, had been harder hit than Toronto in the closure of wartime's munitions industries. Amid the labour revolt of 1919, there was a push not only for sympathetic and general strikes but also for a cash bonus to be paid to veterans. Veterans participated in Toronto's tumultuous May 1919 demonstrations for the eight-hour day, marching under banners proclaiming "We Fought For Democracy, Not For Capitalists," listening to speakers like steeled militant and future Communist Jack MacDonald tell them, "We want the world for the workers, and we are going to have it." One commentator described the proposed $2000 veteran's gratuity as "one grand solution for virtually all the troubles due to unrest, unemployment, discontent and Bolshevism." Many of Toronto's returned soldiers agreed and rallied at one Queen's Park protest, where they were treated to a rabble-rousing speech from J. Harry Flynn, an opportunistic demagogue who quickly established himself as a leading voice of ex-servicemen. "Let us put a peaceful demand," shouted Flynn about the bonus, "and if it is not answered, I say let us take it by force." The panacea of the soldiers' bonus galvanized the formation of the Flynn-led Grand Army of United Veterans (GAUV), which united with Toronto trade unions to attack government agencies dedicated to veterans' "civil reestablishment" for scab-herding ex-servicemen into acts of strikebreaking. Flynn, meanwhile, was making public pronouncements that could be considered pro-Soviet and urging labour not to cringe before capitalism. But the bonus pot of gold at the end of his opportunistic rainbow was not to appear. There would be no $2000 veteran's subsidy granted, or seized, in 1919. Instead, out-of-work soldiers were advised to head to the hinterland. A "Back to the Land" movement, said many employers and not a few farmers, would allow rural producers to "get labour more cheaply." At this the Toronto Great War Veteran's Association took considerable umbrage, arguing that those who had served overseas for four years had not been separated from loved ones and served their country only to be told they could "take employment mucking in the bush," far from the family hearth.[102] Toronto-headquartered Frontier College put a novel spin on the idea that movement to the country could alleviate unemployment, suggesting that municipalities purchase homesteads and employ the jobless in clearing 160 acres and building a house and barn on each improved lot, which could then be sold for a profit.[103]

The crisis of wagelessness that afflicted veterans and non-soldiers alike deepened until, in the fall of 1920, the economy took another turn for the worse, plunging into depression. Across Canada, "work tests" were revived, usually involving stone-breaking and wood chopping. Urban out-of-work outposts, precursors of the militarily-run relief camps of the 1930s, were established, especially in British Columbia and Alberta. These developments were met with the usual protests, including strikes of relief recipients. Ottawa convened two federal unemployment conferences in 1922 and 1924, the first of which, according to historian James Struthers, was called to deflect and deny the national government's responsibility for the rising numbers of out-of-work Canadians.[104]

Toronto employers reduced working time in order not to have to effect mass layoffs, but such band-aid solutions covered the wound of unemployment incompletely and for a limited time. Veterans who had managed to secure work now lost their employment, with estimates being that one in five able-bodied ex-soldiers had been forced into joblessness with the new depression. With national unemployment rates soaring to over ten percent and encompassing 214,000 jobless individuals, the situation in Toronto taxed the public employment bureaus to the break point. Over the winter of 1919–20 these bodies, which favoured the returned soldier, managed to secure 70 percent of all applicants employment, but in 1920–21 that figure dropped to 58 percent. More than three thousand of those registered with the bureaus were "unplaced" and at the height of the crisis that number skyrocketed to fifteen thousand. Federal payments to the municipality of Toronto for the emergency relief of the unemployed over the course of December 1920 to April 1921 totalled $134,128, or almost 40 percent of the funds distributed across the country. Toronto police cells, a home to so many destitute in 1915, but largely empty of these patrons in 1916, began to fill again. By 1925, a record 16,500 people were housed in city jails, many of them ex-servicemen who had been conscripted into the army of the unemployed.[105]

At the Toronto House of Industry, the litany of complaint and the register of inadequacy rose. The poor and unemployed insisted that the outdoor relief doled out to the destitute was woefully insufficient. Social workers claimed that families dependent on assistance were slowly starving. Civic support to the Poor House was challenged as too meagre to begin to address the nature of the unemployment crisis. The *Toronto Star* reported,

> So serious is the situation, on account of the failure of the city to grant sufficient funds to the House of Industry, that the work of the other charitable institutions is being hampered, and the situation is progressing to a point where they will not be able to meet their obligations.

A nurse who regularly visited homes of the Toronto indigent saw children going hungry and concluded that it was "impossible for human beings to live at all on what the city supplies." The plight of the workless, claimed these critics, was reminiscent of the "Dark Ages."[106]

Such charges and allegations were met with the usual arsenal of denial. Officially constituted and often church-affiliated Neighbourhood Workers' Associations claimed that "Everyone should know that no man needs to sleep in the parks or walk the streets in Toronto. There is shelter for him," adding for good measure: "When we encourage begging on the street—which is against the law in the first place—you are encouraging something at the same time that is most deadly for the man." House of Industry Superintendent Arthur Laughlen reassured the public that destitution *was* being dealt with in a timely fashion, relief being provided on the same day an application was received. "People who complain of having to starve while red tape holds up the food they so badly need are not genuine," Laughlen insisted, claiming that such cavils came from imposters.[107]

Left- and trade union-led protests indicated that not all bought into this program of damage control. The Toronto District Trades and Labour Council (TDTLC) organized postwar protests against unemployment in March 1919 and followed this up with routine initiatives throughout the early 1920s. A loose alliance of left-leaning labourites, One Big Unionists (OBU), militant veterans, and nascent Communists advocated for a Dominion-wide unemployment insurance plan, set up a Toronto Unemployment Council, and supported out-of-work harvesters who were on the protest trail, trekking to Ottawa in the winter of 1923–24. The leader of the movement, William Leslie, was convicted of vagrancy in a Toronto courtroom. By this date, the Toronto Association of Unemployed (TAU) had coalesced, committed to supporting picket lines rather than crossing them, and appealing for a general strike to address the needs of both the waged and the wageless. David Thompson notes that the TAU, among the largest organizations of the jobless in Canada over the course of the 1920s, published the *Unemployed Review*, the first newspaper in the country dedicated to the interests of the unemployed. Edited by Frank Fleming, a veteran of the harvesters' trek, the *Review* was hawked on Toronto's streets by the out-of-work and was itself an articulation of the growing consciousness of working-class solidarity that embraced both the waged and the wageless. In spite of organizational advances such as these, the Toronto unemployment movement was not quite able to transcend a plethora of divisions, including long-festering animosities between the British-born and their sense of colonial privilege and immigrant newcomers, who were often castigated by the jobless for taking work that "rightly" belonged to those with ostensible prior claims.

This nativist assertion of white skin privilege wracked the TAU in 1924 as Jerry O'Brien, a veteran of five wars, cultivated a British faction within the unemployed organization that criticized the municipality of Toronto for offering work contracts to Italians rather than former soldiers who were British/Canadian-born citizens of the country. Communists, fighting their way into becoming the leading element within the TAU, eventually ostracized O'Brien and his followers, among whom may well have been the editor of the *Unemployed Review,* Frank Fleming. Fleming fell afoul of the Reds with his tone of "whining Christian gospelling," which manifested itself in the *Review*'s call to "pray to God not to Mammon." This appealed to Communists about as much as O'Brien's patriotic clap-trap. As the Workers' Party dumped Fleming from his editorial post and ousted the divisive O'Brien, they also forced the resignation of the TAU president, securing the post for a trusted supporter, the Reverend A. E. Smith. Smith, who joined the Workers' Party in January 1925, was involved in the People's Church and the Labor Forum and was the Educational Director of the Canadian Labor Party, in which Communists figured prominently. Smith's memoirs recalled how unemployment confronted Toronto's workers in the winter of 1925, with as many as twenty thousand out of work, three to four thousand of whom ostensibly enrolled in the TAU. Accompanying Toronto's mayor, the Orangeman "Honest Tom" Foster, as part of an eight-man delegation to Ottawa, Smith claimed that this was the first time in Canada that a municipal deputation met with the prime minister to confront the Dominion government about its responsibilities regarding the unemployed. Mackenzie King, of course, spouted passages from the British North America Act exempting the federal state from any obligation to contribute to the welfare of the jobless. Communists now urged the out-of-work to march under the "Red Flag" rather than parading behind the Union Jack, which O'Brien and his ultra-respectable nationalist contingent had insisted on carrying to demonstrations. O'Brien and Fleming were but the tip of an iceberg of political differentiation.[108]

At the same time that O'Brien, Fleming, and Communists clashed inside the TAU, for instance, the initial co-operation of mainstream trade unionists and the revolutionary left around the issue of unemployment broke down decisively. The rift had been in the making for some time. Forces within the TDTLC pressed to support only those unemployed who belonged to conventional labour organizations. Unorganized workers who found themselves out of work, such craft unionists argued, rarely joined the labour movement when they managed to secure waged employment. This was to put the cart somewhat before the horse, of course, for in most work sectors where the unemployed could secure an eventual employment foothold, trade unions were anything but the norm. This kind of sectionalist positioning was also almost certainly, for all of its opportunistic appeal to conservative trade unionists, something of a smokescreen, masking animosity to the newly ensconced Red leadership of the TAU. From this combined position of sectionalism/anticommunism, rightward leaning elements in the TDTLC pushed vigorously in increasingly isolationist directions. By 1925, the Labour Council was refusing the unemployed the use of the Labor Temple. From there it was but a short step to arguing that there was nothing to be gained by the trade unions hanging around the public labour bureau and organizing the jobless into the TAU. "Let them help themselves," was the view of one opponent. When President Smith of the TAU appealed to the TDTLC to co-sponsor and help organize a demonstration of the unemployed, his request was unceremoniously rejected. Befuddled by claims that the mainstream trade union movement had done more than enough for the dispossessed, Smith denied that the organization of the out-of-work was somehow the consequence of organized labour's initiatives. It was, he insisted, "the direct result of agitation by the unemployed themselves."

This fracture of ostensible interests separating the waged and the wageless divided even leftists in the 1920s, weakening the revolutionary challenge that might be raised by the dispossessed. This was grasped as early as 1921 when the OBU and other revolutionary militants led a protest of three thousand unemployed. The size of the demonstration threw a scare into the powers that be, but the *One Big Union Bulletin* reflected soberly on the event, grasping that hunger, not class conscious commitment to revolutionary transformation, had animated many of those gathered to voice their discontents. "A panic stricken Capitalist Class see the revolution looming ahead," declared the OBU paper, "The Reds are not so optimistic."[109]

The One Big Unionists no doubt appreciated what was arrayed against them and the hunger of the out-of-work. Barriers to unemployed activism consciously erected by the state were formidable. The Employment Service of Canada (ESC) labour bureaus took on the trappings of agencies of surveillance and discipline. The Toronto unemployed attacked the ESC job creation/placement service as a sham. Few of the unemployed ever managed to secure work through such government agencies. Moreover, when jobless activists refused poorly paid positions offered them under the auspices of the ESC, they found themselves jailed for vagrancy, not unlike the nineteenth-century opponents of the "work test." Frustrated jobless veterans might conduct quasi-organized "dine and dash" acts of guerrilla warfare to ease their hunger pangs, as David Thompson has shown, but they were also prone to riotous tumult that could well be motivated by their antagonism to "foreign others." Their unemployment rate of 20 percent far surpassing the national average, ex-servicemen sought relief in paying rents, leaving them fearful of eviction. They came to loathe the bureaucracy that forced them to chase "around from one place to another, as we have been doing for the last three weeks, with a new report every morning and evening, in the papers that help will be given at such and such a place the next day." Seeking only loans, which they committed to pay back, veterans formed a delegation and went to city hall to seek out Mayor Maguire. Finance Commissioner Ross curtly dismissed the group. "Anybody who thinks that we are going to liquidate his arrears of rent is in error." The former soldiers who decided to organize a 1922 Toronto-to-Ottawa trek in protest of inaction on unemployment fared no better. Three to four hundred veterans hoofed it 220 miles to the nation's capital, only to be sent back empty-handed on the train.[110]

Liberal reformers like Bryce Stewart looked disdainfully on the tendencies of those in power to pass the buck of unemployment to the next generation. "If we wait long enough," he wrote in 1921, "the bread lines and out-of-work doles will cease, unemployment will be gone, men and women will rise out of dull inaction and find joy again in the work of head and hands." Then, all would be forgotten: "The present time will be referred to as the 'hard times of 1920-1921' an unfortunate experience to be forgotten if possible." But Stewart had seen it all before, having written on the 1913–1915 crisis, and he was convinced that "the divine right of unpreparedness" was not going to stave off the next, inevitable downturn:

> Men will pursue their usual ways and in 1925, or 26 or 27 or some other year, the dark ogre of unemployment will again thrust his long arm into the factories and mines and shops and offices, tear the workers from their tasks, bank the fires, hang out the "No Help Wanted" signs and shut the doors against them.[111]

Even as the economy resuscitated somewhat in the years after 1921, the 1920s hardly saw unemployment extinguished. Between 1922 and 1929, the annual average unemployment rate was 11 percent, and 30 percent of all workers found themselves wageless at some point in the year, usually for around eighteen weeks.[112] In 1924, Toronto civic officials lashed out at the influx of single unemployed men descending on Ontario's capital to avail themselves of the largesse of the House of Industry. The mayor insisted that such unwanted outsiders were about to sit down to their last relief meal provided by the city. At an all-candidates meeting during the December 1924 municipal election, Controller Cameron blamed the mayor of Winnipeg for ostensibly shipping out his city's unemployed to Toronto, an allegation that drew catcalls and shouts of opposition. When Cameron was questioned as to why men were sleeping rough, starving, and checking themselves into jail cells, he offered a blunt statement of blame: "If they sleep in box cars, police stations, and parks instead of the House of Industry, it is their fault." Asked if he had tasted the Poor House fare, Cameron deflected his critic by offering up the usual responses: those who needed a bed and a meal should work for them; other municipalities were dumping their out-of-work men on Toronto; and the city could ill afford the costs of sustaining the rising numbers of unemployed, many of whom were ex-servicemen.[113]

By 1925 the presence of beggars on city streets and the ongoing influx of the wageless into Toronto from other municipalities precipitated yet another round of ideological and material attack on the poor. Toronto's chief medical officer, Dr. Charles Hastings, campaigned to rid the city of beggars, whom he considered a variant of the age-old "undeserving poor." Known as an aggressive advocate of improved public health and an enemy of slum conditions, Hastings was also capable of sounding the tocsin of vigilance against the vagrants. He suggested that Toronto civic officials publicize "through the local papers and the Canadian press generally" their intention next winter to terminate "relief to non-residents, or anyone unable to prove their residence, and that, in addition to this, citizens of Toronto be urged not to give promiscuously to men soliciting help at private houses, or to those accosting individuals on the streets, but that they be asked to refer all such persons to the House of Industry, where their case can be properly investigated and where those deserving will receive the necessary food and shelter." Hastings' harangue occurred at a time when George Hamilton, of a government employment bureau, noted that every day between fifteen hundred and twenty-five hundred men were applying for jobs of any kind. For every one hundred, there was work for one of their number. Malnutrition and exposure incapacitated many of those seeking labour, 75 percent of whom, according to Frank Fleming, ousted editor of the *Unemployment Review,* were veterans. Moderate in his views, Fleming still stressed that for all its efforts to relieve the poor, the House of Industry was not able to keep up with the rising pressures on its resources. Hundreds of the unemployed spent their nights huddled in "cold box cars and [on] cement floors," experiencing anything but the pampered existence of the indulged indigent. "Misery and suffering among these men" were all too common, Fleming concluded. The vast majority of the unemployed were genuinely wanting, actively looking for work, and should receive sympathy from Toronto residents. If there was indeed unrest among these poor folk, Fleming suggested, it was the work of "Reds" and "Communists," who were prodding the army of the unemployed to vocalize its discontents and mobilize its ranks.[114]

The red flag had indeed been unfurled among the wageless. The Workers' Party of Canada (later the Communist Party of Canada), born amid the post–First World War downturn, had from its inception been active in forming what James Naylor refers to as "large and militant" Unemployed Associations in Toronto and Hamilton. Capitalism was assailed as the cause of the crisis of wagelessness, and among these advocates of a Soviet Canada, the demand among the jobless was for "work or full maintenance." As we have seen, Communists considered unemployment central to the class struggle, on a par with wage reductions and the open shop as an issue around which revolutionaries organized and cultivated resistance. "Moscow Jack" MacDonald, a Toronto patternmaker who would emerge in the 1920s as one of Canadian Communism's mass leaders, toured the country in the hard winter of 1921, speaking to fellow militants on the scourge of unemployment and laying the groundwork for the formation of the Workers' Party (WP). A short-lived National Committee of Unemployed Workers (NCUW) was established by the WP in November 1922, critiques of capitalism's periodic purges of the working class never being far removed from the revolutionary left's denunciation of the profit system.[115]

By the mid- to late 1920s Florence Custance, a former Socialist Party of North America member and leading figure in the Canadian Federation of Women's Labor Leagues, led the Communist charge against women's joblessness, using the League organ which she edited, *The Woman Worker,* to proselytise for adequate and enforced minimum wage legislation and a national unemployment insurance plan. The first issue of this "Red" woman's journal, in July 1926, carried a lengthy article, "The Story of Ellen Kenealey: A True Story from Life." It detailed the sad case of an unemployed domestic servant who, faced with the prospects of remaining friendless and jobless, swallowed poison as her way out. "I cannot get work," she concluded, "I am better dead than alive." A coroner's jury declared that Kenealey "came to her death ... as a result of carbolic acid, self-administered, ... while suffering an acute despondency on her inability to secure employment." Hundreds of women were in similar straits, registering at the Toronto branch of the Employment Service of Canada in an often futile attempt to gain waged work. Custance laid Kenealey's death at the feet of the "capitalist system of wage labor exploitation," which she insisted was "ruthless with its victims. Workers are cheap these days. Their lives are of little importance." She asked her women readers to "let the story of Ellen Kenealey impress itself upon you," urging them, "Into the union," where they might strengthen "Labor's fight for unemployment insurance."[116]

Nonetheless, the Communist presence in Canadian working-class circles, be they of the waged or wageless kind, was subject to the red-baiting of the mainstream press as well as employers' vehement opposition and the machinations of the state's regulatory relief order. A substantial and influential contingent of dyed-in-the-wool reactionaries ensconced in the most conservative layers of trade union officialdom also never tired of assailing their sworn enemies, the "Reds." Since 1919, this layer of the labour bureaucracy had taken direct aim at revolutionaries in the workers' movement. Two Toronto District Labour Council figures, W. J. Hevey and Arthur O'Leary, launched the *Labor Leader* as the Winnipeg General Strike was winding to a close. The paper, cuddling up to employers and screaming from its masthead fierce opposition to IWWism, One Big Unionism, and Bolshevism, was a strident voice of anticommunism and a proponent of the most entrepreneurial wing of business unionism. The out of-work found little in the way of support within its pages. Repudiated by organized labour because of its ideas and its paymasters, large corporations who footed the bill for its publication, the *Labor Leader* nonetheless survived into the mid-1920s, denouncing Toronto's Communists as servants of Moscow masters and suggesting that Russian Reds were not above threatening good and godly churchgoers with death.[117] As the economic downturn of the early 1920s sapped the strength of the waged and threw more and more of the jobless into the trough of material despondency, conservatizing tendencies could be discerned within the Toronto dispossessed. Tim Buck, a Toronto machinist and perennial Communist candidate for the presidency of the Trades and Labor Congress of Canada, polled 25 percent of the delegates at the 1923–24 annual convention. Thereafter it was downhill, and as the capitalist crisis of the early 1920s abated in 1925–26, the workless, their numbers declining, had a brief reprieve. The red flag, flying listlessly over the thinning ranks of the unemployed, readied itself for the next capitalist crisis. It would not be long in coming. In the next offensive of the outcasts, the reception of this radical banner, prepared in the years 1900–25, was unprecedented.[118]

PART III

"United We Eat; Divided We Starve"

The Toronto Unemployed Movement, 1929–1939

As we enter the 1930s, the obscure history of the wageless and their resistance that we have outlined becomes more familiar. This is a consequence both of how what happened during this decade of discord has been written about *and* of how capitalist crisis registered for so many Canadians of the time in terms of an end of employment.

Study of the crisis of unemployment in Canada in the Great Depression is a staple of modern historiography, and there are excellent, deeply researched mono-graphic accounts and proliferating journal articles on the state and provisioning for the jobless, work camps and their discontents, and the organization of the out-of-work, including much discussion on major events such as the On-to-Ottawa Trek, a protest march that culminated in police attack on unemployed demonstrators in Regina in 1935.[1] Document collections on the "dirty thirties" provide powerful and provocative evidence of the depth of resentment and anger that engulfed the wage-less in the precipitous economic collapse of 1929–35.[2]

A 1930s aesthetic consolidated in the poetics of enforced idleness:

the days of work are gone.
cold and hunger,
and men at missions
waiting,
for bowls of soup.[3]

One idiosyncratic employer, Hamilton's Thomas Dyson Lisson, encouraged the pub-lication of a sales representative's fictional narrative of the messianic fantasy of the son of a rich factory owner aligning with the jobless, forming a Society of Forgotten Men, the purpose of which was to end unemployment:

Forgotten men, from pole to pole
For whom the world does not provide,
Their birthright bartered for a dole
From lust-stained hands that cannot hide
The filth of avaricious grime;
The hands of those who dare to say
That what they do is not a crime,
And sacrilegious, feign to pray,
While vested with a self-made might
Evoke the laws which give them gold,
Forgetful that these men must fight
Else leave their bodies, stark and cold.[4]

Novelist Irene Baird penned what is commonly, if perhaps wrongly, perceived as Canada's first "proletarian" novel about the west coast plight of single jobless men.[5]

Popular historians like William Gray, Barry Broadfoot, and Pierre Berton have written widely read accounts that explore the Great Depression as a crisis of unemployment.[6] Recent work, much of it unpublished, by scholars such as Todd McCallum and Marcus Klee, builds on this past research and writing to craft imaginative perspectives on the working and the workless that place in a new light the always evolving relations and reciprocities of waged and wageless life.[7]

The wageless, then, get some of their due in treatments of the single decade in Canadian history that is most readily associated with an undeniable crisis of capitalism and its human costs in terms of unemployment. It is not hard to understand why. By February 1930 the numbers of unemployed in Canada were estimated to be 323,000, with the rate of joblessness at 12.5 percent and climbing. Sixteen months later, in June 1931, 435,000 of Canada's 2.5 million wage earners were unemployed, or roughly 17 percent. That rate soared to 25 percent by February 1932 and then crossed the incredible 30 percent threshold in 1933. The Dominion Bureau of Statistics estimate was that between 600,000 and 700,000 Canadians were without waged work in 1932, and a year later that number had grown to 876,000. The percentage of the unemployed among trade unionists rose each year from 1929–32, more than tripling from 6.3 percent to 22 percent. Almost a million-and-a-half people were on relief. There was no denying the dimensions of the crisis.[8]

To be sure, the crisis of unemployment in Canada during the Depression years of the 1930s was perhaps most pronounced in the first half of the decade, and as the average annual jobless rate inched downwards in 1936 and then dropped significantly to 12.5 percent in 1937, there was hope of a reversal of the economics of collapse. Its stimulus was thought to be a recovery in the United States, which proved stillborn. Instead of advance, 1938–39 registered a relapse as unemployed rates rose again to 14–15 percent. In December 1938 and March 1939, the quarterly estimates of the numbers of unemployed in Canada, at 472,000 and 494,000 respectively, lagged behind comparable figures for 1934–36, to be sure, but they more than doubled the 223,000 for September 1937 that fed the optimistic but illusory view that the Depression's employment doldrums were lifting.[9]

The problems posed by wagelessness were neither obscure nor unrecognized. H. M. Cassidy and the Unemployment Relief Committee of Ontario stressed that joblessness undermined wage rates, restricted consumption, and lowered standards of housing and other essentials. Cassidy and the Committee then summarized what many mainstream commentators considered to be the contours of a deteriorating socioeconomic order:

> Unemployment has also interfered with the normal mode of life of the unemployed in a dozen and one other ways. It has made for fewer marriages and fewer births, and probably for a greater proportion of illegitimate births; for a greater number of suicides; for wives working and husbands staying at home; for discontent, unrest, and the development of bad habits among boys and girls of the school-leaving age; for overcrowding in the home; for family friction and disagreement; and for an increased number of deportations and the consequent disruption of the plans and aspirations of immigrant groups. It has induced attitudes of discontent, unrest and suspicion of established institutions in many people. The fact of drawing relief over long periods bids fair to develop in many an attitude of dependency. The effects of unemployment upon the unemployed and their families must be to make of them poorer citizens and poorer workers. Our most precious asset, the good quality of our population, is threatened with serious deterioration if unemployment continues.[10]

This statement, of course, wrapped the crisis of unemployment in a plethora of conventional wisdoms around gender, dissent, and good citizenship. Yet, as federal, provincial, and municipal governments toyed with reforms and new initiatives in their ostensible efforts to address the catastrophic impact of rampant worklessness, little was accomplished. Liberal Prime Minister William Lyon Mackenzie King recognized in 1919 that "the fear of unemployment" lay at the root of much of the discontent among working people. In a 1929 statement, King reduced the plight of the out-of-work to infighting among politicians. He considered municipal and provincial pleas for federal aid to buttress their relief efforts as little more than a Tory raid on the Liberal government's budget surplus, which the incumbent prime minister wanted to use to good, self-interested, effect in the forthcoming election. When it came to giving any sitting Conservative government funds "for these alleged unemployment purposes," King told the House of Commons in April 1929, "I would not give them a five-cent piece."[11]

King's replacement as leader of the country, the Tory R. B. Bennett, assumed the office of prime minister in 1930. He at first thought talk of agricultural and industrial crises exaggerated, deploring in 1931 that "people are not bearing their share of the load," bemoaning that the unemployed would not "work their way out of their difficulties rather than look to a government to take care of them." Himself a rich man, Bennett complained that "the fibre of some of our people has grown softer and they are not willing to turn in and save themselves. They now complain because they have no money."[12] Eventually prodded to do more than King to alleviate distress and destitution, Bennett's main concern seemed to be to thwart the Communists that powerful correspondents across the country advised him were an imminent threat. British Columbia's premier, S. F. Tolmie, warned Bennett's Minister of Labour, Gideon Robertson, in 1931, "The unemployment situation is becoming daily more acute and with communistic agitation it is a much more serious question.... The Reds in Vancouver are already talking about revolution." Indeed the Communist Party of Canada (CPC) and the Workers' Unity League (WUL) that it led were organizing a nation-wide campaign for a non-contributory unemployment insurance program, which would fund a minimum level of relief for all Canadians through appropriating money from defence spending and upping taxation on all incomes over $5000 a year. Ivan Avakumovic claims that the unemployed constituted over two-thirds of the membership of the WUL at this time, but that only 5 or 6 percent of the League's adherents were Communists. Nonetheless, there is no denying that Red-led agitation among the jobless had support among masses of Canadians. Following a 1931 national day of protest against unemployment, organized by the CPC, Bennett received a petition signed by almost one hundred thousand Canadians.[13]

This was the background to a memorable suggestion, made in an address at Toronto's tony Royal York Hotel, earning the millionaire Tory Prime Minister his scornful nickname, "Iron Heel" Bennett:

What do they offer you in exchange for the present order? Socialism, Communism, dictatorship. They are sowing the seeds of unrest everywhere. Right in this city such propaganda is being carried on and in the little out of the way places as well. And we know that throughout Canada this propaganda is being put forward by organizations from foreign lands that seek to destroy our institutions. And we ask every man and woman in this country to put the iron heel of ruthlessness against a thing of that kind.[14]

Bennett, however, was behind the times. Toronto civic authority, especially Police Chief Draper's "Red Squad," had been practising what Bennett preached for some time.

The ostensible prosperity of the late 1920s masked the extent to which unemployment returned each winter with a vengeance. Thus, over the course of January–April 1929, well before the stock market crash that for many signalled the arrival of the Great Depression, the out-of-work numbered between 263,000 and 290,000. These official figures of joblessness plummeted in summer months, to as low as 39,000, before rising again in the fall. By 1930, however, seasonal abatements in unemployment had lessened considerably, and by 1932 the numbers of jobless simply increased month-by-month regardless of the weather. There were approximately 50,000 more Canadians unemployed in June 1932 than there had been the previous January.[15]

Toronto followed these trends. In June 1931, of 242,000 wage earners in the city, fully 40,500 were not working. From August to November of 1931, 36,550 unemployed men registered with the Toronto Central Bureau of Employment Relief, 16,664 of them single and 19,886 of them married with dependents. A large number of these men were returned soldiers, 60 percent could be classified as unskilled or semi-skilled, and only one-third of the wageless were native-born Canadians. Of the significant number of immigrants among the out-of-work, roughly half had been in the country less than five years and were thus liable to be deported should they become recipients of public relief. Virtually none of the workless had any tangible property, such as real estate or automobiles, and only a bare 4.4 percent could claim a bank account. Many were forced to turn to institutions of relief, such as the House of Industry, which saw the number of Toronto families drawing from its resources increase from 3,470 in 1929 to over 20,000 in 1932. The almost 63,000 Torontonians drawing relief in January 1932 constituted roughly 10 percent of the population of 631,207, but in specific working-class suburbs like East York, the crisis of unemployment hit harder, with the percentage of residents on assistance approaching 30 percent in January 1934 and surpassing 45 percent in February 1935.

It is all but impossible to make specific comparisons across Ontario's urban landscape of joblessness in the 1930s, situating Toronto's unemployed comparatively. In September 1936, for instance, Toronto ranked fairly high among the province's cities in terms of the maximum monthly relief allowed by specific municipalities, its figure of $58.87 surpassing the ceilings existing in Guelph, Kitchener, Oshawa, Hamilton, and Windsor by anywhere from $6–16. But such amounts were calculated in different ways, sometimes including clothing, medical, and other allowances, and sometimes not, and Toronto figures were distorted by unduly high (and rarely paid out) provisioning estimates for rent, at $20 monthly. What can be said with some certainty is that Toronto's percentages of jobless workers ranked highly in Ontario, while its average relief earnings on public works projects were among the lowest in the cities of the province where industrial capitalism's most concentrated development had taken place. In Windsor such relief earnings averaged $157, in Hamilton $103, and in Toronto a minimalist $54, a reflection, no doubt, of the importance of sweated labour in the Queen City, and the ways in which small employers could pay substandard wages that might then be complemented by allowances of one kind or another. With about 8 percent of the nation's population, Toronto paid out 19 percent of the country's relief bill. To sustain such a massive expenditure, the municipality and its working-class suburban districts relied on funds from the provincial and federal governments and private charitable sources as much as it dipped into its own resources.[16]

It was not until well into the crisis, in 1932, that the Ontario government commissioned an inquiry into how best to deal with unemployment that would aid it in setting benchmarks in the efficient distribution of relief to the needy. Heading up this Advisory Committee on Direct Relief was Wallace Campbell, General Manager of the Ford Motor Company of Canada in Windsor. Conservative Premier George Henry was satisfied that Campbell had played an exemplary role in constructing a system of relief investigation in Windsor that was methodical and thorough. With almost 40 percent of the local population on relief in 1932, Ford managers controlled the relief operation, ran a tight monthly monitoring of all recipients of aid and, with a policeman in attendance, operated one of the most orderly relief offices in the province. Campbell's committee, composed of seven businessmen and a lone figure from the social welfare community, D. B. Harkness, produced a twenty-four-page report in a month. Although the team producing this document contained nary a doctor, nutritionist, public health nurse, or food preparation expert, the resulting statement set standards for food, shelter, and clothing that determined social assistance rates across Ontario until 1944.

As we will see, in Toronto, at various points in time, relief was being gauged on the basis of allocations outlined in the 1932 Campbell Report + percentages of various levels, up to additions of 35 percent. In spite of differential costs of living, in which Toronto was always a place where weekly expenditures were higher than they might be in many other locales, the Campbell Report advocated and promoted standardization, which was always posed in terms of maximum ceilings of expenditure rather than minimum floors of municipal welfare. For the most part, the standards set, which seem to have been arrived at by consulting grocers and the like, were costed out, but not justified by concern with the adequacy of the provisions. Food costs were set at expenditure levels, but there was no evidence that the figures of $5 weekly for a family of five, and $8.25 weekly for a family of ten had been arrived at by taking into consideration nutritional needs. Allowance for shelter was capped at $15 monthly, regardless of the size and nature of the family; electricity costs were never to exceed one dollar a month. Cash relief was frowned on, if not prohibited; relief dependent on standardized investigations, residency requirements, and voucher forms. "Begging," "panhandling," and the general "anxiety caused by the presence of unknown and unattached men in the community" required planned policies so that they would not create social discord or disrupt the relief regime. Moreover, if the unemployed needed to be controlled, so too did municipalities, which were prone to pander to the poor. The Campbell Report called for the creation of Public Welfare Boards, composed of members appointed by the provincial government, to monitor municipal administration of relief, ensuring that it was undertaken with an eye to uniform levels of dispensation and that it was freed from the influence of local political considerations. District relief inspectors were, by the end of 1932, subjecting municipalities to regular visits, determining that the Campbell Report was being honoured and that no community was charging Queen's Park in excess of what was allowed for food, housing, and the necessities, bare enough, of life.

Arguments quickly mounted against the expenditure ceilings set in the Campbell Report. The Ontario Medical Association responded one year after Campbell and his team pronounced on food expenditure that the $5 weekly maximum allowance for a family of five would provide a minimum ration *only* if all of the children were less than five years of age. For most families of this size, food that could sustain health would cost between $6.60 and $7.00 a week, or 25–30 percent in excess of what the Campbell Report set as an expenditure ceiling. A *Toronto Daily*

Star reporter had the arithmetical wit to comment that $5.00 weekly for a family of five worked out to "4 ¾ cents per meal per person," a sum that he suggested could not "safeguard health."[17]

For all of the state's willingness to see Campbell's 1932 document as a definitive statement on need, the report was little more than an ideological edict, one that demanded out of the diversity of relief requirements a forced and mechanical standardization. Driven as much by age-old concerns to limit expenditure related to the destitute, and to impose regimes of surveillance and monitoring that checked the innate tendency of the undeserving poor to ride the coattails of state largesse, the Campbell Report would have a long shelf life within governing circles, where it was a convenient, if rather gilded and socially constructed, authority. It masked the complexity of relief dispensation in a language of administrative procedures, obscuring the essential point that its proclaimed mantra of uniformity was not only never realizable, but had always been little more than a blunt instrument used not for the broad interests of the poor but against them.[18]

As late as 1935–36, with successive provincial governments clinging to so much of the Campbell Report, it was nevertheless difficult if not impossible to realize the call for uniformity. David A. Croll, Minister of Welfare in Mitchell Hepburn's 1934-elected Liberal government, was still complaining, in 1935–36, of a relief administration that he described as "haywire." Some communities had reduced living standards to the famine point, while others, according to Croll, did little but bow down to those who howled the loudest. It was all a "hodge-podge of baffled municipalities, each one separately groping its way blindly, dizzily, without direction or set purpose." Entering influential government office as something of a golden boy of seemingly left sensibilities and labour-sensitive background, Croll was hailed by many in the social work milieu in 1934 as "God's messenger of salvation." Soon he would be hanging in effigy outside of occupied relief offices or from verandahs of relief families beating back the eviction bailiffs, a man reviled and attacked by the dispossessed. His calls for uniformity in relief provisioning as the first step on the road to righting the wrongs of "unfair differentials between relief rates in similar communities" sounded a tocsin of fairness during his first months in office. But Croll would not take

Etobicoke relief office protest, "Army of Occupation" hanging of Minister of Welfare, David Croll, in effigy, March 1935.

York University Libraries, Clara Thomas Archives & Special Collections, *Toronto Telegram* fonds, ASC 19092, *Evening Telegram* Staff.

HON. DAVID CROLL

long to expose himself and his government. As James Struthers concludes, "As soon became apparent, Croll was more concerned with controlling expenditure through systematic procedures for the administration of relief than with raising inadequate allowances."[19] This was a recipe for resistance. It would pit Croll against Communists and anyone else who stood up and fought for improvements in the administration of social welfare.

Reds and the Unemployed in Canada's Great Depression: From Third Period to Popular Front

The Communist Party of Canada (CPC) stepped into this capitalist crisis with a vengeance. Any examination of the unemployed and the resistance mounted against joblessness in Toronto's 1930s inevitably bumps into the leading role of the

Demonstration on "Red Spadina," Toronto, circa 1930–31.

York University Libraries, Clara Thomas Archives & Special Collections, *Toronto Telegram* fonds, ASC19066, *Evening Telegram* Staff.

CPC and its oscillating policies, established by the Communist International (Comintern/CI), but understandably addressed and negotiated in the specific local conditions of Canada in general, and the country's second largest city, in particular. The Party and its leadership, ensconced in Toronto, changed its orientation from what was declared a Third Period (1929–35) to a new, less strident approach, known as the Popular Front (1935–39).

As the Great Depression unfolded, with the scourge of unemployment ravaging everyday life in Toronto, the Communist Party was guided by CI directives that the class struggle globally had entered a new phase known as the Third Period, distinguishing it from a First Period of revolutionary upsurge associated with 1917 and a Second Period of stabilization and relative quietude reaching from the defeat of the German Revolution in 1923 into the later years of the decade. This Third Period was to be one of agitational potential and revolutionary possibility, but only if Communists seized the moment and took up their place at the head of proletarian revolt. Accelerating capitalist crisis and rising working-class militancy were the hallmarks of a new age. Revolution was to be won or lost by a dedicated Communist vanguard, which must shun alliance with compromised alternative leaderships of the labouring masses. These included trade union "fakirs" atop the mainstream craft unions (organized in Canada and the United States in the American Federation of Labor, and gathered together in Toronto in the Trades and Labour Council, or TTLC), much maligned "social fascists" in bodies like the social democratic Co-operative Commonwealth Federation (CCF) or, worse, the demonized forces of international Trotskyism. Such a perspective mandated that Communists adopt not only the most militant tactics, but also the most sectarian and isolating, a trajectory that placed them on an inevitable collision course with both potential allies and sworn enemies such as Toronto's Police Chief, Brigadier-General Dennis Colborne Draper and his "Red Squad"; fervent anticommunist elements in the private charity sector, like the Catholic archdiocese;[20] and the city's labourite mayor in the mid-1930s, CCF advocate and long-time trade unionist, James "Jimmy" Simpson.[21]

One part of the Communist International's insistence that capitalist crisis was unfolding in the Third Period, opening up new avenues of opportunity for revolutionary class struggle, was recognition that, as one 1930 source declared, unemployment was now endemic under capitalism. It had become "normal, inevitable and permanent." As the ranks of the jobless expanded, the wageless grew increasingly cognizant of how unemployment was ravaging cities like Toronto, and of the inadequacy of a class-ordered government response. One disgruntled Toronto "Carpenter" wrote to Prime Minister R. B. Bennett in 1934, irritated with "all your paper talk." The young man railed incoherently but passionately against the rich and their state:

> Why don't you cut off about 2 or 3 thousand dollars from all these big men
> and put men to work out of what your doing is taking all you can get your
> hands on taxing us poor people so as you can make enough money to go to
> Florida for a vacation or England.... What we need is a new government all
> through and us fellows down here are going to see we get it.[22]

The CPC thus took the early lead in organizing those thrown out of work in the first years of the Great Depression and in propagandizing about capitalist crisis and the scourge of joblessness. The Party launched the National Unemployed Workers' Association (NUWA) in 1930, calling for "Work or Full Maintenance" at $25 weekly for the jobless. Tim Buck's published reminiscences outlined the approach of the CPC:

> We demanded a guaranteed minimum wage and unemployment insurance.
> In case of involuntary unemployment, every man or woman should receive
> unemployment benefits equal to not less than ⅔ of the wages that he or
> she would earn if fully employed. Old age pensions should be sufficient to
> live on decently. People should be able to retire at 65. It should be a guar-
> anteed right of every worker to have an annual vacation pay.

Moreover, the NUWA

> would attempt to develop a campaign in the trade union movement to per-
> suade the members to fight in their local unions for the international unions
> to accept, at least, this measure of responsibility for their unemployed mem-
> bers. They should be able to retain their full membership, even voting rights,
> as long as they were unemployed through no fault of their own. Until that
> time, when a worker was unemployed, he lost all his rights in the union.[23]

The arts community was drawn into the cause of the out-of-work, various cultural productions being used to promote protest. Trevor Maguire, a Communist militant who had tramped and worked as a bindle-stiff in the Saskatchewan harvest, and who had served a six-month jail sentence for an ostensibly seditious speech at a Toronto May Day Queen's Park rally in 1922, wrote a one-act play, *Unemployment.*

While putting forward a questionable perspective on gender relations within families wracked by the male "breadwinner" being out of work, Maguire's theatrical representation did present a view of the terrible social costs of economic crisis and the consequent blight of joblessness. The Progressive Arts Club, in which Communists Oscar Ryan and Edward Cecil-Smith were founders, with Jean "Jim" Watts, Dorothy Livesay, and Stanley Ryerson figuring prominently, staged a number of one-act agitprop plays for audiences of the unemployed, highlighting the nature of relief, evictions, being out of work, and deportation.[24]

Communists also pioneered innovative tactics of struggle. They promoted the formation of local Unemployed Councils, the animating slogan of which was "Fight, Don't Starve!" Organized at the neighbourhood level, these councils, according to the Communist newspaper *The Worker*, drew "into the fighting ranks of the working class, new forces who could never be reached by the NUWA—women,

Unemployed benefit performance poster, 46 Cooperative Theatres, Toronto, December 23, 1930.

York University Libraries, Clara Thomas Archives & Special Collections, *Toronto Telegram* fonds, ASC19078, *Evening Telegram* Staff.

youths, and children." "Flying squads" of the jobless were mobilized within districts and around clusters of city street blocks, prepared to travel quickly to specific "hot spots" of confrontation. Canadian Reds such as Tom McEwen, head of the NUWA, saw the army of single unemployed men thrown out of work by the capitalist downturn of 1929–30 as raw recruits for the "struggle in the streets" that would inevitably stamp the new Third Period as one of "class against class." He said of one such combative jobless figure: "The only theory he has is to get a punch at the police [but] that is a very good theory.... He ... wants action ... his type is hard to control, but ... should not be condemned."[25]

Communists in Toronto saw the unemployed as instinctually drawn to angry protest, willing to butt heads with the powers that be; Third Period CPCers thus battled police in a series of open-air meetings, hoping to draw the out-of-work to their revolutionary cause. Defiant of permit procedures and police orders, CPC agitators came to be marked out for often vicious repression by police. A network of counter-subversion linked Toronto's Red Squad to the Department of Justice, the Royal Canadian Mounted Police, and military intelligence,[26] culminating in the arrest, trial, and conviction of CPC leader Tim Buck and seven of his comrades in 1931.

Railroaded to jail under the infamous Winnipeg General Strike–inspired Section 98 of the Criminal Code, the Communists were tried and found guilty as members and officers of an unlawful association. The Communist Party of Canada's illegality was alleged to be its affiliation with the Communist International, which had committed itself to establishing the dictatorship of the proletariat, endorsing violent means to this end, if necessary. Buck and his comrades were also charged with being parties to a seditious conspiracy. Section 98, lambasted by civil libertarians since its passage into law in the climate of Red Scare and fear occasioned by the 1919 class struggle, was nothing more than the state's "get into jail free card," to be played against dissident forces when they threatened the hegemony of constituted authority. In effect, it outlawed any organization that did so much as advocate the overthrowing of constituted authority and declared publishing the views of such an illegal body or representing it as a leader subject to a twenty-year prison sentence. Buck and seven other Communists, collectively known as "The Eight," received sentences of two to five years under two counts of Section 98 and one to two years for seditious conspiracy. Under appeal, the seditious conspiracy convictions were overturned, but the Section 98 sentences stood unaltered. As jurists such as radical lawyer J. L. Cohen complained, Section 98 violated basic standards of British justice, allowing conviction on the basis of association rather than specific acts, or even words uttered or written. But it had served well a state coming to see itself under siege in the early years of the Great Depression, with the discontents of the wageless driving the dagger of threatened insurrection deep into the bourgeois bosom. The state had reason to fear the Communists and their activities among the unemployed. In the first half of 1931, fully twenty thousand joined the NUWA. And, as we shall see, the protests of the jobless and the volatility of this increasingly angry and often rootless reserve army of labour, combined with the convenient capacity of state power to scapegoat "foreign agitators" as the cause of marches, demonstrations, and all manner of resistance, made revolutionaries whose allegiance was to Moscow's Red International a convenient target. Section 98 served its purpose of repression well in 1931. It forced Canadian Communism underground. But by this time it was also dawning on some Canadian Communists that "we have been so active among the unemployed that we have lost sight of everything else."[27]

Between 1931 and 1935 developments internationally and within Canada pushed the CPC to soften its sectarian abstention from involvement with others in the progressive milieu who were committed to fighting on behalf of the jobless, defending the Communists from state repression, and broadening the struggle beyond battles in the streets on behalf of single unemployed men. That said, the residue of CPC attacks on "social fascists" and the suspicion that Communists were not the best partners in broad, united front coalitions of the dispossessed never quite disappeared, in Toronto or elsewhere. Early Third Period sectarianism tended to be remembered.

The first gathering of what was known as the East York Unemployed Workers' Association, for instance, was heralded in *The Worker* under the headline "Beware Social Fascism." Three weeks later, one of the leaders of the East York unemployed was assailed as a Fabian whose advice "never to fight with the police as it never gets you anywhere" was little more than constitutionalist parliamentary cretinism. Activists recalled, decades later, how Tom McEwen tried to undermine their movement, attempting to set up a separate organization and attack one of East York's strongest public speakers at the time, Jim Sutherton, by titling an article, "East York Unemployed Workers Being Misled." As late as the 1934 Ontario provincial election, the Communist Party was running prestigious candidates like the Rev. A. E. Smith against Arthur Williams, a popular leader of the unemployed who would be elected Reeve and then MPP, running on the Co-operative Commonwealth Federation ticket. Eventually, albeit as the Comintern was moving toward the declaration of the Popular Front, Communists in Toronto came to realize that the East York Workers' Association was a powerful and ongoing presence in the struggles of the unemployed, a mobilization that revolutionaries should work within and with rather than against, as did Party member Jerry Flanagan. Collaborations then included a 1936 May Day parade, culminating in a march to Maple Leaf Gardens, where a rally featuring the CPC's Tim Buck and the CCF's Rev. Ben Spence took place.

But, as Patricia V. Schultz stresses in her history of the workers' response to the Great Depression in East York, it was left-wing, non-Communist socialists who held this fragile alliance together. They confronted Communist Third Period sectarianism and a rightward-leaning CCF leadership dedicated to refusing any concession to the CPC, the hard-line social democratic leadership being willing to back up this edict against working with Communists by expelling any organizations that violated the nonco-operation rule. "The average member of the East York Workers' Association was able to rise above the disagreements of the leaders of the Communist Party and the CCF," concludes Schultz, "to join together in struggles both directly relevant to their own particular problems in the township and those of other workers in other places." This was not done without difficulty, however, and across Toronto it was evident to some, by the end of 1934, that the unemployed movement in the city had been handcuffed by Stalinist officials, "who insisted on a hundred percent mechanical, bureaucratic and autocratic domination of the unemployed. Whoever would not see eye-to-eye with Stalinism was duly eliminated." As a result, both the "block" and "ward" organizations of the unemployed under Stalinist auspices were "practically a failure," and in the view of some sceptics "existed mostly on paper." As the Trotskyists who made such criticisms were aware, however, there were signs, with the formation of the Toronto Unemployed Union, of moving forward toward a substantial "mass organization" of the jobless, and the elected Executive of this new body contained CPC figureheads, CCFers, dissident Left-Oppositionists aligned with the Trotskyist Workers' Party, and others unattached to any left-wing political formation.[28]

The final blow to the Comintern's Third Period insistence that parties marching under its banner must lead the class struggle alone was the realization of what had been lost in Germany with the rise to power of Hitler. Instead of building mass resistance to fascism and linking arms with Germany's significant social democratic workers' movement, Communists pursued the folly of their own sectarian policies to the point that they provided Hitler a much easier path to power. The result was the decimation of the labour and socialist movements and a fascist takeover. By 1935 the Communist International had seen the error of these sectarian ways.

Whereas it had lurched to ultra-left positions in 1929, in 1935 it leaped far to the right, adopting the policy of the Popular Front. Unlike the Third Period, in which Communists saw class struggle under the revolutionary leadership of the CI as the only option for working people, the Popular Front embraced cross-class alliances to the point of downplaying the necessity of overt class struggle. In the Third Period Communists built movements of the unemployed, as well as heading up a number of "front groups" that both defended class struggle militants and extended the politics of class confrontation into new arenas—the Canadian Labour Defence League (CLDL), the Workers' Ex-Servicemen's League, the Friends of the Soviet Union, and Women's Labour Leagues—but in the period of the Popular Front such activity waned. While local Toronto Communists no doubt remained active in unemployed agitation, in the later 1930s the issues that had so galvanized Party members to activity on behalf of the jobless in the early years of the 1930s seemed somewhat remote to the concerns of the CPC leadership. Unemployment as a crucial working-class issue virtually disappeared from public propagandistic statements of the Party and appeared hardly at all in annual national convention agendas. The Spanish Civil War and the rising industrial union movement, the Congress of Industrial Organizations, now captivated Communist attention. Although, as we shall see,

Toronto was a centre of relief strikes in 1939, Communist leaders were "increasingly eager to keep the level of militancy under control." Things were thus decidedly different in 1939 than they had been in 1931, with the CPC's cross-class politics now channelling militancy into the parliamentary arena, where the election of progressive candidates might enhance the possibility of "recovery initiatives" that could see the unemployed put to work on large-scale public works projects.[29]

This Popular Front shifting of political gears had been in the making for some time prior to its official proclamation in 1935, and it would last until the end of the decade, when a series of new complications associated with the outbreak of the Second World War necessitated a move away, albeit only briefly, from this programmatic direction. In locales such as Toronto, harbingers of this Popular Front can be discerned as early as 1932, when the Party leadership took the NUWA out of its independent class struggle body, the Workers' Unity League, and renamed it the National Committee of Unemployed Councils (NCUC).[30] This coincided with a broadening of the approach to unemployment, relief, and resistance, which extended the reach of agitation beyond single unemployed men and, in the NCUC's accent on block and neighbourhood councils, drew women increasingly into the class struggles of the dispossessed. Resistance to evictions and relief strikes largely date from this informal 1932 relaxation of Third Period ultraleftism. Struggles in the street continued, but they tended to be less ordered by confrontations with police that seemed orchestrated by ritualistic combat. Instead, the clashes of irreconcilable interests turned on ongoing complaints of the single unemployed, which peaked in the Onto-Ottawa Trek mobilization of 1935 (perhaps one of the Third Period's last hurrahs), eviction blockades, which were concentrated in the years 1932–36, and the increasingly important relief strikes and protests, erupting from 1932–39 and in which the Communist Party played different roles in specific periods. On balance, then, the Third Period stamped class struggle with a new urgency at precisely the time that the lowest points of the Great Depression were reached and mainstream organizations of the working class were most enervated, while the Popular Front and its precursor developments allowed for a widening of the struggles of the unemployed.[31] This invariably opened out into new possibilities of interacting with both the leaders of alternative progressive movements and their mass constituencies, but it also dampened down militancy in its appeal to cross-class sensibilities.

National membership figures of the Communist Party of Canada speak to this trajectory and its meaning. After bottoming out in 1931 as Third Period sectarianism reached its zenith, membership in the Party climbed from its low point of 1,400 to 5,500 in mid-1934. As the Popular Front opened the doors of the CPC

to "anybody ... who wanted to come in," recruits, especially from the unemployed movement, swelled the Party ranks, which doubled from July 1935 to October 1937. With growth rates of from 200–300 a month in this period, the Party boasted 15,000 members by the end of 1937. At this point, the struggles of the unemployed were no longer determined by CPC national leadership to be a priority, but as the case of Toronto establishes and John Manley has suggested, "local cadres continued to mould and lead them."[32]

What all of this suggests is a fresh, albeit complexly layered, perspective on the relationship of capitalist crisis in the 1930s and Communism and the insurgent masses of this notable decade, a contingent of agitators and activists that was always a minority among the dispossessed, be they waged or unwaged. The first point to grasp is that Communism was, throughout the Great Depression and even before its lowering of the material curtain on Canadians of modest means, *always* the *bête noir* of constituted authority, which enjoyed nothing more than attributing all discontent and dissent to the unruly Reds, whom it was imperative to defeat and demoralize. If the Communists did not exist, and if they were not behind *absolutely every* instance of unemployed rebellion, elements within the police, the judicial system, and the state at its municipal, provincial, and federal levels would have had to invent them the better to deny the structural problems inherent in the character of capitalism, which built into its social relations of production periodic crises that unleashed the scourge of joblessness on working people.

Second, official Soviet-aligned Communism and its upper echelons of Canadian leadership was, by the 1930s, undeniably the leading and preponderant force within a fissiparous revolutionary left. But this hegemonic Communism was also compromised in its accommodation to Stalinism, which ensured that policy, set by the Communist International, would oscillate (sometimes quite wildly) and would be determined by the dictates of an ideology which had, since the mid- to late 1920s, sacrificed the programmatic integrity of revolutionary politics on the altar of a limiting vision determined by the ostensible needs of "socialism in one country." If there were times when the shifting contours of Soviet policy seemed to relate to global realities, there was also no mistaking that the prime determinant of decision-making in the Communist International by the 1930s was Stalin's consolidation of power. This reversed the priorities of the Comintern of Lenin's and Trotsky's time, in which advancing the world revolution had always been seen as the only way to secure the victory of the Russian workers and preserve the revolutionary achievements of 1917.

This did not mean, of course, that every member of the Communist Party of Canada was ultimately capable only of acting out this kind of Stalinist compromise, any more than it meant that every unemployed worker who followed the lead of CPC activists in their Toronto ward and workers' associations was a fully conscious revolutionary Red. Rather, Communism and its relationship to the unemployed movement, in Toronto and elsewhere, was a complicated mix in which, at the first level of orientation, a primary CPC leadership set a particular kind of stage on which resistance might be played out. This rather abstract and theoretical articulation was then subject to the gritty practical engagements of a secondary cast of Communist cadre, embedded in neighbourhoods and interacting with local activists, all of whom wrestled with the determinations established by Comintern dictate and its translation to them by a national Party leadership. This produced uneven understandings, carry-overs of old practices, and incomplete realizations of programmatic "turns" as they were carried out on the ground of class struggle. As the conceptual accounting evident in Third Period and Popular Front pronouncements seemed at odds, there was some blurring of stark difference in the arm-twisting of actual mobilizations. This meant, for instance, that the bluster of the Third Period, with its ultra-left and sectarian insistence that only the revolutionary ranks of the Communists could lead the struggle forward in fruitful ways, might well be moderated in local circumstances, where battles in the street established the mettle of seeming "social fascist" misleaders and by which CPC secondary leaders and rank-and-file members came to appreciate the contributions of non-Communist activists. Alternatively, the militancy generated by Third Period "class-against-class" rhetoric and resistance could not entirely be turned off simply because the Popular

Front called for less robust responses and more attention to moderate, seemingly more conciliatory, activities. Communist leaders in specific districts of Toronto might well find themselves, after years in the trenches of jobless activism, pushed to remember the street-fighting tactics that some of their non-Communist followers recalled had gained them advantages in previous, and more confrontational, encounters with power.

In short, Communism operated at complicated levels within the Toronto unemployed movement of the 1930s. These layers of complexity articulated tensions among the international, the national, and the local, frictions arising out of how Red leaderships, locally active Communist cadre, militants from other political tendencies, and the ranks of the jobless movement interacted. All of this, moreover, played itself out within an ensemble of relations forged in the crucible of capitalist crisis, in which state power, again layered in complex and often contradictory ways, involving local municipal councils and police forces, or competing provincial and federal authorities, presented a confusing mix of agents and authorities. But in the swirl of confrontational chaos, there is, ultimately, no denying—from either the vantage point of the multifaceted state or the unemployed workers and their families protesting evictions, demanding better conditions at the House of Industry, or striking for enhanced relief allowances—the importance of the left, and especially the Communist Party, in the making and movement of unemployed protest in Canada's 1930s.[33]

The Single Unemployed and Toronto's Communist Battle for the Streets: Heroes 1914–Bums 1933

The Communist International and its advocates in Canada did not so much *predict* the economic collapse of 1929 and the massive unemployment it unleashed as stumble into the Great Depression with the melange of political positions that comprised the Third Period orientation. Within the Soviet Union, where doctrine and direction were determined, the left turn of 1928–29—which ordered a specific view of capitalism and class struggle—was dictated as much by Josef Stalin's need to vanquish a rightward-leaning rival, Nikolai Bukharin, as it was by any conceptual insight or prophetic program. Well before the stock market crash of October 1929 announced the economy's descent into a ten-year slump, highlighting the many imbalances of the so-called Roaring Twenties, Communists had embarked on their ultra-left crusade to bring class struggle to a fever pitch. However incongruous the material realities of the period—strikes and other indicators of working-class militancy nose-dived over the late 1920s and the CPC itself suffered

Mounted police move crowd of demonstrators along "Red Spadina," Toronto, circa 1930–31.

York University Libraries, Clara Thomas Archives & Special Collections, *Toronto Telegram* fonds, ASC19067, *Evening Telegram* Staff..

losses of membership and influence—the leadership of the Canadian Communist movement was determined to prove its mettle in exposing capitalism's repressive essence. Pointing out in 1931 that there was "no difference in principle between the sadistic brutality of 'Draper's heroes' and that of the Fascist Brown shirts," Stewart Smith's Third Period tract, *Socialism and the C.C.F.*, saw the first step in the march to totalitarianism as "a bloody offensive to smash the labor movement, to break up the Communist Party, the revolutionary trade unions and mass organizations of the working class, annihilating the most active workers, smashing the workers' press, abolishing the right of assemblage and drowning ... every struggle of the workers." Toronto streets, Smith proclaimed with certainty as early as December 1928, would soon be "running in blood."[34]

This aggressive Communist stand exhibited itself most forcefully in a series of violent confrontations with Toronto police, led by Draper's Red Squad, in which Detective-Sergeant William Nursey and Detective Daniel Mann (both men over six feet tall, weighing in at roughly two hundred and twenty-five pounds) figured prominently. Prefaced by a campaign of systematic intimidation and harassment of Communist meetings in public halls, which were required by police dictate to conduct all proceedings in English, these battles were fought over freedom of speech and the right of popular assembly. Theatres and auditoriums which rented premises to the CPC and allowed speakers to address those gathered in their native language, much of the Party membership being first-generation immigrants who spoke Yiddish, Finnish, Macedonian, or Ukrainian, were threatened with their licence to hold public meetings being revoked. But hall managers often either failed to enforce Draper's command that "all proceedings and addresses are to be held in the English language and no disorderly or seditious reflections on our form of government or the King or any constituted authority will be allowed" or found themselves powerless to restrain Communist speakers.[35]

An event at the Standard Theatre on January 22, 1929, revealed a pattern in which authority's intransigence and Communist insistence on the right to meet and speak freely became locked in ritualized combat. At the Lenin Memorial meeting, Max Shur, a Yiddish speaker who had previously run afoul of Draper's English-only edict, rose to address the crowd. He was promptly hustled off the stage by a prominent member of the Red Squad. The audience grew increasingly agitated, and one vocal comrade, Philip Halperin (Halpern), began another speech in Yiddish, was hauled from his seat by police, arrested, charged with disorderly conduct, and made to cool his heels in jail for a night as labour defence activists raised his bail of $1000. Amid cries of "Down with the police!" and "Throw the bums out!," a frightened theatre manager lowered the curtain on the proceedings. Not to be outdone, the redoubtable Communist firebrand Becky Buhay crawled under the muffling velvet and onto the stage. Apologizing for her linguistic limitations, which dictated that she speak in English, Buhay stirred the crowd to applause with her denunciation of the police. Soon, however, she was overcome, dropped her purse and scarf, covered her face with her hands, and reeled backward. Tim Buck, Canadian Communism's *lider maximo,* rushed to her side and caught her as she collapsed. It was rumoured to be the first time in Canada that tear gas had been used to break up a meeting, an allegation later denied by Police Chief Draper.[36]

This blatant attack on freedom of speech and assembly prompted Communists to spearhead a Free Speech Conference at one of their favoured meeting places, Alhambra Hall, claiming support from church groups, trade unions, and social agencies. Determined to defend the right to assemble and propagandize, the Communist Party would run Buck as a candidate for the Toronto Board of Control on a free speech platform. By October 1929, Jeanne Corbin, Secretary of the Free Speech Conference, had pieced together a seemingly impressive list of endorsements, although under scrutiny many of them would prove to be small organizations affiliated directly with the Communist Party, front groups in which the Party was the major decision-maker or union locals in which the CPC had some influence. Draper responded by clarifying his attack. He placed the muzzle not only on foreign languages, but on Communism itself: "If any Communist or Bolshevik public meeting held in a public hall, theatre, music hall, exhibition, show or other place of public amusement, proceedings or addresses, or any of them carried in a foreign language, the licence for such hall etc., shall immediately thereafter be cancelled."[37]

TORONTO'S POOR

Communists now had little option but to fight back. They carried their message to the streets. Between May and September 1929 some thirty-six outdoor meetings, rallies, and impromptu speeches pushed the CPC's free speech cause. Communist militants set up soapboxes at intersections along "Red Spadina" Avenue and Queen Street. Police–Communist confrontations ensued. They were increasingly violent, with the leadership of the CPC, as well as rank-and-file members, routinely manhandled or worse, sometimes arrested and charged with vagrancy, creating a disturbance, or disorderly conduct. Women found themselves jailed, with Buhay, Corbin, and others paraded before judges, while leading and targeted male Communists such as Buck, McEwen, "Moscow Jack" MacDonald, and Oscar Ryan were brutally beaten. The viciousness of these police attacks escalated in August 1929 as battles raged in Queen's Park demonstrations. A series of three August free speech rallies that carried into September and October 1929 kicked off with a demonstration on August 1, 1929, called as part of an International Day of Action organized by Communists in Canada and around the world. Draper let it be known that he had no intention of allowing the Communists to speak at the Queen's Park bandstand, and he further denied them a permit to parade on Toronto's streets. Police confiscated six thousand leaflets announcing the demonstration, arrested CPC members distributing literature outside the Massey-Harris agricultural implements plant on King Street, and took another Red into custody when he was intercepted with a bundle of revolutionary pamphlets. "Chief Draper is determined to smash us," Communist Party spokesman Stewart Smith told the *Toronto Star*, "and we're determined not to be smashed."[38]

Civil libertarians rallied to the cause of the besieged Communists. In the House of Commons progressives such as J. S. Woodsworth and Agnes Macphail opposed the Toronto police edict barring speeches in languages other than English, especially when arrests under such draconian provisions were obviously being used as a pretext to deport dissidents. Toronto Tory Member of Parliament G. Reginald Geary defended Draper's Red Squad:

> The City of Toronto is unalterably opposed to the adoption of the principle
> of Communism in this country. I am informed that the Labor Party in
> Toronto, which owns a building called the Temple, does not permit com-
> munistic meetings to be held within that building. That is to say, organized
> labor, which is quite strong in Toronto, and which commands respect, does
> not choose to allow its building to be used for this same sort of meeting
> even when the addresses are made in English. The Police Commissioners

have decided that it is to the interest of public order to forbid meetings to be held in a language which is not understood.[39]

Buck and the CPC actually sued the Toronto police in the Ontario Supreme Court and, with J. L. Cohen as counsel, won something of a victory.[40] But the most dramatic events in the free speech war of 1929 would take place in public spaces.

Draper's anticommunist fanfare no doubt heightened curiosity about the free speech movement, and newspaper reports estimated the number of those gathered at Queen's Park on the evening of August 1 to be five to ten thousand. This turnout, the vast majority of whom were not Communists, perhaps ensured that arrests would be few—Draper understanding that it would be counterproductive to create martyrs out of the revolutionaries—but it could also have angered the plainclothes officers and Red Squad agents circulating among the crowd. They let their resentments get the better of them. Tim Buck and one of the more inflammatory agitators among the Party's women members, Lily Himmelfarb, approached the bandstand around 7:30 p.m., looking unsuccessfully for the designated Communist speakers; Buck suggested that Himmelfarb appease the restless crowd by commencing the proceedings. No speeches were heard, however. Buck was immediately stopped by the police and beaten severely. Demonstrators were soon being attacked by police, who undertook to clear the park. From different directions contingents of motorcycle cops and mounted police rode their vehicles and horses into those assembled; women, children, and baby carriages scattered for the side streets adjacent to Queen's Park Crescent. With the park cleared by 9 p.m., the thoroughfares of the downtown core were patrolled by police for the rest of the evening. Draper denied that his officers had assaulted Buck, claiming instead that they had taken the Party leader into custody, but released him, whereupon he was set on by angry veterans.[41]

Approximately two weeks later, on August 13, the beaten-back Communists called for another free speech protest meeting at Queen's Park. Well over five thousand showed up, and once again the grounds were guarded by plainclothes cops, mounted police, and the motorcycle corps. As CPC National Secretary Jack MacDonald approached the bandstand to give his introductory speech, he was set on by police. Falling to the ground, MacDonald tried to protect himself and cried for mercy. Undercover police kicked him while other plainclothesmen whaled on him with billies. A uniformed officer grabbed him by the neck and thrust him forward, while another constable seized him by the arm, hoisting him upward. As this happened, MacDonald was then struck in the face by a fist and kicked repeatedly. Attempting an escape, he zigzagged and stumbled toward the relief of a Bloor streetcar, but he was hounded by police who repeatedly pummelled and kicked him. The forty-three-year-old MacDonald, who was never charged with any offence relating to this brutal beating by the cops, had had an exceedingly tough life. He would soon leave the Communist Party of Canada, joining the fledgling Canadian Trotskyist movement, but his health was deteriorating, and he died of a heart attack in 1941.[42]

As MacDonald was being beaten, the crowd was being dispersed violently. Innocent bystanders were shocked at the treatment meted out against those who were only at Queen's Park by accident, deploring "Draper's methods" as "causing riots." Struck by the baton of an officer on horseback, Edward Smith declared that he had "no sympathies with Communists," but he could not condone the actions of the police. "I have been 29 years in Canada," he stated with resentment, "and have never been subject to such an outrage." The liberal use of horsewhips and truncheons came in for public attack, as did comment on the obvious police hatred of the Communists. "Those who looked like Communists were roughly treated," reported the *Star*, it being apparently accepted and understood that Reds were physically identifiable. Whatever the Reds' appearance, there was no mistaking the rancour of the police toward them. "Give it to them," shouted the officers, "They're all yellow." People attacked far outnumbered those arrested, with only seven demonstrators being charged with creating a disturbance or illegal assembly.[43]

The dramatic overkill of the police riot against the Communists generated much criticism as a backlash of progressive repudiation followed the August rout. Labour figures denounced "the Queen's Park riot" as a "brutal, inhuman sample of official violence and the most sordid exhibition of police methods ever heard of," something "unthinkable, awful," in Toronto. Vice-president of the Toronto Trades and Labour Council (TTLC), Jimmy Simpson, addressed a mass meeting at the Labor Temple that unanimously condemned the excessive use of force. A leading pillar of mainstream trade unionism in Toronto, and a labour-sympathetic city councillor, Simpson was poised to become a leading voice in CCF circles and mayor of Toronto in 1935. He was, however, no friend of Communism and despised the Reds he was now forced to reluctantly defend. "We are aggressively opposed to the Communists," Simpson told the Labor Temple audience, "The Labor movement of this city formerly had the Communist Party under control, but the police have adopted a high-handed method and failed to co-operate with us so that we can no longer act. All we can do is protest and urge the safe and sane methods of police administration be inaugurated."[44] The Communists had achieved a sort of victory in their militant, and violently suppressed, advocacy of free speech.

Draper and the police backed away from wildly physical clashes with Toronto's Communists later in 1929, although they managed to contain the ongoing call for free speech gatherings. A Queen's Park rally announced for 8 p.m. on August 27 was derailed by a massive police presence that blocked five thousand demonstrators from entering the park. Mayor McBride was stationed nearby, ready to read the Riot Act should there be a repeat of the violence of earlier thwarted meetings. But with Queen's Park closed by a massive cordon of Draper's ranks, the expected confrontation never materialized, and those assembled sang "The Internationale," booed the police chief and the mayor, and marched south down University Avenue. September saw smaller street rallies along Queen Street, with Communist women mobilizing protests. At one such protest, Rose Shelly kicked off the proceedings, at which Himmelfarb and Buhay were also present. Shelly deferred to police orders to desist from speaking and move along. The way was then cleared for Becky Buhay to take the leading role. As she stepped up on her soapbox to address the growing crowd, Buhay was seized by police, arrested, charged with disorderly conduct, and later released on $500 bail. The defiant Communist yelled to the street gathering of four hundred, "Comrades, we protest against this terrorism. We want the right to free speech!"[45]

To staunch such impromptu free speech gatherings, Draper yet again tried to arbitrarily impose local ordinances that would stifle agitation. He proposed a bylaw that would necessitate securing a permit from the chief constable for any street corner meeting, in effect outlawing Communist propaganda on the grounds that no permits would be allocated to revolutionaries who Draper insisted "carried out their plans in an insinuating way, and in our opinion, against the established constitution in Canada." In response, a large meeting was held at city hall on October 1, 1929, with a range of religious and labour organizations voicing their opposition to Draper's proposed edict before City Council. Salem Bland defended the aims and practices of social gospel activity within Toronto, stressing that it had its origins in "street preaching." He warned that some religious spokesmen would be intimidated if they were required to be "certified by the Chief of Police." If the twelve apostles had been forced to secure permits to preach, Bland mused, the modern Church might never have come into being. The Salvation Army was on hand to recount how the founder of its movement, William Booth, had been persecuted for preaching in public spaces; Salvationists had little faith in the efficacy of jailing those who ministered unto the needs of the poor by speaking in the street. In a more secular vein, the TTLC's Sam McMaster thought it ill advised to suppress free speech meetings, bringing further attention and possible support to the Communists.[46]

In light of such criticism, Draper and Mayor McBride were once again forced to clarify that they did not intend the proposed bylaw as a suppression of religious freedom of speech or the freedom of association of various political societies and groups. Their target was *Communist* freedom of speech. "A wrong impression has gone abroad that the police commission is to stop free speech," declared Mayor McBride. On the contrary,

> What the police commissioners are trying to do is to stop communist meetings. In hearing Dr. Bland and others, I agree that permit is probably not the proper way. But I do appeal to all classes and all creeds to try and stop the Communists. They are not for law and order. We are not opposed to free speech, religious meetings or political meetings, or societies of any kind. I believe in all kinds of meetings in street corners except Communist meetings.

This statement had the virtue of clarifying what was truly at stake, even if it managed to undermine the fundamental principle of freedom of speech and association at the same time as it ostensibly recognized it.[47]

The Communists sought to capitalize on the religious dissent that grew against the suppression of their free speech campaigns in the streets of Toronto. Under the auspices of the Free Speech Conference, they called for a rally in defence of free speech to take place at Queen's Park at 3 p.m. on Saturday, October 12, 1929. Salem Bland and other religious figures were invited to speak and apparently agreed, at first, to appear on the podium with leading Communist Party figures. But as Draper and McBride assured the churchmen that their interests would not be sacrificed on the altar of anticommunism, some of the religious enthusiasm for free speech protest evaporated. To be sure, the CPC had probably not gone out of its way to build a united front of free speech supporters, and inviting Bland and another advocate or two of progressive religious institutions to appear at the meeting was as much of a stunt as it was a serious attempt to build a mobilization of all concerned with the protection of free speech. Jeanne Corbin's challenge to Police Chief Draper that the Free Speech Conference was not merely "a Communist affair" and that any attempt to suppress it would create "a storm of protest such as Toronto has never witness[ed]" was hyperbole at best. The long list of nonreligious speakers scheduled to address the rally read as a who's who of the CPC: Jack MacDonald; Tim Buck; Jack Wirta of the Finnish Organization of Canada; M. Popovich of the Canadian Labor Defence League; H. Englander of the Furriers' Union; Meyer Klig of the Furriers Union; Fred Rose of the Young Communist League; Jeanne Corbin, Secretary of the Free Speech Conference; James Gill of the Earlscourt Labor Party, and Chairman of the Free Speech Conference; Albert Soren, just returned from Russia, where he was sent as a Pioneer Delegate. Draper was not to be intimidated, and he promptly issued an edict banning the proposed Queen's Park meeting on the grounds that it would inevitably result in "a breach of peace, and perhaps a riot, when life and property might be endangered."[48] No doubt, given the established police proclivity for violence.

On the day of the scheduled Saturday protest police set up what was described as an "impregnable" cordon blockading the Queen's Park bandstand and the grounds of the Ontario Legislature. One thousand demonstrators converged on the area but were shut out from getting anywhere near the bandstand. No speeches were given. MacDonald attempted to breach the police lines but was pushed back and escorted from the area by police. There would be no repeat of his brutal and sympathy-arousing beating of a few months earlier. That the numbers attending this abortive free speech rally had declined significantly from those of the summer protests suggests support for the Communists among the general public was fading. If those in attendance were likely more committed to the cause and more inclined to challenge the police and fight back, they simply lacked the numbers to battle Draper's well-outfitted contingent of motorcycle and mounted police, uniformed officers, and plainclothesmen effectively. The police, in actions that bear a striking resemblance to police practices at G-20 Summit protests decades later, simply pushed the crowd down University Avenue, split them at Elm Street, and prohibited a frustrated MacDonald from ever exercising his free speech rights.[49]

A repeat performance unfolded a week later, but on a much smaller scale. Those arrested in the two October 1929 events constitute, again, an identifiable cohort of CPC leaders (Charles Sims, Fred Rose, William Kashtan, and Jeanne Corbin) and the ethnic base of the Party's dominant foreign-language sections (Andrew Holubishen, Mary Holubishen, Ann Polahbneck, Dosir Leibivitch, Edith Chalkof, and Diana Bisghould). The outlier was the Reverend R. E. Knowles, a militant invited to address Communist rallies from the podium, who battled police at the October 19 confrontation and found himself in custody, charged with disorderly conduct and trespassing.[50]

At a superficial glance, the obsession of Draper, McBride, and others at the pinnacle of Toronto's civic authority with suppressing the right of the CPC to exercise its freedom of speech and association seems irrational. Yet as the 1929 protests bled into signs that the economy was about to falter, the threat that streets might prove fertile ground for revolutionary recruitment of the jobless generated fear and loathing of the Communists and their purpose. Part of the reason that certain elements saw the suppression of Communists as imperative was the conviction that the wageless would be drawn to the politics of the red flag. "In Toronto, the capital of the province, [the Communists] are endeavouring in every way to spread their evil doctrines," declared Police Commissioner Judge Emerson Coatsworth in defence of the actions of the cops in savagely dispersing the crowd at one of the August 1929 Queen's Park free speech demonstrations. Anything but "a mere handful of propagandists to be ignored," Coatsworth thought the CPC "a real menace to be put down with the strongest action possible." As "foreigners who have left their own countries," Coatsworth claimed, Communists had come to Canada to "abolish the existing institutions." They sought to foment discord among the discontented, and they had a long history of creating unrest and dissent among the jobless. Coatsworth explained that the revolutionary element needed to be kept in check because "at a time of unemployment they become dangerous." Speaking for himself, Coatsworth intended to "do everything possible to combat this dangerous element," which he insisted had "a serious foothold in Toronto."[51]

Coatsworth was mounting a crudely ideological attack, of course, but he was not entirely wrong. As the crisis of joblessness escalated in the early years of the Great Depression, unemployment became a *cause célèbre* among agitators of the left. Indeed, in the years to come, Communists, as well as a range of other revolutionaries and radicals, among them Trotskyists, social democrats affiliated with the newly established Co-operative Commonwealth Federation, socialists and labourites of various stripes, and anarchists, would propagandize among the unemployed.[52] *October Youth*, the mimeographed organ of Toronto's Spartacus Youth Club, saw joblessness amid capitalist crisis as one of the critical tasks calling out for agitation and action on the part of the revolutionary left.[53] Organizations would be formed, demands posed, demonstrations and marches planned and carried out. A new militancy breathed life and vibrancy into the often enervating experience of dispossession.

The Communist Party led the way, often following Comintern directives to international affiliates to mobilize worldwide days of action against unemployment.[54] Jack Scott remembered that for him, "joining the Communist Party was ... linked directly to the unemployed agitation." And once he joined the Party, "he was always looking for someone sympathetic," those for whom the impact of being out of work might move them in the direction, however preliminary, of revolutionary politics.[55] As in the free speech campaign of 1929, Toronto streets became a battleground, pitting Reds and their rising numbers of supporters against Draper's police, although now the meetings were called to protest rising joblessness and the poor relief measures offered as alleviation.

In March 1930, a large demonstration of more than two thousand Communists, unemployed men and women, and their supporters assembled on Bay Street a few blocks from the House of Industry, where increasing numbers of the jobless were forced to seek refuge. Marching to city hall, the protesters gathered to listen to Tom McEwen speak on the steps. McEwen was immediately arrested, the unemployment rally violently dispersed by police. "Resistance was offered by the Communists and the unemployed," reported the *Toronto Star*, "About a dozen instances ended up in fisticuff encounters between the police and the demonstrators." In the ensuing hand-to-hand combat, eleven were arrested, including Communist soap boxer Rose Shelly and two homeless men, Jack Munro, a resident of the House of Industry, and Harry Coulter.[56] A year later, in February 1931, thirty-eight people were arrested across Canada as free-for-alls broke out in various cities where Communist-led demonstrations of the jobless encountered stern police opposition. In Toronto, three thousand people gathered at the corner of Spadina and Dundas in what had become an annual Communist day of unemployment protest. Police once again broke up the proceedings. The large crowd fought back, throwing bricks and stones at the police, some on foot, others riding horses. It took Draper's gendarmes several hours to disperse the crowd, a dozen of whom were arrested on charges ranging from assault police to vagrancy.[57]

May Days in the early 1930s frequently saw Communists attempt to rally for the rights of the jobless and free speech, although in Toronto, in 1932, the police dominated, "demonstrators never [having] a chance." Officers marched through the assembled Queen's Park crowd, arresting eleven and moving protesters aside. It was not all that different a year later. Free speech/assembly and unemployment protest fused again in 1933, only to have the Red Squad derail a Communist May Day rally announced for Queen's Park. Detective Nursey led the preemptive strike, with eighteen Communist leaders—fourteen men and four women—taken into custody before the event commenced and later released without charges. Police dispersed the remaining crowd rather handily.[58] But this now predictable act of repression prompted the newly formed Co-operative Commonwealth Federation to rally to the defence of the Communist Party, demanding that freedom of speech was not limited only to "legitimate" parties. A week after the actions of the Red Squad on May Day, the CCF called for supporters of free speech to rally at Queen's Park. When they did so they found the main entrance to the bandstand boarded up, but they assembled nearby, with Captain Elmore Phillip calling for all political tendencies to be accorded freedom of speech: "If the Hon. R. B. Bennett can speak from this park, I can speak from this park.... Mrs. Tim Buck can speak. This meeting to-day is no mere stunt. We must establish the right of free speech in Toronto. We have the right of meeting in any public park except Sunday."[59]

As spring gave way to summer in 1933 this escalating demand for freedom of speech, and its fusion with protests of the workless, was challenged by a rising tide of anticommunism.[60] This aggressive reaction was met with a wave of rallies that built on Communist organization of out-of-work servicemen and municipal unemployed councils, embedded in distinct Toronto neighbourhoods. Some of these actions saw members of the CCF and CPC work together, although tensions between the two organizations remained, and some protests were organized unilaterally by one body or the other. Little Communist presence could be discerned, for instance, at the CCF rally in support of the May Day victimization of Communists, who held their own protest later in June. Ewart G. Humphries, at one time president and then secretary of the Red-led National Unemployed Council, addressed eight hundred supporters.[61] Humphries, the Mount Dennis leader of a branch of the York Township United Workers' Association, was an advocate of building broader alliances than had been the norm under the sectarian practices of the early Third Period. In March 1933 Humphries convened a United Workers' Conference, drawing delegates from thirty Toronto organizations, nineteen of them not affiliated to the CPC, into discussions about their common experiences. Out of the pooled knowledge came efforts to build a unified township body, one that brought CCFers and CPCers together with others for whom no formal political alliance was discernible. This kind of activity was emerging as well in other Toronto districts, with the Earlscourt Unemployed Council composed of social democrats, Communists, Trotskyists, ILPers, trade unionists, members of ratepayers and property owner groups, and those affiliated with the Canadian Legion, the British Imperial Association, and the Orange Order. In Toronto Lakeside, CCF rank-and-filers repudiated the obvious antagonism of their national and provincial leaders toward any collective work with Communists to cultivate a "significant degree of unity" with CPC activists. John Manley notes that Toronto's nascent Trotskyist movement, born in part out of hostility to the sectarian isolation of official Communism's Third Period, welcomed such united front initiatives, which were judged a "more correct Leninist approach." Indeed, Left Oppositionists like T. P. Mill were chairing open-air Unemployed Council meetings in Toronto's west end throughout the early summer of 1933, "participating in the struggles of the unemployed for the right of meeting in the public parks." *October Youth* reported that workers fought back at one of these militant gatherings against police attempts to break up the meeting and "For the first time in Toronto Draper's Cossacks were forcibly ejected from a public park by the unemployed."[62]

The pinnacle of this free speech/unemployment protest was reached in August 1933, as three Toronto parks became the stomping ground of demonstrators and their police adversaries. More than a score of separate rallies took place between August 3 and September 1, 1933, many of them happening on the same evening at different venues. These events, ranging in size from several hundred to several thousand, turned Earlscourt Park, Trinity Park, and Allan Gardens into sites of ongoing police-unemployed confrontation. The opening salvo was fired on August 3, with two protest meetings shut down by police. Having been given the bureaucratic run-around at the local police station, city hall, and by the parks commissioner, the Earlscourt branch of the Toronto Unemployed Council lacked a permit to gather on the home turf of their local park but decided to proceed without such a document. Speakers were thwarted by fifteen to twenty officers, a detective ushering the first speaker from the platform, that being a signal for the police to begin dispersing the crowd. The unemployed fought back, noticing in the close quarters of several scuffles that many of the uniformed officers had removed their numbered identification badges, making it difficult or impossible to ascertain which specific cops had exercised undue force. The CCF also tried to assemble that same evening at Trinity Park, insistent that there was "no law stat[ing] that a permit must be obtained to hold political meetings in a city park." Police disagreed and shut down the meeting. Less than a week later, a small riot erupted as the Toronto Unemployed Council, in defiance of police injunctions to stay out of Trinity Park, convened a meeting after a baseball game. On foot and horseback, police charged the crowd, which resisted. When an arrest attempt was made, the officer was swarmed by a group of women who ran him down with baby carriages. The Communist meeting was ultimately broken up, but many of the police reported that they were somewhat the worse for wear, their shins taking a beating in the tumult. Around the same time, a Canadian Labour Defence League protest of two hundred unemployed was driven from Allan Gardens, the forcible dispersal, once again, ostensibly occasioned by the Communist organizers' failure to secure a permit.[63]

Such skirmishes were but a prelude to a much-anticipated bigger battle. August 15 saw two large free speech/unemployment/relief protests, an Allan Gardens rally organized by the Red-led Workers' Ex-Servicemen's League (WESL), and a joint effort by the CCF and the Young Communist League in Earlscourt Park. Each demonstration saw crowds of approximately two thousand come together. The WESL unfurled its banner, "Heroes 1914—Bums 1933," and this action of the unemployed veterans clearly riled the police, who descended on Allan Gardens in large numbers. Corps of motorcyclists and horsemen led the charge. Attacking the banner and those who were waving it over the assembly, police wrestled the support poles away but then found themselves assailed by women, their baby carriages this time parked beneath a tree. Demonstrators and police battled for two hours, with motorcycles used as exhaust fume cannons. The cops, encircling the crowd, positioned their mobile vehicles to direct an endless spray of carbon monoxide at the protesters. Unemployed veterans likened the police action to German use of poison gas in the Great War. In response, John O'Shea, a homeless demonstrator residing in the Wellington House shelter, ostensibly shouted: "We won't throw stones. Get a gun and shoot the ------- like they did in Ireland. The only way to get anything is by showing force." This outburst earned O'Shea arrest for inciting to riot. Four others were taken into custody, charged with obstructing police and assaulting an undercover officer, among them William Lyons, a thirty-six-year-old unemployed ex-soldier.

At Earlscourt Park things were more tranquil, the demonstration going off without a hitch, the speakers unmolested by police, who had obviously decided to invest their repressive capacities in Allan Gardens. The strong show of police force did not dampen the spirits of the WESL, however. The ex-soldiers' association was back at it immediately, as were comrades in the Toronto Unemployed Council. These bodies organized protest rallies at Trinity Park and Earlscourt Park on the nights of August 16–17 respectively. At the former meeting, one thousand strong, the crowd was dispersed as police charged into it on horseback and used to good effect the now familiar "heavy oil smoke from the exhaust" of their motorcycles. But Earlscourt Park was once again an unambiguous victory, the Communists active in that neighbourhood obviously having cultivated effective united front ties with CCFers and many others. The Red-led protest, organized by the WESL and the local Unemployed Council, drew five thousand angry jobless to the park, the vast bulk of whom were neither Communists nor even necessarily Party sympathizers. The police dared not interfere. A. N. Willicombe addressed the massive throng:

> The orderly meeting of 5,000 people tonight proves that the police and not the unemployed had been responsible for the disorders in the past. I think the reasons they failed to break us up is only because the crowd was too vast. This is a great victory for free speech in Toronto.

One night later one thousand gathered in Earlscourt Park, untroubled by police, to hear Maurice Spector of the Trotskyist International Left Opposition address those assembled on "the fight of the workers for free speech and assembly."[64]

Ironically, the police themselves may well have licenced the Earlscourt successes, being reluctant to move on protests where the CCF was playing some role, even if in alliance with the Communist Party of Canada. Draper and his Red Squad, as well as precinct police forces, clearly were targeting those demonstrations of the unemployed led by the Communists and their known "front groups." Thus, a large CCF rally at Allan Gardens on August 26 was allowed to proceed, its message one of work for all and changes to the capitalist economic system. Three days later, when the Communist WESL announced a free speech meeting for the very same Allan Gardens, its attempt to rally was broken up by the gendarmes. At this point some of the sectarian isolation of the CPC's Third Period was wearing thin, and the WESL, as an organization, had close ties to a select group of the more left-wing and militant CCFers. The Ex-Servicemen's League Chairman, Hugh Edmonson, was linked to the CCF and defended the right of all groups to assemble and exercise free speech in city parks. In conversation with the *Toronto Star,* WESL spokesmen stated that the League had determined to "meet anywhere at any time in public parks, until the iron heelism of Chief Draper is stamped out." As if to highlight the differential treatment the police meted out to the CCF and the CPC, at the August 26 WESL Allan Gardens protest, two CCF speakers—Edmonson and T. S. Crain—were allowed to speak but when a third advocate of the unemployed soldiers mounted the rostrum, the police declared the meeting over and dispersed the crowd roughly. There were public and discrediting allegations that the police acted negligently in refusing aid to a girl trampled in the stampede of horses. The unemployed servicemen were back in Allan Gardens the next night and, a few days later, demonstrated again at the same locale. "I was hoping the police would ask us for a permit to speak," the indefatigable A.N. Willicombe thundered, "I have a permit, it is my release from the Imperial Army."[65]

At this point the battle for free speech in Toronto, infused with the militancy of protests against the spreading scourge of unemployment, was won.[66] Draper and the police largely backed away from their attacks on Communists utilizing the streets and parks of Toronto to propagandize in the open air. On September 1, 1933, demonstrations advocating free speech in Allan Gardens and Trinity Park, organized by the CCF and addressed by a representative of the Toronto Unemployed Council, defied the police to deny the right "to hold a public meeting in any park of the city." By the end of September 1933, the Civic Parks Committee had recommended that four parks should be designated open to all public speaking. When the WESL, the Canadian Labour Defence League, and the Toronto Unemployed Council pressured the Committee to expand the list, four more parks were added as free speech venues. Ironically, Trinity Park and Allan Gardens, which had witnessed some of the most pitched battles for the rights of the unemployed and others to congregate and publicly challenge authorities, were not named as sites where public speaking was to be freely permitted. But, importantly, Queen's Park was on the list, as well as Earlscourt Park.[67]

Free speech secured, Communists wasted no time in utilizing this victory in the interests of the jobless. An Ontario Hunger March was being promoted in May–June 1934, with Toronto's Reds promising a turnout of eight thousand from across the province. Some fifty thousand "Hunger March Manifestoes" were distributed in preparation for the end-of-July inundation of Toronto with out-of-work demonstrators. The unemployed of Windsor, Chatham, London, Woodstock, Stratford, Kitchener, the Niagara district, and Hamilton gathered in west Toronto as the protest walk converged on the unemployed strongholds of Long Branch and New Toronto. Civic officials and Police Chief Draper refused the unemployed the right to parade through Toronto to Queen's Park, and skirmishes erupted as police and the jobless clashed. But a newly elected and liberal-leaning reform Premier, Mitchell Hepburn, fresh from a recent landslide victory, agreed to meet a delegation of the hunger marchers, insisting that while Mayor Stewart might choose to "employ a body of Cossacks to ride them down … he cannot prevent the Prime Minister and his Cabinet from giving an audience to these people." The next day, Hepburn and his Liberal Ministers replaced two Tory police commissioners in Toronto with two officially endorsed Grits. The hunger march then proceeded without incident, as five thousand gathered on the Legislature lawns while a large delegation of two hundred met with Hepburn, Attorney-General Arthur Roebuck, and Minister of Welfare David Croll. A procession of speakers urged the Hepburn government to implement a non-contributory unemployment insurance program, increases in cash relief allowances, and a $300 million public works program. Among the speakers on behalf of the jobless were seven of the ten Communist candidates in the recent June 19, 1934 provincial election. Noting that he had failed to convince R. B. Bennett that Ottawa should be footing more of the relief bill, Hepburn listened politely to the hunger marchers' representatives but promised them little. One historian suggests that he charmed the Communist-led unemployed into submission by defending the full and unrestricted right of the unemployed to "meet, speak, and organize in every city and village of the province" and countermanding a City of Toronto prohibition of the marchers' final rally at Queen's Park. Roebuck was cheered when he sent the jobless delegation back to the large crowd awaiting them outside the provincial Legislature with the words, "God bless you in your work. I hope you become strong enough to come [back] and enforce your demands upon any government in power."

The governing Liberals then funded trucks to transport some of the jobless back to their original points of departure.[68]

Workers' Unity League spokesman Fred Collins rightly warned the thousands of unemployed that Hepburn was killing them with kindness. He implored the protesters not to "let yourself be blinded by the soft words, the honeyed phrases, the open arms and proffered friendship" of a government that was in fact a danger to them, and that had offered little, if any, concrete concessions. From his Tory perch atop city hall, Mayor Stewart denounced Hepburn for pandering to "Communists and other subversive elements." His Worship likened Toronto's relationship to the volatile unemployed as "sitting on a volcano."

Croll certainly saw the threatening possibility of an eruption and was hard at work to suppress it. Particularly troubling were the rising relief costs in the blue-collar suburbs of Toronto, locales like Mimico, Etobicoke, New Toronto, Long Branch, Scarborough, and the three Yorks (York, North York, East York), where those on public assistance ranged from 35–45 percent of the entire population. In places like these, Croll found that municipalities were prone to pay out more than was necessary, and to reward the squeaky wheel of unemployed protest with the demanded oil of relief. He resolved to end the situation with a new approach: "Relief

TORONTO'S POOR

to workers, nothing for shirkers." The plan depended on more rigorous supervision and monitoring of the unemployed, who were required to register for relief. Surveillance being tightened up, relief dispensation would then be tied directly to work requirements: an allowance of $40 monthly would be earned for eighty hours of work at fifty cents an hour, paid in cash, and relief recipients could keep any extra money they were able to accrue through paid work, up to one-third of their relief allocation, as long as it was reported.

Over the course of 1934–36 this system, which saw the regulation of the poor intensified with home investigations and constant erosion of relief payments, whose ceilings were set by the 1932 Campbell Report, came under increasing attack by the jobless. Hepburn's "open door" policy to the 1934 delegation of the unemployed was soon replaced by barricades to keep the jobless out of Queen's Park, separated from the premier and his cabinet. On April 4, 1935, almost two thousand unemployed from Toronto and a number of working-class suburbs descended on the provincial seat of government, led by Communists A. E. Smith and Ernest Lawrie. They demanded a 50 percent increase in the food voucher allowance set by the Campbell Report. Not forgotten was the Attorney-General's 1934 invitation. One placard read: "God Bless You, Come Back Again. Here We Are Roebuck!"[69]

On May 1, 1935, Toronto's Communists organized a May Day parade, in which various Unemployed Councils and other organizations centrally concerned with the ongoing challenges posed by those out-of-work participated. Toronto's *Globe* reported an attendance of ten thousand, noting that the Queen's Park rally that completed the march was "the largest outdoor gathering of labor in the history of the city." For the first time since 1929, Communists had been given a permit to use the bandstand and its sound system. Police directed traffic. Thousands of unemployed gathered as Party speakers called on the working class to "Unite and Fight!"[70]

A year later, May Day in Queen's Park drew out the condescending racism and political invective of a "Canadian," writing to the *Mail and Empire* in a way that congealed Reds and relief, the foreign born and alien thinking:

> The huge May Day Communist gathering ... justified itself.... Our politicians, living and dead, who supinely acquiesced in the dumping on our shores of this slum rabble are deserving of the severest censure, not only of our generation, but of the generations succeeding ours.... Everything about Communism is antipathetical to our ideas and ideals.... While easily disposed of as a political menace, it is still a serious social and economic one. Eighty percent of the "Reds" are on relief and will stay there to the last

gasp; many of them will never work again, couldn't even if they wanted to, so undesirable are their employment qualifications. Despite the fact that we are putting the very bread in these foreign-born mouths, they are snarling and snapping like so many curs and doing everything in their power to create dissension and industrial unrest.... In the bandstand Red spouters hold forth at great length—much venting and full dramatics—wooly witted economics, derision of the Diety and Christian religion, exhortations to smash and destroy, boasts and taunts as to future activities. Not a word of protest was raised by the majority of responsible, decent Canadians who listened, fascinated by the fury and the diatribes.... We give you the Communists, an expensive social blight, but not a menace.[71]

It was a different era as Reds moved from the Third Period to the Popular Front. No longer were they necessarily a threatening political force to be suppressed; yet there was also continuity in the sense that Communism remained very much an alien "other," the antithesis of Canada's ostensibly true being. In this shift and continuity, the wageless figured centrally, the single unemployed men whom the Great Depression turned out of the factories and industrial employments of capitalism in

United May Day Conference, Toronto, 1935, possibly Tim Buck (l) and Joshua Gershman (r).

York University Libraries, Clara Thomas Archives & Special Collections, *Toronto Telegram* fonds, ASC19064, *Evening Telegram* Staff.

crisis also proving to be the shock troops of the Communist International's war on the profit system.

The Single Unemployed: Bound for Anything but Glory

If there is a representation of the 1930s that remains imprinted on popular memory, it is that of the single unemployed man, on the move, often riding the rails, in a futile quest for work. Bound for anything and anywhere but glory, the army of the jobless struggled to survive the economic collapse of the Great Depression. The tragedy of capitalist crisis that was the "dirty thirties" is often personalized in terms of a generation of youth which lost, through its wagelessness, the promise and possibility of a future. The 1930s were Barry Broadfoot's "ten lost years," Irene Baird's "waste heritage."

As an icon of the human destruction of the Great Depression, then, the single unemployed man looms large. Too large, in fact, for his longstanding and dominating presence in the imaginary of the 1930s obscures histories of suffering and struggle involving single women and families composed of husbands, wives, sons, and daughters. It skews our understandings of the historical complexity of the diverse impacts of unemployment in ways that concentrate attention on male relief camps, western Canadian riots involving largely the single unemployed, and "treks" of the jobless to Ottawa, where contingents of transient, jobless males might let the powers that be know of their discontents. As important as such developments were and are, there are other stories to tell, and Toronto was one of the most important venues in which they unfolded.

Nonetheless, the single unemployed can hardly be sidestepped in any account of Toronto's dispossessed and the intensity of the capitalist crisis of unemployment in the 1930s. Both the Communist Party and its declared enemies at the pinnacle of power and authority in various levels of the state—federal, provincial, and municipal—tended to see the increasing ranks of desperate, single unemployed men similarly, as the potential shock troops of revolt, the cutting edge of the "dangerous classes."[72] Galvanizing or pacifying this would-be army of redressers was thus of paramount importance.

For those committed to the project of pacification, the sheer magnitude of the crisis of joblessness in the 1930s proved daunting indeed. The ad-hoc nineteenth-century system of poor relief largely remained in existence into the early 1930s, replete with its governing ideology of the deserving/undeserving poor and its mandate to provide only for those who would, metaphorically, "crack the stone." Yet the 1930s was far removed from the 1830s or the 1890s. The tens of thousands who registered with Toronto's Central Bureau of Employment Relief by 1931 were a measure of the quantitative dimensions of the crisis, which taxed, to the breaking point, the capacity of the House of Industry and ancillary philanthropic and religious charities to address the needs of the poor. As inadequacy after inadequacy left the unemployed increasingly agitated, they turned to protest in which the single unemployed often took leading roles. And, unlike their counterparts in the nineteenth century, they could, if they were so inclined, march under the politics of the Red Flag that Communists were more than ready to unfurl.

The House of Industry put up a stubborn front and fought to keep its hegemonic hold over the provision of relief to the poor. In the autumn of 1930, with its Wayfarers' Lodge filled to capacity every night, more than 250 single men relying on its shelter, a House of Industry spokesman reported that "Any homeless man can find a bed here any night of the week" but added the caveat: "If he wants to make sure of a bed, he'll come before seven o'clock at night." No one would be turned away unless they refused the requirement of performing a labour test for their lodging and sustenance.[73]

Between the lines of this claim that all was functioning well for the homeless in Toronto, however, could be read acknowledgement of the pressures now facing the House of Industry. A new wing of the Wayfarers' Lodge was under construction and, according to official statements, would be able to accommodate the rising tide of unemployed and transient applicants for a bed and some modest meals. What was not made clear was that before the completion of this added wing, roughly seventy of the upward of three hundred men who might be crammed into the Wayfarers' Lodge were sleeping on the floor. As construction added thirty-six new double-decker beds at the end of 1931, men continued to have to camp out on concrete. It was also a point of contention in Toronto that 85 percent of those registered at the Lodge "rode the rods" to avail themselves of the House of Industry's largesse. Moreover, anyone looking seriously at the problem of unemployment and transient single males in Toronto knew full well that suggestions of all being right for the workless were little more than special pleading.[74]

Toronto Star headlines proclaimed, "Army of Homeless Huddle in Park, Mission, and Box Car" and "Homeless Steal Warmth from Brick Kilns." Along the waterfront, destitute men sought shelter in railway boxcars, while 450 men were living adjacent to the Don River in and around the Toronto Brick Company. Some of them, described as "homeless, jobless, and penniless wanderers," found working brick furnaces to occupy on frigid December nights, crawling "inside the kilns where hot bricks are cooling off." They did this, apparently, with the blessings of Frank

E. Waterman, general manager of the brick manufacturing concern, who issued orders to his staff that the homeless men were to be accommodated; Waterman even resisted the intrusions of the police. The Don River Valley had a long history of squatting and in the 1910s and 1920s had been home to a wave of Roma immigrants, who established a cycle of encampments that attracted much newspaper interest in the "primitive Gypsies." The particular 1930–31 "hobo colony" of the dispossessed had grown from an original camp of seventy. Its ranks swelled as groups of Finns and Bulgarians—enticed to Toronto with the promise of construction work only to find that no such employment was available—joined the settlement, which expanded beyond the huts constructed from unused bricks into wooden shelters on nearby forested land, tree houses, and lean-tos under the trestles of bridges. The police, Waterman's resistance notwithstanding, broke up the makeshift housing, bulldozing bricks and burning wood, but the determined occupants returned once more, before being finally driven away.

Where to go? Contrary to the House of Industry statement, beds for the homeless were not easy to come by. The Salvation Army was providing eleven hundred beds a night, but this was obviously not enough. Cathedral doorways saw small groups congregate for nightly shelter under arches, while "many stretched out bodies" on park benches might be discerned as evening came. The city's small missions, hostels, and shelters were booked to overflowing and routinely turned away those looking for a place to sleep. On any given night, up to fifteen hundred single transient men might be unsuccessfully looking for a roof over their heads. Nor was shelter the only issue: the Scott Institute, the Everyman's Club, the Maison Club, and other charitable organizations were feeding thousands of homeless men daily. All indications were, by the end of 1930, that the crisis of homelessness was acute. And it was about to get much worse.[75]

A wealthy Toronto philanthropist, J. Allan Ross, funded the operation of two new shelters for unemployed single men, supplementing the facilities of the House of Industry's Wayfarers' Lodge, the Salvation Army, the Fred Victor Mission, and other such institutions. "During the past week," Ross told the *Star* in December 1930, "it has become definitely apparent from the rapidly increasing numbers of men sleeping on newspapers, floors, boards and bricks, that housing facilities are inadequate by some two thousand beds, with an ever greater urgency facing Toronto during December and January." Through his enterprise Wrigley, Ltd., Ross financed the Wellington House hostel, located in an old warehouse. It provided six hundred beds for single unemployed men. He also opened Dundas House out of an empty bakery near Spadina and Dundas. But private philanthropy was only a stopgap solution,

Police officer inspects documents of resting unemployed "hunger marcher," Toronto, July 1934.

York University Libraries, Clara Thomas Archives & Special Collections, *Toronto Telegram* fonds, ASC19079, *Evening Telegram* Staff.

and even Ross's Wellington House was soon taken over by the City of Toronto's Department of Public Welfare.[76] It was destined to become a focal point of discontent, grievance, and protest in the years to come. Ross, in turn, would join with Ford Company executive Wallace Campbell to produce the Campbell Report in 1932.[77]

That the dimensions of the crisis of joblessness in Toronto's early 1930s necessitated a more co-ordinated and organized response than that on offer by the old House of Industry system, supplemented by charity, both philanthropic and religious, was increasingly obvious. This was not merely a matter of good intentions and increased efficiencies. As Paula Maurutto notes in her study of Catholic charities, "Single unemployed men ... were constructed as a potentially unruly mass of layabouts soaking up scarce resources." It was understood that with the numbers of single unemployed men in Toronto growing daily, the possibility of violent protest, should their needs not be met, was quite real. "By keeping stomachs filled with beans, stew, and coffee," reported one newspaper in 1931, Toronto "has prevented riots, perhaps bloodshed."[78]

Laver vs. The Lodge: The Voucher War of 1932–1933 and the Consolidation of a Regulatory Order

Yet the ideological grip exercised by "voluntarism" (with its many deficiencies when confronted with the rise of unemployment in the 1930s to previously unanticipated heights) was tight indeed. It was reinforced by the politics of balkanization that locked Canada constitutionally into a tried and true "passing of the buck" in which the federal state in Ottawa insisted that relief was the responsibility of provincial and local governments, which meant the burden of provisioning fell on municipalities such as Toronto.[79] As the country's second largest metropolitan centre, with an undue weight of relief expenditure, Toronto moved over the course of 1930–34 to centralize control over housing and feeding the army of single unemployed men, as well as the thousands of families reduced to dependency because of the crisis of joblessness. But it did so very much influenced by nineteenth-century understandings that twinned welfare and work, meeting resistance, at every step, from entrenched interests associated with older practices.

An initial step in the direction of building a welfare officialdom was taken late in 1930 with the striking of a Civic Unemployment Relief Committee and its

　　　　　　　　　　　　　　　　　　　TORONTO'S POOR

December establishment of a Central Bureau of Employment/Relief responsible for registering all of those homeless and unemployed in Toronto who were receiving support. This move was a declaration that it was a municipal priority to minimize social spending and maximize control over the unemployed. All organizations involved in providing shelter and food for the poor were expected to co-operate with the Central Bureau, which was ostensibly now making it a condition of relief at all levels that the destitute formally declare their dependency. Organizations like the Everyman's Club, which fed three hundred men a day, worried that this new bureaucracy would have the power to dictate who could be served within its building and who had to be denied. This they did not take kindly. At the Maison Club, presided over by Toronto socialite, would-be journalist, and future player in Ottawa's National Health and Welfare bureaucracy Miss Ivy Maison, one thousand men were served two meals a day at two separate Toronto locations. Backed by churches and women's voluntary organizations, and partially bankrolled by contributions from police and firemen, the Maison Club was one of the philanthropic endeavours that seemed to fly in the face of the regulatory regime that the Central Bureau wanted to establish. Questions were asked of its policy of allowing residents of the Wellington House and the Fred Victor Mission tickets to its mealtimes. Wouldn't such generosity make the single unemployed men who sat, apparently emotionless and speechless, in her soup kitchen at the old St. Lawrence Hall, be reluctant to go out and work in the spring, having been fed all winter? "They'll have to work. We can't go on forever," Miss Maison responded, adding for good measure that her commissary, like the House of Industry and in compliance with the obvious orientation of the Central Bureau, made it a requirement that those who ate had to at least be looking for work. If they refused to hunt for employment, assured Miss Maison, "we take away their meal ticket."[80]

The point of the Central Bureau, however, was that this kind of decision was too important to leave to the likes of Miss Maison. The creation of the City of Toronto Department of Public Welfare in June 1931 marked a new stage in consolidating and centralizing social welfare services, co-ordinating the work of philanthropic initiatives, public bodies like the House of Industry, and the municipal government.[81]

Arguably the most important figure in the Department of Public Welfare was its Commissioner, Albert W. [Bert] Laver. Laver inherited a system in which the municipality, securing funds from other governments, most particularly the province of Ontario, and private sources in the charity milieu, as well as what could be allocated by Toronto's Board of Control, transferred monies to the House of Industry, which then controlled distribution of so-called outdoor relief to destitute families and provided, as it could, for transient homeless men. With 25,000 families and tens of thousands of single unemployed men and women on relief in October 1932, a major battle erupted, pitting Laver against the House of Industry. Estimates were that Toronto was forking over $3,000,000 annually to the antiquated charitable agency, which provided a residence to 150 elderly people, sheltered between 200 and 300 single unemployed men in its casual ward each night, served 2000 meals a day, and distributed daily outdoor relief to 3,500 people. By 1933, when the battle between Laver and the House of Industry peaked, fully one-sixth of Toronto's population, or 126,795 individuals, were being sustained, in part, by the institution's relief procedures.[82]

As early as January 1932, House of Industry superintendent Frances Laughlen charged that Toronto Medical Officer of Health Dr. Gordon Jackson and Laver were colluding to remove responsibility for the distribution of outdoor family relief from the House of Industry. Dr. Jackson had criticized unsanitary conditions in the kitchen, and Laver let it be known that he was no supporter of the institution. By 1933 the acrimonious relations between Laver and the House of Industry were unmistakable, with an Alderman who was also a trustee of the House of Industry denouncing Laver before City Council as having waged a "long and carefully staged assault against the House of Industry, and the methods of operation there." It was claimed that Laver had appeared before the charitable institution's Board less than two weeks after his appointment and declared that "it was his intention to put them 'out of business,' at the earliest possible date."[83]

In this war of commissioner against charitable agency, many complex issues were at stake, among them competing material interests of layers of Toronto's bourgeois and bureaucratic elites. Central to the resulting conflicts, which played an important role in municipal politics, was a change in how relief was to be dispensed, and in particular the possibility of a voucher system. Vouchers, dispensed by the municipality and redeemable by married men for food and other necessities from mercantile grocers or by the single unemployed at the hostels, soup kitchens, or the House of Industry where they slept and ate, would, of course, further concentrate the regulatory authority of Laver's municipal welfare regime. They became central to a sixteen-month debate, often impassioned, that brought the issue of unemployment and its relief into central focus at city hall, in various municipal agencies, and in Toronto election campaign debates of December 1932. At issue were often testy confrontations between supporters of the House of Industry and its opponents, the resulting verbal mud-slinging bringing into the public discourse a wide range of complaints voiced by the unemployed.

A delegation of out-of-work veterans from the Canadian Legion appeared at a Toronto Board of Control meeting in June 1932, demanding that the Department of Public Welfare take over the distribution of outdoor relief from the House of Industry, raising a range of complaints. Getting nowhere, delegation spokesman Jack Parnell sparred with Controller McBride: "Parnell: There are 15,000 men on relief. When they hear of this, they will have something to say about it. McBride: Bring some of them down here. Parnell: I will bring plenty down here." Election meetings regularly ended in mayhem, and the contentious proposed voucher system was often the leading topic of discussion. At an all-candidates meeting at the Harbord Collegiate School, where support for vouchers was particularly strong, Alderman Fred Hamilton declared that he thought it high time "the business should be given to our smaller merchants." "I stand whole-heartedly behind the transfer of relief from the House of Industry," Hamilton concluded. When three conservative Toronto elected officials—Controllers McBride and Ramsden and Alderman J. T. Johnson—defended the House of Industry, its food, and, for good measure, Police Chief Draper at a Riverdale meeting they were drowned out in a cacophony of derision. McBride's audible comment that he always liked "a nice fat, rosy, riot," did nothing to quiet the angry crowd. It had been whipped into a frenzy by a package of tainted meat being thrown on the stage of the all candidates debate, the projectile landing at the feet of the ever-combative McBride:

> The ratepayers, already excited by cat-calls, hoots, jeers, and boos, became uncontrollable. They shouted and cheered, stood on their seats, and jostled one another, crowding toward the platform to view the package.... Con McBride had just stated that the House of Industry supplied pure food when the parcel of meat was flung at his feet.... Mr Cooney (Labour candidate) undid the package and dropped it in disgust.... The package of meat was hastily kicked under a chair by J. T. Johnson, chairperson of the meeting.

"The meeting was the most fiery the ward has seen in many years," reported one newspaper. "Only a squad of able-bodied policemen prevented a riot." [84]

Laver himself often seemed at odds over the issue of vouchers, which he knew had support among varied constituencies, including segments of the unemployed and labour movements. At the wild December 1932 Riverdale electioneering meeting, for instance, both Thomas Cooney, speaking as the Labour candidate, and Alice Buck of the Communist United Workers advocated a voucher system. Similar support for vouchers erupted a few weeks later in mid-January 1933 as a Communist Party–led hunger march united Hamilton and Toronto protesters in the initial stages of an automobile cavalcade to Ottawa. Storming a Board of Control meeting, the jobless jousted with Mayor Stewart, who attacked the leaders of the mobilization as inviting "the unemployed to flock to Toronto, coming in motor cars to lay complaints before us." The spokesman for the discontented marchers piped up, "How 'bout vouchers?" The Mayor responded brusquely, "If you're demanding cash vouchers I say no! All you are looking for is trouble—hunger marches, riding in automobiles." Originally, Laver rejected the voucher scheme, focusing his attack on the House of Industry's central depot. He acknowledged that it posed a considerable inconvenience for the poor, who sometimes had to walk several miles to pick up basic necessitates, only to suffer the humiliating and exhausting trudge home with a sack of relief potatoes and the like on their backs. This was a common complaint, dismissed impolitely by civic officials such as Controller McBride and Alderman Johnson. When attacked for making statements to relief recipients that, "You should not mind going after the food," this duo shot back with retorts that, "Any man who is being looked after by the pogey house should be glad to get it." In February 1933 Laver addressed this issue by advising the municipal Board of Control that it made far more sense to cut the House of Industry out of this practice of centralized distribution, instead setting up a series of municipally run, neighbourhood-based food depots, more accessible to families on relief. Vouchers, then, would not be necessary.[85]

If at times it appeared that Laver was advocating reforms that were also championed by the unemployed themselves or their advocates in the TTLC unions, this should not be misinterpreted as support for the dispossessed. Laver was no friend of the unemployed and their radical leaders, supporting deportation of non-citizen militants who were rocking the regulatory order with defiance and mobilization of protest. Among the policies he endorsed were classificatory schema that designated the *truly* unemployed and the "social problem" cases in which joblessness was ostensibly a consequence of some personal pathology; since the single unemployed, both males and females, were most likely to fall into this latter category they required rigorous surveillance, in which any "moral" failings would be cause for the termination of relief "benefits." Laver had a particular obsession with illegitimacy, insisting that 63 percent of the relief case load could be attributed to immorality and children born out of wedlock, targeting single unemployed women as agents of their own downfall. He advocated birth control and even sterilization for those families taking relief who were judged to be of "low intelligence."[86]

Laver responded to pressure from various non-working class quarters, including demands by the Retail Merchants' Association that the practice of distribution of relief through the House of Industry be discontinued and that a system of individual grocers tendering for relief business "on a competitive basis" be implemented. The merchants, dressing up their opposition to the House of Industry doling out food from a central depot with crocodile tears for those distressed families who were subject to the "unmerited humiliation" of walking great distances to the House of Industry's distribution centre when "they cannot even afford car fare," likely had more prosaic concerns. They well knew that the House of Industry trustees controlled all purchasing and distribution associated with the outdoor relief system, and this constituted a lucrative, and expanding, trade. If they had an easy target in the "inadequate and insufficient" House of Industry monopoly, they nonetheless wanted to spread the profits throughout their ranks, where they felt there was "adequate machinery for handling relief orders." Indeed, the merchants claimed that if they were not given a piece of the action, many of them faced "extinction." Not quite in favour of a reformed voucher system, these small retailers were certainly supporters of Commissioner Laver's crusade to bring the House of Industry's stranglehold over relief provisioning and distribution to an end.[87]

When Laver did eventually endorse a system of vouchers in March 1933, it was evident that his concern was less with the interests of the poor than with the business community and what he perceived as the regulatory rights and responsibilities of his department. Vouchers would be issued by district offices of the Department of Public Welfare, necessitating, of course, that all relief recipients were duly registered with the municipality. These relief tickets would then be presented to grocers in exchange for food. Most importantly, as this radical revision of relief practice was underway, Laver was also advocating a new "work test" to accompany the voucher system. All able-bodied unemployed men receiving relief were required to do two or three days of unpaid labour each week, either clearing the marsh at Mugg's Landing or grading the terrain at Riverdale Park. According to Laver, the number of men that this "work test" would affect approached ten thousand, and the hours of free labour the city would acquire in the process constituted nothing less than a windfall at a time when municipal coffers were less than overflowing. As in the nineteenth century and in our present times, the assault on the morality of the poor was never far from the surface of the debates around such "work for welfare" schemes. Controller Ramsden backed Laver's suggestions, adding that putting the unemployed at hard labour would weed out the undeserving poor. "There are undoubtedly a very large number of imposters," Ramsden said knowingly, "This work test plan would safeguard the worthy, in addition to cutting off the relief lists those who should never have got on in the first place."[88]

The House of Industry, knowing that the voucher system spelled the end of its hegemony in the relief business, fought back with a vengeance, relying especially on powerful trustees well ensconced at city hall. Arguments turned on the economic and the moral. Key spokesmen included C. T. Stark, the House Chairman, and Aldermen Beamish and Day, both of whom were House trustees, Beamish being on the critically important Purchasing Committee of the relief agency. They assailed Laver's lack of experience in buying food in quantity and overseeing its economical preparation. Attention was called to the fact that Laver's plan depended on hiring for wages an entire staff to run the proposed system whereas, at the House of Industry, a "great deal of the labor in connection with the distribution of unemployed relief is also done free by people receiving relief or by wards of the institution." Ratepayers associations got in on the act, defending the House of Industry's use of free labour, either of the kind conscripted from relief recipients or volunteered by members of the community. "The whole tendency of Mr. Laver's department has been to build up too many paying jobs," argued Alex Rhind, President of the Ratepayers Association, bemoaning the apparent discouragement of "private charity and philanthropy." Laver's scheme was simply "not practicable." Complementing such arguments for economy and efficiency were the usual attacks on the unemployed themselves. Stark argued that voucher systems had a long history and had always foundered on the abuse of relief recipients, who could not be stopped from trading their vouchers for cash and then using the money secured to purchase liquor or other undesirable items. Beamish put the case in carefully coded language: "Years ago when the voucher system was tried, it failed because people asked for money, instead of goods, or a class of goods, which was not on the schedule, and not necessarily to sustain life." Dredging up cases of liquor-swilling relief recipients indulged by Laver's department and charging that the commissioner had long coveted the House of Industry's assets, the voucher war took a turn for the worse in March 1933. The invective continued throughout the spring and summer.[89]

It was all for nought. Laver's bureaucratic officialdom was the wave of the future, and the ad hoc relief dispensation of the House of Industry gave way to the regulatory municipal state and its Department of Public Welfare's ostensible expertise. On March 30, 1933, City Council voted twenty to six in favour of adopting the voucher innovations, to be implemented on a trial basis for sixty days as of mid-April. The House of Industry was allowed to retain its responsibility for the distribution of ordinary outdoor relief, especially as it pertained to widows, but the

Department of Public Welfare would now oversee the majority of cases involving families of the unemployed, and single men and women out of work who obviously required the close supervisory eye of the state.

Laver's new regime proved a brutal reconstruction. He retained the Campbell Report's ceilings, leaving the level of food support for relief recipients the same, but he kept the economies of dispensation very much in check, largely by implementing a rigorous surveillance and monitoring apparatus. The food depots he developed across the city were staffed by unemployed white-collar workers whose compensation was their rent relief. And who better to conduct investigations and supervisions of relief families than the unemployed themselves? Ostensibly well versed in the tricks of the chiselling trade, they were recruited in droves to interrogate and report on their counterparts. As the relief rolls expanded to more than twenty-seven thousand Toronto families by September of 1933, Laver was nonetheless able to hold the line on expenditures, largely, as he explained, by weeding out over eight thousand families who failed, under the new system, to qualify for relief. Rigid home investigations and application of an affidavit system supplemented by the energetic prosecution of relief fraud in the courts netted Laver savings of over $300,000 in six months.

Communist "Young Pioneers" at "Hunger Protest," Toronto, 1935.

York University Libraries, Clara Thomas Archives & Special Collections, *Toronto Telegram* fonds, ASC19065, *Evening Telegram* Staff.

Proud of his accomplishment, Laver wrote to Queen's Park that the new regulatory order "has had a moral and deterring effect on would-be imposters."[90]

The ball was now in the court of the unemployed themselves. For all of the bitter divide that separated Toronto's "new age" Department of Public Welfare and the city's antiquated House of Industry in 1933, however, the struggles of the dispossessed would reveal fundamental continuities in attitudes toward, denigration of, and scapegoating of the poor. Laver's approach, as it turns out, would share much with the Wayfarers' Lodge that he had gone to war against in 1932–33.

On the Trail of Harvey Jackson, William M. McKnight, Clifford Mashery, and George Haig: The Single Unemployed Present at Their Own Remaking

It is possible, even attractive, to see Laver, the Department of Public Welfare, and Toronto's new regulatory state as an apparatus of surveillance and governance of the kind heralded in contemporary critical theory as Foucauldian. With its demands for registration, its penchant for classification and control, and its preference for ostensible expertise over the amateurism of voluntary agencies and private philanthropy, the new relief regime conformed perfectly to Foucault's representation of a disciplinary order.[91] This is undoubtedly a part of the story. Where it falls short is in missing the resistance of those subject to the technologies of governance, aimed as they were at remaking the very subject of the dispossessed.[92] The unemployed, especially the single jobless men so targeted by Laver as potential "social problem" cases, were anything but passive and accommodating clients of the Department of Public Welfare initiatives. They were, in the Thompsonian sense, present at their own remaking.[93] Their voices and their acts both structured, in part, how the regulatory onslaught proceeded, and challenged its premises, however hegemonic, at many a turn in the history of municipal relief. In what follows below we present four brief "case studies," which constitute something of a counter file to Laver's officialdom.

Harvey Jackson was a single, twenty-five-year-old unemployed man known to police as a Communist and an agitator. A determined individual, he was pesky to say the least, and he was in on the ground floor of the protests of the jobless in the 1930s, frequenting "labour bureaus, missions, and flop-houses looking for recruits" to the National Unemployed Workers' Association (NUWA). Stephen L. Endicott, historian of the WUL, refers to Jackson as the national organizer of the Communist-led unemployed movement.[94] In March 1930, in one of the earliest delegations of the unemployed to rudely grace a Toronto Board of Control meeting, Jackson was part of a small group, led by notable Red Reverend A. E. Smith, presenting the grievances of hundreds of unemployed gathered outside of city hall to municipal authorities. Police outnumbered the deputation of the jobless protesters admitted to chambers, and twenty officers were astride their horses at the rear of city hall should things take a tumultuous turn.

The proceedings, however, were uneventful. Smith and his entourage informed the Board that relief at the Toronto House of Industry and some local missions was insufficient. Single unemployed men and families on relief were, according to the protesters, slowly starving. To alleviate distress it was mandatory to have allowances paid in cash; to establish trade union wage rates for all labour required of relief recipients; to abolish all work tests; to reduce the number of hours constituting the work week, thereby creating new possibilities for employment; and to name representatives of the jobless to all relief committees. This was not exactly a program designed to secure immediate support within the Board of Control, but the presentation of the unemployed delegation went off without incident, and Smith, Jackson, and others left city hall to join the crowd of hundreds outside.

It was at this point that an unsuspecting Jackson was arrested by police and charged with vagrancy. A poverty inspector working in close collusion with the cops had previously singled out Jackson with a benign offer of waged employment, but the agitator had not reported for his work assignment. Jackson was obviously being made an example of, "one of those ungrateful people who lived off the church mission charity and then complained that they did not get proper food." He found himself sentenced to sixty days in jail, to be served with "hard labour." Adding insult to injury, he got a dressing down from the magistrate, who declared Jackson "just the type who should go to Burwash," an Industrial Farm/Correctional Prison south of Sudbury in northern Ontario where inmates were given a taste of work discipline. The judge was anything but impressed with Jackson, whose unpaid employment was organizing and protesting the lack of waged labour available in Toronto. "Looking for work and praying he does not find it. Just a lazy loafer of the worst kind. The police treated this man with every consideration—even got him a job—and then he fails to come back to get it. Then the next day the police find him as one of the agitators right here in City Hall." Jackson's work for the wageless was put on hold.[95]

With the numbers of unemployed increasing daily by 1932, the kinds of vagrancy charges used to incarcerate Harvey Jackson became commonplace. Many of those convicted drew the ire of judges with allegations that they "refused to work," or that they were "telling other men not to work."[96] Into this volatile situation stepped William M. McKnight, a twenty-three-year-old Irish immigrant to

Canada who refused to be silent in the face of the worsening conditions in the city hostels where he was forced to seek refuge.

In early October 1932, McKnight, then a resident of Wellington House, helped to organize a meeting protesting the quality of the food served in the city's hostels and demanding three square meals a day. Communists apparently played no role in this hostel agitation, although some of those involved may well have been, in the words of the police, "socialistically inclined." Preceded by a petition campaign obviously spearheaded by McKnight that secured the signatures of 350 unemployed and homeless men, the discontented out-of-work gathered at the Church of Ascension to discuss their grievances. Alderman Rogers, known to be sympathetic to the unemployed, was invited to the meeting and apparently agreed to present McKnight's petition to Mayor Stewart. Soon thereafter McKnight was arrested, charged with possession of stolen goods. But the police seemed more interested in the petition of the unemployed that they confiscated when McKnight was taken into custody. It was duly passed on to the ever-vigilant Commissioner Laver. Mayor Stewart was then prodded to take the document under consideration by a McKnight homeless ally, Fred Tyler.

All of this became fodder at a Toronto Board of Control meeting, as the mayor and stalwart voices of reaction, Controllers McBride and Ramsden, backed Alderman Rogers into a corner of capitulation: "In all fairness to myself. I don't want it to go out to the public that I was fomenting discontent." Stewart proposed giving "Mr. Laver ... instruction not to allow anyone to go in and talk to the men unless they have a permit from him. They are liable to cause trouble." McBride, obviously miffed at Rogers's presence at the meeting, snorted that, "It is unfortunate that in everything that comes up, our friend Rogers is connected with it." He endorsed the Mayor's suggestion to restrict Toronto officials in their right to attend public meetings of the unemployed. "There certainly shouldn't be speaking in these institutions," he grumbled incoherently, adding a dig at the protesters, "All they want is to be amused." McBride closed the discussion lecturing Rogers, "If you take an old campaigner's advice you will keep away from such meetings."[97]

McKnight had seemed to get lost in this Board of Control political shuffle, although there are indications he was indeed being closely watched. He was certainly back in the public eye on October 22, 1932, the *Star* publishing a letter to the editor under McKnight's name. It praised the newspaper calling attention to the unemployed, offered qualified endorsement of improvements at Wellington House and Seaton House following publicity of the relief residents' complaints, and suggested the need to monitor the hostels' finances.

As McKnight's letter was posted to the press, things at Wellington House worsened. McKnight ostensibly caused a disturbance at the hostel, refusing to eat the food. Thrown out of Wellington House, McKnight turned up at Seaton House, where more of the same followed. Complaining constantly and disruptively about the daily fare at these agencies, McKnight also committed the unspeakable indiscretion of "refusing to do the fatigue duty required of all hostel inmates ... and to have attempted to arouse discontent among fellow inmates." Now barred from both the Wellington and Seaton establishments, he threatened to take his grievances directly to Mayor Stewart at his home, a practice not all that uncommon among groups of the unemployed. As police got wind of McKnight's utterances, they tracked him down at the Fred Victor Mission, suggesting that he meet with Stewart and Laver the next day. In the meeting that followed, McKnight aired his discontents, insisting that the City of Toronto had a legal obligation to provide him with relief. Mayor Stewart disagreed, letting McKnight know he was a fortunate recipient of charity. "If he could not be satisfied with what he got in any of the hostels he had better go to the Royal York," huffed Stewart. Informing McKnight that accommodations would be found for him at the House of Industry, Stewart and Laver were prepared to wash their hands of the affair, but McKnight refused the offer of food and shelter at the Wayfarers' Lodge. Having overplayed his hand, McKnight was then treated to the full disciplining authority of the municipal state. "Since [McKnight] appeared to be a trouble maker as well as on public charge," Stewart called the police who arrested him, charged him with vagrancy, and, at Laver's request, deported the dissident.[98]

One year later, almost exactly to the day of McKnight's original campaign to improve the diet of the single unemployed at Wellington House, the institution again faced complaint from its residents. There had been a history of men becoming sick after eating tainted beef for dinner. Blame was placed on the preparation of the meat in the kitchen, claims were made that it had been tampered with, and, of course, it was argued that the agency had received and served spoiled grub. Whatever the origins of the problem, hundreds of men had complained of stomach pain, with some violently ill. Laver deflected the discontent, sending some leftover meat to city hall to be tested. A week later Clifford Mashery jumped on a platform as a Wellington House meal was ending and attempted to address the crowd of two hundred single unemployed men. Harry Baker, superintendent of the House, pushed his way through the crowd and confronted Mashery, demanding an explanation of the man's actions. "He answered that he was going to recite or sing. I asked him to get down when it looked like a riot might break out, and he did....

As he was inciting a riot I told him to get out." Mashery was subsequently arrested for vagrancy, arraigned before the "tough on Communists" Judge Coatsworth. Mashery may indeed have been associated with Reds, for he was defended by Onie Brown, well known as the legal counsel for the Ward 2 Unemployed Association. Captain Heron of Laver's Department of Public Welfare testified before Coatsworth that Mashery had more than singing on his mind when he tried to turn the meal hall at Wellington House into his personal soapbox. Earlier in the day, he had been part of an unemployed protest delegation at city hall. Mashery told the Wellington House residents that he had been appointed to find out what their grievances were. To Heron, Mashery was another agitational thorn that the municipal regulatory state wanted removed from its beleaguered side. He told Coatsworth that "the welfare department don't want this man in any of the city's hostels." The judge did his best to comply, finding Mashery guilty of vagrancy, sentencing the first-time offender to one year's probation, and banning him from seeking relief at all city shelters. As Mashery complained that he would be unable to obtain food and lodging, Coatsworth told him to "fend for himself."[99]

Resistance by the unemployed did not always take on the appearance of outright struggle. Jack Scott, a Communist who worked among the unemployed in the early 1930s, remembered that when payment for relief work was reduced by 25 percent, some of the single unemployed simply cut their shovels down in size by a comparable 25 percent: less pay, less work. This was likely an organized, collective form of protest, but it would have masked quite well any sense of common solidarity among the unemployed.[100]

Individual acts of rebellion were also commonplace. Such was the case with George Haig, an unemployed veteran who had been on relief since December 1930. Four years of the food in city shelters finally caused him to crack. In December 1934, after five weeks at the House of Industry, Craig could stand it no longer. He went to the Central Bureau, which had assigned him to the Wayfarers' Lodge, and asked to be transferred to another facility, preferably Wellington House, although, as we have seen above, that institution had its own problems. "He came into my office yesterday," Joseph Torpey, Assistant Director of Relief, told the court, and "said he didn't like the food he was getting, and knocked me out of my chair ... the hospital has taken an ex-ray of my nose." Haig regarded the whole affair as a mere scuffle and noted that plenty of Department of Public Welfare staff were present to protect Torpey if things had gotten really serious. The Crown prosecutor disagreed, commenting that it was "too bad that public officials must be beaten up." Haig, of course, was convicted.[101]

Being on the trail of such single unemployed men as Jackson, McKnight, Mashery, and Haig reminds us that others, such as cops, welfare agents, and politicians, were also on their trail. This often brought them to trial. But these stories also reveal something about the plight of homeless single men and their resentments at what they were forced to endure in establishments like Wellington House.

Indeed, Wellington House was an object of scrutiny in February–March 1935, as John Bruce, president of the Independent Labour Party, convened a meeting of the Toronto Trades and Labour Council at the Church Street Labor Temple. Bruce had done a study of the living conditions at Wellington House, which he described as "brutal and inhumane." He wanted the TTLC to speak out against the institution and to upbraid Commissioner Laver, who had recently whitewashed the circumstances surrounding the death of an unemployed resident of Wellington House, Peter McLean. Bruce's description of life at Wellington House was harrowing:

> Toilet accommodation is in the basement and night pails are used. The men sleep on cots without mattresses or pillows. They are allowed two blankets and if they wish to keep off the wire mattresses they must fold a blanket under them. They must walk up five flights of stairs in their nightshirts after having put their clothes in the fumigator and had a bath. A short while ago, one man died. A number of other men who have received the same treatment are now dead and buried. I can produce evidence of these cases to Commissioner Laver. I have done so and received no satisfaction. There are men in the building who have tuberculosis and other infections mixing with the 640 men in a building that is not equipped as a residence for anyone. There is nothing more abominable in life than this residence. I want to organize labor to sow some action and call a protest meeting in Massey Hall or on the City Hall steps. The food is repulsive and yet human beings have to consume it. They are attempting to discriminate against the men who are giving information to me.

Bruce, no friend of the Communist Party of Canada that had played such an important role in the agitations of the unemployed, spoke in labour circles as a member of the Plumbers' and Steamfitters' Union. He had a long socialist history, alluding to how he had organized protests against unemployment with Socialist Party of Canada activist Ernest Drury as early as 1909. He was adamant that a similar campaign must be initiated again, to make "the unemployed ... articulate." Bruce convinced the TTLC to pressure labourite Mayor Jimmy Simpson to launch an investigation into the issues raised at the meeting, with Simpson agreeing that an inquiry might indeed be in order.

At a subsequent meeting, nine hundred single unemployed residents of Wellington House, Seaton House, and the House of Industry cheered Bruce's litany of complaint about the institutions and bellowed discontent at Laver's lies about the death of McLean. Amid cries of "It was murder," Bruce detailed "the callous and inhuman treatment" that led to the death of the Wellington House inmate, who had been turned out into the street as his temperature rose from 100 to 103 degrees. "Were you in a prison, an asylum, or in the army," Bruce concluded, "these conditions would not be allowed." Predicting that in the overcrowded conditions of city hostels, epidemics could spread like wildfire, resulting in "scores of new pauper's graves," Bruce was responded to by a man in the crowd: "that's what they want." The gathering broke up calling for "the abolition of Wellington House as a civic institution," indicting the municipality of Toronto for its treatment of the unemployed.[102]

Wellington House, its food and its living conditions, would continue to be an object of criticism on the part of the unemployed and their protest movements for years to come.[103] One petition, signed by five hundred of the unemployed and presented to Toronto City Council in the winter of 1937, complained, "Young men and boys and old men are indiscriminately herded together and have to stand around naked because of 350 dressing and undressing in a room not half large enough for that number." Perhaps suggesting the kind of sexual "impropriety" that might spur respectable "Toronto the Good" to action, the jobless pointed out that these conditions were "fast demoralizing those of us who live under them and we wish to impress upon Council the necessity of immediately facing this problem."[104]

At the same time as this petition of protest was circulating, a United Church minister known for his militant support for the unemployed, the Reverend Corey Almack, grew a beard and, with another clergyman, entered Wellington House, the pair posing as single men out of work. The religious duo later issued a report on the city hostel, presenting it to the municipal Board of Control, although they were convinced that civic officials were well aware of what went on at Wellington House, and indeed condoned the ill use of the unemployed. Compiling a long list of what they considered "cruel" and "inhumane" conditions and practices, Almack and his partner addressed issues that had long been confirmed and complained about. Overcrowding meant that forty-four men were sleeping on the floor; beds, to those who could secure them, lacked mattresses; toilet and washing facilities were inadequate; forcing the men into the street during the day placed those improperly clothed, sick and disabled at the mercy of the elements; and the two meals provided lacked sufficient nutrition to sustain men who were expected to be looking for labouring employment. Particularly egregious was Wellington House's expectation that those using its hostel facilities would beg dimes, quarters, and meals on the street to supplement what they were provided. "The officials we approached made no attempt to deny that the men had to 'bum' meals," reported Almack and his collaborator, "One reason for this condition is determination to make hostels as unattractive as possible for the men so they will jump at any job."[105]

As Laver made abundantly clear in a confrontation with a delegation of the unemployed at a Toronto Board of Control meeting in the summer of 1933, it was indeed his department's explicit policy to make life in the hostels anything but accommodating. Almost two hundred single unemployed men had signed a petition complaining about the food, overcrowding, and bedding at one of the city-run hostels on Crawford Street. Their exchange with Commissioner Laver was revealing:

> Unemployed: These men complain of poor meals and overcrowding.
> Laver: Perhaps you don't realize that we have to handle these men so they won't want to come back.
> Unemployed: You mean you don't want to make a sort of "home" for them?
> Laver: That's it—we don't want to make it too comfortable for them.... the conditions are all right....
> Unemployed: And in view of recent complaints you'll make no investigation.
> Laver: No—I'm satisfied things are as good as they can be under the circumstances.

As the *Star* concluded in its capitalized headlines reporting on the "dialogue" between Laver and the unemployed, the Department of Public Welfare's message to the poor was strikingly clear: "TRY NOT TO MAKE JOBLESS COMFORTABLE.... HANDLE THESE MEN SO THEY WON'T WANT TO COME BACK."[106]

If this was the approach to single unemployed men, what was happening to single unemployed women?

Two jobless protesters, march to Queen's Park, Toronto, meeting with Premier Mitchell Hepburn, April 1935.

York University Libraries, Clara Thomas Archives & Special Collections, *Toronto Telegram* fonds, ASC19072, *Evening Telegram* Staff.

Marginalizing the Marginal: Single Unemployed Women

Single unemployed women are the lost subjects of the "ten lost years" of Canada's jobless crisis of the 1930s. Historian Ruth Roach Pierson has rightly called them "a shadowy presence at best" in our understanding of the meanings of the Great Depression. After an extensive exploration of the gendering of work and welfare in the 1930s, Margaret H. Hobbs concluded,

> The situation of workless and often homeless unattached women remained a mystery in the early Depression, although there was an emerging consensus reflected in the press and in the social service records of high levels of unemployment among particular groups of women, particularly stenographers and typists.

CCF Member of Parliament Agnes Macphail noted in 1936, "Young and old unemployed women should be given careful consideration," claiming that, up to that point, such women, and the "serious problem" they posed in the crisis of the out-of-work, had been shunted to the sidelines of social concern. They were, Macphail insisted, absent in discussions around the many "projects to employ unemployed persons on public works and so on." But Macphail's was something of a lone voice. More typical was the tendency to address "single unemployed women transients" as harbingers of moral decay, conduits of social dysfunction and disease. In 1937 one Member of Parliament rose in the House of Commons to decry the moral collapse associated with soaring unemployment: "The problem of unmarried mothers is becoming more acute, the problem of illicit alliances is more acute, … the problem of venereal disease is becoming more acute."[107] It was as if the very presence of single unemployed women violated the conventionally understood "laws of nature."

Single unemployed women largely disappear from view because, in the gendered norms and ideological imperatives of the era, single unemployed women were simply not supposed to exist. Of course, they did: one in four wage earners in Toronto in 1931 was female, and gainfully employed women, as a census category, rose over the course of the decade from 91,780 to 111,334. At the beginning of the 1930s, 84 percent of these Toronto working women were unmarried. It is impossible, even granting the concentrations of working women in female-specific job designations (somewhat more insulated from the economic collapse than manufacturing, where males dominated, and where women constituted just 17 percent of the workforce) such as personal service, clerical, teaching, and nursing, that the unemployment coursing through the Toronto economy did not move a significant number of these female workers into the ranks of the jobless. Conventional statistics suggest that female unemployment in the 1930s was much less than the comparable male figure (in 1931 the respective percentages were 7 and 18), but women's unemployment was notoriously underrepresented in such calculations, precisely because when out of work a woman was socially constructed as not really unemployed but situated within a family, where she was dependent on masculine "providers," be they fathers, husbands, or some other male kin. This social construction meant that single unemployed women were regarded as innately less public figures than their male equivalents: their dependency was doubled by the bind of patriarchy, in which as daughters and/or mothers they were responsibly situated within families, rather than within the state. This meant, as well, that they were looked on as presenting no threat to public order. Single unemployed women who failed to conform to this typecasting or fit into this grid of socialization, even if they were not castigated as "social problem" cases, were marginal social beings.[108]

As Veronica Strong-Boag has argued, then, women "were defined and delimited, not so much by any lesser capacity for work or determination or thought, but by patriarchal custom and male authority."[109] The single unemployed woman was thus an anomaly, a contradiction in the ideological edifice of gender conventions. Leonard Marsh, writing on employment research in 1935, understood the gendered nature of the labour market, recognizing that just under 3.3 million Canadian men were gainfully employed, roughly 60 percent of the total male population. The comparable figures for women were 670,000, or 13 percent. Women, living at home and engaging in domestic labour as wives, mothers, sisters, and daughters, were not recognized as workers, in the sense that their toil was unremunerated. If "home-making," like "housekeeping," were a paid occupation, Marsh speculated, then the extreme divergence in the male-female labour market data would lessen considerably. Nonetheless, Marsh stated bluntly, because women were "home-makers," unemployment was "*primarily ...* a masculine problem," and he was thus able to dispense, all too easily, with the problem of joblessness for young women.[110]

As single women became unemployed, then, they disappeared from view, since they were neither the concern nor the responsibility of the regulatory state. This was the main body "registering" their ostensible presence. Marjorie Cohen notes that small towns, polled by the Canadian Welfare Council for its report on "Schedules of Relief and Assistance in Typical Areas," recorded "no problem of unattached women."[111] If a Toronto Protestant Children's Home report of 1936 was correct in its claim that upward of three million single unemployed women in Canada were on relief, it was certainly the case that such females were not being supported as single women but as part of families that included husbands, wives, and siblings. Women such as L. O. R. Kennedy, Superintendent of the Toronto Women's Employment Office, might protest obvious gendered bias in government relief policies, but such professional women could themselves espouse prejudicial views about single working women, especially if they insisted on finding employment commensurate with their skill and experience.[112] If, for whatever the reason (which was almost always scapegoated as "moral failing"), these shadowy single unemployed women managed to find themselves outside the confines and conformities of the nuclear family, single women who looked for relief were located at the bottom of the socially constructed pecking order of Toronto's early Central Bureau or Laver's later Department of Public Welfare.

They also faced the prejudicial animosity of jobless males who felt displaced as breadwinners. Relief administrators confessed that as they processed applicants they witnessed something of a crisis of gendered identity, one that gave voice to a rising masculine sense of entitlement: "I've seen tears in a man's eyes," reported one official, "as though they were signing away their manhood, their right to be a husband and sit at the head of the table." Too many such deflated men concocted irrational understandings of women taking jobs that such malcontents insisted were rightfully theirs. One disgruntled Toronto man wrote complaining, against a massive weight of evidence, that "women ha[d] captured all the jobs except fatherhood." Too often critiques of single working women descended into moralistic condemnation. Letters to Prime Minister R. B. Bennett in the early 1930s groused that "working girls" only wanted "money, a car, cigarettes, a man every night." A homeless, unemployed veteran found expenditures of single working women deplorable. "[They] always spend their money on shows, etc.," he wrote to Ottawa with disdain, adding for good condemnatory measure, "besides having some Sugar Daddy take them out." This contrasted with the bleak prospects of actual young women entering the depressed labour market. A Toronto African-Canadian woman, Claire Clarke, remembered graduating with distinction from the Central High School of Commerce in 1931, second in her class and the recipient of the Timothy Eaton Scholarship Medal. "There was no placement for me," she remembered, recalling how she trudged up and down King Street and finally landed a job well below her qualifications and outside of her area of training and expertise, making hats.[113]

Indeed, as the crisis of joblessness first hit Toronto in 1930 there was some recognition that the single unemployed woman was struggling in particularly difficult ways. The *Star* editorialized on October 20, 1930, outlining what it called the "appalling" situation destitute young women found themselves confronting: "They can not approach strangers for help with the same freedom as a man. They can not apply for institutional meals as men can. There is apparently no organization equipped to take care of widespread female unemployment." Where hostels existed for single unemployed women (and they were actively discouraged by municipal authority), they were small, private, often religious institutions like the Catholic Women's League Hostel. Three days later, W. J. Greenfield wrote to the same newspaper:

> We hear a lot about unemployed men, but do the majority of us give a thought to the unemployed woman and girl? The man has this big edge. He can go to the St. James Church yard or the Metropolitan and sit on the bench or lie on the grass, as hundreds of them do, but the average woman or girl would think twice before she would do the same. No doubt many have been stopped on the street by fellows who are unemployed. But there are hungry women in Toronto somewhere, and they never ask the citizens for the price of a bowl of soup or the price of a bed for the night. Men can do these things and get away with it, but the woman can't. And the average woman won't who is up against it.

It did not take long, however, for this first short wave of recognition and empathy to devolve into denial.

As Hobbs shows, within months private organizations of women's charity were doubling down on public statements that there was only a "limited amount of destitution" among the single women of Toronto. If there were a few out-of-work "girls" who were "nearing their last penny," the "number was very small." These were welcome words to Bert Laver's ears, and he was more than pleased to shuffle the single unemployed women out of the public realm of responsibility and into the private sphere of charitable care. "No single woman need go unhoused, unfed, or without clothing this winter," Laver pronounced in the summer of 1932. The single unemployed woman was banished to the sidelines of official relief concern. As Maurutto has suggested, the emerging relief apparatus in Toronto in the early-to-mid 1930s was "largely preoccupied with regulating single men, who could threaten the status quo; it was far less interested in the plight of single women."[114]

To be sure, this provided for a small cohort of single unemployed women some space that was never accorded to many male counterparts. Women receiving relief from 1931–35, for instance, had not been required to adhere to work tests; they received relief, depending on their age, in the form of cash or vouchers, allowing them to purchase food and rent lodging in "approved rooming houses," most of which had some rudimentary cooking facilities. For women under forty, who constituted a minuscule relief constituency, relief was paid in cash, something that the most radical advocates of single unemployed men had been agitating for from the outset of the crisis of joblessness in 1930. The supervision of this support was originally in the hands of a special committee of social workers operating out of the offices of the Young Women's Christian Association (YWCA). The Local Council of Women (LCW) was also involved and was approached by the municipality in the early 1930s to care for young unemployed women and provided with a small grant to do so, but forced to seek other funds from the private sector to carry out its informal relief endeavours. Toronto's Women's Teacher's Association supplemented the relief paid to these single unemployed women with a monthly subsidy of $200. Women over forty received their relief in vouchers. By 1932 the administration of all relief for single unemployed women was taken over by the Department of Public Welfare. It continued to pay younger women in cash, issuing vouchers to those over forty. Support was usually on the order of $8.00 a month for rent and $2.00 weekly for food, although the latter amount could theoretically be supplemented if special dietary needs were mandated by illness. This relief, while processed municipally, was provided by the province of Ontario. While barely enough to survive on, unemployed "girls" might get by with the help of generous friends, church congregations, or kind-hearted landladies. Indeed, as Hobbs shows, even with Laver's department taking over responsibility for the provisioning of single unemployed women after 1932, informal relief was being relied on with the YWCA still involved in direct relief.[115]

This fragile order came crashing down in 1935. A February announcement by the Ontario government indicated that the rent allowance for single unemployed women was to be halved to $1.00 a week; cash, once dispensed to the young, was now being discontinued, and all relief would be in vouchers. Moreover, in a deft and devious sleight of hand, the Mitchell Hepburn Liberal government dictated that, as of April 15, in order to receive vouchers those young unemployed women who had for years been receiving cash would have to provide the municipality with "service from the worker amounting to the sum of the voucher." This constituted the implementation of a "work test," for the under-forty women on relief, and it was said to be "rigidly enforced." The Catch-22 in this rewriting of the relief rules was that there were no work projects developed for single unemployed women, leaving this cohort without the capacity to fulfil the provincial government's requirements for aid. At this time the total number of "unattached, homeless, and workless" women in Toronto approached 1,500, with roughly 1250 being over the age of forty. That only 250 or so of the registered single unemployed women in the city were under forty, when fully 64 percent of all working women in Toronto were between the ages of eighteen and thirty-four, was striking proof of how many young unemployed women must have been driven out of their public identification as jobless and into the private confines of an obscured and socially constructed familial dependency. Whatever the possibilities for support and loving relations within families, the personal costs of this coerced dependency must have constituted a terrifying ordeal for thousands of young women. A cynical reading of the February–April 1935 changes in relief dispensation for single unemployed women suggests that the provincial government simply determined to eliminate food and lodging allowances for all women under the age of forty. Their numbers were ostensibly negligible, and they were more properly the responsibility of their families. Young single unemployed women were thus expendable.[116]

In response, disgruntled women formed the Unemployed Single Girls' Association (USGA). Efforts earlier in the decade to form an organization of single unemployed women had proven difficult, according to Minera Davis, a member of the Young Communist League in 1931. Davis later recounted that working with the single unemployed men was an easier organizational road because "we could not get unemployed girls to join up. They were too timid to admit publicly to being unemployed and found the associations, predominantly male, too rough and uncongenial." Nonetheless, women such as North York's Lillian Wilkinson, through her affiliation with the Workers' Unity League, had managed to speak on behalf of unemployed women to Prime Minister Bennett in October 1932, part of a protest delegation that emerged in opposition to the Dominion government's hosting of an Imperial Economic Conference in Ottawa. She bemoaned the situation in North

York, where families of seven were forced to make do on $4 relief weekly, a situation that forced single unemployed young women "on to the streets." Wilkinson ostensibly banged her fist on Bennett's desk, declaring "We women ... are not going to let our children starve for you or any government in Canada." Labelled by Bennett as "bitter," Wilkinson snapped back: "If we are bitter, it is you who have made us bitter. We women can't go on bringing kids into the world just for them to starve."[117]

After years of worsening conditions, some were perhaps more open to signing on to become a part of the out-of-work protest movement. Led by Helen Roberts, this fleeting mid-1930s USGA did what it could to address the worsening conditions of young jobless women. As Roberts recounted, the reduction in rent allowances was forcing unemployed women to move from rooms with cooking facilities to those without. The economic squeeze created an impossible situation: "We can't eat in a restaurant on $2 a week, and it will result in many girls being forced into lives of shame." A Toronto doctor was of the opinion that the unemployed "girls," reduced to diets that were deficient in nutrition, were unable to seek waged employment. Even Laver was distressed. His efforts to get the provincial government to rescind the rent cuts proved unsuccessful, however, and he was forced to concede to Toronto City Council that he could not imagine how rooms for single unemployed women could be secured on the meagre amount now available to them. The YWCA's Ruth Low echoed Laver's concerns, confessing that she was afraid the situation was taking on the trappings of a serious social problem. She extended this into a fear of political mobilization, one that was perhaps related to the formation of the USGA, declaring, "I am greatly alarmed at the growth of radical opinion among the girls with whom I come in contact."[118]

One of those radical "girls" might have been an Australian immigrant, Miss Margaret Lade, who was fired from T. Eaton and Company and forced to live on relief. Lade was active in the United Church-connected Workers' Community League and was a strong advocate of a central employment registry for women that could develop a "scientific approach" to the problem of Toronto's wageless females. She managed to persuade some of the powers that be of the dimensions of unemployment among Toronto's women, which she insisted reached well beyond official figures of twelve thousand in 1933. But Lade ran into a brick wall when she pushed to have the efforts of local women's organizations to alleviate the destitute co-ordinated with government employment and relief offices. This was a gendered twain that, in the determinations of the state, was never to meet.[119]

Helen Roberts and a delegation of single unemployed women met with Ontario Minister of Welfare David A. Croll, but he offered them no concessions.

Croll and the provincial Liberals were, in spite of Hepburn's 1934 election promise to provide a new deal for the unemployed, moving into a post-election stance of relief cuts that would escalate into an all-out assault on the poor.[120]

The attack on single unemployed women's room allowances was an opening volley in this escalating campaign, one that was deliberately designed to further privatize provisioning for the jobless by forcing them into homes rather than hostels, hotels, or rooming houses. As Croll reported in February 1937:

> Last year we notified all municipalities that we were aiming at homes, not hostels, for the single men. That is our idea of the first step towards re-establishing the individual, to get him away from the barracks-like atmosphere of the hostels and back to a normal domestic existence. It is our endeavor to make the single man part of a family group so that he may regain his morale and get away from the regimentation of the hostels. His food requirements may be paid by the relief authorities in the usual way and he no longer has to tramp to a dining room for his meals. That is the first start and a good one on the road to rehabilitation. Adequate appropriations had been made in the relief allowances of all municipalities for single unemployed. The success of the home placement plan in the case of single women has already demonstrated that we are correct in our attitude. The change not only restored the confidence of the relief recipient, but to some degree it lent assistance to the family which provided the lodging.

In this statement was revealed the tragic irony that women, who were marginalized in relief dispensation by a gendered ideology rooted in familial, patriarchal values, would be the original test case for a government scheme to reduce their lodging allocations in order to force them back into private family dwellings. That this was done in the belief that it *could* be done to a small contingent of women who did not pose the political threat of their male counterparts, whose collective, almost militaristic militancy was thought to breed in the conditions of the hostels, illuminated how marginality operated in the 1930s crisis of unemployment. The most vulnerable would be made to pay the most, and do so first.[121]

Evidence of the distress of the unemployed single women mounted. Landlords were harassing women to pay their rent because the Department of Public Welfare was often behind in anteing-up for the rooms. Evictions took place. The voucher system was causing considerable grief, with women complaining of the humiliation of having no cash and having to tally up each grocery purchase to see if their vouchers would cover the cost. With everyone in the store knowing women were on relief, the embarrassment was too much for some to bear. One woman told a *Star* reporter investigating the lot of the female jobless: "Please tell them just how terrible it is to tramp on the streets all the time, when you have to go out week after week, month after month, without a cent in your purse." In addition, the Hepburn government's policies of hiring inconsequential numbers of single women to replace their married counterparts undoubtedly created a backlash against younger, unattached females far out of proportion to any realistic labour market "privileges." "We take the position, as have all previous governments, that if a woman marries, her husband should keep her," announced Hepburn in July 1936, after hiring six single "girls" to replace six women who had concealed their marital status and were subsequently fired from their jobs at Queen's Park. This policy continued into 1939, with the premier assuring those worked up about married women monopolizing salaried positions that, "as soon as a girl marries, who is in the Civil Service, she is automatically out." The Communist newspaper *The Worker* pilloried "this dusty Victorian prejudice" in a 1931 article "About Jobless Women," but among less radical commentators views were not so progressive. So vehement was feeling around married women working that one letter-writer in the *Mail and Empire* referred to them as "scabs in a strike and undersells single women destroying the market for her labour."[122]

If they did find work, often as domestic servants, unemployed women were vulnerable to arbitrary dismissal and abuse, matrons well aware of the plight of these "girls" looking for work, the glut in the labour market, and the necessity of women to keep paid employment, however ill-remunerated and oppressive. In parts of Canada, over the course of the period 1921–36, the number of women working as domestics had more than doubled, but wages in the sector had been halved. It was commonplace for women whose only possible job opportunity was in domestic service to take positions with no wages at all, working for bed and board. Ontario's average servant's wage was the highest in the country, but it was a meagre $6.96 weekly. As women experienced modest job losses in a range of sectors, including feminized professions such as teaching and nursing, and more serious unemployment in stenography and women's manufacturing work, domestic service was increasingly the only paid labour available. A 1935 government memo on "The Domestic Employment Situation in Toronto" indicated that over 4,500 women had been placed in domestic service situations. But the conditions of work and the rate of remuneration were anything but attractive. On the wage scale, domestics were undeniably at the bottom of the heap: the average annual wage for males in

1931 was $927 for forty-one weeks worked; the comparable figure for females was $559 for almost forty-seven weeks; the domestic wage was roughly half of this lower women's annual wage payment.[123]

Many, however, had no choice but to put up with whatever those hiring them dished out. A woman interviewed by Katrina Srigley, Connie Lancaster, immigrated to Canada as a foster child supported in her passage by the Salvation Army. Arriving in Toronto during the Depression, a young eighteen years of age, alone and lacking in education, she had no choice but to seek employment as a household servant. "I had no family to fall back on. I was homeless if I didn't make one, so I started as a domestic." Another Srigley interviewee, a Jamaican woman, Violet Blackman, remembered that "because you were black ... the only thing you could get was a domestic."[124]

In 1932, a working woman wrote a letter of complaint to a Toronto newspaper condemning fellow citizens "who have not felt the pinch of depression as others have," stating that they were "taking a mean advantage of the present state of affairs." Amid claims in popular journals like *Chatelaine* that "domestic service is the one class of job for which vacancies always outnumber suitable applications," and that wages of $20 a month might be secured, women in Toronto struck back with a different set of claims. Writing to the *Evening Telegram* in April 1935, a frustrated applicant to all of the domestic service ads in the newspapers for nine long months reported that "the most I have been offered is $10 per month," adding for good measure, "The great majority offered me only a good home and perhaps a little pocket money." No one, she thought, "could live decently on such wages." One of the discontented women interviewed in the *Star*'s exposé on single unemployed women reported her experiences working for the well-to-do:

I found domestic work the hardest. Some of the women expect too much. It wasn't too bad a few years ago when wages were good, but some of them want you to do all the work, washing, cleaning, waxing, taking care of the children and so on. I had to wash floors every week, do all the washing and ironing, look after two children and do the cooking. That lady fired me. Why? Because one morning when I wasn't feeling well I didn't get down on my knees and dust under all of the beds by hand, after I had already used the dust mop under them.

Among unemployed women canvassed in 1935, their solution of choice to this worsening state of affairs was "unemployment insurance to cover everyone."

This was not in the cards, immediate or otherwise. It flew directly in the face of a powerful ideological push by even the most progressive within the social work community to clearly demarcate gendered boundaries of social assistance, separating "periodic unemployment" (able-bodied men) and the "impotent poor" (women, the aged, and the infirm). By the end of July 1935 Hepburn, Croll, and the provincial government contemplated cutting all single unemployed women from the relief rolls. Modest demands to reinstate cash relief, while undoubtedly popular, were being dismissed by Toronto City Councillors, who dug deep into the well of gendered conventional wisdom to justify their refusal. House of Industry trustee and irrepressible City Councillor John R. Beamish offered his negative assessment of returning to the cash system: "If they are given cash," argued Beamish, "they may spend it on cigarettes and cosmetics and all that." Faced with this kind of condescension, many single unemployed women thought they would just have to join the men and go on a protest trek to Queen's Park or perhaps even to Ottawa. If the Depression had segregated men and women through classifying the jobless as male and the destitute as female, apportioning the responsibility for relief differentially to national, provincial, and municipal authorities, mobilizations of the wageless struggled to break down this divide.[125]

Women of the Toronto On-to-Ottawa Trek, July 1935.

TORONTO'S POOR

Toronto Trekkers

As single unemployed women in Toronto threatened to go "on the trek" at the end of July 1935, jobless protest across Canada had turned decidedly militant. Much in the national news, and causing consternation within R. B. Bennett's federal Tory government, the threat of platoons of single unemployed men fomenting public disorder caused all levels of the state to sit up and take notice. As early as 1931, amid reports from Canada's railways that a transient army was "riding the rods" in search of often unattainable work, politicians cowered at the prospects of "serious riots verging on revolution." "Hungry men can hardly be blamed for refusing to starve quietly," one cabinet minister wrote, noting that the jobless young men on the move could never satisfy municipal relief requirements because they were unmarried and of no known address; they constituted nothing less than a "menace to peace and safety." In 1932 Charlotte Whitton had warned Prime Minister Bennett in a "Report on Unemployment and Relief in Western Canada" that "not less than 100,000 single men [were] roving the country in a shifting army" and there was no "question of more immediate urgency in the relief problem than this."[126] Three years later, with an election looming, with the relief rolls encompassing upward of 20 percent of all Canadians, and with the Communist Party having been agitating among the unemployed for half a decade, the explosive potential of the crisis of unemployment gained new visibility in the spring and summer of 1935.

Federal relief camps in isolated regions of western Canada, where the single unemployed were herded into military-like work locales and paid twenty cents a day for their labours, had long been hotbeds of resentment and animosity. Ironically enough, these camps—there were 170 of them, in every province except Prince Edward Island, and by 1935 some 170,000 single unemployed men had passed through them—were originally conceived as a safety valve. Chief of the Army General Staff, General Andrew McNaughton explained that "by taking the men out of the conditions of misery in the city and giving them a reasonable standard of living and comfort," the government would be removing "the active elements on which 'Red' agitators could play." In actuality, Communists went into the camps where grievances abounded; they found ready audiences for their attacks on the state and its policies. The food and the living conditions were grounds for complaint, as men grumbled about meat "doped with salt petre" and "bedbugs too fresh and eggs not fresh enough." But the most depressing reality of the relief camps was the pervasive alienation, which grew out of the useless make-work that defined so much of everyday life. "What a joke we are," complained one relief camp resident, "We make a ditch one day and then change the plans and find that it is in the wrong place." Another camp worker wrote in his diary that there was no laughter and no hope in the relief outposts. There were also no books or entertainments for the off hours. "Not one cent of public money has been spent … on reading material and recreational equipment," boasted one bureaucrat, who failed to see the forest of grievance growing amid the impecunious trees of neglect. "We are getting nowhere in the plan of life," wrote the relief camp diarist, "we are truly a lost legion of youth—rotting away for want of being offered a sane outlet for our energies." This was a nursery of revolt in which "storm troopers of revolution" might indeed be cultivated.[127]

The rising tide of rebellion arose in the west. Coordinating the upheaval was the Communist-led Relief Camp Workers' Union, which led a series of strikes that erupted in the "slave camps" in April 1935. Soon eighteen hundred of the relief camp workers were flooding into Vancouver. Two months of struggle saw a brief occupation of the Art Gallery, a snake-dancing troupe of the jobless invading department stores, popular "tin canning" of street corners (which netted over $20,000 that was used to buy food and rent public halls for sleeping quarters), and widening support for the jobless demands of real work and real wages and elected committees of the camp residents to be put in charge of organizing the conditions and endeavours of relief labour. When May Day was celebrated in Vancouver in 1935, the striking relief camp workers and their sympathetic supporters swelled the ranks of the Stanley Park gathering to twenty-five thousand. Mayor Gerry McGeer, fearing that his west coast metropolis was up against nothing less than a revolution, sounded the usual reactionary alarm, ordering four hundred uniformed cops and Royal Canadian Mounted Police (RCMP) into the streets to turn back "Communism, hoodlumism, and mob rule."[128]

The single unemployed, growing more volatile by the day, determined to bring their grievances to the national seat of government in Ottawa, presenting a list of demands to Prime Minister Bennett. Prodded to act throughout the early 1930s by Communists whose proclivity for militancy was heightened by Third Period attractions to the supposedly inherently revolutionary tenor of the times, the single unemployed were finally living up to their billing as a vanguard of the class struggle. Unbeknownst to most of them, however, the CPC was in the midst of downsizing its revolutionary rhetoric, adapting to the Popular Front turn, which had been signalled in a Moscow *Pravda* article in May 1934 and was about to be officially proclaimed at the World Congress of the Communist International in August 1935. Party leaders, then, were not entirely keen on the single unemployed unloading bombastically on Bennett. But the jobless were not to be deterred.

TORONTO'S POOR

With a Communist maverick, Arthur "Slim" Evans, leading the way, the west coast unemployed embarked on an On-to-Ottawa Trek, determined to ride the rails to the nation's capital and confront Bennett directly. They managed to get as far as Regina, where two Tory cabinet ministers met with a delegation of the unemployed in mid-June, convincing Evans to constitute a small group of eight representatives that would be whisked off to Ottawa, as long as the remaining transient jobless stayed put in an encampment on the grounds of the Regina Exhibition. The resulting June 22, 1935, meeting with Bennett went badly, with the prime minister insulting the delegation and Evans responding that Canada's head of state was a liar. Four days later Evans and his accompanying group were back in Regina, explaining to the unemployed that their reception in Ottawa had not been to their liking. At a mass meeting on July 2, RCMP charged the crowd, arresting Evans on a speaker's platform. Tear gas canisters flew, and the police fired guns. As the trekkers fought back and then smashed store windows and put the torch to some commercial establishments, 120 of the unemployed and their supporters were arrested. One plainclothes policeman, Charles Millar, was killed, and a trekker, Nick Shaack, later died of injuries he sustained in the riot, which Saskatchewan's premier declared had been precipitated by the RCMP. Bennett was aghast, characterizing the Trek as "not a mere uprising against law and order but a definite revolutionary effort on the part of a group of men to usurp authority and destroy government." But it was his judgmental eye that was blackened in the aftermath of the death and destruction of the Regina Riot: in the 1935 federal election Bennett's Conservatives plummeted, electing a mere 39 members of parliament compared to the 134 they had won in the previous vote. The Liberal Mackenzie King was back in the prime minister's office.[129]

To add a regional punctuation mark to the worsening sentence describing Canada's unemployed, Ontario's Liberal premier, Mitchell Hepburn, cut relief to all able-bodied single unemployed men in the province on August 1, 1935. Over one thousand homeless men were expelled from Toronto shelters, many on one day's notice. The city's relief rolls now encompassed some two hundred thousand individuals. Directed to find work on rural farms, many of the single unemployed, in subsequent medical examinations, were judged either unfit for work or, in over 50 percent of the cases, told they could engage only in duties that required light physical exertion. A newspaper described the eviction scene outside the Sherbourne Street Salvation Army hostel as one of "Dazed, unbelieving groups of men," complaining that they were expected to find their way to farms "which aren't within ten miles of this place," doing so without food and carrying their meagre belongings. Forced to beg

on the streets, many of the homeless men tossed out of missions and hostels in August 1935 found themselves in the courts and jails in the weeks to come, charged with vagrancy and sentenced to thirty days. Mayor Simpson warned that any single unemployed men who refused work and who had been classified as being physically fit would be cut off relief, and Premier Hepburn boasted that 440 of those sent packing from hostels managed to find farm work. Two months later Simpson was forced to do some backtracking, reporting to a Board of Control meeting, "I am told that farmers who took on some of our hostel youths said these young men were not strong enough to work."[130]

Hepburn's relief cuts prompted a flurry of CCF response, the social democratic organization setting up a special headquarters to accommodate the single unemployed, as well as clubrooms throughout the city that would provide shelter and food. But the conditions were deplorable, with beds lacking and the men forced to sleep on cardboard covering bare floors. Bakeries donated bread for sandwiches to the CCF initiative, but this was clearly a stopgap measure. In the months to come, the flow of provincial money into Toronto's relief apparatus slowed considerably. The quality of meals provided at the House of Industry deteriorated even further, with complaints about inedible food increasingly common. One veteran, J. Harrison, appeared with a delegation of unemployed at the Board of Control to voice his disgust. Sour bread and "a horrible mess of macaroni and flour" he considered "rotten" fare. Another ex-soldier, V. Dunn, spoke at a subsequent Board of Control meeting on behalf of the Progressive Veterans. "The House of Industry," he declared, "is the penitentiary of the relief set up for veterans."[131] Throughout 1936–37, unemployed soldiers continued to protest, resentful that the federal government refused to provide pensions that would keep them out of city hostels and off the bread lines. Other single unemployed rallied to Communist-led movements like the Ontario Federation of Unemployment (OFU), petitioning for improvements in the hostels and $5 weekly in cash relief. OFU head Harvey Murphy addressed eight hundred single unemployed men and promised that if civic officials did not make improvements they

Etobicoke placard of unemployed/ relief protest accuses Liberal regime (Mitchell Hepburn and David Croll) of driving workers to misery, March 1935.

would pay a large price. "If they sow the wind," Murphy threatened, "they're going to reap the whirlwind. We intend to go ahead in an orderly manner, but if that fails, they will be responsible for anything that may happen." [132] The bombast drew cheers from the crowd.

As such protests mounted in the summer of 1935 and afterward, there were those well aware of the value of scapegoating the jobless in the context of the politics of fear generated by the On-to-Ottawa Trek and the Regina Riot. At a Board of Control meeting in October 1935, Controller Robbins blasted the notion that conditions and meals in the city's agencies of relief should be improved. This would only invite the hordes of workless from the west to set their sights on the municipality of Toronto as easy pickings. Nothing but trouble would result. "They get in," said Robbins, "and then raise Cain." [133]

Raising Cain was what Communists did best. They had, of course, been active in Toronto among the single unemployed men, just as they were a presence among the jobless in Vancouver and within the relief camps of the British Columbia interior. Communist Party of Canada activists figured prominently in the formation of the Workers' Ex-Servicemen's League in 1933, mounting a persistent fight against the usual hostel complaints, preeminent among them resistance to the "work test." Ex-servicemen were adamant that they would not do "slave labour." Bill Thompson insisted that for the unemployed veterans, "The idea of working for a living is uppermost in our minds. But this 'work test' idea smells of the filthy slave traffic of the days before the American Civil War." Another former soldier wanted to get off the dole, to be sure, but "To work for the sake of getting the rotten meals they dish out for us here," he told a newspaper reporter, "is worse than being in the trenches.... I'd rather starve than give them the satisfaction of working a single hour." At an Allan Gardens meeting of the WESL and the Toronto Unemployed Council, anger was expressed about bed bugs in night shirts and bedding, being forced to cut wood for some macaroni and dry bread, and being kicked out of hostels at 6:30 a.m. with nowhere to go. Form a committee, advised one malcontent, "Let us approach Controllers Simpson and Robbins, the labour members of council, to place this before the Board of Control and find out how the members stand on it. Let us ask them to start a fight to have the 'pogey' houses cleaned up and for three good meals a day." Like the single unemployed women canvassed a few years later, these men wanted a program of "unemployment insurance." [134]

It is sometimes difficult to discern the overt presence of the CPC in the activities of the single unemployed, but in other cases, the inference of involvement is more obvious. One of the most militant Unemployed Associations in Toronto was located in Ward 2, and six of its leading agitators found themselves in court, defended by Onie Brown and the Canadian Labour Defence League (CLDL) in June 1934. Mayor Stewart refused to allow the men to read a statement on behalf of the Ward 2 jobless before the Board of Control, complaining of the menacing manner in which the six approached the table at which City Controllers were seated. "You are just a bunch of agitators," he snorted, noting later that, "I have refused to allow a few agitators to mislead public opinion and stigmatize the unemployed as a whole." As the bickering turned belligerent, the police stepped in, a plainclothesman from the Red Squad being present to put a neck hold on one of the delegation. Fists flew as the Controllers "stirred uneasily in their seats," some "scampering for safety." At their trials, which netted three of the Ward 2 militants vagrancy and obstruction of police charges, fines or jail time, it was brought out that one of the witnesses called to testify on behalf of the defendants, the ex-soldier William Lyons, had previously served thirty days on an obstruction charge arising out of a 1933 Allan Gardens protest. Another man appearing before the court was reminded by the Crown that he had cost the City $2000 in relief since 1931. "The city has been pretty good to you, hasn't it," sneered the prosecutor. "I wouldn't say that," came the reply.[135]

Fracases and retorts were one thing. They could happen, one suspects, because of organization, which provided agitators with the rationale and reach of wider activities among the unemployed, not to mention a sense of righteousness. Communist organizations defending Toronto single unemployed men in the 1930s included neighbourhood Unemployed Councils, which would later be brought together under the umbrella of the Popular Front's National Committee of Unemployed Councils, the Workers' Unity League affiliated National Unemployed Workers' Association, and the Ontario Federation of Unemployment. Leading CPC functionaries active in these bodies included Toronto's Ewart G. Humphries, Harvey Murphy, Fred Collins, Tom King, Ernest Lawrie, and George Harris.[136] In promoting the Unemployed Council movement these Communist agitators sought to instil in the jobless a sense of themselves as part of a vast, Canada-wide movement of the dispossessed, one that involved all of the 1,500,000 Canadians on relief in 1933, when official unemployment rates were recognized to top 25 percent.[137]

An NCUC pamphlet, *Building A Mass Unemployed Movement*, introduced by Humphries, declared:

> Unemployment, want and hunger prevails all over this rich country. Tens of thousands of working people—men women and children—are suffering and are on the verge of starvation because they lack sufficient food, clothing,

and shelter.... As the present crisis deepens and becomes more and more acute, more and more toilers are losing their jobs, their meagre savings and belongings and consequently are needing relief. The huge army of destitute people increases day by day.... What is the policy of the Canadian Govern-ments, federal, provincial and municipal, to this situation of hunger? It has been, and still is that of slow starvation. The workers have been forced to fight for every bit of relief that they receive to-day. For this reason the relief is better in those parts of the country where the workers are organizing, have actually struggled for relief, or where the very threat of struggle has compelled the government to grant relief ... these forms of activities and struggles have resulted in much more bread, milk, clothing and self respect for tens of thousands of unemployed and their dependents. The willingness to struggle and determination to resist all efforts to be classed and treated like outcasts and paupers have brought results and victories, no matter how small. These achievements of the organized unemployed movement have given new courage, new hope, and new self respect to countless men and women who were plunged into silent misery, poverty and degradation by the terrible forces of hunger.

To further this struggle and the organization of the unemployed, Communists proposed a non-contributory unemployment insurance plan; cash relief for all unemployed and part-time workers and their dependents; no evictions or property seizures of those unable to pay rent, interest, principal, or taxes; free medical and health services, and free public utilities and transit services for all unemployed and their dependents; an end to all forced labour and work tests associated with relief; work at trade union rates; elected representation of the jobless on all bodies administering relief; no discrimination against those active in the unemployed movement or youth, transients, strikers, or the foreign-born; free use of public buildings for meetings and activities of unemployed workers and organizations; no deportations of any foreign-born workers, British or otherwise; and unity of the employed and unemployed.[138]

This program animated the activity of Communists among the unemployed. Popular Front proclivities aside, the unemployed agitation in late spring and summer of 1935 supporting the On-to-Ottawa Trek and protesting its brutal break-up in Regina produced an upsurge of activity in Toronto. There had been talk prior to the RCMP-precipitated riot in Regina of organizing a Toronto contingent of the jobless to hook up with the western protesters as they entered southern Ontario and set their sights on Ottawa. A Toronto meeting about the treatment of the BC unemployed drew three thousand and netted a collection of over $1200. With the dispersal of the unemployed marchers in Saskatchewan, talk turned to welcoming any trekkers who could make their way from the prairies to Toronto, and activity was soon directed to raising funds for the support of a march on Ottawa, which would meet up with contingents from Montreal and Winnipeg. Montreal's unemployed protesters were stopped in their tracks by a determined Quebec Provincial Police, whose head, Chief Jargaille, declared unequivocally, "Not a hunger marcher is going to get through. Unless present orders are countermanded, we will arrest every suspect though the prisoners run into the thousands, and fill every jail in Quebec." Jargaille was as good as his word. Flying squads of motorcycle cops and Provincial Liquor Commission officers swooped down on the unemployed, and by mid-July an estimated 230 Quebec trekkers had been placed under arrest, charged with vagrancy or the more serious offence of unlawful assembly. The Montreal mobilization had been derailed. Efforts to trek from Winnipeg fared little better, although Hepburn relied on a disingenuous legal manoeuvre rather than the overt repression employed by Quebec police. Knowing how difficult it would be for the unemployed to walk from Winnipeg to Kenora, and aware that the jobless had secured transportation from the Manitoba metropolis to the Ontario border, the Liberal Premier simply passed a legislative act that made it "illegal for a bus, truck, or automobile to carry passengers for hire within the province unless it had an Ontario licence." A bedraggled 250 unemployed were then forced to walk throughout the night in the "driving rain, mud, and mosquito-infested bush," arriving in Kenora on July 17, 1935. Beaten down, they accepted Hepburn's willingness to commandeer a special train to take the mass of protesters back to Winnipeg, with a delegation of five allowed transport to Ottawa to present their grievances.[139]

Tensions in Toronto were evident amid the anticipation—not to be realized—that thousands of trekkers were about to descend on the Queen City en route to Ottawa. Mayor Simpson was not pleased; nor was he in a mood to appease the local jobless who were committed to doing their part in the trek. He made it abundantly clear that there would be no food provided trekkers and no allowance for them to pitch their tents in any city parks or exhibition grounds. The mayor met with city officials and Police Chief Draper to figure out how to use local bylaws to restrict movement in and out of the city. Toronto trekkers who mobilized a tag day to collect funds to support those marching to Ottawa were subjected to an obscure municipal act governing charities that made it illegal to solicit funds without the authorization of the Department of Public Welfare. Arrests followed as unaware trekkers, with a letter from the Ontario Workers' Federation authorizing them to collect funds for the hunger march, were hauled into court. "We were all together," they claimed innocently, "we were told to go out and get food; we volunteered and went. It was going to help the boys in Ottawa." The indefatigable Onie Brown defended the men but failed to get them acquitted, fines being imposed or, alternatively, sentences of ten days in jail. At the $50 assigned by the court, the convicted were certain to go to jail. Simpson, meanwhile, was on the offensive, insisting that Hepburn's ban on trucks transporting trekkers would be enforced, ranting against revolutionaries and decrying the methods of the Communists:

> I feel that Premier Hepburn regards this as a threat to constituted authority. I regard it as a spectacular method of gaining their ends which is largely engineered by the Communists and into which they are trying to draw others who are sympathetic with the unemployed. In such trying times I do not feel that such spectacular methods are best. They should send their representatives to the seat of authority to make representation on their behalf. I can see that those responsible for the march are determined to override obstruction of any kind. They are challenging law and order and constituted authority. To be weak and vacillating means encouraging a certain type of

individual to revolutionary methods. We cannot allow those men to sleep in the parks. We will not allow any defiance of constituted authority. I am opposed with such wholesale invasions of peaceful cities.

In a final unambiguous statement to the press, Simpson promised, "If they attempt to defy orders they will be regarded as revolutionaries and treated as such."[140]

All of this undoubtedly whittled down the numbers of the Toronto jobless prepared to go on the trek. Communist organizers estimated they would have twenty-five hundred prepared to march, but far fewer than this eventually took to the roadways. Nonetheless, more than two thousand gathered at the Queen's Park bandstand on a Wednesday afternoon, July 17, 1935, to commence the long walk to Ottawa. Numbers dwindled to five hundred as some dropped out, Hepburn's ban on truck cartage and police harassment taking their toll. Most were single unemployed men, although perhaps as many as thirty women and children participated. The small contingent of female trekkers was headed by the "Hunger March" cook, Mary Flanagan, the irrepressible Lil Himmelfarb, Ann Walters, and the fifteen-year-old daughter of a Communist needle trades workers, Louise Sandler, who did her best not to inflame popular prejudice against ostensible "free love" behaviour on the co-ed protest walk. The demands were drawn out of the unemployed agitation of the past years: work with trade union wages; a five-day work week at six hours a day; relief camp workers to be protected under the Workers' Compensation Act; control of relief camps to be taken out of the Department of National Defence's control; an unemployment insurance plan; and abolition of all forced labour and work tests.

Jack Scott, who served as treasurer of the Ontario trek, remembered strong support along the route. Committees composed of CCFers, CPCers and all manner of liberal progressives contributed food and funds, as did motorists who crossed paths with the hunger marchers on Ontario highways. Twenty-two days after they left Toronto, the trekker contingent arrived in Ottawa, 450 strong. They were joined at the city limits by 75 strikers from the Petawawa relief camp and 110 unemployed from Ottawa. Ottawa Mayor Nolan, who had threatened Mayor Simpson that he would sue Ontario's leading municipality for not doing enough to suppress the unemployed committed to marching to Ottawa, and who had cajoled Premier Hepburn to intervene and stop the trek in its tracks, gave the jobless a decidedly cold welcome. No food or shelter would be allowed them. All leaves were cancelled for Ottawa constables, and the RCMP contingent guarding parliament was doubled. Fire hoses were ready to serve as water cannons in anticipation of the necessity to force the protesters away from the House of Commons. Singing "Hold the Fort" as they passed the national legislature, which was now taking on the trappings of an armed citadel, the weary unemployed made their way to the city outskirts, where they camped in Plouffe Park. The jobless spent two weeks in Ottawa before heading back to Toronto. It was retreat or starve since there was no relief available in the nation's capital. Organizers approached Hepburn, hoping that he would provide trekkers with transportation back to the Queen City. He wasn't agreeable. The trekkers managed to get most, if not all, of the women into trucks, their journey home taken on seats rather than on their feet. Many of the largely Toronto ranks of the last leg of the On-to-Ottawa Trek managed, by hook or by crook, to do the same, hitching rides or taking over trains, but the police and railroad bulls did their best to make life miserable for those who had the long walk back to Toronto before them. The hard-core responded in kind. According to Jack Scott, the trekkers made "a nuisance of [themselves]" by snake-walking from one side of the highway to the other, forcing the motorcycle cops who were ordered to keep them on the side of the road to dismount, abandon their rides, and walk beside the unruly unemployed to ensure some kind of orderly march.[141]

Prime Minister Bennett stayed very much on script. No concessions were to be made to the trekkers' demands. In a meeting with a delegation of the unemployed, Bennett attacked and insulted militants, as he had earlier in his meeting with Slim Evans and the west coast trekkers. Miffed at what he considered the hunger marchers' intention to "embarrass the Government of Canada," Bennett labelled the trek demands "extravagant." He reserved his praise for Trekker XXX, who had been evicted from the march at Port Hope, his purpose in walking with the unemployed protest having been discovered to be an exposé of the nefarious designs of the Communist leadership. Reporting for the Hepburn-affiliated *Globe*, Trekker XXX decried the paid revolutionaries at the head of the march, whose sole purpose it was to teach the young single unemployed men to hate and embrace the violent, insurrectionary overthrowing of the government:

> It may well be asked what benefit the leaders of the Communist Party hope to gain from such tactics as I have outlined. The answer is simple. By means of the trek they are enabled to spread their insidious propaganda to the ears of thousands of new listeners, and at the same time work on minds of the members of the trek. The first procedure is to instil in the minds of the men a hatred for all police, for all people with wealth, and for all law and authority.... At the same time they have a definite purpose in mind, for if they can work their followers up to such a pitch that the slightest

interference on the part of the police will bring violent resistance they
will have the opportunity of capitalizing on the so-called "brutality" of the
police. Once they have instilled a hatred of the police and everything standing for law and order in the men it was a short step to convince the men
that the only solution was an armed rebellion against the government.

This kind of "reporting," of course, was political music to Bennett's rather tin ear. It dovetailed perfectly with his jaundiced views on the unemployed and their Communist leadership:

These agitators are out for one purpose, and one purpose only, and that is
to create chaos and unrest. I think the time has come when the Canadian
people should realize that we have in our midst a deliberate effort to
destroy our institutions.... The food in the camps is better than the majority of them have been accustomed to during their whole life.... Our trouble
is that the camps have been so comfortable some of the men have been
too happy to live there and have made no effort to secure gainful employment elsewhere.... They do not talk about overthrowing the government
by force at first, but after they have converted the men to communism they
advocate violent measures in the destruction of our institutions. We will
maintain the right for free speech in Canada, but will not tolerate sedition
and violence.[142]

At Queen's Park, as on Parliament Hill, the jobless had few friends. As the hunger marchers returned to Toronto, Ewart Humphries met with Premier Hepburn to try to cajole the Liberal leader into providing transportation to those trekkers who lived outside of Toronto back to their home bases, as Hepburn had done when the out-of-province jobless protesters were stranded in Kenora earlier in the summer. Hepburn, in a gesture of gallantry, conceded transportation to the handful of women trekkers, but not to the more numerous single unemployed men. Humphries, sensing Hepburn's intransigence, vowed to continue the fight against the cuts in relief. "I've led a workman's army," the Communist told the political commissar, "An army which your class cannot demobilize. I'm proud of it." That evening an open-air meeting at Queen's Park drew the bedraggled trekkers and five hundred of their supporters, addressed by Communist Party figures such as Sam Scarlett, George Harris, "Moon" Mullens, Ann Walters, and Humphries. The crowd then marched to the Ukrainian Farmer-Labour Temple, where they were treated to a banquet and entertainment provided by the Young Communist League. A month later, two thousand assembled in Massey Hall to hear On-to-Ottawa Trek leader Arthur "Slim" Evans regale the crowd for two hours on the Western relief camp protests and the Regina Riot, where Evans laid the blame for "the blood bath" at the feet of R. B. Bennett.[143]

Unemployed march from Long Branch & other Lakeshore municipalities to Queen's Park, Toronto, meeting with Premier Mitchell Hepburn, April 1935.

York University Libraries, Clara Thomas Archives & Special Collections, *Toronto Telegram* fonds, ASC19073, top, *Evening Telegram* Staff.

Depression's Denouement: The Winding Down of the Struggles of Single Unemployed Men, 1937–1939

The Toronto On-to-Ottawa Trek constituted something of a last of hurrah of the militant posture of Communist organizing among single unemployed men. To be sure, the Ontario Federation of Unemployment remained, with George Harris and Harvey Murphy still in positions of leadership. A Single Unemployed Workers' Association (SUWA) advocated for the jobless. But the tone of aggressive demand associated with the Third Period advocacy and activism of the CPC weakened under Popular Front sensibilities, and while much of the content of a program for alleviation of unemployment's deforming features remained in place, the combative militancy of an earlier era seemed to be draining away.

It was not because conditions had improved in the hostels or the circumstances of the jobless had become better. Complaints about facilities such as Wellington House and the House of Industry retained a repetitive familiarity. (House of Industry superintendent Mrs. Laughlen was sure to deflect any criticism that came her way.) Investigations uncovered the same egregious conditions pertaining to food, bedding, and overcrowding, while the Board of Control's defensive denials now constituted stock replies. Calls for cash relief fell on deaf Department of Public Welfare ears, with civic officials carping that handing over money to the poor was no guarantee that they would spend it responsibly on the necessities of life. Facilities and food in shelters were judged good enough, for there was an acute danger that if they were made better transients would be drawn to Toronto from elsewhere and homeless men would never want to leave the posh conditions of their "pogey house." With Hepburn announcing an end to relief for single able-bodied men in the winter and the City of Toronto declaring that it would now provide relief to homeless men only if they could establish a residency requirement of one year's duration, things seemed to go from bad to worse in 1937–38. Hundreds of men were living outdoors in the dead of winter, Reverend Nobel Halton of the Metropolitan Church claiming that they were seeking shelter in "sheds, in holes in the ground, and any place they can find."[144]

By the summer of 1938, fifteen hundred people were known to be sleeping in city parks. They were driven there by the city, an alderman confessing that it was policy to "discourage able bodied men using the hostels once summer arrives." But many of the young jobless were also enticed to Queen's Park, Moss Park, and Allan Gardens by Communist organizers attempting to create a mass constituency that could kick-start the state, federally or provincially, into funding relief projects. Talk of sit-ins proved to be just that—talk. And when militancy was justified in public discussions it was not the CPC agitators among the unemployed who voiced its possibility but figures like Alderman Percy Quinn.

Amid yet another crisis at Wellington House, which was eventually closed for a time due to a lack of provincial funding, the thousand-strong Single Unemployed Workers' Association (SUWA) asked that it be allowed to run the shelter. A spokesman pleaded with the various levels of government to do something to "look after single men who cannot find work.... If we cannot get Wellington House from the city, we hope they can give us some headquarters where we can sleep during the winter." George Harris of the Ontario Federation of Unemployment (OFU) sounded rather subdued as he promised strong measures that would make the Toronto Board of Control "uncomfortable." He prefaced his remarks with a statement that would have been unheard of in 1931 or 1934: "No one with a brain in his head wants to get his skull cracked with a cop's club. We are trying every logical means." Communists, once advocates of militant street confrontation, began to broker welfare services for the poor. SUWA leased space from the Ukrainian Labor Temple on Berkeley Street, attempting to fill the void created by policies of the province and the city that were closing hostels and shutting shelter doors to the single unemployed. By September 1938 the Labor Temple was housing five hundred destitute men, but it was going to have to close its operation when the subletting left-wing Ukrainians moved out the next month. As a last resort, approximately one hundred of the men asked the police to favour them with a mass arrest if the sheriff made good on his promise to evict them from the building, which was regarded as unsuitable for housing such large numbers of the homeless. Harris explained the situation to the chairman of the City Property Committee, arguing that if the unemployed could take over the vacated Wellington House all they would ask of the municipality was that it provide the building free and heat it. In return the Communist unemployed leader guaranteed that the premises would be kept "clean and in proper repair," and that SUWA would take responsibility for feeding the men, providing clothing and other necessities. Tellingly, Harris was prepared to vouch that the homeless residents would be orderly, that all regulations would be observed. Indeed, he went even further, suggesting that a committee of "responsible citizens" be formed to assist the Red-led bodies in the supervision of Wellington House. With the City of Toronto eager to rid itself of the $18,000 annual expense of running the shelter, such proposals managed to secure something of a hearing among civic officialdom.[145] This was Popular Frontism from below.

Popular Front practice conditioned a new willingness on the part of Communists in the unemployed movement such as George Harris and Harvey Murphy to broaden their contacts. Murphy, for instance, worked in the Relief Reform Association in March 1937, a body that convened in the Metropolitan Church and included organizations of the unemployed, labour unions, church groups, and social workers. This widening of activity was all to the good, and the politics of the Relief Reform Association, which included abolition of the hostels and cash relief of $5 weekly for the single unemployed, contained planks that had long been central to the program of militant sectors of the jobless movement. But there was also a layer of moralizing about the brutishness of class experience that was foreign to the more militant stands of Communist-led unemployed movements in the past. In addition, the approach of the Relief Reform Association, dependent as it was on all manner of discussions, broad consensual politics reflected in resolutions, and petitions to City Council, moved dramatically away from the direct action tactics Communists had championed earlier in the decade.[146]

Not that this shift in Communist orientation actually cut radicals, or the unemployed, much slack among their longstanding critics. Department of Public Welfare Commissioner Laver, for instance, responded to the SUWA initiative to house the homeless at the Ukrainian Labor Temple with a Department of Public Welfare report on the conditions at the worker-run hostel. "Most unsatisfactory," was the conclusion, a rare inspection of a shelter that resulted in negative commentary.

Laver could not refrain from giving the Communists a dig, suggesting that they had imported residents at the last minute, to inflate the importance of the temporary shelter. He obviously enjoyed the opportunity to reverse roles and take a poke at the militants who had long been criticizing the city-run mission houses and their abysmal conditions, but he was also able to sound the now conventional refrain that the men inhabiting shelters were not really residents of Toronto, implying that the Labor Temple homeless were either "outside agitators" or those recruited by them. "Some had only been there a few hours," Laver told the *Star*, "They come from all over, from Vancouver to Newfoundland."[147]

Laver's tired claim that the City of Toronto had no real problem providing for the out-of-work, but that the system was being abused by those with an axe to grind, was belied by the realities of October 1938. An overcrowded hostel system was collapsing under the pressures of homelessness and destitution. "Work tests," such as a recently instituted project that demanded of single men two seven-hour stints of labour on the Toronto waterfront's Harbour Commission's lands for their weekly hostel food and sleeping space, only exacerbated a bad situation, fomenting discord. The levelling and grading of the waterfront landscape affected some 900 men, 150 of whom would be working each day. The mayor endorsed the new waterfront work regime, claiming that such labour kept men fit and bolstered their morale. Sidney Brown, an executive member of SUWA disagreed, attacking Mayor Day for forcing the jobless to "work for nothing" and for publicly stating that those who refused such "tests" were freeloaders. According to Brown, the homeless unemployed were fed up with conditions in hostels that they insisted were "worse than jails." Lacking adequate clothing to even walk the streets, and desperate in their need for food and shelter, the jobless "would gladly work if the Mayor will pay wages and enable them to get out of these hostels." At a November 2, 1938, meeting at the Metropolitan Church, 300 single unemployed men passed a motion demanding "work with pay or no work." They elected representatives from each of the main shelters—the House of Industry, Wellington House, and the Salvation Army Hostel—to organize the men lodging at the relief institutions. Evening street meetings were held at downtown intersections, one at the corner of Albert and Yonge attracting 500 unemployed and their sympathizers to hear speakers denounce the inadequacies of relief and the problems with "work tests." A delegation of 15 was appointed to present grievances to the City's Board of Control meeting. When SUWA spokesman N. P. Walton addressed the civic body, reiterating that "We will not work on this scheme [waterfront relief work] unless we are provided with wages," the 100 unemployed accompanying the small official out-of-work delegation "applauded wildly." Mainstream labour movement officials attacked the Harbour Commission "work test" as "practically slavery." The Board of Control, in contrast, warned that men who refused to labour on the waterfront lands would be cut off relief.[148]

Even those willing to submit to this system of chattel servitude could find themselves disappointed when they were locked out of those meagre compensations supposedly earned by submission to the "work test." Jack Parsons put in his seven hours on the Harbour Commission lands and was issued his pink card, which supposedly guaranteed him food and a bed at a City shelter, only to be told when he turned up at the House of Industry that he was out of luck, and that there was no room to be had at the hostel. Advised that he should seek refuge at a police station, Parsons replied indignantly that he had worked for his bed and breakfast and was not a common criminal. Parsons felt aggrieved and insisted that Toronto's Department of Public Welfare, which had orchestrated the "work test," was obliged to provide him lodging for the night. It did him no good. Seventeen other men in similar circumstances had been refused entry to the House over the course of a week. "We have 250 beds here," reported a Miss Sherrin, and "we often have to turn men away." Welfare officer George Stagg confirmed the problem: "Mr. Parsons' story is quite correct," Stagg told the *Star*. "We are at our wits' ends. Things are very bad. We turned about a dozen away on Tuesday night."[149]

Yet, as the 1939 Sixth Annual Convention of the Ontario Federation of Unemployment reported, Mitchell Hepburn and the Liberal government of Ontario were waging a relentless war on the poor:

> We state, without fear of contradiction, that Hepburn, for the past three years has pursued a deliberate policy of cutting social services and that this has reached the point where it presents a grave menace to the health of tens of thousands of our people.... With utter disregard for human values he cuts thousands of our single unemployed youth off all assistance and drives them out onto the highways and byways to become wanderers without domicile. Not content with that he follows it up with the most malignant campaign of slander and misrepresentation in order to appease the public anger that would inevitably arise if the true facts were known. He covers up his callous acts by such ridiculous statements that there is plenty of work but that the unemployed are lazy and won't accept it, therefore in order to make them accept, he cuts off the relief and, presto, they are working.[150]

Hepburn's increasingly bellicose attitude toward the single unemployed was articulated in claims that transient, jobless men had "squandered" relief support and were now refusing to work for their keep. His attacks on the out-of-work for their ostensible penchant for idleness grew increasingly pernicious, the premier claiming that those who would take relief exhibited a decided lack of shame. Reds attacked back but were less in the forefront of repudiation of this state ideology than other forces, such as mainstream trade unionists, veterans, and progressive clergymen. But Communists were still scapegoated and baited. Farmers, for instance, complained that the men being sent to work for them in the late 1930s lacked the endurance and strength to do field labour. Hostel inmates were also not wanted, however, for political reasons. "They say we're a bunch of 'Reds' and bums," reported one unemployed man recently returned from the countryside.

Hepburn continued to attack figures like George Harris publicly, even though he and other well-known Communist leaders were less and less in the limelight of jobless struggles, which seemed smaller and more subdued than previous confrontations. When some single unemployed men set up a picket line outside of city hall, their placards proclaiming, "Pay Wages and Close Hostels," they were quickly chased away by the police, who seized their signs. Hepburn used the non-occasion to deliver an ultimatum to the municipality: impose work tests on all single unemployed men receiving relief and break whatever hold the Communists retained over the jobless. "Toronto should not allow these men to crack the whip over them," Hepburn scolded.

> Certainly the government will not stand for any whip cracking.... We all
> know Harris, their leader—a professional agitator who thrives on situa-
> tions of this kind. The City of Toronto knows my stand, definitely. It's up to
> them. If they quit on this business, then the government steps in, and steps
> in promptly.[151]

It seemed the state was now the political aggressor, with the combativeness of the single unemployed movement softening.

To be sure, bodies like the OFU continued to exist, demanding better living standards for the jobless. The province's forty-two locals boasted a membership of ten thousand registered members in 1939, and they continued to agitate for no cutbacks to relief, a national unemployment insurance plan, the abolition of relief labour, and many other laudable demands. But thought of militant demonstrations and treks seemed a thing of the past. The Single Unemployed Workers' Association, ultimately denied its quest to run Wellington House, took over an old domicile on Duke Street and began accommodating homeless men, who slept in shifts of fifty at the dilapidated residence. Such moves, often defiant of civic authority up to a point, showed a willingness to address the problem of single men being turned out of the city's shelters, but these kinds of actions constituted an entirely different approach than earlier demands to abolish the hostel system and provide cash relief to all homeless unemployed men. Joint delegations of the Executive Board of the Ontario Federation of Unemployment and the Executive Committee of the TTLC now submitted memorandums on joblessness and relief to the Ontario government rather than amassing on the legislature lawns at Queen's Park. Protests against conditions at shelters and hostels had less the feel of direct action and were more likely to be voiced in rhetorical condemnation by bodies like the Toronto Central Labour Club.[152]

The CPC turn to a more subdued, Popular Frontist orientation is evident in RCMP internal reports on revolutionary activity among the jobless. These memos are replete, by 1938, with the recognition that the militancy of the Communist Party was sinking fast with respect to an unemployed movement that, in the view of its agitational vanguard, needed rebuilding along lines that could be supported by churches and mainstream trade unions. Labour defence bodies such as the Canadian Labour Defence League and the Toronto-based Citizens' Defence Committee were being put out to pasture, their work, which had been so central in providing class war prisoners in the 1930s with both moral support and legal representation, wound down and collapsed into the more liberal Civil Liberties Union. It was getting more and more difficult to rally transient and homeless workers to the flagging Single Unemployed Workers' Association. Occupations and militant demonstrations were promoted less and less, and when they did happen, increasingly half-heartedly, they were easily broken up by the police. In September 1938, SUWA had a respectable paper membership of six hundred, but only eighty of these ostensible jobless militants were actively involved in the unemployed movement. Concerned with making the out-of-work a cause in a forthcoming civic election, the CPC was apparently not in favour of "a march on Ottawa and it is not in favour of a sit-down strike or any other such demonstrative action at present." Under the heading, "Agitation Among Unemployed at Toronto Shows Little Result," one RCMP judgment was that

> Organizers of the Single Unemployed Men's Association at Toronto are finding it increasingly difficult to recruit members for their organizations. The Communist Party does not consider the time opportune to take a too active part in this movement and is more or less allowing the unemployed to chart their own course.

With the Liberal Mackenzie King in power in Ottawa, the Communist leadership, taking into account the weakened state of the unemployed movement, apparently did not think "it expedient to embarrass the Federal government at this time." Efforts to form a "Hostel Section" of SUWA in November 1938 were delivered a cruel blow when the organization's president, Talbot Walker, disappeared along with some of the association's assets. The RCMP spies closed the annual book on Communist agitation among homeless, jobless workers in December 1938 with a sad commentary:

> Communist Party activity among the single unemployed continued through-
> out the month, but the tactics of agitating the men to the point of where
> they were ready to take militant action and then restraining them from
> doing so, has caused the men to lose faith in the communist leadership.
> The C. P., realizing this, has placed one of its members who was active in
> the Vancouver disturbances this spring ... in charge of the work among the
> single unemployed, and his task is to keep the men in an organized body
> until the spring of next year.[153]

The small but insightful forces of the Left Opposition echoed the assessment of the RCMP. Toronto's Earle Birney drafted theses that were accepted by a grandiosely named Executive Committee of the Canadian Bolshevik-Leninists for a Fourth International as part of that group's National Political Perspective. Under the heading of "THE UNEMPLOYED," Birney noted that the organization of the jobless had reached its peak under "the Stalinist drive in the 3rd period days when national hunger marches were staged and mass organs were created in certain areas." But these initiatives "collapsed because of 3rd-period ultra-leftism and have not been revived." Writing in May 1938, Toronto's Trotskyists recognized that the "discontent of the large permanent ... army" of the unemployed needed to be harnessed by a Canadian revolutionary party, and that organizing the jobless was a "pressing and fundamental task." But this Left Opposition contingent acknowledged sadly that with the official Communist Party less and less active in the field and "the CCF and the TU's hav[ing] made little attempt to organize" those without work, the once militant movement of the jobless was now languishing, reduced to "local sporadic groups of little effectiveness."[154]

Contrary to the pronouncements of Hepburn in 1938, then, a Communist-dominated mobilization of the unemployed was not the central problem faced by the jobless. Rather, the problem, as it had been for years, was a system that threw people out of work with abandon, and a state—be it at its federal, provincial, or municipal levels—that refused to confront the ways in which the crisis of unemployment destroyed the fabric of everyday life in Canada for so many, among whom the single unemployed were a highly visible and critically important component. At the end of the 1930s, the unemployed movement had come a long way, and it had invested much in agitation, protest, and physical sacrifice. But too much remained as it had always been for the homeless men who could not secure work. Hepburn appeared to be having his way with the unemployed, closing hostels and denigrating the poor and their shortcomings. After a further round of provincial relief reductions in the spring of 1939, conditions in Toronto among the single unemployed worsening because of a cold snap that limited available agriculture labour, the jobless of North York were reduced to requesting licences to beg on the street. "If you can't give us anything to eat," pleaded David Mollison, leader of what remained of the local Unemployment Council, "give us begging permits."[155] This request, a poignant comment on a shameful situation, was denied.

Five months after Mollison's petition, the Second World War was declared. War industries prodded the economy back into production; unemployment lessened and then virtually disappeared. A crisis of the economy was alleviated by a global human crisis, in which, once again, the workers often paid the ultimate sacrifice. For a time, however, the shelters were shut down: Wellington House finally closed its doors for good, and the House of Industry, which dragged on for a few years, was converted into an old age home in the late 1940s. Those who had spent time in such institutions, however, never forgot the experience. They left their mark on a generation of single unemployed men.

Such homeless males were not, of course, the only casualties of the Great Depression's unemployment crisis. They were just its most visible, dramatic, human expression. Families, too, were caught in the tight grip of unemployment's devastating consequences. Among neighbourhoods and kinship networks, Toronto's unemployed waged parallel movements of resistance, particularly in resisting eviction from their homes and bringing into the struggles for adequate relief a tool wielded to good effect over many decades by the waged: the strike. In these expressions of protest and organized opposition to the destructive impact of the jobless crisis of the 1930s, Toronto's poor were often schooled in the arts of resistance by Communists, whose trajectory of struggle took slightly different directions in the change from the Third Period to the Popular Front. Other left groups, such as the CCF, also featured prominently in these battles, as indeed did many working-class people who would have eschewed any labelling of their political positions. In both fighting against evictions and resisting cuts to family relief packages, the district organizing often conducted in Toronto on behalf of single unemployed men set a part of the stage on which ward and neighbourhood councils, associations, and other bodies defended the living standards of the poor.

Much of this activity took place in what Richard Harris has called Toronto's unplanned blue-collar suburbs. As Harris notes, by the 1930s "the industrial satellites of New Toronto, Mimico, and Long Branch, together with the larger and more residential suburbs of York and East York, remained mainly working class in character." More diverse and mixed-class townships, such as North York, Etobicoke, and Scarborough also contained significant enclaves of labouring people, including immigrant neighbourhoods and scattered blocks of "third-class" housing adjacent to suburban factories. This geo-spatial grid meant that Toronto's downtown wards, in which the poor were congregated in particular districts, were ringed by townships and suburban municipalities where unemployed activism would become commonplace. If Toronto's free speech and single unemployed agitation of the early-to-mid 1930s unfolded largely as an urban phenomenon, concentrated around particular friction hotspots such as downtown hostels, "Red Spadina" Avenue, and Queen's Park, protests involving families on relief widened geographically. The western districts of Long Branch, Mimico, New Toronto, and Etobicoke Township, as well as

Map 1: Toronto Ward Boundaries, 1934

Map design: Stephen Gardiner, Trent University.

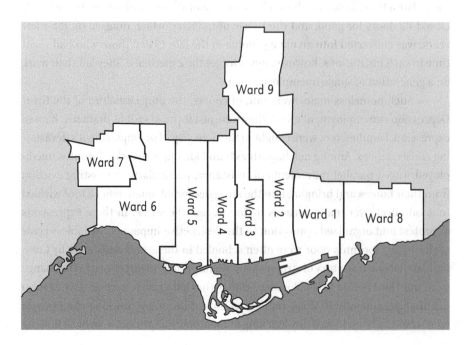

TORONTO'S POOR

the northern and eastern townships of York, North York, East York, and Scarborough, became sites of conflict over evictions and relief worker strikes.[156]

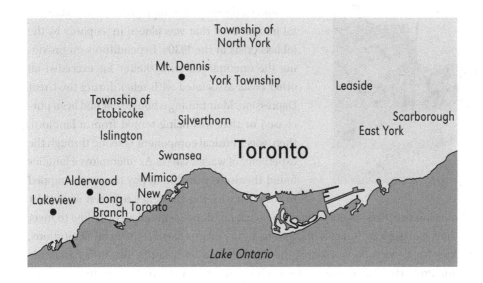

Map 2: Toronto Suburbs

Map design: Stephen Gardiner, Trent University.

	1931	1941
City of Toronto	631,000	667,000
Suburbs	187,000	242,000
Affluent Suburbs		
Forest Hill	5,207	11,757
Leaside	938	6,183
Swansea	5,301	6,988
Mixed Suburbs		
Etobicoke Township (includes Alderwood)	13,769	18,973
North York	13,210	22,908
Weston	4,723	5,740
Blue-Collar Suburbs		
East York Township	36,080	41,821
Long Branch	3,962	5,172
Mimico	6,800	8,070
New Toronto	7,146	9,504
Scarborough	20,682	24,303
York Township	69,593	81,052

Table 1: Population/Classification of Toronto & Suburbs, 1931–41[157]

Cabbagetown,
late 1930s/early
1940s, Toronto.
In possession of
the authors.

Crisis of Unemployment = Housing Crisis

Housing, as we have seen in the above discussion on the single unemployed, was a fundamental human need that was placed in jeopardy by the jobless crisis of the 1930s. Expenditures on providing the unemployed with shelter far exceeded all other costs associated with relief during the Great Depression. Maintaining a house that had been purchased or that was being rented from a landlord, then, was a critical component of living through the experience of wagelessness. As unemployed families found themselves unable to pay the rent, strapped to come up with the difference between what their housing vouchers might provide and what landlords demanded, or failing to meet their mortgage or interest obligations to the city or various financial institutions, they faced eviction. Worsening the situation was lobbying by Toronto's Landlords and Property Owners' Association, a body that routinely tried to put the screws to the Department of Public Welfare to better the prospects of their members, and, by implication, to make life more difficult for relief families, whom many landlords simply refused to accept as tenants. At a 1934 meeting of this *rentier* socioeconomic stratum at the Jarvis Collegiate Institute, for example, the property owners, disgruntled with the Toronto City Council, confirmed that they would enforce all evictions of unemployed families that had fallen behind in their rent, and that they were in favour of not renting to families dependent on relief. Such advocates of acquisitive individualism were not shy: they were known to break down the doors of tenants behind in their rent with axes.[158] The men, women, and children affected fought back, writing an important if largely unrecognized chapter in the history of class struggle.

In 1934, cognizant of a host of problems associated with the critically important matter of housing, the city's Board of Control commissioned Ontario's Lieutenant-Governor, Dr. Herbert A. Bruce, to provide a report on residential conditions in Toronto. Bruce gathered together an impressive and wide-ranging group of social workers, academics, planners, and voluntary organizations, all contributing to the investigation. The report, largely written by architect Eric Arthur and Harry Cassidy, a professor in the University of Toronto's School of Social Work who was a founder of the CCF, active in Toronto's branch of the League for Social

Reconstruction, and an authority on unemployment, has generally been recognized as the most substantial of a number of such inquiries conducted in cities across Canada. It praised Toronto's progressive administration but highlighted the urban blight and social menace of "slum districts." Targeting two to three thousand dilapidated dwellings in Moss Park (Cabbagetown[159]) and the infamous old St. John's Ward, bounded by College/Queen and Yonge/University, known by the 1930s simply as "The Ward," the Bruce report detailed the overcrowded, vermin and bug-infested, dilapidated housing stock of these poor districts. In Moss Park/Cabbagetown the population was dominantly English and Scots, with a smattering of Irish and Macedonians, but The Ward had long been associated with "immigrant Toronto," the city's Polish, Ukrainian, Lithuanian, Jewish, and even Chinese newcomers first establishing themselves there. With roofs leaking, walls damp, paint peeling, floors rotten, toilets blocked in summer and frozen in winter, heat coming from a single stove, and water supply often limited to a solitary tap or an outside pipe, poor housing was a menace to the people's health—children were "ill or ailing all the time" and parents "seldom free from chills and colds." Entire rows of houses were overrun with rats or plagued by bed bugs and cockroaches. Worsening the situation, especially in The Ward, was the commingling of working-class housing and industrial factories and the highly travelled trucking streets and railway lines that served them. Noise, smoke, and odours drowned these deteriorating neighbourhoods (where buildings had largely been constructed before 1874, when local bylaws established the beginnings of regulatory construction codes) in din and suffocated them in soot.

Bruce and his collaborators saw no option but to clear the slums, his report concluding that Toronto must "evacuate those factories and hovels" that were compromising health, morals, and general social welfare. Calling for a broad-ranging reform that would draw on provincial and federal funding, the report was insistent that the "slum districts" of Toronto be replaced with green space and community improvements, coupled with the development of affordable housing for workers in areas outside the city core where industrial employments might be nearby, but not overshadowing residential areas. "We must raze [the hovels] and bury the distressing memory of them in fine central parks and recreational areas," Bruce, Arthur, and Cassidy argued. Leisure, they insisted, must be made an area of human contentment and betterment, not something that, they suggested in the context of 1934, "hangs heavy on the hands of thousands of our citizens, both employed and unemployed." This Toronto beautification plea kicked off a complex set of conflicting campaigns over the question of how low-income housing in Toronto was to be built. As many historians and urban geographers have recently noted in discussions of Regent Park, however, the result was indeed the obliteration of The Ward, but not in the way advocated by the 1934 Toronto Board of Control-commissioned investigation.[160]

The Bruce Report was necessitated by the collapse of the economy, the disappearance of stable, well-paying jobs, the soaring unemployment rates, and the consequent pressures on Toronto's Board of Control and its various relief agencies. In Toronto's 1930s more than 25 percent of unskilled workers and 45 percent of skilled workers started out as homeowners, but with the worsening economy there was a shift away from owner-occupation to renting over the course of the decade. Some might stave off the inevitable loss of homes by taking in boarders and adopting other measures of intensifying domestic labours to bring in much-needed remuneration. Bruce and his collaborators noted that families frequently followed a strategic course of "doubling up" to weather particularly bad economic times, and Richard Harris has pointed out that the number of houses in Toronto taking in two or three lodgers rose rapidly from 236 in 1930 to 823 in 1935. As an acceptable and long-term solution to domestic economic crisis, however, this kind of self-sacrifice and self-exploitation offered little in the way of either security or comfort.[161]

As Bruce and his team of inquiry detailed, the unemployment crisis was simultaneously a housing crisis. The problem was by no means limited to the well known and long recognized "slum districts," such as The Ward. In East York, where future CCF figurehead, township reeve, and Canadian Congress of Labour official Arthur Williams led the powerful East York Workers' Association (EYWA), unemployed activists, possibly working in conjunction with Bruce's broad committee of inquiry, investigated the housing conditions of local relief recipients. Their July 1934 endeavours touched base with officials in the provincial government and Toronto's Department of Public Welfare. Testimony was secured from some of the 2,400 East York families on relief, who provided information on dwellings in various states of disrepair and neglect. "Hundreds of East York families were existing in houses not fit for human habitation," declared John Tonner, Secretary of the EYWA. Several families also reported that because of the insufficient relief provided by authorities, they were now facing eviction. The EYWA report suggested that those who might eventually face being turned out from their homes could be in the hundreds. Among the eviction cases chronicled were an unemployed veteran with a family of six whose rent of $22 monthly, long subsidized by the township at $15, faced a relief reduction to $12 and an unemployed father of four who had just seen his rent raised from $22 to $25.[162]

Toronto's housing problem was thus acute. As Bruce, Arthur, and Cassidy knew well, it hit at Toronto's home-owning working class as well as those who had long been tenants:

> Housing conditions are bad because there are many families which can not earn enough to pay for decent and healthful dwellings. In the lowest income groups of society the insecurity of employment and the inadequacy of wages do not permit the payment of rentals much in excess of $10 to $15 per month in good times. In bad times unemployment may throw the whole burden of rent, together with other relief, upon private charity or the public purse. On the other hand, such are the costs of land, construction, mainten-ance, and, above all, interest, that reasonably decent dwellings of a suitable size cannot be provided on a commercial basis for less than $25 to $30 per month. It is ever less possible for the poorest group to buy, than it is for them to rent adequate accommodation. Home ownership is impossible.[163]

This was the squeeze that Toronto's waged and non-waged workers found themselves in, and for some the situation had worsened to the extent that they were forced to take up residence in the tent colonies that emerged in some of the city's districts.

Eviction was the worst-case scenario of the housing crisis. Tim Buck claimed that by November–December 1930, evictions had become a socioeconomic guillo-tine hanging over the collective head of a working class decimated by joblessness. Metro Toronto, Buck claimed, faced some thirteen thousand dispossession orders, precipitating panic among the unemployed. Probably an exaggeration, Buck's fig-ures can be questioned, but his assessment of the central importance of resistance to evictions by the unemployed movement is undoubtedly true. "In every city of Canada our programme against the crisis boiled down into a struggle against evic-tions, for relief, and to organize the unemployed," Buck claimed. To do this, the CPC and others who joined the growing proliferation of unemployed councils, associa-tions, and leagues created networks of roaming activists, "unemployed workers who pledged themselves ready, at any moment, to go to the assistance of a worker threatened with eviction." Word received at a central office—which might be the home of a particular leader of the neighbourhood jobless or a more formal store-front address—and "the squad would rush off." Sometimes these "flying" militants would be given streetcar tickets, on occasion transported by people who owned cars or trucks. A designated group then telephoned others of the need to support an ongoing eviction protest and to appear at an address where sheriffs were threatening a family and heft was needed to haul furniture back into the home. The anti-eviction committee in Toronto's Cabbagetown was said to be led by an Irishman known as "Hammer-the-Mug." These vigilante bodies, as a 1933 article on evictions in the *Globe* detailed, could muster more than two hundred "members," committed to spend all day camped out on front and rear verandahs, thwarting those who sought to execute the hated warrants of eviction. Communist rank-and-filer Dick

Cabbagetown, late 1930s/early 1940s, Toronto.
In possession of the authors.

Steele participated in a number of these Cabbagetown protests, battling bailiffs with bravado, going so far as to rip the court order from the hands of the sheriff and do a runner with it into a maze of the poor district's alleyways. Steele understood that such actions were merely stalling for time, but they did impress on the masses of the unemployed that it was possible, through solidarity and struggle, to resist. Bill Walsh, Steele's comrade and close friend, concluded, "We believed that if enough people took on the local authorities, someday soon they would be ready to take on the state."[164]

Evictions: "They Shall Not Pass"

Evictions and resistance to them could happen in many ways and involve all manner of scenarios. But a case from the Communist stronghold of Ward 4 involving the family of Nicholas Trach highlights many of the characteristics of evictions and the organized way in which the unemployed movement refused to accept the bad hand dealt to the jobless.

Trach, his wife, who was suffering from a heart condition and sick in bed at the time, and their three children were evicted from a Rebecca Street home in late February 1935. They were $16 in arrears on their rent, one month behind according to the landlords, apparently a couple who derived income from owning properties and letting them out. They obviously cut their tenants no slack, not being inclined to let the rent slide more than thirty days in the dead of winter. Complaining to the Department of Public Welfare, the owners of the Trach house served notice they were going to evict the family from their premises, securing a writ of Execution. For its part, the city welfare agency offered the Trachs accommodation elsewhere, but according to a Ward 4 Unemployed Association spokesperson, the condemned house that was available was "swarming with bugs." As for the landlords, they were prepared to countenance no compromises. They brought bailiffs to the rented dwelling, and the police were on hand in forceful numbers. Trucks were there to be loaded up with the family's belongings, which would then likely be sold to recoup the unpaid rent. The Trach family was in readiness as well, with a contingent of the Toronto Workers' Association on guard at the house, supposedly 100–150 strong. But the police presence and the sheriff's officers and landlady's determination prevailed over the ranks of the unemployed. It nonetheless took something of a battle to secure this victory. Police claimed they were bombarded with "half-pound bricks." The door was broken in and a bedroom window smashed by the landlady, as furniture, clothing, and food were piled into the trucks. Mr. Trach apparently lost his relief registration ticket, which was inside a seized coat. Attempting to remove a washing machine from the bailiffs' truck, Trach was physically restrained and struck. Scuffles ensued between Workers' Association members and police officers. The Trachs were left bereft of their belongings, including the children's clothes and all bedding, and homeless. When twenty friends of the family proceeded to the landlords' home and entered it to register their discontent, police arrived, ordered them to depart, and remained to guard the property.

The Trach eviction occasioned further protest. Claims were made that the bailiffs exceeded their authority and seized family goods that were not on an established list of what it was permissible for such eviction officials to take. It was alleged that in aiding the bailiffs and failing to stop the illegal seizure of specific private family property, the police had violated the expectation of their neutrality, their purpose being limited to "keeping the peace." Captain T. E. Heron of the Department of Public Welfare was not happy with the situation. As he heard of the eviction, Heron, ostensibly concerned that Mrs. Trach was bedridden with a high temperature and under doctor's orders not to put strain on her heart with turmoil of any kind, sent a public health nurse to the domicile, instructing her to try to put a stop to the actions of the landlords. Nothing came of this. In the aftermath of the eviction, it was the extent of the seized family property that Heron addressed. "It's a very serious thing," he told the Toronto Board of Control, "if these bailiffs have gone into a house and left it with the door out and the window broken.... I understand the bailiffs took practically everything in the house, which they are not supposed to do." Among goods prohibited from seizure, apparently, were beds, bedsteads and cradles, bedding, necessary and ordinary wearing apparel of the debtor and his family, and cooking and heating stoves.

Not all city officials were as sympathetic as Heron. With Communist-defender lawyer Onie Brown advising the Trachs and the presence of the Unemployed

Association, Mayor James Simpson and Police Chief Draper were not inclined to be charitable. Simpson, who had already publicly accused the Communists in 1933 of concocting eviction protests and using the city's Unemployed Councils to foment discord and confrontation around the issue for the purpose of personally discrediting him, agreed to have the Trach complaint raised before the Board of Police Commissioner. But he made it clear that he thought the Trach family was ill-used by the Toronto Unemployed Association in a transparent attempt to strengthen the organization of the jobless and bump the stock of the Communist Party of Canada. Chief Draper simply denied the claim that the police had behaved improperly at the Trach eviction, turning the tables by attacking and scapegoating the much-maligned agitators:

> It has been our observation on most of these occasions organized attempt is made by agitators to cause a disturbance and a breach of the peace.... Much abuse has been directed at the police, who must take it and not retaliate. The agitators have told the people not to accept help of the welfare department and defy the authorities. The actions of these agitators often made it necessary for the police to appear on the scene, creating a wrong impression among the evicted people and making their supporters think the police are there to support the bailiffs.

This episode, aside from the failure of the protesters to turn back the eviction, raised many issues that would resurface in the unemployed war against home turnouts that raged in Toronto in 1932–36.[165]

The coming together of Toronto's unemployment and housing crises was evident in York Township in June 1932. On a Friday of that late spring the destitute Thompson family—father, mother, and five children—was evicted from their Kane Avenue home. Thompson had lost his job at the Consumer Gas Company months earlier and at the time of the eviction was $47 behind in his rent. He was supported by the York Township Unemployed Association, in which the militant Ewart Humphries and other Communist activists were involved. Staunchly opposed to housing families in tents, the Unemployed Association swallowed hard and, with no other apparent options, helped the family transport its belongings to Fairbank Park, where the township, anticipating more evictions, had erected large militia tents to accommodate what it knew would be an increasing number of homeless families. The tents, at this point, lacked sanitary facilities, were erected over "floors" of bare earth, and cooking was done on an old stove outside the tent. Water had to be fetched from the edge of the park, two hundred yards distant. But the Thompsons had something, even if it was canvas, over their heads. They were the first family to live in the makeshift shelter. Within a few weeks, the tent city was home to 100 people, and demand was such that a second colony was set up in a vacant field in the township's Mount Dennis district. Charitable organizations and the Red Cross provided food and services. By September almost 60 families were camped out in York Township, encompassing 250 men, women, children, and adolescents. By that date, with winter approaching, the search was well underway for more permanent quarters for the evicted, homeless families.[166]

The arrival of tent colonies in Toronto's working-class suburbs sat poorly with the unemployed movement. In East York, a strong stand was taken against such makeshift provisioning for evicted families. Protests were lodged with the provincial government, Ontario's Conservative Premier, George Stewart Henry, called on to create legislation banning evictions. In the first week of August 1932, the EYWA led hundreds of unemployed on a march through township streets and converged on a local Council meeting where the jobless made it clear that all bailiffs who valued their skins were to keep out of East York. These threats unheeded, the next weeks saw repeated clashes between members of the EYWA and bailiffs and their police protectors. Often, unlike the Trach case from 1935, the unemployed movement was successful in protecting the property of individual families, securing their premises and driving back the bailiffs, or ensuring that evicted households were found reasonable new quarters. In the case of the attempted eviction of ex-veteran Charles Martin and his young family, the unemployed blacksmith refused to vacate his home, which he had draped with a Union Jack, and threatened to manhandle the bailiff if he attempted to carry out the eviction. "Only a bullet would stop us," said Martin. In another attempted eviction the EYWA reported that as the bailiffs carted furniture out the front door "the vigilante committee carried it around to the back and into the house through the rear door." As evictions continued into the winter of 1933, the fifteen hundred-member EYWA continued to protect the unemployed from being put out of their homes. In a January action, one hundred EYWA members attending a meeting heard that a bailiff and five helpers were about to remove the furniture and evict the Whittaker family from an East York residence. They rushed to the address, confronted the bailiff, returned the family's belongings, and declared they were willing to stand guard over the dwelling for a year if necessary. As spring approached in 1933, the EYWA grew to two thousand and continued to resist evictions, often stationing contingents of the unemployed on the front porches and back verandahs of targeted houses. More often than not, the jobless protest actions were successful in re-securing families their homes.[167]

Adjacent to York and East York Townships, where the anti-eviction movement had early and successful beginnings, North York was also a centre of activism, with no less than four organizations of the unemployed pressing demands on the authorities, doing so, according to historian of Canadian communism John Manley, with manifestos ringing with espousals of "the labour theory of value." The Mount Dennis Spartacus Club, established at the York Memorial High School in the mid-1930s, conducted classes on scientific socialism that recruited more than one ardent youth to left-wing politics, activists and future leaders of Canadian Trotskyism such as Ross and Murray Dowson and Sadie Jourard being mainstays of the proto-revolutionary youth group.[168] Eviction blockades became part of this militant response to the crises of joblessness and homelessness, in which living rough and learning radical often proceeded in tandem. It took thirty-one police officers from two townships and a nearby county to subdue a dozen defenders occupying the home of Joseph Pizatto and his wife in late January 1933 when the bailiff descended on the inaptly named Park Avenue address to seize furniture and carry out an eviction writ. When the Pizattos' twelve-year-old daughter, Mary, arrived home from school at 4:30 she found her parents homeless on the street.[169]

Closer to the "slum districts" of Bruce's report, downtown Toronto also witnessed resistance to evictions in 1933. The most dramatic confrontation took place at the Mishka home, where a thirty-one-year-old mother and two of her four children were startled on the first day of June by bailiffs appearing at her door ordering her to pile all the furniture in the back yard. The Mishkas had missed a single rent payment. Mrs. Mishka, informing the bailiff that she was sick and was declining to move anything, locked her door, only to have the determined repo agent break a window, grab a key hanging from a wall, and enter the premises. The first object he attempted to seize was a baby carriage. With Mrs. Mishka and the bailiffs skirmishing, doors were locked, keys fought over, and then some neighbourhood women appeared. "When we saw the bailiffs go into Mrs. Mishka's house, we went right across to help her," reported one of them, "We knew she was very sick and should not be moved. Four of we women entered together and made for the bailiff who had been struggling with Mrs. Mishka. We pulled his hair, punched him, scratched him, and hit him, throwing him out the door." A group of men from the Toronto Unemployed Council then showed up and chased the other two eviction officers from the house. A defence guard of forty unemployed stood vigil over the Mishka residence for twenty-four hours, posting a crayon cardboard sign in the window:

"The Toronto Council of Unemployed Will Fight Eviction Cases." Proud of its successful turning back of another eviction the day before, the Unemployed Council vowed it had three hundred men ready to resist the debt collectors "in every case." Those who would turn people out of their homes and seize their small domestic belongings were warned not to reappear on the street. "The bailiffs will get worse than they got the first time," promised one leader of the unemployed. "We don't like bailiffs down here."[170]

The popular defence of the Mishka home highlighted ways that women might become central players in protests of the unemployed. This, of course, was a logical development in struggles that were directly aimed at preservation of homes, protections of domestic units, and the defence of women, children, and their human rights to shelter, clothing, and living space. An East York eviction of Mrs. Patterson and her family, at least two of whom were grown sons, illustrated vividly the increasingly important place of women in the struggles against eviction. The Patterson eviction had been known about in East York for some time, the home-owning Mrs. Patterson being in arrears on tax payments due on her 598 Woodbine Avenue address for a considerable period, possibly "a number of years." The Board of Control was of the view that "it was in the interests of the city that the matter be brought to a head, and so ordered the eviction." They apparently rejected some kind of compromise proposed by the Department of Public Welfare. On the morning of July 7, 1936, the Reverend D. Wallace Christie and one of Patterson's sons met with Acting Toronto Mayor William D. Robbins to try to stop the sheriff's office from proceeding. The meeting led to confusion and, in any case, officers were on their way to the Patterson home. They found it surrounded by men from the EYWA and the Ward 8 Workers' Association, in which rank-and-file Communists predominated. Twenty women from the neighbourhood stood on the verandah, which was draped with a Union Jack. Mrs. Patterson's threatened eviction managed to bring together Reds and Oranges, for her family ties linked her to the CPC and her neighbourhood affiliations drew in United Empire Loyalists. Both sides of this incongruous network of support were of long historical standing. On the Red side, Mrs. Patterson was the sister of Tom Bell, whose radicalism reached back to the Socialist Party of North America, the founding of the Communist Party of Canada, and revolutionary organizing in Manitoba in the aftermath of the Winnipeg General Strike. Bell ended up a Comintern functionary, working in Moscow for several years, and Party activists in the unemployed movement were not about to let his sister be given the bailiff's bum's rush.[171] Long resident in the neighbourhood, moreover, Mrs. Patterson had many ties with her British neighbours, most of whom would have had little knowledge of her Communist brother.

Sheriff's Officer Jeffrey told the unemployed men and the score of women to move aside, but his orders were of no avail. Insistent that he would "die rather than back down and not execute the warrant," Jeffrey preferred to live in the company of an armed contingent, and he left to return with confreres from the Police Department. A riot ensued, and police reinforcements were called in. Forty-three officers were eventually needed to assist Jeffrey in evicting the Patterson family. The *Star* described the melée:

> Mutters and jeers rippled through the gathering as police arrived but it was not until one of Mrs. Patterson's sons shouted: "We'll resist to the last ditch," that the disturbance burst into flames. Charging down from the flag-draped verandah, where companions lustily sang the National Anthem, an angry mob of screeching women and howling men clashed with twenty police officers yesterday afternoon when a sheriff's eviction order was carried out at the home of Mrs. Patterson.... The resistance grew into a free for all. Women scratched the policemen and bit them ... the men tussled with the constables all over the front lawn. When the squad arrived at the doorway, after much furious battling, they found it barricaded. One of the Sheriff's officers then smashed a pane of glass in the front window and climbed into the living room.

A bailiff and three policemen were injured, along with several of the unemployed. Chivalry apparently dictated against the arrest of women, but twelve men, including both of Mrs. Patterson's adult sons, Hugh and John, were taken off to No. 10 Police Station. Among the Party members arrested were Jack Scott, Phil Hughes, Richard Pratt, and Bill "Barber" Smith. A passerby, swept up in the street fight, was let loose by the cops, but Scott recalled, "We later recruited him to the Party." Before the bloodied arrestees were settled into their cells, Mrs. Patterson's friends brought them a "basket of sandwiches and a gallon jar of tea."

Released later that evening on $500 bail, some of the group proceeded to the corner of Woodbine and Danforth, where a protest meeting was underway. Mrs. Patterson spoke to the crowd: "I'm not a public speaker. I tried to buy my house.... Hard times came. I couldn't pay my taxes. The city wouldn't accept the welfare department offer." The next day a deputation of twenty women from the Ward 8 Progressive Women's Association, some with babies in tow and headed by

Mrs. P. Hughes, wife of a Communist Party member, attended a Toronto Board of Control meeting along with the Reverend Christie and a group of unemployed men led by Robert H. Brown. Plainclothes police and uniformed officers guarded the doors. Mrs. Hughes wanted to know if women would be protected "from abuse and not molested by the police." Another female speaker angrily demanded to know if it was the Acting Mayor's order that the police tear down the British flag. "We are here to protest about it," said Mrs. J. Kemsley, "We are Orange women and we are British." Mrs. Margaret Hambleton recounted being attacked on the verandah by police, who dragged her down the steps. Before fainting, she remembered a lot of cops shouting and "lashing out with their billies everywhere." The leader of the unemployed men, Robert Brown, also protested police violence but drew cheers from the gallery, filled with the jobless, when he told the Board of Control that "Four thousand organized workers from Ward 8" were committing themselves to see that civic officials "treat Mrs. Patterson decently." None of this was looked on favourably by constituted authority. Assistant Crown Attorney W. O. Gibson, well aware that many of those charged after the struggle outside Mrs. Patterson's house were Communists, was outraged by attempts to influence the judicial process and exempt those who had clearly committed criminal acts—a sheriff's officer had been stabbed in the leg!—from punishment. The crowd that resisted the Patterson eviction had, in Gibson's word, been engaged in a "revolution." Such hyperbole aside, even a *Globe and Mail* editorial acknowledged that "public opinion" was on the side of the unfortunate victims being removed from their home. Not responsible for their situation, they should hardly be treated as hard-core "members of the criminal class." But Scott and some of his comrades received twenty days in the Don Jail from the magistrate, ten of the days, Scott figured, because he refused to swear on the Bible.[172]

The Patterson eviction was not your normal eviction blockade. Sandwiches and four o'clock tea served up to the arrested in lock-up, police tearing down a Union Jack, lodge brothers from the Orange Order linking arms with militants of the Communist Party, both groups battling the police, and the evicted a woman homeowner without a husband but with a notable revolutionary brother, who simply could not scrape up her long overdue taxes—this was not the stuff of most of the unemployed protests that proceeded against sheriffs, bailiffs, landlords, police, welfare officers and inadequate relief payments. But it did accent the place of women and Communists in anti-eviction protests. It also went up with a bang and continued with a further bang before the Toronto Board of Control. But it was, by all accounts, a two-day affair. Other eviction resistance had more longevity.[173]

One of the more protracted, convoluted, and successful instances of anti-eviction insurgency took place in Alderwood, as the local Workers' Association guarded the Albany Avenue house of a relief family for almost twenty days in the summer of 1933. A landlord, F. Strang, arrived on the doorstep of a rented domicile when its occupants, the Braithwaite family, were away. The Braithwaites owed Strang $40 in back rent. In their absence, Strang proceeded to move his furniture into the house. Fifty vigilant members of the Alderwood Workers' Association quickly gathered and, ascertaining what was going on, marched the landlord's furniture out to the street quicker than he could get it inside the house. It was all giving the landlord "a sample of his own medicine," in the words of one newspaper headline. Soon Strang gave up and moved some small items to a nearby relative's house. The unemployed stood guard, protecting the vacant Braithwaite residence "from sunset to sundown." While twenty of the unemployed remained at the house, others pressured the local council to assist the family in finding other quarters. J. Bankler, a leader of the organized unemployed in Alderwood, explained to the press that, "We want to work within the law and not do anything rash. We don't want to see this man on the street. He can't repay his rent and the township won't. We are taking up the matter with Council on Monday." With no concessions forthcoming, another squaring off with the bailiffs was likely. It came on July 14, 1933. A bailiff, accompanied by police, arrived at the Braithwaite house, a warrant authorizing the removal and sale of their furniture in hand. Two hundred unemployed protesters surrounded the building and refused the bailiff entry. Knowing retreat was the wisest move, the bailiff announced that the eviction was postponed until the following Wednesday, but promised to have enough police officers with him to enforce the warrant and later advertised the sale of the Braithwaite home furniture. On his return, four hundred Association members had gathered at the Braithwaite home; a large contingent determined to thwart the eviction remained until sunset. Hanging in the window was a large sign: "This House Protected—Alderwood Workers."[174] The eviction and sale never took place.[175]

One thing the Alderwood militants had done that irked police was erect a mock gallows in front of the house on two separate occasions during their July occupation. They then hung in effigy likenesses of the landlord and the sheriff's officer serving the eviction writ. Such theatrical gibbets were a common form of mockery among those resisting evictions, effigy hangings of bailiffs and offensive *rentiers* being an important part of the performative arsenal of poor people's resistance. At the Braithwaite residence, protesters also placed a cardboard casket in front of the house, a large doll laid out in it to symbolize death and starvation. Constituted authority did not appreciate the humour. Police Chief Draper, for instance, took the tongue-in-cheek claims of those resisting a Claremont Street eviction seriously, expressing shocked indignation that agitators at the protest had erected a scaffold from which they ostensibly meant to publicly hang a bailiff.[176] Another officer of the court, directly involved in evictions and protests against them in East York, viewed the unemployed's mock executions of this kind against the hard realities of tenants facing homelessness. "There had been a lot of hanging during the past five years," Sheriff A. M. Gorrie told Reeve Arthur Williams, public spokesman of the East York Workers' Association, "and he had not worried about them. What caused the officer/bailiff sleepless nights, confessed Gorrie, was "the worry of having to go out the next day and put people out of their homes."[177]

Draper's lack of either a sense of humour or a sense of proportion aside, the anti-eviction mobilizations of the 1930s often used shaming rituals to good effect. In Mimico, for instance, J. N. Baxter, a veteran, had been evicted and was unable to find housing for his three children and tubercular wife. He confronted many landlords who simply would not honour relief vouchers, wanting nothing to do with renting to families on relief. The Mimico Workers' Association took up Baxter's cause and, denied a hearing before Mimico councillors, took over the Council Chambers and refused to leave. As Baxter was offered a house in Etobicoke, owned by one of the councillors, but with "windows out of place and in need of plastering," the Workers' Association thought this shady dealing, suggesting local officials were shirking their responsibilities. To shame their elected representatives into behaving better, the Association came up with a novel proposal. Since Baxter, who had served his country in the First World War, was not to be provided suitable accommodations, the veteran's family would be housed in a tent by the War Memorial in Prince of Wales Park. "We will place the Mimico Council on a banner and charge that" Baxter had been forced to live in a tent "through the negligence of council," said the Chairman of the Workers' Association Housing Committee. "We have the tent and we will guard the tent and keep it there until Mimico Council secures a house and guarantees to look after all other cases." Within a day the Mimico councillors managed to find homes for two of the three families on relief that were without shelter.

Similar militancy and success were exhibited at the same time by the Long Branch Workers' Association, aided by unemployed reinforcements from Lakeview, Alderwood, New Toronto, Humber Bay, and Islington, all of whom were affiliated with the Lakeshore District Federation of Workers. They stopped the eviction of seventy-eight-year-old Percy Bellamy, his wife, and three children. Hanging the proverbial effigy from a makeshift gallows, the unemployed guarded Bellamy's house and prevented hydro workers from climbing poles to disconnect the relief family's electricity. A year later, in mid-March 1935, an evicted Etobicoke worker newly housed by the Mimico Council was disgusted by the conditions he found in his family's relief digs. "The Medical Officer of Health condemned the house as unfit," he complained to those who had placed him in a dwelling where the sink was gone, the roof leaked, and bed bugs were crawling all over the place. To shame the Council and throw a little panic its way, the ungrateful new tenant brought some bed bugs with him to the Mimico Council. The Mimico Workers' Association then moved the man, his wife, their children, and the family's domestic belongings and furniture into a vacant house without the owner's permission. The squatters were protected by one hundred unemployed men from the Lakeshore district, forty of whom stayed inside the house with the family, covering the outside of the residence with signs and placards.[178]

As the anti-eviction mobilizations accelerated in 1934–35, various unemployed/workers' associations adopted new and creative tactics in widening the resistance. In mid-April 1934, when three New Toronto relief families living on Sixth Street faced eviction, the unemployed erected billboards on the lakeshore calling the jobless to come to the defence of those about to be made homeless. The bailiff, who had announced that he would enforce the evictions that weekend, feared an angry crowd. He thought discretion the better part of valour and stayed away. The New Toronto Workers' Association maintained its protective presence over the course of Saturday and Sunday, continuing to guard the threatened relief families and forestall the evictions. The energetic EYWA rallied two hundred unemployed to a noon-hour blockade of the eviction of Vincent Mielen, his wife, and their six children on March 14, 1935. Knowing that a city relief officer and a landlord's representative were to descend on the Mielen residence Saturday morning, the EYWA spent Friday evening posting signs on township hydro poles: "Wanted—500 men at 9 AM Saturday to prevent an eviction at 16 Crewe Avenue." With hundreds of unemployed outside their house, the Mielens were emboldened to stand their ground, refuse any furniture removal, and await the outcome of negotiations between EYWA representatives and the evictors. In the end, arrangements were made to allow the family to stay put.[179]

East York and York townships had become centres of Toronto's anti-eviction mobilization. As relief allowances for unemployed families were being cut back in the autumn of 1935, the township welfare officer in East York estimated that as many as two hundred families had been given notice to vacate homes they could no longer afford to occupy under the curtailed rental allowances. East York Workers' Association President Arthur Williams warned of how the poor of the district were facing "wholesale evictions." In York, the numbers facing dispossession were fewer, at about one hundred, but the toll of the relief rent reductions was nonetheless devastating. In a brief presented to Ontario's Minister of Welfare, David A. Croll, the York Council attributed the rising rate of eviction to four main causes: 1) the lack of homes that could be rented by families on relief; 2) landlords' reluctance to rent to relief recipients; 3) inability of relief-dependent families to make up the difference between their monthly rent allowance and what landlords charged; and 4) an influx of relief families from other municipalities. York Council suggested to Croll that the relief rates be raised and that no families be allowed to move from one municipality to another until provisions were made to shelter them. Even the South York Liberal Young People's Association got in on the anti-eviction act, telling Hepburn that they were prepared to take direct action on behalf of an invalid mother and her seven children who were facing eviction on account of an unpaid tax bill. "If worst come to the worst," declared the Young Liberals, "the members of our Association are prepared to picket the house and prevent the Bailiff from entering."[180]

In the winter of 1936, evictions in East York stretched the social fabric of civil society to the tearing point. Five hundred relief-dependent families, some two thousand people in total, were on notice that they were to be ousted from their homes. A mother of three had been looking for new accommodations all over the township, but nothing was available. "Houses are scarce," she told the *Star*, but the situation was worsened because "landlords won't even rent to people on relief." Another worried potential evictee pointed out that her current rent was $20, but under the new government policies of restraint, the family was only receiving $8 in rent allowance. Trucks were organized to drive the streets in "Paul Revere" ridings to mobilize EYWA members to resist evictions, shouts of "Eviction" announcing that people should rally to the defence of those about to be ousted from their homes. East York councillors, led by Arthur Williams, were unusually receptive to the need to defend those on relief from the bailiffs and, on at least one occasion, adjourned an official Council meeting to follow Williams to an anti-eviction rally. Bailiffs received little leeway in East York, and eventually, in 1937 the township Council ruled that any sheriff's officer removing people from their homes had to be licenced, the fee being $25. In addition, the required posted bond was set at $1000, which civic officials thought would be prohibitive. When four individuals applied for the bailiff licence, councillors refused to grant documentation for a two-month period.[181]

In York Township, Councillor C. J. McMaster reported in April 1936 that, "My telephone was ringing all last night with alarms that the bailiffs were coming to all sorts of families. I told them to keep their doors locked and the bailiffs out because there is a shortage of houses. The situation is terrible." On the first of May it was estimated that one hundred York eviction notices would reach their due date. Veterans warned that if something was not done to stop the proposed removal of people from their homes, "it may be very hard to keep law and order." East York's Arthur Williams worried in the first week of June 1936 that he would not be "surprised if bloodshed ensued." Even the local sheriff, A. M. Gorrie, feared the worst, writing to Queen's Park and Ottawa that conditions were grave in his district. "It will be impossible for me to enforce five East York writs unless my officers are given protection of a considerable force of uniform policemen," Gorrie reported. Faced with crowds of hundreds determined to protect relief residents from being removed from their homes, Gorrie had come to the conclusion that to try to carry out evictions in East York was to court "riot and bloodshed." Yet the situation was such in East York that after a year in which some 475 eviction notices had been served, it was still the case that 450 more were threatened.[182]

Winter evictions drew the particular ire of organizations of the unemployed, as did harsh treatment of veterans of the First World War. In York Township in early April 1936, a veteran's family of six was forced into an icy cold street. Furniture, piled at the curb, was soon covered with snow and remained in a deteriorating state for twenty-four hours. The ex-soldier and his wife and children trudged through the slush to spend the night at a friend's house. Veterans' associations denounced the actions of the bailiffs, who called on the police to aid them in the eviction. A member of the Canadian Legion expressed regret that he and others had not heard about the coerced removal of the ex-serviceman and his family soon enough to mount an offensive against it. "There will be trouble in this township if things like this happen in the carrying out of evictions," he prophesied, adding for good, loyalist political measure that, "It is counteracting our drive against Communists by giving them ammunition."[183]

The most dramatic defence of veterans' homes came in East York in June 1936. At this point, the EYWA led the way in organizing massive demonstrations to stop township evictions. On the morning of June 5, 1936, at 7 a.m., men with large signs had paraded through East York streets, rallying the unemployed to defend people's homes against the bailiffs. Hundreds of ex-servicemen assembled in front of the residence of a former comrade, George Durant, taunting the bailiff, who arrived at 9 a.m. By this time the Durant crowd had swelled to between three hundred and four hundred, and four other homes threatened with eviction were being guarded by the EYWA. A confrontation was narrowly avoided as Arthur Williams and an East York Councillor negotiated with officials at Queen's Park to stay the evictions. Ten days later, the families threatened with forcible removal were still safe and ensconced in their homes, guarded by EYWA. Draped across the Durant family's front-yard fence was a large sign: "THEY SHALL NOT PASS."[184]

The struggle against evictions that raged in Toronto and its working-class suburbs in 1932–36 constituted nothing less than a war of the dispossessed waged against the propertied, the powerful, and the politically callous. It signalled the determination of the unemployed, be they in the ranks of single jobless men or embedded in families, that the suffering associated directly with the human consequences of the Great Depression would not be tolerated. Ewart Humphries, the Communist leader of the militant York Township Workers' Association, perhaps deserves the last word on the Toronto eviction war of the 1930s.

In late July 1936, a defiant Humphries attended a York Council meeting, angered by the recent eviction of a veteran and his large family. "The unemployed are not a bunch of dogs who will run away with their tail between their legs because Premier Hepburn opens his mouth and issues a few warrants," Humphries thundered, noting that the eviction of the ex-serviceman had only proceeded because not enough people knew about the family's plight. "If the unemployed had known about the case … they would have been there to prevent the eviction and all the police and warrants you want wouldn't have stopped them."[185] Humphries had come to the Council meeting fresh from jail, out on bail after having been rounded up by police in a midnight raid, charged with participating in relief disturbances in the district. Indeed, as other unemployed protests of the 1930s indicated, to stop evictions the unemployed were not only prepared to fight at the site of home removals. They were also, in the words of the Mimico unemployed in 1935, willing to refuse their own relief work in what constituted nothing less than a job action of the jobless. "We are not looking for trouble," one spokesman declared, but "most of the men [will] leave their relief work to stop any family from being put out. We told officials last spring that if the bailiff came in we would throw them out, and the same still holds."[186] As the crisis of unemployment unfolded in Toronto's 1930s, the solidarity of the dispossessed expressed itself in a variety of ways, bringing together the single unemployed and relief-dependent families. If protests against evictions might take the form of sit-ins, dissent among relief recipients often expressed itself in ways that drew on an age-old weapon in the class struggle, the strike, as well as in occupations and even hostage-takings.

The Jobless Take Job Action: Early Relief Strikes, 1932–1933

Entering the Great Depression, Canada's mainstream American Federation of Labor unions were largely moribund. Trade unions, incarcerated in the limiting ideology of craft sectionalism and the enervating practices of business unionism, suffered membership loss over the course of the late 1920s and, with the economic collapse of 1929–30, militancy all but disappeared within the conservative, conventional labour movement. This was one part of the push, associated with the Third Period, to form separate, Red-led unions, which the Communist Party organized under the auspices of the Workers' Unity League (WUL).[187] Most of the strikes in Canada in the opening years of the 1930s—perhaps as much as 90 percent of the total of all work actions—were led by Communists.[188]

Not surprisingly, then, when unemployed workers took up the strike as a tactic against the work requirements of relief, and in support of families suffering cuts in their support or other oppressions and grievances, they were often led by Toronto Communists. Workers' Associations in various city districts were headed by Communists, as we have seen in the case of Ewart Humphries in York Township. In Long Branch, where relief workers were especially militant, the Communist Ernest Lawrie was one of the most arrested men in Toronto in the 1932–36 years. Yet other Workers' Associations were, on occasion, hostile to the CPC and its presence in the overall unemployed movement. Tensions among Communists, CCFers, and others never really disappeared throughout the 1930s, although many organizations of the jobless, like EYWA, managed to find ways that activists of different political stripes could work together.

Rumblings against unfair practices in the relief system of York Township were growing louder and more public among the district's four thousand relief recipients in late June and early July 1932. In return for food vouchers, those without waged employment were required to work one day a week on municipal projects. At a series of meetings, the jobless groused about conditions and talk turned in the direction of demanding cash wages for their "work test," which would allow the poor to purchase household necessities, such as blankets and kitchen utensils. After the holiday weekend, six hundred York relief workers downed tools, disrupting work at the local sewage disposal plant in Mount Dennis, garbage collection, and the grading underway at several parks. Reeve A. J. Gray wasted no time in telling the relief strikers that there would be no food vouchers issued to any men refusing to do their work allocation. A few days later the township erected a barricade at the sewage works to keep relief strikers from entering the grounds and disrupting full-time waged workers. It was becoming increasingly obvious that the work done by relief recipients was sustaining York Township's public works, and strike leader William Broadhurst rallied the ranks by proclaiming, "The work by the unemployed is absolutely necessary. If the unemployed stay away from the disposal plant we can force the township to take action in the matter." The problem, as was so often the case in relief dispensation in the 1930s, was that various levels of government were, conveniently, at odds. The township, which doled out relief, ostensibly had to turn to the provincial government to ascertain if government relief could be paid in cash wages as opposed to vouchers. Provincial authorities, in turn, claimed their hands were tied and that they could not endorse cash payments for relief labour because "the present agreement [did] not permit this without the consent of the Dominion government." Later in the Depression, this kind of bureaucratic run-around would have been old hat to unemployed activists, but in 1932 it no doubt had a novel ring to it. On the fourth day of the strike, the York unemployed declared a week-long truce, allowing the various levels of the state to get their respective acts together and rule on whether or not the jobless doing relief work could be paid cash wages. In return, the township conceded that it would provide food vouchers to the strikers, even though they had not fulfilled their obligation to undertake "some useful labour."[189]

Two weeks later, the provincial government ruled that it would pay cash relief, but only up to 20 percent of the total compensation voucher. This the relief strikers thought insulting, and twelve hundred voted to resume the strike. "No cash, No work," they stated unequivocally. There were, however, breaks in the ranks. A number of relief workers opted out of the strike, crossing picket lines that were now "manned," increasingly, by women. Up to 50 percent of the relief strikers in some sectors were going to work, although in many areas of municipal relief employment the solidarity of the strike was stronger. When one of the strikebreakers told women on a relief work picket line to "go home and do your dishes," an irate mother snapped back, "We haven't any dishes to do. We never eat." With the entire York Township police force assembled at municipal work sites to monitor pickets, with the municipality issuing orders to relief workers that they must attend to their assigned tasks, and with evidence that relief workers were being brought in from other Toronto districts to "scab" and undertake the necessary labour to keep York's sewage disposal plant and other work sites up and running, tensions ran increasingly high. On July 27, 1932, seventy strikers ambushed a dozen strikebreakers at the sewage plant, forcing them to back into a muddy creek. Two strikers were arrested and charged with assault and intimidation. One of them was living in the township's Fairburn Park tent colony. In order to avoid further violence, the strike was called off, but the vote to do so carried by only a slim majority. As other Workers' Associations, such as the organization in Mimico, determined to struggle to achieve cash payment for relief work, the York Township strike wound down, but not without divided views, criticisms of leaders, and considerable discontent.[190]

Two relief strikes in the spring and fall of 1933, one in Lakeview and the other in Etobicoke, revealed the growing tensions and animosities arising out of the relief system. They also showed how, in particular circumstances of struggle, such actions could escalate beyond a simple downing of tools to other, increasingly militant, protests.

In Lakeview, the precipitating factor in the calling of a relief strike was a cut in the wage rate on public works projects to 17.5 cents an hour. The battle, which lasted two months and involving eleven hundred relief recipients, was both protracted and creative in its adoption of new and newsworthy tactics. Supported by other Workers' Associations, the strike, commencing in April, was soon being heralded by large signs constructed over the Lakeshore Highway proclaiming that "hundreds of Lakeview men were being driven into starvation." Motorists, reading this message, were then required to run a gauntlet of "collection stations" in which the unemployed, armed with buckets, collected funds for food and other necessities.

Five weeks into the strike, the Lakeview Workers' Association voted unanimously to take its members' children out of school in order to put pressure on the township to provide relief recipients with decent wages. This tactic, an uncommon one that would resurface in the later 1930s, caused considerable consternation among the unemployed, many of whom were reluctant to remove sons and daughters from their classrooms, especially in June exam time. The school strike never materialized. Nevertheless, the jobless were forced to adopt militant tactics when local politicians refused to countenance any thought of concession. "One reason we cut the wages," a reactionary reeve declared, "was to try and make them find work."

On June 7, 1933, David B. Harkness, a key Ontario government relief official, attended a mass meeting of the Lakeview unemployed and relief strikers. Adamant that he had no authority to act in ways that would alleviate their distress, Harkness' pleas that he could do nothing angered rather than placated the crowd. The relief official became a virtual captive of the strikers, three of whom guarded him throughout the evening, escorting him to the house of a striker, where an executive committee of the job action was meeting. One hundred men and women waited outside the house in the pouring rain, ensuring that Harkness would be unable to beat an easy and hasty retreat. Whenever Harkness needed to exit the meeting to make a phone call, he was accompanied by his unemployed guards. His automobile, parked nearby, was surrounded by determined women, who vowed "to secure, by violence if necessary, food for their hungry families."

In spite of his claims to be powerless, Harkness was indeed negotiating with the relief strikers, and he eventually announced that the Ontario government would immediately begin to cover the full cost of emergency vouchers while the township and the strike committee negotiated an acceptable settlement that would bring the relief protest to an end. A local reverend friendly to the unemployed and active in the mobilizations of the jobless was designated to distribute the emergency relief vouchers. This was a major victory for the strikers, some of whose families were reputed to be nearing starvation. Relief striker militancy in forcing Harkness to make an important concession was not, however, translated into effective talks with civic officials. The next week of the strike saw rising frustration as the Lakeview Council prevaricated and failed to produce any resolution to the conflict. After an unsuccessful June 16, 1933, meeting at the township hall, a disaffected crowd stomped from the building, with some pausing to smash windows and shatter a front door. There was an attempt to drag one of the more offensive local authorities, Reeve Pallett, into the street. On June 20, the strike was called off, some headway having been made. Two hundred men and women endorsed the proposal to stop the strike, and when this decision was announced to a huge crowd gathered outside near Lake Ontario there were loud cheers for the "new relief schedule."[191]

A few months later, with winter approaching, the Etobicoke Unemployed Associations of Alderwood, Humber Bay, Westmount, and Islington formed a central committee to better pursue demands arising out of grievances with the administration of relief. The central committee drew up a list of strike issues. A central demand was for a 50 percent increase in relief support, but there were many other complaints. Relief workers wanted an end to the Council's insistence that relief work must be undertaken for all relief vouchers, not just those redeemable for food, which was a more common expectation. The Etobicoke unemployed also wanted to be paid in cash, not vouchers, and for their children to be granted relief support from birth rather than at six months.

The strike commenced in late October 1933. Council refused to meet with a delegation of the relief workers, calling on police to keep all protesters out of its chambers. Insisting that the administration of relief was the sole prerogative of the Welfare Board, Reeve Clarke explained that Council had no intention of interfering in a matter over which it had no authority. Tellingly he justified the police blockade with the statement, "The police had a perfect right to refuse admittance. We closed the meeting because they threatened to raid us and bring 500 men." One day later, work on the Etobicoke public works projects ground to a halt. The strike, encompassing hundreds of relief workers, was well organized and honoured by the vast bulk of the unemployed. In Alderwood, only two out of approximately 200 relief workers showed up for work. The Chairman of the Welfare Board blustered the usual challenge that without work there would be no relief vouchers, and the strikers countered with a threat to take their children out of school.

D. J. Monteith, the provincial Minister of Labour, soon convened a round table of strikers, government officials, and the Welfare Board. With the latter refusing to provide fuel to striking relief families as temperatures dropped, the first negotiating point was to get the delivery of wood and coal reinstituted. Montieth and provincial relief official Harkness tried to pressure the Welfare Board not to continue to put families and their health at risk, but it was to no avail. "We are taking no direction from Queen's Park," declared a defiant Etobicoke welfare administrator. Eventually, sixty members of the central committee marched to the home of township relief officer A. M. McDonald, who, panicked by the anger of the crowd, summoned the police. After a tense standoff, McDonald, in phone consultation with the Welfare Board, agreed to provide fuel to eight destitute families, but his commentary and posture were increasingly belligerent. "They were supposed to be in dire need," he explained to the press, "so I thought I had better issue the orders. It was a put-up job and the men didn't need it at all, in my opinion. We are not going to make a general issue of fuel." Insulted and angry, the relief strikers began to cut down trees to heat their homes. They added one more condition that had to be satisfied if they were to return to work: that McDonald be removed as the local relief officer.

As October closed, the strike leaders met with the Etobicoke Council, mediators from the provincial government being present. Three hundred men, women, and children paraded outside of the municipal building where the negotiations were taking place, their placards reading, "Give us our daily bread." Police officers guarded the Council chambers, while motorcycle cops patrolled the Lakeshore Highway. But the Etobicoke Council and Welfare Board were not to be moved. "I have never dealt with a striker in my life," said an intransigent Welfare Board member, "and I don't intend to now." The Board was insistent that the relief strikers' central demand to work only one day for the entire relief supplement was simply non-negotiable. "There can be no compromise whatever on this point," was its blunt response. As negotiations continued for days, relief strikers clashed with small numbers of relief workers who had crossed their picket lines, seizing tools and driving those at work away from public works sites. On November 1, 1933, strike leader Buck O'Brien proposed an end to the strike after the Board agreed to a compromise in which, depending on the size of a relief worker's family, the unemployed recipient would work a minimum of one day and a maximum of three days for a package constituting the necessities of life; infants were to be recognized as dependents from date of birth; six weeks of fuel was to be distributed immediately to all relief recipients on their return to work; and representatives from each of the Workers' Associations were to be seated on the Central Welfare Board. A significant holdout related to the reviled relief officer, with the Welfare Board refusing to discharge McDonald. But there was a commitment to investigate allegations of inhumane and haughty treatment of relief recipients. All told, this constituted a significant victory for the protesters, yet many relief strikers remained unhappy and were prepared to fight on. The decision to terminate the strike was reached, but only after much debate. The ultimate vote to end the strike was 85-40, with O'Brien tilting the scales toward a return to work with a forceful speech accenting what had been achieved. Alderwood's and Westmount's contingents were militant supporters of holding out for more and continuing the job action, while the sentiment for settlement was stronger in Humber Bay.[192]

These early relief strikes established that militant tactics, including virtual hostage-taking of officials, secured results. They outlined a series of demands that would resurface throughout the 1930s. And even if threatened strikes of school children did not materialize, they first pointed in the direction of such a tactic. Local officials were sometimes quite adamant in their insistence that they would not broker relief administration with "strikers," but this stubbornness would fade somewhat as relief job actions became commonplace. The out-of-work demonstrated that they could and would take job action. In securing representation on the Etobicoke Central Welfare Board, moreover, the Lakeshore relief strike struck an important symbolic victory for limited self-representation that, while never fully achieved in the 1930s, was a significant principle that articulated the poor's willingness to stand up for themselves. In that process, the leadership of the unemployed was, of course, a critical issue.

A "Red" among Relief Recipients: Long Branch's Ernest Lawrie

One part of the divide that revealed itself among the York Township relief strikers of 1932 was undoubtedly related to ill will generated by the presence of Communists in the mobilization of the unemployed. As the relief strike unfolded, a conference was organized by the Lakeshore District Workers' Association at the Eastwood United Church. Delegates from forty-five Toronto organizations attended, with the purpose of discussing conditions of the unemployed and their suggestions for improving the relief system. From the outset, it was apparent that significant opposition existed toward the Communist Party of Canada, and the presence of the Young Communist League (YCL) at the church meeting became a point of contention. The Chair of the meeting, Reverend Allen Ferry, announced that his Church Board had instructed him that if the YCL were seated, the Church would no longer be available and its minister would have to resign from his chairing responsibilities. The vote to exclude the young Communists carried, but the vote, 45–29, was a statement that in spite of significant animosity to "Reds," there was also considerable support for them. The conference came up with a series of demands, many of which were undoubtedly either inspired by or supported by the CPC: a non-contributory unemployment insurance plan; a six-hour day and five-day week; immediate cash relief; workers to be paid at trade union rates; and an end to evictions. Delegates from the East York Workers' Association attended the Eastwood United Church conference and were later attacked for their ostensible affiliations with Communists. Police pressured school authorities to justify why they allowed EYWA to hold meetings on civic properties like the Danforth Park School when the organization obviously harboured Communists. The vice-president of EYWA, William Walker, was forced to publicly deny that the association was a Communist body. Less than a year later both the Alderwood Workers' Association and the New Toronto Workers' Association severed ties with the Lakeshore District Workers' Association, a broad front of all organizations of the unemployed located west of Toronto along the Lakeshore. Centred in Long Branch, the Lakeshore relief solidarity campaign was launched by Ernest Lawrie, a Communist who was pioneering a robust and combative jobless movement, attempting to expand his locale of struggle into a wider district organization. But in Alderwood and New Toronto, Lawrie's well-known Communist Party membership was a stumbling block to collaboration, and unemployed organizations in these districts claimed they would only consider being a part of the central organization if Lawrie resigned as President.[193]

Long Branch, under Lawrie's leadership, nonetheless became known as a centre of unemployed activism. The district, a working-class suburb in Toronto's western sprawl, was an early site of a relief camp operated by the national Department of Defence. Ontario's camps, numbering thirty-seven in total, accommodated just over fifty thousand single unemployed men in the early-to-mid 1930s, most of these work sites in remote areas of northern Ontario such as Kowkash, Vermillion Bay, and Pagawa. Paid a mere twenty cents a day, relief camp workers were, as the British Columbia case and the On-to-Ottawa Trek it spawned indicated, a constituency receptive to militant actions. Some 359 strikes, riots, demonstrations, and disturbances took place in Canada's relief camps over the course of the 1930s. In Ontario, there were barely thirty events of this kind that warranted official reports, largely because camps in the central Canadian heartland tended to be isolated and were often insulated from the ideas of dissent brought to them by activists in the organized unemployed movement. The relief camp strike at Long Branch was, arguably, one of the "major" outbreaks of this kind of out-of-work discontent in the province.[194]

Eight hundred men toiled at Long Branch's militarily-run work site, their resentments rising over the course of the summer of 1933. Demanding a wage of thirty-five cents an hour, the eight-hour day, and coverage under the Workers' Compensation Act, the relief campers struck in mid-September. General E. C. Ashton, the commander responsible for the District 2 work camps located in the vicinity of Toronto, addressed a committee of thirty-five men representing the strikers, who were being refused lunch unless they returned to their labour. Ashton was not prepared to enter into negotiations, stressing that the camp was one of many run by the state and its armed forces. "What is done in one camp is done in all," the General declared emphatically, "We are not to keep men and feed them if there is to be no return in work, so instructions have to be issued to stop feeding." Ashton issued a curt ultimatum: if the strikers continued to refuse work assignments, they would be expected to leave the camp. When the relief strikers rejected this option, condemning the "filthy hostels in the city" as lodgings they refused to go back into, Ashton issued orders to lock down the kitchen, planning on simply starving the strikers out of the camp. His authority buttressed by a mobile force of almost forty RCMP, provincial police constables, and Toronto cops, Ashton managed to keep a rump group of twenty-seven strikebreaking relief campers at work. The scabs, who were put up in a brick building, were marched past their striking counterparts each morning en route to breakfast. Their police guard was heavy. The relief strikers, having to witness this daily spectacle of turncoats headed to the table, had their spirits buoyed and their stomachs assuaged by truckloads of food brought into the camp by Communist and social democratic bodies like the Workers' International Relief Association, the Ex-Servicemen's League, and the CCF. The Toronto Trades and Labour Council and many union affiliates also supported the Long Branch relief strikers, protesting the use of relief labour on public works and calling for trade union wages for all camp residents.

Defeated by the relief strikers' resolve, Ashton and the Department of Defence simply closed down the camp. On September 21, 1933, five hundred men turned in their blankets and dispersed. But two hundred refused to leave, insisting they would go to jail rather than seek refuge in the disgusting hostels/shelters many of them had already experienced first-hand. For its part, the city agreed that it would do its best to provide food and shelter for any of the single unemployed men who made their way to Toronto, but that it would not allow itself to become "the gathering point for everyone out of work." Some of the relief strikers were indeed put up in Toronto shelters like the Fred Victor Mission, where they found the beds hard as rocks and the nightshirts crawling with bed bugs. At the House of Industry, the former relief campers were forced to chop and cut wood for some macaroni, dry bread, and cocoa. After 6:30 a.m. the residents were put out into the streets with nowhere to go. Soon the discontented men were organizing again, this time at a meeting of seven hundred unemployed in Allan Gardens. Actively involved in the agitation, which threatened to converge on city hall with a set of demands, were members of the Young Communist League and the Toronto Council of Unemployed.[195]

A few months later, the Long Branch Workers' Association led a relief strike in February 1934 to restore water services that had been cut off for three families whose breadwinners were out of work and could not scrape together the required $5–8 deposit. Pressuring Ontario's Conservative Premier Henry to reconnect the discontinued water, the Long Branch unemployed won their demand after only three days of a strike. Amazingly united, the relief strikers faced a solitary refusal to honour picket lines, with another worker blustering that he would indeed work when his turn to appear on a municipal project came up. Both of these workers who broke ranks with the Association were subsequently expelled from its ranks. Water service being disconnected for relief families remained an issue in Long Branch into the summer of 1934. Women, armed with buckets, pots, and pitchers, organized brigades, marching to the home of a medical officer of health, demanding that he issue an order rescinding the termination of water services. When families whose water had been cut off circumvented the Long Branch village clerk, mobilizations of the jobless struck relief work sites to defend the families who had taken direct action from any retaliatory measures on the part of civic authorities. Strikes such as these often won the reconnection of water services and established, for the first time, that the Long Branch unemployed who defied work orders to protest would receive relief in spite of their refusal to undertake specific designated labour tasks. Two Long Branch Workers' Association leaders, Lawrie and Vice-President M. Costello, were arrested in the midst of one May 1934 relief strike, charged with causing a disturbance and assault of a relief tool shed time-keeper. Lawrie managed to get the charge against him dropped, but Costello was convicted. The water services for relief families, however, were operative.[196]

Lawrie was back in the mix of things in November 1934. A common front of Workers' Associations in East York, York, and Long Branch led by CCF militant Arthur Williams, Communist firebrand Ewart Humphries, and the irrepressible Lawrie fomented discord by occupying relief offices and taking a government official hostage. The uprising of the jobless commenced on October 25, 1934, as five hundred EYWA members took over the local relief office and held its leading official, James Malcolm, captive. The protesters demanded that Malcolm concede a number of points and issue them with required necessities: mattresses, stoves, and

household utensils. Claiming that he was powerless to do so, Malcolm found his office occupied by two hundred demonstrators who refused to let him leave. David Croll, Minister of Welfare in the Hepburn provincial government, was eventually contacted by Arthur Williams, but Croll had little liking for the East York agitator, whom he accused of instigating "riotous assemblies" of intimidation. Eventually, however, the show of resolve and force won the day for relief recipients, who were granted most of their demands: no reductions in food relief; mattresses and bedding; no more evictions; winter fuel schedule to start immediately. Malcolm was allowed to leave the building in which he had been held, escorted to his car by police. According to the *Globe* his departure was rowdy: "It was with great difficulty that he made his way down the narrow stairway to the main floor, as every nook and corner of the offices was crowded with bystanders and sympathizers. With the crowd he was subjected to much hissing and booing." Apparently the only casualties of the day were suffered by police, who discovered the air had been let out of their tires.[197]

Inspired by the successful actions of EYWA, its Long Branch equivalent occupied the local relief office at noon on November 1, 1934. Guarding entrances in and out of relief officer J. S. Tiffin's workplace, the two hundred men, women, and children were adamant that Tiffin was to remain under their "care" until he came up with bedding, mattresses, and household necessities. A new appointee of the provincial government, Tiffin faced this onslaught of relief recipients, speaking for 216 families, on his first day at work. Negotiations with Croll went nowhere and, under police pressure, the unemployed occupation came to an end, a badly shaken Tiffin leaving the building with an escort of uniformed officers. The following day the same scenario of occupation, hostage-taking, and unsuccessful termination of the protest was enacted again at the York Township Welfare Office, when Hugh Colon, assistant relief commissioner, was held by two hundred protesting men, women, and children for two hours. Less than a week later, with Ewart Humphries as their spokesman, the York jobless crammed into the relief office once again, four hundred strong, occupying the welfare premises throughout the afternoon until police forced an evacuation.

Croll, obviously getting fed up with the taking over of his offices and the confinement of his relief officials by demonstrators, whom he undoubtedly knew were led by Communists, put his foot down. The police issued summons for six of the Long Branch Workers' Association leaders, with Ernest Lawrie heading the list of those designed "disturber[s] of the peace," those who would:

> incite persons to commit indictable offences, and offences punishable on summary conviction and to commit breaches of the peace to cause discontent and dissatisfaction among her majesty's subjects and to promote feelings of ill will and hostility between different classes of such subjects to the evil example of others in like cases offending, and against the peace of our lord the King, His Crown and dignity.

Undaunted by the pomp and solemnity of such a writ of criminal allegation, the Long Branch unemployed and their leaders buckled down to petition local residents in ways that would build sympathy for families on relief. They claimed children would be taken out of school in protest and cars on the Lakeshore Highway would be levied a surcharge to raise money to pay for the items relief families were desperately needing. Led by the Canadian Labour Defence League, the Long Branch unemployed also spearheaded a campaign to defend their arrested leaders, calling at Lakeview meetings for the dropping of all conspiracy charges. In a late November 1934 trial a judge found "absolutely no evidence" that the six indicted Workers' Association leaders had conspired to incite violence. After the not guilty verdict, the Long Branch unemployed launched a "charity drive" for relief families. Erecting signs along the side of the road, and parading through the street with pots and pans, they solicited money from cars passing through the village.[198]

The New Toronto Workers' Association animosity to Lawrie as a Communist had either abated by March 1935, or rank-and-file relief demonstrators were more willing to abide his presence and organizational acumen. At this point, Hepburn's Ontario Liberals were waging a war of cutbacks against relief recipients, and Croll was working himself into a lather about aspiring Lenins agitating among the jobless and making his life generally miserable. A special force of twelve relief investigators was established to "make it tough on cheaters." Such actions led to riots, the storming of welfare offices, occupations, and a rash of relief strikes.[199]

One of the most militant and expansive actions took place in New Toronto where, in March 1935, the unemployed threatened a Gandhian campaign of passive resistance if sufficient food voucher support was not forthcoming to feed their children. Led by women, one hundred relief demonstrators invaded the New Toronto relief office, pressured the local Council to restore a ten percent cut in the relief allowance, and managed to convince local officials to twist the arm of David B. Harkness of the Ontario government's Relief Committee. With Harkness adamant that he would not be coerced by those illegally occupying government offices, the police were called in and cleared out the New Toronto demonstrators. Two hundred unemployed were back the next day. This time, their occupation was more sustained. Families took fifty children out of school and set them up in the seized relief office, while sympathetic merchants and an array of organizations representing the jobless sent in food. As an eight-piece orchestra played, men and women square dancing about, with others helping children do puzzles or passing the time in a game of euchre, the proceedings were taking on the atmosphere of a block party. Orders to vacate the relief office were of no avail. A. McDougall, president of the New Toronto Workers' Association, defied the police: "Come and put us out if you want the place cleared," he replied with a challenge, "We are determined to meet a Government official immediately, or we shall take such dramatic action as is necessary to bring them out." New Toronto Police Chief Padgett feared a bloodbath and decided, for the time, to avoid a direct confrontation. Hearing of threats to the unemployed occupying the relief office, jobless men and relief families from across the Lakeshore district began to congregate outside the building where the protest was ongoing. Alderwood, Long Branch, Mimico, Humber Bay, and Lakeview all sent reinforcements. The massive and growing crowd burned Welfare Minister Croll in effigy. Emboldened, those who had occupied the relief offices for two days marched out, paraded across the street, and took over another edifice—the police station! Sleeping in the cells, the demonstrators made no bones about their disgust with various hierarchies of power: "In jail they give us many things we are refused. The only representative they will send us is the state police. Our own Council are too weak-kneed to bother with us. They have washed their hands of the whole matter."

Significant numbers of those inside the New Toronto lock-up were from other districts of Toronto. This irked local officials to no end, conjuring up the political nightmare of outside agitators descending on New Toronto, invading its police headquarters, no less. Provincial relief officers and New Toronto officials determined to end the embarrassment. "When unemployed from other centres started to come in and make a disturbance, it was high time they were put out," explained New Toronto Chairman of the Police Committee, C. J. Bennett. Eventually, after thirty-six hours, thirty-three officers from New Toronto and neighbouring municipalities retook the police station, and the occupiers joined one thousand supporters in the streets. Then followed the victimization. Officers circulated throughout the crowd, arresting leaders of the siege. One of the eleven men taken into custody (no women were targeted in spite of their prominence in the proceedings) was Long Branch's Ernest Lawrie.[200]

Lawrie obviously had a way of popping up like a bad penny, at least as far as relief officials, police, and politicians in the Ontario government were concerned. This would happen again, in November–December 1935. Once more, the mobilization involved the three districts of East York, York Township, and Long Branch. Although Lawrie was no longer the president of the Long Branch Workers' Association, having been replaced by P. Dyer, the cast of characters, with Arthur Williams, Ewart Humphries, and Lawrie occupying prominent places among the dissidents, with various police chiefs, relief officers, local reeves, and David Croll as their chief adversaries (Hepburn was replaced by Acting Premier Harry Nixon), ran true to form.

Things were particularly bad in East York, with some thirteen thousand on relief, subject to the reductions of $1–$3 in the food allowance and the dismantling of a special diet program that had allowed doctors to write notes for relief families in which members, for a variety of health reasons, might require extra rations of bread, eggs, and milk. EYWA voted to wage a relief strike in protest, and on November 5, 1935, five hundred men walked off their jobs grading roads and landscapes on Woodbine Avenue and in Todmorden Park. When ten relief workers employed in the relief office struck in sympathy, East York retaliated by ending the cash relief system and reverting to relief vouchers. Angered by this overt attack, the relief strikers and others in EYWA mounted a school strike, pulling their children out of classrooms and vowing that they would stay out until payment of relief in cash was reinstituted. A resounding success, the school strike featured one thousand determined boys and girls walking out on their teachers, spontaneous child picketing of the schools, and a public march of seven hundred school kids and four thousand East York unemployed. The striking children carried banners demanding warm clothing and adequate footwear, often sporting arm bands reading, "On Strike." Within two days the East York Council agreed to reinstate a system of cash relief and the children returned to their classrooms. But the strike against the relief reductions continued, with the township council blocking delegations of the unemployed from coming into its chambers and addressing it, the jobless parading before police, chanting "Force council to meet with us."[201]

A week into the strike, 500 workers occupied the township relief offices. Winning the concession of a meeting next day between Council and a delegation of the strikers, the occupiers left the building at midnight. Croll, however, was keeping his distance, and little came out of the deliberations. Fed up with the proverbial run-around, 300 East York unemployed stormed Council chambers, clashing with police. Their way cleared by a woman and a small child who managed to sneak past a police guard of the municipal offices, 150 angry men and women pushed their way into the Council's rooms, sitting in. They let their co-demonstrators into the building by opening windows. The police, who were outmanoeuvred and outnumbered, called on reinforcements from various Toronto townships and when Police Chief Faulds issued an order for the crowd to vacate the premises, physical confrontations with the police broke out.[202]

Croll had determined to tough it out against the East York militants. Meeting with the municipal council, he sounded the battle cry of "no surrender," and then upped the ante. Not only would there be no restoration of the 10 percent relief cut, but all cash relief on East York public works projects was summarily terminated. Relief work being done in constructing skating rinks for the winter, straightening the Don River, monitoring of school intersections, and grading Woodbine Avenue was perfunctorily wound down. Police forces were buttressed with recruits from outside the municipality. It was nothing less than a declaration of war against the unemployed and their militant relief strike action. At mass meetings in two local schools, the EYWA determined to stay the course, the votes to continue the strike being 811 to 11 and 479 to 0. Local politician and leader of the unemployed Arthur Williams protested the flooding of his district with outside police officers, brought in and paid for by other agencies, whose sole purpose was to break the relief strike. Since a number of the police came from York Township, where the unemployed movement was strong and led by Ewart Humphries, Williams took time out of the East York battle to speak at a meeting of York's Mount Dennis unemployed, urging them to strike in solidarity, so that their police forces would be kept busy on their home turf and could not invade East York with impunity. Knowing that a defeat for the East York strike would be a savage blow to all of Toronto's unemployed, Humphries concurred. He advocated that a number of other municipalities commence militant unemployed actions.[203]

In Long Branch, this had been happening anyway. Building since early October, a protest mobilization aimed at restoring cutback relief support to some 230 Long Branch families peaked in late November. The newly arrived president of the Workers' Association, P. Dyer, railed against the "new" cash relief system implemented by the Long Branch Council that dictated that the poor receive less food at the same time that they were required to work for every cent of relief provided. Dyer wrote to the local Council on behalf of the Association, stressing that "the 'full cash relief' program inaugurated Nov. 16 is degrading, demoralizing, humiliating, deprives recipients of their self-respect, and the right to gainful employment and reduces us to a state of serfdom." Meetings of delegations of the unemployed and Long Branch Councillors produced only impasse. On December 2, 1935, one hundred relief workers struck. They quickly enticed a contingent of relief workers guarded by police from New Toronto, Islington, and Long Branch to throw in their lot with the strikers. The local council responded with a blunt "No Work, No Relief" policy.[204]

In East York, Williams refused to believe the local council would force thousands of women and children into starvation. At a mass rally in support of the East York and Long Branch strikes held at Massey Hall in early December 1935, Williams told those assembled: "When they say that they are going to cut off relief they are only trying to intimidate us. It is more than any government dare do. They dare not risk the starving of thousands of people." Yet the relief was stopped. Relief strikers in East York taunted and jeered those who crossed their picket lines. Clashes with police resulted in six arrests. A few days later in Long Branch, Dyer and another Association leader were taken into custody charged with obstructing police. The cops must have been surprised Ernest Lawrie was not again in their cells. With families facing the starvation Williams could not countenance, and police forces swollen with recruits from across Toronto protecting relief strike breakers, the East York and Long Branch strikes began to peter out.

A CCF campaign to utilize private charitable donations from businesses, churches, and other sources simply could not meet the demand. At a December 12, 1935, meeting of four hundred Long Branch unemployed, Lawrie resurfaced with a rousing speech attempting to rally the relief strikers to continue their struggle:

> I will never go back to work under the same conditions I left if I have to
> do 10 years in jail instead, because the only reason I went to work was to
> get the men to go out on strike. I have been locked up in jails all over the
> country, but I have never been convicted. If we are not willing to accept the
> meagre allowance of the authorities, we are threatened with jail, we and

our children with starvation, and we are met by council which announces it will meet trouble with trouble. When we meet the members, they bring out the riot squads for protection—even when meeting a deputation of two they did this.... We have suffered yet there has never been any damage here by the unemployed.... This is not an accident, it is the peaceful attitude of the recipients. The unemployed are not afraid of the police, although the police on at least one occasion showed fear of the strikers. They knew better than attempt to start anything. They waited, and when we had scattered, they returned with three carloads of police and arrested two men. We are not afraid of the police, and you may give them that message right now. It is the police, not the unemployed, who incite riots.

Four days later Lawrie was part of a delegation of East York/Long Branch relief strikers that met with Acting Premier Nixon and the ever-present David Croll. Nixon offered no concessions and put the blame on "professional agitators" for the problems associated with the relief strikes. Lawrie retorted that Nixon was a "professional agitator" during the last provincial election. As Nixon denied the allegation, Lawrie labelled the politician a liar. A few days later the relief strikes, some of the longest in

Lakeview relief marchers asleep by roadside outside Reeve E. D. Maguire's house, Clarkson, April 1938.

York University Libraries, Clara Thomas Archives & Special Collections, *Toronto Telegram* fonds, ASC19071, *Evening Telegram* Staff..

duration in Ontario's economic collapse of the 1930s, were formally declared over. The unemployed went back to their relief jobs so that their children could eat; they did so under protest and with a few minor concessions to their credit. Williams tried to put a positive spin on the defeat: "It is not true that the strike has collapsed. We have simply decided to postpone further action."[205] Christmas, 1935, was not shaping up well for the unemployed of East York and Long Branch.

Reds, Riots, and Raising the Relief Rates: March–May 1935

Communists like Lawrie would lead other struggles as well. By the spring of 1935 the provincial government of the newly elected Liberals, led by Premier Mitchell Hepburn, was truly fed up with all such agitators. Hepburn and his Minister of Welfare, David Croll, launched an all-out attack on the Reds whom they labelled as entirely responsible for fomenting grievances among the unemployed.

In York Township the jobless were increasingly discontented. A delegation of nine unemployed, seven men and two women, met with welfare official R. B. Geggie at the Rogers Road relief offices in York on the afternoon of March 28, 1935. Geggie had police protection present. Demanding that evictions end, and that recent cuts to the relief rates be reversed, the spokespersons for the poor grew impatient as the relief official was constantly on the phone with Queen's Park, where someone in the government advised the local figure to merely record the complaints of the unemployed and forward them to the appropriate provincial authorities. Dissatisfied with this, the delegation refused to leave Geggie's office until their demands were met. The police ended up forcibly removing two men, and the entire small contingent left the building, where they joined a demonstration of seven hundred.[206]

The rebuffed delegates addressed the throng, which grew as word spread throughout the community of the treatment meted out to the jobless at the hands of Geggie and the police. Soon one thousand men and women were surging forward, storming the building where Geggie sat protected by police. Women apparently led the assault on the building, male youths figuring prominently in the street fighting. Police batons were met with rocks, bottles, and other missiles, windows shattering, showering those inside the edifice with glass. Protesters and police were locked in hand-to-hand combat, battles continuing until the dinner hour. Several officers and numerous demonstrators suffered injury. The *Star* described the event:

> Urged by women, [the crowd] made a rush at the side door, smashing it in, while glass continued to fly in all directions.... Police drew their batons and fought with the men through the shattered door, preventing them from

gaining entrance. Riot squads arrived from headquarters and charged the crowd driving it along Rogers Road and down the street. A group of youths blocked the path of police and a free-for-all-fight followed, in which police wielded their batons and the youths hurled stones and bottles and wielded fists. Small fights were waged along the side streets. Several fights raged on verandahs in nearby homes.

Thirteen were arrested, including one juvenile, charged with assault, obstructing police, and inciting a riot. By 6 o'clock the violence had subsided, but police patrolled the neighbourhood. The unemployed, undaunted, formed a fresh crowd and gathered to hear a protest address by James Shapcock.[207]

Police Chief Faulds quickly blamed the disturbance on Communist agitators. The Reds, Faulds claimed, were exploiting the unemployed and encouraging confrontations with the police simply to get publicity:

> It is time the public should be informed about what is actually going on in York township. A group of six to twelve agitators in the township receives its instruction from Toronto and the organization there gets instruction from Moscow. Secret meetings, at which only a small number of persons are present, are being held in the township, at which plans for mass demonstrations are laid. They take the form of preparing disturbances calculated to force the police to make arrests, all of which aims at public sympathy. But over 95 percent of those taking part in these demonstrations are genuine unemployed who are ignorant of the manner in which they are being exploited by these Communist leaders.

Two weeks later, Faulds justified the use of physical force by his officers against the unemployed, drawing on the ideological arsenal of anticommunism. "This gang is agitating all over the country, and the sooner the government gets them by the neck and ships them back to Russia in a cattle boat the better."[208]

Outside the cloistered ranks of the police, the criticism ran in the other direction. "The attitude of the police was entirely uncalled for," argued Dr. Luke Teskey, "That our police would use billies and strike defenceless women is something that we cannot tolerate. These people were only asking for something to which they are perfectly entitled." Members of the Mount Dennis Ratepayers' Association met the evening following the riot and denounced the police brutality. "Get the men work," declared Martin Davey of the Silverthorn Property Owners' Association, "and start immediately to stop the riots by proper method—removing the cause." There were calls to have Arthur Roebuck, Provincial Attorney-General, release those arrested unconditionally.[209]

Sympathetic Councillor C. J. Cashman stood with the unemployed and claimed the people of the township were in support of the protesters and their demands that evictions be stopped and relief rates raised. For its part, the York United Workers' Association explained that demonstrations were the only way the jobless could better conditions for themselves, spokesman John Denton pointing out that, "If it were not for demonstrations we would not even have the allowances which they gave us at the present." When a stubborn Reeve Stuart addressed a post-riot crowd of the unemployed and attempted to argue that the township's jobless were being manipulated and exploited by agitators, he was shouted down. Police remained stationed in the relief offices.[210]

Local struggles such as those waged in York Township spring-boarded into wider mobilizations. In early April, three thousand men, women, and children marched on Queen's Park to demand that the Hepburn government raise relief rates. Led by Communists A. E. Smith of Toronto and Ernest Lawrie of Long Branch, organizations from as far west as Oakville marched separately and then fused these feeder parades into one massive march composed of Workers' Associations from Long Branch, Mimico, New Toronto, East York, York Township, and Toronto proper. Songs rang along the route as the protesters paraded under the banner, "United We Eat. Divided We Starve." Police prepared for the onslaught. A cable barricade was erected on the front lawn of the Legislature. Inside uniformed officers protected all doorways and patrolled the halls. Queen's Park resembled a fortress, Premier Hepburn explaining:

> They sent us a demand—not a request—that they be allowed to speak from the floor of the House. Of course, we couldn't allow that, but when we refused that demand we heard rumors of the threats they made. We have it on good authority they threatened to force their way in and create as much a disturbance as possible.

But to placate the protest Hepburn agreed to meet a small delegation of twelve people from the various Workers' Associations. Two cabinet ministers, Croll and Roebuck, would also be present with him during the meeting. The meeting, which lasted for three hours, was not one of like minds. The unemployed wanted relief rates raised by 50 percent; money to be made available to purchase household necessities like bedding; a stop to evictions; higher rent allowances; and amnesty for those recently arrested at unemployed protests in York Township and the New Toronto police station occupation. Hepburn was adamant that there would be no raising of relief, the Liberal Premier taking his cues from his Conservative prime ministerial counterpart: "I was at a relief conference … with Premier Bennett, when he said the standard of living of the unemployed was rapidly reaching that of those getting wages. That was the reason he cut down payment to the province. We took up the slack." Indeed, Hepburn implied that the jobless were doing fine under current relief administrations. Protests, demonstrations, and disturbances were unheard of in many Toronto districts, he said slyly, suggesting that where there was the smoke of conflict, there was likely the fire of Communist agitation. Against claims of child malnutrition, both Croll and Hepburn were insistent that the province had investigated thoroughly any such possibility and had never found "one case." Croll took on the issue of evictions and passed the buck to the municipalities, whom he bluntly said were "shirking their responsibility in finding housing for the unemployed." Hepburn conceded that evictions posed a serious problem and noted that he was willing to arrange a conference with municipal authorities to address the issue. Similarly, the head of the Ontario government and Croll agreed that the lack of bedding among Ontario's relief-dependent poor necessitated a response on the part of the state. They made a vague commitment to accompany the jobless on a tour of their living quarters; twenty thousand mattresses were later distributed across the province. Roebuck got in on the act by categorically stating that, as Attorney-General, he would refuse to intervene in any judicial processes arising out of local criminal charges; magistrates could not be told how to run their courts. All in all, it was less than a mixed bag of consequences for the unemployed; the jobless got some small concessions to sleep on, to be sure, but the bulk of their demands were rejected and deflected by the three wise men of Ontario's governing Liberal Party.[211]

If the Workers' Associations' April 1935 march on Queen's Park netted the poor some minor achievements, it was also used to accumulate ideological capital in the camp of the state. Minister of Welfare Croll's response to the meeting was not so much to recognize that conditions among those receiving relief were deplorable, but to lambaste the working-class districts of Toronto for "playing ball" with Communist agitators and, in giving in to their demands, escalating social conflict and generating civic turmoil:

> Lately there have been demonstrations and disorders in certain muni-
> cipalities. Let me assure you that those incipient riots did not occur

spontaneously. They were well organized and before they were staged legal advice was obtained by those who promoted them. I am well aware of these parades and make-believe sieges were covertly organized by two-cent revolutionaries. They have occurred in municipalities where the relief allowances are the most generous in the province, places where municipal government has substantially collapsed.... I attach no blame to the unemployed for being upset. No matter what your income, whether it is through clipping coupons or in vouchers, it is a bitter blow to take a cut. Nevertheless, if vote-greedy councillors had given us even a little co-operation, we should have witnessed none of the regrettable outbursts. But the council has done even worse. They played ball, not with relief recipients, but with troublemakers.... It is significant that the demands made of the city council of Toronto, upon the relief administrations of all the Yorks ... are couched in exactly the same words, and set out exactly the same demands.... Those Lilliputian Lenins are not good hardy radicals with a broad vision, but niggardly obstructionists with delusions of grandeur.... They have learned that by constantly damning the government you can get quite a name for yourself among the vocal firebrand.[212]

Croll's rant contained reference to like happenings in the Niagara Falls area. There, in Crowland, nine hundred of the peninsula town's three thousand residents, many of whom were ethnic, immigrant workers, were on relief. As in Toronto, their complaints reached fever pitch in the spring of 1935. A massive relief strike rocked the small town. The demands were indeed similar to those raised in Toronto's working-class districts, as were the riots, street confrontations with strike breakers, and arrests. But the situation of the Crowland relief strikers was, if possible, even more dire than the conditions facing the Toronto unemployed. Repression was heavy indeed. Strike historian Carmela Patrias attributes what she calls the "unparalleled harshness" of the civic and provincial response to the strike to the ethnic composition of urban Crowland. Relief strike rioters were tear-gassed and the jail terms assigned to those arrested lengthy. Faced with starvation, the poor of Crowland survived only because of the help they received from Workers' Associations across the province. In an effort to keep children from suffering malnutrition and worse, the relief strikers sent forty-one of their sons and daughters to Toronto on April 24, 1935. The Communist-led National Unemployed Council made arrangements to billet the children with members of Toronto's various Workers' Associations; the youngsters were fed at the Ukrainian Farmer-Labor Hall. Mayor Simpson, perpetually in a huff about the CPC and its willingness to make trouble for him, was enraged that the Crowland relief strike was being imported into his city, where it might well incite confrontation. "This is a threat to constituted authority, but we've got nothing to do with it and won't invite trouble by interfering," whined the CCF mayor.

Hepburn was not inclined to stand back and let things unfold with respect to the Crowland children. With a Toronto parade of Crowland relief strike children calling attention to the plight of the poor, Hepburn threatened to have the parents of the hungry boys and girls arrested for violating truancy regulations and, after the youngsters failed to show for a scheduled meeting with the premier, they were bussed back to Crowland at government expense. Soon thereafter, the Crowland municipal authorities, intransigent in their opposition to the strikers but unable to control the situation, called on Hepburn and the provincial government to step in and squash the protests. The government wielded a particularly heavy hand of coercion and refusal, insisting that if relief strikers continued to boycott work they should be cut off all support. Communist agitators were indeed on the scene, the old stalwarts of the Toronto movement, Ewart Humphries and Ernest Lawrie, being on the ground floor of agitation, working with some local comrades. When, along with the Crowland leaders of the relief strike, the Toronto Communists came as part of a delegation to negotiate with Hepburn, the premier was having no truck with the Reds. "Lawrie and Humphries aren't coming in today, that is all there is to it," he ruled, "And we aren't seeing any of those who are under arrest at the moment. The trouble with you people is that you've come under the control of those spell-binders from Toronto. You and the reeve here would have gotten on very well if it hadn't been for them." It was an old state refrain.

One Crowland militant, Mrs. Steven Holiday, wasn't buying it:

> I advise every comrade to lay down his shovel and walk out. If it means bloodshed we are not the only ones. They are only trying to starve us. Hepburn tried to scare me today by telling me not to listen to agitators. Why should we turn down our comrades? If they want to put us in jail let them do it. We are not Communists; we are only fighting for our bread.

After six weeks of struggle, the Crowland relief strike was broken, leaving a bitter taste in the mouths of the unemployed and intensifying Hepburn's loathing and scapegoating of Red agitators. Two of the Crowland relief strike leaders, Frank Haslam and William Douglas, both known Communists, went to jail for fifteen months, convicted of inciting to riot and being members of an unlawful assembly.[213]

Less momentous confrontations also punctuated the social relations of relief in the Toronto area in April and May 1935, among them developments in Mimico and Alderwood. In the former, turmoil resulted when the unemployed were refused the right to address the town council, delegations being turned away on a number of occasions. Finally, on April 24, 1935, the jobless contingent's patience wore thin. Demanding trade union wages for relief recipients working on a municipal works program, forty jobless protesters assembled in the town hall and refused to leave, threatening to occupy the building overnight. Police were called and a fight broke out:

> Screams of women mingled with the clamour of the men as wives rushed to assist their husbands when they saw them struggling with police. Seats and chairs were thrown about in the chaos which developed in the hand to hand fight. Police helmets were trampled and one or two chairs smashed. One constable was knocked unconscious while struggling with three men. Reinforcements arrived from the New Toronto police force after the hall had been cleared.

A key combatant, George Welch, was arrested in the melée, charged with vagrancy, and released on $100 bail. Welch, a Communist, would be targeted by Hepburn's government more than a year later, one of a number of militants arrested in the dead of night as the premier took aim at Red agitators among the unemployed. In Alderwood, at the same time Welch was being arrested for the first time in Mimico, 225 families were on relief. The jobless fought to be paid in cash wages for relief work rather than receiving vouchers and demanded that they receive more money for food than was the normal allowance. They struck a relief construction site and attempted to parlay this local job action into a wider district mobilization, a general strike that would encompass more than 3000 relief workers across a spectrum of Toronto municipal works projects. In East York, relief mothers demanded clothing for their children's new school year, rejecting sweaters that were offered because they were "visible a block away" as charitable apparel. They promised picket lines at the homes of township councillors if the issue of their youngsters' clothing was not addressed immediately. Apparently, this escalating kind of demand, as well as the threat of extending the struggle into a general strike, had positive consequences, for vouchers were replaced with cash payment in a number of Lakeshore District townships.[214]

Indeed, the struggle to secure cash wages for relief work and do away with the voucher system was largely won by mid-1935, with Croll announcing major reforms in the administration of relief that August. Municipalities could choose whatever form of payment they preferred, but the province no longer objected to cash payment and, indeed, gave indications that it preferred to do away with the voucher system. "Cash relief is past the experimental stage in this province," Croll explained. "During the past twelve months nearly eighty million dollars had been expended on work and cash programs and 70 percent of Ontario municipalities have participated in the scheme." According to Croll cash payments avoided "paternalism— an ailment which afflicts government today." But if this seemed a good thing, and a concession to the demands of the jobless, it was paired with an overhauling of relief administration in Ontario that constituted nothing less than an overt attack on the poor. Relief administration was to be tightened up at the municipal level, which was now granted more power to dispense support to the unemployed. A package of reforms was implemented, the purpose of which was to develop more rigorous accounting of who was granted relief. Croll explained to a conference of the Ontario Municipalities Association that there had to be a new spirit animating relief administration, one that would "purge relief lists of those who have no right to public assistance. In dozens of municipalities surveys of relief rolls are taking place, to the end that cheaters and idlers are eliminated." The government's long-standing "No Work, No Relief" policy remained in place, an entrenched position that served as a material means of controlling relief recipients rebelling against low rates or protesting through strikes and other actions a broad array of grievances. In the later 1930s, this tightening of relief administration would, however, continue to generate protests among the unemployed.[215]

Upping the Ante: The Hepburn Offensive and the Militancy of the Unemployed, 1936

In the late winter and spring of 1936, the Hepburn government cut relief drastically, reducing family allowances 10 percent and eliminating the single unemployed from support entirely. Federal funds to the provinces were being pared back. Croll and Hepburn thought "Need, not greed" needed to be the watchword in Ontario, and with signs of a modest economic recovery a campaign was introduced to "houseclean" the relief rolls by the end of March 1936. Croll wanted to purge the "chisellers—families who have made relief their career." To demonstrate that the state was even-handed in its cutback crusade, and that it could attack business as well as the wageless workers, the Minister of Welfare announced that "no longer would the government subsidize the starvation wages paid by unscrupulous employers" and that anyone who was working full-time but who required supplementary relief to support a family would also be purged.[216] The jobless responded by organizing one of the largest relief strikes since the beginning of the Great Depression. Involving ten Toronto suburban working-class municipalities, the strike took in thousands of families receiving relief and escalated from job action to occupations and hostage takings. Hepburn responded with an intensified campaign of attack, the rhetoric of red-baiting reaching new heights and arrest totals climbing.

A centre of the resistance storm of 1936 was York Township, where relief picket lines were established by militants associated with the CPC, the CCF, and the Trotskyist Workers Party, among others. Almost immediately after the cutbacks to relief came into effect, fifty relief workers in York refused to undertake their work duties collecting garbage. Within a day, all relief work sites in the township were being picketed. "We are going to stop every bit of work," promised Humphries. Wives supported their striking husbands wholeheartedly. "You'll have more to contend with with them [the women] than you will with the men," Humphries's wife warned, adding, "The women aren't going to stand for it." A York reeve claimed that the township had no option but to implement reductions in relief when the federal government cut grants to the province, which then passed the losses on to municipalities. From provincial relief officer R. B. Geggie came the commitment that whatever actions the unemployed took in downing tools, they must understand that the government's policy was not to cave in to such intimidation: striking relief workers would be declared unemployable and suffer the consequences, which included a further cut in relief support and the termination of cash payments, with vouchers reintroduced.[217]

Geggie's announcement was met with a widening of the struggle. Meetings of the unemployed were called in all three York townships as one thousand vowed to "strike to the finish." A strike committee of twenty-eight delegates from York, North York, and East York was constituted, representing some thirty-six hundred relief families. Plans were made to confront Hepburn at Queen's Park, and pressure was put on A. J. Gray of the Department of Municipal Affairs to provide emergency vouchers for the now destitute single unemployed. They were told, however, that there was "no more money" for transient single men without jobs. To protest this abandonment, the single unemployed of York set up an encampment on a vacant lot, dubbing their settlement "Red Square" or "Croll Village." Those relief workers defying the strike were shamed with public "outings" of humiliation, posters being circulated under the heading "SCAB LIST," numbering the strike-breakers and listing name and address. Meanwhile, the unemployed in New Toronto, Mimico, Alderwood, Humber Bay, Lakeview, and Long Branch were discussing the possibility of striking in sympathy with their York counterparts. Support was also building among non-relief elements of the community, with clergymen calling for the removal of Hepburn from office because of his indifference to the suffering of relief families. "The people are starving," declared one minister, "If we were plunged into another war tomorrow, these young men who have been cut off relief would be the first ones called."[218]

A delegation of York unemployed and Council members met with Hepburn and Croll on June 10, 1936. The discussion was one-sided and accomplished little except to further drive a wedge between the township council and the unemployed. Hepburn insisted that if York needed more funds for relief, it would have to raise the levy on taxpayers. Having implemented the Hepburn cuts to relief, York councillors were now faced with a relief strike that was expanding and an inability to resolve the obvious material crisis. On June 16, the North York unemployed joined York relief workers in striking, setting up pickets at all township work sites. Lakeshore District Workers' Associations convened, set up a central strike committee, and, after a series of deliberations, joined the relief strike at the end of June. Relief families in Lakeview (two hundred), Mimico (three hundred), Humber Bay, Westmount, and Alderwood (three hundred), and, later, Long Branch, expanded the numbers of strikers, bringing the total of families involved to over five thousand. The demands of the Lakeshore District strikers included a return to the 1935 relief rate schedule;

reinstatement of the single unemployed on the relief rolls; and the elimination of the "budget system," which required that part of the earnings of all relief families be deducted from their total package of support. As this was happening, the federal government announced a 25 percent cut to all relief support to the provinces for the summer months of July, August, and September, further shrinking Ontario's relief allocation from $892,000 to $700,000. Seven hundred unemployed marched on Queen's Park, where a crowd of over two thousand quickly assembled. A group of young men carried a model of the shacks constructed in what they had dubbed "Croll Village," and the protest on the Legislative lawns heard speeches from CCFers A. W. Woods and William Broadhurst, and Communists George Harris, Stewart Smith, Sam Scarlett, and Humphries, who claimed Croll and Hepburn would not meet with them because they were "afraid to face the working class."[219]

As the York males picketed work sites, women took their own initiatives. They held a mass meeting in "Red Square," whereupon they decided to "storm the relief office." "When we go on the war path we force attention and nothing brings these men to come to time so quickly as a crowd of angry women," said Mrs. McGregor, who chaired the women's assembly. Informing Geggie that they would be coming, McGregor promised nothing less than a "show down." The situation was worsening daily as Lakeview merchants ended a practice of extending credit to the jobless. They now insisted on receiving either cash or food vouchers for sustenance, implementing a "No voucher, no food," regime. "We have carried these people for years," a grocer spokesman said, "and we just can't carry this on any longer." With food gone from many households, the York women decided that their only options were to continue to have the government and the relief office "powering" them until they starved, or fight back. On June 24, 1936, women, many of them with baby carriages, occupied Geggie's office and refused to let him leave until he restored the relief. As they sat down on the office floor, their husbands and other unemployed men brought the women soup and sandwiches. The standoff ended hours later as a reeve negotiated with the occupiers and authorized Geggie to issue emergency relief vouchers to those families without food. York Council, having weathered this initial attack, soon posted a police officer at the relief office.[220]

In Lakeview, the women were also militant in their resistance to the relief reductions. Their township council was less sympathetic than the civic officials in York, and with the outbreak of the strike enforced a rigid, "No Work, No Relief" policy. Lakeview women then surrounded the home of Reeve Dennison, demanding that emergency vouchers be issued. The reeve was not at home, however, and the next day the women reconvened at the relief office. They confronted relief officer R. S. Moore at this desk, held him prisoner for twelve hours, and generally laid siege to the administrative apparatus of welfare. With the women keeping guard over Moore and occupying his offices, a group of unemployed from the newly formed Lakeview General Workers' Association waited on Dennison, who dug in his heels in reiterating Council's policy of "No Work, No Relief." Given the Lakeview Council's very cold shoulder, the strikers joined the occupation and helped to plaster the relief office walls with posters and hang Croll in effigy from the building. Still sitting in at midnight, the resolve of the women-led occupation twisted the arm of Dennison, who agreed to issue food vouchers for a full week to the unemployed strikers and their families. In Mimico, a similar outcome resulted from a relief office occupation, although there the Council was more bellicose in its claims that there would be no more concessions, and strike leaders expressed open fear that violence would erupt and dampen support for the unemployed among non-striking members of the community. Meanwhile, rumours circulated that the Lakeshore District unemployed were sending their children to Lake Ontario picnic grounds to beg for food.[221]

Not all Councils followed a hard line against the Lakeshore relief strikers. In Ernest Lawrie's stomping ground of Long Branch, for instance, the Deputy Reeve continued to issue food vouchers to the strikers, defying provincial government guidelines and supporting the job action of the poor:

> God bless them. I hope they get some action from the authorities because we can't. I think that they are justified in striking. How are they going to live when they are cut in relief, while food prices are at war time levels? Potatoes are 55 cents a peck—a luxury for unemployed. Bread is 11 cents, and milk is almost beyond their reach, I hope they are successful.

Long Branch relief strikers, in turn, agreed to maintain sports playing fields during the strike.[222]

The York-led Lakeview District strike was entering its fifth week in early July 1936, threatening to spread to other Toronto municipalities and the province at large. Things came to a head on Monday, July 6, 1936. Two thousand York unemployed rallied at midday, marching to the relief office. Fifty women, many with crying babies clutched in their arms, crashed the front door of the building, clashing with a police guard, who used his baton to strike some of those struggling to get past him to the second-floor relief offices. But the lone officer was no match for the now enraged women, who chased him up the stairs. Taking refuge behind the closed door of the relief office, the retreating guard found no respite. The women tore the door from its hinges, surged into the offices, and hurled chairs at the cop, who suffered further physical assault. "It's the last of my tie," the constable whined looking down at his torn neckwear, "It's ripped from my neck. I'm sure lucky I'm still in one piece." Meanwhile, the women secured the office suite, taking relief officer Geggie and thirteen assistants hostage. As police reinforcements arrived, battled, and failed to disperse the occupation, the hallways of the building filled up with the unemployed strikers. Separately, a strike committee was meeting with the York Township Council and its chief negotiator, Reeve Magwood. As the afternoon gave way to evening, the occupation, now sustained by relief strikers bringing ladders and climbing into relief office windows, grew festive. Estimates placed the unemployed and their supporters at four thousand, and the York women who had played the lead role in the occupation were reinforced by a contingent of North York women who brought the good news that they had won a special provision of food vouchers after they occupied a council meeting that afternoon, refusing to let civic officials leave the premises until they agreed to issue emergency relief. As the York negotiations were proceeding, a rope was produced, with the women singing from the building, "We'll hang Geggie to a sour apple tree." As Reeve Magwood entered the building to see firsthand the state of the occupation and ascertain that Geggie and his staff were physically safe, Ewart Humphries told the township official that he did not know how long the relief striker crowd would remain peaceful. Soon it was apparent that Magwood, too, was being refused exit. He was told to get township councillors to the site and negotiate an end to the occupation by making certain concessions to the demands of the relief strikes. At 10:30 at night, the reluctant and undoubtedly fearful municipal officials arrived. Over the next ninety minutes, in sweltering heat, the unemployed and the York Township councillors "negotiated." Just after midnight, the ten-hour siege of the York relief offices ended. Council conceded all of the demands of the relief strikers: the single unemployed were reinstated on the relief rolls; married men could earn $10 weekly without suffering reductions in their relief allowance; vouchers would be discontinued on relief work, payment provided by cash; and the relief scale was restored to levels prevailing in May 1936. Militancy had won the day.[223]

Two days later, Etobicoke relief strikers took a page out of York's confrontationist handbook. They kidnapped Reeve W. A. Armstrong and Relief Officer C. Grubb and held them prisoner in the boiler room of Sir Adam Beck School for the better part of twenty-four hours. The women leading this action forced Grubb to take their picture with them even as he refused. A pot of tar for a tar and feathering was present in the boiler room, as was a rope with a hangman's noose. The unemployed filled the school, sang songs, and played cards, sleeping in hallways on mats and mattresses. Constables from New Toronto, Mimico, Long Branch, and across the province reinforced Etobicoke's uniformed officers. But as word spread of police amassing at the school, the unemployed sent truckloads of supporters from York, North York, and various Lakeshore municipalities. As police prepared to storm the school, Etobicoke councillors, undoubtedly aware that a bloodbath might be in the making, agreed to several concessions to the relief strikers, and the hostages were released. The full demands of the strikers would be considered at a further date. A "weltering and unshaven" Reeve Armstrong left the Etobicoke school occupation obviously shaken, but clearly somewhat more aware of the desperate conditions of the unemployed. He agreed to accompany a delegation of the relief strikers to Queen's Park, where the case of the unemployed could be presented to Premier Mitchell Hepburn.[224]

Hepburn was by now in no mood to listen. A veteran *Star* reporter had informed the angry premier that well-known Communists were behind the increasingly militant actions of the unemployed. Mitch had had enough of agitators in general and hostage takings in particular. Immediately after the Etobicoke "settlement" Hepburn convened a day-long emergency meeting of his inner circle to discuss recent relief disturbances. He emerged from the Cabinet-confab stern-faced and hard-lined. "No longer are municipal and provincial officials to submit to humiliation," the premier ruled. The Highway Department was ordered to revoke the licences of any trucks used to carry "agitators" throughout municipalities, fomenting trouble. Arrest warrants were issued for the Etobicoke and York relief strike leaders. Two spectacular midnight raids were conducted by twenty-nine York County officers and members of the Ontario Provincial Police. They rounded up the militants as they slept in their beds, netting ten unemployed leaders in Etobicoke and seventeen in York. Heading the latter list was Ewart Humphries. Those taken into custody along with Humphries ranged in age from twenty to sixty-four. The Ontario Unemployed Council leader and well-known Communist firebrand Harvey Murphy was also sought but was not at home during the nocturnal raids. He turned himself in to authorities a day later. The majority of the twenty-eight men detained—no women were arrested in spite of their obviously leading roles in the militant occupations—were held on the charge that they forcibly seized and confined individuals and had assembled unlawfully. The biggest catches, Humphries and Murphy, were released on $2000 bail, a figure levied against a number of those arrested.[225]

Many of those taken into custody were Communists, including at least two militants from the Trotskyist Left Opposition group, the Workers' Party. And it was the revolutionary left that Hepburn's repression was out to squash, as well as the impact of Reds among the unemployed. In the day-long government meeting determining what to do about the escalating militancy of relief demonstrations and protests, cabinet ministers heard lurid reports about clandestine Communist meetings in which the jobless were to be used as cannon fodder in the insurrectionary war against the state:

> At a meeting in their Adelaide St. headquarters last week, the Communists plotted to incite an ever-widening circle of relief troubles which would culminate in a giant riot at Queen's Park, according to a detailed report of their plans laid before the Hepburn cabinet yesterday by a government operator.... The Communists at last week's meeting planned to ask a permit to demonstrate at Queen's Park, the report stated. If the permit was refused, they planned to demonstrate anyway, "because they had to get a riot." To the extent of the Communist plans, as laid before the cabinet, decided Premier Hepburn to order the wholesale arrest last night "to end mob rule in Ontario." ... The jobless were to be used as "fronts," the radicals to remain in the background, it is said.

Hepburn was supposedly in possession of a Communist Party directive detailing the actions to be taken in utilizing the unrest among the unemployed to promote confrontation. Much emphasis was placed on supposed orders to keep actual Party members "inconspicuous," stressing that while they might speak at rallies and demonstrations they should "not appear or take active public part in any action which the unemployed may take." Townships such as York, North York, East York, Scarborough, and Long Branch were alluded to in this report as places where secondary-level Communist Party cadre, rooted in the organizations of the unemployed, could remain in their locales, but other Communists were to be prepared to be foot soldiers of the revolution, holding themselves "in readiness to go to any part of the province at all times." Hepburn's government operator, a spy in the service of the state, obviously had an inside track on information about Communist Party planning, but he concocted his report with the usual mix of mundane information and sensationalist, ideological posturing. Stewart Smith responded to the publication of this secret report with nonchalance. "We have publicly opposed the government's relief cuts for months and have made it known every step taken by our party in the unemployed movement to advocate opposition to the relief cuts," stated Smith. "So if they had some stool pigeon around, he could not know anything not known by as large a body of opinion as it is possible for us to meet."[226]

Hepburn's heavy-handedness did not squelch militancy in the Lakeview district. Three months later, in October 1936, a crowd of women once again held a relief officer and two of his staff hostage, demanding the reinstatement of 135 family men on the municipal relief rolls. They had been terminated for refusing to work on a municipal waterworks project for 30 cents an hour, striking instead for the rate of 45 cents. After a two-week strike, the women surged into the relief office, wired the door shut, and traded barbs with Relief Officer Moore, who refused to either put the men back on relief or issue them emergency food vouchers. The occupation ended only on the arrival, just before midnight, of carloads of provincial police. As the women left the building, the police were forced to stand guard over municipal water pipes, as the strikers made noises about damaging them in retaliation.[227]

The midnight arrests of Communist leaders and local activists ordered by the Hepburn government were undoubtedly meant to intimidate the unruly unemployed. But this hardly drove the militants into cowering retreat. Ewart Humphries, swept up in the summer 1936 arrest raid in York, was elected to the township council as a known Communist when he was out on bail facing Hepburn's charges. In Scarborough, another Communist, Jimmy Wilson, was also elected as a councillor. And in the end, all of those targeted in Hepburn's repressive assault on the unemployed movement never faced trial. Put through the wringer of many pre-trial court appearances, the group, defended by noted radical attorney J. L. Cohen, opted for trial by jury and pled not guilty to "forceful seizure" and "unlawful assembly." Since many, if not all, had not been physically present within the occupations or involved in the hostage-takings, to convict them for having been illegally involved in the events that so angered Hepburn would have stretched the pliant laws against the poor and the dissident even past their normal break point. On December 15, 1936 Crown Attorney McFadden announced the dropping of all charges. Roebuck, obviously on a collision course with Hepburn, was not in favour of the all-out war on communism and the unemployed. "These men are not criminals," he explained, adding for good, paternalist effect: "They were just excited and poor people. I thought it wise and in the public interest that the trial should not go on and I told them to go in peace and sin no more." When Cohen was asked what happened, he smiled. "The book is closed," he said knowingly.[228]

Lakeview Militancy and a Hepburn Ambush, 1938

Grievances against the provincial government and the administration of relief in Toronto's many townships were, however, anything but settled. Claims of an economic recovery in mid-1936, evident in Ontario's relief rolls dropping below three hundred thousand for the first time since the fall of 1932, proved empty. As the Mackenzie King federal government cut back on relief support to Ontario and other provinces, the ostensible buoyant economy burst its rather small recovery bubble. With hundreds of thousands still on relief in Ontario in March 1938 and the number of jobless dependents climbing, the province's burden of support payments, compared to its federal counterpart, rose from 38 to 46 percent of total costs. Hepburn was pressured by Ottawa to cleanse the relief rolls of the "large numbers of unemployables and charity cases." The undeserving poor, it was insisted, were the province's responsibility. The material writing was now on the wall of class relations, scripted to produce a late 1930s clash between Toronto's unemployed movement and Hepburn's administration of relief.[229]

Indeed, 1936 ended with East York's Arthur Williams at loggerheads with David Croll. The Hepburn government was demanding that specific locales where relief expenditures were judged to be out of control must pass bylaws levying a special tax assessment, raising funds to cover the costs of various allowances. Refusing to do so could result in councillors being liable to fines of $500 each. Williams resigned from the East York Relief Committee in protest and pointed out that municipal councils in which Liberals predominated were being treated differently than those like Windsor (Labor), York (Conservative), and East York (Socialist), where non-Hepburn supporters were in positions of decision-making. Croll countered with dismissal. "Mr. Williams clings to his old tactics of appealing to mob rule. He apparently hasn't grasped the point that an executive office demands tactics somewhat different to a soap box." The irony was that contrary to the Welfare Minister's depiction of Williams as a left-wing agitator, the CCFer was, at this point, being criticized by activists in the EYWA for holding back the relief protests, and for utilizing his considerable personal authority against dissident voices in the unemployed movement.[230] There were clearly those who wanted to fight back with more vigour against the Ontario government's cuts to the administration of relief.

To the west of East York, in Lakeview, militant actions were in the making. In the spring of 1938, there were almost 1,200 people on relief in Lakeview. The unemployed in the district, through concerted protest, had raised relief rates in December 1937. They made the case, acceded to by the local relief officer, R. S.

Moore, that the level of allowance established under the Campbell Report in 1932 was inadequate under the circumstances prevailing five years later.[231] On April 15, 1938, however, Hepburn announced yet another round of relief cuts. Given this 25 percent reduction, relief recipients were forced back to a scale of allocations that had been established in 1932. A week after the announced slashing of relief, 200 Lakeview unemployed members of the General Workers' Union met to plan a course of resistance. They were addressed by Ed Lace, president of the organization and a Lakeview resident for six or seven years. Married and the father of six children, Lace had a long work history, including stints as an agricultural labourer in the United States and a well-paying job as a foreman for a hydro project. His last employment was in a New Toronto plant, where he had been discharged for union organizing. Suffering from stomach ulcers, a consequence of an inadequate diet, Lace urged the Lakeview relief workers to strike for wages that would allow them to purchase the food they lacked. "We are going through with this if we have to go to jail," he thundered. The Workers' Union Vice-President, Fred Bailey, an ex-soldier who had come to Canada in 1930, had tried unsuccessfully to get work in the mines of British Columbia but was told he was too old. Known in the Lakeview district as something of a workers' intellectual, with a firm grasp of economic theories and social questions, Bailey also had a reputation for standing up for the downtrodden and was pegged by authorities as an agitator. Like Lace, he also accented the necessity of resolute action, required by the inadequacies of relief provisioning: "It is simply beyond human endurance to do four days' work on this amount of food. It is a walkout because we are not getting enough food to nourish us and our families." Bailey's wife Evelyn concurred, stating later that the family of five was subsisting on $5 a week in relief. The household, which lacked money, credit, and food, was overwhelmed with bills and had only managed due to the kindness of organizations of the workless. But Mrs. Bailey was adamant that, as a mother, she was not about to "stand by and see her children go hungry." Anticipating that leaders such as these might find themselves behind bars, the Lakeview relief workers used their meeting to elect back-up spokesmen, urged the women of the relief families about to go on strike to join the struggle, and petitioned the Department of Highways to create a public works project widening the Lakeshore Drive that would provide the unemployed with "living wages."[232]

Lakeview Council would support this call for the widening of the Lakeshore, but it was not terribly enamoured with the relief workers' job action. When the strike commenced on April 21, 1938, Reeve E. D. Maguire refused a request to accompany the strikers to Queen's Park, impatiently explaining that he had already approached the government, which reaffirmed that the relief scale was to remain at its reduced level. "You created the condition you now find yourself in by walking out," Maguire lectured the unemployed. "If you want to do work required of you, you'll get relief. It's strictly up to yourselves." McGuire's policy was the provincial government's command: "No Work, No Relief."[233]

During the first week of the strike, women gathered in vacant lots to hear news of what was transpiring in talks between the township council and the provincial government. Often they kept their children out of school as part of their protest, collecting donations from passersby and nearby shopkeepers. On the evening of April 26, 1938, strike leaders Lace, Bailey, William Finch, and George Kellett were given a ride to a council meeting by township relief administrator R. S. Moore. The meeting was long and boisterous, with Reeve Maguire leading the charge against the relief strikers' demands that emergency food vouchers had to be issued immediately to stave off starvation. Bailey vowed that he would "spend 12 months in jail" before putting in "another year on relief," insisting that "something will have to be done and done right away." Moore and the delegation of four unemployed leaders drove back to the local Lakeview relief office, where a crowd of three to four hundred had assembled by 9:30 p.m. As the leaders of the relief strike got out of Moore's car, four women jumped in: Evelyn Bailey, Dorothy Cooper, and Edith Daigle plopped themselves in the back seat, while Elizabeth Meeker sat in the front with the relief officer. A crowd surrounded the vehicle. Refusing to leave, the women told Moore to open his office and issue emergency food vouchers. When he declined, he was told to drive them to the home of Reeve Maguire, a request that was also denied. As police arrived, Moore was asked what was going on. He replied: "Just a bunch of hungry people." As Moore calmly smoked his pipe, one of the women in the back seat fell asleep. But the stalemate went on for three hours, with a large crowd ignoring police officers' warnings that Moore could not be held captive in his vehicle indefinitely. Finally, well after midnight, as Lace negotiated with police to have a meeting with Reeve Maguire the next day, Moore was allowed to drive off and go home to bed. The following night Maguire's home was picketed by hundreds of protesters, eighty of whom marched six miles in three hours to get there and sixty of whom joined the evening demonstration after a day of monitoring struck relief work sites. More than forty men, women, children, and infants stayed the entire night, sleeping beside the roadway. Maguire's neighbours provided the striking relief families with a small meal.[234]

Reeve Maguire not being at home, the Lakeview relief strike protesters decided to march to Queen's Park, a three-hour trek. Women and children were

Lakeview relief protesters march to Reeve E. D. Maguire's house, Clarkson, April 1938.

York University Librar-ies, Clara Thomas Archives & Special Collections, *Toronto Telegram* fonds, ASC19070, *Evening Telegram* Staff.

transported in an open flatbed truck. No police were waiting for them on the Queen's Park lawn when they arrived, an unusual and surprising occurrence. As the unemployed entered the legislative buildings, however, they were surrounded by a detachment of provincial police, in and out of uniform. Heading them was General A. V. S. Williams, Chief of the Ontario Provincial Police (OPP). Williams conveyed the rather shocking news that Premier Hepburn was willing to see all of the contingent rather than a select few. Well, almost all. Excluded were any non-residents of Lakeview, which meant that the president and secretary of the OFU, Harvey Murphy and George Harris, both high-ranking Communists, were barred from meeting with Hepburn. In addition, all going in to see the premier had to provide name and address. Duly accounted for, the Lakeview demonstrators were taken to the premier's suite, where they found a large and illustrious body awaiting them: Attorney-General Gordon Conant; OPP Chief Williams; Provincial Secretary Harry Nixon; Minister of Mines Paul Ledu; the Lakeview Relief Officer, R. S. Moore; and a collection of ministers, deputy ministers, and officials. After five minutes of waiting in this august company, the relief strikers were treated to Hepburn's entry. He immediately adopted a confrontational stance, interrupting the Lakeview dem-onstrators as they tried to plead their case. It was barely possible for the unem-ployed to get a word in edgewise. Hepburn denied all charges or had others speak against them. It was an aggressive repudiation. Thirty minutes into this fiasco, half a dozen OPP officers blocked the doors of the chambers within which Hepburn was haranguing the unemployed. One of the women present "dared," in the words of a shocked newspaper report, to "arrange" her baby's clothing (a euphemism for changing diapers) "on the cabinet table," an indecorous act described as nothing less than "utter defiance of Parliamentary customs and constituted history." The weapons of the weak seemed able to overturn centuries of convention with a well-timed and well-placed wiping of an infant's bottom.[235]

At one point in the proceedings, Hepburn turned to George Kellett, a Lakeview relief strike leader. The premier began to harangue Kellett, demanding to know if he was one of the men who had "captured the relief officer." Hepburn further dredged up allegations of Kellett having stolen money from Ontario's Department of Agriculture, for whom he worked three years earlier; the charges had been unproven in any court, although Kellett was fired from his public sector job, and he, his wife, and three children became dependent on public assistance. Hepburn called on J. O. Fraser, Commissioner of Loans on the Farm Development Board, who had attended the meeting at the premier's request, to identify Kellett. That done, Hepburn had the Lakeview protester placed under arrest by General Williams on the revived three-year old theft charge. One by one, Hepburn then ordered the arrest of Lace, Bailey, and Finch, having called on Moore to identify any individuals who had kept him in his car. They were charged with assault and unlawful assembly. Charges under the Truancy Act were also laid against Bailey, Elmer Meeker, John Noble, and Albert Carey, militants marked out for involving their children in the struggle. Alf Miller, a trucker who had transported some of the men, women, and children from Lakeview to Queen's Park, was charged with carrying passengers without a licence and had his driver's permit and vehicle plates confiscated. Hepburn dismissed the delegation with a stiff rebuke:

> There is not going to be mob rule in this province. There are going to be
> no more summonses. Instead, there will be arrests. My advice to you is to
> behave like decent citizens. I am going to warn you again that there will be
> no more tactics like holding the relief administrator in his car.

Subsequently, the four women who had actually detained Moore were issued summons and charged with unlawful assembly and assaulting the relief officer.[236]

Hepburn's ambush shocked Toronto. The *Globe* considered the arrests, coming as they did in Hepburn's chambers, to which he had invited a delegation of the unemployed to air their grievances, as nothing less than one of the most sensational incidents to have occurred at Queen's Park since just before the First World War. The relief strikers were sickened at the premier's heartlessness. Opposition parties criticized Hepburn and expressed "amazement" that he would admit individuals to government Cabinet rooms only to call on police to arrest some of them. One Member of the Provincial Parliament insisted that the premier had erred in not "recognizing the system whereby people express their grief through their representatives ... his actions were certainly a very curious form of hospitality." Church groups, labour organizations, and unemployed workers' associations across Toronto lined up to denounce Hepburn. At May Day rallies in 1938, Hepburn's treatment of the Lakeview relief strikers was singled out for condemnation. The Communist Party was less in evidence than it would likely have been in earlier years of the 1930s, however. Its Canadian Labour Defence League was now effectively defunct, and the CPC formed a committee headed by five of its number active in different municipalities (George Harris, Jimmy Wilson, A. E. Smith, George Welch, and Frank Russell), but it was the CCF carrying the bulk of the defence load. It arranged bail for three of the four men arrested, for instance, all of whom were released on $2,000; Kellett, obviously very much in Hepburn's sights, was denied the option of freedom. The TTLC voted to support the Lakeview relief strikers with a cash grant, and the Labour Council managed to secure the services of former Attorney-General Arthur Roebuck to defend the Lakeview militants, Roebuck and Croll having had a falling out with Hepburn over the Premier's handling of the 1937 auto workers strike in Oshawa. CCFer E. B. Joliffe acted as co-counsel.[237]

If the layers of society critical of Hepburn's violation of British understandings of a sense of fair play were notably wide, Reeve Maguire applauded the arrests of the four men and four women. "I am particularly glad to have it broadcast that no body of people can take the law into their own hands," he pontificated. For his part, relief officer Moore posted a notice informing all on relief that they were to be back on their jobs, and Council made it clear that the "No Work, No Relief" regime had not been toppled by the Lakeview protests. The relief strike, faced with such intransigence and a court battle ahead, petered out, Lakeview families staving off absolute destitution only with the aid of Workers' and Ward Associations across Toronto, on whom they felt they could no longer impose. The strikers, who went back to work in mid-May, agreed to relief being issued daily until June 1, 1938, thereby alleviating some of the immediate distress. Thereafter relief payments would be only every two weeks and would be at a rate pegged to the Campbell Report allowance levels of 1932.[238]

The trial of the eight Lakeview defendants began on June 7, 1938, in Brampton, perhaps because of ongoing renovations at the local courthouse, a convenience that distanced the inflammatory proceedings from proximity to the defendants' homes and neighbourhood resentments. One of the women, Edith Daigle, was excused after being hospitalized with appendicitis. Hepburn assigned Crown Counsel W. B. Common, the Deputy Attorney-General, as prosecutor, and Roebuck used every available opportunity to let the jurors and the public know that this was a "state trial," conducted at great expense and at the behest of the premier's office. He claimed that the central issue in the trial was the political "right of an individual to petition the Crown without being terrorized by Crown officials." But Common was fairly effective in having Roebuck's defence limited. Still, the trial managed to expose the conditions of the relief families. Elizabeth Cooper, the mother of four children between the ages of six and eleven, testified that her electrician husband lost his job, and the family could not survive on less than $12.50 for fifteen days. She added that if the government needed examples of malnourished children it could look at her youngsters. Elizabeth Meeker, whose husband was one of the fathers charged by Hepburn under the Truancy Act, was the mother of eight children, six of whom still lived at home in 1938. Unable to live on past rates, Mrs. Meeker noted that the $5 reduction placed her family in dire straits. When asked by Roebuck what her intentions were in keeping Relief Officer Moore captive in his car, she replied forthrightly: "We said we were staying only till we got our voucher signed that night." Ed Lace also placed the accent on how families were closer to starvation and addressed the cruel situation that fathers forced to work had to feed themselves more in order to secure their wives and children relief provisioning, ensuring that mothers, sons, and daughters necessarily had less to eat: "We were faced with a direct form of starvation," Lace testified, "The more a man worked, the more he took off the table at home.... it takes more to feed a working man than a man not working."[239]

As the trial wound to its close, the judge dismissed all charges of assault, realizing that no such offence had been committed. What remained was the charge of unlawful assembly. Shut out by the judge from bringing into his defence the acts of Hepburn immediately before the arrests took place, Roebuck tried to marshal sympathies for the unemployed, contrasting the power of the state and the lack of power of the accused:

> A state trial is a great expense, as you know. These things are not done
> without money, charged to the county.... We are not here to decide

whether these people should or should not be in the position they find themselves. What position they're in … we accept it. We are not to decide any dispute between them and the Township of Toronto…. Your problem is whether or not the accused conducted themselves in such a way as to disturb the King's peace tumultuously. First thing we find is that they are on relief. It is a relief that men work for—not on the basis of wages, because there is a variation of wage according to the members of the family. They are not working at light work. I know how hard the work is, and I don't think I would care to shovel continuously all day…. It was work that required more sustenance than ordinary work. The diet they received was not sufficient for them to do the work and maintain their strength. They had an undoubted right to complain to the proper authorities. It is the serious duty of every public office to listen with patience to complaints…. They did not ask for charity. These men are not drifters. They are citizens of the community. They asked for work and wages so they need not burden their fellow citizens, and could look the community in the face. Whether wisely or unwisely, they decided to stop work. Then we find them with no money in the house and no food for the children. They had gotten themselves in a jam. The recipients did not bring an armed concourse in their appeal to the township council…. Then the question arose very vividly, how to eat in the morning? When they arrived at Lakeview there was a crowd assembled. Everybody was asking, "Will we eat?" Mothers in the crowd, anxious for their children, came to Mr. Moore and asked if their children would be fed. In the spirit of protest and anxiety, they climbed into Mr. Moore's car. Is there any man on the jury who wouldn't give a mother a loaf of bread, if she came to your home, even in the small hours of the morning? You would listen to them and hear their story. There is nothing wrong in their pleas…. An emergency voucher had been arranged two-and-a-half years before by Mr. Moore, and it was reasonable for these people to expect somebody would have common sense enough to do it again. During the entire interval Moore did not sound the horn, the recognized symbol for people to get out of the way. We have indisputable indications that Moore did not stay because of threats. He could have stayed because of the decency in his own heart, or because of fear. I prefer to accept the first. This is a state trial. You may feel this is a small police court trial, but it is not. It ranks along with treason and sedition and those other political offences which men get sent to jail for long sentences.

Roebuck's defence, so different than the kind of arguments that would have been made in the Third Period by the CPC, sacrificed much in the interests of tugging at the jurors' sense of the blatant inequality separating the prosecution and the defendants. Crown Counsel Common was having none of it:

> This is not a political trial in any sense whatsoever. It is a criminal proceeding. You are not, under any circumstances, trying the poverty of these people. It has nothing to do with the issues in this case, whether people are affluent or poverty-stricken. This is no perplexing question of relief. Its adequacy or inadequacy are not the issues here.

Common managed to turn the pertinence of poverty, relief's inadequacy, hunger, and want into non-issues, and Roebuck's arguments failed to convince the jury. As Elizabeth Meeker wept, all of the defendants were found guilty of unlawful assembly.

Roebuck's pleas for empathy had not, however, been totally in vain. The jury recommended mercy for the men and guided the judge with an even stronger recommendation to exercise leniency in sentencing the women. The men were handed down jail terms of two months; the women were given suspended sentences and told to keep the peace for a year, the judge lecturing them: "I trust that the long and arduous trial will be a lesson." But the story did not end with these convictions and this judicial pedagogy. Two weeks after the sentencing of the main defendants on unlawful assembly convictions, the vindictive charges under the Truancy Act were dismissed against Fred Bailey, Elmer Meeker, John Noble, and Albert Carey. Defence lawyers proceeded to appeal the original verdict of guilty and succeeded in having all convictions overturned by the Ontario Court of Appeal. Not to be outdone, Hepburn's Attorney-General's office appealed to the Supreme Court of Canada, but on January 16, 1939, this higher body refused leave to appeal the case. The Lakeview militants "quietly rejoiced" at this legal news. Fred Bailey reported that he was "naturally elated at the decision of the Supreme Court," adding, for explanation, "There may be those who disagree with the methods we used during the demonstration, but our situation left us no alternative. We will continue to press for work and wages." The Lakeview General Workers' Union leaders, Fred Bailey and Ed Lace, were still, at the time of these court decisions, earning their relief on township public works projects. Their co-defendants were, if possible, even less fortunate. William Finch had been hospitalized for two weeks, while George Kellett never managed to quite escape the Hepburn dragnet: he was in jail, serving his sentence on the three-year-old theft charge that the Premier had successfully resurrected to inflict on one of the unemployed whose agitational temerity had encouraged "mob rule."[240]

Closing Out the Decade: Relief Strikes and the Call to Abolish Relief Work

By 1939 there were signs of economic recovery in Toronto and elsewhere, but unemployment would remain a factor to grapple with until the Second World War brought slumping material conditions to an end and necessitated conscripting workers to fight in a global conflict. It was not until well into 1940 that the national unemployment rate dipped to below 10 percent; it was not until September 1940 that the total of individuals on direct relief in Canada dropped to below 300,000, with the figures for 1939 fluctuating between highs of over one million in February, March, and April, to between 585,696 and 976,528 in other months.[241]

Before this decline in the level of unemployment and the numbers of jobless dependent on direct relief, however, many municipalities in Ontario continued to experience a relief crisis, with the 1932 Campbell Report scale setting a benchmark that was then enhanced by upward of 30–35 percent. Hepburn once again decided this was too much, and in the spring of 1939 he announced yet another 10 percent reduction; he also threatened to take single unemployed men off the relief rolls once and for all. Toronto, where the cost of living was higher than elsewhere, was to be accorded no privileges, and Eric Cross, Croll's replacement as Minister of Welfare, declared that "the scale of relief we are willing to support is to be the same all over the Province," setting a maximum that was 25 percent above that recommended by the 1932 Campbell report. Toronto and its surrounding blue-collar environs were very much in the government's bad books: by 1939 this regional enclave was drawing one-third of all provincial relief expenditure, up drastically from the 19 percent of 1933. When a team of Ontario relief inspectors scrutinized 939 ostensibly randomly-picked relief case files in Toronto, already screened by local relief administrations, they concluded that only 33 percent of those investigated were without irregularities or violations of relief conditions. These provincial reinvestigations resulted in almost 150 of the relief clients having allowances cancelled, reduced, or suspended for a variety of violations, including unreported income and ownership and use of a telephone. Hepburn and Cross were adamant that Toronto needed to clean its relief house, insisting that the cuts would not be rescinded.[242]

The response to this 1939 singling out of Toronto for its lax administration of the dole was immediate and wide-ranging protest. The Toronto Welfare Council organized a mass meeting attended by 250 opponents of the government's policies. Labour unions flooded welfare officials with resolutions and communications demanding that the relief rates be bumped upward not downward, calling for a schedule that would conform to nutritional guidelines established by the Ontario Medical Association in 1937, boosting food allowances to 50 percent above those recommended in the Campbell Report.[243]

The most dramatic expression of outrage against this provincial curtailment of relief support was an explosion of relief strikes in York, Scarborough, and three other municipalities. In East York, the Council refused to implement Hepburn's reduced scale. Aware of the militancy of past relief strikes, civic officials in York township and other districts often aligned with the unemployed, stressing that Hepburn's policy of relief reduction would cause untold distress. York Deputy-Reeve C. J. McMaster accused the provincial government of blackmail, saying "The relief recipients will refuse to work and then we will have to hire 50 more men in the works department. This is going to cost us more money than if we continued the higher relief. The government told us they would cut our grants if we didn't come down." When three hundred relief workers in York, doing their stints collecting garbage, cleaning streets, and working on other municipal projects, did strike they were supported by the Civic Employees' Union, which had always been opposed to having relief work done in these job sectors. Council refused even to address the question of whether the provincial government's "No Work, No Relief" stance would be followed, and fear was expressed that relief cutbacks would result in riots and mayhem, as had occurred in the past. Anger grew when it was learned that Hepburn refused to take part in a federal relief works program that would have taken many of the family men dependent on relief and put them to work for conventional wages. Demands for the abolition of relief labour became part of the York unemployed movement's call for change in the administration of social welfare.[244]

The York relief strike of April 1939 was quickly followed by a second walkout in Scarborough, where Communist Councillor Jimmy Wilson led 375 members of the township's Relief Union in their downing of public works project tools. Wilson knew well that provisioning for the unemployed paid dividends in Scarborough: relief labour was saving the township approximately $22,000 a year. The inevitable strike would only push Scarborough to hire more municipal workers at wage rates far in excess of what was being paid out in relief compensation. Services like garbage collection would "be crippled." Unlike in York, however, Scarborough's civic officials were not big supporters of relief strikers. Before the unemployed had a chance to take job action, Scarborough's council cut special clothing allowances and ordered a monthly investigation of all persons receiving relief, intending to whittle down the relief bill. Reeve Clutterbuck would be a resolute opponent of the unemployed. He was outraged at the suggestion that relief recipients should get an open clothing voucher, claiming that those "who provide and not those who receive, should determine such a question." Welfare recipients who refused to undertake their work stints caused Clutterbuck even more consternation, and he would be in the forefront of implementing the "No Work, No Relief" policy. "We realize it is a hardship to take a 10 percent cut," he said, "but it is a government edict and no fault of council." The jobless, however, were determined, and struck on April 5, 1939, demanding no cuts and an abolition of relief labour. They defied a Police Chief order of "no picketing," taking their placards to the homes of Reeve Clutterbuck, who was constantly monitoring relief strikers' acts, and Councillor Dr. Jones. When, after almost a month of the relief strike, Councillor Wilson opposed the move to cut all relief recipients refusing to take up work orders, his counterparts on the township governing body argued that he should be removed from his civic post, disqualified as a member of Council. By May 1, 1939, there were signs of a weakening in the ranks of the Scarborough unemployed; police managed to intimidate the strikers into not conducting a public parade. On May 4, the Scarborough relief strikers threw in the towel in exchange for an agreement with Clutterbuck that they would only have to work for food relief, rather than for shelter and fuel as well as nourishment.[245]

At this time, a number of relief strikes fought over the course of April and early May 1939 wound down. Led by the York walkout, these battles unfolded throughout the Lakeshore district and involved Scarborough, New Toronto, Long Branch, Etobicoke, and Mimico. Often municipal Councils were opposed to implementing the Hepburn government's ordered relief reductions but did so under protest. Some civic officials, even if reluctant to cut relief, responded to strikes with vigorous enforcement of "No Work, No Relief," a policy slogan that increasingly took on the trappings of a messianic ideology. The relief strikes of the spring of 1939 were thus somewhat unified in their purpose: resistance to the cutback and the demand that the single unemployed not be dropped from all relief consideration. This general purpose evolved into calls for the abolition of relief labour in its entirety.

The only municipality to refuse to fall into line with the province's dictated reduction of relief was a stronghold of unemployed activism, East York. Despite the Liberal Ontario government's threat to claw back East York's relief grant, the Council there stood its ground. Appreciating how inadequate the relief levels first laid out in the 1932 Campbell Report were, in the context of 1939, East York Reeve

John Warren thought that as a guideline (which the government insisted it was), the outdated document was "hopelessly inadequate and should be thrown in the nearest wastebasket." There was, in fact, considerable turmoil because various municipalities were determining rates of relief based on the Campbell Report +, a wildly disparate set of percentage plusses ranging from a low of + 5 to a high of + 39. Dorothea Crittenden, subsequently the Deputy Minister of Community and Social Services (1974–78) in the Ontario government, and the first female deputy minister in Canada, was a statistician working in the Ontario civil service in 1937. She bemoaned the lack of consistency in the rates, claiming, "It was awful. It was Campbell + 5, Campbell + 10.... It was all over the place."[246]

East York thus continued, throughout the turmoil of relief strikes in 1939, to pay its relief recipients based on a formula determined by the Campbell report's 1932 scale + 35 percent, when the government wanted to peg the plus rate at a ceiling of 25 percent. Calling Hepburn's bluff, East York managed to ride out the storm without government retaliation, which angered other municipalities such as York. These constituencies believed that the province should be true to its word that it intended to create uniform relief rates across the province. This problem was only exacerbated when municipalities contending with strikes continued to provide relief to those who were refusing work because the province did indeed enforce the "No Work, No Relief" dictate. York, for instance, was read the metaphorical riot act by the province, which issued an ultimatum that it must cut relief to all strikers by 15 percent the first time the men refused labour orders, and the second time that they would not report for work they were to be cut off relief entirely. A divided York Township Council was caught between fear that relief strikers would respond to further reprisals with violence and resentment that "law and order" was at issue and the municipality had to decide if civic officials were the governing authority or the strikers were running the show.[247]

As for the York Township unemployed, they had long objected to being used as what they referred to as "scab labour" on municipal works projects. This was increasingly an issue in 1939 as the Council was forced to approve $12,000 in additional spending on permanent employees in the public works department, a result of a decision of the Ontario government that relief work should not be used for the collection of ash and garbage. As early as 1935, the York jobless affiliated with the Silverwood United Workers' Association had been ready to declare a strike in protest against "Cash relief workers ... being used as scabs against regular employees." They pointed out, as well, that such a practice made no allowance for an "increase that may be received as relief." This and other resentments fuelled an increasing agitation on the part of the relief labourers of Toronto's working-class districts in April of 1939.[248]

In Mimico, the hard-line of the municipality's Mayor Waites in adhering to the "No Work, No Relief" injunction prompted the unemployed to picket his home. Chased away from the mayor's residence by the police, the jobless returned the next day. They also threw up pickets around various public works projects. The Council, locked in session for six hours debating how to respond to the relief strike, determined to remove thirty-two families from the relief rolls, barring the heads of these households from ever returning to work. Waites blamed the proverbial agitator for the troubles in his jurisdiction: "These strikers are just agitators and trouble makers. We don't want them back, even if they decide to work." As the province ruled against Mimico's vindictive prohibition of strikers from future relief work, Waites and his council simply did an end run around the edict, stipulating that strikers could return to work "if and where they are needed." Which wasn't likely to be anywhere in Mimico Township very soon. Subsequent pleas on the part of victimized Mimico strikers fell on deaf council ears. Communist leader of the strike in Mimico, George Welch, protested, but to no avail: "The men have been viciously discriminated against because they exercised the age-old right of workers to fight for a higher standard of living. If you cut off all relief you won't weaken the struggles of the working class. Don't think that we will lie down."[249]

Welch spoke as the relief strikes of 1939 were defeated. In the last week of April, however, there was still some fight left in the movement. On April 24, 1939, seven hundred jobless gathered and marched on Queen's Park, demonstrating their discontent with Hepburn's relief cuts and the administration of support for the destitute. They converged at three different locations, the streams of protesters drawing on relief recipients from Mimico, New Toronto, Long Branch, Alderwood, Lakeview, East York, York, and Scarborough. The crowd, having no formal meeting with the premier or any members of his cabinet scheduled, chose a delegation of twenty, which tried to get into the legislature via a back door. Blocked by police, the relief workers nonetheless had some support among politicians, one of whom called on Hepburn or Minister of Welfare Cross to meet with the unemployed. Instead, an interview was arranged with A. E. Horton, provincial Director of Relief. The men and women who met with Horton pushed for the restoration of the 10 percent relief cut, the reinstatement of single unemployed men on the relief rolls, and a work-wages program for relief recipients. Eva O'Rourke, married to a disabled and jobless man, and the mother of seven children, had been on relief for five years. She made an impassioned plea to Horton. "The mothers are really desperate," she explained, "My children went all day yesterday with a cup of cocoa and a slice of bread each. I sent five of them to school this morning without food because I couldn't get my voucher until noon." Cross was unfeeling: relief, in his view, was adequate; the issue of mal-nutrition of children was being manufactured by agitators; children on relief were better off than those children who came from working families, and he pointed out that they received free medical care. Saving his spleen for known Communists, like unemployed leader George Harris, Cross simply refused to hear anything from men of this dissident stripe, alleging that the jobless were merely pawns in the hands of such unscrupulous agents. He got into a shouting match with York Township relief strike leader Tom Montague, who, in his anger, pulled some First World War medals from his pockets and told Horton he was not going to take "any lip" from a young fellow like him. At the end of four hours, Minister of Welfare Cross simply closed down the discussion, informing the delegation there would be no changes made to government policies: the cutbacks would stay.[250]

This provincial intransigence was soon translated to township councils. In York, as the relief strike dragged into its fourth week, tensions between the muni-cipality and the strikers grew. Reeve MacRae replaced the cash system with vouch-ers, penalizing the unemployed for having the audacity to take job action. MacRae had apparently boasted that the first time a man refused work he would be put on vouchers; thereafter work refusals would result in being cut off relief entirely. Council meetings were treated to women pleading for the well-being of their fam-ilies, claiming that if they must steal to keep food on the table, they would, and complaining that children could not be sent to school hungry. Strike leader George Marriott reported on May 1, 1939, "The leaders of the strike are anxious to avoid trouble. But it is hard to prevent hungry men. They would have seized the relief offices this morning but for cooler heads. On Wednesday 300 men will have been refused relief vouchers. Watch for trouble then."[251]

The trouble coming, however, proved to be in sustaining the strike. One hun-dred men tried a subterfuge, but this kind of tactic could be nothing more than stalling for a bit of time. They signed an agreement that, in return for being issued a $2 emergency food voucher, they would return to work. On receipt of the food ticket, which was good for two days, the men tore up their agreement and their work cards and vowed to continue the strike. Pickets were set up around the homes of York civic officials particularly vociferous in their opposition to the strike: Reeve MacRae, Deputy-Reeve Stuart, and Councillor Thorburn. This was a last stand. With the province unrelenting in pressuring townships like York to adhere to the "No Work, No Relief" policy, and with relief families inching slowly but surely toward starvation, a vote was taken on May 4, 1939, to end the York relief strike. Some fifteen hundred York unemployed decided to terminate their job action, although the decision was by no means unanimous: many wanted to continue the strike, and some argued that violence should be their last resort. "I'd hate to see men's heads smashed in when it would not mean a return of the relief cuts anyhow," Tom Montague told the strikers, "However, if you decided to stay out and heads are going to be smashed, I'll get mine broken in leading you." By 5 p.m. on May 4, the York relief strikers were back at their labours, food vouchers were being issued, and the last widespread relief mobilization of Toronto's Great Depression was over. The New Toronto relief strikers had returned to work on April 28; Etobicoke's strike petered out on, of all dates, May Day, as relief workers returned to their work at the same rate they had been receiving when they struck. Mimico's strike lasted slightly longer but resulted in the harshest measures of repression.[252]

Hepburn's "No Work, No Relief," rooted in age-old understandings of who was worthy of state aid and who was not, and how and when such allowance should be dispensed, prevailed at the end of Toronto's 1930s. On the one hand, this revealed striking continuities in the policies and practices of the state, which stigmatized the wageless and continued to mark them in public and humiliating ways. On the other, the resistance of the jobless to this state of affairs was a monumental shift in the nature of class relations as workers and their dissident, often Communist, leaders grappled with new ways of challenging capitalist understandings of what the poor should be doing during times of crisis. That Communists had shifted gears over the course of the 1930s, moving from the Third Period to the Popular Front, explains a part of what happened as the 1939 relief strikes unfolded in ways somewhat different than past protests. For Communist leadership of the unemployed was more cautious and less combative than it had been in 1934–35, or earlier in free speech campaigns.[253]

That said, the militancy that the Communists encouraged in the early to mid-1930s, in spite of often being built on an unsure foundation of sectarianism, was never really able to be exorcized from the popular memory of the class struggles of the dispossessed. That is precisely why the jobless harkened back to recollections of 1935 and other combative benchmarks in their 1939 relief strikes. There was a fundamental continuity, as well as an evolution, in the approach of the relief workers to their resentments of the administration of provisioning. Even as overt militancy and the style of physical confrontation characteristic of early years waned in 1938–39, the unemployed developed increasingly sophisticated positions in their analytic and political understandings. The 1939 relief strikes, the outcome of a long process of gestation in which struggles of the wageless developed over the course of the changing relief administrations of the 1930s, proved to be as much about the abolition of the relief labour system as they were about specific cutbacks on the part of the Hepburn government. The demand for waged work and programs that moved the relief recipients out of age-old variants of "cracking the stone" and into productive socioeconomic relations embedded in civil society had now been raised decisively. This central tenet of unemployed protest advanced in seven league boots in Toronto's 1930s, as workers marched, protested, occupied, and even took hostages to make their essential points. In the future this demand for work programs that integrated the jobless back into the economy of waged labour would figure forcefully in the ongoing resistance of the dispossessed.

Unemployed community garden sod-turning ceremony, harbour lands south of Fleet Street, with Welfare Commissioner A. W. Laver and other civic, welfare, and Queen's Park figures examining earth, November 1939.

York University Libraries, Clara Thomas Archives & Special Collections, *Toronto Telegram* fonds, ASC19076, *Evening Telegram* Staff.

PART IV

"A Hopeless Failure"

The Limitations and Erosion of the
Modern Welfare State, 1940–2015

oronto's 1930s had been tumultuous times. The Communist free speech and unemployed protests, the treks and tribulations of the single unemployed men and women, eviction blockades, strikes of the jobless on public works projects, and occupations of relief offices and hostage-takings of their officials and administrators constituted an unprecedented uprising of the dispossessed. These militant actions galvanized tens of thousands of poor people in Toronto and its blue-collar suburbs; they won more than their fair share of immediate, albeit small, victories. In calling attention to the abysmal conditions of those out of work and the inadequacies of the relief system, as well as demonstrating in combative ways that this would not be accepted without the costs of social upheaval, such protests paved the way for the post–Second World War consolidation of what many refer to as the modern welfare state. This process was neither smooth nor welcomed universally, however, and its making was highly contested. Moreover, the welfare state that did emerge was by no means an effective and comprehensive institutional response to either joblessness or poverty. Between 1945 and 1970 the ad hoc nature of relief provisioning, as it had been lived and challenged in the Great Depression, gave way to a more systematic and institutionalized socioeconomic order. To be sure, this state-orchestrated change regulated[1] and provided for the poor, although with respect to care and sustenance never in ways that were adequate. Resistance on the part of the dispossessed continued, of course, but the material conditions were such that social struggles comparable to those of the 1930s were less likely to erupt.

The Uneven Origins of an Incomplete Welfare State

In the twenty-five years following the Second World War, Canada put in place a combination of universal income security and contributory social programs that redefined both how joblessness and economic need would be lived and how they related to understandings of citizenship and its entitlements. Unemployment insurance, family allowances, old age pensions, and medicare were but some of the universal programs that combined with needs-based welfare provisioning to link national, provincial, and municipal states in a new socioeconomic order whose purpose was to leave behind the volunteerism of the House of Industry, replacing this nineteenth-century lack of system with a twentieth-century welfare order.[2] An apparatus of social safety nets had come to be recognized

James Harris, Robertson Street, Toronto, African-Canadian worker unemployed for six months before being hired by the city to clean up Sherwood Park, February 1958.

York University Libraries, Clara Thomas Archives and Special Collections, *Toronto Telegram* fonds, ASC19084, Proulx, *Toronto Telegram*.

as a pivotally important component of government, even if this protective meshing contained glaring holes. The angry occupations and protest placards of the 1930s had prodded and pulled a mindset that recognized the necessity of addressing unemployment, homelessness, nutritional standards and other issues related to poverty into mainstream politics. That the welfare provisioning created in the aftermath of the Great Depression provided an ostensible buffering layer of protection, supposedly freeing the poor and disadvantaged from falling too far into the abyss of destitution, was a central component of the liberal ideology and rhetoric of the era. One strength of Western capitalism was now proclaimed to be its unimpeachable record of providing ever-rising standards of living in a much-heralded age of affluence. Another claimed achievement was that those who could not climb the ladder of upward mobility in this social success story would be protected from the worst excesses of a free-fall into absolute want. That poverty existed within this plenty, however, and that the welfare state that was evolving continued to reproduce some of the rhetoric and practices of its nineteenth-century predecessors would nonetheless be evident in any serious scrutiny of the post–Second World War era. The constraining and controlling approach to the dispossessed as actual human subjects that was commonplace up to the 1930s thus continued.

Much changed, then, but much also seemed immune to meaningful transformation. What did shift decidedly in the postwar period of seeming affluence was the material investment in state-dispensed welfare. Canada's governments laid out increasing sums on health and social programs, approaching 24 percent of their total expenditure. By 1950 the cost had climbed to $1 billion dollars; twenty years later that figure was approaching $9 billion. In Ontario, the amount expended on broad social programs associated with education, health, social services, culture and recreation was over $10 billion by 1980, or nearly two-thirds of all provincial spending, and this did not take into account the federal government's funnelling of immense sums into social security areas in cities like Toronto. The province spent roughly $800,000 annually on narrowly defined, welfare-type social assistance during the 1920s, but the levels of expenditure on such programs soared to over $230 million by 1970; the percentage of the provincial population dependent on welfare in some form jumped during this same fifty-year period from less than .5 percent to over 5 percent. And in the twenty-five critical years of growth of the welfare state from 1945–70, social assistance spending in the Ontario government budget grew by three-and-a-half times. Again, especially since the passage of the 1958 General Welfare Assistance Act (GWA), federal contributions to this social security budget were not insignificant. Municipalities like Toronto saw their share of relief costs under the GWA halved, from 40 to 20 percent. The slack was taken up entirely by the availability of federal unemployment funding assistance.[3]

For all of this expansion, however, those working to administer the system were witness to its uneven and limited development. A 1977 report of the Social Planning Council of Metro Toronto acknowledged "a sizeable increase in Ontario's welfare budget since 1961." But this increase was not a consequence of welfare allowances getting larger. Rather, the expansion of the province's welfare order was a consequence of an expanding population of those in need, with a large increase in the number of single mothers with dependent children and those experiencing major health problems and disabilities. Larger and larger caseloads in these areas accounted for 98 percent of the expansion of the welfare order. And the growth that had taken place was both inadequate and administratively chaotic, the report concluding: "Examination has shown a continual shortfall opposite any measure of adequacy. We do not know how allowances are derived. Periodic increases have been haphazard and follow no discoverable logic. Allowances have grown, one may presume, inconsistently over the years in response to various social and political pressures."[4]

The rise of this limited welfare state nonetheless provided a good part of the oil that greased the wheels of Keynesianism, a conscious attempt, theoretically and practically, to address, within capitalism, Marx's insight and the Great Depression's undeniable lesson. Periodic crises were destined to disrupt an economic regime of accumulation ordered by the imperatives of profit. The British economist John Maynard Keynes responded directly to the crisis of joblessness in the 1930s. He argued that in conditions of economic collapse and high unemployment, the state should use its authority and resources to offset the fall in demand for goods and services that accompanied the dislocations of depressions and recessions.

Government spending in particular and fiscal policy in general, then, could be deployed to stabilize the cyclical fluctuations of an economy orchestrated by private, apparently market-dominated, interests. Seeming proof that Keynes's theory worked was the Second World War experience. The years 1939–45 demonstrated how capitalist economies could be brought out of debilitating depression through the production of armaments, mobilization and outfitting of troops, and massive expenditure on the infrastructure of war. In Canada, the armed forces absorbed the jobless like a sponge: the personnel of war expanded from 9,000 in 1939 to 107,000 in 1940 to 779,000 in 1944. Correspondingly, the number of Canadians "without jobs and seeking work" went from 529,000 in 1939 to 63,000 in 1944.[5]

What would happen, however, with the coming of peace? The answer was provided, for many, in the title of a 1941 pamphlet: *Can We Avoid a Post Armament Depression?* Keynesianism, or perhaps what Alvin Finkel has labelled crypto-Keynesianism, offered, especially for the growing government bureaucracy, a more palatable response.[6] If, metaphorically, a crisis of capitalism might be averted by spending on guns, might not such crisis be avoided with a cessation of hostilities by putting money into the production of butter? Given the continuity of wartime expenditure in the post–Second World War years of ostensible peace, through the massive funding directed to the military-industrial complex, the choice was never, in the Western capitalist economies of the 1945–70 period, a simple one of guns or butter. Both kinds of spending could and did easily take place. But the butter component of the Keynesian metaphor was, in good measure, the material foundation of both a postwar settlement with organized labour that institutionalized collective bargaining for the first time in Canada and a postwar settlement with the poor, which institutionalized, again for the first time, the Canadian welfare state. For Keynesianism rationalized higher, unionized wages for the employed working class, which would underpin rising consumption and stimulate demand for capitalist production, just as it validated increased spending on a wide array of social insurance initiatives, which would have the important consequence of maintaining spending, and averting domestic turmoil, even in the midst of recessionary downturns. This was done in a variety of ways.

A critically important component of this development was the universal programs that allowed the liberal state to bypass addressing frontally systemic inequality, funding and providing security for all Canadians rather than coming to grips with a class society in which need was pronounced among particular populations (the many) and absent in others (the few). The welfare state was thus a kind of "automatic stabilizer" that paid dividends, not so much as charity and as a liberal safety net for those at risk of spiralling irrevocably downward, but rather as a buffer zone insulating productive capitalism from its periodic crises and staving off the social unrest that inevitably accompanied economic downturns. Amid widespread fear that Canada would be precipitated into an inevitable postwar recession or depression, social security issues assumed unprecedented significance in the early to mid-1940s. Canada's leading social welfare authority, Harry M. Cassidy, reported that, in a summer 1942 trip across Canada, he was repeatedly told "workers and farmers look forward to something far better than the relief doles of the 1930s. Soldiers and sailors are saying that they will insist upon work or decent mainten-ance." Surveys conducted by the Canadian Institute of Public Opinion confirmed Cassidy's impression: "to the average Canadian man and woman the men in the fighting forces should be assured of one thing in the post-war world, and that is economic security." For Cassidy, governments of Western democracies like Canada were on notice that the old ways of addressing the poor and their relief were no longer acceptable:

> Unless they can provide for their citizens a large measure of social secur-
> ity they will face, at the least, resumption in more acute form of the social
> struggles of the 1930s, with the ever-present possibility that these conflicts
> will lead to violence. Mass unemployment, privation, and frustration are
> conditions that are not compatible with peaceful change and the solution of
> the domestic troubles of Canada and her allies by the democratic process.[7]

This recognition drove the reconstruction agenda.

Economist John Kenneth Galbraith has suggested that Canada was among the first of the advanced capitalist countries to embrace Keynesianism. Frank Scott, founder of the League for Social Reconstruction, observed in 1945 that, "a central government which could not provide three square meals a day to the hundreds of thousands on relief ... now pours its billions annually among the astonished cit-izens and calls forth miracles of production from old and new enterprises."[8] But the triumph of Keynesian thought and the realization of the Canadian welfare state took place haltingly and incompletely. Ontario as a province and Toronto as its cap-ital city would be cases in point. Developments were not without setbacks, and to the extent that achievements were registered, they were always something less than an unambiguous commitment to the poor. State policy always seemed balanced on a precarious fulcrum, in which the rhetoric of reform was necessarily tempered by the reality of adversarial interests. Among them were fundamental oppositions of classes and entrenched differences among power blocs, be they economic or polit-ical, one longstanding expression of which would prove to be tensions over social security separating the provinces and the federal government.[9] Nuances of inter-pretation such as these acknowledged, the 1940s in Ontario nevertheless saw wel-fare provisioning beginning to be institutionalized in ways that marked a departure from earlier, informal practices.

In a 1944 Speech from the Throne, the Mackenzie King–led federal Liberal government announced that its postwar domestic policy would be animated by "social security and human welfare." Ostensibly committed to establishing national minimums of social security in the areas of employment, housing, health, and nutrition, Mackenzie King promised to battle unemployment and protect Can-adians from the debilitating consequences of old age, accidents, and ill health. As the historian Jack Granatstein has argued, the pioneering social security legislation that followed the announcement of the Liberal government's priorities in 1944 was driven by "the fear of postwar unemployment, depression, and possible disorder." And to assuage those of the business community who remained ill at ease with this program of welfare accommodation, Mackenzie King offered "an attractive—and expensive—package" of assistance to captains of industry and employers of labour. As a way of softening capitalism's contradictions, Keynesianism was always a costly undertaking, and one devised to benefit capital at least as much as labour. It was, in the phrasing of the social-democratic publication *Canadian Forum,* "the price Liberalism [was] willing to pay to prevent socialism." In this sense the arrival of the welfare state, however limited, paid solid political dividends in that its attention to social security was easily and conveniently turned to ideological purpose, promot-ing the view that a genuine concern for the welfare of *all* citizens was democracy's trump card, played to good effect against the emerging Cold War enemy of Com-munism. Under the heading "Social Security a Democratic Objective," Cassidy was quick to remind those grappling with how to chart welfare reform that, "It was the upward thrust of the poverty-stricken workers and peasants of Russia that led to the Communist revolution of 1917 and the rise of the international Communist party to carry the torch of the class struggle throughout the world." In Leonard Marsh's social-democratic *Report on Social Security for Canada* (1943), the case was made that a postwar reconstruction would consolidate productive efficiency, wealth, and political strength, all decisive weapons in the war against Communism: "Social security payments are not money lost. They are investments in morale and health, in greater family stability, and from both material and psychological viewpoints, in human productive efficiency.... It has yet to be proved that any democracy which underwrites the social minimum for its citizens is any weaker or less wealthy for doing so."[10]

· That the welfare state could begin to be constructed in the 1940s was, of course, not just an ideological project. The initiative also rested on the firm foundation of material possibility. As James Struthers has pointed out, "the financial implications of placing the diets of 10,000 Torontonians on a nutritionally adequate basis in 1944 bore no relation to the cost of doing the same thing for 120,000 relief recipients in the 1930s." One 1942 estimate of the cost of meeting an adequate dietary standard for Toronto's relief recipients put the expenditure, which required increases in a range of areas from 20 to 70 percent, at just less than $200,000. Three years earlier, with the relief rolls swelled by a factor of almost seven, the cost would have been over $1,350,000. Toronto's Welfare Department staff of 311 serviced a monthly caseload of 77,000 at Depression's end, but by the late 1940s its pared down workforce of 200 dealt with relief roll numbers of 6,300. Social security could be addressed meaningfully *only* when capitalist crisis abated: government allowances for the poor, after 1941, were necessarily concerned with an extreme end of a spectrum of joblessness that had extended much more widely a few years before; able-bodied men, in the 1940s, were off the relief rolls and engaged in the war effort, either at the fighting front in Europe or the productive front in Canada. Youth and single women were not dependent on the dole, public works, relief camps, or families; in the "full employment" economy of wartime, they earned wages and more than paid their way. Two labour historians described the new situation:

> Resource and mass-production industries geared up for war production and hired anyone with a body temperature of 98.6 degrees. By 1941, full employment made it possible for the federal government to introduce unemployment insurance, contributions to which provided a nice nest egg for the costs of war. One year later the "manpower" shortage was so severe that major companies scoured the country for female recruits and the government set up child-care facilities and introduced special tax concessions for working women. By 1943, the labour market was so tight that government denied workers and employers in essential industries the right to quit or fire at will.[11]

In this context, those addressed by the consolidating welfare state would be the old, the disabled, and women and children lacking the presence of a so-called "breadwinner." The national unemployment rate, which stood at 9.2 percent in 1940, had been halved by 1941, and by 1944, with the Mackenzie King Liberals expected to begin to deliver on their social security promises, it stood at a meagre 1.4 percent. For the remainder of the 1940s, it would average less than 2 percent. Ontario, Canada's industrial-capitalist heartland, fared well. Over the course of the relatively prosperous years from 1946 to 1974 the average annual provincial rate was only 3.3 percent, leading one economic historian to conclude that "the spectre of mass unemployment was absent during the entire period."[12]

This kind of comment no doubt exaggerated well-being, but it addressed the extent to which the relative prosperity of this postwar period made possible new understandings and material advances in the area of social assistance. At the foundation of welfare provisioning's renewal and reinvigoration in Ontario was a final accounting of some old scores, registered in a decade and more of debate and public protest involving the infamous 1932 Campbell Report. This document, as we saw in our previous discussion of the 1930s, had set "standards" of relief so low that militant demonstrations on the part of the poor were ongoing, forced time and time again to go over the same ground established in the early years of the Great Depression by a quickly produced, ill-conceived, and poorly informed document. A Toronto committee composed of Dr. F. F. Tisdale, Dr. Alice Willard, and Miss Marjorie Bell confirmed in 1941 that the "present relief allowance is not sufficient to permit families to secure food adequate for health," suggesting that a minimum of $10 weekly was needed.

Finally, in 1943, a new report, conducted by nutritionist Dr. E. W. McHenry, determined that the benchmark + established by the Campbell Report (in the early 1940s that + was now 60 percent, factoring in inflation and other issues) for dietary sufficiency to sustain a "typical" family of five was inadequate. Against the provincial ceiling of $8.00 weekly mandated in 1943 by the Campbell Report + 60 percent, McHenry's study acknowledged that the recommended maximum in Toronto would have to be over $11.00. This hefty increase still put the official ceiling of relief support below that advocated by the labour movement and Toronto Welfare Council–sponsored and endorsed studies, such as the 1939 publication *The Cost of Living*, which looked at nutrition in the city's low-income families. That report concluded that more than $13.30 would be required to adequately feed a family of five. McHenry, a director of the University of Toronto's School of Hygiene, was critical of *The Cost of Living* conclusions, however, because he claimed mothers could be better trained to buy and prepare food more efficiently, both in terms of cost and nutritional value. Refusing to trust in the capacities of poor women to feed their families "scientifically," McHenry proposed that "restaurants at which nutritious meals could be economically provided" would be preferable to cash relief. Short of forcing the poor to eat at state institutions, McHenry wanted relief payments for food to be accompanied by specially prepared pedagogical cookbooks and ongoing education in the culinary science of food purchase and preparation.

The University of Toronto nutritionist's orientation endeared him to a state apparatus always willing to blame the victim. McHenry was brought on board by Mitchell Hepburn's Liberal provincial government to challenge a broad coalition of welfare activists, led by women social workers radicalized by the Depression experience. This united front of the Toronto Welfare Council, Women Electors, Local Council of Women, Co-operative Commonwealth Federation (CCF), Communist Party (CP, and renamed the Labor Progressive Party, or LPP, in response to a *de facto* wartime outlawing of Communism), Toronto Trades and Labour Council (TTLC), and Mayor Fred Conboy had pushed decisively in 1941–42 to up the rates, successfully pressuring Toronto City Council to agree to a 20 percent cost-of-living allowance increase for relief recipients.[13]

Premier Hepburn was not pleased. The Ontario government refused to shell out any additional funds for Toronto's relief bill, leaving civic officials to shoulder the $108,000 increase. Minister of Welfare Farquhar Oliver was of the opinion that Toronto, with 17.5 percent of the provincial population but 43.5 percent of the relief expenditure, was "definitely out of line with the other municipalities in Ontario," suggesting that the metropolitan centre had "too many straw bosses ... clamouring for publicity." If McHenry's report had indeed raised the rates, it did so in ways that were acceptable to the state precisely because the elevation of a mythical average registered advantageously in terms of its practical application in the changed conditions of the 1940s. The "typical" family of five as a domestic unit of relief administration was no longer anything approximating a norm under the conditions of so-called "full employment." McHenry's maximum weekly food allowance of $11.00 would be paid out rarely. Upward of six in ten relief recipients in Ontario in 1943 were single unemployable women living alone, often old and infirm, and ineligible for any program of support other than direct relief. The McHenry report actually *lowered* the recommended ceiling of food relief for such women, dropping their weekly payment from $2.40 to $2.22. Amid the ideological hoopla of what newspapers referred to as an ending of the "underfeeding of relief recipients," McHenry's report, even as it seemingly hoisted allowances upward, did so unevenly, as some recipients lost out in the supposed increase. On balance, McHenry's revised schedule almost certainly held the line on the costs of relief provisioning, providing guidelines for maximum compensation that were shared by the province and municipalities such as Toronto. These latter local jurisdictions, moreover, were more than adept at defining need stringently and keeping the narrow construction of food relief uppermost in their considerations of who did and who did not comprise the deserving poor. In this sense, also, McHenry's schedule allowed liberal concern with feeding the poor adequately to displace other considerations of housing, clothing, and jobs, all of which moved to the sidelines of consideration.[14]

The same could be said for the Mothers' Allowance Commission, which between 1939 and 1943 reduced its provincial caseload of support from twelve thousand to eight thousand, shaving a million dollars off its costs, doubling the number of investigators who monitored relief recipients, and upping the vigilant visits of such families to four a year. For women who were the state's designated relief recipient grouping, employable men supposedly being removed from the relief rolls

Unemployed picket Unemployment Insurance Commission, National Employment Office Building, Toronto, March 13, 1961.

York University Libraries, Clara Thomas Archives and Special Collections, *Toronto Telegram* fonds, ASC19093 Pete Ward, *Toronto Telegram*.

by their coverage under the Unemployment Insurance Act of 1940, need was never divorced from behaviour. Drinking liquor, evidence of lax attitudes toward personal hygiene or housekeeping, indulgences in entertainments, friendships and visitors of the questionable sort, and sexual activity might all be cited to curtail allowances or remove women entirely from relief support. Even after a Conservative government headed by George Drew increased Mothers' Allowance payments by 20 percent, the maximum monthly benefit for a woman with three children was only $54, whereas various agencies estimated that the minimum such a domestic unit would need in Toronto was between $86.60 and $117.57. The squeeze on relief recipients only tightened as wartime double-digit inflation hovered around the 15 percent mark.[15] As the welfare state consolidated unevenly, the possibilities for the poor, ironically, often seemed to constrict.

One part of this tightening was the postwar fading of commitment among Ontario's governing conservative elite to the provisions of social security, especially its non-contributory dimensions. With war's end, the Great Depression's social dislocations pushed to the background of recollection, and the province's welfare caseload dwindling to perhaps 5 percent of the figures from the mid-1930s, the push to address social security needs orchestrated by Cassidy and other welfare/policy experts began to be deflected in the upper echelons of the provincial state. Burne Wismer Heise, Deputy Minister of Ontario's Department of Welfare, University of Toronto-educated and a former Children's Aid Society administrator, spoke for the social work reform constituency inside the Queen's Park bureaucracy, advocating for the creation of a coherent social assistance system. He was charged with developing a Welfare Units Act, but as he completed this task and the legislation was being prepared in 1948, Heise found himself outflanked by powerful figures like the provincial treasurer and future premier, Leslie Frost. Frost and Welfare Minister William Goodfellow had no liking for an expansive welfare state, which they felt eroded the independence and self-reliance they equated with small-town, rural Ontario values. Goodfellow steered the Welfare Units Act through the legislature, but along the way the bill was gutted and the growing disconnect between the needs of welfare administration as envisioned by Heise and Goodfellow led to the former's resignation. He was replaced by James "Jimmy" Band, an accountant whose climb up the social policy ladder had commenced in the 1930s as a relief inspector dedicated to the strict supervision and rationalization of allowance distribution. With Band at the helm, and there for the long haul (he would rule the Welfare Department for almost twenty years), progressive reconstruction of Ontario's social security system stalled and sputtered and the hopes of radical reconstruction nurtured by social work professionals in the early 1940s came, in the words of historian James Struthers, to "a bitter and pathetic end."[16]

This history of institutional and policy frustration was mirrored in Toronto. The fundraising functions of organized private philanthropy in the city had been the purview of the Community Chest, dominated by businessmen. Toronto's Community Chest merged with the Toronto Welfare Council in 1943, seemingly liquidating the private charity wing of welfare provisioning into a public planning body. But the consequence of this merger was the Council's increasing subordination to the views of its financial wing, which sought to keep the body restricted in what it could advocate. A decisive and destructive role was played by Edgar Burton, the president of Simpsons and chairman of Toronto's Community Chest. Burton was angered when, during a strike at his firm, he found disgruntled workers distributing information from *The Cost of Living* on a picket line. Outraged that his workers could compare their wages to the social minimums outlined in a Welfare Council–funded study, Burton embarked on a late 1940s campaign to suppress the popular primer, known in labour movement circles as "the Redbook" because of its bright, crimson covers. In the end, the Toronto Welfare Council declined to reprint *The Cost of Living*, much to the chagrin of the trade unions, which had found the Redbook a compilation of useful data. Instead, the Council sponsored the publication of a consciously more neutral statement. Ten years after its original appearance, *The Cost of Living* was replaced by *A Guide to Family Spending in Toronto* (1949), a sometimes sanctimonious and always restrained report that followed the McHenry-like assessment that "incompetency on the part of the homemaker was the problem to be addressed," rather than "any income policy of the wider community." Trade unions found little to like in the new Welfare Council publication, but Personnel Departments of industrial firms were devotees of its functionalist message.[17]

Things were little better on the housing front. A number of the 1930s hostels, lodgings for the single unemployed, had been closed down in the early 1940s, among them the notorious Wellington House. The House of Industry was turned into an old age home. St. Lawrence Hall, opened during the Great Depression to shelter ex-servicemen, was again re-opened as a homeless shelter in the late 1940s, run by Father Hunnisset, whose declared mission of "Soup, Soap, and Salvation," earned him the sobriquet "ring-master," a denigration of his insistence on making the homeless sit through an evangelical circus in order to get food and lodging. Canada as a whole was gripped by an acute housing shortage during the war years that continued to worsen into a national housing crisis in 1946–48. Veterans' groups, trade unions, and other constituencies, including businessmen in a variety of sectors, pressured the state to provide low-income housing and expand the horizons of housing policy and development. Conditions in Toronto were so bad that Mayor Robert Hood Saunders took out paid advertisements in newspapers across the country. Headed "WARNING," these August 29, 1947, declarations advised anyone thinking of coming to Toronto to stay away. Saunders gave notice to "non-residents of this city, that there is no housing accommodation here. This corporation will assume no responsibility or provide no assistance in locating quarters for any person contemplating moving to Toronto." Outside of the long-established Fred Victor Mission, where conditions were little better than they had been on the eve of the First World War, scores of men lined up at 6:30 p.m. to sleep on the floor and share two taps for drinking water and four often overused toilets. Small wonder that a Toronto coalition of academics, social democrats, social workers, Communists, and small business interests established the Citizen's Housing and Planning Association (CHPA) to lobby for public housing. Slum clearance of "The Ward"—first advocated strenuously in 1934—resulted, followed by the creation of public housing in the nearby Regent Park, which accepted its first tenants in 1949 and by the 1960s was residence to ten thousand people.[18]

Housing availability, which might take more than a decade to come to fruition, was one thing, soaring costs another. At the end of the war, welfare recipients were limited to allowances of $27.00 monthly for rent, a figure that, by 1946, was widely recognized as inadequate. With double-digit inflation sometimes increasing the cost of living by as much as 25 percent in a single twelve-month period, housing costs absorbed larger and larger amounts of the total allowances families received. Since food was one of the few necessities within the bundle of goods comprising the welfare package that managed to be apportioned with inflation taken into consideration, skyrocketing rents were often supplemented by resources meant to be directed to nutrition, with the obvious debilitating consequences. In 1957, Toronto's Assistant Welfare Commissioner, Robena Morris, admitted that training relief mothers to plan meals economically and cook food efficiently would not be easy when "a portion of the food allowance was used to pay rent or other necessary expenses." But as a good welfare bureaucrat, she remained adamant that no one need go hungry "if welfare money was spent wisely."

Prudent budgeting, however, wasn't really providing answers to many of the Toronto dispossessed. Well into the 1960s the poorest of Toronto's relief dependents found themselves unable to make ends meet in the perennial rent-food squeeze, going hungry to keep themselves off the streets. Lillian Thomson, head of Toronto's largest social work agency, noted in 1961 that among destitute families, "Money for food, fuel, and clothing [is] being diverted to keep a roof of sorts over the family's head. The wolf is at the door all right, but he's looking for the rent." A fifty-three-year-old widow, living alone in a cold, top-floor, Parkdale rooming house, spent $40 of her $57 monthly allowance on rent, leaving her 45 cents a day for food. She lived on bread, porridge, and soup, and was "hungry a lot of the time." By the close of the 1940s, two-thirds of Toronto's relief tenants were dependent on the maximum provincial rental allowance as well as a City subsidy, this supplementary municipal aid totalling almost $175,000 annually. Unable to make both the food and rent ends of their budgets meet, families dependent on social assistance either cut their caloric intake, moved into squalid slum housing, or both. Over the course of the 1950s and early 1960s, the situation deteriorated further, with Toronto's welfare administration actively seeking to limit its contribution to rental support to no more than $50 monthly for a family of five, even though the market rental rate for a one-bedroom apartment was $100.

At the end of the 1950s, a Social Planning Council of Toronto study of welfare caseloads revealed that more than 2500 families needed private charitable subsidies for basic budgetary items—clothing, food, shelter—from agencies such as the United Appeal. For every dollar of public welfare assistance, another forty-one cents of private aid was required. Housing costs, for the vast majority of families on this combined public-private relief, constituted one-half of domestic expenditure. It was commonplace, in the early 1960s, for families to subsidize inadequate rent allowances with their food relief cheques, staving off eviction, but forcing them, eventually, to turn to churches and the Red Cross for meals. Children of families reliant on welfare could often be found outside of the Scott Mission, lining up at lunchtime to get a sandwich. If landlords were gouging these poor tenants, Toronto's welfare administration was squeezing what it could out of the poor at the other end. With shelter costs rising 42 percent over the course of the 1950s, and with a major expansion in welfare caseloads, Toronto managed nonetheless to spend 40 percent less on rent supplements than it had in 1949.[19]

If there was a legislative poster boy for the emerging 1940s welfare state, it was the federal Unemployment Insurance Act (UIA), a bill passed into law in August 1940, a direct consequence of the struggles and demands of the jobless of the 1930s. Under the Act, unemployment insurance benefits were to be paid to workers who found themselves out of work, were unable to find suitable employment, and were ready and able to take up a new job. To qualify for payments, a worker must have made contributions to the program for at least 180 days during the two years immediately preceding his or her claim. Benefits were calculated according to the contribution made, which was determined by the level of earnings. Originally stipulated to be 34 times the average weekly contribution of claimants without dependents, and 40 times the contribution of those with families to support, the benefit schedule was adjusted throughout the 1950s and 1960s so that the rate was roughly 50 percent of earnings for those with dependents and 37 percent for those without. Many occupations were at first excluded, from domestic service to teaching, most logging and lumbering employments, and civil servants; employees with annual salaries of $2,000 or more were also barred from drawing UIA benefits.

Over time, exclusions of specific occupations lessened, and Canadians covered by the UIA grew from 42 to over 50 percent of the labour force. Both employers and workers paid into the fund, as did the federal government, and over the course of the so-called "full employment" 1940s the UIA kitty grew enormously. The contributing, insured population was between 2 million and just under 2.6 million. But annual claims on the fund were modest, especially in the war years of 1942–44, when the benefits paid were between $353,000 and $3,277,000. Even at the end of the decade, in 1949, the year's payout in benefits was $65,351,000. While no doubt a hefty sum, this was less than the Insurance Fund's initial income, in 1941, of $68.2 million, made up of contributions from employers and workers of $23.4 million each, with an additional $9.7 million from Ottawa. Over the course of the years 1940–57, the state overestimated levels of unemployment and the subsequent benefit payouts, with the result that the Unemployment Insurance Fund had reserves of $871 million. Administered by an Unemployment Insurance Commission, operating out of sixteen hundred federal offices opened across the country in the early 1940s, staffed by three thousand civil servants, the costs of running the unemployment insurance program in the early years of the Second World War exceeded $5 million annually. Unemployment had become a state industry.[20]

Nonetheless, the limitations of this industrialization were profound. Most telling, for the dispossessed, was that unemployment insurance was only a recourse for those who had employment that was covered by the 1940 Act. As Struthers notes,

> the 1940 plan was, in fact, a cautious piece of legislation that initially covered slightly more than 40 percent of Canada's total civilian labour force and provided an inadequate benefit ceiling of $62.40 a month for a maximum of thirty-six weeks. It was at best a scheme designed to tide wage-earners over temporary and short term spells of joblessness, not a prolonged or deep depression.

In practice, the late 1940s and 1950s would see Ottawa and the provinces wrestle over precisely the definition of who was and who was not "unemployed," with Ontario and its counterparts straining to restrict their relief role to the wageless who were demonstrably unemployable through disease and disability, old age, or gendered responsibilities. The able-bodied jobless, regardless of their eligibility under the UIA, were judged the responsibility of the federal government, which, not surprisingly, refused to see the problem in the same way.

This impasse, reproducing older federal-provincial-municipal arm-twisting of the 1930s, might be negotiated as long as unemployment was kept in check. But as soon as the official jobless rate crept upward, to 4–6 percent, as it inevitably did, the pinch on the poor was felt most acutely at the local, municipal level. Since women and children would often qualify for assistance only if there was no "employable" man on the scene, the rules of welfare contributed to familial breakdown. Social workers employed by the City of Toronto were traumatized in the winter of 1952 as jobless men unable to secure unemployment benefits appealed to them. The welfare staff found it emotionally stressful to have to "refuse assistance to people who appear destitute.... Fathers ... have left the home in order to place

Unemployed protest, "Dogs Have Homes but Not the Unemployed," Toronto, February 1954.

York University Libraries, Clara Thomas Archives and Special Collections, *Toronto Telegram* fonds, ASC19082, Whyte, *Toronto Telegram*.

their families in an advantageous position of securing financial help." In Toronto, the Welfare Department, the Neighbourhood Workers' Association (the city's largest private welfare agency), the Red Cross, the Scott Mission, the Department of Veterans' Affairs, and the Salvation Army all found themselves besieged by the desperately poor. They had little to offer. Out of a total Toronto welfare budget of $1.6 million in 1955, the city spent barely $26,000 on aid to those it designated "employable." Casual labourers, many of them newly arrived immigrants, who needed a helping hand to weather a particularly bad patch in lives of intolerable insecurity, became embittered when they confronted layers of bureaucracy that could do nothing for them. One Neighbourhood Workers' Association report noted that such newly arrived Canadians could not fathom how, in the midst of affluence and an established welfare state, "they should not have either work or assistance.... [Their] greatest burden is a frantic fear of deportation." For the dispossessed, the welfare state must often have seemed a distant and detached body.[21]

In the Shadow of the Great Depression, War, and the Emerging Welfare State: Episodic Struggle in the 1940s, 1950s, and early 1960s

The 1940s consolidated much, but an adequate and compassionate system of provisioning for the poor was certainly not put in place. To the extent that a welfare state emerged in the 1940s, it was limited and constructed on a foundation of conventional and constraining wisdoms.[22] Nonetheless, the combination of relative affluence, so-called full employment, declining numbers of relief recipients, and halting but often dramatic state initiatives in the provisioning of social security, cultivated a sense of well-being, even if this was not generalized throughout the entire social order. The emerging Cold War consensus tilted the ideological winds of the 1940s against the kinds of protest mobilizations that had been commonplace in the 1930s. With the growing and often quite rabid climate of anti-communism, the prospects of Reds leading such demonstrations and organized resistance lessened considerably as the postwar era gave way to the 1950s. In any case, the ranks of the dispossessed thinned noticeably from the troubled times and crisis of joblessness of the Great Depression. Toronto's officially recognized indigent population in 1942 was a not insignificant 10,000, but it would further fall to below 6,500 by decade's end. Such figures constituted an overwhelming, absolute decline when compared to those on the relief rolls ten to fifteen years earlier. The 1940s were not the 1930s.

Many were no doubt pleased with this new state of affairs. This has caused most historians and social commentators to view the 1940s, especially the latter half of the decade, as a period of complacency. One historian has suggested that "most Ontarians were in no mood … to create a socialist heaven on earth, especially one directed by bureaucrats. They wished only to drive their new cars down one of Ontario's many new expressways or mow their suburban lawns." Donald MacDonald, the leader of Ontario's Co-operative Commonwealth forces, claimed that "Everybody just wanted to relax."[23] But for those without new cars and suburban lawns relaxation, perhaps, was not easily attainable.

Certainly, organized labour was not relaxed. Some might characterize it as frenzied in the late 1940s. Canadian trade union history was made in the years 1945 to 1948. A labour revolt, building on advances registered in a Second World War protected mobilization, rocked industrial relations. This won workers major gains that translated into the long-fought-for right to bargain collective agreements with bosses who had to negotiate with labour organizations they had struggled to keep out of their workplaces for generations.[24]

There was no comparable uprising of the dispossessed, but war veterans were a determined and feisty lot. When they found themselves without jobs and, especially, without homes in the 1946–47 housing crisis, they organized Homeless Veterans' Leagues and occupied abandoned buildings. A union activist, Communist, and LPP organizer, Henri Gagnon, led a Montreal Squatters' Movement composed mainly of ex-servicemen and their families. They occupied abandoned homes that had previously been used as gambling dens or camped out in military barracks. Gagnon was able to call on Canadian Seamen's Union members to protect the squatters from vindictive gaming bosses who wanted to recapture their lucrative dens; the public tended to sympathize with the homeless veterans, the press christening the occupations a "Robin Hood" initiative. On the west coast, veterans took aim at loftier, if derelict, digs. The stately Hotel Vancouver, home to the wartime Department of National Defence, was unused after the federal government's lease on the building expired. The Citizens' Rehabilitation Council of Greater Vancouver (CRCGV), trade unions, the CCF, and the LPP demanded the hotel be used as a temporary shelter to alleviate the crisis of homelessness. Frustrated with what appeared to be an endless cycle of negotiations and discussions, the LPP threw a picket around the old building on New Year's Day 1946. Communist veteran Bob McEwen led a contingent of the Canadian Legion's New Veterans into the hotel lobby and within a week fourteen hundred people "registered" to take up accommodations at the Georgia-Granville address. With public opinion very much on the ex-servicemen's side, the state backed away from a confrontation. The returned soldiers were even saluted by a Liberal Member of Parliament, who thought that after seizing many towns in Europe in the name of freedom, the Canadian vets could liberate a hotel at home. The occupation soon turned into an agreement to secure funds to refurbish the Hotel Vancouver so that the CRCGV could operate it as a temporary hostel, which it did for two years. But the militant origins of this public housing venture were never entirely eclipsed. When the CRCGV tried to raise the rates, some of the tenants organized a rent strike.[25]

Toronto's veteran protests around the 1946–48 housing crisis probably lacked the "newsworthy" panache of Montreal's and Vancouver's squatter wars, pitted as they were against gamblers' dens and once-posh hotels. But as rents soared and controls on them were lifted, ex-servicemen took a page out of the book of 1930s protests and established picket lines to block the eviction of soldiers' widows. In the Toronto working-class suburb of Mimico, the site of so many activist initiatives on the part of the unemployed in the 1930s, veteran Sam Colberry led homeless families in the occupation of the municipality's city hall. As police rallied to disperse the protest sit-in, Colberry rounded up a contingent of lacrosse fans attending a local match and convinced them to set up barricades of resistance. Soldiers, Colberry insisted, were not about to be bullied by anyone, including baton-wielding cops.[26]

One measure of the late 1940s Toronto housing crisis was the showing of Ross Dowson in the January 1, 1949, municipal election. Running for the city's top post and campaigning openly on behalf of the Trotskyist Revolutionary Workers Party (RWP), Dowson's platform took discussion of Toronto's housing crisis in truly radical directions. The RWP candidate lost no chance to pillory the mainstream Liberal and Conservative politicians for their "criminal failure to do anything about the housing shortage," lambasting "the vicious rent gouging of … workers forced to live in … ramshackle emergency housing projects." Calling for an end to all construction of theatres, banks, and cocktail bars, Dowson promised to restrict Toronto development to "essential buildings," using city hall's control of permits to ensure that developers channelled their activities in socially useful directions. He stood for "the improvement and extension of emergency housing; no evictions; for rent control of emergency housing under the supervision of … tenant's committees." As mayor of one of Canada's leading cities, Dowson promised to pressure the Dominion government to divert resources now earmarked for war and destruction into "low rent government housing projects, hospitals, schools, and nurseries." Positions such as these earned Dowson the vitriol of Toronto's business interests, both the *Financial Post* and the *Globe and Mail* bending their editorial pens in anticommunist diatribe. But the revolutionary approach to housing helped secure Dowson 23,777 votes, almost 20 percent of the total mayoral tally.[27]

Dowson's strong and decidedly left-wing advocacy of the dispossessed in the 1949 Toronto election notwithstanding, revolutionaries kept their heads relatively low over the course of the late 1940s and 1950s, the Cold War being a rather chilly climate for dissent. This had an undeniable impact on mobilizations of the poor and the unemployed, whose militant activism in the 1930s often advanced under the leadership of Communists, CCFers, and others on the left. Protests of the jobless in subsequent years have received little attention, and our knowledge of poor people's mobilizations in the immediate postwar period is limited. An exception is an unpublished study of British Columbia by David Thompson, who details how Communist veterans of 1930s struggles like Fred Collins pioneered postwar protests by organizing a Vancouver Unemployed Action Committee and an East End Tenants' Defence Committee in 1949–50. These mobilizations prompted demands for cash relief and curbs on rent hikes. They were followed by the emergence of the Lower Mainland Unemployed Committee, renamed the British Columbia Federation of Unemployed, agitations that grew out of a 1958–62 economic downturn.[28] No doubt organized protest, like the welfare state itself, was uneven, and its episodic nature in these years has led some to believe that grassroots anti-poverty organizing did not exist before the 1960s except in the highly troubled 1930s.[29] But as a London costermonger told Henry Mayhew in the mid-nineteenth century, "People fancy that when all's quiet, all's stagnating. Propagandism is going on for all that. It's when all's quiet that the seed's a growing."[30]

Unemployment protests and, indeed, organized mobilizations of the jobless surfaced in the 1950s and early 1960s. These initiatives happened at *precisely* the point that official statistics indicated a bump in the numbers of the out-of-work to 4–7 percent of the labour force. This occurred twice over the course of the period reaching from the early 1950s into the early 1960s. First, when a Korean War–induced inflationary cycle truncated with the end of the conflict in 1953, culminating in a mild recession that saw the jobless rate double from 2–4 percent. The mid-1950s saw an easing off of this joblessness, and when the federal government passed an Unemployment Assistance Act in 1956, Ontario led a group of four provinces that chose to remain outside the legislative agreement, which brokered ways the national and provincial governments might act together to alleviate the costs of aiding the jobless. With the provincial jobless rate at a modest 2.3 percent, and hovering below the national average, Ontario's premier, Leslie Frost, thought he could stay an abstentionist course and extract a better cost-sharing formula with Ottawa. If things took a turn in the wrong direction, Ontario could obviously opt in to the agreement. A recessionary downturn in 1957–58 did indeed worsen the employment situation, and the percentage of males without jobs seeking work climbed to almost 12 percent. The economy tanked in 1958–62, prodding Ontario to align itself with Ottawa's loosely-worded Unemployment Assistance Act. But the main consequence of this legislation seemed to be to divert possible unemployed benefits to so-called unemployables. A Prime Minister's Conference on Unemployment was convened in October 1960, in which industry spokesmen voiced concerns about unemployment's potential to disrupt domestic tranquility and its capacity to undermine faith in the superiority of the Western, capitalist democratic way of life. Rising rates of joblessness, said R. M Fowler, president of the Canadian Pulp and Paper Association, provided "comfort for our enemies and a poor appeal to the uncommitted nations."[31]

Union of Unemployed Workers, Toronto, January 1954.

York University Libraries, Clara Thomas Archives and Special Collections, *Toronto Telegram* fonds, ASC19080, Madison Sale, *Toronto Telegram*.

By the winter of 1960–61, the numbers of the out-of-work were rising. The official unemployment rate topped 7 percent. A massive surplus in Ottawa's Unemployment Insurance Fund "shrank away to nothing" as annual benefit payments rose from $210 million in 1956 to almost $500 million in 1962. Reserves in the fund, which peaked at hundreds of millions of dollars in the mid-1950s, dropped dangerously between 1959 and 1963, crashing below the symbolic $1 million barrier. In this context an ill-advised movement to reinstitute 1930s-like "work for relief" programs, popped up, justified by political figures across the country who resorted to age-old characterizations of the undeserving poor. With provincial premiers like Quebec's Jean Lesage, Manitoba's Duff Roblin, and British Columbia's W. A. C. Bennett worrying aloud about "professional relief recipients" and "a class of people whose only occupation was receiving unemployment assistance," the idea of restoring the "work test" gained ground in a number of small Ontario municipalities and within the Ontario Welfare Officers Association. But in the changed context of the postwar settlement, implementing "work for relief" programs had little traction.

Stopping the movement in its tracks was the now powerful labour movement. Welfare Minister Louis Cecile warned Ontario's Conservative Premier, John Robarts, that "vocal groups, particularly labour unions [were] vigorously opposed" to any revival of "work tests." Emerging public sector unions, not yet the centre of power they would become in later decades, nevertheless took strong stands against a program that would "create unemployment for regular municipal employees." In Ottawa, the federal bureaucracy was no more inclined to endorse "work for welfare" panaceas. For a variety of complicated reasons, including mistrust of the provinces and local municipal relief administrations, the governing Diefenbaker Conservatives had no stomach for the proposed "punitive approach to relief recipients," which smacked of "old Poor Law concepts." Those among the general population who could recall the humiliation of relief practices in the 1930s wanted nothing of any "labour tests." The *Toronto Star* summed up the consensus consolidating in opposition to the late 1950s/early 1960s "work for relief" initiative: "Our wealthy society has the obligation to provide [the unemployed] with work at a living wage. Failing this, it has the obligation to support them and their families decently— not in exchange for forced labor, not as a matter of charity, but simply as a matter of right."[32]

And yet precisely this kind of support was *not* forthcoming from the incompletely consolidated Canadian welfare state. In Toronto, these 1950s and early 1960s employment crises gave rise to almost mushroom-like mobilizations of the out-of-work. A Union of Unemployed Workers led by A. L. Davis surfaced in the 1952–54 years. It combined demands for work with chauvinistic appeals to "Stop Immigration," scapegoating newly-arrived immigrants as the cause of joblessness among established, native-born Canadians, some of whom were "suffering hunger because of unemployment." But it also played a role in an On-to-Ottawa motorcade calling for cash relief for those unemployed not covered by the UIA. This movement apparently did not survive the decade, for when the economy dipped again in the late 1950s, leading to rising rates of joblessness by 1958 that continued to grow into the winter of 1960–61, a newly-formed Metro Association for Unemployed Workers appeared. It took umbrage at the ill-considered remarks of Toronto reeve Norman Goodhead, who claimed in a public statement that Canada's unemployment problem was the fault of "fat and sloppy" workers who refused pick and shovel jobs. During a North

Unemployed motor cavalcade, "On to Ottawa," Toronto, May 1954.

York University Libraries, Clara Thomas Archives and Special Collections, *Toronto Telegram* fonds, ASC19081, Glen Platt, *Toronto Telegram*.

Metro Association of Unemployed Workers, "Jobs For All," Toronto, May 1961.

York University Libraries, Clara Thomas Archives and Special Collections, *Toronto Telegram* fonds, ASC19088, Cooper, *Toronto Telegram*.

York municipal election campaign, the Metro association of the jobless hounded Goodhead. They crashed his speaking engagement meetings waving picks, shovels, and signs proclaiming, "Dump Goodhead," greeting his every word with a chorus of boos. Dissatisfied with the performance of the local UI bureaucracy, the Unemployed Workers picketed the program's Spadina Avenue offices in March 1961. An emerging provincially organized unemployed movement led two mid-December 1960 protest rallies at the parliament buildings in Toronto and Ottawa. Industrial centres like Peterborough and Windsor, hard hit by job losses, mobilized a twenty-four-car motorcade to the national capital, demanding "distribution of government-owned food surpluses to the unemployed and needy, federal help with hospital and medical plans for the unemployed, and an increase in family allowances." A delegation of the Toronto jobless protested at Queen's Park before meeting with Leslie Frost's Conservative Minister of Labour, Charles Daley. More likely to be led by left-wing, trade union-affiliated forces, this 1958–62 unemployed movement differentiated itself from its predecessor in the early 1950s by refusing to typecast immigrants as "job-stealers," advocating the necessity of seeing newly arrived Canadians as part of the working class and just as deserving of work, wages, and allowances as their counterparts with more established roots in the country.

As unemployment rates cracked the 10 percent barrier for many groups of workers and rose to over 16 percent for youth, socioeconomic tensions were exacerbated by the slumping Canadian dollar. Its fall from financial grace generated an acute and publicly aired controversy between Canada's populist-inclined Conservative prime minister, John Diefenbaker, and the more puritanical tight-money manager of the Bank of Canada, James Elliott Coyne. The jobless came out in force to register their discontents, prodding Diefenbaker to consider massive public works projects to deflect the resentments of the out-of-work. Notwithstanding an attempt to spend government money to siphon unemployed discontent, Diefenbaker's campaign trail in the 1962 election was littered with ugly, often violent confrontations with placard pumping protesters. Two

Unemployed picket Unemployment Insurance Commission, National Employment Office Building, Toronto, March 13, 1961.

York University Libraries, Clara Thomas Archives and Special Collections, *Toronto Telegram* fonds, ASC19094, Pete Ward, *Toronto Telegram*.

Metro Association of Unemployed Workers protest Reeve Norman Goodhead's remarks about "fat and lazy" workers, Toronto, November 1960.

York University Libraries, Clara Thomas Archives and Special Collections, *Toronto Telegram* fonds, ASC19083, Hunt, *Toronto Telegram*.

Unemployed
Diefenbaker pro-
test, "March To
Ottawa," Union
Station, Toronto,
April 23, 1961.

hundred unemployed marched into a Vancouver Tory rally of seven thousand yelling, "Hello
John, Where Are Our Jobs?" In the melée that followed, fists flew, blood flowed, and Diefenbaker
sputtered from the podium that he would not
be silenced by a mob of "organized anarchists."
Other Diefenbaker protests rallied unemployed
workers from Hamilton, St. Catharines, and
Toronto, who congregated at an Ottawa park
before heading to Parliament Hill and meetings
with the federal Minister of Labour, Michael
Starr. Among their placards were signs reading,
"Hungry 30s—Hungry 60s."[33]

Clearly, there were those activists on
behalf of the dispossessed who remembered the
protest mobilizations of the Great Depression. That said, a confluence of developments both lessened the level of mobilized dissent *and* fragmented such struggles
as did manage to break out of a postwar quietude that, in general, stifled somewhat uprisings of the poor. First, while poverty and joblessness continued to exist
throughout 1945–62, and while periodic crises pushed the economy into recessionary downturns, the level of absolute need and the acuteness of capitalist collapse in
the postwar period hardly bore comparison to the experience of the "dirty thirties."
Second, for all its incomplete and uneven development, the emerging welfare state

TORONTO'S POOR

eased a part of the burdens of deprivation in the 1940s and 1950s, at least for some of the dispossessed. Third, this welfare state's social construction and material consolidation of a great divide separating so-called employables (mostly able-bodied males) and unemployables (mostly females, many of them elderly and infirm) fractured the reciprocity of interests that often surfaced in 1930s struggles of the dispossessed, and that was evident in resistance to evictions and relief struggles of all kinds. Between out-of-work males, ostensibly covered under the Unemployment Insurance Act when jobless and protected by unions and their collective bargaining rights when at work, and unemployable women, locked out of the labour market because of their age, health, or responsibilities for children, stood an institutionalized allocation of state resources: relief on the one hand, unemployment insurance on the other, with very little in the way of mechanisms or programs of support that might bridge what now constituted the established allowance barriers. This state-ordered division subjected marginal populations to further isolation, deepening subordination in highly gendered ways. At the most basic of levels, women in need of welfare assistance were subject to the intrusive and sanctimonious moral regulation of the state, while barely one-third to one-half of all employable men, in the

Women unemployed protest, Queen's Park, Toronto, February 1961.

best of all possible worlds, could avail themselves of the protections and securities of unions or UI. Those who fell between the cracks, and there would be many, had nowhere to turn.[34] Fourth, these separate gender spheres inevitably structured such mobilizations of the unemployed as did arise. It appeared that organizations of the jobless in the immediate postwar period were overwhelmingly male, and possibly a subsidiary of the male-dominated, and increasingly influential, but also growingly conservative, leadership of the mainstream labour movement. By the early 1960s, women were indeed present in demonstrations of the jobless in greater numbers than had been common in the 1952–54 jobless protests, but it is likely that they took a backseat to a more influential cohort of male figureheads.[35] Fifth, and relatedly, a militant, radical leadership of the dispossessed, so visible in the 1930s, was undeniably inhibited by the Cold War climate and the conservatizing impulse of the vigorous anticommunism of the 1945–60 era. All of this, combined, meant that the dispossessed seemed in retreat in Toronto. With a return to economic buoyancy in the mid-1960s, official unemployment rates dipped to below four percent, a critical threshold that was not seriously breached until the 1970s. To a casual observer, it may have looked like the poor had disappeared.

Metro Association of Unemployed Workers picket Unemployment Insurance Commission Office, Toronto, March 1961.

York University Libraries, Clara Thomas Archives and Special Collections, *Toronto Telegram* fonds, ASC19085, Pete Ward, *Toronto Telegram*.

TORONTO'S POOR

A Sixties Turn: The Just Society, the New Left, and the "Discovery" of the Poor, 1965–1975

This illusion of the disappearance of the dispossessed fuelled the "discovery" of poverty amid plenty in the affluent but socially progressive later 1960s. With the publication of Michael Harrington's widely read *The Other America: Poverty in the United States* (1962) and Lyndon Johnson's declaration of an "unconditional War on Poverty" in his 1964 State of the Union address, the poor became a topic of wide discussion. In Canada, Jenny R. Podoluk's 1968 Dominion Bureau of Statistics–generated account of the country's low-income population provided a skeletal outline of the dimensions of poverty and how this was related to factors such as age and gender.[36] Affluence drove progressives of various stripes to insist that, for the first time, solutions to poverty could and should be found. The Ontario Federation of Labour (OFL) produced a study that set the poverty line at $3000 for a family of four, suggesting that seven hundred thousand of the province's people were living in abject destitution, and over a million were mired in poverty. Insisting that for the first time in history the means to eliminate mass poverty were available, the OFL report called for an all-out assault on the causes of need and want among those groups overrepresented among the poor: the unemployed and the underemployed; older workers and pensioners; the disabled and the sick; native peoples and immigrant newcomers; school drop-outs and the undereducated; small farmers and migrant workers. Bumping the minimum wage of one dollar an hour upward, constructing more low-income housing, raising the unemployment benefit rates, and developing job training for those displaced by automation were but some of the OFL's suggestions.[37]

As a Conservative-governed Ontario under John Robarts sidestepped such calls for action, the Lester B. Pearson and Pierre Elliott Trudeau–led Liberals in power in Ottawa embraced them, up to a rhetorical point. With much ideological fanfare, Canada's national War on Poverty would proclaim its commitment to the full utilization of government resources in the battle to eliminate material want. Yet little in the way of tangible funding support found its way into the pockets of the poor, especially the Indigenous peoples whose abysmal living conditions in northern communities or southern urban centres were routinely identified. The most visible achievement of Ottawa's loudly heralded War on Poverty was the passage of the Canada Assistance Plan (CAP) in July 1966. But this new legislation changed little and constituted yet another round in federal-provincial arm-twisting over jurisdictional responsibility and management. As CAP-induced guidelines within the Toronto Welfare Department indicated, caseworkers administering needs tests to the poor were to be less concerned with eliminating poverty's debilitating consequences than they were fixated on bureaucratic manipulation of the costs of relief. These were never to exceed the allowable maximum for families of particular sizes and were to be massaged so that federal inputs were pushed and provincial contributions kept in line with past practice.

With Ottawa cajoled by Ontario and other provincial allies into providing more social security largesse through CAP, and with the province enjoying an unprecedented economic boom, welfare benefits rose, seemingly, 15–20 percent in 1967–68. But this global leap masked the province's rigid imposition of maximum ceilings of support, which the Toronto Social Planning Council pointed out fell well short of the actual cost-of-living needs of the city's poor. New Democrat Stephen Lewis referred to CAP as a "bitter disappointment," calling for a guaranteed annual income of $4000–$5000 for a family of four, a standard that would alleviate distress among relief recipients and buttress the well-being of those now being identified as "the working poor." Even if, by the end of the 1960s, social assistance allowances for a family of four had increased by 100 percent over the course of the decade, this still left those in need receiving only 60 percent of what was required in housing, food, clothing, and other necessities. The attitudes of politicians, welfare administrators, and case workers often remained mired in nineteenth-century maxims, ordered by the virtuous imperatives of acquisitive individualism and fear and loathing of the undeserving poor. John Robarts wanted nothing to do with anything approximating a guaranteed annual income, which, he shuddered, might "encourage ... 'professional' welfare families.... How far does one go in making sure that they do not reproduce themselves."[38]

A Senate Special Committee on Poverty, appointed at the end of November 1968 and headed by David Croll, the Welfare Minister in Mitchell Hepburn's Ontario cabinet for much of the latter half of the 1930s, concluded that the problem of poverty was "the great social issue of our times." The "professional poor," according to Croll's report, did not choose poverty, nor was it their intent, Robarts' views notwithstanding, to reproduce themselves in order to live off the welfare system. Indeed, *Poverty in Canada: A Report of the Special Senate Committee* (1971) asserted that the "social-welfare structure so laboriously and painstakingly erected in Canada over the past forty years has clearly outlived its usefulness.... The welfare system is a hopeless failure." Insisting that one in four Canadians lacked sufficient income to maintain a basic standard of living, and that Unemployment Insurance, Social Assistance, Family Allowances, and Old Age Security were falling far short of what was required to elevate this 25 percent of the population above the poverty line, the Senate investigation placed a great emphasis on the existence of the "working poor." Sixty percent of those living in poverty, Croll's report claimed, were not receiving welfare. Calling for a bill of rights for the poor and a guaranteed annual income of $3500 for a family of four, the Senate statement also hinted at the need for participatory democracy, for social assistance reform that would grant the poor "a voice in what is to be done and how it is to be done":

> If the poor are being rapidly alienated from the mainstream of Canadian society, it is not only because they are excluded economically but because they are excluded from participation in the decisions that affect their own lives.... Five million fellow-Canadians, a veritable army of the dispossessed, cry out for action that will free them from the trap of poverty. They ask to be treated with the decency and dignity due to fellow human beings, and if their voices are becoming insistent, it is understandable in the light of their experiences.

With rhetorical flourish, Croll and his Committee warned that a failure to address poverty would cost Canada a high price in "lost humanity," arguing that, "We must move from welfare strategy to income strategy; from services to money; from helplessness to hope; and from despair to destiny." This was to be the priority for the 1970s, "a project that will stir the world's imagination and command its respect."[39]

This was heady stuff, and it coincided with and adapted easily to Trudeau's vague but politically shrewd 1968 call for a Just Society, one component of which was the determination of what constituted a "minimum standard of satisfactory living—not a subsistence standard, but one which allows for dignity and decency."[40] Moreover, in conducting hearings across Canada over the course of 1969–70, in which hundreds of witnesses appeared before it, and receiving over one hundred briefs, the Senate Committee on Poverty undoubtedly galvanized anti-poverty groups and stimulated both organization and discussion relating to the poor. The emergence of these campaigns of poor people in the mid- to late 1960s was not just a response to Ottawa initiatives, however, and they grew out of overlapping but distinct streams of mobilization.

In Peterborough, for instance, the United Citizens (UC) evolved out of roots that reached back to labour militancy in the industrial union upsurge of the 1940s if not before. A Peterborough Unemployed Workers Unity organization, connected to the left-led Canadian Labour Defence League, first surfaced in 1933, advocating for cash allowances to replace the voucher system, blocking evictions, and leading the usual array of relief protests. The leading figure in the United Citizens, a body that linked the unemployed and welfare recipients, challenging the officialdom of social assistance administration with rare use of a 1969 appeal process, was Ray Peters. Peters, a United Electrical Workers (UE) activist, almost certainly had close ties to Communist militants who had charted that union's development. UC emerged out of the unemployment crisis of 1958–62 and was reputedly the oldest welfare rights organization in Ontario. Responding to the constant attacks on supposed "welfare chiselers and cheats," Peters apparently coined the term "corporate welfare bums" to highlight how Canadian big business avoided its fair share of taxes, profiting from government loopholes in ways that far outstripped individual abuses of the welfare system by the poor. David Lewis would later turn the phrase to good effect in his 1972 election manifesto, *The Corporate Welfare Bums.* UC and Peters were still active well into the 1990s, opposing the deregulation of the housing market and government proposals to discontinue rent controls.[41]

Poor people's organizing intersected with 1960s youth radicalism and the New Left. With the formation of the Student Union for Peace Action (SUPA) in December 1965, Canada's student radicals promoted participatory democracy and championed a number of youth projects aimed at mobilizing for peace and nuclear disarmament, developing a rigorous analysis of power and how it operated, and advancing the interests of the most disadvantaged groups in society, among them native peoples and the urban poor. In the case of the latter, SUPA sponsored the Kingston Community Project. Young radicals lived in poor neighbourhoods, talked to the residents about their concerns, and offered suggestions on how best to protect their rights as tenants or pressure city hall to undertake necessary safety measures on dangerous streets and develop needed park space.[42] SUPA's activities prompted Lester B. Pearson and the federal government to fund youth, under the auspices of the Company of Young Canadians, to undertake similar activist projects, in which anti-poverty organizing also developed. Well into the 1970s, with Opportunities for Youth and Local Initiatives Projects, the Just Society state bankrolled, and, to some extent, therefore, controlled, aspects of anti-poverty organizing.[43]

Out of the Kingston Community Project emerged a cohort of young New Left women, some of whom were barely eighteen years old when they first engaged in community organizing. One of them, Sarah Spinks, would be involved in the Toronto Community Union Project at Trefann Court, a poor district east of Parliament Street adjacent to Regent Park, Moss Park, and Cabbagetown, scheduled for redevelopment in the late 1960s. By the end of the decade, Toronto's newly created

Ward 7 included three public housing projects—Regent Park North and South and Moss Park—as well as three areas designated for urban renewal: Trefann Court, Don Vale, and Don Mount. These low-income districts, when considered as a whole, sustained owner-occupied dwellings, rooming houses, and tenant-occupied residences. Average family income was well below that of Toronto as a whole, between $290 and $360 monthly, compared to $415 for the city average. A Toronto Social Planning "Don District" study reported in 1970 that "high levels of poverty" were evident in the area, with tenants, in particular, living well below the official poverty line, on less than $3,000 yearly; fully 19 percent of them were unemployed. If some neighbourhoods were well maintained, just west of Parliament Street Toronto's Skid Row had a disproportionate population of single and elderly males, transients, and the seemingly permanently jobless. It also sustained one of the city's major "red light districts." These neighbourhoods, targeted for redevelopment, began to organize in the mid- to late 1960s. Poor homeowners and renters were concerned about coerced expropriation, low levels of compensation, and the destruction of neighbourhoods that, however poor, had provided homes and sustained sociability networks for decades. They established a variety of ratepayers', residents', tenants' and neighbourhood groups, associations, and organizations, many of which gained from the involvement of young New Leftists and socially progressive community caseworkers/activists like Spinks, even as political differences emerged in the midst of struggles to defend working-class interests. It was this milieu that springboarded urban reform politician John Sewell to municipal prominence. It also raised the profile of an academic urban politics gadfly and future publisher, James Lorimer, whose weekly articles in the *Globe and Mail* pilloried the consistently arrogant and condescending decisions of Toronto civic officials "in the interests of private development, and against the interests of ordinary citizens and less affluent neighbourhoods." Lorimer would later write an account of living in one of Toronto's east of Parliament neighbourhoods, *Working People* (1971), in which he recounted the trials and tribulations of the "working poor."[44]

Toronto's St. James Town district, bordered by Bloor Street East (north), Wellesley Street (south), Sherbourne Street (west), and Parliament Street (east), currently one of the most densely populated urban districts in Canada, was central to this story of redevelopment and the displacement of poor residents and tenants. With a population of under 1,000 in 1961, St. James Town skyrocketed to 11,462 in 1971, a period that saw several high-rise residential towers mushroom throughout the neighbourhood. Many were bankrolled by the Meridian Property Management group, a North American consortium of construction, finance, and insurance companies that found itself butting heads with New Left community organizers and various tenants' organizations. As the rooming houses were razed and poor rental housing was increasingly bought up by the Meridian conglomerate for demolition, protests and mobilizations mounted, with John Sewell and urban reformer Jane Jacobs often involved in controversy and anti-development campaigns. Jacobs managed, with the help of pink Tory Toronto mayor David Crombie, to stop the levelling of a number of St. James Town Victorian residences, using a little-known provision in the City Code that prohibited demolishing buildings that were not protected by fencing. With houses about to be bulldozed, demonstrators, prompted by Jacobs, dismantled the wooden fencing, a city inspector was summoned to the property and ordered a halt to the demolition, Crombie called provincial housing authorities, and the construction of three high-rise apartment buildings was derailed. Toronto eventually bought up the buildings, preserved them, and created high-density "infill" affordable housing in what remained of residential backyards in the Dundas-Sherbourne area. Sewell was enmeshed in battles that erupted along Bleecker and Ontario Streets in south St. James Town, culminating in militant tenants' organizations protesting at city council meetings, seven hundred strong, proposed rent strikes, and confrontations with police as Meridian-orchestrated evictions put poor families on the streets. In one battle, chronicled in an Opportunities for Youth–funded video, "Free Bleecker Street—1974," cops and demonstrators clashed, leading to four arrests.[45]

Arguably Toronto's largest, militant, and most effective anti-poverty organization in this period was the feminist Just Society Movement (JSM), a body "organized by the poor, for the poor," which utilized Trudeau's words to call the state's bluff on alleviating poverty. Conceived as a "union of poor people," the JSM noted that the plumbers' union had less than one thousand members to back its demands for $6.00 an hour, but there were hundreds of thousands of impoverished men, women, and children to support "demands for a ... JUST SOCIETY." A presence within the welfare milieu during the years 1968–71, JSM was founded and led by young single women dissatisfied with their treatment under the Mothers' Allowance program. Doris Power, Suzanne Polgar, and Susan Abela were mainstays of the organization, which set up two downtown Toronto offices to advise welfare applicants of their rights and how best to negotiate the social security bureaucracy. Committed to 50 percent representation of poor people on the Ontario Welfare Council and the Toronto Social Planning Council, a $3.00 an hour minimum wage, a bump in welfare benefits, a comprehensive government-funded day care program, and participation of welfare recipients in the administration of relief and the training of caseworkers, the JSM launched itself with ten full-time workers, "all of whom are poor." Soon the organization, with a base of six hundred and two hundred members who actively attended meetings, was putting out a newspaper, *Community Concern*, and garnering considerable media attention for its creative protests at welfare offices.

Welfare officials were particularly outraged when the JSM showed up at their public offices and set up card tables, dispensing juice and snacks to relief recipients, throwing in advice on rights and entitlements, their presence a reminder that callous treatment of the poor would be recorded. In July of 1970, the group exposed the discriminatory practices of the Ontario Housing Corporation, sitting in at the subsidized apartment of a single mother with two special needs children who was facing eviction because of her failure to pay a $30 rent hike. Two dozen police officers eventually cleared the premises of the JSM, with two paddy wagons used to haul the demonstrators away. Likely drawn to New Left ideas—Power and Polgar were described as "very political animals ... involved in abortion rights and other political causes" and Abela's activism stemmed from her struggle to receive welfare as a single mother at the same time as she was attending Ontario College of Art—the JSM leadership was nonetheless founded by and functioned in the interests of welfare recipients. Yet it soon connected with the New Left collective Praxis: Research Institute for Social Change, led by an American social worker expatriate, Howard Buchbinder. Praxis provided office space for JSM meetings and, like left-wing elements in the New Democratic Party, helped bail those arrested at the JSM's actions out of jail. JSM also had a New Left sensibility toward the state and its financial capacity to co-opt radical criticism, refusing to take any money or formally appear before the Toronto hearings of Croll's Senate Poverty Committee. Instead, 150 JSMers flooded into the posh ballroom of St. Lawrence Hall, loudly denouncing the proceedings as a deceitful sham, insisting that poverty did not need to be studied and that capitalist power and oppression were the real enemies that demanded scrutiny. "We demand that this farce stop," the angry JMS contingent declared, insisting that the committee bring "the owners of the mining companies and the automobile companies and the growing list of American subsidiaries" before it to answer how they "contribute to poverty in Canada."[46]

A year later, four of Croll's Poverty Committee staff—Ian Adams, William Cameron, Brian Hill, and Peter Penz—resigned, convinced that "the Senate Committee was not going to live up to its mandate" and that it was rewriting the evidence presented in unilateral and transparently political ways in order to obscure "the actual production of poverty in Canada." Adams and his fellow workers decided, in the aftermath of the JSM's rudely effective intervention, that if "the roles played by the tax system, corporate autonomy, collective bargaining and the rest" were to be "systematically eliminated from the drafts" that they had prepared, then they would submit their resignations and offer to the public *The Real Poverty Report* (1971), an "analysis of the economic system that keeps people poor." Antagonistic to the corporations, the state, conservative business unionism, and the monopoly capitalism that orchestrated welfare and wages, *The Real Poverty Report* was a New Left document that could not stifle its contempt for the Establishment that had drawn radical critics of poverty into the research project of a Senate inquiry sustained by one million dollars in public funds. Its closing paragraph was a slap in the face to the politics of complacency. Adams and his colleagues disputed the claim that poverty could not be eliminated because to do so required funds that were not available. "The Senate of Canada costs about $5 million a year to run," wrote Adams and his co-authors. "This is $5 million a year too much." That money should be "distributed each year to five poor people, so that they, too, could be introduced to the pleasant sensation of being millionaires; the office space should be rented out to those who would make good use of it; and the bagmen should be returned to the arms of the interests they have served so well." This was undeniably "in the public interest," concluded *The Real Poverty Report,* because it would ensure the prevention of "any future reports on poverty by the Senate of Canada, leaving the subsidy of fantasy to others."[47] The state's accommodationist hand, feeding New Left researchers like Ian Adams, was publicly bitten.

The culmination of this late 1960s/early 1970s mobilization of anti-poverty forces took place in Toronto in 1971 as five hundred activists attended the first National Conference of Poor People's Organizations. Praxis's Howard Buchbinder, one of the gathering's organizers, recalls that the coming together of these groups was unprecedented, allowing the JSM to connect with other like-minded movements across the country. Calling for a radical redistribution of profit, those attending the conference formed the National Anti-Poverty Organization (NAPO). The JSM, obviously influenced by Praxis's participatory democracy orientation, issued a statement on the need to struggle to achieve "greater and greater amounts of control within our respective communities," be this extended in food co-operatives or community health clinics. Powerful opposition to this agenda, the JSM insisted, would be forthcoming from "the corporate power structure," and "We must prepare now, to fight very soon." This statement, however, was one of the last issued by the JSM. As funding opportunities for radical activists dried up in the early 1970s, as friction emerged among those within the JSM who wanted to narrow the organization's work to specific goals related to poor people's immediate needs rather than striking out at symbolic points of capitalist power, and as the state, at various levels, attracted willing figures from the JSM like Suzanne Polgar and Susan Abela onto bodies like the Toronto Social Planning National Welfare Council, the Just Society Movement, like so many New Left–inspired and –connected initiatives, waned.[48]

The mid- to late 1960s Canadian War on Poverty, in which Toronto was a decisive battleground, had been fought in many ways, and not without outcomes that were sometimes beneficial to the poor and some of the jobless. But there was also no mistaking the extent to which fine words rather than expansive welfare were the weapons of choice for governments and social security bureaucracies. With the demise of the JSM and the shelving of both the official Senate inquiry, *Poverty in Canada*, and the dissenting statement of a breakaway New Left contingent, *The Real Poverty Report*, there was a sense that poverty could now be challenged in an ongoing era of affluence. The problem was that capitalism, which organizations like the JSM and publications like *The Real Poverty Report* saw as the system that *produced* poverty, was about to go into crisis overdrive. In the years from the 1970s to our own era, the boom times of postwar capitalism came crashing down. Periodic crises pushed unemployment levels upward. Rampant inflation ate away at the purchasing power of both wages and allowances. State revenues constricted. What the state had given in seemingly never-ending largesse, it could take away. A postwar settlement that had secured collective bargaining rights for the employed and limited, inadequate, but nonetheless institutionalized, social assistance for the unemployed and the unemployables was, in this new climate of ostensible neoliberal post-Keynesianism, expendable. The short-lived Canadian War on Poverty gave way to a more protracted, ongoing war, one waged against unions and the entitlements of the poor.[49]

Men's Hostel, Central District Office of the Department of Public Welfare, Toronto, March 1961.

Hard Times: Capitalist Crises, Ideological Initiative, and the State Assault on the Dispossessed, 1973–2015

The 1945–70 period, for all its unevenness and the limitations of the compromises/settlements with the organized working class and the poor, was Western capitalism's most sustained period of affluence and social security. Now known as the Fordist accord, this orientation toward class relations was also an extremely successful (for capital and the state) regime of accumulation. The social relations of output and social security were premised on the recognition of relatively high-wage unions in the mass production sectors of largely male employment and the expansion of the state apparatus of welfare provisioning. These vehicles of accommodation, whatever their considerable limitations, undoubtedly helped keep the lid on overt class struggle, which repeatedly threatened to break out of acceptable bounds. Of central importance in this process of containment were the Cold War's anticommunist domestication of protest and the role of the state in mediating and incorporating dissent through complex layers of industrial pluralism/legalism and ever-sophisticated techniques of surveillance and governance of populations likely to erupt in resistance. All of this was possible because it was bankrolled by capitalist expansion, growth sustained by a rising profit rate that, in Canada, was minimally 15–20 percent annually for much of the period stretching from the 1940s into the 1960s. In some manufacturing sectors, the average annual rate of profit topped 45 percent in the flush of "postwar prosperity" in the early 1950s. This was a period in which the idealized norm of the "baby boom," male "breadwinner," suburban working-class family consolidated, described in 1958 by mainstream historian A. R. M. Lower: "Today ... the five-room bungalow [is] the object of life, and every woman in sight [is] pregnant."[50]

The profitability of the so-called Fordist era could not last. It began to falter in the late 1960s, and by the 1970s capitalist economies worldwide were locked into a profitability crisis that saw returns to capital decline substantially amid the soaring inflation rates, declines in growth, and rising unemployment of "stagflation." The fragility of these Western capitalist political economies was revealed most starkly in November 1973, when their dependency on critical oil reserves was exposed by the Organization of the Petroleum Exporting Countries (OPEC), located in Africa, Latin America, and the Middle East. OPEC instituted limitations on production and embargoes that drove the price of crude upward in what was the first of many "oil shocks" that destabilized the political economies of the advanced capitalist nations. In Canada, as elsewhere, the crisis of the 1970s grew out of this first "oil shock" but extended well beyond it into a generalized fiscal crisis of the state.

This crisis, in turn, unleashed an attack on the organized working class. Pierre Elliot Trudeau pirouetted from his war on francophone radicals and advocates of independence in the 1960s, culminating in his implementation of the War Measures Act during Quebec's October Crisis in 1970, to a declaration of hostilities against the labour movement. Trudeau's Anti-Inflation Board (AIB) policed Wage and Price Control initiatives that curbed the former far more successfully than the latter. As the trade unions mounted a challenge, with almost twelve million working days lost to strikes in 1976, including a million in a Canadian Congress of Labour–led symbolic one-day national protest on October 15, Trudeau was asked how far he was prepared to go keeping labour leaders in line. "We'll put a few union leaders in jail for three years and others will get the message," Trudeau quipped with confident cynicism. And he was almost as good as his cocky word, with Jean-Claude Parrot, militant head of the Canadian Union of Postal Workers (CUPW), eventually sentenced to a jail term (of three months, not three years) in 1979 for defying government back-to-work legislation. Administrators at the AIB were granted extensive powers to impose onerous penalties on those unions resisting government guidelines on how much collective agreements could grant the waged working class. The mid- to late 1970s thus announced a new, and vigorous, state war on the Canadian labour movement.[51]

The results were soon evident. One estimate suggests that between 1975 and 1978, Canadian wages declined by almost 8 percent, which was also where the official unemployment rate rested. More than a million jobless walked the streets in 1978, and among young workers, the unemployment rate was between 12 and 18.5 percent. In Metro Toronto, the number of suicides was up 15 percent, caseworkers convinced that there was a "direct correlation between the suicide rate and the jobless rate. It's not just being out of work, it's the social alienation that goes with joblessness and the hopelessness of ever find a job that is pushing people to suicide."[52]

All crises, although endemic to capitalism and routine in their periodic nature, are not the same, a point made with vigour in Leo Panitch and Sam Gindin's recent study, *The Making of Global Capitalism*.[53] Panitch and Gindin stress that the slump of the 1970s, occasioned by profit's decisive downturn, was fought on the terrain of a class struggle in which the working class was relatively strong and combative, and capable of mounting resistance that curbed capital's capacity to intensify the rate of exploitation of labour through managerial and technological innovations. The economic downturn of the 1970s prompted capital and the state to abandon the Fordist regime's fundamental accord, taking direct aim at labour's strongest link, the unions. Recalcitrant workers needed, in the eyes of capitalists and the state, to be disciplined. Crisis was the mother of a necessary repression, one that was first lowered on organized labour but that also soon came down on the heads of those more vulnerable workers who lacked the protections of unions and the security of stable jobs.[54]

From the late 1970s into the early to mid-1980s, rising unemployment, which had reached the unprecedented post-1930s rate of 11 percent in 1982, also kept workers' demands in check, and surging inflation eroded real wages. In combination with capital's retrenchment, evident in a willingness to face down worker demands in hard-fought strikes, and the state's utilization of all of its authority, including the capacity to pass back-to-work legislation in the public sector, such developments revealed a new truculence on the part of labour's opponents, who dug in their heels in defiant insistence that the terms of trade in the class struggle were now reversed. The number of strikes waged over the course of 1982–85 declined significantly, down 30 percent from comparable figures for the 1970s. Not since the early 1960s—amid recession and a serious rise in joblessness—had the number of days lost to class conflict been so low. This trend continued over the course of the next decades, from 1985 to 2006, as shown by Thom Workman. He notes that in 1995–97 the number of strikes annually was less than 300, compared to 1970s figures that regularly approached 1000. Over the course of the period 2000–2005, work stoppages per year were often in the range of 200, and in 2006 the strike total in Canada was a meagre 126. Employers reaped tangible benefits: in 1984 almost 300,000 workers were bound by collective agreements that called for a wage freeze or an actual pay cut. Journalists in newspapers like the *Financial Post* recognized that capital was transforming the nature of collective bargaining as master agreements were torn up, wages were pegged to profitability, and two-tier contracts established differential pay packages for new employees. In this context household savings were eroded, falling from a high of roughly 20 percent of family income in 1982 to 10 percent in 1994 to the dangerously low level of 2 percent in 2005. Small wonder that by 2006, the average household debt in Canada had climbed 75 percent over a decade.[55]

This was the climate that nurtured neoliberalism, an ideological parallel to the reversal of class struggle that took place in the 1970s and 1980s. The dominance of the notion that the free market must determine wages and a Keynesian order of welfare accommodation must be cut back in a downsizing of government emerged out of the crisis of profitability in the 1970s, rather than such ideas being the orchestrating impulse behind the changes of this era.

Indeed, the Unemployment Insurance program, in tatters by the late 1960s, finally reached the point of insolvency in 1972 as Canada was entering the global economic downturn. Changes were made as UI was revamped to widen the contribution base, extend surveillance of beneficiaries, raise the wage income ceilings on which weekly premiums were paid, and restructure the original inputs into the fund so that labour and capital each paid 50 percent. The federal government lessened its responsibility, contributing only when the rate of unemployment surpassed

4 percent. Such revisions to the UI Act were clearly meant to ease the burden on the state and shift responsibility onto the shoulders of workers and their employers. But the dimensions of the crisis of unemployment that would unfold over the course of the 1970s, and especially the 1980s, were staggering and overwhelmed projections on the part of the employment officialdom in Ottawa.

As a crisis of solvency worsened throughout the 1970s, further modification of the UI program was necessitated as early as 1976, the state determining that joblessness was not being made sufficiently punitive. The waiting period to collect UI benefits was doubled, benefit rates were cut back, and the funding formula determining the level of state contribution to the program was altered, decreasing Ottawa's economic responsibility. The net effect of all of these changes was to shift more of the economic responsibility for the costs of UI onto wage earners and to make the benefits of the UI program less and less adequate. Things only worsened over the course of the 1990s. The widening coverage of the unemployed was reversed as less than half of Canadians without jobs found themselves qualifying for benefits, a decisive decline from the 83 percent eligibility of the 1980s. Forced to work longer before they could collect smaller benefit payments for shorter periods, Canadians on UI were, by the mid-1990s, in one of the least generous unemployment systems of the advanced capitalist economies of the world. Only Britain, Japan, and the United States offered an unemployment benefit package that was judged worse than Canada's, where allowances were ranked sixteenth among the world's nineteen leading industrialized nations. But even this was not enough to resolve the growing crisis of unemployment social security.

As went UI, so went the broader process of welfare assistance and family allowances. In 1977, the Social Planning Council of Metro Toronto noted that throughout the 1970s social security provisioning in Ontario had been characterized by "restraint." "Almost all increases in the adequacy of allowances," noted one report, "[were] achieved prior to 1970. In fact some of the gains achieved since 1970 have been eroded even though the federal government granted substantial increases in Family Allowances since 1974." As a February 1981 joint project of the Ontario Welfare Council and the Social Planning Council of Metropolitan Toronto noted, restraint as a government practice if not a declared state policy was rooted in the post-1975 climate of economic malaise. In a published statement entitled "And the Poor Get Poorer," the two councils revealed that in Ontario, social development expenditures grew over the course of the 1970s but were "strongly curtailed by the provincial restraint program" after 1975; that the welfare system protected "employers in the low wage sector by providing a secondary source of income to workers faced with job insecurity and poor working conditions"; and that in an era of rampant joblessness "restrictions on Unemployment Insurance eligibility ... by the federal government" distorted "income security planning at the provincial levels" where, nonetheless, "the overwhelming majority of people receiving social assistance [were] sick, disabled or elderly adults and their dependents and women raising children alone." This devastating report, accenting just how Ontario "carried out its restraint program to a significant degree at the expense of income mainten-ance programs" established that before the heralded neoliberalism of the 1980s and 1990s was a widely touted ideological imperative, the politics of welfare provision-ing had been gearing down in the immediate post-1975 context of economic crisis.[56]

"And the Poor Get Poorer" also noted that the benefits of social assistance programs had been "pegged below minimum wage levels to encourage short-term recipients to return to the workforce and to ensure that the working poor continue working." This insight accented the reciprocal relationship of the waged and the wageless, highlighting the significance of real wages in a period of seemingly out-of-control inflation and of setting minimum wage levels as a conventional bottom below which remuneration could not plummet. In the early 1980s the wage, both as an expression of earning power and a recognized minimum floor sustaining the "working poor," was under sustained attack. Both organized labour, guarantor of the high wage, and those relying on the minimum wage in the absence of union protections, felt the lash of a political thrashing unleashed on the dispossessed in an era of insatiable demands that both the employed and the poor pay the costs of economic crisis.

As the economy crashed in sharp recession in 1981–82, two hundred thou-sand full-time jobs evaporated, the official unemployment rate topping 13 percent in what was, within the living memory of most people, an all-time high; inflation was also at the unheard of figure of 12 percent, with interest rates rising astro-nomically to 21 percent. This combination of skyrocketing rates of joblessness and upwardly spiralling costs of everyday life was unprecedented, pushing the federal government, followed by the provinces, to intensify its war on unionized workers. The wages of "protected labour" took a nosedive. The postwar upward curve of real wage advances was reversed, and strikingly so. Over the course of the 1950s and 1960s, real wages in Canada had grown by 35 and 29 percent respectively. In the 1970s and into the 1980s that growth was roughly halved to 16 percent. More dra-matic still was that this reversal then accelerated into overdrive in the later 1980s, with the result that for the remainder of the twentieth century, real wages bot-tomed out into a stagnation that flat-lined at less than zero percent growth. For the "working poor," many of whom were stuck in non-union, low (often minimum) wage jobs, this assault on the purchasing power of their paycheques was devastating. A 1974 Canadian Council on Social Development Conference devoted to discussion of income supplements for the "working poor" suggested that in Metro Toronto upward of thirty thousand families were dependent on the often minimum wage employment of those whose paid labour did not lift them above welfare/officially recognized poverty lines. Those arbitrary designations ranged from annual incomes of $2340 for a single individual to $6232 for a five-person family. Scraping by on budgets that could be carved out of such modest yearly earnings, poor people's meagre resources were able to buy less and less of life's necessities. The real value of the minimum wage plunged by as much as 30 percent between 1975 and the early 1990s.[57]

With organized labour in retreat, the recurring crises of the 1980s, 1990s, and the 2007–2008 subprime mortgage meltdown constituted nothing less than an all-out assault on the remnants of working-class power, and an especially vicious and accelerating attack on the poor and the dispossessed.[58] Complementing the destructive amendments to the Unemployment Insurance Act were a series of other cutbacks and changes that either eroded the principle of universality or left allowances and benefits to the wageless precarious or materially lessened. Federal cost-share payments to the Canada Assistance Plans for three provinces were capped in 1989 and then discontinued altogether in 1996. The latter termination replaced federal funds earmarked for provincial assistance programs with block grants for health, education, and welfare. In this decentralization of welfare funding, Ottawa watered down rules of allocation and reduced national standards, cutting up to $7 billion in aid. De-indexation of family allowances and child tax credits between 1984 and 1991 upped the tax burden on society's poorest taxpayer contributors, resulting in a $3.5 billion loss to low-income Canadians. Ontario, under the Mike Harris "Common Sense Revolution" waged a particularly brutal war against the poor, following on the heels of British Columbia's 1983 attacks on public sector unions and various low-income constituencies, which BC's Social Credit labelled "special interest groups." In 1995, Ontario partially dismantled legal aid and non-profit, co-operative housing programs while promising to cut drug plans for the welfare poor and senior citizens and remove rent control. Harris's Conservatives were committed to tax cuts for the province's well-to-do citizens at the same time as they were dedicated to reducing welfare benefits by over 20 percent. These and many other similar developments, often made or promised in the name of privatization and removing restrictions to capital accumulation, threatened to reverse the evolution of social security in Canada, driving it back to positions that existed at the beginning of the 1930s.[59]

Indicators suggest that the quickening pace of economic crises have materially drawn organized labour and the poor/dispossessed unprotected by unions closer together in terms of the worsening circumstances of the *entire* working class, yet there was little indication that this reciprocity of class interests was recognized and acted on by labour's most powerful unionized sectors. Aside from the generalized worsening of conditions for all workers, be they waged or wageless, employed or dependent on state allowances, an insightful suggestion of the narrowing of the separation of these sectors of the working class is provided by Robert J. Brym. Brym shows that in 1987–2000, with conditions worsening for both unionized and unorganized workers, a longstanding "inverse relationship between the unemployment rate and weighted strike frequency nearly disappeared." The historical effect of the business cycle on wage militancy seemed, in the hard times of the 1980s and 1990s to have come to an abrupt halt. Brym argues that the campaign against the unions and the entitlements of the poor and the dispossessed had largely been won in a one-sided class war reaching from the 1970s into the opening decades of this century. By cutting budgets for a wide range of government assistance programs and passing laws and taking stands that regulated and restricted what unions could do, the state played a decisive role in tilting the terms of trade in the class struggle toward capital. Emboldened by the ideological and material climate relentlessly structured in their favour, employers increasingly faced down organized workers and battled to victory after victory. As unions went into retreat, the dispossessed faced the onslaught of state-orchestrated austerity, confronting repeated cutbacks to allowance programs and erosions of all manner of entitlements. For both organized labour and the poor, then, worsening conditions characterized their experience of a post-1975 capitalism that seemed to lurch from crisis to crisis. They found themselves, as part of the same class under attack, in similar straights.[60]

Instead of a militant co-operation of the forces of the waged and the wageless, however, what too often happened was actually a widening gulf between these reciprocal components of the beleaguered working class. Roberts and Bullen noted in a 1984 publication that, "Although unions showed themselves capable of mounting an unprecedented 100,000-strong protest in Ottawa against runaway interest rates in 1981, they have done virtually nothing to organize the unemployed or even to advance demands for a shorter work week to provide employment." For all that organized labour had achieved since gaining collective bargaining rights in the late 1940s, these commentators concluded, the "road to labour's just society" had led to little in the way of changing the fundamental political and economic structure of Canada. The gap between the rich and the poor was actually wider in the early 1980s than it had been in 1945.[61] When coalitions of the unions and the dispossessed did emerge amid the capitalist crises of the last quarter of the twentieth century, as happened in British Columbia's Solidarity mobilization of 1983, the ensuing struggles might well be exhilarating. Outcomes, however, often fell far short of the desired mark, sometimes tragically so. The Solidarity debacle might be characterized as an intensification of class struggle that promised victory for a militant and united working class, only to be followed by a tragic divisiveness as the trade union tops exposed their penchant for accommodation, if not their outright reactionary disdain for all but the dues-fed officialdoms of a complacent labour bureaucracy.[62]

This confluence of capitalist crises, a one-sided war waged against the organized working class and the poor/dispossessed, and the failure of a class struggle leadership to emerge and effectively fuse resistance to the myriad forces that threatened the waged and the wageless paved the way for social upheavals in Toronto's 1990s and 2000s. The "hopeless failure" that the 1971 *Report of the Special Senate Committee on Poverty* judged Canada's limited and uneven social security

Line-up of unemployed, Metro Welfare Office, Adelaide Street, Toronto, circa 1968–69.

York University Libraries, Clara Thomas Archives and Special Collections, *Toronto Telegram* fonds, ASC19089, Russell, *Toronto Telegram*.

system had certainly not improved by the 1980s and 1990s. The return, even the revenge, of the dispossessed, was long overdue. In the Ontario Coalition Against Poverty, Toronto's economically disenfranchised struggled to resist hard times and "fight to win" in the ongoing, and crisis-intensified, war against the poor.

PART V

"Fight to Win!"

The Ontario Coalition Against Poverty and the
Return/Revenge of the Dispossessed, 1985–2015

The 1960s, 1970s, and early 1980s, for the most part, were decades of Liberal Party rule. That dominance ended with the 1984 federal election as Conservatives seized the reins of power. With separatists in Quebec coercively quieted and the trade unions in relative retreat, Brian Mulroney led an attack on what he labelled waste and bloated bureaucratic government into the prime minister's office. While it would take some time to become truly transparent, the ultimate target of this attack would turn out to be the poor, whose numbers were growing and whose destitution was worsening with each passing year of the 1980s.

Mulroney campaigned for the job of leading Canadians out of the deficit spending the country was mired in, ostensibly thanks to the Liberals. Mulroney stumped the electoral trail with lots of finger-jabbing at the practices of the past, playing perpetually the role of concerned guardian of the public purse, one with a supposedly caring eye out for the deserving poor. Against the privileged beneficiaries of state officialdoms cultivated by Liberal patronage, Mulroney was a scathing critic who mixed political abstractions in powerful rhetorical commitments, claiming to be watching out for the taxpayer and materially providing for everyone's favoured constituency, retirees dependent on fixed-income pensions. Liberal patronage, Mulroney thundered, had cost the country almost $85 million, a sum that, had it been properly invested in the welfare of all Canadians, could have provided "every senior citizen on the supplement an extra $70 at Christmas." Instead, Liberal Prime Minister John Turner's first act as head of state had not been "to help the unemployed or the elderly but to reward fellow liberals." For all of this bluster, however, Mulroney and the Conservatives were careful not to venture too far off the track of parsimonious budgeting. "We'd like to help everybody, but we just can't afford the high costs." Deregulation, privatization, and individual initiative were increasingly the buzzwords of Conservatives on the make.[1]

Marauding through the 1980s and into the 1990s:
The Many-Sided Attack on the Poor

As much as Mulroney might gesture toward the unemployed and the elderly as rightful beneficiaries of state largesse wasted by the governing Liberals, he was not about to commit to any expansion of social programs. On the contrary, "the tragic process of swedenizing Canada," he proclaimed, "must come to a halt." It was not hard to see why Conservatives fixated on restraining expenditure rather than confronting the needs of the poor. As the welfare rolls expanded nationally from 1.3 million people in 1976 to almost 3 million in 1993,[2] the cries mounted predictably to downsize government, implement restraint, and resolve the fiscal crisis of the state on what amounted to the underfunded backs of the poor. With Mulroney sweeping to a stunning electoral landslide in 1984, the Conservative seat count of 211 lapping the combined Liberal (40) and New Democratic Party (30) totals three times, the true colours of the Tory pallet of painting poverty out of the picture of governance and its responsibilities were highlighted. Barbara Greene, an Ontario caucus member, was appointed by Mulroney to chair a House of Commons subcommittee on poverty. She used that powerful position to press parliamentarians to lower their sights as to what constituted a poverty line so that more Canadians could be placed above, rather than below, such an arbitrary designation. "Our Government does not view Canadians as victims," declared one prominent Tory in 1989, "and does not see it as the role of government to perpetuate weakness and dependency."[3]

The ideological fixation on self-sufficiency translated into the age-old arm-twisting around federal-provincial responsibilities for welfare provisioning. One of the Mulroney government's early initiatives was to negotiate the 1985 Agreement on Enhancement of Employment Opportunities for Social Assistance Recipients (SAR) with the provinces. As Sylvia Bashevkin notes, the SAR arrangement offered Ontario and other regions the possibility of developing programs, including work-for-welfare schemes, that could draw on federal funds, but whose ultimate purpose was part of broad federal policies aimed at "reducing spending, tightening eligibility rules, ferreting out fraudulent users, and imposing penalties on welfare recipients who were defined as eligible for workfare but who refused to participate in such programs."[4]

In Ontario, SAR prompted the establishment, in the immediate context of a coalition Liberal-NDP government, of a Social Assistance Review Committee (SARC) that drew on the expertise of anti-poverty activists, heard from people in fourteen cities, and received over 1500 submissions. In its 1988 report, *Transitions*, the Committee provided a massive set of 274 recommendations that, in the words of George Ehring and Wayne Roberts, "lifted the veil of secrecy that shrouded the extent of poverty in the province." SARC exposed the existence of 400,000 children living below the poverty line and accented the ways in which the elderly, Native peoples, and the disabled experienced need disproportionately. Much comment focused on the working poor. Households dependent on female "providers" were identified as increasingly economically precarious. In 1961, 13.2 percent of poor families were characterized as headed by a woman, but by 1985 this figure had climbed to 36.5 percent. Given the longstanding disparity between male and female wages, the concentration of women in poorly paid, non-union, and insecure job ghettoes, women's historically conditioned responsibility for children, and the emerging tendency for women's unemployment rates, by the 1980s, to surpass those of men, the rise in poor, female-headed families increased the absolute numbers of those Canadians living below the poverty line and ensured that a growing percentage of them would be children. While undoubtedly a major achievement in calling all of this to public attention, SARC was, of course, reiterating much that had already been voiced in the Croll Report and by its left critics, led by Ian Adams, in the late 1960s and early 1970s. More tellingly, while the *Transitions* report called for some $2 billion to be infused into a welfare system that was declared costly, wasteful and a dead end, it also bought into the federal government's overall policy agenda of self-sufficiency. Seemingly left-leaning committee members pushed the value of "investment" in social assistance that could pay long-term "dividends," promising to turn "welfare cheques [into] pay cheques." This kind of language mollified business interests. Yet it also played into the historic differentiation of the deserving vs. undeserving poor, even as left NDPers such as former McMaster University professor Richard Allen made statements to the contrary. "There are not deserving and undeserving poor," Allen declared in 1990, "There are only people in crisis and need." Anti-poverty activists in the late 1980s picked up on the possibilities of the moment and managed to pressure out of the seemingly favourable situation substantial increases in welfare rates. Between 1988 and 1992 the problem of homelessness, while remaining acute, was being addressed, with the provincial Liberal government supporting the construction of approximately 1500–2500 Ontario social housing units a year in the latter half of the 1980s. With the New Democrats elected in 1990, this push to create low-income rental accommodations continued. The promise of Ontario's SARC, then, seemed great as the 1980s gave way to the 1990s.[5]

The sad reality was that the potential of the moment was derailed. It was stopped in its tracks by three converging developments in the political economy.

Provincial and federal governments turned the taps off state support for the poor, a serious economic downturn in the early 1990s both worsening the situation materially and providing further pressure on various levels of the state to dig in the iron heels of austerity. Peterson's Liberals not surprisingly prevaricated and stalled on making substantial changes to the increasingly costly system of welfare provisioning, their commitment to raise the rates plateauing at funding increases of a relatively modest 10 percent. By the time, in 1990, that the initial phase of the *Transitions* report was about to be implemented, taking the support of the poor to an entirely different level, things fell apart. The recession of the 1990s was looming, the NDP was on the verge of assuming the governance of Ontario (an unbelievable event that nevertheless saddled the province's first social democratic state with a ballooning deficit that Bob Rae, Floyd Laughren and the now reigning and inexperienced New Democrats could not fathom how to manage), and Ottawa was backtracking on its provincial commitments to social assistance programs.

The federal Tory budget, delivered in February 1990, was announced in the *Toronto Star* under the headline, "Budget Batters the Poor." Critical to the Conservative assault on social assistance was Mulroney's revision to the Canada Assistance Plan (CAP) legislation that regulated cost-sharing agreements between Ottawa and the provinces around social assistance funding. Since 1966, CAP had established that the two levels of government would each contribute 50 percent to the total benefits package expended. Faced with provinces like Ontario following the recommendations of its SARC report and upping welfare rates by as much as 25 percent so that the poor living on social assistance would not have to survive below recognized and designated poverty levels, the federal government decided to draw a line in the sand. It established a ceiling of 5 percent on increases in provincial welfare provisioning that it would provide to the country's three richest provinces, Ontario, British Columbia, and Alberta, claiming that they could and should give more than they were accustomed to kicking in on social assistance spending. In effect, this cap on CAP told Ontario that if its relief rolls were rising and its SARC-induced intention of upping the rates was to happen, Ottawa would contribute to the new reality only up to a 5 percent increase. Any bump in expenditures beyond this—and it was clear that such an increase was going to be huge—would have to be paid for by the province. This ended up costing the Ontario treasury dearly at the very time that it was diving further into deficit and the economy was seriously slumping, constricting revenues. Anti-poverty activist John Clarke has suggested that with rising caseloads, Ontario's welfare budget jumped 40 percent in 1991 alone, leading to increased expenditure of $4.9 billion. Conservative estimates are that Mulroney's

1990s rewriting of the CAP agreement drained $10 billion from the Ontario treasury between 1990 and 1995; Ottawa's contribution to social assistance costs in the country's largest province plunged from 50 to 29 percent.[6]

By the 1990s, then, Canada's governing elites had declared the dispossessed liabilities the state could no longer afford to sustain. It was all too apparent that the country was in a recessionary free-fall threatening to push the panic of depression downturn to lows well beyond that of 1981–82. Official unemployment rates surpassed 10 percent in the summer of 1991, and a left think tank estimated job losses at 435,000 for a twenty-month period. Unemployment insurance, the federal government's largest single social program, came under increasing attack for what was proclaimed to be "widespread cheating" and "the deadening effects of long-term dependence." But it was the material burden of the program that was perhaps of most concern, driving the fiscal crisis of possible state insolvency. The costs of providing unemployment payments to those eligible soared from $9 billion in 1982–83 to a whopping $19 billion in 1992–93. Capitalism's accelerating periodic crises were obviously taking their toll. Even conservative commentators, like the pro-free trade Tom d'Aquino of the Business Council on National Issues, signalled alarm in October 1990, claiming that the Mulroney government had "lost control of spending." The C. D. Howe Institute criticized the federal Tories for what it castigated as "irresponsible policies," aghast that Mulroney and company managed to let the "level of debt to GDP" rise to 55 percent, a shocking deficit-producing escalation that was "almost double its level at the beginning of the previous recession" of the early 1980s. With the economy about to register its first trade deficit since the 1960s in September 1991, the ill health of Canada was diagnosed from abroad: *Euromoney*, a guide for global fiscal conservatives, judged Mulroney money manager Michael Wilson among the three worst ministers of finance in the world. Nonetheless, there were those who had cause to be pleased. The political economy of capitalist crisis and its restructuring of material reality, over which Mulroney, Wilson, and the Conservatives found themselves presiding, produced a widening gap between the haves and the have-nots over the course of the 1980s and 1990s. Canadian income was redistributed away from the dispossessed to the extent that they had much of a secure grasp on wages and social assistance, and into the coffers of the well-to-do. One estimate suggested that this income transfer amounted to a staggering $5.4 billion.[7]

In this climate of crisis and cutbacks, the newly empowered Ontario NDP shifted gears, abandoning its SARC pledge to raise the social income of welfare recipients and the working poor so that no one would have to struggle to make ends meet. As premier, Bob Rae charted the new course of social democracy's waning commitment to the poor. Handcuffed by a huge provincial deficit, Rae and the more fiscally-minded of his NDP cabinet choked down resentment at Toronto's relief roll expenditure, which climbed 83 percent in 1991, necessitating unprecedented cuts to city programs, prodding the ad-hoc anti-poverty coalition Fightback Metro! into existence. "Welfare isn't working," Rae told a student audience in 1993, "Simply paying people to sit at home is not smart." Such words translated into budget battering, the NDP announcing a $313 million chop to its Ministry of Community and Social Services, headed by Tony Silipo, who issued a White Paper on social reform. Aptly named *Turning Point*, it proclaimed the social democratic government about to "dismantle welfare as we know it." Silipo went so far as to propose the idea of fingerprinting welfare recipients as a way of cracking down on welfare fraud. A year later, Rae was pontificating on CBC Radio about "mutual responsibility" and how everyone in society owes each other "the willingness to work." This at a time when the official unemployment rate fluctuated between 9 and 12 percent. Not to worry, however, the Ontario NDP government was willing to help "parents whose children are over 12 to prepare them to enter the workforce." Canada's most prominent social democrat was sounding and acting like Scrooge. Behind closed doors, the Rae government was said to be setting up an intensive, methodical system for investigating welfare fraud; proposals were being made to sanction any welfare recipients who failed or refused to participate in mandated training and counselling, or even the more punitive possibility of assigned work activities, penalties ranging from $100–$200 monthly. The SARC insistence, which the late 1980s NDP had endorsed with enthusiasm, that welfare recipients were not shirkers and bums unwilling to work but people unable to do so, including children and many single mothers; that the bulk of those on social assistance did not linger and cheat but went off the dole to assume waged work as soon as they could, often within three months; and that welfare rates were anything but generous, forcing people to live below the poverty line—all of this seemed forgotten in the economic and political crisis of social democratic governance in 1993–94.[8]

Just as the Trudeau Liberals paved the way for Mulroney's Conservatives federally, as the 1970s gave way to the 1980s, so too, then, did Rae's NDP clear the provincial path for Mike Harris and the Tories in the mid-1990s. Silipo's fingerprinting scheme and Rae's welfare rhetoric of 1993–94 accelerated into attacks on welfare fraud that were soon the hallmark of the virulently anti-poor provincial regime elected in the mid-1990s, half of its members coming from the suburban sunbelt surrounding Metro Toronto. Much of the Harris ideology, laid out in his

1995 playbook, *Common Sense Revolution*, placed runaway welfare expenditure very high on the provincial Conservative hit list. "The facts are staggering," declared the Conservative revolutionaries, "In the recession of 1982, just a dozen years ago, total welfare costs in Ontario were $930 million. Coming out of the current recession, we have four times as many people in the welfare system and our costs are more than 6 times higher—an astonishing $6.3 billion a year." The Harris government's response was a decisive tax give-back to the rich and an initial, draconian 21.6 percent reduction in the welfare rates. As Margaret Little has pointed out, with single mothers constituting a sizeable block of welfare recipients, a constituency that exploded in Ontario from 84,300 in 1987 to almost 200,000 in 1994, Harris's "common sense" restructuring of the welfare order was nothing less than an uncivil war waged against poor women and their children.

Aside from simply reaching into the pockets of the poor and lifting one in every five dollars of social assistance received, the provincial state also moved into aggressive new modes of regulation and retribution. The moral monitoring of single women-headed households intensified, case workers were cajoled into heightened scrutiny of clients, and community members were encouraged to report suspect activities on the part of welfare recipients. A much-ballyhooed telephone fraud line was set up in the summer of 1995, with the Tories promising $15 million in welfare savings if the public would inform on the "cheats" and "swindlers" who were living off the people's purse and abusing the system. A year-and-a-half later, as Little reports, a mere ninety-two "snitch-line" allegations had been reported to police, of which barely 10 percent resulted in formal charges of fraudulent acts. The capstone on this cleansing operation was Bill 152, legislation passed by the Harris government in 1997, a welfare "reform" initiative that heightened the now routinized surveillance of the poor and enhanced the capacities of the state and its caseworkers to harass and intimidate relief recipients and redefine eligibility for benefits. Bill 152 also reintroduced, against decades of actual common sense repudiation, the notion of the "work test," seemingly defeated by the struggles of the unemployed in the 1930s. Welfare was being taken back to its nineteenth-century Poor Law roots, Bill 152 declaring that relief constituted "temporary financial assistance to those most in need while they satisfy obligations to become and stay employed." "Cracking the stone" was seemingly back on the policy table, prompting Ontario's historian of unemployment and social assistance, James Struthers, to reflect on the dismal historical failure of workfare as a response to capitalist crisis and joblessness. But rational argument was not registering in Harris's Ontario Toryland where an Orwellian-named Tenant Protection Act virtually eliminated rent controls and facilitated evictions. The provincial premier's response to the growing army of the urban homeless was to terminate three thousand provincial units of subsidized housing in one fell swoop and, adding to the carnage, phase out seventeen thousand units of non-profit and co-operative housing. Not a single government-assistance Toronto housing unit was created over the course of 1997–2000, in spite of a torrential flood of need on the part of low-income tenants. With the dispossessed dying in Toronto streets, virtually on the Queen's Park doorstep of Mike Harris, the architect of the "Common Sense Revolution" offered perplexed condolences. "Isn't it sad," said Harris on hearing about the mounting toll of street deaths in Toronto, "that these people just seem to want to be homeless."[9]

Homelessness in Toronto was arguably the most striking and visible of the many ways in which the lives of the dispossessed were affected adversely in the 1980s and 1990s.[10] As a number of commentators have suggested, a crisis in housing and shelter, with the zenith of despair being without regular lodgings and depending on city hostels and private charities, was one of poverty's most telling markers. Through the rise of homelessness over the course of the 1980s, the public was constantly made aware of the presence of the dispossessed, if it would only see. Two women who took the time and trouble to look, also listened, talking to the homeless. Their compilation of the voices of those living rough in Toronto concludes:

> *Street People Speak* is a testimony to the life threatening reality of low-income, unemployment and the lack of affordable housing. The bureaucratic band-aid barricades built around the poor are not working, because of these systemic economic conditions which perpetuate poverty and homelessness. Toronto's social service system, reputedly one of the best in Canada, is barely working. No one is free from the threat of homelessness and all the consequent physical, psychological, and social scars which the homeless suffer. As a society, we pay a price for the clutter of institutionalism which is not designed to meet human needs, nor to solve the systemic conditions which trap the vulnerable in our society.[11]

The dimensions of Toronto homelessness in the 1980s and 1990s were truly astounding, conditions worsening year by year. More than 25,000 individuals and family units, constituting a total of 45,000 people, were admitted to Toronto's homeless refuges in 1986, the bulk of them single men. The Metro Toronto Commissioner of Community Services reported in 1987 that in spite of an increase of 260 percent in beds available since 1982, existing shelters were filled beyond capacity, necessitating placing some families in commercial hotels/motels. Social service agencies claimed a "tremendous pressure for shelter from couples, two-parent families, and single-father led families." In the nine years from 1988 to 1996, as Anne Golden and others associated with the Mayor's Homeless Action Task Force discovered, 170,000 different individuals passed through the Toronto shelter system. Overnight stays in various missions, hostels, and shelters jumped approximately 20 percent between 1998 and 2000, a not surprising development given the escalating numbers of eviction applications. In 1997, Toronto's annual count of applications to remove tenants from their homes exceeded 23,000, and this yearly total increased by 9 percent over the next year and 12–14 percent in the following twelve-month period. The Toronto demography of those dependent on emergency shelter reflected the shifting nature of social assistance and the ways in which the problem of homelessness, always destructive enough for single men, was now generalized throughout the social order, with children suffering especially. Families accounted for 46 percent of hostel users in 1996, while increasing numbers of women, upward of 30 percent by the end of the 1990s, were seeking refuge in emergency shelters.[12]

This worsening situation grew out of a two-pronged development. On the one hand, as the poor, including the working poor, became poorer, driven to the wall by rising rates of unemployment, declining real wages, and stripped down social assistance benefits that were further eroded by inflation, more of their limited funds had to be expended on the critical and primary consideration of housing. One definition of poverty, often utilized by Statistics Canada, is household expenditure of more than 30 percent of income on housing. From 1976–86 the proportion of Toronto tenants spending 30 percent or more of their income on rent rose from 23 to 27 percent, and of those city residents on General Welfare Assistance, 77 percent devoted 40 percent or more of their monthly income to housing costs. On the other hand, as the state responded to its fiscal crisis, it targeted expenditures shoring up the poor's access to housing for reduction or outright elimination, just as it jettisoned support for and commitment to low-income social housing.

Among the social programs first on the Mulroney chopping block in 1985 were several ad hoc housing initiatives aimed at ameliorating the destructive impact of the stagflation of the 1970s/early 1980s and the sharp economic downturn of 1981–82. Low-income housing could no longer count on the federal support that sustained co-operatives and social housing ventures throughout the 1950s, 1960s, and 1970s. The market took its long-awaited revenge. Over the first half of the 1980s, nine thousand affordable Toronto units were lost to demolition/gentrification, casualties of the rising tide of federal support for the privatized development of residential housing. With federal funds not forthcoming, Toronto's municipal Not-for-Profit Housing Corporation scaled back in the 1980s. Hampered by increasing annual accumulated debt, it underwent a reorganization resulting in fewer on-site project offices and tighter budget controls as well as an overall downsizing that reduced the number of low-income housing units available, possibly by as much as 10 percent. With the erosion of the social housing project, more and more of Toronto's working poor and relief recipients were forced into increasingly substandard housing, much of it far distant from the downtown core they had inhabited for generations. Cabbagetown's transformation was a case in point. In 1971 its average household income was 25 percent lower than that of the Metro Toronto average as a whole; in 1996 that same income was 25 percent higher. Many of the poor had been driven out, the old downtown Toronto core experiencing a net loss of fifty-three thousand people over the course of twenty-five years, while the city as a whole grew by hundreds of thousands. Low-income housing, including boarding houses that might accommodate eighteen to twenty people, had given way to the renovated Parliament Street carriage house of small, affluent families. As this scissors-like squeeze of rising poverty and declining housing possibilities cut into the social fabric of poor Toronto neighbourhoods, there was little space left for anything but nuclear families with both adults working professionally.[13]

At the end of the 1990s, *Breaking the Cycle of Homelessness: An Interim Report of the Mayor's Homelessness Action Task Force* concluded that the conditions of life for the homeless in Toronto were threatening indeed, yet the dominant public discourse around being poor had taken a 1990s detour into calloused indifference. Long-time anti-poverty activist Jean Swanson suggests that the shifting contours of this Canadian political economy and how the dispossessed fare within it can be discerned by looking at two federal reports on poverty that appeared in 1970 and 1994. The first, *Income Security for Canadians*, was, like the Croll Report, dedicated to establishing for all Canadians an "adequate income on which to live," espousing the need to enlist the country's abundant material resources "in support of social objectives." It recognized the inadequacy of the welfare order, which subjected relief recipients to humiliation, untenable bureaucracy, and arbitrary denial of benefits. Many people "genuinely in need do not get enough," it concluded. Those Canadians unable to support themselves, said the 1970 government statement, "have a right to assistance." In 1994, the tone and substance of the federal statement *Improving Social Security in Canada* exhibited less care and more calculation. There was no sense in this latter document that the economy should serve human ends. Rather, those who found themselves out of work or in need of assistance were to "retool," adapting to their circumstances by embracing and developing "independence, self-confidence, and initiative." The welfare system was not so much inadequate as the victim of "waste and abuse." Programs like Unemployment Insurance encouraged "repeat users" and discouraged "adjustment." Benefits and allowances of all kinds "trap[ped] people." If particular environments were unlikely to yield waged employment, then those who lived in them should explore "self employment or mobility." As Lynne Toupin, Executive Director of Canada's National Anti-Poverty Organization, told journalist Walter Stewart in 1995,

> If three years ago someone had told me that we would see what we are
> seeing today in terms of poor-bashing, I would have said, 'You're dreaming'.
> But it has happened with a rapidity that alarms me, and one of the things
> we have to deal with is the idea that the people who are poor are somehow
> to blame. It has become a very mean society.

The state's changing language of how to address the poor and its approach to how to provide for them were, of course, parts of a larger project. Evident in the media, government legislation, and the stereotyping common in popular culture, this "blame the victim poor-bashing" undoubtedly put the dispossessed of the late twentieth century on the defensive.[14]

Sheila Baxter begins her first-hand account of women and poverty in Vancouver by acknowledging the ways in which the self-esteem of the poor have been and continue to be eroded, resulting in resignation. Women with whom she talked wrote down their thoughts: "Welfare sucks./My solution to poverty is suicide./I will always be poor, unless I get the help I need./I am sure that I will always be poor." The women featured in Baxter's book often feel "stuck in a game of Russian roulette," with their "*biggest* problem" being the attitude society shows toward them when they become poor or sick. As the out-of-work and destitute were yet again separated into socially constructed categories of deserving and undeserving, and as capitalism continued to be beset by accelerating economic crises, with actual need becoming greater, those officially recognized and sanctioned as rightful recipients of material help were deliberately and definitively declared to be fewer and fewer. The social, systemic dimensions of poverty then became lost amid the personalizing of responsibility for people being wageless. In this sanctimonious winnowing, which defined much of the state's orientation toward welfare in the 1980s and 1990s, lay a significant, and longstanding failure, reaching back to the Poor Law mentality of the nineteenth century. As Pat Capponi concluded in her 1999 book, *The War at*

Home: An Intimate Portrait of Canada's Poor, "The system is now set up more for the purposes of judging the worthiness of the poor than for providing services to all those who clearly need them."[15]

All of this scratched and gouged its way into the lives of the dispossessed in particularly nasty ways. The sociologist James Rinehart provides one assessment of this in his foreword to Patrick Burman's 1988 study of how the alienated jobless experienced unemployment in London, Ontario:

> Like characters in a Franz Kafka novel, the jobless often apprehend themselves in these settings as being at the mercy of powerful, manipulative, and unfathomable persons and forces. As individuals search for work, they come to realize how indistinguishable they are from their fellow unemployed, impressing upon them a consciousness of being abstract commodities no one wants to purchase. Institutions like Canada Manpower, which ostensibly were established to provide a necessary service, are seen by their clients as sources of frustration and degradation. In bureaucratic encounters, the jobless are stripped of individuality, their uniqueness ignored. External attributes such as age, physical appearance, and credentials are scrutinized, reified, and crammed into particular niches in the occupational world. As the period of joblessness drags on, there is among these informants an agonizing sense of being trapped in a maze in which the exit seems more and more remote.

Burman's unemployed discussants were thus conditioned to internalize the poor-bashing that Swanson has chronicled was so central to the everyday life of Canada in the 1980s and 1990s. They accepted the judgment of those whose purpose it was to subordinate them, describing themselves over and over again to Burman as "being nothing," "being on the receiving end of everything," "being participants in a script written by others." This is the powerlessness that power wants from the dispossessed. It is bred into the ossified bone of the limited and uneven welfare state that was, throughout the last quarter of the twentieth century, being dismantled. Recurrent capitalist crises and the provincial and federal governments that they crippled hacked away at the few entitlements the poor managed to secure over the course of decades of battle. As Capponi writes, this is the "powerlessness which so much defines [the poor's] everyday existence, ... exacerbated and prolonged in each social service contact." It is a powerlessness that grows through "shame and humiliation."

Even one of modern Canada's most militant anti-poverty activists, John Clarke, notes:

> The truth is that oppression never fails to leave its mark on its victims.... The full weight of Poor Law tradition and philanthropic judgements bears down on poor people and holds them back from organized resistance. To be laid off and collect unemployment insurance is not, generally, seen as a badge of distinction; but the unemployed worker who exhausts those benefits and has to turn to welfare undertakes the modern equivalent of passing through the doors of the workhouse. A stigmatization takes place (and this is no accident) that discourages collective action.

That said, as Rinehart concludes, "There is nothing inevitable about this political quiescence, as evidenced by the activities among the unemployed in other eras." The "politics of exclusion" and the experience of isolation, marginalization, alienation, and even self-loathing that can overtake the dispossessed and mire them in passivity can only be transcended by mobilizations of the poor, other segments of the working class, and their supporters. Organization and resistance, and the possibility of a *social movement* that challenges capital and its periodic crises and stands up to the state, which functions as a manager of the consequent social dislocations, are the only antidotes to the generalized immiseration of the working class that produces the demoralization of the dispossessed. This uphill fight to bring the wageless together into a force of opposition that might unite them with the waged began to gain momentum over the course of the 1980s.[16]

Mobilizing against the Marauders: Reviving Poor People's Agitations in the 1980s

As we have suggested, the organizations and mobilizations of the dispossessed certainly fluctuate in their intensities, bottoming out in certain historical periods and rearing their collective heads much higher in other confrontational moments. The short but intense burst of anti-poverty organizing in Ontario associated with the Croll Report and its Just Society Movement (JSM) critical rejoinder culminated in the 1970s emergence of a coordinated National Anti-Poverty Organization. But the strength of anti-poverty activism still registered largely in specific locales, such as East Vancouver, where the Downtown Eastside Residents Association (DERA), with leaders like Bruce Eriksen, Libby Davies, Jean Swanson, and Jim Green, consolidated an effective presence from its founding in 1973 into the 1990s.

Green, running for mayor in 1990, managed to win 45 percent of the vote. In Ontario, the anti-poverty movement of the late 1960s and early 1970s had stalled somewhat by the time of the 1981–82 economic recession. There was no DERA equivalent in Toronto, nor anywhere else in the province.[17]

With the uncertainty of the crisis looming, social worker, community activist, Praxis-founder, and JSM member Howard Buchbinder posed questions that emerged out of the 1970s. "If the fiscal crisis of the state intensifies," Buchbinder implied there would be "increased pressures on workers, clients, and administration alike." Yet in 1981, it is important to understand, few could appreciate how devastating the economic downturn in Ontario would prove to be, nor how recurrent crises from 1982 to the present would lend the relative prosperity of the 1945–75 years a halo-like golden glow. Buchbinder wondered what lay ahead: "a more progressive or a more reactionary cadre of service workers?"; "a more militant or a more passive client group?"; "more money or less money ... diverted to [the poor] ... in the interests of 'stability'?"[18] Full answers to Buchbinder's queries would require many chapters and address the ebbs and flows in various developments. We concentrate on briefly chronicling the response of the dispossessed themselves, who struggled in Ontario over the course of the 1980s to develop local organizations of the poor and to sustain a militant response to what was a relentless assault on their well-being.

As John Clarke has shown, the downturn in the Ontario economy in 1981–82 catapulted "a whole new layer of unemployed workers and jobless youth into poverty." With the further deterioration of the material circumstances of those who were already poor, this led to a "burst of organizing activity." Clarke suggests that under the 1930s banner "We Refuse to Starve in Silence," a host of "democratically structured bodies planted influential roots in their respective communities." Some of these organizations undoubtedly drew on past experiences of anti-poverty community organizing and, in a few locales, such as Peterborough, specific associations and committees already existed and revived under the tragic stimulus of worsening conditions. But for the most part, new collectivities of activists emerged out of the cuts to social assistance and programs that constituted the dismantling of the welfare order, now the front line of combat in the war against the poor. Across Ontario some thirty-five municipalities saw instances of this self-activity of the dispossessed: London's Union of Unemployed Workers; Kitchener's Mothers and Others Making Change; and North Bay's Low Income People Involvement were but some of the poor people's organizations that mobilized, raising militant demands defending past entitlements and refusing to bow and scrape as recipients of charitable "gifts."[19]

In Toronto, the central body was the Union of Unemployed Workers (TUUW), but as in the 1930s, the blue-collar suburbs of Scarborough, Etobicoke, East York, and North York also witnessed the creation of new initiatives on the part of the unemployed and the poor. Clarke, an immigrant to Canada from the United Kingdom, lost his London, Ontario factory job in the collapse of the early 1980s and was a moving force behind the 1983 creation of a local Union of Unemployed Workers. Speaking under the pseudonym of "Jim" when interviewed by Patrick Burman in the mid-1980s, Clarke espoused a collectivist stance against the grinding destructiveness of capitalism's periodic crises and their purposeful erosion of the working-class's sense of self. Burman outlined Clarke's position: "the roots of the present crisis lay in the objective contradictions between capitalism's world-wide search to maintain its rate of profit and the interests of communities and the working class." Clarke claimed that business and government were intent on demoralizing the unemployed, intimidating them. "Large numbers of people who are scared, looking for work, not ever knowing what is expected of them" were, in Clarke's words, increasingly reluctant to be "pushed around and carried by blind forces." This is why Clarke put his energies into organizing the Union of Unemployed Workers, a body whose purpose it was, in part, to ensure that the dispossessed did not succumb to isolation and what Burman described as "the marginalizing currents of capitalism." Clarke concluded: "The essential thing I come back to is a sense of your person. Don't let them grind you down. Don't let them give you the impression you are all alone, don't let them atomize you.... You didn't make the situation, but you can have a hand in changing it." From this global and abstract perspective, which drew on rich streams of Marxist analysis, Clarke and other 1980s activists mobilized against the marauders.

The Union of Unemployed Workers set up a London drop-in centre with a regular listing of available jobs and provided information/advocacy around welfare rights and the unemployment insurance system. Often an alternative to the staid Unemployment Help Centre of the conservative London District Labour Council, which functioned as a "service" for "clients," the UUW embraced principles of co-operation and was determined to make waves publicly, protesting in ways that the mainstream trade union officialdom would never have condoned. The UUW organized rallies and picnics, looked consciously to models of 1930s unemployed activism, and picketed and protested noisily. It occupied the offices of the mayor of London and set up a tent city in an adjacent park to voice its discontent with the decision to withdraw welfare benefits from those taking upgrading courses at the community college; some of the members of the militant jobless group were jailed briefly as a consequence of the sit-in. An initial attempt to rally the province-wide forces of the jobless occurred in 1983, as groups advocating for the interests of the unemployed converged from a number of Ontario centres, demanding work and wages. The London and Toronto Unions of Unemployed Workers joined forces with a Scarborough group known as the Poverty Eliminators in 1986, successfully pressuring the welfare bureaucracy to provide a clothing allowance for children subsisting on welfare. With a large vision, then, Ontario's Unions of the Unemployed tackled issues affecting the jobless, however seemingly small. Sometimes drawing on material support from the trade unions, these bodies nonetheless saw themselves as "filling a vacuum created by unions' neglect of laid-off members and the unemployed-at-large."[20]

Also important was the spectre of homelessness stalking the land, and particularly Toronto, in the wake of the 1981–82 economic downturn. The tragic case of Drina Joubert, a forty-one-year-old woman who died of exposure while living in an abandoned, rusted truck inside of a garage at the back of a Sherbourne Street rooming house in December 1985 brought to the attention of the public how desperate conditions for the Toronto poor had become. Joubert, a successful fashion model in South Africa, immigrated to Canada in 1970 and was provided for by her mother. That support dried up in 1983, however, and as her mother faced debilitating health problems, Joubert lost her apartment and became homeless. Suffering from depression and alcohol dependency, and often banned from women's shelters like that operated by the All Saints Anglican Church because of her erratic behaviour, Joubert had no choice but to live rough amid the seeming affluence of Toronto's gentrifying downtown core. Neighbourhood youths like thirteen-year-old Benjamin Young checked in on Drina regularly. Beric German, a Rooms Registry social worker and member of the Toronto Union of Unemployed Workers, also had contact with Drina, who often came into the All Saints drop-in where German worked. It was Ben who discovered Joubert's lifeless body in the cab of the abandoned truck. Young then found German at the All Saints Church, conveying the information that the homeless woman had died. When the police arrived, one officer suggested to German that keeping the death quiet would be a good idea. "I don't think so," replied German, who promptly contacted Toronto's media. Soon Joubert's death was front page news, and over the next six weeks another homeless woman and two men living on Toronto's streets would also expire in the winter cold, their bodies discovered in alleyways, stairwells, and alongside heating vents. "We've been warning the politicians that this was going to happen," German told one newspaper reporter, "There's just not enough places for people to live in this city."[21]

Drina Joubert's death, although but one of at least nineteen cases of homeless people succumbing to exposure over the course of 1984–85, crystallized growing concerns and resentments at civic complacency. Fourteen organizations formed the Affordable Housing Not Hostels Coalition; the TUUW called for an inquest, which was subsequently convened by the coroner's office. On the day before the hearings commenced, a memorial was held for Joubert at All Saints Anglican Church. One hundred and fifty people then marched under a "Housing Not Hostels" banner to Nathan Phillips Square, where they demanded the building of more affordable housing. At the inquest itself, presided over by Coroner Dr. Murray Naiburg, social workers conveyed a bleak picture of women's shelters, which routinely turned away anywhere from five to thirty homeless females every night. German detailed how rooming and boarding house landlords discriminated against women, whom they refused rooms on the grounds that they caused trouble with male lodgers or prostituted themselves. Other expert testimony explained how single adults under the age of sixty who were not "mentally or physically disabled" found themselves ineligible for subsidized housing, and how Joubert, in particular, whose major issue was alcohol, would have been unlikely to qualify for housing assistance. These problems—in provisioning and with respect to individual cases like that of Joubert— were exacerbated by gentrification, with low-cost housing disappearing in the face of demolitions and conversion renovations. For Joubert herself, life on the street was a nightmare of hostel doors being closed to her, rooming house invasions of her privacy, hospitalizations after police found her nearly dead in a snow bank, and beatings by young thugs who broke into her truck and assaulted her. The coroner's jury concluded that Drina Joubert had died accidentally, but that the causes of her death were identifiable as "alcoholism, mental illness, and homelessness," with the welfare system having failed to deal with these problems. Recommending government funding of programs that would specifically employ caseworkers cognizant of the needs of homeless women, the jurors also stressed the need for "long-term housing options" accessible "to women who are homeless and in crisis."[22]

In her life, Drina Joubert had clearly mattered all too little. Her death, however, helped spur provincial action. The government of Ontario promised to build three thousand units of social housing across Ontario in 1986, and one year later $31.5 million was earmarked for new emergency shelters and homeless relief. At All Saints Anglican Church, the hostel that had closed its doors to Joubert on the night of her death, new facilities were created that improved conditions for the homeless, expanding the capacities of the church shelter to address the needs of women. Preparations were in the works to open a new building behind the church that would provide sixty-one units of subsidized housing for single women and men. According to Carmel Hili of the Christian Resource Centre, Drina Joubert's death mobilized activists whose demands "opened up housing benefits for single people and stopped stigmatizing them as being lazy and having no right to social housing." Every single adult in the province was now eligible for subsidized housing.[23] If a derogatory view of the dispossessed would clearly never be eradicated, returning with a vengeance in the years of reactionary assault on the poor in the mid- to late 1990s, Drina Joubert's sad demise nonetheless helped ease up on the stereotyping of the poor that had gained momentum with the economic slump of the early 1980s. In conjunction with the specific and somewhat unique political conjuncture of the mid- to late 1980s, of which the establishing of SARC was one expression, the lot of the poor in Toronto seemed poised on the edge of possible improvement.

Anti-poverty activism, as one expression of this possibility, accelerated with the openings presented by the creation of SARC in 1986. The initiative for the welfare review came under the Peterson-led coalition Liberal-NDP government, with social democratic services critic Richard Johnson pressuring and manoeuvring the dominant Liberals to strike a committee and appoint Family Court Judge George Thomson as Chair. Thomson and Johnson then paved the way for the review committee to hire National Anti-Poverty Organization leader Patrick Johnston as its research director. In the midst of these developments, which cultivated the possibilities for a progressive report, a number of Ontario organizations of the poor and the unemployed grasped that the times were propitious for demands to raise the welfare rates. As the committee studied and inquired, activists representing eleven municipalities mobilized and engaged in discussions on the need to campaign for a 25 percent increase in social assistance rates. Out of the ongoing communications and meetings emerged the March Against Poverty Committee, which drew on the unemployed treks of the 1930s to orchestrate a series of jobless walks converging on Queen's Park in 1987, 1988, and 1989. Central to this strategy was the London Union of Unemployed Workers, which under Clarke's leadership was emerging as a militant centrepiece of a provincial protest movement. The 1987 and 1988 marches commenced in London and Hamilton respectively, giving rise to supplementary actions to raise the welfare rates, including a petition drive and picket lines. At first, David Peterson refused to meet with protest marchers, but his Olympian disdain mobilized support for the anti-poverty cause, which was now drawing on trade union support as well as building bridges to groups like the Ontario Coalition for Better Child Care, the Ontario Coalition for Abortion Clinics, the Co-operative Housing Association of Ontario, and the United Tenants of Ontario.[24]

The culmination of this mobilization was a three-pronged 1989 hunger march that commenced simultaneously in Windsor, Sudbury, and Ottawa on Good Friday and, after sixteen days on the roads of Ontario, arrived at Queen's Park on the 8th of April. Described by two commentators as "the brainchild of anti-poverty activist John Clarke," this final On-to-Toronto trek was a resounding success. It raised the profile of protests about the poor and helped to extract concessions from the provincial state. Continuing the struggle to raise the rates by 25 percent, the walking demonstration pressured the Peterson provincial government to implement the recommendations of the 1988 SARC report of George Thomson on issues of hunger, homelessness, and poverty immediately. The march itself was small—a core group of thirty activists led the way—but it garnered considerable support. Now out of government, former NDP coalition partners with the Peterson Liberals were cajoled to get on board the anti-poverty bandwagon by MPP Richard Allen, the new social services critic in Bob Rae's parliamentary opposition. Allen, a compassionate and principled social democrat with a social gospel bent, impressed activists by the extent to which he "went to the wall" to provide resources for the fragile coalition of militant poverty eliminators, squeezing funds out of the reluctant pocket of NDP leader, Bob Rae, who was anything but enthusiastic about plans for the protest. The poor revelled at the NDP support that came the way of the mobilization, which was an extra-parliamentary coalition-building experiment that now embraced the official party of social democracy, the labour movement, the unemployed, feminist organizations, church groups, and many others. Allen walked with the trekkers for a few days on each of the separate marches and when, in April, the converging cohorts of marching militants approached Queen's Park, SARC Chair George Thomson joined "with the poor to press for government action." By this time three to four thousand were assembled at Queen's Park, making the event the largest anti-poverty rally in Ontario since the 1930s. Bob Rae addressed the crowd, seeming to take credit for the demonstration. "A great number of people were enormously offended by that," John Clarke remembered, and at least one coalition group apparently wrote a letter to Rae attacking the misrepresentation of his role. More importantly, however, the Peterson Liberals were forced off the fence. Just over a month later, Social Services Minister John Sweeny announced a package of $420 million in new money for Ontario families on social assistance, and there were other important concessions to the jobless, including allowing the out-of-work to keep unemployment insurance benefits if they managed to find some part-time work earning them limited wages.[25]

The Liberals understood that the crisis of the welfare order was creating new waves of resistance. Beyond throwing money into the sagging welfare order, David

Peterson also co-opted former National Anti-Poverty Organization head and SARC Research Director, Patrick Johnston, hiring him as a social policy analyst and integrating him into his inner circle. But the premier, MPP for London Centre, nonetheless had little liking for the militant voice of the London Union of Unemployed Workers. In the summer of 1990 Peterson, with two years remaining in his governing mandate, called a snap election, thinking he could rout the Conservatives and the NDP. Things turned out differently, and as he took to the hustings to garner votes, Peterson was assailed by a motley crew of malcontents, among them public sector workers, teachers, environmentalists, doctors affiliated with the powerful Ontario Medical Association, and, of course, the poor and their emerging movement. In London, anti-poverty activists disrupted Peterson's hometown nomination meeting with the cry that would hound the premier across the province, "Down with the Poverty Premier!" Peterson was imprudent enough to yell back, "Get a job!" and television cameras captured the slight but wiry unemployed agitator, John Clarke, being roughly escorted from the hall by Liberal Party muscle.[26] By this time, discussions were underway about forming a new anti-poverty organization, what would eventually come to be the Ontario Coalition Against Poverty (OCAP). Toronto braced for the return/revenge of the dispossessed.

Marching to Mobilization: The Beginnings of OCAP

The 1930s-style hunger marches mobilized over the course of the late 1980s by the Unions of Unemployed Workers and other community activists crystallized growing discontents with the Peterson Liberals. With a taste for the theatrical, two hundred poor and jobless assembled at Queen's Park in April 1990 and dumped hundreds of pairs of worn out and smelly footwear on the legislative grounds, suggesting that the head of the provincial government needed to "walk a mile in their shoes." As Peterson announced an election for September 6, 1990, a province-wide network of activists coalesced to work against the re-election of the "Poverty Premier." Militants among the jobless and welfare recipients hounded Peterson across the province, confronting him on twenty-seven separate occasions. Their raucous extra-parliamentary protests helped turn a sleepy summer parliamentary contest, which was wrongly thought to be little more than a Peterson runaway, into an at times quite robust political debate, in which hostilities toward and anger at the complacency suffocating the poor surfaced in rowdy exchanges. Advocacy organizations of tenants, poor people, and the disabled banded together under the *nom de guerre* Adjust Ontario, campaigning around a five-point program for improving the lives of Ontario's dispossessed. The Ontario Coalition for Social Justice (OCSJ) united trade unionists and popular forces affiliated with a variety of social movements in a similar coalition that aimed its sights at the Mulroney Conservatives in power federally.[27]

This was the climate of agitation and activist challenge that spawned OCAP. Discussions among activists got off the ground early in 1990, culminating in the founding convention of the organization in November 1990. From the moment of its inception, OCAP was immersed in controversy and conflict. Two different strategic orientations wrestled for dominance on the floor of the anti-poverty coalition's first, defining, convention. At issue were opposing views on how best to challenge poverty and work on behalf of the dispossessed. The more conservative contingent, which may have represented as much as one-third of those gathered, wanted to form a "concerned citizen's" organization that would engage in respectable lobbying in the interests of the poor, welfare recipients, and the out-of-work. Others, including John Clarke, pushed for the creation of a militant body, based in poor communities and willing to take up "disruptive forms of collective action as the basic strategy of resisting poverty." Drawing on his experience in the London Union of Unemployed Workers, Clarke put forward views that would come to encapsulate OCAP's understanding of its approach, and that resonated with others on the activist left-wing of the anti-poverty movement. Poor people's organizations, these militants claimed, must always be "looking for the best way available to engage the enemies of the unemployed, to cause them pain, to hurt their cash flow or disrupt their workings, and in this way force concessions out of them." This was the direction eventually adopted at OCAP's founding conference, although it would, at first, operate out of a base that was restricted to Toronto's poor downtown core.[28]

The agitational essence of OCAP's approach was always paired with a commitment to achieve better conditions and treatment for the poor, squeezing improved benefits out of a welfare state understood to be inadequate and under attack by various ideological opponents, some of whom were among the most influential pillars of government. From its inception, OCAP adopted what was called a Direct Action Casework approach. In defending the rights of the poor, OCAP understood its role as something different than securing social work-like incremental improvements in the lives of the dispossessed. Rather, to be most successful OCAP had to sustain positive achievements of the kind that can be wrestled out of the state and transferred as material benefits to the poor. But this had to be done in combination with challenges to the state as a fundamental agency of capitalist exploitation and oppression, through militant actions and ongoing critique, never letting the poor forget that they are subjected to dispossession and that this process of subordination and the vast social inequalities it spawns and deepens daily privilege the few and preserve the profit system. The project, then, was to win benefits for the poor, but never in ways that would mask or obscure the origins and meaning of poverty as a social rather than an individual phenomenon. OCAP believed, and continues to believe, that militant action both secures such gains *and* demonstrates how the system as a whole produces the very dispossession that it then demands individuals somehow transcend in lives of acquisitive individualism. As Clarke notes:

> Very early in our history, we realized that our actions must demonstrate that concrete victories are possible. To simply campaign and protest on the broader issues would be of limited value if it could not be also shown that immediate and individual grievances can be tackled effectively.... All of the thousands of actions we have organized—delegations to welfare and disability offices, actions at immigration centres, pickets of abusive employers, direct challenges to landlords and housing authorities—have been about building a capacity for poor communities to defend their members and aim to instill in people a sense that resistance brings both meaningful results and leads to bigger possibilities.

In this dialectic of taking on the needs of the dispossessed both as a defensive stand for rights and entitlements and an offensive attack on the wider systems and structures responsible for socioeconomic inequality, OCAP necessarily found itself on an activist, Direct Action escalator.

The ground floor of casework led to higher floors of welfare administration, policy formulation and their shortcomings and, ultimately, "to conflict with the political institutions" of capitalist governance. Among those whose causes—individual and collective—were taken up by OCAP's Direct Action understanding of casework were welfare recipients, the homeless, those sustained by disability payments, immigrants, refugees, those about to be deported, targeted penny capitalists like "squeegee merchants," and victims of specific oppression such as trans people and sex trade workers.[29]

OCAP member Norman Feltes explained the process in a posthumously published 2002 article:

> We undertake every week the "cases" of individual poor persons and we see them through the hostile bureaucracies of the welfare system, public

housing, and the immigration process.... OCAP wins most of these cases (immigration and refugee cases, a federal jurisdiction, are the most difficult) and, apart from the good achieved for individual claimants, the good achieved for OCAP among its supporters in the poor is considerable. Our cases, not only the victories, build our movement. Except among the court cases, OCAP's tactics in these actions follow a flexible sequence of escalation of pressure on the agency. Individual cases have been settled at each step of the process. We may begin by contacting the agency by phone or letter and then by the client visiting the official accompanied by an OCAP representative. If denied a satisfactory settlement (or perhaps even serious consideration) at this stage, we may follow with a group visit, passive intimidation, and a veiled threat. Faced with further denial or delay, we may picket and, finally, we may conduct a mass invasion and disruption of the office. Somewhere in the process the case is usually settled in our favour.

Direct Action casework thus combined practical, material assistance to the poor, along with a pedagogy that militancy wins. Jonathan Greene, in his unpublished study of OCAP, has suggested that the Coalition wins upward of 90 percent of its welfare cases and perhaps as much as 70 percent of the more difficult immigration/asylum contests. Victories come because OCAP is willing to push the envelope, and top-heavy institutions have come to appreciate that tangling with the anti-poverty organization is more trouble than it is worth. Thus, often the "threat of an in-house demonstration is enough to get bureaucratic balls rolling miraculously smoothly, making stuck accounts suddenly unstuck."

A little satire might also get results. In 2002, OCAP fought for a nineteen-year-old nine-month pregnant woman who was struggling with welfare officers to secure needed financial support to which she was entitled, allowing her to purchase bottles, bibs, a comforter, and a crib for her baby, obviously due imminently. The welfare office, astoundingly, sent her to a doctor, requiring a physician's note confirming her pregnancy, before it would provide social assistance. The apparently cash-starved MD demanded payment on the spot before he would consider providing the necessary documentation. An OCAP caseworker intervened with a curt note: "I presume that this whole matter is a joke and that someone in your office is offering a satire on inflexible bureaucracy at its most ludicrous and damaging." Within hours the young mother-to-be had her start-up funds. Such successful arm-twisting not only secures the poor entitlements; it also wins recruits to OCAP. When a terminally ill cancer patient secured a new dental plate through OCAP picketing the Ontario Disability and Social Services' insurance provider, the client was "anxious to be involved in case work actions on a regular basis."[30]

OCAP's willingness to stretch understandings of casework and how it might be used to defend the interests of the dispossessed is perhaps most revealingly showcased in a late 1990s instance of coming forcefully to the aid of a small group of East Coast sex trade workers who had been pushed off their street corners by a film shoot that was fencing off parts of the downtown core along Jarvis and Sherbourne Streets. Local businesses were being compensated for the loss of commerce by the accommodating cinematic corporation funding the location filming. Valerie Scott of the Sex Workers Alliance of Toronto approached OCAP with the complaint that the women, who had demanded like treatment by those doling out cash for lost trade, had been laughed at rather than offered fair remuneration for their foregone earnings. OCAP responded, in alliance with sex trade workers and others, with two actions. At an outdoor filming, the anti-poverty body showed up en masse, outfitted with pots and pans, creating such a ruckus that filming proved impossible. The protest then moved indoors, as OCAP members and supporters marched on a Jarvis Street house being used for an indoor shoot, invading the premises and making such a nuisance of themselves that the cops had to be called in to remove the protesters. With their pockets empty the demonstrators retreated, and it looked like the women who had been shunted off their corners were destined to be stiffed by the corporate filmmakers. The next day, however, a courier turned up at OCAP's office, dropping off an envelope with $1600 in cash. John Clarke remembers meeting the four sex trade workers at the Kennedy Subway Station at the end of the Bloor-Danforth line and handing over the money, small compensation that was nonetheless undoubtedly much appreciated.[31] This was casework with an attitude, a pursuit of the seemingly impossible that nonetheless managed to demonstrate that fighting to win indeed yielded results.

OCAP's work was conducted without an elaborate bureaucracy. There was little in the way of any officialdom, and organizing was most often undertaken and sustained by the volunteer work of members-at-large who received no salaries, wages, or benefits. Many such OCAP members were themselves on some kind of social assistance, meaning that they knew intimately the plight and complaints of the poor. This allowed OCAP as an organization to mount some of its most successful campaigns. Members contributed decisively to discussions within the OCAP Executive and at the organization's general meetings and were instrumental in creating a consensus on how anti-poverty activism could move forward and sustain direct-action momentum. A large number of the tasks associated with OCAP's ongoing work, such as preparing food, doing outreach, distributing leaflets, postering, speaking at events, and preparing for and effectively carrying out casework assignments were taken on by the membership. Members designed propaganda material such as flyers and posters, maintained OCAP's website, which was a crucial means of communicating what the meaning of OCAP was and what it was doing, and helped write and physically put together OCAP publications. Members often helped out in the office during the day, answering the phone, responding to emails, and offering advice and support to people asking for help regarding welfare, housing, and immigration. And it was this activist, volunteer membership base that took risks and faced arrest during militant actions premised on a willingness to "fight to win."

Armed with this orientation, sustained by this volunteer cadre, and helped out by precarious trade union funding and the material support of a small corps of committed, employed leftists, OCAP marched into the 1990s defiant in its demand that the dispossessed deserved far more than what was on offer from contemporary capitalism. John Clarke was one of only two full-time OCAP workers, remunerated at the poverty-line level of roughly $20,000 a year, this duo of paid organizers elected annually. Establishing offices in the downtown Toronto core and a reputation that it could effectively go nose-to-nose with the grinding bureaucracies with which the poor routinely battled, OCAP slowly gained street credibility among the dispossessed, who found they could count on the coalition to be there when needed. OCAP was, in its beginnings, a movement in search of a constituency, for while its membership was overwhelmingly composed of the unemployed, the destitute, and the desperate, the dispossessed as a significant layer of Ontario's working class never joined the new organization en masse. Nonetheless, OCAP activists— who came from virtually all walks of life, including students and professionals, the unemployed and trade unionists—were firmly of the belief that their campaigns were empowering the poor, whether or not those who benefited were even aware of how their lives and life chances were being improved by the "fighting to win" strategy. With possibly two to three hundred members in the mid-1990s, OCAP could rally ten times that number if circumstances demanded, and soon it found itself, in Jack Layton's words, needing "larger and larger halls for its weekly meetings." As various struggles unfolded, OCAP was forced to "adapt to the changing political regimes in government," often having to confront governing powers with "progressive credentials that were openly or tacitly supported by many of the unions and social movements we might take as our allies." Within a capitalism wracked by periodic crises, OCAP found that the "prevailing agenda of reducing social entitlement and increasing the rate of exploitation of working people has remained in place under every political party and at every level of government."[32] But OCAP first got on the political map as an anti-capitalist voice of the dispossessed by taking on Mulroney and the federal Conservatives.

Mulroneyville, NDP Welfare Cheats, and Operation Desert Gypsy

A little more than eight months after its inauguration late in the autumn of 1990, OCAP captured public attention with bold bravado. The Conservative Party held a national policy conference at the Metro Toronto Convention Centre, scheduling the meetings from August 6–11, 1991. Mulroney and his free marketeers had gained notoriety in the late 1980s by signing a Free Trade Agreement with the United States. The trade deal generated national opposition and considerable discussion centred on how American corporate interests were demanding that Ottawa cut back on its "generous social programs," the better to level the playing field for capital to flow from the United States into Canada. By 1991, after years of the ruling federal Conservatives tearing away at the social safety net of the country's welfare provisioning, the unions, church groups, Aboriginal organizations, women's associations, and anti-poverty/homeless activists were more than ready to take a stand. OCSJ assumed the lead in mobilizing these constituencies to mount summer protests against the Mulroney marauders, planning a series of marches and

Mulroneyville residents with effigy of Mulroney, Toronto, August 1991.

OCAP Archives.

demonstrations for each day of the Conservative conference. Perhaps the most news-catching of the protest statements was OCAP's "Mulroneyville," the making of a tent city at the foot of the CN Tower symbolizing the plight of the poor and homeless affected by the federal government's reductions and eliminations of social programs. Modelled on the Hoovervilles and Bennettburghs of the Great Depression, Mulroneyville was to be a hobo village that, unlike its 1930 counterparts, was not located on the margins of the metropolis but directly in its visible centre, where it could not be ignored by either Tory delegates or the media.

OCAP gained pre-convention press by looking after conventional business. It sought and received permission from the Metro Neighbourhood Services Committee to set up the tent village. OCAP also had to negotiate with the powerful tenant, CN, which demanded extra security in the form of two off-duty police officers whose moonlighting wages totalled $2,200. OCAP agreed to put down a $4,000 security deposit, as well as providing portable washrooms and lighting. In spite of opposition at city hall, Mulroneyville went ahead, albeit in a scaled down way: the social services committee provided propane barbecues but limited the tents to twelve in number and the total population of the makeshift city to twenty-four overnight residents. With a street grid layout consisting of Cut Back Avenue, Pogey Alley, and Layoff Lane, Mulroneyville also boasted a mock cemetery, with tombstones recording the names of factories closed down across Canada because of the Free Trade Agreement and the numbers of jobs lost as a consequence. A makeshift post office encouraged people to send letters to Ottawa demanding Mulroney's removal from office. David Kidd of Central Neighbourhood House organized food for Mulroneyville, and several agencies offering services to the poor of Toronto's downtown core provided meals throughout the day. For six days and nights anti-poverty activists and a small exodus of people fleeing the streets and day shelters camped out in Toronto's most talked-about tent city.

As Tory Convention delegates passed by and through Mulroneyville on their way to the Metro Toronto Convention Centre, they got an earful of the diatribes of the poor, as well as actually laying eyes on homeless individuals. One Conservative nonetheless described the tent city as "a $3 protest," and others were quick to insist that the residents of Mulroneyville were professional agitators, paid to sleep in the small tents. *Toronto Star* writer Jane Armstrong couldn't quite decide whether the tent city protest was a flop or a "brilliant demonstration against seven years of federal cutbacks," but she recognized how effectively Mulroneyville got under the Tories' skin, stealing national headlines and gaining countrywide recognition. The *Calgary Sun* responded to Tory walks down Cut Back Avenue with a denunciation of the media's culpability in raising Mulroneyville to national news and being duped by OCAP. Red-baiting John Clarke and David Kidd, the *Sun* journalist painted them as Communists and the architects of Mulroneyville as interested in nothing so much as "the total destruction of Canada and free democratic nations."[33]

If the Tories were targeted, the provincial NDP was not let off the hook, nor did it deserve favourable treatment. OCAP had emerged out of anti-poverty activism aimed at David Peterson in the 1990 election. It took a while for the shock to die down that the NDP had come to power for the first time in Ontario, and, indeed, for the first time anywhere in Canada east of Manitoba. Bob Rae's New Democrats, with nineteen seats in the legislature in the summer of 1990, elected seventy-four candidates as MPPs in September, besting the Liberals (thirty-six) and the Conservatives (twenty) by a long shot. OCAP wasted little time marching on Queen's Park to demand that the NDP "Keep the Promise on Poverty," although this, as we have seen, was not to come to pass. As the social democrats met in a party convention, OCAP set up a soup kitchen to symbolize the persistence of poverty.[34]

By 1992, however, those at the NDP helm suddenly realized that with the economy paralyzed and mass unemployment throwing society off-balance, their precarious government had been treading water in increasingly troubled seas for too long. A kind of panic overtook Rae and his inner circle. As battles raged inside the governing social democratic party, with left-wing advocates of maintaining social assistance like Marilyn Churley often reduced to tears, the writing on the welfare wall was becoming increasingly strident. In the end, having gutted the public sector unions with a so-called Social Contract that essentially abrogated collective agreements, voiding negotiated wage increases, institutionalizing unpaid "Rae Days" of workers' leave, and allowing the reopening of any wage contracts deemed necessary in the government's bid to reduce its compensation obligations by $2 billion, the NDP had no stomach for revving up its state engine in a discordant war against the poor.[35] But the sound of a potential marauding motor was threatening enough.

Rae, for instance, took Community and Social Services Minister Tony Silipo's December 1993 statement that with respect to Ottawa's shrinking contribution to Ontario's growing social assistance bill, it was going to be necessary to "look at all options," one better. In March 1994, Rae named welfare rates as one of the areas the NDP was considering in terms of necessary economizing; he made even more threatening noises around "welfare dependency" and the possibility that some of those in the province on social assistance would have to enrol in training programs that would facilitate getting them off public support. Ontario's social assistance programs were the "most generous" in Canada, Rae added, with a sense that this was something that could not last. Alongside such public pronouncements, Silipo was promising to get tough on "welfare cheats," and newspaper headlines proclaimed loudly that the province was getting set to "TARGET WELFARE FRAUD CASES," at a $50 million saving. Rae's government was proposing to lay out $20 million to hire 270 investigators who would work in municipalities that would, again, be funded to weed out those working the system abusively. When Silipo tried to promote the NDP's plan to crackdown on "welfare cheats" at a Town Hall meeting in Toronto on April 19, 1994, OCAP and other anti-poverty groups came out in force to give him a dissident's welcome. The Ontario Cabinet Minister was booed every time he tried to get a word out, and demonstrators climbed onto the stage to prevent him from speaking. Eventually, after ten minutes of enforced silence, Silipo tired of the protest and "turned on his heels and left," giving the boisterous crowd a blessing of sorts. "Have a nice meeting," he muttered in disgust, before climbing into a waiting limousine.[36]

Soon the NDP would not be going to such meetings as members of the government, the 1995 defeat to Mike Harris and the Tories just around the corner. Federally, Brian Mulroney was already gone and the Liberals, headed by Jean Chrétien, were back in power in Ottawa, having won a majority government in 1993. But the 1990s was a different era. Like Mulroney before him, Chrétien had his restraint sights set on the poor. He told a Metro Toronto Board meeting in early 1994 that his government was intent on "reinventing social programs," but his inventiveness took a rather tired course. To an applauding audience, he preached the now conventional doctrine of "welfare dependency," bemoaning that "it is unacceptable that people refuse to work when there is work available.... Too many people can't quit welfare or social assistance because there are too many disincentives." Chrétien's Minister of Employment and Immigration, Lloyd Axworthy, told a student audience that the days of bumming around on social assistance after leaving school were over. Unemployment insurance rates, cut previously by the federal Tories in 1992, were scheduled to be hacked again in July 1994. Chrétien and Axworthy proposed $5.5 billion in cuts over three years, as well as requiring longer work periods before collection of benefits would be allowed and shortening the insured period. Amid riotous confrontations in New Brunswick and Quebec, in which Chrétien was rushed into buildings by protective security guards and burned in effigy by angry crowds, the Liberals continued down the road of welfare restructuring. Secretary of State Sergio Marchi announced that he would be working with the provinces and his colleagues in other federal ministries to crack down on immigrants and

320   **TORONTO'S POOR**

refugee claimants who were defrauding the welfare system. Among the worst abusers, Marchi claimed, were Somalis, many of them residents of Toronto. This new welfare policing initiative was indelicately code-named with the racist appellation "Operation Desert Gypsy." Buttressing this package of poor-bashing was the Liberal Finance Minister, Paul Martin, who promised "Major, major cuts which are going to affect every sector of our society.... We have told the provinces that they have two years in which to complete with us the end of this process. And that at the end of the two years we will be taking massive amounts of money out of the federal-provincial structure." Several months later, Axworthy announced that a parliamentary standing committee was about to traverse Canada to consult with various citizen's groups and interested parties about the state of the country's social programs and the government's proposals for reforming them. He urged anti-poverty organizations and trade unions not to withdraw from the process, but to participate and "respect the pressures that the country is under fiscally." Before this committee began its tour, however, an eighty-nine-page Cabinet discussion paper was leaked to the press. Titled *Improving Social Security in Canada,* the document indicated that the federal government had already determined that it was going to freeze transfer payments to the provinces for social assistance programs, regardless of what the peripatetic committee heard and determined. The decision had been made, for instance, to cut a further $3 billion from the Unemployment Insurance (UI) plan beginning in 1997.[37]

Anti-poverty activists in Quebec who had mobilized in 1993–94 to defend the poor against provincial cutbacks and imposed workfare turned their attention to the Chrétien Liberals and their new austerity order. The militant Comité des sans emploi (CSE) mobilized the unemployed in the southeast sector of downtown Montreal, with Richard St. Pierre, a housing worker in the Jeanne-Mance projects, playing a leading role. In the summer of 1994, la Coalition pour la survie des programmes sociaux formed, composed of trade unions and various organizations that worked with the jobless and relief recipients. In spite of fears that its direct action tactics would culminate in violence, the CSE was asked to join the larger, labour-led coalition, a condition being that if the CSE was going to consider utilizing direct action it first meet with the larger group, allowing a collective position to be taken. CSE members concurred.

For both the Coalition and the CSE, the main issue in the summer of 1994 was Axworthy's travelling parliamentary commission. Thoroughly discredited at this point, the commission was nonetheless scheduled to meet in Montreal in December 1994 at the Hotel Du Parc, where it would hear deputations from unions and organizations of the poor. Both the Coalition and the CSE agreed to boycott the proceedings, to encourage all other groups and unions to do likewise, and to hold a direct action demonstration as Axworthy and other parliamentarians convened their Montreal hearings. OCAP was trying to build alliances with a number of Quebec groups in the hopes of organizing protests around the Axworthy Commission, and St. Pierre and John Clarke crossed paths in a meeting in an Ottawa bar. They began working together, travelled to Detroit, Michigan, where there were the beginnings of a movement to oppose welfare restructuring and were generally in agreement about the necessity of a strategy of militant fight-back on the part of the dispossessed. But for all that Clarke and St. Pierre hit it off, there remained many in the Montreal unemployed movement who wanted little to do with OCAP and thought it best to go it alone in their struggle against Chrétien, Axworthy, and the attack on UI.[38]

Axworthy's travelling commission checked into Toronto's Royal York Hotel on November 22, 1994. A protest was organized by "representatives from labour, women, students, and anti-poverty groups." As the parliamentary commission heard testimony inside, three hundred demonstrators, OCAP supporters among them, heard speeches of denunciation outside the posh, establishment hotel. John Clarke addressed the crowd last. Aroused by Clarke's oratory and moved by his concluding invitation to join him in taking their resentments inside, the crowd stormed the doors of the Royal York. Finding their way to the ballroom where Axworthy was presiding over the hearings into unemployment and social programs, Clarke and the contingent of protesters disrupted the proceedings for thirty minutes, with people chanting "Shame, Shame," and "Fight Back!" Bullhorn in hand, Clarke faced those who had made their way to provide briefs and testimonials to Axworthy and his assembled parliamentarians. "We are perfectly aware this consultation process is flawed," they said as the OCAP spokesperson bellowed in response: "This is a done deal to cut billions from social programs.... And we are here to tell you that the people of this country are mobilizing to fight you every step of the way."[39]

As *Toronto Star* journalist Rosie DiManno was ranting against Clarke, OCAP, and the tiresome activists, whom she depicted as acting "rudely and crudely on our behalf," screaming and spitting and snarling and sneering, the protest received extensive coverage on French television via CBC and was also featured on Radio-Canada. St. Pierre later recalled seeing "everything that happened in Toronto" and being exhilarated by "a very angry demonstration" against the cuts. With Axworthy's commission scheduled to arrive in Montreal in a matter of days, militants gathered around an anarchist collective in which anti-poverty activist and St. Pierre friend Alexandre Popovic was a member, and started talking about disrupting the hearings. Rumours floated about that others, including a radical section of the Montreal student movement, were intent on crashing the Hotel Du Parc and disrupting the proceedings. The militant CSE was in favour of such an action but felt committed not to violate its agreement with the larger Coalition to confine its direct action to the outside of the hotel. Radicals thus agreed to postpone any storming of the proceedings until after the main demonstration was over. The day before Axworthy's arrival in Montreal, the CSE "evicted" MP Elana Bakopanos from her office, protesting the federal government's cuts to social programs. Piling the office furniture outside in the rain, one hundred militants marched down St. Denis Street, blocking traffic for several hours before they burned Axworthy in effigy. It was a preface to the next day's activities.[40]

Between one and two thousand gathered outside the hotel. OCAP members and supporters joined the CSE. Small groups of protesters approached St. Pierre and the CSE to let it be known they were going to storm the hotel after the public demonstration wound down. Tension rippled through the crowd as mainstream elements worried about getting caught up in the rumoured violence. As people filed away, finding their seats on buses about to depart, Popovic announced on a bullhorn, "The demonstration is finished but we are continuing." Marshals from the main rally worked with private hotel security forces and Montreal police to try to stop the crowd from entering the hotel and confronting Axworthy, but it was to no avail. Not even knowing where Axworthy was, the crowd surged upstairs before those coming up the rear realized that the proceedings were being held in the basement. Eventually, 150 people poured into the hearing, overturning tables, sending microphones, coffee mugs, and glasses of water flying, with MPs scrambling to get out of the line of fire. One small woman, about to give her presentation on behalf of Solidarité Populaire Québec, was approached by members of the media and the large, mainstream Coalition and asked to condemn the actions of the militants who broke up the meeting. She refused to do so. "I am afraid there are people who have come to the conclusion that the dice are loaded against the poor in the Axworthy reform programs," Madeleine Parent told the *Montreal Gazette* politely and knowingly. For his sins, St. Pierre was given a ten-day jail sentence for overturning a table inside the Hotel Du Parc ballroom and prohibited from participating in any public demonstrations. As the CSE was getting phone calls and letters from anti-poverty groups across Canada supporting and praising its militant stand, certain mainstream types began typecasting the group, treating it as something of a pariah. St. Pierre and the Comité des sans emploi were given the heave-ho from the moderate Coalition, even though the militant protest was being heralded as an "electrifying" response to Axworthy's public relations scam.[41]

Protests followed the Axworthy Commission across Canada, but none had the intensity, anger, or news coverage of the actions in Montreal and Toronto. In 1996, with the Axworthy hearings report presented to the federal Liberal government, the Chrétien government made good on its restructuring commitments. The Canada Assistance Plan (CAP) was terminated, replaced by the Canada Health and Social Transfer Plan. Provinces and territories, now given a block grant for health, education, and welfare, were forced to apportion resources as they saw fit. No longer were provincial governments required to provide social assistance to all of those in need. Regional states could now determine the eligibility requirements for those on welfare, just as they could impose "work tests." This gave rise to a rash of provincial cuts to health, education, and welfare programs; the hounds of state surveillance of the poor were unleashed. If politicians of the right, like Alberta's Ralph Klein, seemed to be champing at the bit to strike out at the dispossessed, it was also true that social democrats in power became avid poor-bashers. Well before the type was set on the Axworthy report, for instance, British Columbia's NDP premier, Mike Harcourt, was on the trail of the much-maligned "welfare cheat." Harcourt appointed a special Social Services Minister to "crack down on what [he] called 'welfare cheats and deadbeats.... We want to catch these varmints'."[42] In Ontario, as OCAP came up against the Mike Harris Conservative "Common Sense Revolution," things went from bad to worse in the mid-1990s.

Revolution from Above, against Those Below: The Poor Fight Back

When it came to the Ontario government's plans to thin out the relief rolls by hitting hard at so-called welfare fraud, Bob Rae's biggest fan was a Trudeau-hating former teacher turned on by the promise of tax cuts and repulsed by the soaring provincial deficit, which reached the unheard of sum of $11 billion in the early 1990s. Mike Harris responded to the NDP's proposed hiring of hundreds of investigators to clamp down on social assistance fraud with rare words of endorsement: "If it truly deals with welfare reform, with removing from the rolls those who are ripping us off, those who are staying home and doing nothing because they want to do nothing," Harris huffed, "then that will be good enough for me."[43] With Michael Deane Harris heading the provincial Tories, once the proud leaders of pace-setting Ontario in the 1960s days of John Robarts but reduced to a mere seventeen seats in the legislature in the late 1980s, central Canadian Conservatives took a hard turn to the right. Harris, destined to lead the Tories and their "Common Sense Revolution" to a decisive June 1995 electoral victory in which the Conservative seat count more than quadrupled from twenty to eighty-two, while the NDP collapsed from

seventy-four to seventeen seats, had his eye on the ostensibly pampered poor from the moment he stepped into the Legislature as premier.

Individual adults on welfare were welcomed to life under the Harris Tories with income reductions from $663 to $520, which, after paying for rent, left little more than $100 to live on for the month. Single mothers were especially hard hit, being forced off the Family Benefits Act (FBA) and eventually into Ontario Works, introduced in 1997 as a key legislative plank in Harris's workfare regime. As the National Child Benefit was clawed back, it only worsened a bad situation for women and children. Central to what constituted an emerging crisis, however, was the dismantling of the social housing system, which, once gutted by the Tories cancelling the construction of affordable housing in Ontario, was downloaded onto increasingly impoverished municipalities. All told, the Tories were gouging almost $2 billion out of their budgeted social assistance to welfare, child care, and social housing.[44]

OCAP wasted no time getting into the fray. Elected in June 1995, Harris faced OCAP protests in July. On Saturday, July 29, 1995, two thousand people marched on Queen's Park, some of them from communities outside of Toronto. John Clarke addressed the crowd, laying the groundwork for later actions. If the poor were to be attacked, then they must do their best to make the province ungovernable. "We have to be prepared to take on the authorities," Clarke argued, adding for good

OCAP demonstration leaving Regent Park for Rosedale, August 23, 1995.

OCAP Archives.

measure, "and go to jail if necessary." The crowd dispersed, pledging to return when the Legislature was in session in September. OCAP supporters are fond of saying that while unionized workers can show their strength and make their demands by "not being where their employer wants them to be, ... the poor can only have power by being where they're not supposed to be." In the summer of 1995, that was in one of Toronto's toniest of neighbourhoods, Rosedale. Less than a month after OCAP's first anti-Tory Queen's Park mobilization, it rallied between eight hundred and one thousand residents of the Regent Park housing project to march a short distance north where the dispossessed got to see, many of them for the first time, the true wages of capitalist sin. Amid the mansions of Rosedale, OCAP raised the indelicate reality that if social assistance rates were to be cut and taxes for the rich scaled back, this constituted nothing more than a massive income transfer, from the poor to the rich, that amounted to approximately $1 million taken from Regent Park and other residents of Toronto's poor downtown core and placed directly in the pockets of wealthy homeowners in posh districts. Later, in the fall, OCAP returned to Rosedale on Halloween, conducting a "trick or treat" house-to-house visit in which the dispossessed conducted, in Clarke's words, "a very concrete demand for our money back." One of the stops on the first OCAP Rosedale tour was the house of Lieutenant-Governor Hal Jackman, scheduled to read the Speech from the Throne as the Ontario Legislature reconvened in September 1995.[45]

TORONTO'S POOR

This time, OCAP was not alone. Between five and seven thousand people assembled in September 1995 to take issue with the Tories. Organized by the labour movement of Toronto and North York, working in conjunction with the "Embarrass Harris" campaign, the demonstration was supported by unions, Native people's organizations, feminists, environmentalists, and anti-poverty groups, OCAP prominent among them. Clarke was one of the rally's featured speakers, and he struck a chord of militancy. "This government is going to become a government behind sandbags," he predicted, "They will be a group of people who can't go out on the street without being confronted and being silenced by us." Clarke's rousing words were met with cheers of approval and, with other speeches continuing, some in the crowd, OCAP members no doubt among them, began to dismantle the police barricades separating the entry-way to the legislature and protesters. Militants in the crowd swarmed the steps leading to the two-dozen police guarding Harris and his cronies. Beaten back by police batons and pepper spray, the demonstrators failed to gain entry to the legislature. A standoff resulted as the forces of the larger rally melted away; an hour later the police advanced on the two hundred remaining dissenters, pushing them off the steps and dispersing what was left of the crowd.[46]

Months later, a February 1996 protest of cuts to education saw anti-poverty and student groups come together in a militant march that proceeded under the banner, "Education is a Right!" Two hundred protesters dismantled barricades, stormed the legislature's doors, and fought their way into the lobby of the provincial parliament buildings. There, according to outraged reports in the press, they "smashed three-century old windows, severely damaged the white oak doors, and ... vandalized the walls, overturned furniture, damaged equipment and stole items from desks," to the tune of $20,000 in damages. Two university and two high school students were slapped with a number of charges, including a century-old archaic and draconian criminal offence of "intimidating the legislature." If convicted, the students, aged eighteen to twenty-four, faced up to fourteen years in jail. Cautious student organizations at the centre of the educational rally pointed the finger at OCAP and other anti-poverty organizations, as well as at labour militants, for hijacking the demonstration and turning it into an act of "government bashing." Yet while OCAP did endorse the rally and members were present at the protest, the group played little, if any, role in the physical damage that drew outrage in some quarters and barred the vindictive teeth of the state. Crown Counsel later stayed the charges of government intimidation. Over the next ten months, OCAP joined with labour-organized protest against the Harris Tories. Queen's Park was turned into a battleground pitting striking trade unions like the Ontario Public Service

Employees Union (OPSEU) and labour mobilizations like the ostensibly General Strike–promoting Days of Action against the government and the riot squad of the Ontario Provincial Police (OPP), whose unenviable task it was to "protect" the legislature and its ruling Common Sense revolutionaries. The most violent clash involved OPSEU's March 18, 1996, picket protest, which saw the OPP riot police themselves run amuck, their excessive and undisciplined use of force prompting further protests, denunciations from trade union officials, and a public inquiry. The largest protest, involving well over 100,000 people (with estimates reaching as high as 250,000), took place on October 26, 1996, as the Toronto Day of Action concentrated a province-wide wave of resistance to the Harris government's policies into a singular mass rally of unrivalled size.[47]

OCAP's presence in the growing anti-Harris mobilization was securing it a reputation as a militant and increasingly radical voice on the left. If these large demonstrations gave OCAP a particular kind of forum, in which it could publicly assail the ways in which the dispossessed were being subjected to vicious attack, smaller, often theatrical actions also effectively highlighted just what the poor were up against in 1990s Ontario.

At this time, Metro Council established a consortium of companies to pioneer a new Client Identification and Benefits System (CIBS), one component of which was the "biometric scanning," or fingerprinting, of those on social assistance. Over the next two years, the City of Toronto worked with Royal Bank, Unysis, and Great-West Life to develop CIBS which, it was claimed, would "ensure the integrity of the social assistance program," saving upward of $30 million. On May 13, 1996, the Metro Council's plans to introduce fingerprinting of Toronto's 105,000 welfare recipients came to a head at a Human Services Committee meeting. Dozens of OCAP members were in attendance. A forty-one-year-old single mother, Maria Ingrosso-Cox, argued, "If this government was to suggest fingerprinting only Black Canadians, the Jewish community, Aboriginals, homosexuals, Catholics or any other sector of society, it would not be tolerated." But stigmatizing and discriminating against the poor was now part of mainstream political fare, and fingerprinting, with its connotations of criminalization, was apparently acceptable. OCAP member Gaétan Héroux addressed the Committee, explaining why the poor were so vehement in their opposition to fingerprinting. Allocated five minutes, Héroux spoke for three. He then announced that in the remaining time available to himself and his OCAP colleagues, who had come to the council chambers armed with ink pads and paper, city councillors and civic officials would themselves be fingerprinted. In the mêlée that followed, an enraged Councillor Gordon Chong, fond of relating how he and his mother had been on social assistance when they first came to Canada, assailed Héroux, who was incredulous that Chong insisted that he would have no problem with his mother being fingerprinted. TV cameras captured an angry Chong telling Héroux to "fuck off." Kelly O'Sullivan, an OCAP member, managed to secure the fingerprints of Heather McVicar, General Manager of Toronto's Social Services Division. A month later, Metro Council voted twenty-two to eight to move forward with its fingerprinting program. "The choice is clear, it's scan or scam," argued Norm Kelly, neoliberal councillor and former chair of the History Department at the finishing school for Toronto's rich and famous, Upper Canada College. A Parkdale Community Legal Services memo that informed the city that the clinic would be advising clients of their right to refuse fingerprinting prompted a Metro Council motion to request that the Province of Ontario "amend welfare regulations to make biometric identification mandatory." A score of OCAP members watched the proceedings from the council gallery. They rose on occasion to hold up a placard of a clenched hand, middle finger extended, reading "SCAN THIS." All indications were that the CIBS plan was on its way to implementation when Royal Bank pulled the plug on its involvement, citing an inability to come to "suitable financial terms." Unable to reconstruct adequate corporate partnerships, Toronto gave up this particular ghost equivalent of the Scarlet Letter, abandoning biometric scanning in 1999.[48]

If it wasn't the finger, it was the fish. A few days after the Tories chopped welfare rates by 21.6 percent in 1995, the misnamed Minister of Community and Social Services, David Tsubouchi, put his well-heeled foot in his mouth. Facing questions in the legislature about how welfare recipients would be adversely affected by the cuts, Tsubouchi suggested that if those on assistance were feeling the pinch they could always buy cheap canned tuna at 69 cents a tin or, alternatively, if the price was higher they could bargain with shopkeepers, especially if the product packaging seemed to be a little the worse for wear. Tsubouchi, who had undoubtedly never haggled with a supermarket clerk in his life, nonetheless seemed confident that bargains could be secured, if only the poor took the proper initiative. "Even if it's not priced at 69 cents," the MPP claimed, referring to a dented can of tuna, "quite often you can make a deal to get it for 69 cents."[49]

A month later, on Saturday, November 4, 1995, fifty OCAP members, many of them welfare recipients, turned up to shop for groceries at a Yorkville Loblaws supermarket. Each one of them carried a 21.6 percent coupon adorned with Tsubouchi's image. Having filled their carts, the OCAP shoppers lined up at the registers and, when payment was due, presented their coupons. Befuddled and perhaps bemused cashiers were forced to call for the manager who, after refusing to bargain with the crowd, insisting that prices were firm and had been established by head office, called the police. Chaos reigned for over an hour, and it took thirteen police and a paddy wagon to cart away five OCAP demonstrators who insisted on their Tsubouchi-given right to haggle. Charges against the five accused were later dropped as the Crown faced an OCAP lawyer, Peter Rosenthal, prepared to subpoena Tsubouchi as a witness and argue that those before the courts were only following instructions of the government's own minister.[50]

Once again indicating that it was willing to step outside the box of constrained, conventional protest, OCAP turned up on Tsubouchi's Markham doorstep on Saturday, May 25, 1996. Two busloads of OCAPers took a drive to the affluent suburb, connecting up with York Region anti-poverty activists and marching on Tsubouchi's home to protest ongoing cuts to social assistance and mandatory workfare programs. The protest ran into a well-armed blue wall of fifty OPP and York Regional Police Force officers surrounding the minister's home. Targeting individuals within the government and demonstrating at their homes was unpopular with both trade unions and mainstream anti-poverty organizations, which either threatened to withdraw financial support from OCAP or issued proclamations of pique. "Personally, I think picketing someone's house is in bad taste," declared the Chair of the York Region Child and Poverty Action Group, Fitz Matheson, adding that such actions were "distasteful."[51]

Homelessness and the Freezing Deaths Inquest, 1995–1996

Distasteful, for OCAP, wasn't the half of it in terms of the worsening situation of Toronto's dispossessed. Homelessness was arguably the most acute expression of a growing crisis that by late 1995 had seen the numbers of men and women living on Toronto's streets increase by 43 percent in nine months. City-run hostels were "filled to busting these days," said Seaton House shift supervisor Byron Godfrey in October 1995. With men sleeping on the floor, conditions deteriorated rapidly in the overcrowded emergency shelters. With all forty-five of the city's homeless refuges filled to capacity, Toronto Councillor Dennis Fotinos, chair of the municipal Human Services Committee, commented that the demand for hostel beds was greater than at any time since the Great Depression. Toronto's Out of the Cold program, initiated every November by the city's churches and synagogues, faced unprecedented pressures, with the program's founder, Sister Susan, reporting worriedly to the press, "I can tell you everything has tripled, the amount of suffering is immense." As four homeless men—Brent Simms, Eugene Upper, Mirsalah Kompani, and Irwin

Anderson—died on the frigid streets in January–February 1996, the crisis of homelessness reached what political scientist Jonathan Greene has called "a transformative moment," both for the poor and for OCAP. Metro Council approved a $600,000 crisis fund to address the growing army of the dispossessed who, unable to secure beds in shelters, were living in alleyways and parks, begging on the streets during the day and early evening. But it seemed but a drop in a material bucket demanding so much more.

Anti-poverty activists pressured civic authorities to force the military to allow its buildings to be used to house the homeless, while community-based social workers demanded an expansion of funded services for the poor. The Canadian Armed Forces eventually opened the doors of the Moss Park Armoury, volunteers providing the homeless with cots, food, shower facilities, and medical attention, all on a "no questions asked" basis. Anti-poverty organizations and Councillors Olivia Chow and Jack Layton pressed for an inquest into the deaths of the homeless, which was scheduled by the City Coroner for June 1996. Twenty-eight social agencies and organizations, including OCAP, formed the Toronto Coalition Against Homelessness (TCAH), which included workers from various drop-in centres, community health clinics, and legal aid offices in the city's downtown core, such as Gaétan Héroux. Leading TCAH figures, later to play important roles in the inquest, were Beric German, now an AIDS outreach worker, and Cathy Crowe, a street nurse, both of whom would later go on to help found the Toronto Disaster Relief Committee

(TDRC). OCAP had no quarrel with the inquest demand, but it also saw the need for an immediate protest and led a rowdy storming of Seaton House, condemning conditions at the hostel and attacking the welfare-slashing destructiveness of the Tory "Common Sense Revolution." Meanwhile, TCAH selected University of Toronto mathematician and lawyer Peter Rosenthal to represent it at the inquest, although the Committee would ultimately be denied standing. A feisty, rough and tumble advocate, Rosenthal was well known on the left for his willingness to battle against powerful forces and conventional wisdom in the name of social justice.[52]

TCAH prefaced the formal inquest with a public inquiry panel at Toronto's All Saints Church on May 25, 1996. The six panellists included NDP MPP Peter Tabuns; actor Sarah Polley; Steve Lane, a recipient of Ontario social assistance who had been associated with the Toronto Union of Unemployed Workers in the 1980s, later joining OCAP, and subsequently serving as part of the group's Executive for a number of years; and journalist Michael Valpy. Roughly 250 attended the event. Testimony provided by the homeless, by advocates of the poor, and by friends and supporters of the dispossessed was harrowing, indicative, in the words of Fred Martin of the Good Shepherd Mission, "of a seriously troubled society." In a formal report, the panellists concluded that they were "overwhelmed by the stories of suffering and death ... heard during ... the day," and Valpy later wrote in the *Globe and Mail* of how the Tory provincial government cuts to welfare "hit Toronto's poor—and particularly its homeless—like a bomb." He relayed reports of the horrendous conditions in a hostel system clearly overextended and incapacitated, where assaults, fear of disease, robbery of personal possessions, the impossibility of sleep, and the presence of seriously disturbed people in need of specialized care made emergency shelters dangerous environments. Some of the homeless responded to this situation rationally, choosing not so much to sleep on the streets as to shun environments where they might well be even less safe for a night than they would be in a park.[53]

The inquest, which was presided over by Dr. Murray Naiburg, the same coroner who had conducted the inquiry into the death of Drina Joubert more than a decade earlier in February 1986, exposed the shift in political climates that a brief ten years had witnessed. While the coroner's jury, as it had in Joubert's inquest, recognized the central place of homelessness in causing the deaths of Messrs. Upper, Kompani, and Anderson and recommended increased government support of programs that would enhance the living conditions and life chances of the dispossessed, the inquest itself was often indicative of the 1990s aggressiveness of all arms of the state in flexing the muscles of poor-bashing. Naiburg did his best to stifle discussion, ruling that he did not want a "roving inquiry" into the issues facing the homeless, including, ironically, housing. Beric German, for instance, had been a pivotal "expert witness" at the Joubert inquest in 1986, but in 1996 Naiburg vetoed any "testimony according to the Gospel of St. Germain," a nasty put-down of the anti-poverty activist. As the lengthy, twenty-three-day hearings were colloquially referred to as "the housing inquest" or the "Freezing Deaths Inquest," Naiburg shut down witness after witness who tried to relate the deaths of the homeless men to the need for more affordable housing. The one exception, pushed by TCAH, was getting Melvin Tipping, a friend of Eugene Upper, a veteran of living on Toronto's streets, recognized as an expert witness on homelessness. Most of the testimony that was allowed, however, was of the kind that stressed that as the men succumbed to exposure, hostel beds were available for the taking; that hostel users like Eugene Upper and Irwin Anderson, a sixty-three-year-old Aboriginal man, "refused help" from those "trying to get them into a positive lifestyle." When an Aboriginal community worker who had known Anderson appealed to testify about how the First Nations man had lost his apartment after declining to pay rent once threatened with eviction, Naiburg again refused to hear the evidence, saying in the absence of the jury, "Irwin Anderson was the author of his own misfortune." In the case of Mirsalah Kompani, an Iranian landed immigrant in Canada since 1991 who had earned an engineering degree in the United States, key testimony was provided by Dr. Stephen Stoki, a Newmarket physician who had treated the homeless man earlier in the 1990s. Stoki recalled contacting immigration officials because he was of the opinion that Kompani was in the country illegally and was abusing the welfare system. Neither Kompani's sister nor brother appeared at the hearings, not knowing until days after the inquest that their sibling had died in a makeshift lean-to under the Gardiner Expressway months before, his shoes tucked under his arms, hands frozen to his face. An autopsy was not possible for several days until the body thawed, it being described by the chief coroner as "a solid block of ice." Having identified the body, and through medical records found a physician willing to offer testimony, could not the authorities have located Kompani's next of kin?[54]

Such questions were not priorities for Naiburg, who no doubt suffered through Peter Rosenthal's five-hour summation to the jury. Rosenthal stated the case for the six social agencies granted the right to appear before the inquest by Naiburg, whose first major ruling was to deny the Toronto Coalition Against Homelessness, the lawyer's main client, legal standing. TCAH nonetheless played an important role at the inquest, mobilizing the poor to be in attendance at the hearings, filling the courtroom, which made it clear to the jurors that homeless people were not abstractions and that they cared about the outbreak of deaths on Toronto's streets. The committee served lunch to the homeless who came to the inquest, providing sidewalk meals on a daily basis. Rosenthal appealed to the jurors to understand that homelessness, rather than individual failings, had caused the deaths of Eugene Upper, Irwin Anderson, and Mirsalah Kompani. What Rosenthal wanted to come out of the inquest was increased social assistance for homeless people with mental health and alcohol problems; government commitment to provide affordable housing; resolution of the inhumane conditions at city hostels; the creation of an office to address complaints of homeless men and women dependent on social assistance; increased funding for drop-in centres, hostels, outreach programs, and detox centres; and the creation of a program of "wet hostels," where the homeless could drink, in moderation, so they would not be shut out of refuge simply because they were alcohol dependent.

Naiburg was having none of it. He clearly wanted no repeat of the Joubert inquest. He asked the jurors to find that the cause of the men's deaths had nothing to do with homelessness. "Their altered mental states or mental illness were the reasons they died," he pronounced confidently, adding: "Adequate housing is of great concern to us all, but this inquest is not the place to address it." In this positioning, Naiburg was reiterating positions put forward during the hearings by Mary Ellen Hurman, legal counsel for the Coroner's Office. She suggested in her summation that Kompani had great survival skills because he had survived on the streets of Toronto for several years. A juror shouted in response, "But he's dead!"[55]

This punctuation to the proceedings summarized, in many ways, the disjuncture between the "official" and the "popular" representation of what was at stake in the deaths of homeless men. Jurors rejected the Coroner's Office insistence that housing and social assistance levels were irrelevant, and instead largely followed Rosenthal's lead in recommending widespread changes to how the homeless were treated. Prefacing a long list of fifty-four recommendations, the jurors acknowledged that many factors may well have contributed to the deaths of Eugene Upper, Irwin Anderson, and Mirsalah Kompani, but their immediate concern was to urge "all levels of government and society at large to make a concerted and serious effort to alleviate the burden of this group of people to allow them to live in dignity." Affordable housing was needed, said the jurors unambiguously, and funding for programs of outreach for Native people, homeless people, and people afflicted with addiction or mental health issues should be increased not cut back. Sweeping changes to the organization and everyday management of hostels was mandatory, and the jurors even recommended experimenting with "wet hostels," a position that drew swift editorial rebuke from the *Star*. "The idea of Metro taxpayers funding a 'wet hostel' where alcoholics can come in from the cold and drink safely," the newspaper scoffed, "is a tough one to swallow." Safe "crackhouses," funded by the state, might be next, intimated the paper. Compared to 1986, 1996 was a leaner, meaner political climate. Unlike the Joubert inquest, the hearing into the deaths of Upper, Anderson, and Kompani was largely ignored by governments and what remained of the trimmed-down welfare bureaucracy.[56]

It was left to the Toronto Coalition Against Homelessness, with which OCAP was affiliated, to protest. TCAH organized pickets and demonstrations outside of the inquest hearings, denouncing the restriction of testimony. It issued a poster, depicting a homeless man living in a bus shelter, emblazoned with the words: "PEOPLE WHO LIVE IN GLASS HOUSES ... SHOULD THROW STONES." Over the course of the late 1990s, homelessness continued to plague the poor of Toronto. With social assistance rates eroding year by year, eviction applications increased (by 25 percent in 1996 alone), hostels remained filled to overcrowded capacity, and the homeless continued to die on the streets. Among those in Toronto on welfare of some kind, more and more of their income was expended on housing. The percentage of those paying more in rents than they received in shelter allowances doubled, rising from 33 percent in August 1995 to 68 percent in February 1996. A Toronto tabloid headlined the finding, "Homelessness at 30-Year High" in October 1997. During the megacity mayoral campaign of 1997, North York's Mel Lastman responded callously to the extensive coverage of homelessness in Toronto. The death of a homeless woman, Linda Houston, who succumbed to a heart attack in the bathroom of an all-night gas station near Yonge and York Mills, made front-page news. "I haven't seen anybody in North York that's homeless," Lastman told a CBC interviewer, "and I haven't heard of anyone except a woman who won't come in out of the cold." OCAP promptly delivered a wreath bearing Linda Houston's name to Lastman's campaign headquarters, demanding the building of more affordable housing.[57]

Lastman, about to be elected mayor in November 1997, barely had time to ditch the OCAP wreath before police discovered the decomposed body of Mary Louise Sharrow, a thirty-three-year-old Aboriginal woman living in a homeless encampment hidden among the trees on the banks of the Don River. More than a dozen people called the forested settlement their home. Mary (also known as Marie) and her husband Peter had lived in a teepee-like structure constructed of twigs, tree branches, mud, and a mustard-coloured tarpaulin for two years, under conditions that *Globe and Mail* columnist Jan Wong found depressingly squalid. Mary, who had participated in an OCAP housing protest in April 1997, was apparently the victim of a massive heart attack. Buried in a shallow grave just beyond her makeshift lodgings,

Mary Sharrow was a reflection of how the homelessness of racialized men and women of Aboriginal and Métis origins, living in urban settings, entailed a dispossession from shelters, rooming houses, and social services once available to the inhabitants of marginal metropolitan spaces. As such, Native peoples, the object of an original colonial dispossession, found themselves subject to repeated waves of dispossession and displacement.[58]

Six weeks after the discovery of Sharrow's body, Michael Faithorne, a forty-one-year-old homeless man, was found frozen to death in a stairwell in the Parkdale area. Before the year was out another homeless victim succumbed to hypothermia, huddling for protection from the elements under a tarp in a Scarborough ravine. His name was never released. OCAP marched to Queen's Park, dropping off two wreaths at the Legislature. "We'd like a commitment," the anti-poverty organization said, "that those wreaths will be put up in Harris's office as a reminder of his own shameful behaviour."[59]

Squats and NIMBYs: OCAP Escalates the Struggle

Toronto's homelessness crisis hit youth particularly hard. One of the fastest growing demographic sectors relying on hostels in the 1990s were the young, whose lives on the streets took an especially mean turn under the ideological

OCAP office, Parkdale, 4 Mac-Donnell Avenue, 2000.

OCAP Archives.

climate of social assistance cuts, mandatory workfare, and other retributions of the "Common Sense Revolution." Almost 20 percent of the city's "officially" designated homeless population in the mid-1990s was composed of children/youth under the age of eighteen. Many were cared for by single mothers or parents who had lost housing, but thousands of others were young people alone, most of whom lacked waged employment, many of whom were escaping familial abuse, and some of whom battled drug addiction or relied on sex trade work to survive. Entering the 1990s, the Salvation Army estimated that twelve thousand adolescents and youths were living on Toronto's streets when it cost $11,000 yearly to sustain a single bed in an emergency shelter. This was about as much as it would have required to rent a modest one- or two-bedroom apartment at the time. By 1997, as a report issued by Metro hostel systems manager John Jagt and Commissioner of Neighbourhood and Community Services Shirley Hoy made clear, increasing numbers of homeless youth were seeking beds in emergency shelters. Between 1992 and 1998, youth use of city hostels increased by 80 percent.[60]

Throughout the winter and spring of 1996, fifty homeless youth were squatting in two three-storey apartment buildings at 88–90 Carlton Street, a stone's throw away from Maple Leaf Gardens. The privately owned structures, occupying prime real estate, had been vacant since the early 1990s when their owners, allowing them to lapse into a dilapidated state, ceased renting to tenants. The buildings were without electricity and running water, and their doors and windows had been boarded over, but the determined youths managed to secure entry, probably by hoisting a ladder into the backyard, scaling a fence, and then ascending to a second-floor window and removing its board covering. For months, the youths inhabited the abandoned apartments. Police evicted them on May 4, 1996 and, with nowhere to go, some of the homeless youth set up an OCAP-supported encampment in the Peace Garden at Nathan Phillips Square, demanding of Mayor Barbara Hall that she either allow them to return to the Carlton Street squat or arrange for them to live in another of the city's many unused, abandoned buildings. Hall, of course, refused. She offered the homeless youths beds in overcrowded, dingy, and dangerous shelters. The protesters stood their ground, and their tent city was broken up by police on May 10. Eleven young men and women were arrested, charged with trespass, and then released. A spokesman for Tourism Toronto expressed concern about homeless people camping out beside city hall, a noted attraction for out-of-country visitors to the Queen City. "Toronto's safe clean image is a selling point for the city's tourism trade," he said, expressing hope that "the events of the past week are just a bleep." If this were to be the beginning of a trend, he concluded in reference to the unsightly presence of the poor on the doorsteps of civic officialdom, "it could really damage the tourist industry."[61]

One of the homeless youth evicted from the Carlton Street squat, and a participant in the protest at Nathan Phillips Square, was Sean Keegan. Less than three weeks after being forcibly removed from the vacant apartment buildings, Keegan's body was discovered by police in an underground parking garage stairwell on Homewood Avenue, one block east of his old squat. Shot to death, Keegan was one of three people murdered by a man targeting sex workers.[62] OCAP was determined to make sure that the crisis of youth homelessness, and Keegan's death, be something more than a bleep.

Ten months later, at 10 a.m. on the morning of March 5, 1997, twenty-one OCAP members, many of them homeless, returned to 88–90 Carlton Street. They quietly took over one of the two again vacant apartment buildings, informing the media of their intention to occupy the site in protest against the lack of facilities for the homeless. Police arrived and ordered the squatters to depart or be arrested and charged with trespassing. After a three-and-a-half hour standoff, with the squatters standing pat, police broke in, placed the protesters under arrest, and escorted them from the building. For OCAP it was an obscenity "that there are 258 empty buildings in Toronto while people freeze to death on the streets." At a press conference outside the building, OCAP announced its intention to return and open the buildings to use for the homeless. Calling for a "Use It Or Lose It" bylaw that would allow the city to take ownership of abandoned buildings that were unoccupied for a specific number of years, Sue Collis, an OCAP organizer, warned that militant anti-poverty activists and the homeless themselves would use "whatever means necessary" to liberate the Carlton Street apartments from landlords who shuttered their properties, content to sit on rising real estate prices that would eventually "earn" them tidy profits. "Our right to be here comes from the fact that homeless people are dying," she declared decisively.[63]

On April 19, 1997, OCAP returned to Carlton Street. The protest was organized to coincide with the spring closing of the Out of the Cold Program. At noon more than three hundred people gathered at Allan Gardens. On entering the park, they found artist-erected monuments memorializing homeless men and women who had died on the streets. On the northwest side of the park, just across from Homewood Avenue where Sean Keegan had been murdered, a large piece of grass, the size of a coffin, was cut and rolled up leaving the brown earth exposed. Accompanied by representatives from trade unions, social justice organizations, and youth agencies, OCAP and the homeless marched to 88–90 Carlton Street. There they confronted

338

police, on foot and horseback. John Clarke addressed the militant crowd. "If the law says that people have to die on the streets when buildings are still empty," Clarke yelled, "then I say it must be defied." When OCAP members attempted to remove the plywood covering the windows with a crowbar, a struggle with the cops broke out. Protesters shouting "Police Out, Homeless In," swarmed the padlocked front doors of the buildings. Arrests ensued, with Clarke charged with counselling to commit an indictable offence and he and Gaétan Héroux taken into custody for break and enter. Charges against four others, including MacDonald Scott, who would later join OCAP, were subsequently dropped. When Clarke and Héroux went to trial, they faced conviction for the lesser crime of public mischief under $5000. They were found guilty, but Judge David Cole granted the two OCAP activists an absolute discharge on the grounds that they had been guided by "altruistic motivation." The City of Toronto subsequently purchased the Carlton Street buildings and by 2006 had constructed a twelve-storey social housing apartment complex for low-income people.[64]

88-90 Carlton Street demonstration, Toronto, April 19, 1997.

OCAP Archives.

OCAP activist Gaétan Héroux's day job was, at the time of the Carlton Street protest, coordinator of a weekend drop-in centre operated by Central Neighbourhood House (CNH), a multiservice agency that had long been located on East Downtown Toronto's Ontario Street. Indeed, the CNH drop-in centre had been a centrepiece in OCAP's mobilization of homeless and poor people around the 88–90

Carlton Street protests. The centre provided food and shelter to low-income and homeless people, but CNH also boasted a long history of advocating for the poor of the area, which by the 1990s had experienced decades of gentrification, with consequent realignments of the district's class make-up. Temporarily displaced from Ontario Street because of renovations to CNH's main building, the drop-in centre had relocated to Parliament Street. Ready to return to the CNH building in the summer of 1997, Héroux and others affiliated with the drop-in service were confronted with an announcement by the CNH's Executive Director that the long-anticipated reintegration into the now refurbished CNH building on Ontario Street was not going to happen, and that an alternative location was needed. CNH was in fact bowing to pressure from Toronto Councillor Pam McConnell, neighbourhood residents' associations, and upscale businesses, all having joined in a campaign to keep the CNH drop-in centre out of their backyard. They were also doing their best to thin out other unseemly social service agencies/institutions—Council Fire, 416 Drop-In for Women, the All Saints Church Open Door Drop-In and the Friend-

ship Centre[65]—all of which were accused of servicing drug dealers, prostitutes, and others of unsavoury and unwanted character. Knowing that relocating the drop-in centre would ultimately kill the program of aid to the poor, and unable to convince the CNH Board to resist the lobbying efforts of local property owners and their political allies, Héroux announced his resignation as CNH drop-in co-ordinator. To facilitate the agency hiring a replacement, Héroux agreed to stay at his work until the end of October 1997.[66]

OCAP mobilized to resist the Not-In-My-Backyardism (NIMBYism) of the property-proud, gentrifying well-to-do and their campaign to weed out services that might attract the socially outcast to their renovated neighbourhood. Postering hydro poles in the East Downtown, OCAP called on the dispossessed to rally on August 5, 1997, and march to the doorsteps of their counterparts, the now protesting possessors. "YUPPIE RESIDENTS BACK OFF!' proclaimed the OCAP poster, which then explained:

> Yuppie residents have made it their mission to attack the poor and homeless in

YUPPIE RESIDENTS BACK OFF!

Yuppie residents have made it their mission to attack the poor and homeless in the area. More interested in their property values than they are in human life, two resident groups (Toronto East Downtown Residents Association — TEDRA and Seaton Ontario Berkeley Residents Association — SOBRA) are trying to shut the doors on vital services in the neighbourhood. The already massive cuts to welfare and affordable housing have left tens of thousands of people with no alternative to hostels and drop-ins like the ones in this neighbourhood. Now these residents groups would see the drop-ins/day shelters driven from the area and people left in utter destitution. This attack, backed by some local politicians, is clearly part of a larger pattern to force the poor from the downtown core in order to make room for yuppie condominiums and retail development.

On August 5th, the Ontario Coalition Against Poverty will be leading a march to the homes of these yuppies to challenge their plans! If they find the face of poverty so unpleasant that they want to drive it from the neighbourhood, we will take it right to their doorsteps and deliver the message that they keep their hands off of our services! Join us on the 5th and give these residents a taste of their own medicine!

Tuesday August 5th
7:30 PM
Allan Gardens
(Sherbourne and Gerrard)

ONTARIO COALITION AGAINST POVERTY: (416) 925-6939

the area. More interested in their property values than they are in human life, two resident groups (Toronto East Downtown Residents Association—TEDRA, and Seaton Ontario Berkeley Residents Association—SOBRA) are trying to shut down the doors on vital services in the neighbourhood. The already massive cuts to welfare and affordable housing have left tens of thousands of people with no other alternative to hostels and drop-ins like the ones in this neighbourhood. Now these residents groups would see the drop-ins/day shelters driven from the area and people left in utter destitution. This attack, backed by some local politicians, is clearly a part of a larger pattern to force the poor from the downtown core in order to make room for yuppie condominiums and retail development. On August 5th the Ontario Coalition Against Poverty will be leading a march on the homes of these yuppies to challenge their plans. If they find the face of poverty so unpleasant that they want to drive it from their neighbourhood, we will take it right to their doorsteps and deliver the message that they keep their hands off of our services.[67]

On seeing this announcement, a group of residents in the gentrifying East Downtown were enraged, denouncing the inflammatory tone of the poster and decrying OCAP's "terrorist tactics." They targeted Héroux, well known among the poor of the East Downtown, for attack, claiming to have seen him postering for the OCAP rally. In a July 24, 1997, letter to Toronto Councillor Pam McConnell, copied to Héroux's boss at CNH, Staff Inspector Bill Blair, Mayor Barbara Hall, and Toronto politician Jack Layton, a member of SOBRA demanded police protection and called for Héroux's head:

[We] saw Gaétan Héroux pasting the attached flyer on the hydro poles at Sherbourne & Dundas. He has continued throughout the SOBRA and TEDRA areas. The facts in these flyers are grossly overexaggerated and highly inflammatory; the tone is extremely violent and he is inciting riot. We have witnessed first hand that he is capable of violence, vandalism and anti-social behavior. We view the flyer as a threat that he is targeting our homes. We request that on August 5th, considerable numbers of police officers be available for our protection. The regular foot patrol is not sufficient. We also request that Gaétan be removed as an employee of Central Neighbourhood House immediately. We support TEDRA's request that a police investigation of OCAP and their activities be conducted. This organization is a political animal trying to achieve their objective through terrorism. It is time to stop these tactics.[68]

This demand that Héroux be sacked was echoed by other letters from SOBRA, TEDRA, and the Central Cabbagetown Residents Association. Called into the CNH executive director's office, Héroux was asked if he intended to participate in the OCAP march. Replying that he was indeed going to be a part of the demonstration, he was fired on the spot, informed that he would be paid until the end of October.

The entire CNH staff was then contacted, the executive director expressing concern about how the proposed OCAP demonstration was damaging the agency's reputation with funders and materially and adversely affecting its ability to offer services. Facing intense criticism and scrutiny about the protest, CNH had appealed to OCAP not to demonstrate at people's homes, but the request was rebuffed. Claiming that CNH was "battling the public misperception that CNH or by extension our staff had some role in organizing" the OCAP protest, the executive director insisted that no flyers advertising the August 5 event would be allowed on CNH property, and no promotion of the protest would be permitted; that OCAP was no longer welcome to use CNH space for meetings or to make use of any of the agency's resources; and that "Staff are strongly encouraged not to participate in this protest." CNH staff that chose to participate in any demonstration taking place outside neighbours' homes were informed that they were "in conflict with staff code of ethics and could face consequences with regards to their employment."[69]

The opposition to OCAP's direct challenge to NIMBYism neither started nor stopped with CNH. There had long been chagrin among some OCAP supporters for the anti-poverty group's militant willingness to demonstrate at individuals' houses, a tactic that had first been used in 1995 when Bob Rae's residence was picketed and that would be repeated in later years, when welfare officers and cabinet ministers could be singled out. Trade union leaders, who often signed cheques that went to OCAP, were particularly uncomfortable with this willingness to make the personal political. In the aftermath of the "Yuppie Residents" action, mainstream elements grew more and more reluctant to be associated with OCAP. The All Saints Church, which opened its doors to OCAP's general meetings, would ban OCAP from using its premises after the August 5, 1997, protest. Daniel Robillard, Director of the All Saints Community Centre, likened OCAP's approach to "Nazi roundups." Toronto's liberal/social democratic Councillor, Jack Layton, who often took strong stands on behalf of the homeless, intervened to try to deter OCAP from following through on its promise to take protest to the yuppie doorsteps of the East Downtown. OCAP, however, stood its ground, stating that its "tactics flow from the concept that if the poor are going to have power, that power is going to have to be a question of collective action. We have the capacity to create a crisis for the other side through mobilization." With SOBRA and TEDRA establishing "witness programs" that targeted sex trade workers with the intent of working with police to terrorize and banish women from their long-established routes of street solicitation, the situation worsened. One sex worker was severely beaten by a police constable and barred from appearing within specified Cabbagetown-area boundaries for eighteen months. Residents Association members attended the woman's court dates and "smirked as the judge rendered his decision." OCAP called for a

> celebration of resistance on Cabbagetown streets involving all the poor and homeless, sex trade workers, recent immigrants and others who have been systematically excluded and banished from this community.... We have to show our readiness to defend the rights of people ... to live without fear where they see fit, and to move towards the creation of neighbourhoods where inclusiveness, diversity, and compassion hold sway rather than property values.

As Andrew Cash would later comment in *Now Magazine*, the "live-and-let-live understanding between the street society and the residents of the reno-ed vintage homes worried about their housing values" had collapsed, upending a "finely-balanced" East Downtown "ecosystem." What was resulting was a "vigorous tug of war that's ugly to behold."[70]

The August rally went off without a hitch. Two hundred obviously hardcore OCAP members and supporters gathered in Allan Gardens. After listening to a round of early evening speeches, the demonstrators marched to the homes of residents and the street sites of businesses that had taken the lead in publicly attacking services vital to the survival of the homeless, calling for their removal from the neighbourhood. A large contingent of police officers was on hand, overseen by Bill Blair, the cops shadowing the demonstrators as they wound their way through the East Downtown. Given what was lost because of these residential protests, in which property value and complacency trumped the quite limited services and assistance for the poor, two hours of protest was a small price for the affluent of Toronto's East Downtown to pay. The CNH drop-in centre, for instance, long a mainstay of the agency's support for the neighbourhood poor, shuffled from relocation to relocation between 1997 and 2003 before finally, predictably, shutting its doors. The largest weekend drop-in centre in Toronto, which had provided food and shelter for some of the city's poorest people for more than three decades, was forced out of a neighbourhood that had long sustained it and was eventually closed down. In its absence, property owners affiliated with SOBRA met regularly at the Ontario Street building of CNH, where they continued to strategize how best to sanitize their neighbourhood of the irksome presence of poor people's social services. The *Globe and Mail*'s Margaret Philp addressed OCAP's militancy and its radical tactics of bringing the war on poverty home, to the doorsteps of those who opposed having their front and backyards sullied by evidence of the poor's existence. "Most anti-poverty activists say OCAP has overstepped its bounds in the past few months," Philp reported, noting that some suggested that the "coalition has become too strident to be credible." That said, Philp acknowledged, "most all agree, like it or hate it, OCAP has played a pivotal role over the years in drawing public attention to epidemic levels of poverty and homelessness." *Star* reporter Susan Kastner captured something of what was happening in the summer of 1997:

> It was a hot embattled summer for the people who call themselves OCAP. All summer, every few weeks, they took their "actions" to the streets; streets on whose sidewalks many of them live but are less and less welcome. A jumble of ragged men and women without homes, without clean clothes, often without teeth, they lay claim to unused downtown buildings, demonstrated against neighbourhood heartlessness, official brutality, blind bureaucracy, raised money for the neediest around them. As business reports rang with news of economic cheer, as homelessness spiraled upwards, the anger in the streets was growing, the people without teeth seemed to signal that they were fed up with being toothless.

One of the commentators Philp interviewed for her article offered insight into why OCAP had come to symbolize the return/revenge of the dispossessed: "If things get worse, I can see that their credibility will increase among the homeless. If people die on the streets this winter I see that the message that OCAP brings to that community of the homeless and the poor will resonate. They offer quick solutions and definite action."[71]

Indeed, things did get worse. Barbara Hall, running for mayor of the new Toronto megacity against Lastman, told Gail Swanson of the *Star*, "We're scared because we know homelessness isn't just more visible. It's more chronic, and it's getting worse. We know it's not going to be a nice winter out there on the streets of

our city and there will be more deaths." City officials predicted that there would be a 67 percent increase in the number of people using emergency shelters by Christmas 1997, while statistics revealed that over the course of a year from October 1996 to October 1997, the numbers using hostels, missions, and shelters had grown from 3,970 to 5,350. Indeed, the situation from 1996 to 1997 gave no sign of improvement. Service providers and politicians sang the same sorry tune: "All of our shelters are overburdened. People are desperate." "The worst situation we've had since the 30s when people slept in shantytowns in the Don Valley park system." With shelters turning single people away because beds were lacking, Metro Hostel Services, running out of Toronto hotels to rent for homeless families, were relocating those in need of shelter to motels in Trenton, Burlington, and St. Catharines.[72]

More Deaths, More Protests, More Complacency (and Worse)

Homelessness in Toronto was now so obviously a crisis that even newly elected poverty-denying Mel Lastman had to strike a Mayor's Task Force on Homelessness. As the four-person investigation headed by the United Way's Anne Golden proceeded, rents continued to rise, vacancy rates approached zero, and the shortage of hostel beds in emergency shelters was so acute that it was projected that two thousand people would be living on Toronto's streets by the summer of 1998.

Toronto's Hostel Services head, John Jagt, complained in May 1998, "As of today I don't have a single room left for mothers with children," and the fourteen hundred beds available for men alone were all taken. The poor were sleeping in parks in large numbers, while tent encampments in the Don Valley, at city hall, and along the Lakeshore under the Gardner Expressway were growing. Meanwhile, the cost-cutting Tories at Queen's Park were proposing to download the expense of maintaining Toronto's fifty thousand social housing units onto the municipality. With forty thousand on the wait list for social assistance housing, families were anticipating a twelve-year wait before they could secure residences. Nothing improved except the weather between January and June 1998: city shelters, their beds taken, tightened eligibility requirements; downtown spaces like Allan Gardens, city hall, Metropolitan United Church Park, and Moss Park sprouted encampments of the homeless, some of which were broken up by police. Gaétan Héroux saw signs of destitution everywhere: sleeping bags drenched by a previous night's rain abandoned on grates and sidewalks; clothes packed neatly in garbage bags and stowed away under a bush or in a back alleyway; the streets clogged with beggars.[73]

It was in this context that two front-line service providers, AIDS outreach worker Beric German (who also worked with the homeless utilizing emergency shelters and had known Drina Joubert) and a highly regarded street nurse, Cathy Crowe, spearheaded the creation of the Toronto Disaster Relief Committee (TDRC).

TORONTO'S POOR

The Committee mobilized broadly among activists working with the poor and within the social housing milieu, such as Héroux, Steve Lane, Sherrie Golden, and Maurice Adongo; researchers, academics, and lawyers, among them David Hulchanski and Peter Rosenthal; and a host of others, including those on social assistance themselves, artists, writers, priests, politicians, progressive real estate developers, and AIDS activists. Under this broad umbrella gathered those who thought homelessness in Canada a violation of basic human rights. The committee wrote the State of Emergency Declaration, presenting it to a crowded assembly of several hundred people in the Church of the Holy Trinity in downtown Toronto on October 8, 1998. Calling on governments to spend an additional 1 percent of their budgets, or roughly $2 billion a year, on affordable housing, TDRC declared:

> The homeless situation is worsening daily at an alarming rate, as the factors creating it remain unchecked. Any delay in firmly and massively responding will only contribute to compounding the present crisis of suffering and death which is already an epidemic which no civilized society can tolerate.

At a press conference, University of Toronto professor Ursula Franklin announced, "Homelessness is a national disaster. We have the legal and technical means to end it." The TDRC plan, quickly dubbed "the 1% Solution," demanded an immediate relief fund to sustain additional emergency shelters, support programs, and a national housing initiative. As the Church of the Holy Trinity meeting broke up, one hundred people marched to city hall to successfully secure the passage of a Community and Neighbourhood Services Committee motion declaring homelessness a state of emergency, and approving funding for an additional four to five hundred emergency shelter beds.

Newspapers like the *Star* offered a week of coverage and unequivocal headlines—"Plight of the Homeless: A National Disaster"—assigning a reporter to cover homeless issues full-time. Men continued to die on the streets of Toronto—three in October 1998 alone—and both TDRC and OCAP stepped up the campaign to make homelessness a recognized social crisis. With the Declaration of National Disaster to be voted on by City Council on October 28, OCAP and TDRC organized a pancake breakfast at Metro Hall and rallied some five hundred homeless people and their supporters to fill the gallery of the council chambers. As the Toronto City Council discussed the Declaration, the homeless grew restless and tired of the pontification, chanting "Vote Now! Vote Now!" Truncating the lengthy speakers list, Council voted fifty-three to one to endorse the TDRC Declaration, stipulating that homelessness was a National Disaster and calling on governments in Ottawa and Toronto to provide a relief fund that could be used for immediate humanitarian aid to the homeless, in the same way that floods, earthquakes, hurricanes and their distress were alleviated. Council also approved the addition of 350 hostel beds for the Toronto emergency shelter system, promising that five new shelters would be opened by the end of December. Lastman later announced that Toronto would host a two-day national summit on homelessness in the New Year, the event coinciding with the release of Anne Golden's Mayor's Task Force on Homelessness report. All of this came too late for the homeless victims who succumbed to suicide and hypothermia as the city's 4,000 hostel spaces filled to capacity. City Councillor and future NDP leader Jack Layton proclaimed, "We're in a grim situation here." Dr. Richard Fung of the Emergency Ward at Toronto's downtown St. Michael's Hospital appreciated Layton's assessment, having an idea of just how bad circumstances were for the Toronto dispossessed. By his count, one hundred homeless men had died in Toronto between 1996 and 1998.[74]

On the morning of November 5, roughly one week after Toronto had declared homelessness a National Disaster, a small contingent of OCAP activists walked through the unlocked doors of the vacated Doctor's Hospital Brunswick Avenue building in the city's west end. They pushed by security guards, barricaded themselves in a room on the first floor, and began to unpack sleeping bags, makeshift toilets, and enough food to last through the weekend. A large banner was unfurled from the window: "SHELTER IS OPEN." Demanding that the city open a facility immediately to alleviate the overcrowding of hostels and lack of availability of beds, OCAP entered into negotiations with civic official Joan Campbell. Campbell insisted no shelter expansion could take place before December 1, and when the occupiers refused to leave the Doctor's Hospital voluntarily, police moved in and arrested thirteen and charged them with trespass and unlawful assembly. TDRC came to OCAP's support the next day, demonstrating in front of the again empty Brunswick Avenue building, calling for the immediate opening of new shelters. Sticking to her guns, Campbell claimed no shelter at Doctor's Hospital could be opened before December, but one week later the Fort York Armoury in the west end opened its doors to the homeless for the first time in its history. The Armoury, the site of Canadian Armed Forces military training, accommodated 150 people and continued to operate as an emergency shelter into January 1999. TDRC pressed for the Armoury to remain open and called for the east end Moss Park Armoury to be similarly converted into an emergency shelter. The demand was rejected on the grounds that there was "capacity in the system to bring people in for the night." Three weeks later an unidentified man died as he slept under layers of old sleeping bags and a tarp, his final resting place a heating duct grate visible from the Queen's Park office window of Premier Mike Harris.[75]

On the eve of Mayor Lastman's Homeless Summit, OCAP led a large and rowdy protest at a Toronto Community and Neighbourhoods Committee meeting. More than two hundred protesters, many of them homeless, marched to city hall on March 23, 1999, filling council chambers to register their discontent that six hundred hostel beds at three shelter sites were due to be terminated as of May 1. A local ratepayer's association from Riverdale was also in attendance, its project being to close down an emergency women's shelter on Pape Avenue. A classic case of NIMBY-ism, the Riverdale petition was justified in language that drew the understandable ire of the OCAP homeless:

> Increased crime, litter everywhere, drunkenness. Every donut shop and greasy spoon in the neighbourhood has become licenced, and a great-diminished quality of life. As it should be noticeable by now it is all in our backyard. Would it not be easier to bull dose down South River Dale and erect Regent Park Phase Two. We have nothing whatsoever against the homeless. My wife and I constantly support the food bank. These opinions are not just mine. I have here not just petitions from my backyard.

As Council Chambers echoed with boos and catcalls to this screed, Councillor Pam McConnell struggled unsuccessfully to quiet the crowd, pleading that she wanted "people to be able to feel free and comfortable to express their opinions on both sides of this issue." John Clarke rose to insist that to "present bigotry as community interest and dialogue" was unacceptable, and called on the committee to keep hostels open. "VOTE! VOTE! VOTE!" chanted the crowd, with Clarke refusing to leave the podium and dozens of protesters blocking the doors, thwarting an attempt to recess the meeting giving councillors a chance to flee. Police were eventually called to clear the chambers and scuffles resulted, but order was eventually restored, and arrests avoided. The committee waffled on the issue of hostel closings, reducing the number of beds at the Pape Avenue women's shelter from thirty to eighteen and passing a motion to allow the city's hostel services to open an emergency refuge if shelter occupancy climbed above 90 percent occupancy.[76]

The Doctor's Hospital shelter, which opened in December 1998 and provided 80–100 homeless men and women a respite from the elements for months, closed its doors on April 12, 1999. OCAP and TDRC were there to protest. As spring gave way to summer, the shortage of hostel beds only worsened. John A. Jagt, Director of Toronto's Hostel Services, confessed, "This is a crisis. We've never been in this kind of position at the beginning of the summer. We're not on top of it, we're chasing it." Frustrated at what he perceived to be the hopelessness of the situation, Jagt told *Star* reporter Cathy Dunphy, "I don't see any light at the end of the tunnel." As the temporary shelter at the Canadian Armed Forces Fort York Armoury closed its doors in June 1999, Jagt turned a portion of Metro Hall into an emergency shelter for 150 people. Nineteen days later, the National Defence Department of the federal government announced that the City of Toronto was leasing the Armoury for six months and establishing an emergency shelter that would, coincidentally, take in 150 of the homeless, who would share the facilities with army trainees. Anti-poverty activists in TDRC forced the opening of shelters in residential neighbourhoods where older government buildings were available, but local property owners wanted to nix the presence of hostels for the homeless in their backyards. It was a fight on every front to simply tread water against the high waves of homelessness.[77]

The release of Anne Golden's Mayor's Homeless Action Task Force report contributed to a growing pessimism, its 105 recommendations revealing a system in crisis that the Task Force was reluctant to name as such. Two of its pivotal suggestions, calling for the building of more affordable housing and increasing shelter allowance funding for welfare recipients, were never acted on. Lastman's National Summit on Homelessness, similarly, lashed out at the federal government for its failure to provide adequate resources for the poor, but little in the way of positive response was forthcoming. Jagt reported in the fall of 1999 that the city's 2,350 beds for single men and women were "totally full." New shelter openings and seasonal programs like the religious volunteer service Out of the Cold promised modest relief, but many of the dispossessed faced the new millennium unsure of whether they would have a roof over their heads as temperatures dropped below 0 degrees.[78]

Squeegees, Soliciting, and the Safe Streets Act: OCAP Continues to Counter

Death stalked the homeless on cold nights as they slept over grates, in alleyways, or in ravine encampments, or visited them in the crowded hostel rooms where they lay, with many others, coughing and complaining, on stiff cots. In the Toronto of commercial transactions and 9-to-5 business undertakings, its presence was limited. But the dispossessed did not only retire to their rough makeshift lodgings or the emergency shelters and sleep, sometimes even die. During the day they wandered the streets, which were their workplaces, from which the unwaged might squeeze a few coins that translated, over hours, into the dollars that would get them through another hour, another twenty-four hours, another week. With the street as their source of accumulation, however modest, the poor of Toronto begged and panhandled as the dispossessed have always done. Increasingly, however, by the late 1990s, especially among homeless youth, the art of squeegeeing grew popular as a paying pastime of the poor. The occupation consisted of standing at street corners and in intersections, a pail of soapy water nearby, armed with a tool composed of a flat rubber blade that could be wielded to scrap off the sludge that accumulates on the windshields of cars, irksomely so in the Canadian winter. Although a squeegee could, and often would, be utilized by a homeless person of any age, those offering this service and expecting some compensation for their efforts were soon labelled "squeegee kids," although OCAP preferred the term squeegee merchants. Their

Hands Off Street Youth! poster, August 22, 1998. OCAP Archives.

growing presence on the streets of Toronto, first noticed around 1996, had grown by 1998 into a festering sore point with those who wanted not so much to erase poverty as to exorcise its irksome visibility among the comfortably well off.[79]

As the crisis of homelessness deepened, the dispossessed were under intensifying attack. By the end of 1996 Toronto's Chief of Police, David Boothby, was on a rampage against the poor, promising to clean the streets of "welfare cheats and panhandlers." Boothby had no time for beggars. "We have a system of assistance so that people don't starve to death," he explained, yet panhandling was being turned into a business. It was all "annoying, intimidating, and a nuisance." Calling for special laws that would equip the police to deal effectively with the growing army of "squeegee kids" and the roving bands of beggars, Boothby cultivated support among downtown merchants and within City Council, where Kyle Rae called for a crackdown on squeegeers and panhandlers. "I want them off residential strips," Rae fumed, "Businesses and residences made it clear that they're not welcomed.... They are fighting over turf, they're intimidating (store) customers, and they're intimidating drivers. It's unacceptable activity." Those sleeping in public parks were soon added to the list of miscreants who needed to be moved along and out of sight. OCAP, drawing on the public's revulsion toward the ethnic cleansing of the Yugoslav Wars of the 1990s, labelled this social cleansing. By May of 1998 the police were becoming increasingly aggressive in their harassment and targeting of the homeless, who found themselves ticketed for all manner of petty offences, "soliciting business on a road, impeding traffic, jaywalking, operating a bicycle without a bell, abandoning material on a sidewalk that can be considered litter." Toronto civic officials tried to introduce a new by-law banning squeegeeing and panhandling, especially near bus stops, liquor stores, and banks. As lawyers warned of enforcement nightmares, Toronto councillors grew apprehensive and voted the new bylaw down by a narrow margin.[80]

Mayor Mel Lastman then went on the attack, declaring war on the squeegee fraternity and their panhandling cousins. With the Toronto *Sun* emblazoning its July 23, 1998, front page with "MAYOR! IT'S WAR ON SQUEEGEERS," Lastman insisted the hostilities had begun, and the police would be doing their utmost to "get squeegee kids off the streets," they being "beggars, that's all they are." Mike Harris instructed his Crime Control Commission to get tough on the squeegees, prodding it to come up with a law that might deal with the squeegee/panhandling nuisance. Police Chief Boothby pressed the provincial Attorney-General to devote some immediate attention to the panhandling problem. A Community Action Policing program was introduced in Toronto to the cost of $1.9 million, bankrolling a "zero tolerance policy" that had police moving through the downtown core in the hopes of pushing the poor out. Harris's provincial Safe Streets Act came into effect in November 1999, passing a third reading in the legislature before it recessed for the December–January holidays. The Act banned "aggressive panhandling" and made it illegal to solicit money at "bus stops, taxi stands, and automated banking machines." To target the street corner squeegee, the Highway Traffic Act was amended, criminalizing stopping or approaching "a motor vehicle with intent to offer, sell or provide any product or service." Violators could be fined up to $500 for each infraction, and repeat offenders faced $1000 fines and six months in jail. Nineteenth-century vagrancy laws were now back on the books, dressed up in the coercive garb of an automated, automobile age. OCAP challenged the "police targeting" of squeegee merchants and others, Sue Collis explaining: "Our philosophy is really if they want to fight in the streets, we're prepared to fight in the streets, and we've more than demonstrated that. But if they're going to take that fight to the courtroom, then we'll meet them there, and we'll win there too." Facing $200 fines, squeegee workers were grateful for OCAP's support, and over an intense battle

throughout 2000 over one thousand poor and homeless people, many of them youths, were successfully defended in the courts from prosecution under the Safe Streets Act.[81]

OCAP was also quick off the mark in organizing direct action resistance to this kind of draconian assault. On January 26, 1997, one hundred demonstrators gathered outside of the Eaton Centre. Armed with whistles and plastic cups for coin donations, they marched through the mall soliciting shoppers. The march concluded outside Toronto Police Headquarters, where speakers denounced the Chief of Police for proposing further criminalization of the poor. As the war on beggars and the squeegees ramped up in the summer of 1998, OCAP promised to focus on tourist attractions, threatening mass panhandling actions. Aprille Rhomer spoke for OCAP at an emergency meeting of Toronto's Protective Services Committee, convened to discuss the proposed city by-law against begging. "I can promise you that if such a by-law is passed we will organize mass panhandling and mass squeegeeing in front of opera houses, theatres, and restaurants," Rhomer threatened, adding that OCAP would be relentless in blocking "sidewalks and … aggressive about our demands … we will shut down every tourist attraction in this city." OCAP followed this up with a mass squeegee assembly at Queen and Spadina, a favoured locale for police to ticket and harass squeegeeing youth. With city council voting down the coercive bylaw, police simply stepped up their attacks on panhandlers and those soliciting funds with squeegees. OCAP continued to mount protests, aligning with groups such as Active Resistance and Anti-Racist Action to promote a Saturday

afternoon "HANDS OFF STREET YOUTH" demonstration on August 22, 1998. The protest, organized to coincide with a weekend anarchist conference in Toronto, drew one thousand people who were invited to gather at Alexandra Park near Bathurst and Queen, bringing "banners, signs and lots of attitude." Led by large mocking puppets, protesters marched along Queen Street West where much of the police harassment of homeless youth had been happening, finally convening in front of 52 Division of the Metro Toronto Police. *Star* columnist Royson James commented on OCAP's "new in-your-face-attitude and campaign aimed at improving the lot of the city's outcasts," and how it was helping the poor to be heard amid the deafening din of public attack.[82]

The 1999 Safe Streets Act had, of course, made the streets anything but safe for the homeless. When Attorney-General Jim Flaherty popped up in Toronto's historic Skid Row district, calling a snap press conference in early November 1999 to announce the details of the proposed legislation, OCAP rushed to the site, confronted Flaherty, and chased him out of the neighbourhood. As the *Star* reported, the Attorney-General had to cut short his proposed tour of the gentrifying district as an OCAP-led contingent of homeless men and women "drowned out" Flaherty's proposed speech, forcing the cabinet minister to walk "briskly to his car to shouts of obscenities."[83]

A year later, with the Safe Streets Act in effect and enforced, OCAP decided to counter with the creation of what it called a Safe Park in Allan Gardens, establishing a space where the dispossessed could gather unmolested by cops and their barrage of orders and prods and pushes to move along, reinforced by the irksome issuing of tickets demanding court appearances. The park had a long history as a site of unemployed protests, reaching back to the 1930s and earlier, as well as being used by the homeless as a sedate resting place, driving the residential association NIMBY-ists to fits of rage. Prior to the OCAP occupation, Allan Gardens was a flashpoint illuminating the racist, police targeting of black men. In one park sweep, cheered on by local homeowners, the cops rounded up sixty-five black men who were hanging out, playing soccer and dominoes, forced them to their knees, searched them, assigned $3000 in loitering tickets, and told the black population of Allan Gardens not to come back.[84]

OCAP's proclamation that it intended to establish a safe encampment of the homeless in Allan Gardens threw city hall into a panic. Civic officials had no idea of how to handle the volatile situation and feared riotous tumult if police and the poor clashed. OCAP attempted to secure city approval for what amounted to a tent city in Allan Gardens, but the request was refused. "We are not going to give our seal of approval," said Mayor Lastman, who then equivocated, "We are saying you can't do it and you shouldn't be doing it but we know they're going to do it and will be there with 300 to 500 people and I don't want violence." If Lastman's statement was difficult to decipher, OCAP's John Clarke was both determined and clear: "If we are attacked in the course of trying to maintain our community, we'll defend ourselves." One of the property-proud SOBRA leaders, who had campaigned to have Gaétan Héroux fired from the drop-in where he worked with the poor of Toronto's Downtown East, now speaking as chair of the Neighbourhood Forum, argued that OCAP's Safe Park was little more than a provocation to confront and battle with police. She insisted that the whole enterprise was just another OCAP "terrorist tactic." With police standing by, committed to enforcing city bylaws on park use, Mayor Lastman reiterating that sleeping in Toronto's parks was prohibited, tents not being allowed, and OCAP declaring that it was prepared to stand its ground, the Safe Park got started on August 7, 1999.[85]

There was bound to be safety in numbers, and OCAP had secured commitments from downtown social service agencies, trade unions, churches, and militant Mohawks at the Tyendinaga reserve near Belleville with whom they had established connections. Much preparation and discussion with a variety of people preceded the event. In the mid-afternoon, food and other necessities were brought into Allan Gardens from the OCAP office on Sherbourne Street, and a crowd of more than 500 assembled. Among those present was NDP leader Alexa McDonough. Shawn Brant

from Tyendinaga and Sue Collis, an OCAP organizer, served a lunch of fried fish provided by OCAP's Aboriginal allies. More than 1000 homeless and low-income residents of the neighbourhood were eventually fed. Large blue tarps were hung from trees and makeshift washrooms set up; blankets and supplies were handed out, and tents erected. A banner declaring "SAFE PARK" was hung at the Allan Gardens entryway, and yellow tape marked off the park's perimeter. With police and the media attending in force, evening descended and 150 homeless men and women, anti-poverty supporters, and activists bedded down for the night.[86]

The Safe Park was concerned not only to provide an alternative to the Safe Streets Act-patrolled public spaces where the poor normally spent their days and nights. It was also meant to call attention to the inadequacy of the city's overcrowded emergency shelters. Not surprisingly, John Jagt, spokesman for the city-run hostels, was quick to announce that there were plenty of beds available as the OCAP sleep-in at Allan Gardens unfolded. But others contradicted him. At Seaton House and the Fort York Armoury shelters, supervisors reported that no beds were available. "Last night we were full," said one front-line worker, "We're always full."[87]

The Safe Park was full as well. And it was proving difficult to sustain it. OCAP's small contingent of full-time workers was strained to the limit to provide meals for the residents, and cool evenings and rainy weather complicated matters greatly, there not being enough blankets and other supplies to go around. Activists were in the park for days, often without much in the way of sleep, John Clarke

TORONTO'S POOR

among them. A decision was made to wind the protest down after a few days and close things out on the following weekend, the protest then having lasted roughly a week. Civic officials and the police, however, had other plans, informing the media that some drama was in the making. The swarm of reporters and news vehicles that descended on the Downtown East park awakened some of those sleeping, who also noticed the police assembling and obviously readying themselves for an onslaught. At 5:50 a.m. on August 11, 1999, with the majority of the camp asleep, ninety police officers, some of them decked out in riot gear, entered Allan Gardens. Safe Park residents were given ten minutes to leave or face arrest. Many complied but some did not. "You had ample time to talk to us," an enraged Gaétan Héroux snapped at the police, "Why are you doing this now when people are tired?" The *National Post* described the ensuing mêlée, which saw one of its reporters mistaken for a protester and arrested, later to be released without charge: "Scuffles broke out as officers wrestled the unruly protesters to the ground. Paddy wagons pulled up, and dozens of people were handcuffed and dragged into the back of the vans, kicking and flailing.... Parks crews went to work immediately, clearing out the remaining tents, tarpaulins, and litter that was left." The arrest tally totalled twenty-seven, with criminal charges of assault police, obstruct police, mischief, and trespass. Much was made in the media that John Clarke was not in the park at the time of the break-up. After fifty hours with little sleep, the OCAP activist had gone home to get some rest and spend a few hours with his children. In the end, the majority of charges laid against the Safe Park protesters would be dropped and only a handful of the allegations of criminal conduct pursued. Mayor Lastman's office praised the police and deplored the behaviour of a corps of "professional protesters" who had ostensibly led the homeless astray again.[88]

OCAP responded by upping the ante. In an August 18 letter to Lastman and the Toronto City Council on behalf of OCAP, Stefan Pilipa attacked the rampant commercialization of everyday life in the city and the attempt to sweep the poor off the streets in order to placate powerful business interests. He warned that,

> For every dollar that does not go to providing for needs for the home-
> less, we will take another two dollars from the precious cash registers of
> Toronto's merchants and developers. We will directly attack the reputation
> of this city as a place to visit, invest in or potentially host the Olympic
> games. We guarantee that large numbers of tourists will leave Toronto this
> summer with stark images of the homeless loudly interfering with their
> enjoyment of what the commercial traps have to offer.[89]

OCAP's demands included an end to the targeted policing of the poor; termination of derogatory remarks, commonly made by the mayor and other civic officials, that criminalized squeegee merchants, panhandlers, and homeless men, women, and youth; an additional five hundred shelter beds; a Charter of Rights for hostel users, and an end to arbitrary bans; changes to welfare administration that groundlessly denied support; revision of housing policies to ensure that evictions would be used only as a last resort; and the elimination of zoning regulations that threatened low-income housing.

Less than a month after putting Lastman and city hall on notice, OCAP mounted a highly effective theatrical challenge to the ongoing street harassment of the poor that was legislated by the Safe Streets Act and tied to the plethora of commercial interests of Toronto's political economy, including the lucrative and powerful cultural industry. On September 9, 1999, it greeted the celebrity-worshipping fanfare of Toronto's International Film Festival (TIFF) with a mass panhandle in front of Roy Thompson Hall. TIFF's much-heralded opening was a showing of Canadian director Atom Egoyan's newly released film, *Felicia's Journey*. As seventy-five OCAPers turned up amid the starlets, swanky producers, and swarm of cinema aficionados, they hoisted their placards in front of the parade of limousines, banged tin cups in solicitation of funds, and generally did their best to make the issue of homelessness register with those for whom poverty was a rather distant abstraction. The favoured chant of the evening was, "The films may be nice, but the homeless pay the price." Police on horseback kept most of the protesters at bay, across the street from the red-carpeted entryway to the gala film, while private security guards and uniformed officers monitored those demonstrators who managed to get closer to the front of the hall. According to a CNN "ShowBiz" report, the OCAP visitors "made enough noise to put an end to the red-carpet treatment of the stars." The celebrities, who were denied their usual extended period of preening and fawning, were "quickly ushered into the screening" via an alleyway. Some even dug into their pockets for the poor. One homeless demonstrator was given a cheque for $100, which he promptly donated to OCAP. For his part, Egoyan deferred to the protest, addressing the film audience before the screening and dedicating the evening's showing to the homeless. "There are serious problems in this province," he told the packed house, "I urge [Premier Mike] Harris to address the erosion of social issues ... right away." As *Star* reporter Catherine Dunphy concluded, the protesters did not stop the TIFF show, "They made the show." OCAP had scored a major publicity hit and promised to be back at a forthcoming Cabbagetown "Word on the Street" arts and literary festival.[90]

Ottawa Bound and Bringing the War against
Poverty Back Home to Queen's Park

OCAP organizers had an appreciation of the historical struggles of the dispossessed and often alluded to what mobilizations of the jobless had managed
to accomplish in the past with various protests. Aware that, as Clarke wrote, "the
unemployed agitation of the 1930s shook Canadian society to its roots," OCAP was
cognizant of how the On-to-Ottawa Trek of 1935 had gained the wageless both
sympathy and public promotion of the need for fundamental social reforms.
As the crisis of homelessness worsened over the course of the late 1990s, OCAP
activists discussed mobilizing a cavalcade of buses to Ottawa, demanding that
Liberal Prime Minister Jean Chrétien meet with a delegation of the dispossessed.
In conjunction with anti-poverty activists in Montreal's Comité des sans emploi
and militants in the Mohawk community of Tyendinaga, and supported by trade
union funding from the Canadian Union of Postal Workers (CUPW), OCAP made
its first trek to Ottawa on February 10, 1999. Calling on "the Federal Government
[to] return all cuts to Income Support Programs and increase the Federal Budget
for Social Housing by 1% in order to eliminate homelessness," OCAP's demands
echoed those of the Toronto Disaster Relief Committee, but did so in more direct
action ways.[91]

OCAP wrote to Chrétien in January 1999, insisting on a meeting to discuss the
national crisis of homelessness. With the prime minister refusing such a discussion,

a crowd of three hundred rallied in downtown Ottawa on February 10 and marched toward Parliament Hill. After blocking the street for forty-five minutes, the protest advanced on the legislative buildings, where it was confronted by a barricade of police vehicles set up by Ottawa-Carleton police forces and the Royal Canadian Mounted Police (RCMP). Pushing the cars, scrambling atop their hoods, and tussling with the cops, the demonstrators soon faced the intimidating formation of two rows of the RCMP riot squad. Joe Clark, leader of the federal Conservatives, tried to address the protest, happy for the chance to get in a few licks against the ruling Liberals, but the homeless wanted little to do with him and ended up in a shoving match with the long-time politician. Headlines across the country fixated on Clark being pushed and jostled during a protest labelled "nasty" and "unruly." The NDP MP for Vancouver East, Libby Davies, whose roots lay in anti-poverty activism, came out of the legislature and led a small deputation of six protesters inside the parliament buildings, where they were allowed to hold a press conference. OCAP's Sue Collis denounced Chrétien for refusing to meet with the homeless, noting that he opted instead to turn the day's events into "a police issue. That's 100% the wrong way to go." NDP leader Alexa McDonough also criticized the prime minister, telling the House of Commons that he should have met with the delegation, listened to the desperation of the homeless, and responded to their pleas. "Instead," McDonough huffed, he "brings in the riot squad." Eleven arrests that resulted from the February 1999 Ottawa OCAP demonstration were ultimately vacated when John Clarke agreed to plead guilty to the charge of obstructing police as long as all charges against ten other demonstrators were dropped.[92]

Nine months later, OCAP returned to the scene of the crime. On Wednesday, November 17, 1999, after having been fed venison stew and accommodated for the night at the community centre of the Tyendinaga Mohawks, five busloads of largely homeless OCAP members and supporters rolled into Ottawa, their numbers buttressed by another bus from Kingston. Finding the road to the parliament buildings blocked by a police barricade, the anti-poverty protesters vowed to take their message of the need for more government support for social housing to the legislature. The demonstrators, attempting to breach police lines, were treated to blasts of pepper spray, the first time this stinging repellent had been used against dissidents on Parliament Hill. A newspaper described the tumultuous confrontation:

> With blasts of pepper spray the police fended off a surly crowd of anti-
> poverty activists and the homeless ... who were protesting shortages of

> low-income housing.... The group advanced toward the Peace Tower wielding hockey sticks and placards. About 150 RCMP officers in riot gear of helmets, shields, and batons met them as they neared the Parliament Buildings. Protesters pelted the officers with metal cans and other debris, while yelling obscenities.... The leading edge of the crowd jostled the barricades set up in front of police and attempted to raise them above their heads. That set off the first blast of pepper spray.... A half hour later, with the protest showing little sign of subsiding, the police sprayed again, this time hitting about twenty people.

After an hour's battle, the OCAP forces retreated to their buses. Assailed by the press for the anger manifested in the Ottawa demonstration, John Clarke responded that, if what had taken place was indeed ugly, "dying in an alleyway, or in a bloody park, of exposure, is a great deal more ugly." A month later the Chrétien government announced a National Homeless Initiative, funded for three years at $750 million, the money being spent on assisting municipalities to establish shelters, food banks, and other services for the poor.[93]

Yet the dying did indeed continue. On Thursday, May 4, 2000, TDRC held a demonstration at Queen's Park to protest the death in late March of a young, twenty-year-old homeless woman, Jennifer Caldwell. Originally from Vancouver, Caldwell had made her way to Toronto and could find no other lodgings than a patch of ground on the Don Valley ravine, adjacent to the posh neighbourhood of Rosedale. There she constructed a makeshift lean-to under a footbridge, living rough for three months according to street nurse Cathy Crowe. Something went awry, and her living space was engulfed in flames. When firefighters arrived, they thought the blaze a bushfire, but poking their pikes into the debris they struck the soft tissue of an incinerated body. TDRC estimated that Jennifer Caldwell was one of twenty-one homeless men and women who had died in Toronto since November 1999. Over the next months more would expire.[94]

On March 27, 2000, OCAP issued an open letter to Ontario's premier, Mike Harris. Tired of various levels of the state ignoring the worsening situation of the poor and refusing to meet with advocates of the dispossessed, OCAP served notice that it would march on the legislature on June 15, with the intention of addressing politicians on the crisis of homelessness and the debilitating impact of the erosion of social services and rates of welfare assistance. The open letter, demanding in tone and unabashed in its condemnation of Tory policies, made it clear that the voice of the dispossessed was not to be suppressed:

Your government has caused more than enough misery in this province. Welfare programs have been so cut to the bone that even those still able to access them are reduced to a wretched state of sub-poverty.... With this letter we serve notice that we intend to both rekindle and transform this struggle against your government. For several years now we have been at the forefront of the resistance to the measures you have inflicted on the lives of poor people and the homeless.... We intend to see mobilization against you and all that you stand for taken to a level that is powerful and disruptive enough so your government can no longer proceed with its agenda. On June 15, we will be marking this new course with a march on the legislature. This time, however, you will not be able to ignore us ... while we make speeches outside. This is because we are demanding of you, as premier, the right to address the legislature in session so that those who have been profoundly damaged can bring just call for redress before the entire assembly of the provincial government.

The June 15 demonstration was also driven by specific demands: 1) reinstatement of the 21.6 percent cuts to social assistance inaugurated by the Tories in 1995; 2) repeal of the Tenant Protection Act that removed rent controls, resulting in thousands of evictions across the province, and the subsequent escalation of homelessness; and 3) repeal of the offensive Safe Streets Act, which had so obviously been used to criminalize the poor. OCAP's militant call to march on the legislature and to demand that it admit a delegation of the dispossessed to address legislators on the state of the poor garnered wide support. TDRC, the Metro Network for Social Justice, the York University Faculty Association, the St. Catharines Labour Council, the Canadian Union of Postal Workers (CUPW), the Canadian Automobile Workers (CAW), and the Canadian Union of Public Employees (CUPE), among others, endorsed the action.[95]

OCAP's June Days would unfold under the banner, "Fight to Win!" Preparations for the Queen's Park action included visiting and organizing homeless men and women at Toronto's shelters and soup kitchens. Thousands of leaflets were distributed throughout the Downtown East, and posters were plastered about the city. Word spread across Ontario, but it did so unevenly, with left-wing activists very much on board while others, anticipating a public battle, were more guarded. Within labour organizations, even among those like the CAW, which was contributing monthly tithes to OCAP's shallow coffers, there was anxiety among the trade union tops, whose public pronouncements of support for the anti-Harris

Mother feeding baby marches on Queen's Park, Toronto, June 15, 2000.

OCAP Archives.

mobilization never quite registered in an all-out mobilization of the ranks. On the morning of June 15, fifteen hundred people assembled in Allan Gardens, eating, talking, listening to speakers, milling about. The crowd, a motley crew if ever there was one, contained the homeless and the professoriate, the seemingly meek and the obviously anything but mild. After a lunch served by OCAP, the army of the dispossessed and their supporters set off for Queen's Park, where OCAP and others had stated that the intention was to address the legislature. Gaétan Héroux's parting words to those filing out of Allan Gardens constituted a forceful reminder, "Don't be shy!"

Two hours before the anti-poverty protest approached Queen's Park, dozens of helmeted, well shielded, baton-wielding police set themselves up in riot formation in front of the legislature. They had steel barricades before them and an equestrian corps of officers behind and at their flanks. Their commanders had not been stingy with the pepper spray. The demonstrators, prepared for the worst, did not exactly come unprepared, although later newspaper reports on the armed nature of the combatants, with the accent on Molotov cocktails, in the plural, was a media/cop fabrication. But the OCAP contingent did carry a paraphernalia of protection: goggles, bandanas soaked in vinegar, bicycle helmets, the odd spoked wheel to slip over a horse's hoof and disable mounted police, even a large soiled mattress.

With the large crowd at a standstill on the edge of the Queen's Park lawn, John Clarke and a small OCAP delegation of five walked to the police barricades.

There the group was told that the six protesters would not be allowed to address the legislature, this being a privilege only granted heads of state. OCAP's position was that it couldn't care less about such protocols, and it was time for the government to hear, first hand, from the homeless. Anything but naïve, the militants in OCAP did not expect to be accommodated by Harris and the legislature, but they did think it possible, as Clarke later explained, and as has happened historically, that some deal could have been brokered, allowing a small group to meet with either the premier or a relevant cabinet minister. Nothing of the sort, however, was going to be conceded. Once this news was conveyed to the remainder of the protesters, demonstrators began to move toward the police lines.

What ensued was nothing less than a riot, but one in which the police themselves were most decidedly out of control and in which events took a turn that surprised OCAP. John Clarke recalled:

> We were astounded.... They moved to clear the grounds of the legislature. They rode horses into the crowd, and they began what the riot police refer to in their technical terminology as "punch outs"—that is, full speed baton charges into the crowd.... I imagine they anticipated there would be a rout—people would flee the grounds. What actually happened is that there was a battle. People stood their ground and people fought back. It wasn't organized, it wasn't planned that there would be a confrontation, but once

TORONTO'S POOR

they began the confrontation, there is no question that the people we brought to Queen's Park did not turn their backs.

It is crucial to understand that no attempt was made by the cops to contain the crowd behind the barricades. Indeed, the steel barricades were not forcefully secured and were easily lifted and pushed aside, almost purposively so. With the conventional barrier separating police and protest gone, cops and the crowd were thrown upon one another. As protesters approached the "blue wall," the police acted precipitously. The blows they meted out to the marchers were rebuffed and occasionally returned. There was no loudspeaker order to disperse. Pepper spray filled the air. Tin-can noise-makers were thrown by protesters, and the police were also pelted with relatively harmless "paint bombs" (defensive in their intent, they splatter on plexiglass shields and face protectors, making it difficult for the police to see clearly those they are pursuing or want to beat). Isolating individuals who had made themselves repugnant in their resistance, groups of cops wrestled single figures to the ground and then whaled on them with batons, kicking at their prostrate bodies. Mounted police rode through the crowd, pushing it back, battering those attempting to hold their ground or protect comrades. Understandably, horses were then struck by demonstrators, and at least one was disabled by a bicycle tire slipped under a hoof and pushed up the animal's shin. A few in the increasingly angry crowd began breaking up interlocking bricks, using the projectiles to halt

Riot police retreat from flimsy barricades, Queen's Park, June 15, 2000.

OCAP Archives.

the charge of the gendarmes. Critically important in understanding the police riot was the singular fact that no arrests were made as the cops battered on protesters. Those on the ground suffering police assault often simply covered their heads and curled up in defensive balls. Small crowds of demonstrators circled the police and yelled for them to stop and arrest the individual if a crime had been committed, but this did not happen. Cries of "Shame!" and worse rang out. For all of the subsequent press hyperbole about arsenals of explosives being detonated, there was in fact very little of this. To the best of our knowledge, one incendiary device imploded on the steps of the Legislature. No other "bombs" were sighted.[96]

The police undoubtedly had the best of the battle, armed and protected as they were with batons, shields, and horses, although OCAP's forces certainly got in their licks. OCAP and its homeless constituents and outraged supporters made their way back to Allan Gardens. By this time, the police were posing for the photo ops that would confirm their abuse at the hands of the demonstrators. The physical toll was hardly devastating, with cops putting on display for the media scraped knees and bumps and bruises on shins. Scratched and whacked horses caused much postured anguish. But the count of police injured tallied up, in the immediate aftermath of the Queen's Park confrontation, at twenty-nine. As the bedraggled OCAP forces reassembled in Allan Gardens, the cops ringed the park and began to pick off individuals and arrest them, following with more arrests shortly thereafter, twenty-nine in all. Tit for tat. With more police injuries coming to light over the next days, with the filing of "injured on duty" forms, further arrests were made, again bringing the scorecard of police injured/protesters arrested, to a like number, forty-two cops vs. forty-five demonstrators charged. On July 20, OCAP's John Clarke, Gaétan Héroux, and Stefan Pilipa were arrested, charges claiming that they were the leaders responsible for the riot. Coercive bail conditions were imposed, including prohibition of communication with any OCAP member, participation in protests, demonstrations, or marches of any kind, and restrictions on movement, including a ban on being within fifty metres of Allan Gardens. Even the *Globe and Mail* thought this was all a bit much, editorializing that such bail conditions were "unreasonable," giving the impression of "an act of court sanctioned political repression." Crown Attorney Vincent Paris, however, pushed for a decisive containment of the OCAP activists, whom he described as "a cancer," a denigration reinforced by Police Chief Julian Fantino's mid-July reference to the protest tactics as "domestic terrorism." OCAP's lawyers managed to get these draconian bail terms rescinded in a mid-September 2000 Ontario Supreme Court ruling, but Clarke, Héroux, and Pilipa existed under the guillotine of serious criminal charges for years.[97]

TORONTO'S POOR

Riot police,
mounted police,
protesters,
Queen's Park, June
15, 2000.
OCAP Archives.

Globe and Mail columnist Rick Salutin astutely commented on the "Press Riot" that followed the Queen's Park June 15, 2000, protest. Newspapers carried lurid caricatures of an anti-poverty mob, armed "with smoke bombs and Molotov cocktails," lobbing poor man's grenades into the police ranks, lighting the streets ablaze in their retreat. Official poverty crusaders, like Liberal MPP Gerard Kennedy, gave the journalistic rampage good copy, commenting for the press in the midst of the Queen's Park tumult, "This is not the face of the poor and the homeless. This is the face of a few idiots." Kennedy later stated in a press release that the protesters came with the "intention of inciting the police," a theme that commonly ran through mainstream media accounts. John Barber of the *Globe and Mail*, for instance, wrote on the day after the riot that OCAP organizers were "a nasty bunch," who "came with the intention of inciting violence." John Clarke, in particular, was singled out for supposedly wanting the "political theatre" and "spectacle" of a violent confrontation between the poor and the police. There were, to be sure, columnists and commentators in the conventional press who countered such views, among them the predictable—such as left-leaning figures like Michael Valpy, Judy Rebick, and Naomi Klein—as well as the oddly out of sync. In the latter category was Dalton Camp, an old-style "Red Tory" who found the sledgehammer response of the "Common Sense Revolution" off-putting in its complacent dismantling of democracy and its mean-spirited austerity. Camp, often writing tongue-in-cheek, recognized that for the poor the optics were not good, and it did not help that so many of their spokespeople and agitators were "unkempt and ill-dressed, even for a riot." To be sure, he acknowledged, in a democracy, "those who have a beef against the government should use the institutions provided for citizens' complaint and redress." But, added Camp tellingly, "who said this was a democracy?" "There is historic evidence that mobs have changed the minds of their masters," Camp insisted, and if the dispossessed had rioted against the Harris government, as unsettling as this may be to "editorial boards and letter writers to the press," it might just reflect tragic necessity. This recognition that the harsh reality of homelessness and poverty was finally bringing the chickens home to roost in Ontario also came across in journalistic reports of how quickly the police and protest turned ugly. Richard Brennon of the *Star* noted that, "It was stunning, the speed with which the protesters and the police officers alike were grimacing with rage." It was the "anger etched on the faces of both sides," that Brennon remembered most vividly, even as he was pepper sprayed by police. Staff-Sergeant Brian O'Connor, a member of the riot squad, had never experienced what he saw on the faces of the homeless in Queen's Park. "There was a fury in these people, an intensity.... It's frightening. It was hand-hand-combat. Very short—intense, very violent. [The protesters] didn't appear to feel the blows." This was the revenge of the dispossessed.[98]

Shayesteh Mohammadian, one of the June 15 defendants and an OCAP member, summed up what had happened at Queen's Park, stressing that witnessing the police riot and her subsequent arrest had done nothing to change her commitment to fighting against poverty. Her understanding of the conditions under which the poor lived, what caused them, and the necessity to mobilize for the rights of the dispossessed remained unshaken as she read a statement in court:

> I would like to make it clear to everyone that what happened on June 15, 2000, ha[s] not changed my views on poverty. Its causes, and the necessity to fight it. I am not a woman of violence, but will continue to fight it as a political activist, as a rights activist, as I have done for many years, starting in Iran. Decent dignified housing is a right, a basic human right, not a privilege, and I am absolutely convinced, and more determined than ever before, that I must fight for it. No rights have ever been offered to the people on a silver tray. Every one of them is a hard won achievement. Make no mistake about it! Had it not been for the struggles of the people, of the have nots, we would still be living under the cruel, exploitative, conditions of the 17th, 18th, and 19th centuries.

What happened on June 15 was, for Mohammadian, "nothing but another page of the history of class struggle."[99]

The fallout from the Queen's Park police riot did not end for years. In order to facilitate prosecution of the protesters, Toronto police executed warrants at fourteen of the city's media outlets and on July 11, 2000, seized negatives, digital images and videotapes compiled by journalists covering the demonstration. Fearing that they would be perceived as little more than an arm of the state, the *Star*, the CBC, and other print and electronic media attempted to quash the police seizures. Media claims that the warrants infringed their Charter of Rights guarantees cut no ice with the courts, which ruled against the fourth estate, bolstering police claims that the seized evidence was needed to identify and prosecute perpetrators of the serious offence of rioting in front of the Ontario Legislature. More than three-dozen other protesters faced 250 criminal charges, with court appearances that dragged into 2002–2003. Among the fourteen homeless men arrested, many spent time in jail; some were unable to make bail and offered guilty pleas simply to speed up the process and lessen their incarceration time, which approached six months. One of these homeless men and OCAP members, James Semple, would later recount how he was forced to spend six months in jail awaiting trial because he had been refused bail. Of the remaining two dozen or so protesters facing "participating in a riot" charges, most plea bargained or had the charges against them dropped. But Crown Prosecutor Paris waited more than eighteen months, an inordinate delay, before dropping most of the charges against those who had at least sufficient means to wait him out.

June 15 defendants in front of old City Hall.

OCAP Archives.

The trial of Clarke, Héroux, and Pilipa began in January of 2003, lasted four months, and cost $1 million. Defended by lawyers Peter Rosenthal, Bob Kellerman, and Jeffrey House, the OCAP activists were slapped with serious charges involving maximum sentences of two to five years of jail time. Héroux and Pilipa, in court for their alleged "participation in a riot" faced possible two-year sentences if convicted, while, in Clarke's case, the Crown's charge that he had "counselled to assault police" carried a maximum five-year jail term. The charge was almost unprecedented in modern times, because, in effect, it criminalized speech. Clarke and his lawyers later determined that precedents for these kinds of charges almost always reached back to the 1930s, when the state used the courts to try to silence the Communist Party. After the gruelling court proceedings, the jurors were unable to reach a unanimous verdict. Jurors' emotional distress during their deliberations necessitated the hospitalization of one of their number, who was discharged. Other jurors suffered panic attacks, migraine headaches, and various forms of personal anxiety, all of this brought on by the failure of the jury to come to a decision.

With the court panel deadlocked, presiding Justice Lee Ferrier declared a mistrial. Toronto's Chief Prosecutor, Paul Cover, then decided to drop the charges against Héroux and Pilipa, but to continue the crusade against Clarke, proceeding to a second trial. Thirty OCAP activists promptly shut down Attorney-General Norm Sterling's office for an hour and a half. With proceedings beginning in October 2003, Rosenthal argued convincingly that Clarke's rights as an accused had been violated by the Crown's failure to prosecute his charges in a reasonable time. Justice Harvey Spiegel dismissed all counts against Clarke, and the Queen's Park police riot was finally put behind OCAP.[100]

In the period between the June 2000 protest at Queen's Park and the final termination of the legal assault on John Clarke and other OCAP activists in October 2003, a great deal of political water flowed under the anti-poverty mobilizing bridge. Traditionally reliant on trade union funding support, and with some in its ranks (Clarke among them) seeing OCAP as something of a left conscience of an organized labour movement that it sought to galvanize into a more militant, oppositional stand, OCAP's willingness to "fight to win" in this period scared some conventional working-class leaders. At OCAP's birth at the beginning of the 1990s, Clarke had written,

> The real power to defeat the corporate onslaught is not to be found in community organizing but in the millions of working men and women organized in their workplaces by trade unions. The way forward for social movements,

therefore, depends on how effectively they can forge a link with the power of the organized working class, while, at the same time, encourage within the union movement a far bolder and broader outlook of mobilization and struggle that includes social movements.

Many in OCAP would not share Clarke's view. But his fundamentally dialectical understanding of the relationship of organized labour—both its multitudes in the ranks and its layers of leadership—to social movements of militant struggle, often led by the left, offered something of a blueprint for how to approach the politics of resistance in a non-revolutionary age. It was no less valid a position in 2002 than it had been when first published in 1992.

That said, what OCAP experienced between 1995 and 2003 complicated matters because as it was forced, with the ongoing and intensifying war against the dispossessed, to fight back with increasing militancy and unequivocal combativity, it constantly ran into the domestication of the Canadian trade union movement, which proved less and less able to mount even the most defensive, economistic, and limited of struggles. Trade union leaders began to backtrack more publicly, after Queen's Park, away from the practice if not necessarily the purpose of OCAP. The trade union funds kept coming to OCAP in the immediate aftermath of the June

2000 protest, to be sure, but they now came, not so much with strings attached, but with fairly transparent warnings. Sid Ryan, president of CUPE-Ontario, handed over a cheque to support the defence campaign of Clarke and others in 2000, but he did so, one suspects, in part because he had been raked over the coals by militants in his union ranks for disassociating himself from OCAP as the battle on the legislature lawn was being pilloried in the press. Even as he forked over the money, Ryan could not refrain from an equivocal statement about "Clarke's tactics," buying into the mainstream harangues. It was not all that different with the CAW's Buzz Hargrove who, while he endorsed support for the June 15 defendants, distanced himself from the protest. Indeed, had the two powerful union leaders truly wanted to mobilize their ranks to be at OCAP's Queen's Park rally in significant numbers, the cops could not have rioted as they did. The size of the demonstration would not then have been between one and two thousand but would instead have approached ten thousand. That, and not the symbolic presence of the CAW's "Union Train," with its banner calling on all concerned to "Get On Board," would have given the police cause to pause. But the union presence at Queen's Park in June 2000 was tepid rather than tumultuous.

In a 2003 interview, Stefan Pilipa, when asked how the OCAP trials "relate directly to the labour movement," responded:

> For the labour movement as it is, or as it should be? It is hard to imagine many contemporary labour leaders taking any sort of dramatic or disobedient political action that could subject them to prosecution in the criminal courts. Yet, a labour movement worthy of the name inevitably comes in conflict with both employers and states on a nearly constant basis as it battles for improved social conditions and higher wages, and resists a widening capitalist agenda that necessarily undermines the well being of the vast majority of the population.... Our trial is a direct expression of how the law can be used to intimidate those who would resist, and the trade unions need to take direct action.

Clarke agreed:

> the response of the major, powerful, working-class organizations to this very serious threat to our rights is nothing remotely close to what it could and should be. We need to bring home to the political decision makers that a considerable price will be paid for acts of this kind of

John Clarke
fundraiser: Stefan
Pilipa, Peter Rosen-
thal, Naomi Klein,
and Bryan Palmer
at Tranzac Club,
Toronto, October
7, 2003.

OCAP Archives.

legal persecution. If that is not the response, we can only expect more
public-order show trials in the period ahead. And, while they have come
for OCAP now, they will come for others in the future, especially if we are
dispensed with rather easily.[101]

"The Long Retreat is Over"

The curtain of legal repression that lowered on OCAP in the summer of
2000 was meant to decapitate the organization, demoralize its membership, drain
the anti-poverty movement of resources by eating up its meagre funds in costly
courtroom charades, and intimidate its respectable supporters. OCAP responded
by refusing to be cowed into submission, and it launched one of its most ambi-
tious campaigns of economic disruption. With a significant number of its members
facing criminal charges, and with key activists and leaders targeted by the state,
OCAP vowed that "The Long Retreat is Over," and initiated a province-wide mobilization of a Common Front involving some eighty organizations dedicated to defeating the Harris government *and* attacking the business and financial interests that
orchestrated much of the Tories' repugnant poor-bashing state policy. The idea of
the Common Front, never fully realized, was to unite militants in the student movement, the trade unions, the environmental and anti-poverty sectors, and among
refugee, immigrant, and First Nations communities, drawing these opponents of
capitalism's business-as-usual attitude to the crises foisted on the poor into resistance through a variety of direct actions.

The urgency of mounting a militant resistance was highlighted by the ongoing crisis of homelessness and the increasingly dangerous nature of street living in Toronto. In addition to depressed immune systems due to living on the streets and in hostels with a lack of sleep and proper nutrition, overcrowding in the shelters meant that the homeless were susceptible to disease. Tuberculosis (TB), in particular, was an ongoing threat, with 30 percent of Toronto hostel inmates and 24 percent of shelter staff testing positive for TB. Those who chose to live on the streets were not unaware of how the congested shelters were conduits of disease. Between September 2000 and July 2002 an outbreak of tuberculosis in two of Toronto's largest men's hostels, Seaton House and the Maxwell Meighen Centre, infected dozens of residents and took several lives. As conditions in the hostels and day shelters worsened, the homeless who shunned them for the streets died, often of hypothermia, sometimes at the hands of attackers.[102]

Conditions in city shelters actually seemed to be deteriorating in the opening years of the twenty-first century, to standards associated with the nineteenth-century House of Industry. A video in the possession of TDRC depicted the horrific conditions at an overnight shelter, where up to 140 homeless men and women crowded on a concrete floor to pass a sleep-interrupted night before being woken at 5:30 a.m. and ushered out of the building at 7 a.m. There were no shower facilities, and the men's washroom consisted of two urinals, one of which was usually backed up, and a single toilet. The *Star* described the scene:

> The bodies are jammed together, men and women, on the floor in a windowless basement. A man coughing stumbles around sleeping bodies, trying to find room on the floor for his mat and sleeping bag.... There's a blur of bodies—dozens in sleeping bags, others wrapped in blankets, still more on the metal chairs talking at a table. The bright lights stay on all night.

Superimposed on some stills of the video that appeared alongside the *Star* article was a drawn-to-scale 4.5-metre square, representing the space that the United Nations stipulates should separate beds in refugee camps. In Toronto's emergency overnight shelters, there were three or four persons occupying that 4.5-metre grid. Yet the Conservative provincial government's Minister of Social Services, Brenda Elliott, who oversaw 80 percent of the costs of running shelters in Ontario, dismissed the TDRC video's significance. Hostels, declared Elliott, were not meant to be "Holiday Inns." In May 2003, a "Shelter Inspection Report: A Report of Conditions in Toronto's Shelter System" documented the crisis in the city's shelter system, with outbreaks of tuberculosis, infestations of bed bugs, inadequate food, chronic overcrowding, ill-equipped hygienic facilities, and routinized theft and violence. Rick Wallace, one of the authors of the report, and a former United Nations worker, testified that "Some of the conditions in Toronto shelters are worse than in refugee camps in Rwanda, in terms of space, sanitation, and preventative health care practices." Such assessments drove some community workers to demand a revamping of the province's social housing program. They urged addressing the cramped conditions of squalor that defined shelter living, establishing an Ombudsman's office to process complaints and effect change, and called for the development of new shelters and opening the doors to buildings like the Fort York Armoury that had been and could continue to be used to provide much needed beds for those living on Toronto's streets.[103]

The Tories, however, were listening to none of this. Perhaps, thought OCAP, the Common Sense Revolution's inability to hear and see evidence of the crisis of homelessness could be impressed on them by putting one of their number on the street himself, at least symbolically. One of the Common Front's first, and arguably most controversial, actions was the mock eviction of Ontario's Finance Minister, Jim Flaherty, from his Whitby constituency office. On June 12, 2001, a group of fifty OCAPers and some radicals from the CAW's flying squad, used to provide support for strikes across the province, and in this case apparently acting on their own initiative, invaded Flaherty's Whitby headquarters. Mimicking the behaviour of sheriffs serving eviction papers in the 1930s, the protesters took the office furniture and files and dumped them on the sidewalk. They plastered "Defeat Harris" posters on the windows and graffitied walls with slogans. Files and flyers were scattered about the rooms. Newspapers reported the mock eviction with outrage, labelling the protest the work of vandals, revelling in quoting from one scrawled obscenity on an office door: 'F___ your corporate pride." Mohawk militant Shawn Brant promised that the Flaherty eviction was the beginning of a Common Front campaign, in which "both the numbers and the intensity of the actions will be increased,"

Flaherty mock eviction, Whitby, June 12, 2001.
OCAP Archives.

while Sue Collis proclaimed the demonstration "the first skirmish in an all out war." Whitby police were quickly called to the scene, arresting a number of people in the street and later intercepting a chartered bus that was transporting demonstrators back to Toronto. More arrests followed, for a total of nineteen people charged with unlawful assembly, causing a disturbance, and mischief over $5000, assault, obstruct, and resisting police. Among those facing charges were Brant, Collis, and four June 15 defendants, including John Clarke. The June 15 defendants, under indictment for their part in the previous year's Queen's Park confrontation, were singled out for special treatment. Labelled as "terrorists" by the Crown Attorney, Clarke and Sean Lee-Popham were denied bail, forced to cool their heels in jail for several weeks. Lee-Popham and A. J. Withers two of the June 15 defendants, were ultimately given strict bail conditions, which included house arrest. Lee-Popham's bail was set at $70,000; Clarke was released on a $40,000 surety with conditions that prohibited him from attending any demonstration. Collis was soon out of police custody but was jailed for ten days a week or so later when she was arrested after addressing a crowd gathered to commemorate the anniversary of the June 15, 2000, protest at the Ontario Legislature.[104]

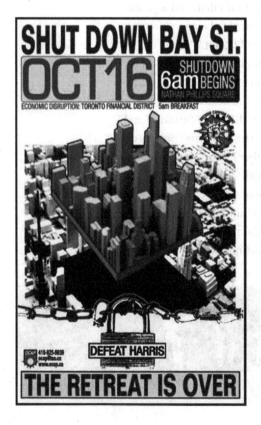

Controversial Common Front poster—Shut Down Bay Street! October 16, 2001.

OCAP Archives.

Buzz Hargrove, president of the powerful CAW, was incensed at the Flaherty eviction. He was particularly agitated that some CAW militants were visibly involved in the demonstration and were charged by the police. Seeking to dissociate the CAW from the action, Hargrove spoke out publicly against it and sent a letter of regret to Flaherty, offering to meet with him to talk about his union's relationship with OCAP. Hargrove subsequently sat down with the province's Tory Minister of Labour, Chris Stockwell, to discuss the Whitby demonstration. While Hargrove had to call for the release of Clarke and the granting of bail conditions for him, given that some CAW members faced similar charges, the Flaherty eviction wrote *finis* to the CAW funding for OCAP. In July 2001, the CAW National Executive Board officially announced that it had voted to terminate its financial arrangements with the anti-poverty organization. OCAP responded with an immediate appeal to trade unionists, community activists, and all of those fighting the Harris government, explaining how materially crippling the CAW's short-notice withdrawal of its annual support of $10,000 was to its capacity to organize and resist. Defending the need to take militant stands, OCAP found Hargrove's offence at an action that "may have damaged some of Flaherty's furniture" galling and "out of touch with the tasks that face" all of those desirous of building a movement that could defeat the Tories. "The political thugs at Queen's Park just don't understand the language of fair play and respectability that Buzz wants us to use on them," OCAP said, "but, when they know we're ready to fight back just as seriously as they're prepared to attack us, that's when they'll understand us perfectly ... that's when the defeat of the Harris agenda will be on the table."[105]

The culmination of the Ontario Common Front initiative was OCAP's Tuesday, October 16, 2001, march through Toronto's financial district. Assiduously prepared, the action was announced in a poster proclaiming "Shut Down Bay Street," "Economic Disruption. Toronto Financial District," "Defeat Harris," and "The Retreat Is Over." Over the course of the late summer, OCAP distributed thousands of these posters, which depicted an aerial view of Toronto's downtown, in which a financial district inset, highlighted in red, was lifted out of the topography so as to float above the Toronto skyline. In the immediate context of 9/11, in which the terrorist bombing of New York's Twin Towers levelled the metropolitan landmarks, some construed this poster as callously calling for the bombing of Toronto's downtown, even though the actual image had been created and distributed well before the September attack on lower Manhattan. Some called on OCAP to cancel the proposed October march to Bay and Adelaide Streets, the immediate post-9/11 climate being one of an intensifying crackdown on all dissent. OCAP met with Common Front-allied organizations calling for a tactical retreat but refused to be cowed and determined to proceed with the intended day of disruption in the financial district.

Tensions mounted as October 16 approached. Businesses in the financial district emailed employees, warning them of the possibility of violent clashes. People were reminded to carry security passes and advised not to interact with protesters. Private security forces were beefed up, and parking and access to certain buildings were restricted. Two busloads of dissidents from Montreal and Quebec City, who had arranged to be billeted at All Saints Church, were met as they arrived in the downtown core by Steve Irwin, a Toronto police officer from the Intelligence Squad, and dozens of uniformed cops who ostentatiously videotaped the protesters as they stepped out of the buses. Police Chief Julian Fantino vowed the demonstrators would not be allowed to bring their protest to the financial district. To add muscle to this rhetoric, Fantino dispatched five hundred Toronto officers, many of them in riot gear, to the perimeter of the financial district, a core contingent that was reinforced by hundreds of cops brought in from York, Peel, and Durham regions and a platoon of OPP officers. This army of safe street occupation took up positions around 3 a.m., two hours before OCAP had announced it would serve breakfast to the homeless.[106]

As hundreds of demonstrators filtered into Nathan Phillips Square on a rainy morning on October 16, the crowd grew to 2,000–2,500. Some, like the Quebeckers coming from All Saints Church, had been followed by police vans. Arriving at the Square, demonstrators encountered an imposing and intimidating line of riot police ringing the protest. The cops demanded, illegally, to search the arriving demonstrators, refusing entry to the Square to any who declined to be processed by the police. The Quebec group took the position that it was unwilling to be searched, as did many other individuals and small groups of arriving protesters. Blocked from entering Nathan Phillips Square, they gathered in an adjacent parking lot. Some protesters who complied with the search were detained for having protective gear such as goggles, balaclavas, bandanas, and vinegar, a commonly used repellent for pepper spray or tear gas. They were herded into paddy wagons and held for up to seven hours before being released without charge. In dividing the ranks of the protest, the police no doubt thought they had conquered it. In fact, they had created a two-headed serpent, with more than a thousand people inside the Square and hundreds milling about its outskirts.

The tactic that OCAP had decided on for the demonstration was a snake march, in which the rally broke out of the orderly pattern of most protests, characterized by a march proceeding with direction toward a specific end-point. Snake marches defy such order. They zig and zag in different directions and follow no logic of progression, making them exceedingly difficult for the police to predict and thus effectively contain. As the marchers left Nathan Phillips Square and its surrounding environs in two distinct groups, there was almost no communication between the isolated bodies of protesters. With very little knowledge of the Toronto topography and unaware of where the financial district was located, the Quebec group decided to depart first and actually moved in a southwest direction, away from the targeted Bay and Adelaide core. Some of the cops had to follow, leaving fewer to shadow those inside Nathan Phillips Square, who began to march downtown. The Quebec marchers soon found themselves lost, having no idea where they were going, but neither did the police. Meanwhile, the main body of the march was wandering the streets of downtown, seemingly aimlessly, playing a cat and mouse game with the frustrated police, who had trouble figuring out what was going on. Startlingly, the Quebec-led snake marchers managed to break through a police line and found themselves, to their surprise, smack in the middle of the financial district. After an hour of seemingly directionless, quick-paced traversing of streets adjacent to the financial district, the Nathan Phillips Square marchers also managed to break through police lines, joining forces with their Quebec counterparts, and the march was united.

As OCAP members later explained, the snake march threw the police into "an absolute quandary." Those detained in paddy wagons heard the police radio reports and registered the extent to which the forces of law and order were perplexed to the point of incapacitation:

> At one point, they decided we were going to the Stock Exchange, so they moved a whole pile of cops down to the Stock Exchange. Then they decided we weren't, so they pulled them away. Then they decided they were again, so they pulled them back. And then they had a conversation in which they said, "They're not coming to the Stock Exchange, but we can't leave again because someone in the media is going to get the idea we don't know what we're doing."

In constant phone communication with his troops in the midst of this chaos, Fantino at one point reportedly slammed down a receiver with a disgusted retort, "There is nothing we can do to stop this." A superintendent later offered a less anguished, more candid comment: "Our difficulty was the size of the boundary we had to protect. A gap was left open and they were able to get through." Of course, this was not the public proclamation, which came later, Police Chief Fantino acknowledging that his forces had failed to keep the snake march out of the financial district. "We may not have been able to achieve everything that we had hoped," he confessed, adding with pique, "but OCAP failed miserably and the forces of good won today." For OCAP, the highlight of the day was when the Deputy Chief of Police, being interviewed by CITY TV, declared, "There is absolutely no way that these people are going to get to the corner of Bay and Adelaide." Television cameras then focused in on a crowd of two thousand protesters standing victoriously at Bay and Adelaide.[107]

The snake march, lasting more than five hours, was a visible reminder that there were those who were not willing to be silenced amid capitalism's persistent crises. The counter-climate of terror waged against dissidents and scapegoating others of all kinds in the aftermath of 9/11 was, for a few hours, put on the defensive.

Cries rang out in the financial district: "Capitalism, No Thanks. We'll Shut Down Your Fucking Banks!" Onlookers in business suits were admonished to, "Join us.... You're in jail!" As traffic snarled in Toronto's always congested downtown core, Ontario Common Front activists from Kingston blockaded the Don Valley Parkway and the 401, bringing what demonstrators called the "just in time" economy of Ontario to a halt. But violence, even against property, which the rich so deplore and fear, was almost non-existent. Several buildings "suffered" at the hands of spray-painting graffiti artists, whose slogans of choice included "Eat the Rich," "Smash the Banks," and "Affordable Housing"; newspaper boxes were turned over; and some police car windows were smashed. A Montreal militant, Christopher Arsenault, managed to make his way to the roof of the Royal York Hotel, where he spray-painted "Stop Murder" on a United States flag before putting it to flames. He and a co-conspirator in this act of desecration were later arrested, although rain ensured that the Stars and Stripes failed to burn, and hotel property was never in danger of catching fire. All told, forty people were arrested on a variety of charges or held on breach of peace, and Fantino claimed that police confiscated sticks, rocks, two-by-fours, gas masks, and what was described as Molotov cocktail ingredients. He neglected to mention plastic bottles of vinegar.[108]

It is difficult, if not impossible, to ascertain the economic hit sustained by the financial backers of the Mike Harris regime that OCAP's snake march targeted. Conservative estimates put the cost of the day's disruption at $200,000, while activists suggest hundreds of thousands of dollars, perhaps as much as one million. Mayor Mel Lastman wasn't about to understate the damage, however, as he fumed publicly, apoplectic at OCAP's affront: "We'll sue the thugs," he promised, claiming that the city's cost of policing the event was $200,000. Lastman also encouraged businesses to go after OCAP for any damages they could claim relating to loss of commerce resulting from the demonstration. None of this came to pass and, in the end, the protest's significance was largely, if powerfully, symbolic. The snake marchers revelled, if only for a few hours, in a visible anti-capitalist statement. The icing on the cake was that the mobilization, launched under the banner, "Defeat Harris," took place on October 16, 2001, the very day that newspaper headlines proclaimed that the hated Tory leader was stepping down as premier. Perhaps, many in OCAP must have thought, they had played some small role in driving the Common Sense counterrevolutionary from office.[109]

Ernie Eves replaced Harris as the head of the Ontario government, but the Tories needed to choose a new leader and go to the polls. They met at the Metro Convention Centre in March 2002. On the first night of the leadership conference,

March 22, five hundred OCAP-Ontario Common Front anti-poverty activists assembled at Moss Park and, at 7 p.m., began a snake march. Heading toward the Metro Convention Centre, the unpredictable throng wound through downtown Toronto streets, ending up in front of the boarded-up Mission Press building at Dundas and Yonge. Dozens of protesters stripped the plywood shuttering off the front door, and sixty-five people, many of them homeless, occupied the third floor. A banner was hung from a window, reading "Build Housing Now." OCAP had no intention of squatting at the site permanently and planned to vacate the occupied premises the next day at noon. Police, however, refused to negotiate and demanded the activists and homeless depart immediately. Streets were closed off, and riot and mounted police moved in, breaking up the crowd gathered outside the building, and fired tear gas canisters into the occupation. Squatters were forced to leave the building one at a time, targeted by police laser guns, made to lay face down on the concrete, handcuffed, and hauled off to paddy wagons, where they languished for as much as seven hours before being processed and charged at the police station. Following this overdone mass arrest, twelve other protesters were taken into police custody the next day. The Ontario Common Front legal team spent two days bailing out the arrested squatters/protesters.[110]

At noon the next day three hundred rallied to protest the arrests. The group assembled in Allan Gardens and planned to march past the Mission Press building and make its way to the Conservative leadership convention at the Front Street Metro Convention Centre. An aggressive corps of riot police and bicycle wielding cops contained the crowd, restricting movement. As scuffles ensued, arrests were made. Eventually, the crowd, almost matched in size by the police ranks, made its way toward the Metro Convention Centre. At the same time, an Ontario Federation of Labour (OFL) rally against the Conservative government's agenda was taking place at the Front Street hotel. Concerned about the optics of protesting against the Tories when OCAP and the Common Front were also doing so and worried that their respectable reputation would be sullied if a confrontation with the police developed, the OFL had co-ordinated their protest with the police, intending to be long gone by the time the militant homeless arrived. But with the police perhaps unable to contain the Common Front crowd as effectively as they had hoped, the cops informed the OFL hierarchy that the Allan Gardens protest was getting dangerously close. The trade union tops then called it quits on their protest, and the marshals herded the OFL members away from the rally site in a hasty retreat. The Allan Gardens protest converged on the Metro Convention Centre, speakers denounced the Tory government's attacks on the poor, and the day's proceedings came to a close.

A rift was now evident in the Ontario Common Front. The labour bureau-crats had signalled that they wanted nothing to do with Common Front actions, where they might find themselves rubbing shoulders with the dispossessed in ways that threatened their sensibilities. This had been in the works for a long time, but OCAP's militancy since the Queen's Park police riot was now evident for all to see, and many within the trade union hierarchy saw the anti-poverty group as a serious liability. Organizations within the Common Front also began to backtrack, rethink-ing their commitment to the campaign to challenge the Tories through financial disruption and militant direct action. The mass arrests at the Mission Press occu-pation had brought home to many in the Common Front that OCAP was serious in its call to "Fight to Win," and the repercussions of going all-in for such a campaign scared many away. By the spring of 2002, the Ontario Common Front was in tatters. Even though it broadened its direct action to Sudbury, Peterborough, Hamilton, Guelph, and Ottawa through its Common Front mobilizations, OCAP learned that it was too small and marginal a force, on its own, to sustain a militant amalgama-tion of other social justice coalitions and organizations, united in a direct action attack on the servile state and the powerful capitalist interests that back it. Nor could it realistically garner support and retain ties to rank-and-file workers battling their ossified leadership, which remained "unwilling to put union resources into any extra-parliamentary fightback campaign." Nonetheless, recognizing its limita-tions, OCAP remained committed to a program of both fighting and winning, even if it recognized how much such a necessarily protracted battle had to be waged uphill, against the odds.[111]

Squatting with the Pope and the Tenants of Tent City

In the summer of 2002, Toronto was aflutter with news of a papal visit. Pope John Paul II was coming to the provincial capital after indulging in a few days of apparently much-needed rest with the Basilian Fathers of Strawberry Island in Lake Simcoe. He would then settle in at Morrow Park, the motherhouse of the Sisters of St. Joseph, and grace the World Youth Day Ceremonies at Downsview Park and the Canadian National Exhibition Grounds. OCAP decided to piggyback off the Pope's celebrity status to promote an understanding of the homeless crisis. Announcing that it would seize an unidentified empty building during the Pope's visit, OCAP explained that with international eyes on Toronto during the Catholic Youth Day events, and with humanitarian sensibilities running high, it would be difficult for civic officials to ignore the housing crisis and for the police to act toward the poor and squatters with their usual brutality. "We see the Papal visit as an opportunity

Queen Street
march to the Pope
Squat, Toronto,
July 25, 2002.
OCAP Archives.

to literally get our foot in the door," OCAP declared in an open letter released July 22, 2002. With millions of dollars spent on the papal visit, sixty thousand low-income Torontonians were awaiting social housing, often for as long as a decade. Conditions in the city's emergency shelters failed to meet minimum standards established for refugee camps by the United Nations, and five hundred evictions were happening weekly, forcing thousands to live on the streets. OCAP thus called on the homeless and their supporters to rally on July 25 at Parkdale's Masaryk Cowan Park. Outraged that Mayor Lastman would speak openly of his desire to "sweep" the homeless from the streets of Toronto during the Pope's visit, OCAP put forward a set of immediate demands: a massive drive to inspect and repair unsafe and substandard housing; an end to evictions; the abolition of the Housing Tribunal, a rubber stamp for landlords; restoring the cuts to social services instituted under the Conservative government in 1995; raising the minimum wage to $10 hourly; restoration of rent controls; and the building of two thousand units of social housing every year. "We have to stand up for ourselves and turn this situation around," OCAP declared defiantly.[112]

OCAP had scouted out the poor Parkdale neighbourhood to come up with an appropriate building to seize. With information provided by Bart Poesiat, a well-known tenant organizer in Parkdale, the anti-poverty organization settled on 1510 King Street West as a suitable site for the occupation. It did not, for obvious reasons, broadcast the exact location of the action. The ownership of the building, a three-storey one-time rooming house that had been empty since October 2000 when the last paying tenant left the building, was difficult to decipher. There was a history of squatting on the site as recently as 2001, according to an inspector's report that claimed, "Widespread damage has been done.... The building is being used by vagrants, causing damage and resulting in unhealthy conditions as there is exposed electrical wiring, open sewage, obstructed fire escapes." What OCAP would soon ascertain as it marked 1510 King Street West out for the Pope Squat was that, as of summer 2002, no one was living at the address, the building appeared to be abandoned, both the province and the municipality had a hand in responsibility for the property, and it was necessary to keep the King Street target under wraps as the police monitored OCAP's threat to occupy space for the homeless. Detective Constable Branko Novinc of the Intelligence-Anti-Terrorist and Threat Investigation of the Toronto Police Service approached OCAP and proposed holding discussions regarding the Pope Squat action. OCAP replied to Novinc with a polite and reasoned statement that it had decided on the occupation to challenge civic complacency around homelessness and the housing crisis, meaning no disrespect to anyone's religion. OCAP further hoped that "authority can behave reasonably during this event." The organization noted, "If there are no tasers, laser sights and riot clubs this time around, we won't miss them." While OCAP stipulated that it did not "automatically refuse to speak to the Police," it was more important that they communicate with the political power whose responsibility it was to deal with social issues, the provincial and municipal governments, either of which was very likely to have a "considerable interest in the property that is the focus of this initiative." OCAP was thus copying the letter to Premier Ernie Eves and Mayor Mel Lastman. It closed by thanking Novinc for "the consideration we know you will give these comments. No doubt, we shall have further dealings on this matter in due course."[113]

On the evening of Thursday, July 25, 2002, hundreds of people gathered at Masaryk Cowen Park. At the nearby Canadian National Exhibition grounds, the Pontiff received his youthful pilgrims. But in Parkdale hip-hop music blared from a portable sound system, Tyendinaga Mohawk Territory residents served a dinner of venison stew, and speakers talked of the injustice of the housing crisis and the dire straits of the homeless. Across the street, the festivities were solemnly observed by a sizable helmeted police corps, among whom could be spotted a Catholic priest wearing a bulletproof vest. Anarchists joked that the gendarmes might be looking for divine intervention, but it wasn't likely to be forthcoming that evening. OCAP, headed by drummers and a saxophonist, led the boisterous, good-natured crowd

Large crowd outside Pope Squat, Toronto, July 25, 2002.

OCAP Archives.

into Queen Street, chanting "Fight for Housing, Fight to Win" and "What Would Jesus Say? Build Housing Today." Stopping outside an abandoned building where two female tenants had died in a fire several years earlier, the crowd was welcomed by Parkdale residents, who cheered it on from sidewalks and second-storey windows. The protest march wended its way through the neighbourhood and eventually found its way to 1510 King Street West, where a crew of squatters had already entered the building the night before. As a 'No Trespassing' sign was torn from a fence and plywood was popped out from inside a window, a huge banner was unfurled, and an OCAP speaker declared the Pope Squat open. Leaflets were distributed among the crowd, listing a schedule of planned events at the squat in the days to follow, including movie screenings, clean-up and repair bees, and a Saturday street festival. The police, uncertain as to what to do, stood by and watched as small groups were formed to fan out throughout neighbourhood streets and alleyways to forage for furniture and other items useful to those now occupying the building. A few days later, OCAP called for a "radical garage sale," in which supporters were asked to clear all of their unused possessions out of apartments and homes and bring them to the King Street occupation, where people could barter or sell, the proceeds and unwanted goods to be donated to the Pope Squat.[114]

The dilapidated address taken in the Pope Squat had a complicated history. The original owner, Mississauga-based 459105 Ontario Ltd., had gone belly-up and no longer existed, the provincial government having cancelled its status, an extreme, last recourse, response. Work orders on the property had been piling up since 1995 when an inspector found the owners guilty of failing to provide tenants with heat and light. The city had the hydro reconnected, at a cost of $5,200, and billed the owners, who ignored the demand to settle the account. This ritual was re-enacted in 1996, 1997, and 1998, with the slumlords continuing to stiff the municipality. Toronto took out liens against the property worth approximately $16,000. Tenants, of course, were still paying their rent to the company, even though, in 1998, the plumbing was so dysfunctional that they were without water. Toronto paid another $2,000 that it could not collect. Eventually, the tenants moved on or were moved out, and the city informed the deadbeat corporation that it owed almost $40,000 in back taxes. Threats were made to seize the building and sell it to clear the arrears, but this never happened.

By the time OCAP occupied the building, conditions inside had deteriorated so badly that the squatters lived under a tarp in the backyard rather than set up living quarters inside. An industrial-size portable toilet was provided by trade union supporters, and hundreds of OCAP activists and their allies, homeless people, volunteer tradesmen, and the squatters themselves began to rip out mould-spawning carpet, water-soaked drywall, and other threats to health and safety. A month of hard, loving work turned the place around: water and electricity were restored, dumpsters of refuse were carted away, floors, handrails, and walls were cleaned and repaired, the holes in the roof patched and leaks stopped, and outside vegetable gardens thrived and bloomed with flowers. Michelle Landsberg visited the building as the refurbishing was taking place. She was shown around "the model suite" by twenty-year-old squatter Lisa Kocsis. The Toronto journalist thought it a "perfect example of functioning anarchy." Whoever wanted to work showed up and put in their hours. Whoever lived at the squat and put first dibs on a finished room got to live there. Local fast food restaurants allowed unfettered use of their washrooms, and neighbours brought water, food, and equipment. "It's messy, and the house is still half-wrecked, and you wouldn't want to live there if daily hygiene is an important part of your lifestyle," Landsberg concluded, "but 15 people have a roof over their heads and a home address." Finally, the syndicated columnist stressed that this "slow, hard collective work of reclamation" was rebuilding self-confidence among homeless youth, so beaten down by condescension and worse.

With no owners coming forward to protest that their property was subject to trespass and damage, the police seemed stymied. The King Street squat was now becoming something of a Toronto event: 250 people crammed the backyard one evening to hear Ron Hawkins Jr. and the Lowest of the Low perform and be present as Naomi Klein and Avi Lewis previewed their film on police violence in Argentina. Soon 70 organizations had endorsed the Pope Squat, including Buzz Hargrove and the CAW, which promised a cheque of $50,000 if all three levels of government made commitments to provide the necessary funds and infrastructure to turn the occupied King Street building into social housing for the homeless. Support also came from CUPE, TDRC, the Student Christian Movement, and the Metro Network for Social Justice. Martin Long, president of the Toronto local of the Elementary Teachers Federation of Ontario (ETFO), praised the OCAP organizers for "taking the matter into their own hands." Even Thomas Walkom, usually no supporter of OCAP's methods, reported that the militant anti-poverty organizers now got to "wear the good guy mantle," the Pope Squat illustrating "the disgraceful manner in which … authorities who claim to want to end homelessness allow viable housing to rot." As the city and the province fiddled with the homeless virtually burning in a property-conscious hell, OCAP deserved praise, according to Walkom, for filling "the gap." Its demands for "Ottawa and Queen's Park to pony up money for social housing" and for a "return to provincial rent controls" were not even radical, argued Walkom.[115]

Following a July 31 OCAP press conference demanding Toronto and the Ontario government step up and convert 1510 King Street West into socially useful housing, city hall passed a motion calling on the province to transfer title of the property to Toronto for the purpose of creating affordable housing. The motion, in the spirit of the Pontiff's visit and his pilgrims' devotion, began with an expression of lofty sentiments: "Whereas, in celebration of the visit of Pope John Paul II to the City of Toronto, bringing with him the message of justice and 'love they neighbour,' and Whereas, in honour of the Pilgrims who visited Toronto with their hope and faith for a better world." Councillor Chris Korwin-Kuczynski from Parkdale-High Park nonetheless took aim at OCAP, adding an amendment stipulating that the transfer of title and affordable/social housing conversion was only to take effect if OCAP and the squatters vacated the building immediately. "You have to make a stand," said the civic official, "This can't become a trend; anarchy can't decide the future of things." Korwin-Kuczynski clearly feared that if OCAP were not exorcized, the radical anti-poverty activists might just target some of the other thirty-five Parkdale buildings that had been identified as vacant. OCAP responded that if it were to leave the property, it would only be on the transfer of title *and* a guarantee that the two dozen King Street squatters would all be housed.[116]

What followed would certainly have made pontiffs and pilgrims animated by the spirit of loving thy neighbour and faith in a better world blanch. The City

Council motion to have the province transfer title of the King Street property to the municipality proved as vacuous as its rhetorical preamble. OCAP and the squatters stayed put. Councillor Olivia Chow worked with OCAP to prepare a brief making it clear that the province could assert its ownership of 1510 King Street West. That document sat without response on the desk of Attorney-General Dave Young. Behind the scenes, the province completed paper work that had long been in arrears and that finally and legally allowed it to take possession of the building, doing so, however, largely in the name of the original mortgage holders. That done, the assault on the Pope Squat began. Fire marshals and cops broke into the building on October 25, 2002, with Fire Prevention Division Chief Jack Collins ruling it unsafe for human habitation. A fire alarm was broken, electrical wiring was in poor condition, and there were cracks in the walls and fire doors. These violations supposedly constituted "an immediate threat to life." The water and electricity were ordered shut off. A week later, police were given the crucial go-ahead and raided the Pope Squat on November 1, tasked with removing the residents. Some of the OCAPers and squatters did not go quietly, and three were arrested, including squatter Sam Tassew. All those occupying the building were offered transportation to city shelters, but none took up the city's offer. A crew of city workers boarded up the building, and a security guard was left to guard the premises. That evening an emergency meeting at the Parkdale Activity-Recreation Centre determined to take back the Pope Squat the next evening. One hundred people marched on the King Street property. As a helplessly outnumbered security guard looked on impotently, OCAP members, former squatters, and other homeless people and supporters broke the locks on the front door and pried plywood off the windows.

The squatters' victory was short-lived. Mass arrests were threatened, and the Fire Marshal manoeuvred, with the result that the squatters were forced to vacate the premises, believing that, if certain conditions of improvement were met, they would be allowed to return. Nothing of the sort happened. A security firm was hired to keep watch over the address, running up a $12,000 bill in a matter of weeks. The mortgage holders of the property eventually sold it for $500,000 to Antonio and Filomena Sciscente, who also owned other buildings in Parkdale, the municipality cancelling all back taxes and any outstanding leases, perhaps to ease the sale of the property on the open market. The new owners secured funding from the federal and municipal governments to renovate 1510 King Street West. While OCAP's insistence that social housing be created was thus thwarted, the property reverting to privatized ownership, the King Street complex now houses two dozen low-income people in single bachelor apartments. Brilliantly executed, OCAP's Pope Squat broadened understanding of homelessness, exposed municipal and provincial ineptitude and disingenuousness, and, perhaps most importantly, brought under the bright light of scrutiny the contradictions at the core of a profit-driven system of private property, in which viable housing stock deteriorated and sat unused while the poor languished or lost their lives because they had no access to shelter.[117]

As the Pope Squat was calling attention to the crisis of homelessness, a more long-standing and larger squatting occupation was coming under attack. More than one hundred homeless men and women were living in a shantytown known as Tent City. Located on a piece of polluted land adjacent to Toronto's waterfront, Tent City's origins reached back to at least the early 1990s, when squatters first utilized the site. In December 1997, thirty to forty homeless youth squatting in the abandoned Canadian Malting Factory at the foot of Parliament Street and Lakeshore Boulevard were threatened with eviction by the city. The factory, especially its concrete grain elevators, was an innovation when constructed in the 1920s, and the building's stark functionalism was supposedly important in the history of Toronto's modernist architecture. Thus, when abandoned in the 1980s, the Malting Factory, while scheduled for demolition, was given a stay of execution, declared a heritage site, with vague plans for its conversion to parkland or a museum. Bureaucrats no doubt began to ponder how to get rid of the squatters, prompting harassment and talk of eviction. Known as the Rooster Squat because of a large painting on the side of one of the abandoned factory's concrete silos, the young residents of the former Malting Factory had other thoughts, however, and declared their intention to defend themselves and their occupied space should the city and police try to remove them. They contacted OCAP, and Beric German negotiated with the youth, Councillor Jack Layton, and the city to bring trailers donated by the Canadian Foundation for World Development to the lot, where they were converted into livable units. The squatters occupied these makeshift dwellings for a time but eventually moved out in the summer of 1998, and the trailers were removed. Over the next eighteen months, thirty to forty more homeless men and women set up a shantytown on a 5.3-hectare lot next to the Canada Malting Factory. The land, owned by Home Depot, was well known by the Ministry of the Environment to be "contaminated with heavy metals, including lead and arsenic, which can increase the risk of cancer." Citing "immediate risk to human health and ecological health at the site," the Ministry pressured Home Depot to get rid of the squatters, who were told in November 2000 that an eviction was imminent. OCAP provided support, but German and TDRC took the lead in organizing around Tent City, arguing that if it was to be broken up, this could only happen if its inhabitants were provided with safe, affordable housing. Emergency shelters, overcrowded and dangerous, were not considered an option, and the squatters were defiant that they would not submit without resistance. "I'll fight if I have to fight," declared Nancy Baker at a rain-soaked press conference. "This is my home."[118]

Home Depot wasn't prepared to go to war over a piece of polluted land, especially a battle that organizations like OCAP would make sure was fought out in the public relations realm. Round one in the struggle over Tent City went to the dispossessed. TDRC did what it could to make conditions passable for the squatters, bringing in prefabricated homes, outdoor toilets, generators, and wood stoves. Food, blankets, clothing, and tools were donated. There was the usual toing and froing as civic officials, TDRC, and others tried to come up with a "solution" for the homeless of Tent City, but little was happening except that the squatters and their "community" were getting a fair bit of airplay. An aspiring author, Shaughnessy Bishop-Stall, in an age-old version of literary slumming, lived in Tent City for a year, adopting the habits and living the rough life of the shantytown. Bishop-Stall's book presents a chronicle of acute urban poverty and homelessness, albeit in ways that often sensationalize and pander to the worst kinds of ideological typecasting. It is also disturbingly complacent in its stress on individual failings, detailed in an almost voyeuristic fixation on personalities that are pathologized, playing into avoidance of the structures of power that both create and criminalize the poor. But it was perhaps a summer 2002 exposé in the *New York Times* that finally shone a light of exposure on the existence of Toronto's down and out. Their conditions were detailed with brutal and broad brushstrokes, painting a stark picture of a province and a city beset by inequality and bedevilled by a political economy of mean-spirited accumulation, the underside of which is the making of the dispossessed:

> Some of the city's 6,000 homeless have resorted to living on undeveloped land. A shantytown is swelling on the shores of Lake Ontario … in the shadow of Canada's richest banks. The 80 residents have squatted on … land that is soaking in mercury and lead. Dogs rummage through garbage. Outhouses donated by charities have a stench. There is no running water save for a single hose shared by everyone, and no electricity. In the winter, people warm themselves over wood stoves. The first baby was born in the shanty town last month, but was taken away by government authorities because the parents used drugs and lived in a shack.… The poor have been left behind in an otherwise bustling housing market. Pan-handlers have also become more plentiful outside Toronto's fashionable stores and hotels. Less than 1 percent of Toronto's low income housing units stand vacant,

TORONTO'S POOR

and apartment rents have risen 35 percent in five years. The number of units that can be rented for $455 a month or less has decreased by nearly two-thirds since 1998, city officials say. At the same time, welfare payments fell—by 21 percent since 1996—because the Ontario provincial government was running deficits and cut spending on things like housing, welfare, and transport austerity. This city built almost 24,500 units of public housing from 1984 to 1996, but fewer than 100 units were built in the next five years. The waiting list is long and growing: in shelters, the number of beds is up sixfold in three years, to 4,100 and occupancy is 95 percent.... Tent City and growing homelessness suggest that the quality of life in Toronto, as in many other Canadian cities, is beginning to fray under the financial and demographic strain.

As went the *New York Times,* so followed the *Toronto Sun* and the *National Post,* both publishing pieces that referred to "Toronto's shame" and Tent City as a "patch of hell."[119] Mayor Lastman and the City Council were not pleased.

Neither was Home Depot, which clearly began to feel some heat. On Tuesday morning, September 25, 2002, without warning, Shadow Security, hired by the hardware franchise, entered Tent City and evicted the 110 squatters then living there. Backed by police who observed, an army of security guards, some dressed in blue, others in white, sporting black gloves and flak jackets, armed with guns and megaphones and accompanied by trained dogs, emptied the encampment. Each was photographed as he or she exited. The lot was then secured, the existing fence being reinforced and topped up by three feet of layered chain-link crowned with razor wire. Gates were installed. Tent City took on the appearance of a "gulag." The men of Shadow Security formed a wall. They had no names, only badge numbers. Their commander informed the displaced that they would be allowed to come back into the now effectively fenced and guarded lot, one at a time, to collect as many of their belongings as they were able to carry out in one trip. As this "retrieval" process ran its slow course, the periphery of the camp was bulldozed and spread with gravel, the Shadowmen protected from toxins by white jumpsuits. Eventually, the full twenty-seven acres was entirely levelled, its tents, shacks, discarded furniture, and piles of reclaimed building materials junked, the result a barren wasteland. The *Sun*'s front page proclaimed proudly, "TENT CITY, POP: 0." This did not happen without protest. TDRC was on the scene almost immediately, Beric German bellowing in a bullhorn. A crowd of protesters materialized as the Shadow Security guards went about their business to cries of "Shame! Shame!" and "*Homeless* Depot!

Homeless Depot!" But as the TDRC pushed for the dispossessed to be housed at a local community centre for a few days, put up in suburban motels, and eventually receive rent supplements and support workers to help them find housing, the longstanding occupation of the Toronto waterfront was finally, after more than a decade, brought to an end.[120]

If the visible statement of poverty and homelessness that Tent City constituted was written off the face of Toronto's waterfront by powerful interests, OCAP was determined to make sure that issues of social provisioning and housing did not disappear from the public discourse. On August 23, 2003, eleven months after the razing of Tent City, five hundred OCAP activists, homeless people, and others gathered in Yorkville's Cumberland Park. They came for a feast of venison, provided by OCAP allies among the Bay of Quinte Tyendinaga Mohawks, complemented by other delectable offerings brought by a variety of supporting organizations. The purpose was to bring the poor to the rich, so that those who dine so often at Morton's Steakhouse or the Four Seasons, where bottles of wine can go for as much as $3,500, might get a whiff of how the other "half" eat. After dinner, the OCAP-led crowd marched in a disciplined phalanx throughout Yorkville, dispersing at Bay and Bloor. This army of the dispossessed carried no weapons, save the unmistakable armour of its homelessness and its insistence that this social fact should not be hidden from history and that it would continue to be present in the politics of

Yorkville "Poor People's" Feast, Cumberland Park, Toronto, August 23, 2003.

OCAP Archives.

TORONTO'S POOR

the future. This was too much for constituted authority. The police denounced the protest, and the announcement of the OCAP dinner prompted Mayor Mel Lastman to visit Yorkville, ensuring that the cops had things under control. When the OCAP march was uneventful, the disappointed and plentiful police allowed the ranks to thin at Bay and Bloor and then charged remnants of the crowd, striking out with their batons and arresting four protesters. "It was a futile and ugly attempt to undermine our victory," OCAP claimed, adding that, with a municipal election in the offing, it had every intention of dogging those who denied the poor a living income and affordable housing. "We said in Yorkville that 'they are rich because we are Poor.' We can't end poverty until their wealth is taken from them and the means by which they obtain it is eliminated."[121]

Miller Time: Streets to Homes and the Death of Paul Croutch – Two Faces of Social Cleansing

OCAP played a key role in a Downtown East demonstration a month after the Tent City eviction. It was heavily monitored by Toronto bicycle police, buttressed by reinforcements from Barrie, York Region, and the OPP. Targeting a building on Parliament Street to be occupied, OCAP marchers were prohibited from getting near the possible squat site by cops lining the streets, forming a gauntlet through which the demonstration was forced to pass. OCAP then broke up and reassembled at a vacant Parliament Street house the city was preparing to sell, occupying it briefly before the riot police appeared, charged into the building, and forced the squatters to flee. Actions like this continued for years, morphing into a sustained opposition to reform Mayor David Miller's Streets to Homes initiative.

Miller, a card-carrying social democratic NDPer before assuming the mayor's office, served on Toronto City Council, elected in the Parkdale-High Park constituency. He ran against riches-to-riches future Conservative Party provincial premier hopeful and later mayoral successor to Rob Ford, John Tory. In the November 2003 civic election, Miller topped Tory, winning 43 percent of the vote to his closest opponent's 38 percent. A seeming progressive, Miller would cultivate the kind of non-partisanship that Mel Lastman found it congenitally impossible to muster, appointing the legendary and revered urban reformer Jane Jacobs and the Pink Tory David Crombie to head up his transition team. Miller, an advocate of social housing, was hailed by some early in his mayoralty as promoting and expanding low-income housing stock and widening possibilities for the poor and the homeless. Given the extent to which social housing programs had atrophied to the point that no new low-income, subsidized housing was being built in Toronto, Miller is often praised for turning things around on the affordable housing front. He convened a summit on housing in late February 2004, in which municipal, provincial, and federal officials addressed the sorry state of affordable housing in Toronto. Out of this came $24 million in provincial funds to build nine hundred units of housing for low-to-middle income people. Under Miller as mayor, a long-dormant development project to build thousands of units of housing adjacent to the Don River was revitalized, and Dalton McGuinty's Liberal provincial government, elected in 2003, later earmarked almost $400 million for affordable housing, the bulk of which went to Toronto. Miller is thus heralded in some quarters for putting the city of Toronto on track to increase affordable housing annually, and a massive Regent Park renewal was initiated. But the promise of change on this front was more rhetorical than real.

Regent Park's revitalization was noteworthy, and it no doubt improved Toronto's social assistance housing stock. But for many anti-poverty activists, what happened in Regent Park shed light on the Miller regime's housing policy, illuminating its less than progressive features. New housing units were indeed created, but shelters, hostels, and rooming houses were razed. Much of the acclaimed "bump" in social housing stock, for instance, was not *additional* accommodation as it replaced facilities routinely accessed by the homeless. Regent Park's redevelopment exposed the problem with this orientation: it caused dislocation for its poor residents, the fifteen-year $1 billion enterprise tearing down 2500 public housing units, replacing them with a total of 5100 units, only 1779 of which were on-site subsidized housing. Combining social assistance housing with private condo-owning units, the Regent Park renovation aimed at creating "a mixed income neighbourhood," clearing the slums of the older, deteriorated housing project, an endeavour that fit comfortably and well with the gentrification of Toronto's Downtown East that had been ongoing for decades,[122] and that continued under the post-Miller mayoralty of Rob Ford.

At the end of Miller's regime, Build Toronto, an ostensibly "arms-length" real estate and development corporation tasked with generating value from the city's real estate assets, signed a 2010 memorandum of understanding (MOU) with civic officials suggesting that between 2010 and 2015,

Housing Now banner, squatted building, November 10, 2003.
OCAP Archives.

TORONTO'S POOR

1250 units of affordable housing (80 percent rental/20 percent ownership) would be built. With Miller gone and the Ford brothers in the municipal saddle (Rob Ford's brother Doug sat on Build Toronto as the mayor's representative), the entire project stalled, the Fords resistant to telling developers that they needed to include affordable units in their construction plans. As of 2015, the Miller affordable housing legacy seemed in tatters, with only 12 of the projected 1250 affordable housing units completed. Councillor Ana Bailao, who chaired the Affordable Housing Committee, was clearly frustrated in 2015 with Doug Ford's replacement on Build Toronto, John Tory's appointee, Denzil Minnan-Wong, attributing the inability to complete old commitments to a failure to establish "realistic" goals for the building of affordable housing. "Ya, … there's no accountability in terms of only 12 units being done," groused Councillor Bailao, "So now what?"[123]

No doubt the housing crisis worsened when Ford replaced Miller. But in actuality, Miller's contribution to bettering the lot of the homeless had been complicated by his introduction of a Streets to Homes program that was championed as having taken hundreds of homeless people from living rough to having habitable homes. Yet Streets to Homes, an American-style initiative promoted by George Bush's homeless czar, Philip Mangano, also had another side to it. This campaign targeted homeless people who were living on the streets, especially the one hundred or so men and women camping out nightly in and around Nathan Phillips Square. Miller made it a priority to force these people from the downtown core, passing a February 2005 bylaw criminalizing camping out in and around city hall's public square. Coupled with this edict, an effective act of eviction, City Council began to cut back on outreach services like Street Patrol, which it was claimed encouraged the homeless to continue lives of vagrancy. Streets to Homes, while having a sound rhetorical ring to it, was thus also a project of social cleansing, in which the poor were driven off the streets and tourist-attraction squares of central Toronto and herded into substandard slum housing far distant from the city's downtown. Over a decade, Miller's Streets to Homes program displaced more than two thousand people to suburban squalor, isolating at-risk individuals from key (and familiar) downtown support networks and social services essential to their daily lives, like meals programs and health care. The beneficiaries of this liberal-sounding act of displacement were downtown commercial merchants, civic officials, the powerful tourism industry, and despicable suburban slumlords, at least one of whom had been served with one thousand complaints about premises rented out to low-income tenants in a one-year period. Streets to Homes, in effect, funnelled the dispossessed from the highly visible streets and parks adjacent to Toronto's tourist hot-spots, political hub, and central business district to distant and dilapidated accommodations. Social assistance funding was drained away in exorbitant rents, leaving the poor "housed" but essentially abandoned.[124]

This process of social cleansing was reinforced and exacerbated in two ways. First, under Miller, the city built social housing to be sure, but it did this largely away from the downtown core, and within that older habitat of the homeless it also closed five major hostels and undertook renovations at Seaton House, all of which curtailed the availability of beds and meals to the homeless, saving the city and the province $4 million. Second, police stepped up harassment under the provisions of the Safe Streets Act, issuing a record number of tickets for petty public space violations under Miller's reign. In 2007 alone, over 10,500 such ticketed infringement notices were handed out by the cops. OCAP earned Miller's enmity by opposing the Streets to Homes undertaking in a rowdy protest at City Council in February 2005 and by continuing to be a thorn in the municipal administration's side. Direct actions and ongoing propaganda against Toronto allowing shuttered buildings to sit dormant and decaying when the homeless were without shelter did not sit well with city hall. At the same time that Miller's Streets to Homes program was in full swing, for instance, OCAP and other advocates of affordable housing were fighting a "Use It Or Lose It" campaign, pressuring City Council to expropriate a privately owned Parkdale building at 1495 Queen Street West that had been vacant for eight years. A fire had left two low-income tenants dead, the large boarding house gutted, and the residents of its fifty-one rooms homeless. Pressured by anti-poverty activists, the City eventually paid Copper Crow Property Management $420,000 for the abandoned building in 2006. Five years later, a Parkdale Community and Recreation Centre-run apartment complex of twenty-nine low-income housing units was opened, christened Edmund Place in memory of Edmund Yu, a homeless man gunned down by Toronto police in 1997. Streets to Homes thus worked on the level of erasure, removing many of Toronto's homeless from the downtown core, but throughout Miller's mayoralty, OCAP and the homeless people it fought to defend continued to struggle. Unfortunately the homeless also continued to die.[125]

One of those homeless was Paul Croutch. Estimates of the numbers of homeless people who died on the streets of Toronto between 1995 and 2005 approach one thousand. Anti-poverty activists have tried to memorialize this loss and, where possible, record the names of those who succumbed to homelessness. For several years in the 1990s, a memorial was organized at Nathan Phillips Square by the Street People's Association, but Miller's Streets to Homes program marked a specific attempt to break the relationship of homelessness and the public space surrounding city hall. More recently, a memorial has been set up outside of the Church of the Holy Trinity, which is nestled behind the Eaton Centre. The names of hundreds of homeless men and women who have died on Toronto streets are listed, and a memorial service is held every second Tuesday of the month to remember this human loss. The funerals of the homeless are often held at the Rosar-Morrison Funeral Home & Chapel on Sherbourne just south of Wellesley, in the heart of the old Skid Row district of Toronto's East Downtown. For many of these services, only a handful of people have been in attendance. The bills are often paid by the City's Welfare Department, the dead buried in unmarked graves in a cemetery in Toronto's north end. The pauper's graveyard of the nineteenth century thus continues to exist and for the homeless is often their final resting place. The names of the homeless who have succumbed to the elements or to disease or the violence of the street rarely register in polite society, and if their deaths are newsworthy, they appear only as passing tragedies, conveniently marginalized as of only local and fleeting concern. The death of Paul Croutch in the summer of 2005, however, was different: it made national news. If Miller's Streets to Homes program was social cleansing at its ostensibly benign best, Croutch's death was an expression of its murderous worst.

Croutch, a fifty-nine-year-old homeless man dealing with mental health problems, was once a newspaper editor and businessman, but his life spiralled out of control and he was reduced to homelessness. He was sleeping in the rain on a bench in Moss Park during the early morning hours of August 31, 2005. The park, which Croutch often used for shelter, is adjacent to the Moss Park Armoury, where reservists with the Canadian Army's Queen's Own Rifles regularly trained. These uniformed soldiers in waiting often taunted Croutch and other homeless men and women, "shouting derogatory and abusive comments." On the evening of August 30, 2005, three reservists, at least two of whom had been drinking heavily, had an altercation with an unidentified man hanging about a bus shelter who may or may not have been Croutch. "I hate fucking bums, why's he dissin' me," one railed as he was seen being restrained by a buddy. "I'm going to kick his ass. I'm gonna take him on," threatened the aggressor. Later that evening the three young soldier trainees, Jeffery Hall (21), Brian Deganis (21), and Mountaz Ibrahim (23) entered Moss Park and Hall and Deganis viciously assaulted the sleeping Croutch, "kicking him like a football." When a homeless woman, Valerie Valen, came to Croutch's defence, she too was attacked by all three reservists, who told her that "bums were not welcomed in the park ... tell your friends the Park is ours. We own it." Assailing the homeless as "addicts, hookers, bums," the three civilian soldiers hurled verbal abuse at Valen, haranguing her that she and her kind had "no right to be in the park," that they were "all a useless waste of skin." Sticking his dog tags in her face, Deganis spat out venomously, "This gives us the right to kill all the homeless bums, crackheads [and] whores." The three reservists then re-entered the Armoury grounds, piled into Deganis's truck, and fled. Croutch was taken to St. Michael's hospital with six broken ribs, a ruptured spleen, and acute trauma to the head. He died later that morning.

Police kept the murder somewhat under wraps, the media not being informed until September 3, a day after they and the National Investigation Unit of the Canadian Armed Forces arrested Deganis, Hall, and Ibrahim. TDRC organized a September 8 demonstration in front of the Moss Park Armoury, which had often provided shelter, safety, and food to the homeless, demanding that Attorney-General Michael Bryant address the nature of the homeless man's murder. Protesters formed a line in front of the Armoury, with individuals holding large letters that spelled out "H A T E C R I M E." Speakers called for the Armoury to be dismantled as a training centre for soldiers, the facilities to be used instead as a shelter for the homeless or turned into affordable housing. The gathering then moved to the park bench where Croutch had been killed and laid flowers on it.

One of the demonstrators, Croutch's ex-wife Marilyn Howard, was brought to Toronto from Dawson City, British Columbia, by TDRC. She spoke at the Armoury memorial protest, attended a large 130-person service for her ex-husband at the Salvation Army Gateway shelter, and later met with officials in the Attorney-General's office to plead that the murder be prosecuted as a hate crime. Outreach workers, employees of Street Health, signed affidavits supporting this argument, sustaining it with statements confirming that they had witnessed uniformed soldiers taunting and abusing Croutch in the past, and Valerie Valen's testimony was unambiguous in its indication of the hate animating the reservists' assault on Croutch. But while crimes against religion, race, and sexual orientation can be prosecuted as hate crimes, the Attorney General was adamant that "class" conditions of poverty and homelessness did not fall within the categories constituted as potential justifications for criminal prosecution on the basis of hate. The poor could be criminalized in so many ways, yet attacks on the poor could not, apparently, be criminally prosecuted for exactly what they were.

Even the judge, when sentencing the convicted trio in 2008, acknowledged the hate of their crime. "The accused had a hatred of homeless people," said Justice Ewaschuk in a filled courtroom, viewing "them as human garbage to be evicted from Moss Park." Croutch, beaten "savagely," had "no chance of survival" when attacked by his assailants, who "literally stomped him to death," using the homeless man "as a combination punching bag and soccer ball." Against Ms. Valen, whom the judge told the jurors had acted the Good Samaritan and without whom the apprehension of the killers could well have been impossible, the convicted exhibited an inhumane and "elitist" cruelty. "They mocked her, toyed with her, kicked her legs out from under her. The effect was to totally humiliate Ms. Valen," who, like Mr. Croutch, was regarded as nothing more than "human garbage." The convictions came about when the accused cut a deal, midway through the trial, plea-bargaining their second-degree murder charges down to manslaughter. Deganis and Hall received jail terms of ten years for their killing of Croutch and an additional year, to be served consecutively, for the assault on Valerie Valen. Ibrahim was handed down a twelve-month sentence for accessory after the fact to manslaughter and assault causing bodily harm to Valerie Valen. Given time served pending trial, the total sentence that Deganis and Hall would serve for their vicious and deadly attack might come to no less than three and a half years and no more than seven years. Ibrahim, for all of his complicity, physical battering, and ugliness toward Valen, would be inside a cell for only a few months. The price of a homeless life seemed cheap indeed; the acknowledgement of hatred of the homeless undeniable, but something the legal order had a great deal of trouble acknowledging.[126]

A Women's Squat

The cheapness of human life and the lack of attention paid to adequate living conditions in this period was also addressed by the Women Against Poverty Collective, which led a 2007 protest/occupation of a vacant house in the Downtown East, accenting how homelessness for women had lethal consequences. Homeless women were anywhere from two to ten times more likely to die than housed women, depending on the age group.[127]

On June 3, 2007, roughly three hundred supporters of the Women Against Poverty Collective gathered in Cawthra Square on Church Street, just north of Wellesley. Fiery speeches highlighted how the Toronto housing crisis was exacerbating the general problem of violence against women. Increasing numbers of women were living with their children in overcrowded shelters as they engaged in often futile searches for affordable housing. Many such women were trying to extricate themselves from abusive relationships and often had to return to unsafe homes because they were unable to relocate themselves and their sons and daughters. Single homeless women also routinely faced violence while living on the streets. On the conclusion of the Cawthra Square speeches, the crowd, led by women, with male supporters in the rear, took to the streets, chanting, "They gentrify, we'll occupy!"

The protestors stopped at the Hayden Street subway entrance, located near Bloor and Yonge. A month earlier, Bly Markis, a thirty-three-year-old homeless woman, had been brutally murdered at the site. Kathy Hardill, a long-time anti-poverty activist and nurse practitioner in the Downtown East, addressed the crowd, pointing out that the best way to honour the memory of Markis and other young women who had succumbed to violence, treatable infectious diseases, and hypothermia because they were forced to live on the streets was "to do what we are doing here today. Which is to fight back!" Protesters then moved on and made their way to a vacant house at 4 Howard Street, between Sherbourne and Bleecker. Four OCAP women had entered the building earlier and hung a banner from the second story window, "Housing For Women by Women Now."

As women pitched tents in front of the squat and hung a clothes line from two trees, police gathered in force. By 7 p.m. the skies opened, drenching the occupied site with rain. The cops were joined by a contingent of mounted police, and the protest tents and clothes line were torn down, the Women Against Poverty Collective ranks physically forced across the street, and the OCAP squatters inside the vacant building arrested, escorted out in handcuffs, hustled into a paddy wagon, and driven to the police station, charges of break and enter and mischief laid. Horses were then used to disperse the crowd, which was physically pushed down Howard Street, its fragmented parts eventually making their way back to Cawthra

Square. Seven weeks later, on July 27, the Crown dropped all charges against the four women arrested. In November 2011, 4 Howard Street was one of a number of buildings slotted for redevelopment, with the proposed land use to include a four-tower condominium complex with an adjacent three-story multi-use commercial agglomeration.[128]

Raise the Rates! The Special Diet Supplement

In 2005, OCAP began one of its most successful and important campaigns to raise welfare rates in Ontario, utilizing the system's possibilities to expand the material provisions available to poor people. This initiative focused on the special diet allowance, which was available to all Ontario Disability Support recipients and all Ontario residents receiving welfare assistance. The special diet allowance provided for a maximum of $250 monthly if a health care figure, such as a nurse practitioner or a doctor, filled out a form stating that a client needed a special diet due to one of forty-one illnesses or medical conditions stipulated on a form, which further detailed specific sums associated with particular diseases or health issues. OCAP astutely realized that hundreds of thousands of people on social assistance, whose welfare rates had been slashed by the government to the point that proper nutrition was unlikely to be maintained over time, making the poor vulnerable to disease and deteriorating health, might well access this special diet income supplement if they

Mass hunger clinic, Queen's Park lawn, Toronto, October 3, 2005.
OCAP Archives.

could be organized. It thus used the special diet possibilities to address the steady erosion of welfare rates taking place in the post-Mike Harris era of Liberal govern-ance under Dalton McGuinty. OCAP's monitoring of the decline in welfare rates suggested that in 2010 dollars, a person on General Welfare Assistance in 1994 was receiving just over $900 a month. Factoring the Harris government's cuts, the rates fell to $690, and under McGuinty and the Liberals the monthly welfare provision-ing deteriorated further to $585. With one worker in six in Ontario subsisting on the minimum wage, the province was becoming a low-income ghetto. The special diet allowance, little known before 2005, and bureaucratically deflected by officials turning away those welfare recipients who tried to apply for it without an adequate knowledge of the Welfare Act's provisions, was OCAP's wedge in a door that they wanted to open wide to Raise the Rates.[129]

OCAP's Dennis Black kicked things off in February 2005, renting out a social events room of a Regent Park-area Toronto Community Housing high-rise apart-ment. Flyers distributed throughout the building earlier in the day announced that OCAP would be holding a special diet clinic that evening at 7 p.m. Kathy Hardill and Ann Egger, two nurse practitioners who worked in a nearby community health centre, would be in attendance, helping those on social assistance eligible for the diet supplement. Interested residents trickled into the evening session, and over the course of two hours, some sixty people had special diet forms filled in and signed by Hardill and Egger. The following afternoon, OCAP received a call at its office from a mother who had attended the clinic, reporting that her welfare worker had accepted the special diet forms for her, her husband, and their four children, validating an additional monthly payment of $1500 for the next year. Grasping what this might mean for the Toronto dispossessed, OCAP immediately set to work building connections with a group of sympathetic doctors, nurses, and others with health expertise, who formed a group, Health Providers Against Poverty, that began organizing a series of special-diet "Hunger Clinics" across the city, twenty in total. The Ontario Common Front contributed its support as well, and clinics were also organized in other communities, including Belleville, Kingston, Peterborough, Guelph, Sudbury, Kitchener, and Ottawa. OCAP was getting more than one hundred calls a day from people on social assistance, asking how they could access the spe-cial diet supplement.

On May 12, 2005, OCAP rallied 400 people to an Allan Gardens protest, calling on the McGuinty government to grant all 760,000 people receiving social assistance in the province of Ontario the $250 special diet monthly allowance. Welfare recipi-ents from as far away as Ottawa were bussed in to participate in the event. After a festive meal, the crowd marched to the Bay and Wellesley office of Sandra Pupatello, Minister of Social Services, where they found the entire building on lockdown by police order. No one was allowed in or out of the Macdonald Block complex of the Ontario Government Buildings. Thwarted in its effort to see Pupatello, the protest broke up, with 140 people making their way to a Regent Park community centre clinic where volunteers and nurses helped them fill out special diet forms that were then signed by health practitioners. Not surprisingly, a backlash was brewing. By mid-July 2005 Toronto welfare and civic officials reported that the number of people receiving the special diet allowance had grown from 6,000 to 10,000 over the previous six months, and the list of those successfully accessing the supplement was expanding daily. The city tried to curtail this stampede in August 2005 by stipulating that only doctors could sign off on the special diet allowance, but this restrictive measure was beaten back by public resistance, which pointed out that it contradicted the Welfare Act. Pupatello, describing OCAP as "rogue advocates," deplored "a campaign out there to misuse the intent of … special diet allowances." She announced that the province was in the process of reviewing special diet provisioning because the program was being abused, the integrity of its intent having been compromised. She also complained that patients were intimidating doctors, an allegation borne out by physicians calling OCAP at its office, irate that people were apparently threatening them if they refused to sign the special diet form. "We can not have physicians in a position," Pupatello fumed, of being coerced into signing forms "if in fact these people do not meet those medical conditions."[130]

OCAP responded to Pupatello with a massive "Hunger Clinic" on the front lawn of Queen's Park on October 3, 2005. More than thirty medical workers, including nurse practitioners and doctors, volunteered to help more than one thousand people on social assistance access the special diet supplement. Low-income people from the Toronto districts of Etobicoke, Scarborough, Jane-Finch, Parkdale, and East Downtown congregated at the legislature, their numbers reinforced by others arriving by bus from Belleville, Kingston, Peterborough, Northumberland, Kitchener, Midland, and Sudbury. Makeshift offices with portable walls, tables, and chairs were set up in front of the parliament buildings, so that health care providers could assess the applicants and sign their forms, with food and drink provided to the large crowd, members of which waited several hours to be processed by medical personnel. "The premise of the clinic today," said family physician Dr. Patricia Melinzer, "is that poverty is a medical condition and helping people access adequate funds to afford a nutritious diet is a medical intervention." This position was not accepted by the provincial government, which moved quickly to slash the stipulated supplement for the illnesses and conditions listed on the special diet form. In addition, new regulations made it difficult for people to access the special diet allowance, and for those who insisted on following through there were requirements of disclosure, which angered those defending the privacy of individuals, such as people who had contracted HIV/AIDS. Anti-poverty activists fought back with demonstrations organized throughout the province, including in Sudbury, where Cabinet Minister Rich Bartolluci's office was guarded by police.[131]

On Saturday, November 26, OCAP led a march of six hundred people on the luxurious Sutton Place Hotel, where Pupatello rented an apartment, subsidized by a $20,000 government housing allowance. A militant contingent occupied the hotel lobby, determined to pressure the Minister of Social Services to meet with it and hear complaints about the cuts to the special diet program. But Pupatello was not going to appear. The crowd eventually dispersed. Three days later, twenty OCAP women made their way to the Finding Common Ground Working Together to Reduce Domestic Violence conference, where the Liberal Cabinet Minister was delivering a keynote address. The anti-poverty activists were stopped by security, however, blocked from entering the meeting. Hearing of this, one thousand conference delegates voted to allow the OCAP women entry and give them time to speak. After listening to the women, many of whom relied on the special diet, outline the significance of the supplement and the difference it made to the lives of their families, the delegates were sufficiently impressed with the impassioned speeches that they raised $700 for OCAP's Raise the Rates campaign and then issued a press release supporting its demands for the restoration of the special diet allowance. Pupatello, who refused to meet with the OCAP women, beat a hasty retreat through a back door.[132]

The Raise the Rates campaign protesting the Liberal government's slashing of the special diet supplement continued into 2006. A February 10 action saw fifty OCAPers crashing the Toronto Housing Tribunal, a court-like hearing which processed evictions, meeting in the city's north end. Chanting "We won't be quiet until we get our special diet," the protesters brought proceedings to a halt. As police threatened arrests, the demonstrators refused to leave, the standoff eventually closing the doors of the eviction assembly line for a day, saving thirty families from being legally removed from their homes. Tenants' unions and youth collectives affiliated with the Ontario Common Front and based in Belleville, Guelph, and Kitchener-Waterloo similarly shut down a Guelph Housing Tribunal for part of a day. Five of the thirty anti-poverty activists were arrested, six police cars and a dozen cops descending on the protest. In Peterborough, forty protesters connected to the Ontario

Common Front disrupted the Ontario Housing Tribunal for a day in late March 2006. Liberal politicians also came under fire, with Tenant Action Group (TAG) protesters, outfitted in gas masks, invading the Belleville constituency office of Ernie Parsons, MPP for Prince Edwards-Hastings, demanding the reinstatement of the special diet allowance. TAG had been one of the more active and militant organizations in the province-wide fight for the special diet, helping almost one thousand people in its region access the supplement. The office was forced to go on lockdown, and five TAG members were arrested, charged with illegal assembly, breach of the peace, and mischief under $5,000. TAG organizer Sam Khun plead guilty to charges in exchange for the Crown dropping its cases against the four other accused and was sentenced to jail for forty days as a consequence of his leading role in the Belleville direct action.[133]

Ongoing Toronto protests against the cuts to the special diet program included a March 15 rally of six hundred people in Metropolitan Park, organized by the Hunger March Coalition, which included OCAP and the Downtown Fight Back Campaign. This demonstration was followed by a hunger march that snaked its way through the downtown core, endorsed by forty organizations representing unions, health providers, social agencies, churches, and others. Three weeks later,

Hunger march leaves Metropolitan Park for Queen's Park, Toronto, March 15, 2006.
OCAP Archives.

hundreds of people joined OCAP in an April 8 night march through Rosedale, protesting cuts to the special diet and demanding raises to the welfare rates. Later in the fall, on October 24, 2006, about fifty OCAP members and supporters, many of them Somali women, marched into the Metro Toronto Convention Centre, where the provincial Liberal Party was holding a lavish fundraiser. Crashing the party and confronting McGuinty, the anti-poverty activists videotaped the affluent supporters as they sat uncomfortably at their expensive tables. Security and police eventually herded the protesters out of the ballroom. OCAP and Health Providers Against Poverty continued to offer special diet clinics, despite the difficulty people now had in getting the maximum $250 monthly allowance. In spite of the program being rewritten to curb access, Toronto's City Services Committee reported that a record thirty-one thousand individuals were still collecting the dietary supplement at the end of 2007. Two years later Auditor-General Jim Carter released a five-hundred-page report that contained a discussion of welfare and disability recipients receiving the special diet allowance. Carter's document called attention to the astronomical rise in payouts resulting from the growing numbers of Ontario social assistance clients receiving the income supplement, the costs of which had soared, reaching tens of millions of dollars. The report called on the province to investigate the "abuse" and "welfare fraud" that it claimed lay at the heart of this explosion of expenditure, an ideological posture that managed to obscure to the point of denial the devastating impact of the global financial meltdown of these years.[134]

In particular, Carter demanded investigation of Dr. Roland Wong, whom it was alleged had exaggerated patients' allergies "so they could access special diet allowances" and failed to adequately document other patient conditions in his record keeping. Dr. Wong was one of the few Toronto doctors willing to work productively with OCAP and routinely held "Hunger Clinics" in his Chinatown office, seeing eighty to one hundred low-income people a day, advising them on their needs as they related to nutrition and processing their special diet forms. In many cases, Dr. Wong assigned each member of the family the full $250 monthly allowance, ensuring that thousands of Toronto's dispossessed, the majority of them women and children, were able to maintain nutritional diets and thereby prevent a plethora of illnesses and medical problems. Over several years Dr. Wong filled out thirty-four thousand special diet forms, the compensation totalling many millions of dollars. Clamouring for Dr. Wong's head was then mayoral candidate Rob Ford, who told the *Canadian Medical Association Journal* in 2010 that, "A doctor is there to be a doctor, not to advocate for the poor, or to be the official Opposition in government through taxpayers' money." Ontario's College of Physicians and Surgeons eventually conducted a six-month investigation into Dr. Wong's practices, the hearings beginning in October 2011. Dubbed "the Robin Hood Doctor" by the Toronto media, Wong was found guilty of professional misconduct in December 2012. The Chinatown doctor's "primary purpose" of "helping patients" whose welfare assistance was not sufficient to allow them "to purchase healthy food" was said by the College to be "misguided." Paid $60 to fill out each patient's forms, the doctor to the dispossessed collected fees of over $700,000 in 2008 alone, and over the years he had billed the Ontario government $1.8 million through the special diet program. This outraged state officials and welfare bureaucrats, but they never addressed the obvious needs of Dr. Wong's thousands of clients. The College's sentence, which went into effect in 2014, required Wong to pay fines/fees of $60,000, stipulated that the family physician must take training in medical record keeping and a course of instruction on the completion of special diet allowance forms, suspended him from practising medicine for six months, and appointed an official to monitor his doctoring and billing when he did return to his practice. OCAP lawyer Peter Rosenthal, representing Dr. Wong at inquiries and hearings, pointed out that it was Dr. Wong's poor patients who would have great difficulty in finding physicians to minister to their many maladies, and who would really suffer from the suspension meted out. Asked as to his remorse, Dr. Wong replied: "Regrets? Only that the government doesn't help the poor." He stressed how many of his low-income patients had benefited from the special diet allowance. And Dr. Wong's welfare patients and OCAP certainly supported him in the face of his colleagues' claims that he had been misdirected in his medical judgments and practices. OCAP was incensed that Dr. Wong was facing punishment, arguing instead that he should be given "a medal and the keys to the city." Michael Hurley of the Ontario Council of Hospital Unions (OCHU) declared in a press release that Dr. Wong

> practiced medicine professionally with great compassion. He signed off
> on forms so that poor people with medical conditions, like diabetes, could
> access supplementary funding for fresh fruit and vegetables. When his
> efforts and that of other[s] ... drove up the cost of [the special diet allow-
> ance available to Ontario residents on social assistance] ... the government
> pushed back, hacking back the program.

For Hurley and the OCHU, the disciplinary hearings conducted against Dr. Wong were "another step in that push back."[135]

As this state reaction to the OCAP-initiated special diet campaign ramped up, the anti-poverty organization continued to fight back. Between 2007 and 2009, OCAP fought several cases in which special diet allowances were refused by the welfare bureaucracy on the grounds of a number of technicalities. A large group of welfare recipients had their special diet forms rejected and their allotment reduced because Dr. Wong had signed their forms at one of his many "Hunger Clinics." On December 8, 2009, the day after the release of Auditor-General Carter's report that first targeted Dr. Wong, a demonstration of OCAP and Somali women from the OCAP Women of Etobicoke occupied the main lobby of the Ontario Works and Ontario Disability Support Plan offices, located on the 12th floor of Metro Hall. The mid-day protest sat in, clogging the entry to the government building and chanting "We won't be quiet until we get our special diet." It took the arrival of dozens of uniformed officers as well as the police Emergency Task Force and threats of mass arrests to clear the building. In February 2010, the Ontario government informed municipalities and ODSP officials that they had the right and responsibility to evaluate and reject diagnoses of health providers, a directive that suggested fraudulent filling in of the special diet forms and abuse of the plan. A few months later, with the provincial government prepared to table its 2010 budget, OCAP released a statement publicly denouncing the province for attacking people receiving social assistance:

> In the face of government accusations of widespread fraud, we must emphasize that it is not fraudulent for hungry people to apply for the Special Diet—it is a necessity in a system that forces people to live in poverty to decide from month to month whether to pay the rent or put food on the table. The dramatic increase in people accessing the Special Diet is not an indication of fraud: it is an indication of a hunger problem and a looming health crisis in this province. It should raise alarm bells for the Health Care system that people living on Social Assistance in this Province are living with poor health as a direct result of poverty conditions. There are huge health consequences when people cannot afford to buy healthy and nutritious food, when they cannot afford to avoid the food that they are allergic to and when thousands are living with the extreme stress of trying to survive and support their families in dire circumstances. Poor people suffer from poor health—this is a fact that the government ignores at their own peril.

With the governing Liberal Party of Ontario holding a fundraising event at the Metro Convention Centre on the evening of February 25, 2010, OCAP geared up to disrupt the $950 a plate event, at which Premier Dalton McGuinty would be speaking. As guests arrived in limousines at 7 p.m., fifty OCAP supporters and security guards clashed on one of the convention centre's large escalators. Well-heeled Liberal Party patrons and partisans became a captive audience of bullhorn speeches, lasting about thirty minutes before the protest moved outside.[136]

Three weeks later, anticipating that the government attack on the special diet program was gaining momentum, OCAP aligned with the Ottawa Under Pressure Collective to occupy the national capital office of Madelaine Meilleur, who had replaced Pupatello as the Minister of Community and Social Services in the Ontario government. The protest seized Meilleur's office and took over the sidewalk outside, demanding a 40 percent increase in welfare rates and the termination of Liberal government attacks on the special diet allowance. As the cops were called, a large banner was unfurled from the roof of the office building. By the end of the month, however, the McGuinty Liberals had resolved to end the costly success that OCAP had achieved with its special diet mobilization. On March 25, Dwight Duncan, Ontario's finance minister, announced during his budget speech that the special diet allowance was being eliminated, replaced by a new food supplement program that had yet to be fully worked out, but that the government claimed would be in place by the summer of 2011. A day later, twenty OCAPers confronted Duncan during a live recording of a Television Ontario (TVO) segment. With banners unveiled and loud demands made that the welfare rates be raised for the province's 760,000 needy people and the special diet supplement be reinstated, the usually staid television taping was turned into a chaotic scene.[137]

A subsequent OCAP protest at Allan Gardens on April 15 rallied seven hundred people who marched to the offices of the Ministry of Community and Social Services, which was immediately put on lockdown. OCAP speakers stressed that only three times in Ontario's history had the government actually cut welfare rates, under Mitchell Hepburn during the Great Depression, in the 1990s as part of Mike Harris's Common Sense Revolution, and now through the McGuinty administration's jettisoning of the special diet program, which translated into a 3 percent reduction in the incomes of the province's poor. On May 20, OCAP orchestrated a Toronto-wide protest of MPPs, six constituency offices being the site of spirited demonstrations. In Ottawa, St. Catharines, and Oakville, similar actions took place. Glen Murray, MPP for Toronto Centre, an urban affairs specialist, formerly mayor of Winnipeg, and the first openly gay politician to be elected as the leading civic official of a major North American city, was irate that a protest was called for his office. He phoned OCAP to berate organizers, angrily asking, "How dare you protest my office?" and claiming that he was a friend of the poor. When a delegation of anti-poverty activists and poor people arrived at Murray's office on May 20, however, the friend of low-income families was nowhere to be seen, and his office was obviously shut down for the day. Liberal MPP Shafiq Qaadri's office was marched on by a contingent of OCAP and a group of Somali women. They were met by a blue wall of police and told by Qaadri's office workers that they had been advised to keep the doors locked. Five months later OCAP Women of Etobicoke crashed a Qaadri fundraising event, getting the MPP to read a letter of protest on the floor of the provincial legislature.

Protests continued into the summer. A Raise the Rates action on July 21 included further indication of how devastating the cutting of the special diet program had been to Toronto's poor. Three hundred people gathered outside the government buildings of Macdonald Block, with eleven participants, including OCAP members and allies and labour movement supporters, delivering to the Liberal Party headquarters an invoice for money owed to the poor. When one of them hung a banner from the window and attempted to address the crowd outside, police intervened, arresting the entire group for trespassing. Those charged included Anne Abbot, a non-speaking wheelchair user, and her communication assistant, Lenny. Abbot later filed a human rights complaint against Toronto Police Services. "I went to the demonstration to demand the special diet not be cut and that welfare and ODSP rates be raised by 55 % for those on social assistance," she declared forthrightly. She then explained how the police had treated her: "I was arrested and the police called me 'a pawn' because I am disabled. I am not a pawn. Disabled people fight until they win enough money to eat healthy food and pay our rents." All of the trespassing charges were dropped three months later with the OCAP militants agreeing to make donations to a government charity. In the winter of 2011, the Liberal government announced its new food supplement program, which greatly reduced the amount people could receive for special diet needs and tightened up the procedures that had to be followed, in which new forms addressed the medical requirements for the allowance to be accessed. Everyone receiving the special diet had to have the new forms filled out by July 31, 2011, and if they failed to do so, they lost their food supplement. Thousands of poor people were affected, many unable to meet the new and more stringent government eligibility requirements, others simply blocked by their failure to find a doctor to fill out the new forms.[138]

On July 23, 2011, OCAP and CUPE Ontario organized a barbecue in Allan Gardens. More than one thousand attended and were fed and listened to speeches denouncing the attacks on the poor in general and the dismantling of the special diet program in particular. That day a large banner was unveiled, proclaiming "United We Eat. Divided We Starve." This call for solidarity reached through decades of struggles of the dispossessed to highlight one of the slogans of the unemployed in the 1930s. Diet allowances had, of course, been a part of relief provisioning in the Great Depression. The struggle to maintain them in 2005 was both embedded in understandings of past struggles and mobilized out of a sense of how militant direct action had to meld with astute pressure, applied to specific areas of welfare provisioning, that might garner material gains for the dispossessed. This had always been OCAP's approach, and in the special diet agitation it generated concrete advances for welfare recipients, be they single individuals without homes or low-income families. In October 2005, Sandra Pupatello, then Minister of Social Services, admitted that people on social assistance could not afford to eat well on the amount of money they were receiving. "I'll be the first one to stand up and tell you that I don't believe people can live healthily with the amount of money [they] receive on welfare," she acknowledged.

OCAP pried open the possibility that all of Ontario's poor could access the income-enhancing special diet allowance. Its campaign, supported by a few health care providers, like Dr. Wong, who were willing to utilize the system to sustain healthy diets for the poor, provided the stimulus that saw expenditure on the social diet program put millions of dollars in the hands of the dispossessed. In 2002, Ontario allocated $5 million in special diet allowances. Six years later, in 2008, that figure had skyrocketed to almost $70 million. The overall costs of operating the program climbed from $6 million in 2001–2 to $220 million in 2009–10, and these overall costs were projected to further multiply to $750 million by the 2015–16 fiscal year, with the outlay on the supplement alone rising 40 percent from 2008–9. It was the "Hunger Clinics" organized by OCAP and supporters like Dr. Wong that for the first time in more than a decade restored something of the welfare rate cuts that had slashed low- or non-income people's capacity to feed themselves. Through this campaign, OCAP was able to interact with and organize poor people in ways that they had never managed to do in the past, proving what the dispossessed already knew—"We don't need a doctor's note to tell us we are hungry." This outraged a state for which welfare provisioning was as much about surveillance and regulation as it was the maintenance of health and well-being. This antagonized apparatus struck back with a vengeance, drawing on age-old understandings of the undeserving poor that, once again, suggested that those in need were resorting to abuse of the system and fraudulence to gain access to allowances that even the welfare state recognized needed to be in place. And so the special diet, on the books for decades, but now

accessed through the organization of poor people to understand their rights, had to be cut back and redefined, even if it could not quite be terminated. OCAP took justifiable pride in what the special diet campaign had secured for the poor. But as John Clarke later recognized, "it is instructive to note that this effort might have taken back—at its high point—about 10 percent of the yearly welfare income loss of the last 15 years."[139] Even this modest reparation was too much for the state to stomach, not only because of the hundreds of millions of dollars potentially involved but also because of *how* this reappropriation happened: as a mobilization of militant protest and assertion of basic rights, as part of the direct action of the poor themselves, as yet another expression of the revenge of the dispossessed.

Turning on the TAP: Toronto Against Poverty

As OCAP struggled to raise the rates around the special diet allowance, poverty as a widespread social problem was placed more squarely before the public, a political issue that demanded attention. At the beginning of the twenty-first century, poverty reduction had gained traction globally, with Tony Blair's Labour Party promising to reduce poverty by 25 percent over five years ("25 in 5"). In Canada, Newfoundland and Labrador developed a provincial poverty reduction plan in 2006, and Ontario's Premier Dalton McGuinty promised on the hustings that if re-elected in the fall of 2007 he would introduce anti-poverty legislation during his next term

TORONTO'S POOR

as head of the provincial government. MPP Deborah Matthews, Minister of Youth and Children's Services, who would later chair the Cabinet Committee on Poverty Reduction, co-ordinated the activities of a number of Toronto-based organizations and social agencies, committing the next Liberal government to anti-poverty measures if only mainstream activists would line up with the McGuinty campaign.[140]

David Miller's municipal regime was reluctant to confront the provincial Liberals, engaging in what would have seemed, in the parlance of bourgeois democracy, "government to government" contestation. Engaged in negotiations with the ruling provincial Liberals around the renewal of the City of Toronto Act and a Provincial-Municipal Fiscal and Service Delivery Review, Miller and his entourage at city hall simply had no taste for an all-out war with McGuinty and his team about issues central to the lives of the urban poor. Yet the public crisis of homelessness and increasingly visible poverty was such that what was judged necessary and politic was a "third party community organization" that would demand legislation and anti-poverty reforms, taking some of the heat off Toronto's beleaguered municipal social assistance apparatus. Miller's civic officialdom could then stand in the wings, acting as "a silent partner," but offer sustenance to the seemingly community-based provincial critics.

Toronto's Community Development and Recreation Committee (CDRC) thus convened a special meeting on May 3, 2007, to discuss "income security issues." Sixteen organizations provided briefs and presentations, out of which emerged a Cross-Community Action Table (CCAT) that would soon crystallize into a Blairite "25 in 5 Network". Its steering committee originally included John Stapleton of the Metcalf Foundation and representatives from the Stop Community Food Centre and the Income Security Advocacy Centre. Other largely liberal organizations soon came on board, among them the Wellesley Institute, the Ontario Association of Food Banks, and St. Christopher House (now renamed West Neighbourhood House). The city of Toronto was soon providing the 25 in 5 Network with office space and seconding two civic employees who worked for the poverty-reduction initiative as administrative staff. Key members of 25 in 5 were closeted with Deborah Matthews, whose role was to consolidate commitment to a Liberal government poverty-reduction program in return for electoral support for McGuinty.

The icing on this cake of co-optation was Ontario's 2008 Poverty Reduction Act, the passage of which ensured that the support of a number of moderate organizations and agencies went to the Liberals, whose price of admission to their inner circle was the containment of social unrest. The 25 in 5 Network abstained from mobilizations animated by OCAP-like demands to raise the welfare rates and aggressively promote the need for more social assistance housing. As Matthews toured the province in the spring and summer of 2008, holding seventy-five community meetings on the issue of poverty reduction, a liberal consensus quickly coalesced in mainstream, moderate social agencies that attempting to obtain immediate increases in social assistance remuneration in general, and welfare rates, in particular, was "misguided," nothing more than a "lost cause." Carol-Anne Hudson and Peter Graefe concluded in 2011 that such bodies "believe an immediate increase is not a political winner with the existing government, and moreover would spark a backlash against social assistance in the broader population if implemented without other changes." Beric German, writing for RABBLE in September 2008, noted that, under conditions of growing poverty, "some organizers encourage people to take to the streets," while others "try to contain the troubles, arguing that polite deputations will have better outcomes." With McGuinty announcing that his government would be unlikely to meet its poverty reduction targets, the stage was clearly set for a clash of anti-poverty activists, who were now divided as to how best to work on behalf of the poor: those like OCAP, who had long invested their energies in a "fight to win" commitment to public street protests and direct action versus those, such as many in the 25 in 5 Network, who preferred the practice of quiet meetings behind closed doors with officials who had the ear of political power.[141]

The more radical forces had indeed been coalescing, knowing that a fall election was going to put poverty on the campaign map in the summer of 2007. An early meeting took place at the Parkdale Activity-Recreation Centre. Representatives from OCAP, Toronto Disaster Relief Committee (TDRC), No One is Illegal, the Disability Action Movement Now (DAMN), and the Canadian Automobile Workers attended. Discussions focused on the need to target and protest against the Liberals' social policies, and whether or not a province-wide campaign should be mounted. Most thought such a wide-ranging protest was beyond the capabilities of the organizations on board with the tactics of militant resistance, but it was agreed to form a coalition, Toronto Against Poverty (TAP), dedicated to mobilizing local resistance. The CAW played a key role in providing the personnel and resources that sustained TAP, with Steven Watson of the union's Education Department and Jim McDowell, an auto worker from Local 1285, seconded to the militant anti-poverty activist network.

TAP's agitational orientation culminated in a four-prong feeder march/protest, to take place September 26, 2007, one month before the provincial election. OCAP and No One is Illegal constituted the first leg of the march, rallying at the Metropolitan Church at Queen and Church Streets. A second contingent, composed of forces associated with TDRC and various labour and community groups, assembled in Ramsdon Park on Yonge Street several blocks north of Bloor. DAMN and its allies gathered outside the Macdonald Block, relatively near Queen's Park at Bay and Wellesley, where it was arranged that they would be joined by a student contingent coming from University of Toronto's Hart House. Demands to be made as the various components of the protest came together at Macdonald Block and then flooded onto the front lawn of the legislature, were: 1) an immediate raising of social assistance rates by 40 percent; 2) construction of affordable housing; 3) increasing the minimum wage to $10 an hour; 4) lowering of tuition fees; and 5) province-wide implementation of a "Don't Ask, Don't Tell" policy for non-status migrants accessing government services.

More than one hundred organizations endorsed the protest, with estimates of the crowd ranging from a conservative media suggestion of four hundred to organizers' claims of an attendance of fifteen hundred. Hundreds of curious onlookers, drawn to the militant crowd surging through the downtown core during lunch hour and marching on Queen's Park, upped the numbers involved considerably. The police were out in force, some decked out in riot gear, others on horseback. A line of officers stood behind steel barricades, shielding the legislature from a feared attack.

The crowd was peaceful, albeit militant. Speakers denounced the social policies of the Liberal government and highlighted the extent to which poverty was a central issue in the election. Demonstrating that not all anti-poverty activists had been co-opted into the moderate 25 in 5 Network, the rally struck a note of defiance, proclaiming there were those who refused to be divided by the government, the better to be conquered on issues associated with poverty. Loree Erickson, speaking for DAMN, insisted that, "Throughout history poor and disabled people have been pitted against poor non-disabled people. People with disabilities have been pitted against one another fighting for all too few scraps provided for us. We're here today to say that the divide and conquer technique isn't going to work anymore.... Enough is enough." TDRC's Beric German reminded those gathered outside the Legislature that while those inside had recently voted themselves a 25 percent pay increase, they were not of a mind to up the rates for social assistance recipients, promising that the politicians who heard the shouts of "Shame" today were going to "hear us more in the future."[142]

McGuinty's re-election and the subsequent back-peddling on the Poverty Reduction Act, in conjunction with the curtailment of the special diet program, spelled ongoing misery for Toronto's poor and homeless and unemployed. In the aftermath of the 2007–8 financial meltdown, with the half-decade that followed it one of increasingly shrill cries for cutbacks in government social assistance, it was not surprising that the special diet supplement was reconfigured in an age of austerity. With OCAP and other organized expressions of anti-poverty activism demanding a raising of all rates, "fighting to win" and the revenge of the dispossessed that this slogan articulated spread quickly to other fronts, including restoration of different rates and defending shelters and services needed by poor and homeless people.

Another Demolition Job:
The Community Start Up and Maintenance Benefit

The special diet allowance was not the only program the McGuinty Liberals tried to put on the chopping block. In the spring of 2012, the provincial government announced a new formula for funding homeless programs serviced by Ontario's municipalities. Toronto, under the new system, was slotted to receive $91 million, a $21 million cut from what the city had been apportioned over the previous year. Emergency shelter funding was also capped, meaning that the municipality would be responsible for the full costs of any sudden increase in demand for shelter beds, which could come about for a wide variety of reasons, including inclement weather, natural disasters, economic meltdowns, or pressures arising from contractions in the delivery of other kinds of social assistance. The province was adamant that what was needed was a "whole new approach to dealing with housing," in which there was apparently an increasing need for flexibility in how municipalities utilized the highly regulated funds. Jim Millow of Ontario's Ministry of Community and Social Services conceded that the new approach was being driven by the province's "very serious fiscal crisis," insisting that, "we simply have to find a way to balance things, particularly in a ministry like ours, where there is a huge pressure with a growing caseload.... It would have been nice not to have done this, but I think it can be explained very much in line with the broader vision." The cuts were to be implemented on January 1, 2013, with the elimination of the Community Start Up and Maintenance Benefits program (CSUMB).[143]

CSUMB provided single adults on welfare and Ontario Disability and families similarly assisted with start-up funds of $799 and $1500 respectively, every two years. This allowance, which like the special diet had equivalents in the relief provisioning of the Great Depression, made it possible for people to outfit accommodations if they were forced to relocate or set up an entirely new living environment. Purchase of necessities like bedding, cooking utensils, furniture, and the like, or paying the first or last month's rent demanded by landlords if tenants took possession of new rental accommodations, could be offset by the funds. So too could expenses incurred by emergencies, among them ice storms, power blackouts, fires, or other natural calamities that destroyed property or provisions, necessitating replacements and demanding cash layouts. According to OCAP research, some sixteen thousand Ontario residents were relying on funds from CSUMB every month. The cutting of this social program was therefore going to have a decisive and debilitating impact across the province, further undermining the capacity of poor people to weather the repeated storms of economic crises, constituting a generalized lowering of the social assistance rates.[144]

Under its Raise the Rates banner, OCAP mobilized against the cuts to CSUMB. Working with the Canadian Union of Public Employees Ontario (CUPE) and various community groups across the province, OCAP promoted the necessity of keeping the start-up funding alive. In the fall of 2012, Kitchener, Sudbury, Ottawa, Kingston, Hamilton, Niagara Falls, and Toronto all held community meetings, marches, rallies, mass clinics, and barbecues to raise awareness of how devastating the elimination of start-up funds would be to poor people. A weeklong, Ontario-wide protest involving more than thirty-five actions was organized from December 7–12, 2012, calling on the government to reconsider its decision to close down the program. Trade unions worked closely with OCAP so that the demonstrations were sufficiently funded and well organized. OCAP summarized what took place:

> CUPE continued to provide organizational and communications support as the week unfolded. The Public Service Alliance of Canada (PSAC), Ontario Region, provided material assistance and encouraged its local activists to be part of the week. The Ontario Federation of Labour (OFL) supported the organizing in key ways and helped mobilize for local actions.... Delegations to Ministry offices took place in Oshawa and the Sault. In Ottawa, a roving delegation visited five MPPs. Meetings with MPPS were held in Sarnia and Halton. The Peel Poverty Action Group occupied the office of leadership candidate Harindar Takhar. Teachers held a bake sale outside a $500 a ticket cocktail party put on by Kathleen Wynne. Health Providers Against Poverty went to the office of Dr. Eric Hoskins, MPP to ask him about his role in eliminating the CSUMB only to be met by cops. Jane-Finch Action Against Poverty in Toronto mobilized a contingent to the door-step of Mario Sergio's office and were disrespectfully met with a locked door and a note. The Kingston Coalition Against Poverty (KCAP) mobilized at the office of John Gerretson. Sudbury Coalition Against Poverty (S-CAP) mobilized at a city council meeting and was able to get the council to pass a resolution

opposing the cut to CSUMB. Later in the week, joined by the North Shore Tribal Council and Local S-CAP members, militants marched on the office of David Oraziette. Drawing on the strength and experience of our First Nations allies, this march succeeded in shutting down the trans-Canada Highway. OCAP held an overnight campout at the office of a leadership candidate, Glen Murray, about 40 people, five homeless people, and allies joined by OFL President Sid Ryan, and Executive Vice-President Irwin Nanda, slept there. Murray, himself, put in an appearance, and informed us that he supported the position that the CSUMB should not be eliminated.[145]

Four days before the CSUMB program was to be terminated, the Ontario government provided an additional one-time fund of $42 million to provincial municipalities, providing a brief reprieve.[146]

OCAP's actions twisted the austerity arm of the state, forcing it to cough up some material concessions. But the victory achieved was little more than a stopgap measure, and one that provided only minimal support. On January 1, 2013, the City of Toronto replaced the Start-Up benefit with the Housing Stabilization Fund (HSF). People on social assistance could access allowances from this source only with great difficulty, however, and there were curbs on the limited funds available. Many Ontario municipalities simply stopped offering the Start-Up benefit because the funds available from the province were no longer attached to a specific program. OCAP continued to campaign for the return of the Start-Up income supplement throughout 2013.[147]

Hostels under Attack: OCAP Fights Back

Late in the autumn of 2011, OCAP received a phone call from a School House Shelter (SHS) worker informing them that the hostel was about to be shut down. SHS was run by Dixon Hall, a United Way-affiliated non-profit agency offering a range of community services. Located at 349 George Street, School House had been operating as a "wet hostel" since 1999, when Dixon Hall took over the program from the city. A decade later, with the program running at a deficit and the century-old building needing major structural repair, estimated to cost $300,000, the hostel was obviously a precarious undertaking. In addition, Dixon Hall was increasingly focused on permanent housing for low-income people. For a variety of reasons, the municipality of Toronto balked at picking up the bill for the expensive repairs allowing the School House program to operate on a 24-hour basis. As a somewhat unique men's shelter, School House was one of only two "wet hostels" in the city

based on a harm reduction model. Homeless men paid $7 a night and were allowed
to consume a dozen beers a day while sheltered at the fifty-five-bed facility. The
doors opened at 4 p.m., and the men were expected to be out of the building by
10 a.m. the next day. On weekends, the hostel was open during the day. All of this
was coming to an end, however, and in November 2011 Dixon Hall quietly stopped
admitting men to the shelter and began the long process of trying to find permanent housing for its long-term clients.[148]

OCAP, concerned with the closure of an established shelter and the loss of
fifty-five beds, spoke with School House Shelter residents and front-line workers,
as well as with City Councillor Kristyn Wong-Tam. It also discussed the situation
with other agencies, which disagreed with the closure of the "wet hostel" but were
reluctant to criticize or meddle in the affairs of another institution. OCAP soon concluded that there were few bodies that would fight to keep School House Shelter
open. It understood that at least a part of the willingness to close down the hostel
was based on the ongoing gentrification of the Downtown East. Writing to Toronto's
Director of Hostel Services, Ann Longair, OCAP pilloried those who would rational-
ize the closing of School House because "it is better for people to have housing than
be put in shelters" as a "cynical diversion from the real issues by a municipal government that knows very well the scale of the housing crisis even as it sells off its own
public housing stock. It is a key element of the agenda of upscale redevelopment in
downtown east."[149]

Forming an alliance with the Toronto East Downtown Stop the Cuts Committee, the Toronto Harm Reduction Coalition, and other organizations, OCAP

helped launch a Save the School House Campaign in March 2012. Demonstrations protested outside the homeless facility, advocates of the shelter explained why a "wet hostel" was necessary, and the municipality was pressured to take over the program. If School House was in fact closed down and its doors locked, OCAP threatened "to mobilize the community to take it back," fighting to keep the shelter open. OCAP also clashed with left-leaning Councillor Wong-Tam whose views that the program should be shut down because of insufficient monitoring of alcohol consumption defied statements made by Dixon Hall and shelter workers about the running of a "harm reduction" hostel. With the Dundas and Sherbourne area plastered with "Save the School House" posters, demonstrations, and barbecues at the shelter drew crowds of five hundred and more. On May 22, a large protest delegation attended the Community Development and Recreation Committee meeting at city hall, asking to speak on the School House closing. Denied a forum, the OCAP protesters disrupted the meeting and Giorgio Mammoliti, Chair of the Committee, had security eject them.[150]

Globe and Mail headlines the next day proclaimed, "PROTEST UNLIKELY TO SAVE UNIQUE SCHOOLHOUSE SHELTER." The *Sun's* Sue-Ann Levy argued that the closure of the hostel was a "slam dunk." Levy assailed the campaign to save School House as but "the latest *cause célèbre* by OCAP terrorists," quoting Mammoliti as the authoritative voice on why the shelter needed to be shuttered: "They want to keep this shelter open, for what? ... They want to keep all their pet projects even though both the left and right on council agree shelters should not exist." Yet OCAP and its allies continued to fight. On June 26, 2012, City Council's committee room was filled with advocates of the School House, among them homeless men, front-line workers, union locals representing workers in the neighbourhood, social agencies, and OCAP members, all of whom spoke out against the closing of the hostel. A rally at Moss Park on August 23 stressed that the closure of shelters and removal of social services from the East Downtown displaced the poor and the homeless from neighbourhoods and surroundings they had lived in for decades, while developers and gentrification priced homes beyond low-income residents. The demonstration then marched to an empty lot at the corner of Dundas and Jarvis, where Great Gulf Homes' Pace condos was planning to construct a forty-six-storey condo tower. OCAP distributed cans of beer to the crowd. Police watched the illegal consumption of alcohol on the street, a purposeful protest that highlighted just why a "wet hostel" was a necessity. Closure of a space like School House would force many homeless men who were dependent on alcohol to drink in back alleys, parks, and streets, where arrest, debilitating intoxication, and succumbing to the elements were routine.[151]

OCAP's pressure played a role in keeping the School House open, as did the city of Toronto's failure to abide by its promise to house all of the shelter's clients. By late October 2012, fifteen men remained in the program. Only nineteen of the original fifty-five School House Shelter residents found housing. Many had simply left amid the uncertainty of the hostel's future, leaving for other shelters or departing Toronto; some were barred for bad behaviour. Once the men were no longer in the program, the city's commitment to finding them housing evaporated. On October 31, a staff report recommended that the School House remain open as an emergency shelter, with its beds reduced from fifty-five to forty, and that fees associated with the shelter and drinking be discontinued, effective January 1, 2013. Acknowledging that between 2009, when Dixon Hall first notified Toronto's Hostel Services of its intention to close down School House, and 2012, the increasing demand for shelter beds justified keeping the facility open, the Community Development and Recreation Committee voted on November 14, 2012, not to close the facility. Dixon Hall agreed to continue to operate the School House Shelter, albeit not as a "wet hostel." Saving School House Shelter, then, had come at a crucial cost, since the elimination of a harm reduction run hostel that allowed residents to drink meant that more men would indeed consume alcohol on the streets, and some would die as a consequence.[152]

In the winter of 2013 city hostels were full, people were being turned away, and occupancy rates were running at 96 percent, well above the 90 percent level that all agreed constituted overcrowding. For some demographic sectors—most notably women and couples—shelter occupancy rates approached 99–100 percent. To call attention to the deplorable lack of shelter beds and the worsening crisis of homelessness, fifty OCAP protesters set up an emergency shelter outside of the mayor's office at Toronto city hall on February 15. With the exception of Adam Vaughan, city councillors refused to meet with the protesters during the ten-hour standoff. Vaughan promised to call for an emergency debate on the homeless crisis at the next city council meeting. Mayor Rob Ford indicated he would oppose such a discussion, claiming that there were "more than enough beds" available for those needing shelter accommodations. OCAP, vowing to stay until civic authorities stopped "lying about the situation and pretending that there are enough beds to meet the needs that exist," was warned that if it did not leave, protesters would be ejected and subject to criminal charges. Liisa Schofield replied on behalf of OCAP that, "We're going to stay no matter what." At 10 p.m., police moved in, and twenty-eight people were arrested and charged with trespass.[153]

Vaughan attempted to put the homeless crisis before Council on February 20, 2013. "The cycle of this winter has put people at extraordinary risk," he argued,

"The clear indication we're getting is that this is a crisis, people are in harms way, and the city is failing to take care of them, and that constitutes a crisis." Vaughan noted that the Peter Street Referral Centre was cramming seventy people inside its space, with many of the homeless sleeping on the floor. The motion to discuss homelessness, which itself entailed much debate, failed to secure the two-thirds majority required, falling short by six votes. From the gallery, OCAP members heckled Council, shouting that it had "Blood on its Hands": over the course of 2012 and into the two brief winter months of 2013, forty homeless people had died on the streets of Toronto. Council Speaker Frances Nunziata was forced to recess the meeting and clear the gallery. A petition with one thousand signatures, many of them from homeless people, called on the city to open more shelters, and OCAP announced that it would occupy Metro Hall, turning it into an emergency shelter. John Jagt, Director of Toronto's Hostel Services in 1999, had declared the site a temporary hostel in the past, with Council voting to grant Jagt the authority to turn suitable buildings into emergency shelters without seeking permission from the city should occupancy rates at hostels rise above 90 percent.[154]

OCAP and its allies, including a number of homeless men and women, descended on Metro Hall at 11 a.m. on March 7, 2013. They unfurled a large banner, "GRAND OPENING METRO HALL HOMELESS SHELTER" on the front steps of the building. Scuffling with police officers and security, the protesters made their way inside, determined to remain until the city opened another hostel for the homeless. Rob Ford blasted OCAP for creating "a false sense of crisis," describing the seizure of Metro Hall as "nothing more than a cheap publicity stunt." The OCAP occupation ended twelve hours later as dozens of police officers moved in and arrested more than forty of the protesters for trespass. Charges from both occupations were later dropped for all of those taken into custody, with the exception of OCAP's John Clarke, who was found guilty, paid a small fine, and was put on probation for six months. A twenty-two-page report gave the city's hostel system a thumbs-up, claiming that the 3,836 beds in fifty-seven shelters met the needs of the homeless. This assertion was repudiated at a March 18 Community Development and Recreation Committee meeting, with Councillor Joe Mihevc stating unequivocally: "Yes, we have a problem. We don't have enough beds to meet the demand." Social workers and anti-poverty activists echoed Mihevc's insistence that what existed was not enough, prompting Council to vote unanimously to buttress the existing number of shelter beds with 172 emergency or "flex beds," normally used during cold alerts. As OCAP explained, this band-aid solution was in no way going to resolve the crisis. It meant little more than "putting down mats on the floor of already overcrowded shelters and pushing the capacity well beyond 96 percent." With the Church-run Out of the Cold program due to shut down in the spring, as it always did, more people would be looking for beds when there were even fewer spaces available. As winter eased, the homeless crisis continued, and in the summer shelter occupancy hovered between 94-100 percent for different demographic groups.[155]

One of the main constituencies for whom homelessness presented particular dangers, including violence, was women. In the summer of 2013, OCAP targeted an abandoned rooming house at 230 Sherbourne Street, vacant for six years, and an adjoining lot, once the site of similar accommodations that had been bulldozed for redevelopment. It was at this address that Drina Joubert had frozen to death almost two decades earlier. OCAP demanded that the Sherbourne Street complex of unused properties be developed as affordable housing and named Drina House. An occupation of the lot, at which OCAP set up an encampment on September 26, 2013, was broken up by police, and the struggle to address women's homelessness intensified.[156]

As the "Drina House" mobilization was underway, a young homeless woman, sitting on the steps of Street Health, a social agency located near Dundas and Sherbourne, was sexually assaulted by two men during dark, early morning hours. Video cameras outside the agency captured the attack on tape, which was turned over to the police. Police failed to follow up on this evidence and did not alert homeless women in the vicinity that an attack had occurred. In early October a delegation of women delivered a letter to Philip Abrahams, responsible for hostel services, complaining that shelters in the city had been oversubscribed for seven months, with occupancy rates commonly at 99 percent. The women's protest called on Abrahams to immediately open a shelter and set up a twenty-four-hour safe space for women and trans people fearful of violent attack on the streets. A night watch was organized. OCAP women postered the Downtown East with images of the male assailants who had sexually assaulted the young woman in late September, also dropping off the leaflet to social agencies offering services to the homeless.

Later, on November 25, the International Day for the Elimination of Violence Against Women, an open letter was sent to the city calling for protection of homeless women who were facing the threat of violence on a daily basis because of the lack of shelter beds for them and the failure of the city to provide affordable housing:

> We are writing you ... to demand that the City take immediate action to
> address the shelter crisis and the tremendous violence experienced by
> homeless women every night.... For women, the state of the city's shelters

is particularly devastating. Women's shelters are operating at 97% capacity or higher every night, even with the use of "flex" beds.... The crisis in the shelter system is continuing to worsen with each passing day.... It is also certain that without action more women will be victims of assault and violence and unable to access help or safety because of this crisis.

Endorsed by a wide range of organizations and individuals, including Toronto Rape Crisis Centre/Multicultural Women Against Rape, the Redwood Shelter (a safe haven for women and children fleeing abuse), Native Women's Resource Centre, Regent Park Community Health Centre, and Street Health, this OCAP-initiated letter helped prod Toronto's Community Development and Recreation Committee to recommend the immediate opening of a temporary, thirty-bed shelter for women that would transition into a permanent hostel able to accommodate almost double that number of beds in the future.[157]

Six months later, Toronto City Council officially approved establishing two twenty-four-hour drop-in centres for women and trans people in the east and west downtown districts. But getting the drop-in facilities set up dragged on to the point that, one year later, on the eve of another International Day to stop violence against women, the centres still did not exist, the city citing bureaucratic delays as the reason for a lack of progress. On November 25, 2014, after a rally and march, five OCAP women occupied a downtown city hostel administrative building, refused to leave, and demanded to speak with an official. Outside, more than one hundred people rallied and insisted that the city follow through on its commitment to safe space and shelter. After two hours the police moved in without warning, arrested the protesters, and violently removed them from the building. The arrested women, who were charged with forcible entry and mischief, reported being assaulted, verbally abused, and subjected to misogynistic harangues during their time in police custody. Months later, in March 2015, charges against the women were dropped in exchange for hours of volunteer community service.[158]

With John Tory defeating the Ford brothers in November's 2014 civic election, OCAP addressed the new, clean-cut Conservative Mayor about the dangers of the city's apparent indifference to the worsening conditions in Toronto's shelters:

The Daily Census that was issued by the City, on December 2, reveals a deepening homeless crisis. The Co-ed shelters are reported at 99% capacity, those for women at 95% and the family shelters are now at 97%.... Moreover, these estimates include "flex beds," placed in common areas, that only

compound the overcrowding problem.... It is now twenty months since the
City Council voted that shelter occupancy was to be kept at or below 90%.
We are entering the second winter in which this supposedly binding instruc-
tion has been completely disregarded.

The letter called on Tory to receive a delegation of poor and homeless people, but
before any meeting could be arranged four men would die, succumbing to Toronto's
winter. With word of the second of these deaths, OCAP occupied the front lobby of
Mayor Tory's office. Fifty protesters demanded, yet again as such demonstrators
had in the past, the opening of the Moss Park Armoury as an emergency shelter.
OCAP also sharply criticized the City Medical Officer's failure to issue an extreme
cold alert as the mercury dropped to frigid temperatures. John Clarke railed against
the failure to open emergency warming centres and temporary shelter beds. "If you
don't provide people with even emergency shelter beds, that's the last thing you give
a human being before you abandon him, and we're not going to see people abandoned on the streets of this city."

Tory wasn't about to meet with OCAP, but he was, unlike his predecessor
Rob Ford, cognizant of the need to put forward a caring public relations front. He
ordered the immediate opening of two warming centres, announced the city was
leasing two motels to house some of the homeless, and set up a task force on community housing to be led by former mayor and Liberal MP Art Eggleton.[159] But to
OCAP this signalled a recycling of the old personnel of the state's resilient dodging of
fundamental change. Eggleton was a key cabinet minister in Jean Chrétien's federal
Liberal government, which had killed the National Housing Program in 1993 and
cut hundreds of millions of dollars in transfer payments to the provinces earmarked
for social assistance of the poor. Tory, whatever his media-friendly image, was wedded to a Conservative Party agenda that, in Ontario, had a destructive history of
slashing welfare rates and abandoning the construction of seventeen thousand
affordable housing units.

As OCAP protested, city councillors sidestepped. In a repetition of a centur-
ies-old variant of passing the responsibility back onto the poor, the dispossessed
were presented as suffering on the street not because they were without work,
wages, and the material foundations of human welfare (of which housing was crucial) but, rather, because they had other problems that afflicted them as individuals. This was, once more, a benign variant of arguments that reached back to the
1830s, the House of Industry, and the long history of Poor Law prejudice. "This cry
of beds, beds, beds is a dated strategy that is not really solving problems that our

homeless face," declared Councillor James Pasternak, Chair of Toronto's Community Development and Recreation Committee. "We can open up thousands of beds, but unless we are working with the homeless in areas such as mental health and addiction, we will not be able to solve the problem."[160]

But the reverse, surely, was true, calling into question posing the matter in such a way. Without beds, and all that they symbolize, how can poor people's mental health and addiction problems possibly be addressed, let alone solved? Indeed, as we complete this book, Toronto City Council, under the astute but unashamedly capitalist-conscious leadership of Mayor John Tory, has rallied around what has been called an "austerity consensus." This consensus unites the right and the ostensible left in an acknowledgement that the politics of pragmatism must prevail, and to get things done there must be unity around creating a progressive Toronto that is also a Toronto always willing to grease the wheels of development.[161] Central to this agenda is a continuation of the Streets to Homes program first initiated under liberal-social democratic Mayor David Miller.

John Tory, who understands that spending a few million to ease the political fall-out attendant on homeless people dying on the streets in Toronto's cold winter, as they did in January–February 2015, is money well spent, has managed to rally seeming left-wing councillors to what is, in effect, an intensification of the program of social cleansing. A recent report of the General Manager of Toronto's Shelter, Support, and Housing Administration (SSHA) entitled "Infrastructure and Service Improvement Plan for the Emergency Shelter System," submitted to the Community Development and Recreation Committee of City Council, acknowledges that shelter use in Toronto between January 2011 and January 2015 increased by 11 percent. Overcrowding in the hostels and the rising numbers of homeless are registering with the Tory administration. The 2015 Shelter System report charts a three-pronged agenda that many will applaud: move a portion of long-term shelter users into socially-assisted housing; open additional space and increase capacity in the shelter system as it is currently constituted; and relocate shelter facilities in outlying areas of the city. This seemingly progressive approach is, in fact, a clearing away of the human impediments to the gentrification of the city's core. The homeless will be removed from high-profile areas of unsightly concentration and maximum visibility, dispersed throughout the city in isolating locations where the poor will be allowed to slowly and quietly atrophy. At the same time as, to use a nineteenth-century phrase, "the paupers are shovelled out," the infrastructure that has sustained them, however inadequately, is on the chopping block, as a network of urban drop-in centres, street-level social assistance, food banks, soup kitchens, emergency shelters, and other facilities in the downtown neighbourhoods of Toronto's poorest intersections, such as Dundas and Sherbourne, are to be scaled-down or closed, paving the way to further condominium-driven gentrification. Thus the "George Street Redevelopment" project, with its adjacent forty-six-storey Pace Condo Tower, is twinned with the downsizing of shelter bed capacity at Seaton House and School House shelters (400 beds); hundreds of homeless people will necessarily be relocated. Emergency refuges such as the Hope Shelter (124 beds) at McCaul and College Streets are set to close in April 2015 and other shelters, having been allowed to slip irreversibly into dilapidation, are undoubtedly going to be shut down as well. Hostels leasing their properties are finding that owners are selling out, cashing in on the seemingly insatiable inflationary Toronto real estate boom; the result is that more facilities traditionally used by the homeless are having to move.

Toronto's SSHA notes that as of early 2015 "fifty-three per cent of all shelter beds are concentrated in three downtown wards," while twenty wards have no emergency shelter beds at all. It therefore targets these supposedly "underserved locations outside of the downtown core" as Toronto's districts that must be "prioritized for new shelters." This has the ring of fairness and concern about it. But it manages to miss the forest of homeless people's needs for the trees of development profit. As OCAP's John Clarke comments, there are no responsible "proposals for how you can possibly meet the survival needs of people you dump outside the city core. Where will you locate drop-ins and support agencies? How will you overcome the fact that people will be left to fend for themselves in parts of the city where distances between service providing facilities are measured in miles instead of blocks?" Deploring this "exercise in social cleansing," Clarke notes that "this forced relocation plan" will result in the plug being pulled on "existing facilities before firm arrangements in 'underserved suburbs' are even in place." This, suggests Clarke reasonably, will only "increase the risk" of homeless people continuing to die on the streets. As the OCAP organizer rightly concludes:

> We must build the broadest community and union alliance to challenge [the relocation process] and be ready to occupy facilities to prevent them being locked up or to take the necessary action to open new space. We must fight to prevent the driving out of homeless people. It is an exercise in reckless social abandonment that will not stop at targeting those forced onto the streets. Those in public housing and other low income tenants will also continue to be slated for removal at an increased pace. This is

really about challenging the notion that Toronto should be a City where the investment needs of developers, bankers and business owners get to prevail unchecked.[162]

Indeed, this class agenda and what it speaks to in terms of human needs is the fulcrum on which Toronto's long and rebellious history of the dispossessed has always balanced.

PART VI

Conclusion

"Bread I Want, and Bread I Will Have"

T

he poor *have* always been with us. This is not, however, because scripture dictates their presence, decreeing that somehow they *must* exist. Poverty, moreover, is not, in spite of what certain politicians are apt to say, a lifestyle choice, adopted by those who choose to live within its constraints. The dispossessed are here now as they have been throughout history, in such great numbers because what they are deprived of helps to sate the craving of the few for unbridled accumulation. It is the appetite for unrestricted and expansive acquisition on the part of a small contingent of society that ensures those many layers "beneath" it will have less and less. The powerful require the conditions that displace people, creating and extending a regime of iniquitous relations that marks the waged and wageless as forever apart from those who own and control, not only places of employment (factories and fields, mines and mills), but also institutions of regulation and retribution (schools and welfare offices, prisons and police divisions). And from this ownership and control coffers are filled and a regime of accumulation sustained.

Capitalism as the ordered-by-profit system that ultimately sustains this systematic and unbalanced ecology of inequality is crisis-ridden. It conditions economic crisis into its survival cycles, needing the periodic collapse of productive life in order to lower the costs of this edifice of acquisition, shore up profitability, and keep the machinery of dispossession going. Without capitalist crisis, profits weaken, and production stagnates, becoming a dead weight that cannot realize a maximum benefit for the few. More and more smaller capitalist enterprises compete unproductively on the edges of the market. With capitalist crisis, new technologies of production displace irksome collectivities of workers and marginal employers, and the poor are precipitated into public spaces, where they are excoriated for not having work, wages, and the wherewithal to support themselves and their families. Their presence as a reserve army of the unemployed serves as a reminder to those employed, be their wages high or low, that resistance at the point of production might well drive the waged into the unenviable ranks of the wageless. Crisis disciplines the destitute, the working poor, and the seemingly union-protected, ostensibly high-waged, "middle-class" worker. It depresses the absolute wage remuneration and assails the protections of the social wage, those safety nets of provisioning and entitlement that have been struggled for over centuries of conflict, culminating in unionization and collective bargaining rights, on the one hand, and welfare systems on the other. Capitalism thus relies on crisis to sustain it. An ideological hegemony is strengthened as the dispossessed are demonized and the consolidating ranks of the privileged are given new justifications for their right to accumulate and govern. Possession's insatiable needs condition dispossession's denials of necessities. Crisis reorders the relationships of class society, further consolidating and concentrating power. Power rationalizes its own existence.

Something like beds for the homeless, in a society such as this, registers weakly against a skyline of high-rise condominiums and office towers, alongside streetscapes of fashionable boutiques and urbane bistros. The banks, the assembly lines, the sweatshops—their bottom lines dwarf considerations of those evicted, mangled, and exploited, of those sleeping under the viaducts and lining up at food banks. And yet these experiences, as the lived grievance of dispossession, can never quite be exorcised from the visible relations of inequality, cleansed from a body politic many necessarily see as soiled.

As long as the dispossessed *are* dispossessed, as long as a segment of our society is without adequate housing, clothing, nutrition, and security, all of which depend on a living wage or social assistance rates that provide for the capacity to exist in ways that reach beyond poverty, there will be those who demand beds and so much more. With capitalism and its periodic and inevitable crises thwarting the material ability of widening circles of the poor to access the absolute requirements of life, destitution and homelessness *are* inevitable. The increasing evidence and glaring visibility of human suffering, and ultimately unnecessary death, inevitably gives rise to resistance, protest, rebellion. The revenge of the dispossessed, a measure of our humanity, cannot, finally, be suppressed. It erupts periodically and in more intensified and sustained ways, through mobilizations and challenges to the established (dis)order of a brutalizing and impersonal political economy. If this rebelliousness champions changes that promise a resurrection of what is worthwhile in humanity, its suppression and repression expose the systemic inequality and shameful inhumanity of a civil society ruled by acquisitive individualism rather than appreciations of collective, common good.

Toronto's history of the poor, spanning more than two centuries of dynamic development, provides copious examples of how the recurring consequences of economic crises repeatedly and routinely reduce many to dire circumstances, including homelessness. As this happens, the ruling order ratchets up its ideological din. It demands an end to indulgence, insisting that the dispossessed themselves are alone responsible for their worsening lot. Many are castigated as undeserving of aid which, should it be offered, is better given as the gift of charity rather than be made a required responsibility of the state. This is not merely an artifact of nineteenth-century thought, with its Poor Laws and Houses of Industry. Rather, this complacent attitude toward poverty and its debilitating consequences runs through our history. The language with which the poor are castigated changes, of course, and the policy considerations articulated in legislation are posed in increasingly sophisticated ways. But for all that seems so different, so much remains the same. Positions first evident in the 1830s have a stubborn continuity, surfacing again and again, even in our own times, notable for their retreat into a mean-spirited insistence that markets not democratic states should provide for the poor, who must do their own bidding if they are to rise out of destitution and carve themselves a piece of the good life.

None of this—economic crises, joblessness, deprivation, homelessness, and the misery of wants and needs unfulfilled—has been accepted by Toronto's dispossessed, who have been anything but resigned. Over the course of two centuries, the dispossessed have resisted the demands of their better-off so-called superiors that they be compliant and content with a little. They have demanded relief in the 1830s and the 1930s; they have petitioned and marched, occupied and fought in the streets, leading collective struggles for "work and bread" in the late nineteenth century, and demanding shelter, special diet considerations, and sustenance in the opening years of the twenty-first century. Campaigns of the jobless and the destitute have surfaced in the 1890s, the 1920s, the 1960s, and the 1990s. The activists that led them and in some cases continue to mobilize the legions of those seemingly left behind remain very much a part of our political landscape. These people have come from all stripes of the political spectrum, although more often than not they have located themselves as leftists—socialists, communists, anarchists: anticapitalists all.

"Fight to win," not just as a slogan, but as a practical banner under which walk a wide range of activities, has again and again been raised by the poor, announcing there will be no lasting social peace until there is a widening understanding of social responsibility and recognition of human rights. Struggles waged in this manner, be it in the 1870s, the 1950s or now, have not, to be sure, created a truly just social order, establishing unequivocally the rights of the poor to housing, adequate health care and nutrition, and access to meaningful work and secure and sufficient wages. But militant campaigns of resistance and those who have worked overtime to make them happen have pressured the state and won improvements in social provisioning. This practical political intervention, waged by and in the name of the wageless, has bettered the lives of hundreds of thousands of people. It has, over hundreds of years and more, been fundamental in setting standards of universal entitlement that make it increasingly difficult for ruling authority and the apparatus of governance to either avoid or obfuscate the debilitating consequences of economic crises or the all too regularized impoverishment of a significant sector of the population.

Those who have organized the varied and persistent movements of the poor and the unemployed have not been given an easy ride. Beaten by police, hauled before the courts on countless charges, jailed, vilified in the press and denounced from the pulpit, fired from work, and blacklisted by employers—in spite of this harsh treatment and relentless attack, uncompromising, often radical, advocates of the dispossessed have continued to struggle. They have written leaflets and pamphlets, educated and lectured, advised and agitated, working tirelessly on behalf of those who obviously have too little and need more. In the process, what is wrong with a society that lets buildings sit vacant while the homeless lack basic shelter, and that encourages and expands inequality while depriving masses of people of proper nutrition, basic health care, and access to waged employment is brought, time and time again, into the limelight of public scrutiny.

Just as the poor have always been with us, then, so too has opposition to the social fact of being poor, of suffering unemployment, homelessness, and hunger. In the early summer of 1816, the agricultural labourers of East Anglia in England revolted. They had lived in the jaws of crisis for too long. They demanded, as did their Canadian urban counterparts in the late nineteenth century, "bread or blood." With poor relief kept at abysmally low levels, the game laws restricting access to the bounty of the forests that the poor considered "common property," clergymen countenancing acceptance of their worsening lot, and facing the menacing repression of the lash, or worse, the gallows, a distressed rural population rose up, insistent that hunger could no longer ravage the labouring poor. William Dawson declared that he had been "working for a long time for a small allowance, and ... he would either have a remedy or lose his life." At one confrontation, a crowd demanded a baker give up his loaves so the poor could eat. Remonstrating with the rebels to be more restrained, lest they unleash authority's anger at "Persons so tumultuously and riotously assembled," a local reverend condemned "Depredations or Violence." But Dawson was unmoved by such criticism, however divine its origins. "Here I am," the dissident agricultural worker declared, "between Earth and Sky—so help me god. I would sooner loose my life than go home as I am. Bread I want and Bread I will have."[1]

These words of defiant demand defy so much. They refuse accommodation and reject fear. They challenge easy and empty conciliation. They are categorical in not settling for too little. Above all, they animate action. They constitute a vocabulary of insistence that has written chapter on chapter in a too often unread and unappreciated book chronicling the resistance of the dispossessed, people who have repeatedly put struggle into the pages of the past. These words of "Bread I want and Bread I will have," remain with us still, constituting a legacy of living and longing for liberation from an unjust, crisis-ridden order that reverberates resiliently over the course of the long, rebellious history of Toronto's dispossessed.

Notes

FOREWORD

1. Any number of reports will do to make the case, as when Credit Suisse in its Global Wealth Report in 2015 noted that the richest 1 percent of the world's population now owns half the world's wealth. See for example Emily Peck, "The 62 Richest People on Earth Now Hold as Much Wealth as the Poorest 3.4 Billion," *Huffington Post*, www.huffingtonpost.com.

2. See Kathryn J. Edin and H. Luke Shaefer, *$2.00 a Day: Living on Almost Nothing in America* (Boston: Houghton Mifflin, 2015).

PART I

1. "Vigil Held for Homeless Men Who Died During Toronto Cold Snap," www.cp24; "Homeless Man Dies at Toronto Shelter during Extreme Cold," metronews.ca.

2. Marcus Gee, "Suburban Homelessness an Often Neglected Problem," *Globe and Mail*, January 15, 2015. See also Jenny Yuen, "Homeless Man Killed in Fire Fondly Remembered," *Toronto Sun*, January 14, 2015.

3. Konrad Yakabuski, "What's So Smart about Unaffordable Housing?" *Globe and Mail*, January 26, 2016; Jeffrey Simpson, "Ignoring the Poor Impoverishes Politics," *Globe and Mail*, January 30, 2015. We cite Yakabuski and Simpson because they establish that even among mainstream conservative and liberal commentators, the issues of poverty and homelessness in our times have registered in important ways. For a more radical commentary which accords more with our views see John Clarke, "The Fight against Street Deaths in Toronto," Socialist Project E-Bulletin No. 1077, February 6, 2015, www.socialistproject.ca.

4. For the kinds of cultures of prejudice that have historically primed the pump of poor-bashing and deepened animosity to the so-called "undeserving poor" see the varied discussions in Judith C. Blackwell, Murray E. G. Smith, and John S. Sorenson, eds., *Cultures of Prejudice: Arguments in Critical Social Science* (Peterborough, Ontario: Broadview, 2003), esp. 107–74; Jean Swanson, *Poor-Bashing: The Politics of Exclusion* (Toronto: Between the Lines, 2001); Gareth Stedman Jones, *An End to Poverty? A Historical Debate* (London: Profile Books, 2004); Michael B. Katz, *The Undeserving Poor: American's Enduring Confrontation with Poverty* (New York: Oxford University Press, 2013).

5. Bill Curry, "Provinces Take On Ottawa over Funding for Job Training," *Globe and Mail*, February 11, 2015.

6. See for instance, Bryan D. Palmer, "The Riot Act: Reviving Protest in Ontario," *Canadian Dimension* 34, September–October 2000, 28–32; Palmer, "Repression and Dissent: The OCAP Trials," *Canadian Dimension* 37, May–June 2003, 12–15.

7. Others did write of OCAP in their blended roles as scholars and activists. See Norman Feltes,

"The New Prince in a New Principality: OCAP and the Toronto Poor," *Labour/Le Travail* 48 (Fall 2001): 125–55.

8. For an accessible statement on capitalism and poverty see Cy Gonick, "Poverty and Capitalism," in *Poverty and Social Policy in Canada*, ed. W. E. Mann (Vancouver: Copp Clark, 1970), 66–82.

9. In this latter appreciation of the role of the organization, leadership, *and* agency of the dispossessed we share the perspective of Frances Fox Piven and Richard A. Cloward, as developed in their rightly acclaimed *Poor People's Movements: Why They Succeed, How They Fail* (New York: Pantheon, 1977). Our focus on one locale, and our detailed presentation of the actual struggles of Toronto's poor over the *longue durée*, however, means that our account has a different texture than many other studies. The historical and socially specific approach that we have adopted, congruent with Piven's and Cloward's orientation, allows us to develop understandings of resistance quite rich in detail. Our concern with bringing to life the actual struggles of the poor distances us somewhat from the state-centred or discourse-oriented approaches of many scholars who have produced excellent studies of welfare reform. Michael B. Katz notes, "The history of welfare looks very different when the historian perches on the shoulder of a poor person and looks outward than it does when the story is told from the perspective of governments, agencies, or reformers." Katz, *In the Shadow of the Poor House: A Social History of Welfare in America* (New York: Basic Books, 1986), 293.

10. Ernest Mandel, *Marxist Economic Theory* (New York: Monthly Review, 1968), I: 359–60; Alexander Keyssar, *Out of Work: The First Century of Unemployment in Massachusetts* (Cambridge: Cambridge University Press, 1986), 47; Cy Gonick, *Out of Work: Why There's So Much Unemployment, and Why It's Getting Worse* (Toronto: James Lorimer, 1978), 39; Murray E. G. Smith, *Global Capitalism in Crisis: Karl Marx & the Decay of the Profit System* (Halifax: Fernwood, 2010), 65–66.

11. James C. Scott, *Seeing Like a State: How Certain Schemes to Improve the Human Condition Have Failed* (New Haven: Yale University Press, 1999), 1.

12. See, for instance, Steven High, *Industrial Sunset: The Making of North America's Rust Belt, 1969–1984* (Toronto: University of Toronto Press, 2003); Aaron Brenner, Robert Brenner, and Cal Winslow, eds., *Rebel Rank-and-File: Labor Militancy and the Revolt from Below during the Long Seventies* (New York: Verso, 2010); Jefferson Cowie, *Stayin' Alive: The 1970s and the Last Days of the Working Class* (New York: New Press, 2010).

13. For an illuminating discussion of the tendency of the rate of profit to fall see Smith, *Global Capitalism in Crisis*.

14. See, among many possible statements, Bryan D. Palmer, "'Taking It': Ontario Workers' Struggles," in *Lectures in Canadian Labour and Working-Class History*, ed. W. J. C. Cherwinski and Gregory S. Kealey (St. John's, Newfoundland: Committee on Canadian Labour History, 1985), 183–98; David Rapaport, *No Justice, No Peace: The 1996 OPSEU Strike against the Harris Government in Ontario* (Kingston: McGill-Queen's University Press, 1999); David Camfield, "Assessing Resistance in Harris's Ontario, 1995–1999," in *Canadian Public Policy in an Age of Global Capitalism*, ed. Mike Burke, Colin Mooers, and John Shields (Halifax: Fernwood, 2000), 306–17; Bryan D. Palmer, "Showdown in Ontario: Build the General Strike," *Canadian Dimension* 30, May-June 1996, 21–26; Palmer, "Halloween in Harrisland: Teachers, Bureaucrats, and Betrayal," *Canadian Dimension* 32, January-February 1998, 29–32; Palmer, "Where Ya at, General Strike?!" *Canadian Dimension* 32, September-October 1998, 20–24.

15. The above paragraphs draw on quotes from "Manifesto of the Communist Party," in Karl Marx and Frederick Engels, *Selected Works* (Moscow: Progress Publishers, 1968), 36–46; Karl Marx, *Capital: A Critical Analysis of Capitalist Production* (Moscow: Foreign Languages Publishing House, n.d.), 1: 20; Marx, *Grundrisse: Foundations of the Critique of Political Economy*

(Rough Draft) (Harmondsworth: Penguin, 1973), 749–50.

16. Karl Marx, *Wage-Labour and Capital/Value, Price and Profit* (New York: International, 1933), 45.

17. See Bryan D. Palmer, "Social Formation and Class Formation in Nineteenth-Century North America," in *Proletarianization and Family History*, ed. David Levine (New York: Academic Press, 1984), 229–308.

18. Marx, *Capital*, 568, 612–16. See also Marx, *Grundrisse*, esp. 483–509.

19. The literature that could be cited is immense, and for London alone is benchmarked between 1850 and 1890 by the pioneering sociological inquiries of Henry Mayhew and Charles Booth. For other useful commentary see Raphael Samuel, "Workshop of the World: Steam Power and Hand Technology in Mid-Victorian Britain," *History Workshop Journal* 3 (1977): 6–72; Gareth Stedman Jones, *Outcast London: A Study in the Relationship between Classes in Victorian Society* (Oxford: Oxford University Press, 1971); and for France, Louis Chevalier, *Laboring Classes and Dangerous Classes in Paris during the First Half of the Nineteenth Century* (New York: Howard Fertig, 1973); Robert Stuart, *Marxism at Work: Ideology, Class and French Socialism during the Third Republic* (Cambridge: Cambridge University Press, 1992), 127–79.

20. Michael Denning, "Wageless Life," *New Left Review* 66 (November-December 2010): 79–81; J. C. L. Simonde de Sismondi, *Nouveaux principes d'économie politique ou de la richesse dans ses rapports avec la population* (Paris, 1819), II: 262, 305; I: 146, quoted in Stedman Jones, *An End to Poverty?*, 151; Catharina Lis and Hugo Soly, "Policing the Early Modern Proletariat, 1450–1850," in Levine, *Proletarianization and Family History*, 163–228; Max Weber, *General Economic History*, translated by F. H. Knight (New York, 1961), quoted in G. E. M. de Ste. Croix, *The Class Struggle in the Ancient Greek World* (London: Duckworth, 1981), 262; Edith Abbott, "The Wages of Unskilled Labor in the United States," *Journal of Political Economy* 13 (June 1905): 324.

21. See Bryan D. Palmer, *Canada's 1960s: The Ironies of Identity in a Rebellious Era* (Toronto: University of Toronto Press, 2009).

22. For discussions see Greg Albo, Sam Gindin, and Leo Panitch, *In and Out of Crisis: The Global Financial Meltdown and Left Alternatives* (Oakland: PM Press, 2010); Bryan D. Palmer, "Profits of Doom: Spectres of Capitalist Crisis," *Labour/Le Travail* 67 (Spring 2011), 189-202.

23. Paul Campbell Appleton, "The Sunshine and the Shade: Labour Activism in Central Canada, 1850-1860" (master's thesis, University of Calgary, 1974); Steven Langdon, "The Political Economy of Capitalist Transformation: Central Canada from the 1840s to the 1870s," (master's thesis, Carleton University, 1972); Gregory S. Kealey, *Toronto Workers Respond to Industrial Capitalism, 1860–1892* (Toronto: University of Toronto Press, 1980); Gregory S. Kealey and Bryan D. Palmer, *Dreaming of What Might Be: The Knights of Labor in Ontario, 1880–1900* (New York: Cambridge University Press, 1982).

24. As a brief introduction see Robert H. Babcock, *Gompers in Canada: A Study of American Continentalism Before the First World War* (Toronto: University of Toronto Press, 1975).

25. A recent unpublished study, completed as we were finishing our parallel examination of Toronto, addresses struggles of the unemployed nationally in the years 1875–1928, concluding as we do that the left-led movements of jobless protest that are associated with the Great Depression had a long period of gestation. See David Alexander Thompson, "Working Class Anguish and Revolutionary Indignation: The Making of Radical and Socialist Unemployed Movements in Canada, 1875-1928" (PhD dissertation, Queen's University, 2014). We are grateful to Professor Thompson for sharing his manuscript with us. For the Cold War in Canadian unions see Irving Martin Abella, *Nationalism, Communism, and Canadian Labour: The CIO, the Communist Party of Canada, and the Canadian Congress of Labour, 1935–1956* (Toronto: University of Toronto Press, 1973), and for a general

treatment of the Cold War see Reg Whitaker and Gary Marcuse, *Cold War Canada: The Making of a National Insecurity State, 1945–1957* (Toronto: University of Toronto Press, 1974).

26. See, for instance, James Struthers, *The Limits of Affluence: Welfare in Ontario, 1920–1970* (Toronto: University of Toronto Press, 1994).

27. For accounts of union density and decline, on which much is now written, see Michael Goldfield, *The Decline of Organized Labor in the United States* (Chicago: University of Chicago Press, 1987); Wythe Holt, "Union Densities, Business Unionism, and Working-Class Struggle: Labour Movement Decline in the United States and Japan, 1930–2000," and Michael Goldfield and Bryan D. Palmer, "Canada's Workers Movement: Uneven Developments," *Labour/Le Travail* 59 (Spring 2007): 99–132, 149–78. For the general assault on the working class see Leo Panitch and Donald Swartz, *From Consent to Coercion: The Assault on Trade Union Freedoms* (Toronto: Garamond Press, 2003).

28. See Bryan D. Palmer, *Solidarity: The Rise and Fall of an Opposition in British Columbia* (Vancouver: New Star Books, 1987).

29. See, for instance, George Ehring and Wayne Roberts, *Giving Away a Miracle: Lost Dreams, Broken Promises, and the Ontario NDP* (Oakville, Ontario: Mosaic Press, 1993); Thomas Walkom, *Rae Days: The Rise and Follies of the NDP* (Toronto: Key Porter Books, 1994).

30. Mike Davis, *Planet of Slums* (London: Verso, 2006); Davis, "The Urbanization of Empire: Megacities and the Laws of Chaos," *Social Text* 22 (Winter 2004): 9-15; Joseph Gugler, ed., *Cities in the Developing World: Issues, Theory and Policy* (Oxford: Oxford University Press, 1997). For an older work see John Iliffe, *The African Poor: A History* (Cambridge: Cambridge University Press, 1987).

31. Jason K. Hall and Loretta E. Bass, "The Effects of Global Interaction on Poverty in Developing Countries, 1991–2005," *Journal of World Systems Research* 18 (Summer 2012): 236–65; Shaohua Chen and Martin Ravaillion, "Absolute Poverty Measures for the Developing World,

1981–2004," *Proceedings of the National Academy of Sciences of the United States of America* 104 (October 23, 2007): 16757–62.

32. John Bellamy Foster, Robert W. McChesney, and R. Jamil Jonna, "The Global Reserve Army of Labor and the New Imperialism," *Monthly Review* 63 (November 2011), monthlyreview.org; Marx, *Capital,* I: 644–45; Davis, *Planet of Slums,* 178. Early comment on the growing significance of the informal sector appeared in Manfred Bienefeld, "The informal sector and peripheral capitalism," *Bulletin of the Institute of Development Studies* 4 (1975): 53–73, and the importance of the informal sector in terms of African class formation runs through the discussion in Bill Freund, *The African Worker* (Cambridge: Cambridge University Press, 1988).

33. See, for instance, Stuart Hall, Chas Critcher, Tony Jefferson, John Clarke, and Brian Roberts, *Policing the Crisis: Mugging, the State, and Law and Order* (London: Macmillan, 1978).

34. See Leo Panitch and Sam Gindin, *The Making of Global Capitalism: The Political Economy of American Empire* (London: Verso, 2012); Joshua B. Freeman, *American Empire: The Rise of a Global Power—The Democratic Revolution at Home* (New York: Viking, 2012).

35. This has gendered and racialized dimensions, as is evident in the work of Leah F. Vosko and others. See Vosko, *Temporary Work: The Gendered Rise of a Precarious Employment Relation* (Toronto: University of Toronto Press, 2000); Vosko, ed., *Precarious Employment: Understanding Labour Market Insecurity in Canada* (Montreal & Kingston: McGill-Queen's University Press, 2006); Vosko, *Managing the Margins: Gender, Citizenship, and the International Regulation of Precarious Employment* (Oxford: Oxford University Press, 2010); Gregory Albo, "The 'New Economy' and Capitalism Today," in *Interrogating the New Economy: Restructuring Work in the 21st Century*, ed. Norene J. Pupo and Mark P. Thomas (Toronto: University of Toronto Press, 2010), 12; Christopher Hermann, "Labouring in the Network," *Capitalism, Nature, Socialism* 17 (2006): 65–76.

36. Ricardo Antunes, "The Working Class Today: The New Form of Being of the Class Who Lives From its Labour," *Workers of the World: International Journal on Strikes and Social Conflict* 1 (January 2012): 7–18.

37. Frantz Fanon, *The Wretched of the Earth* (New York: Evergreen, 1966); Davis, *Planet of Slums*, 206.

38. See Guy Standing, *The Precariat: The New Dangerous Class* (London: Bloomsbury Academic, 2011).

39. David Montgomery, "Working People's Responses to Past Depressions," in *Workers in Hard Times: A Long View of Economic Crises*, ed. Leon Fink, Joseph A. McCartin, and Joan Sangster (Urbana: University of Illinois Press, 2014), 56.

40. Marx, *Capital*, 640–44.

41. The "underclass," an early twentieth-century sociological designation that would be excavated in Robert Roberts, *The Classic Slum: Salford Life in the First Quarter of the Century* (Manchester: Manchester University Press, 1971), is not unrelated to the continuity of precariousness in proletarian life.

42. Peter Hayes, "Utopia and the Lumpenproletariat: Marx's Reasoning in 'The Eighteenth Brumaire of Louis Bonaparte'," *Review of Politics* 50 (Summer 1988): esp. 458.

43. Frederick Engels, *The Condition of the Working-Class in England in 1844* (London: Swan Sonnenschein, 1892). Six years earlier Engels had written in correspondence to Laura Lafargue and August Bebel in ways that suggested a jaundiced view of seeing "barrow boys, idlers, police spies, and rogues" as sources of support for socialism. He referred to "numbers of poor devils of the East End who vegetate in the borderland between working class and lumpen proletariat." Engels to Laura Lafargue, February 9, 1886; Engels to August Bebel, February 15, 1886, in Karl Marx and Frederick Engels, *Collected Works*, vol. 47, *1883–1886* (New York: International, 1995), 403–10. See also Stedman Jones, *Outcast London;* Arthur Morrison, *A Child of the Jago* (London: Methuen, 1896).

44. Karl Marx, "Economic and Philosophic Manuscripts of 1844," in Karl Marx and Frederick Engels, *Collected Works*, vol. 3, *1843–1844* (New York: Lawrence and Wishart, 1975), 284.

45. Among many passages that might be cited see Marx, *Capital*, 653–54, and the following discussion of "The Badly Paid Strata of the British Industrial Working Class," 654–63, "The Nomad Population," 663–67, and "The British Agricultural Proletariat," 673–712.

46. See also Peter Linebaugh, *The Magna Carta Manifesto: Liberties and Commons for All* (Berkeley: University of California Press, 2008).

47. See Karl Marx, "Proceedings of the Sixth Rhine Province Assembly. Third Article Debates on the Law on Thefts of Wood," in Marx and Engels, *Collected Works*, vol. 1, *1835–1843* (Moscow: Progress, 1975), 224–63; Teo Ballvé, "Marx: Law on Thefts of Wood," territorialmasquerades.net, Peter Linebaugh, "Karl Marx, the Theft of Wood, and Working Class Composition: A Contribution to the Current Debate," *Crime and Social Justice* 6 (Fall-Winter 1976): 5–16; Erica Sherover-Marcuse, *Emancipation and Consciousness: Dogmatic and Dialectical Perspectives in the Early Marx* (New York: Blackwell, 1986). Marx has recently been criticized within literature on transnational and global labour history for placing undue emphasis on the waged worker and disregarding the wageless, some of whom are cavalierly and moralistically dismissed as the lumpenproletariat. Such critique draws one-sidedly on Marx's writings on the 1848 class struggle in France, culminating in the defeat of an 1848 Revolution. See, for instance, Marcel van der Linden, *Workers of the World: Essays Toward a Global Labour History* (Leiden: Brill, 2008), 10, 22–27, 267, 298; Van der Linden, "Who Are the Workers of the World? Marx and Beyond," *Workers of the World: International Journal on Strikes and Social Conflicts* 1 (January 2013): 55–76. Unease with Marx's seeming dismissiveness of the so-called lumpenproletariat has long been evident among Africanists and was posed forcefully in Peter Worsley, "Frantz Fanon and the 'Lumpenproletariat',"

in *The Socialist Register, 1972*, ed. Ralph Miliband and John Saville (London: Merlin, 1972), 193–229. Our view is that Marx's undeniably caustic comments on the lumpenproletariat in his writings on class struggle in France grew out of his acute disappointment at the ways in which *some* of the dispossessed gravitated to reaction in a moment of potential revolution in 1848. But such comments, as we have suggested above and as other writers demonstrate, must be placed alongside many other writings that express great empathy for those whom capitalism has assailed in ongoing acts of dispossession. For a still highly useful discussion of the lumpenproletariat see Hal Draper, "The Lumpen-Class versus the Proletariat," *Karl Marx's Theory of Revolution, Volume II: The Politics of Social Classes* (New York: Monthly Review, 1978), 453–80. In the 1960s/ early 1970s in Toronto the issue of the working class as counterposed to the lumpenproletariat was suggested in one New Left polemic with respect to community organizing in downtown, core neighbourhoods. See Marjaleena Repo, "Organizing the Poor—Against the Working Class," *Transformation* 1 (March-April 1971). During the 1990s and early 2000s, echoes of the pejorative depiction of the lumpenproletariat could be heard in Shaughnessy Bishop-Stall, *Down to This: Squalor and Splendour in a Big-City Shantytown* (Toronto: Vintage, 2004).

48. Wal Hannington, *The Problem of the Distressed Areas* (London: Victor Gollancz, 1937), 233–50, in which an organizer of the Communist Party's National Unemployed Workers' Movement in Great Britain asked, "Is there a Fascist danger among the Unemployed?"

PART II

1. William Graves, "Diary," in *Ontario Historical Society Papers and Records,* vol. 43, *1951,* ed. Donald F. McQuat, 10, quoted in Donald B. Smith, "The Dispossession of the Mississauga Indians: A Missing Chapter in the Early History of Upper Canada," in *Historical Essays on Upper Canada: New Perspectives*, ed. J. K. Johnson and Bruce G Wilson (Ottawa: Carleton University Press, 1989), 43.

2. Peter Kulchyski, *Like the Sound of a Drum: Aboriginal Cultural Politics in Denendeh and Nunavut* (Winnipeg: University of Manitoba Press, 2005), 88. See also the discussion in Glen Sean Coulthard, *Red Skin, White Masks: Rejecting the Colonial Politics of Recognition* (Minneapolis: University of Minnesota Press, 2014), 62.

3. We have not detailed extensively the particular condition and forms of resistance of Toronto's urban poor of Indigenous/Aboriginal/ First Nation (terms we use interchangeably, although cognizant of how contemporary scholarship is parsing differentiations) or Métis origin. This would take a separate study. Nonetheless, it is useful to recognize that the original pre-Confederation Euro-capitalist ideology of an ostensible right to dispossess First Nations peoples because land in North America was supposedly unowned and undeveloped—*terra nullius*—is not unrelated to a similar modern ideology of urban improvement that justifies contemporary gentrification and rationalizes the obliteration of urban spaces where the poor and the dispossessed (some of whom have Indigenous/ Aboriginal/First Nations or Métis origins) have historically established a presence. That much of this presence involves people and spaces that are undeniably Indigenous suggests an ongoing colonization, what Coulthard sees as a frontier of dispossession driven by capital's claims of *urbs nullius.* See Coulthard, *Red Skin, White Masks,* 175–76; Bonita Lawrence, *"Real" Indians and Others: Mixed Blood Urban Native Peoples and Indigenous Nationalism* (Vancouver: University of British Columbia Press, 2004).

4. For a recent discussion of managing the migrants that accents the role of the developing layers of the state over the course of the nineteenth century see Lisa Chilton, "Managing Migrants: Toronto, 1820–1880," *Canadian Historical Review* 92 (June 2011): 231–62.

5. A classic statement is Smith, "The Dispossession of the Mississauga Indians," 23–51, but for more recent views see Victoria Jane Freeman, "'Toronto Has No History': Indigeneity, Settler Colonialism and Historical Memory in Canada's Largest City" (PhD diss., University of Toronto, 2010); Deanne Aline Marie LeBlanc, "Identifying the Settler Denizen within Settler Colonialism" (master's thesis, University of Victoria, 2014).

6. J. M. S. Careless, *Toronto to 1918: An Illustrated History* (Toronto: James Lorimer, 1984), 11; Smith, "The Dispossession of the Mississauga Indians," 23–51.

7. Industrial-capitalist Toronto in the late nineteenth century is the subject of Kealey's pioneering account of workers confronting the disciplines of the new order: Gregory S. Kealey, *Toronto Workers Respond to Industrial Capitalism, 1860–1892* (Toronto: University of Toronto Press, 1980).

8. Henry Scadding, *Toronto of Old: Collections and Recollections Illustrative of the Early Settlement and Social Life of the Capital of Ontario* (Toronto: Adam, Stevenson & Company, 1873), 228–29.

9. Albert Schrauwers, "The Gentlemanly Order & the Politics of Production in the Transition to Capitalism in Upper Canada," *Labour/Le Travail* 65 (Spring 2010): 9–46.

10. See David Gagan, "Land, Population, and Social Change: The 'Critical Years' in Rural Canada West," *Canadian Historical Review* 59 (1978): 293–318; Gagan, *Hopeful Travellers: Families, Land, and Social Change in Mid-Victorian Peel County, Canada West* (Toronto: University of Toronto Press, 1981); and for later reflections Gordon Darroch and Lee Soltow, *Property and Inequality in Victorian Ontario: Structural Patterns and Cultural Communities in the 1871 Census* (Toronto: University of Toronto Press, 1994); and for the experience of workers on the land, Terry Crowley, "Rural Labour," in *Labouring Lives: Work and Workers in Nineteenth-Century Ontario*, ed. Paul Craven (Toronto: University of Toronto Press, 1995), 17–41.

11. Gary Teeple, "Land, Labour and Capital in Pre-Confederation Canada," in Teeple, ed., *Capitalism and the National Question in Canada* (Toronto: University of Toronto Press, 1972), 43–55; Graeme Wynn, "Notes on Society and Environment in Old Ontario," *Journal of Social History* 13 (Fall 1979): 51–52; Peter A. Russell, "Upper Canada: A Poor Man's Country? Some Statistical Evidence," in *Canadian Papers in Rural History*, vol. 3, ed. Donald H. Akenson (Gananoque, Ontario: Langdale Press, 1982), 138–44; Patrick Shirreff, *A Tour Through North America: Together with a Comprehensive View of the Canadas and the United States, as Adapted for Agricultural Emigration* (Edinburgh: Oliver and Boyd, 1835), 363–65, quoted in Schrauwers, "Gentlemanly Order," 27, 29–30; Schrauwers, "'Money Bound You—Money Shall Loose You': Micro-Credit, Social Capital, and the Meaning of Money in Upper Canada," *Comparative Studies in Society and History* 53 (2011): 1–30; John Clarke, *Land, Power, and Economics in the Frontier of Upper Canada* (Kingston and Montreal: McGill-Queen's University Press, 2001), esp. 266–72; Leo A. Johnson, "Land Policy, Population Growth, and Social Structure in the Home District, 1793–1851," *Ontario History* 63 (March 1971): 41–60; with Goderich quoted in Leo A. Johnson, *History of the Country of Ontario, 1615–1875* (Whitby, Ontario: Corporation of the County of Ontario, 1973), 66.

12. Johnson, *County of Ontario*, 68; Karl Marx, *Capital: A Critical Analysis of Capitalist Production*, vol. I (Moscow: Foreign Languages Publishing House, n.d.), 766–73.

13. Johnson, "Land Policy," 57–59.

14. Bryan D. Palmer, "Social Formation and Class Formation in North America, 1800–1900," in *Proletarianization and Family History*, ed. David Levine (New York: Academic Press, 1984), 247; Donald H. Akenson, "Ontario: Whatever Happened to the Irish?" in Akenson, ed., *Canadian Papers in Rural History*, vol. 3, 111, 204–356; H. C. Pentland, *Labour and Capital in Canada, 1650–1860* (Toronto: Lorimer, 1981), 96–129, esp. 109; Stephen A. Speisman, "Munificent Parsons and Municipal

Parsimony: Voluntary vs. Public Poor Relief in Nineteenth-Century Toronto," *Ontario History* 65 (March 1973): 37; Kenneth Duncan, "Irish Famine Immigration and the Social Structure of Canada West," in *Studies in Canadian Social History*, ed. Michiel Horn and Ronald Sabourin (Toronto: McClelland and Stewart, 1974), 140–63; Ruth Bleasdale, "Class Conflict on the Canals of Upper Canada in the 1840s," *Labour/ Le Travailleur*, 7 (Spring 1981): 9–40 esp. quote from *St. Catharines Journal*, 13, which refers to "unemployed labourers," a use of the term predating the general identification of named unemployment to the latter half of the nineteenth century, as outlined in Peter Baskerville and Eric W. Sager, *Unwilling Idlers: The Urban Unemployed and Their Families in Late Victorian Canada* (Toronto: University of Toronto Press, 1998), 3–6; John C. Weaver, "Crime, Public Order, and Repression: The Gore District in Upheaval, 1832–1851," *Ontario History* 78 (September 1986): 186; William Thomas Matthews, "By and for the Large Propertied Interests: The Dynamics of Local Government in Six Upper Canadian Towns during the Era of Commercial Capitalism, 1832–1860" (PhD diss., McMaster University, 1985), 41–45.

15. Albert Schrauwers, *"Union Is Strength": W. L. Mackenzie, the Children of Peace, and the Emergence of Joint Stock Democracy in Upper Canada* (Toronto: University of Toronto Press, 2009), 189; Eugene Forsey, *Trade Unions in Canada, 1812–1902* (Toronto: University of Toronto Press, 1902), 20; F. H. Armstrong, "The Reformer as Capitalist: William Lyon Mackenzie and the Printers' Strike of 1836," *Ontario History* 59 (September 1967): 187–96; Paul Romney, "On the Eve of the Rebellion: Nationality, Religion and Class in the Toronto Election of 1836," in *Old Ontario: Essays in Honour of J. M. S. Careless*, ed. David Keane and Colin Read (Toronto: Dundurn Press, 1990), 205–6; Geoffrey Bilson, *A Darkened House: Cholera in Nineteenth-Century Canada* (Toronto: University of Toronto Press, 1980), 63; Rainer Baehre, "Paupers and Poor Relief in Upper Canada," Canadian Historical Association, *Historical Papers* (1981): 72. Discussion of the economic crisis of 1836–37 appears in Colin Read and Ronald J. Stagg, eds., *The Rebellion of 1837 in Upper Canada: A Collection of Documents* (Toronto and Ottawa: Champlain Society and Carleton University Press, 1985), xxix–xxx, with a number of relevant documents following. Note as well Donald G. Creighton, *The Commercial Empire of the St. Lawrence* (Toronto: Ryerson Press, 1937), 288–320.

16. W. L. Mackenzie, *The Constitution*, July 26, 1837, quoted in Schrauwers, "Gentlemanly Order," 10.

17. See Schrauwers, *"Union Is Strength,"* especially 56–65, and for a useful more general statement, Michael B. Katz, "The Origins of the Institutional State," *Marxist Perspectives* 4 (Winter 1978): 6–23. Note also John C. Weaver, *Crimes, Constables, and Courts: Order and Transgression in a Canadian City, 1816–1870* (Montreal and Kingston: McGill-Queen's University Press, 1995) and for the spectacle that could be exploited by the presence of such institutions, Janet Miron, *Prisons, Asylums, and the Public: Institutional Visiting in the Nineteenth Century* (Toronto: University of Toronto Press, 2011).

18. Russell C. Smandych, *Upper Canadian Considerations about Rejecting the English Poor Law, 1817–1837: A Comparative Study of the Reception of Law* (Winnipeg: University of Manitoba, Canadian Legal History Project, Faculty of Law, 1991), 36.

19. Quoted in Baehre, "Paupers and Poor Relief," 65–66; and, for Jarvis and the anti-begging ordinance, "House of Industry, Old City Building," *Toronto Daily Star*, March 18, 1929.

20. Contrast Baehre, "Paupers and Poor Relief," 57–80 and Russell Smandych, "William Osgoode, John Graves Simcoe, and the Exclusion of the English Poor Law from Upper Canada," in *Law, Society, and the State: Essays in Modern Legal History*, ed. Louis A. Knafla and Susan W. S. Binnie (Toronto: University of Toronto Press, 1995), 99–129; Romney, "On the Eve of the Rebellion," 192–216; Smandych, "Rethinking 'The Master Principle of Administering Relief' in Upper Canada: A Response to

Allan Irving," *Canadian Review of Social Policy* 27 (1991): 81–86.

21. *The Statutes of the Province of Upper Canada* (Toronto 1837), 80–82, reprinted in S. D. Clark, *The Social Development of Canada: An Introductory Study with Select Documents* (Toronto: University of Toronto Press, 1942), 232–33.

22. Quoted in Baehre, "Paupers and Poor Relief," 74.

23. These early figures and the House of Industry's First Annual Report are cited in *Sixtieth Annual Report of the House of Industry, City of Toronto, 1896–1897*, 5–6.

24. Henry Scadding, *Toronto of Old*, ed. F. H. Armstrong (Toronto: Oxford University Press, 1966), 214; Maxine Kerr and Donald Booth, *The St. Patrick's Benevolent Society of Toronto: A History* (Ottawa: Providence Press, 1995), 29; Mary Larratt Smith, *Young Mr. Smith in Upper Canada* (Toronto: University of Toronto Press, 1960), 11–12; Jarvis to Boulton, August 20, 1847, quoted in Careless, *Toronto to 1918*, 73.

25. *History of Toronto and the Country of York Ontario...*, vol. 1 (Toronto: C. Blackett Robinson, 1885), 325; Speisman, "Munificent Parsons," 38–39; *Report of the Trustees of the House of Industry, City of Toronto, 1852*, 8.

26. Richard B. Splane, *Social Welfare in Ontario, 1791–1893: A Study of Public Welfare Administration* (Toronto: University of Toronto Press, 1965), 71; Careless, *Toronto to 1918*, 100.

27. James Buchanan, *Project for the Formation of a Depot in Upper Canada with a View to Relieve the Whole Pauper Population of England* (New York, 1834), quoted in Baehre, "Paupers and Poor Relief," 70, and for documents relating to Buchanan, see Charles R. Sanderson, ed., *The Arthur Papers Being the Papers Mainly Confidential, Private, and Demi-Official...*, vol. 1 (Toronto: Toronto Public Libraries and University of Toronto Press, 1943), 16–17, 229–31; Schrauwers, *"Union Is Strength,"* 192. On the Baldwin family and reform see Michael S. Cross, *A Biography of Robert Baldwin: The Morning Star of Memory* (Don Mills, Ontario: Oxford University Press, 2012).

28. An important older statement is Stanley B. Ryerson, *Unequal Union: Confederation and the Roots of Conflict in the Canadas, 1815–1873* (Toronto: Progress Books, 1968), while newer analytic sensibilities and perspectives emerge in many of the essays in Allan Greer and Ian Radforth, eds., *Colonial Leviathan: State Formation in Mid-Nineteenth-Century Canada* (Toronto: University of Toronto Press, 1992). Note, also, older studies, such as Paul G. Cornell, *The Alignment of Political Groups in Canada, 1841–1867* (Toronto: University of Toronto Press, 1962) and William Ormsby, *The Emergence of the Federal Concept in Canada, 1839–1845* (Toronto: University of Toronto Press, 1969).

29. See Jeffrey McNairn, *The Capacity to Judge: Public Opinion and Deliberative Democracy in Upper Canada, 1791–1854* (Toronto: University of Toronto Press, 2000); Carol Wilton, *Popular Politics and Political Culture in Upper Canada, 1800–1850* (Montreal and Kingston: McGill-Queen's University Press, 2000).

30. J. H. Aitchison, "The Development of Local Government in Upper Canada" (PhD diss., University of Toronto, 1953), esp. 656–57; Splane, *Social Welfare in Ontario*, 40, 72–79; Matthews, "By and for the Large Propertied Interests," esp. 306–78, which deals with the consequences of the 1857 commercial collapse.

31. Splane, *Social Welfare in Ontario*, 43–51. There is much on Langmuir in Edward McCoy, "The Rise of the Modern Canadian Penitentiary, 1835–1900" (PhD diss., Frost Centre for Canadian and Indigenous Studies, Trent University, 2011). Chilton, "Managing Migrants," 252–56 has useful information on emigration agents and subsidizing the transportation costs of immigrants making their way to Toronto in these years.

32. The carpenter is quoted in Judith Fingard, "The Winter's Tale: The Seasonal Contours of Pre-Industrial Poverty in British North America, 1815–1860," Canadian Historical Association, *Historical Papers* (1974), 74–75, but the entire article is now a classic statement on poverty, early Canadian unemployment, and charitable relief of the poor. In the period that Fingard addresses, nascent capitalist developments

jostled uneasily with older social and product-ive relations rooted in pre-capitalist economic formations. In some ways, the seasonality of winter and the employment crises that came with its onslaught would be exacerbated by intensified capitalist crises in the latter half of the nineteenth century.

33. Peter G. Goheen, *Victorian Toronto: 1850–1900* (Chicago: University of Chicago, 1970), 75–76.

34. Bryan D. Palmer, *Working-Class Experience: Rethinking the History of Canadian Labour, 1800–1991* (Toronto: McClelland and Stewart, 1992), 87.

35. Kealey, *Toronto Workers Respond to Industrial Capitalism*, 3–34, suggests the importance of the 1840s and 1850s as pivotal decades in the transition to industrial capitalism. On the Irish the views of Pentland, *Labour and Capital in Canada* and Akenson, "Ontario: Whatever Happened to the Irish" provide perspectives that probably need to be blended into one another rather than counterposed polemic-ally. For class struggle in this period an older, unpublished work still repays examination: Paul C. Appleton, "The Sunshine and the Shade: Labour Activism in Central Canada, 1850–1860" (master's thesis, University of Calgary, 1974). For an introduction to the nature and dimensions of working-class activ-ity see Bryan D. Palmer, "Labour Protest and Organization in Nineteenth-Century Canada, 1820-1890," *Labour/Le Travail* 20 (Fall 1987): 61–84. Inequality and class differentiation are addressed substantively in Michael B. Katz, *The People of Hamilton, Canada West: Family and Class in a Mid-Nineteenth Century City* (Cam-bridge: Harvard University Press, 1975).

36. See, for instance, discussions in Baskerville and Sager, *Unwilling Idlers*; John Garraty, *Unemployment in History: Economic Thought and Public Policy* (New York: Harper and Row, 1978), esp. 4, 109–28; Alexander Keyssar, *Out of Work: The First Century of Unemployment in Massachusetts* (New York: Cambridge Univer-sity Press, 1986).

37. J. I. Cooper, "The Quebec Ship Labourers' Benevolent Society," *Canadian Historical Review* 30 (December 1949): 338–39; Fingard, "Winter's Tale," 74–75, 89; Baskerville and Sager, *Unwilling Idlers*, 23–24.

38. Rev. Henry Scadding and John Charles Dent, *Toronto: Past and Present: Historical and Descriptive: A Memorial Volume for the Semi-Centennial of 1884* (Toronto: Hunter and Rose, 1884), 212–13; Strachan to Hutcheson, Toronto City Council Papers, quoted in D. C. Masters, *The Rise of Toronto: 1850–1890* (Toronto: Univer-sity of Toronto Press, 1947), 80.

39. Jennifer L. Bonnell, *Reclaiming the Don: An Environmental History of Toronto's Don River Valley* (Toronto: University of Toronto Press, 2014), 79–97; Jesse Edgar Middleton, *The Muni-cipality of Toronto: A History*, vol. I (Toronto: Dominion Publishing, 1923), 264.

40. The above paragraphs rely on *Report of the Trustees of the House of Industry, City of Toronto, 1852*, 8; *Report of the Trustees of the House of Industry, City of Toronto, 1853*, 8; *Report of the Trustees of the House of Industry, City of Toronto, 1854*, 9; *Report of the Trustees of the House of Industry, City of Toronto, 1861*, 9; *Report of the Trustees of the House of Industry, City of Toronto, 1864*, 10; Speisman, "Munificent Parsons," 39–49; and Splane, *Social Welfare in Ontario*, 47–51, 79–84, which draws on, among other sources, Langmuir's annual reports in Ontario's *Sessional Papers*. See as well Careless, *Toronto to 1918*, 100; C. Pelham Mulvany, *Toronto Past and Present until 1882* (Toronto: W. E. Caiger, 1884), 63–69.

41. Ontario, *Sessional Papers* (1881), no. 8, 15, quoted in Splane, *Social Welfare in Ontario*, 49; Michael B. Katz, Michael J. Doucet, and Mark J. Stern, *The Social Organization of Early Indus-trial Capitalism* (Cambridge: Harvard Univer-sity Press, 1975). A recent study, documenting the extent to which the old connections of master and man remained embedded in craft production, understates the extent to which the long and complex process of proletarian-ization had affected the social relations of production and the social organization of early industrial capitalism. See Robert Kristofferson, *Craft Capitalism: Craftworkers and Early*

Industrialization in Hamilton, Ontario, 1840–1872 (Toronto: University of Toronto Press, 2007), and contrast it with the perspectives outlined in Katz, *People of Hamilton, Canada West,* and the later study of Katz, Doucet, and Stern, *Social Organization,* and Bryan D. Palmer, *A Culture in Conflict: Skilled Workers and Industrial Capitalism in Hamilton, Ontario, 1860–1914* (Kingston and Montreal: McGill-Queen's University Press, 1979), especially the discussion of the producer ideology, 97–123.

42. Kealey, *Toronto Workers Respond to Industrial Capitalism;* Palmer, "Labour Protest and Organization in Nineteenth-Century Canada," 73; Gregory S. Kealey and Bryan D. Palmer, *Dreaming of What Might Be: The Knights of Labor in Ontario, 1880–1900* (Cambridge: Cambridge University Press, 1982).

43. *Globe,* January 26, 1877, as cited in Michael Cross, ed., *The Workingman in Nineteenth Century Canada* (Toronto: Oxford University Press, 1974), 196 and in James Struthers, *No Fault of Their Own: Unemployment and the Canadian Welfare State, 1914–1941* (Toronto: University of Toronto Press, 1983), 7; *Globe,* February 27, 1874, as cited in Splane, *Social Welfare in Ontario,* 16.

44. For a broad discussion see Baskerville and Sager, *Unwilling Idlers.* McKiernan is quoted in Peter DeLottinville, "Joe Beef of Montreal: Working-Class Culture and the Tavern, 1869–1889," *Labour/Le Travailleur* 8/9 (Autumn/Spring 1981/82): 17.

45. Richard Anderson, "'The Irrepressible Stampede': Tramps in Ontario, 1870–1880," *Ontario History* 84 (March 1992): 33-56; Diane Bisson, *Compassion Builds a House: The Legacy of Caring at Providence Centre* (Scarborough: The Centre, 2000), 30, 37, 68, quoting *Globe; Annual Report of the House of Industry, City of Toronto, 1877,* 3; *Annual Report of the House of Industry, City of Toronto, 1878,* 5–6. This period saw repeated concern expressed by trustees of the House of Industry that other Ontario municipalities were dumping their poor on Toronto, especially in the depths of winter. See *Annual Report of the House of Industry, City of Toronto, 1877,* 3; *Annual Report of the House of Industry,*

City of Toronto, 1879, 6. Perspectives on the late nineteenth-century war on the tramp can be developed through a reading of a range of commentary, including Marx's discussion of "The Nomad Population," in *Capital,* vol. 1, 663–67; Frank Tobias Higbie, *Indispensable Outcasts: Hobo Workers and Community in the American Midwest, 1880–1930* (Urbana: University of Illinois Press, 2003); Jim Phillips, "Poverty, Unemployment, and the Administration of the Criminal Law: Vagrancy Laws in Halifax, 1864–1900," in *Essays in the History of Canadian Law: Nova Scotia,* vol. 3, ed. Philip Girard and Jim Phillips (Toronto: University of Toronto Press, 1990), 128–62; David Montgomery, *Citizen Worker: The Experience of Workers in the United States with Democracy and the Free Market during the Nineteenth Century* (New York: Cambridge University Press, 1993), 87–88; and Edmund Kelly, *The Elimination of the Tramp by the Introduction into America of the Labour Colony System Already Proved Effective in Holland, Belgium and Switzerland, with the Modification Thereof Necessary to Adapt This System to American Conditions* (New York: G. P. Putnam, 1908).

46. The preceding two paragraphs draw on "Felix" to *Palladium of Labor,* January 26 1884, cited in Baskerville and Sager, *Unwilling Idlers,* 35; James M. Pitsula, "The Treatment of Tramps in Late Nineteenth-Century Toronto," Canadian Historical Association, *Historical Papers* (1980): 116–32; "The Support of the Poor," *The Canadian Presbyterian,* January 7, 1881; "Tramps and Waifs," *Globe,* March 22, 1887; *Annual Report of the House of Industry, City of Toronto, 1885,* 6. One part of the inner history of wood-cutting as a "labour test" involved the Board of the House of Industry subcontracting the delivery of cordwood and the transportation of cut wood sold to clients to the Rogers Coal Company. The owner of this enterprise, Elias Rogers, was involved in a price-fixing ring in the coal industry in the late 1880s. See Careless, *Toronto to 1918,* 143.

47. *Report of the Commissioners Appointed to Enquire into the Prison and Reformatory System in the Province of Ontario, 8 April, 1891,*

111, 682–85. See also the comments on "work tests" in *All Saints Church Parish Magazine*, V (December 1895), 138.

48. Splane, *Social Welfare in Ontario*, 86; *Fifty-Seventh Annual Report of the House of Industry, City of Toronto, 1893–1894*, 12.

49. *Fifty-Ninth Annual Report of the House of Industry, City of Toronto, 1891–1892*, 6, 9, 11.

50. The above two paragraphs draw on *Fifty-Fifth Annual Report of the House of Industry, City of Toronto, 1891–1892*, 9; *Fifty-Eighth Annual Report of the House of Industry, City of Toronto, 1894–1895*, 6; *Fifty-Ninth Annual Report of the House of Industry, City of Toronto, 1895–1896*, 11; Pitsula, "Treatment of Tramps in Toronto," 131–32; "Talking of the Law," *Toronto Evening Star*, January 10, 1896; "House of Industry Still in a Bad Way Financially," *Toronto Evening Star*, February 19, 1896; *Report of the Commissioners Appointed to Enquire into the Prison and Reformatory System in the Province of Ontario, 8 April, 1891*, 113, 145, 68–85, 698.

51. "The Labor Test," *Toronto Evening Star*, May 16, 1896.

52. Editorial, "The Unemployed," *Globe*, February 12, 1891; *All Saints Church Parish Magazine*, V (December 1895), 138; Thomas Conant, *Upper Canada Sketches* (Toronto: William Briggs, 1898), 195.

53. Pitsula, "Treatment of Tramps in Toronto," 130.

54. "Around a Stove. Daily Gathering of Queer People at City Hall. Men out of Employment and Those Seeking Charity. How They View Officials and How Officials View Them," *Toronto Evening Star*, February 22, 1896.

55. "Stone Test Scares Them. Tramps Object to Work for Food and Lodging," *Toronto Evening Star*, December 21, 1897.

56. B. Rosamund, *House of Commons Journals* (1876), App. 3, 200, quoted in Steven Langdon, "The Emergence of the Canadian Working Class Movement, 1845–1875," Part II, *Journal of Canadian Studies* 8 (August 1973), 21. For relevant discussions in the Toronto-based *Ontario Workman* see "Number and Condition of the Unemployed," December 18, 1873; "The Unemployed," February 5, 1874.

57. David Alexander Thompson, "Working Class Anguish and Revolutionary Indignation: The Making of Radical and Socialist Unemployment Movements in Canada, 1875–1928" (PhD diss., Queen's University, 2014), 63–67; Jean-Philip Mathieu, "'C'est le people qui est mâitre; nous sommes les mâitres à Québec': La grève des ouvriers des travaux publics, juin 1878," *Labour/Le Travail* 70 (Fall 2012): 132, 135–36. The moral panic around the 1878 Quebec City agitations was no doubt conditioned by recollection of the Paris Commune events of 1871, which were widely reported in the Canadian press and conjured up the spectre of communist insurrection. See Alban Bargain-Villéger, "The Scarecrow on the Other Side of the Pond: The Paris Commune of 1871 in the Canadian Press," *Labour/Le Travail* 74 (Fall 2014): 179–98.

58. Debi Wells, "'The Hardest Lines of the Sternest School': Working-Class Ottawa in the Depression of the 1870s" (master's thesis, Carleton University, 1982). Much of the discussion of unemployed demonstrations in this thesis is summarized in Baskerville and Sager, *Unwilling Idlers*, 30–33. For political context see as well Bernard Ostry, "Conservatives, Liberals, and Labour in the 1870s," *Canadian Historical Review* 61 (June 1960): 93–127.

59. See, for instance, *Ottawa Herald*, February 23, 1880; *Ottawa Daily Free Press*, February 23, 1880, among dozens of newspaper accounts that might be cited.

60. Quoted in Wells, "'The Hardest Lines'," 98, and cited in Baskerville and Sager, *Unwilling Idlers*, 33. For general discussions of racism and national chauvinism see David Goutor, "Drawing Different Lines of Color: The Mainstream English Canadian Labour Movement's Approach to Blacks and Chinese, 1880-1914," *Labor: Studies in Working-Class History of the Americas* 2 (Spring 2005): 55–76; Goutor, *Guarding the Gates: The Canadian Labour Movement and Immigration, 1872–1934* (Vancouver: UBC Press, 2007). But see as well Peter Campbell, "'Not as a White Man, Not as a Sojourner': James A. Teit and the Fight for

Native Rights in British Columbia, 1884–1922," *Left History* 2 (Fall 1994): 37–57.

61. *Annual Report of the House of Industry, City of Toronto, 1878*, 5–6; "Tramps and Waifs," *Globe*, March 22, 1887.

62. Kealey and Palmer, *Dreaming of What Might Be*.

63. Phillips Thompson, *The Politics of Labor* (New York: Belford, Clarke, 1987), 186–88; and the discussion of Thompson in Baskerville and Sager, *Unwilling Idlers*, 171–72. See also Russell Hann, "Brainworkers and the Knights of Labor: E. E. Sheppard, Phillips Thompson and the Toronto *News*, 1883–1887," in *Essays in Canadian Working-Class History*, ed. Gregory S. Kealey and Peter Warrian (Toronto: McClelland and Stewart, 1976), 35–57. The Knights of Labor stimulated many approaches to the problem of unemployment. See, for instance, G. B. DeBernardi, *The Equitable Co-Operative Association for the Employment of Idle Labor by Mutual Exchange* (Sedalia, Missouri: J. O. Parmerlee, 1888).

64. Bettina Bradbury, "The Home as Workplace," in Craven, ed., *Labouring Lives*, 417, citing *Bureau of Industries*, 1888, 42; Greg Kealey, ed., *Canada Investigates Industrialism: The Royal Commission on the Relations of Labor and Capital, 1889* (Toronto: University of Toronto Press, 1973), for a small sampling of the testimony; Charles Lipton, *The Trade Union Movement of Canada, 1827–1959* (Toronto: NC Press, 1973), 90.

65. *Ottawa Free Press*, February 27, 1880; Wells, "'The Hardest Lines'," 95; Baskerville and Sager, *Unwilling Idlers*, 33 and 40, quoting *Globe*, February 21, 1891; and, for a useful recent discussion of the Ottawa black flag protest and the meaning of this symbol, Thompson, "Working Class Anguish," 68–72, 91.

66. The above paragraphs draw on the same sources, listed here. An image of the black flag, "Work or Bread" demonstration adorns the cover of Baskerville and Sager, *Unwilling Idlers*, where the event of February 11, 1891 is discussed, 39–40, 238, citing and quoting "Work or Bread," *Globe*, February 12, 1891; *Globe*, February 13, 1891. The cover illustration from the *Globe* is dated February 19, 1891, but

we locate the image in *Globe*, February 21, 1891. See also Lipton, *Trade Union Movement of Canada*, 90, with improper dating; Russell G. Hann, Gregory S. Kealey, Linda Kealey, and Peter Warrian, *Primary Sources in Canadian Working Class History* (Kitchener: Dumont, 1973), 9–10. We draw explicitly on "The Black Flag in Toronto. Hungry Men March the Streets and Demand Work or Bread," *New York Times*, February 12, 1891; Editorial, "The Unemployed," *Globe*, February 12, 1891; C. Wesey, "Letter to the Editor," and "A Glimmering of Truth," *Labor Advocate*, February 20, 1891; Thompson, "Working Class Anguish," 90–92 and 85, which cites Phillips Thompson's role in urging "quiet, orderly conduct" on the unemployed, referencing "Two Flags Today," *Evening News*, February 12, 1891. On Canadian contemporary reporting of the Paris Commune, see Bargain-Villéger, "The Scarecrow on the Other Side of the Pond," 179–98.

67. Thompson, "Working Class Anguish," 140.

68. "Asked for Work, Got Sympathy. The Mayor Said There Would Be Plenty When the Flowers Bloomed," *Toronto Daily Star*, February 16, 1894. On William Holmes Howland's reform mayoralty see Desmond Morton, *Mayor Howland: The Citizen's Candidate* (Toronto: Hakkert, 1973); Gregory S. Kealey, *Toronto Workers Respond to Industrial Capitalism*; and Christopher Armstrong and H. V. Nelles, *The Revenge of the Methodist Bicycle Company: Sunday Streetcars and Municipal Reform in Toronto, 1888–1897* (Toronto: Peter Martin, 1977). Thompson, "Working Class Anguish," 92, notes that Mills had suggested, following the example of British protests of the unemployed, that the demonstration march through "aristocratic quarters." This course had been followed in the protests of the unemployed in February 1891.

69. "Clergy Asked to Aid. The Unemployed Appeal to Ministers and Rich Men," *Toronto Daily Star*, February 17, 1894. For a United States discussion of how the Depression of the 1890s prompted nativist attack on foreigners and Catholics see John Higham, *Strangers in the Land: Patterns of American Nativism, 1860–1925*

(New Brunswick, New Jersey: Rutgers University Press, 1955), 68–105.

70. "Crack! Crack! Crack! Beams Creaked and Plaster Fell Under the Weight of a Wild Time at City Hall. The Unemployed Demand That the City Supply Them with Work at Once. Little Hope Held Out to Them," *Toronto Evening Star*, February 27, 1894.

71. The above paragraphs draw on "Ald. Lamb Alone Came. Sole Aldermanic Representative before the Unemployed. Isaac Mills Warns the Men Not to Commit Violence. One Man Wants to Organize," *Toronto Evening Star*, February 28, 1894; "The Band Didn't Play. The Unemployed's Music Fails to Materialize. The Procession Starts for Col. Sweny's but Turns Round and Returns to City Hall. The Police Turn Out," *Toronto Evening Star*, March 15, 1894. On the Macdonald scheme see Thompson, "Working Class Anguish," 117–19; Middleton, *The Municipality of Toronto*, vol. 1, 344–47. There is much on Macdonald's numerous and often outrageous interventions in city politics in Armstrong and Nelles, *Revenge of the Methodist Bicycle Company*, a text that outlines a canal scheme remarkably similar to the one Macdonald was floating in 1894 surfacing during E. E. Sheppard's mayoralty bid of 1892 (84).

72. Thompson, "Working Class Anguish," 76–77, 93–94, 96–99.

73. On Jury and Thompson see Kealey, *Toronto Workers Respond to Industrial Capitalism* and Kealey and Palmer, *Dreaming of What Might Be*, which also has brief mention of Darlington, 202, 392. The comparisons of Jury, Thompson, and Darlington related to the 1894 protests of the unemployed are posed in Thompson, "Working Class Anguish," 83–86, 92–94. Jury is profiled in the Phillips Thompson-edited *Labor Advocate*, February 13, 1891, where he is positively described as a staunch labour reformer often castigated in the capitalist press as a demagogue and an agitator.

74. We draw on the useful discussion in Thompson, "Working Class Anguish," 92–96, 119, but offer a slightly different reading of the evidence he has marshalled. On Stowe and the Labour Exchange see Emily H. Stowe, MD, "The Unemployed—An Open Letter from Dr. Emily H. Stowe—The Labor Exchange—Growth of the Movement—An Opportunity for the Laborer," *Globe*, March 31, 1897. Our thanks to Veronica Strong-Boag for bringing this letter to our attention.

75. That unemployment was, by the 1890s, recognized as intrinsic to capitalism, was one thing. That the state would actually address unemployment meaningfully was quite another. See Peter Baskerville and Eric Sager, "The First National Unemployment Survey: Unemployment and the Canadian Census of 1891," *Labour/Le Travail* 23 (Spring 1989): 171–78.

76. "Need Not Hunger If They'll Work. Superintendent Laughlan [sic] of House of Industry Willingly Feeds the Industrious. He Has a Work Test—It's Work.... Soup, Fuel and Grocery Orders Result," *Toronto Daily Star*, January 28, 1908. On the amount of stone that had to be broken and its weight see Dennis Guest, *The Emergence of Social Security in Canada* (Vancouver: UBC Press, 1980), 37. Haymarket's story is told in two important studies: Paul Avrich, *The Haymarket Tragedy* (Princeton: Princeton University Press, 1986), and James Green, *Death in the Haymarket: The Story of Chicago, the First Labor Movement, and the Bombing that Divided Gilded Age America* (New York: Pantheon, 2007). The unemployed who carried the black flag in Toronto's 1891 protest did so a mere four years after the execution of the Haymarket anarchists. Toronto radical Phillips Thompson recorded his sense of the climate surrounding this first North American Red Scare at the time: "the entire press gave rise to a furious, insensate howl for blood and vengeance.... The case was prejudiced against men on trial for their lives." He condemned "the hideous brutality which found in the death sentence of the ... convicted Anarchists a subject for ghoulish rejoicing and heartless jests." Thompson, *Politics of Labor*, 167.

77. For discussion of socialists and "the degenerate and dangerous class," where quotes such

as those in the above paragraph appear, see Ian McKay, *Reasoning Otherwise: Leftists and the People's Enlightenment in Canada, 1890–1920* (Toronto: Between the Lines, 2008), 208–11. Thompson, "Working Class Anguish," 150–209, is an unrivalled discussion of the pan-Canadian development of unemployed protests and the socialist movement in the 1907–15 years.

78. See the important statement on Toronto radicalism in the 1890s in Gene Homel, "'Fading Beams of the Nineteenth Century': Radicalism and Early Socialism in Canada's 1890s," *Labour/Le Travailleur* 5 (Spring 1980): 7–32. For one accessible collection of writings by a Canadian socialist of this era that commented on unemployment and capitalist crisis see Ian McKay, ed., *For a Working-Class Culture in Canada: A Selection of Colin McKay's Writings on Sociology and Political Economy, 1897–1939* (St. John's: Canadian Committee on Labour History, 1996), esp. "The Secret of Poverty," "The Scourge of Unemployment: A Critique of Goldwin Smith," and "The Right to Work," 34–39, 47–52, with quotes of Colin McKay against Smith, 49–50. There is much on Smith and the 1880s and 1890s, as well as the later development of the SPC, the SDPC, and the Toronto unemployed in Thompson, "Working Class Anguish,"123–28, 150–256, but see as well Wayne Roberts, "Goldwin's Myth: The Nonconformist as Mudwump," *Canadian Literature* 83 (Winter 1979): 50–71.

79. For an introduction to Toronto's economic transformation in these years and the condition of the working class see Michael J. Piva, *The Condition of the Working Class in Toronto—1900–1921* (Ottawa: University of Ottawa Press, 1979). See as well Leonard C. Marsh, "The Problem of Seasonal Unemployment: A Quantitative and Comparative Survey of Seasonal Fluctuations in Canadian Employment" (master's thesis, McGill University, 1933), 134–35; and for women workers Marsh, *Canadians In and Out of Work*, 273–79.

80. Robert H. Babcock, *Gompers in Canada: A Study in American Continentalism Before the First World War* (Toronto: University of Toronto Press, 1974), esp. 44, 53; Palmer, "Labour Protest and Organization in Nineteenth-Century Canada," 82; Martin Robin, *Radical Politics and Canadian Labour* (Kingston: Queen's University Industrial Relations Centre, 1968), 117; *Labour Gazette* IV (July 1903–June 1904), 614; Thompson, "Working Class Anguish," 150. A thorough study of Simpson's early years is Gene Howard Homel, "James Simpson and the Origins of Canadian Social Democracy" (PhD diss., University of Toronto, 1978), which discusses the December 24, 1903 unemployment protest, 167–68. For a different perspective on Simpson in this period that nonetheless relies on Homel see McKay, *Reasoning Otherwise*, 193–98.

81. Thompson, "Working Class Anguish," 177, 229; Piva, *Condition of the Working Class in Toronto*, 69, 71–74; *Labour Gazette* VIII (July 1907–June 1908), 962–63; "Toronto Free Employment Bureau," *Labour Gazette* IX (July 1908–June 1909), 1343; "Need Not Hunger If They'll Work," *Daily Star*, January 28, 1908.

82. Thompson, "Working Class Anguish," 174–76, 228–29; Phillips Thompson, *Labour Gazette* VIII (March 1908), 1056; Phillips Thompson, *Labour Gazette* VIII (April 1908), 1198.

83. *Globe*, March 17, 1908, cited in Piva, *Condition of the Working Class in Toronto*, 74; "Hot Talk in Muddy Park. Orators of the Soap-Box Order Harangue a Crowd on the Waterfront. And Talk of Taking Forcible Possession of Contents of Warehouse," *Toronto Daily Star*, January 5, 1909. On Gribble and Drury see Thompson, "Working Class Anguish," 165–70.

84. "Ugly Temper of Idle Men. The Unemployed Gathered Swiftly this Morning into Army at City Hall. Blocked Street but Had to Move On," *Toronto Daily Star*, January 13, 1909.

85. "To Get Work for Idle Men. Heard Deputation Today. The Speaker Dropped the Violent Tone When They Entered City Hall. A Large Force of Police on Hand to Guard against Any Disturbance," *Toronto Daily Star*, January 14, 1909.

86. "Stuck a Pin in Ald. J. J. Graham," *Toronto Daily Star*, January 18, 1909; Thompson, "Working

Class Anguish," 179; Phillips Thompson, *Labour Gazette* IX (February 1909), 829.

87. "A Preacher to the Unemployed. Rev. Dr. Eby Roused the Crowd to Very High Pitch of Enthusiasm. Then Speaker Got Hot and Proceeded to Abuse the Civic Authorities in Angry Terms," *Toronto Daily Star,* January 21, 1909. On the social gospel see Richard Allen, *The Social Passion: Religion and Social Reform in Canada, 1914–1928* (Toronto: University of Toronto Press, 1973). McKay, *Reasoning Otherwise,* 472, refers to Eby's 1909 Church of the Revolution, noting its connection to the Social Democratic Party of Canada and the encouragement of early socialist feminism.

88. "A Preacher to the Unemployed," *Toronto Daily Star*, February 15, 1909; Phillips Thompson, *Labour Gazette* IX (February 1909), 829; Thompson, "Working Class Anguish," 154, 165–70, 174–81, with 175 citing *Toronto Star,* March 10, 1908 indication of the existence of the Unemployed Association.

89. The above paragraphs draw on "Brutal Treatment of the Unemployed," *Toronto Daily Star,* February 15, 1909; Thompson, "Working Class Anguish," 179–80, and for a broad and illuminating discussion of immigration and the unemployed in the 1880–1919 period, chapter 5, "Whiteness Unwaged: Empire, Immigration, and the Unemployed, 1880–1919," 210–56, with specific comment on deportation and the 1907–9 slump, 223–24.

90. Thompson, "Working Class Anguish," 181, quoting Alex Lyon, "Amongst the Unemployed of Toronto," *Western Clarion,* January 30, 1909.

91. The above paragraphs draw on "Vagrants Sent Where They'll Have to Work. House of Industry Too Easy for them and They go to Prison—Early," *Toronto Daily Star,* February 8, 1910; "More Stone Breaking. Casuals at House of Industry Must Crack Double Quantity," *Toronto Daily Star,* January 25, 1910; "Toronto a Mecca of Tired Tramps. Tramps Flock Here, and the Associated Charities Want Steps Taken to Keep them Working. Also Asks that Province Make a Grant to the House of Industry," *Toronto Daily Star*, December 21, 1910; Phillips Thompson,

Labour Gazette IX (February 1909), 829. A toise was a unit of measure for length, area, and volume originating in pre-Revolutionary France and commonly utilized in nineteenth-century North America. It corresponded to roughly eight cubic metres.

92. Piva, *Condition of the Working Class in Toronto,* 75–86, presents a good summary of the Toronto situation, as does Ontario, *Report of the Ontario Commission on Unemployment* (Toronto: A. T. Wilgress, 1916), with particular reference to 77–78, 201–2; Baskerville and Sager, *Unwilling Idlers,* 176–84; "100,000 Jobless: The Forgotten Depressions of 1908–1916," in *The Canadian Worker in the Twentieth Century,* ed. Irving Abella and David Millar (Toronto: Oxford University Press, 1978), 73–76; Struthers, *No Fault of Their Own,* 12–16; Bryce Stewart, "Unemployment and Organization of the Labour Market," American Academy of Political and Social Science, "Social and Economic Conditions in the Dominion of Canada," *The Annals,* 107 (May 1923), 286–93; *Eighty-Fourth Annual Report of the House of Industry, City of Toronto, 1920–1921,* 7, 10.

93. The above paragraphs quote and draw on Ontario, *Report of the Ontario Commission on Unemployment,* 77–78, 201–2; McKay, *Reasoning Otherwise,* 209; James Naylor, *The New Democracy: Challenging the Social Order in Industrial Ontario, 1914–1925* (Toronto: University of Toronto Press, 1991), 18–19, 80; Barbara Roberts, *Whence They Came: Deportation from Canada, 1900–1935* (Ottawa: University of Ottawa Press, 1988), 44; Baskerville and Sager, *Unwilling Idlers,* 176–84.

94. *Labour Gazette* XV (July 1914–June 1915), 464–65, 666–67.

95. Thompson, "Working Class Anguish," 192–94, 244.

96. Struthers, *No Fault of Their Own,* 12–16; Stewart, "Unemployment and Organization of the Labour Market," 286–93; "100,000 Jobless," in Abella and Millar, eds., *Canadian Worker in the Twentieth Century,* 73–76.

97. Naylor, *The New Democracy,* 18–19, 80; Roberts, *Whence They Came,* 44; Baskerville and Sager,

Unwilling Idlers, 176–84; Ontario, *Report of the Ontario Commission on Unemployment*, 77–78, 201–2.

98. "Preferred the Jail to Any Other Place. Aged Vagrant Insisted on Being Sent Across the Don, and He was Obliged," *Toronto Daily Star*, December 18, 1912; "Refused to Work, but Took Meals—Jailed. George Bust was Defiant in Police Court—Received a Lesson. Couldn't Find Work. Wouldn't Crack Stone at the House of Industry for His Breakfast," *Toronto Daily Star*, February 5, 1915.

99. See *Twenty-One Years of Mission Work in Toronto, 1886–1907: The Story of the Fred Victor Mission* (Toronto: Acton Publishing, 1907); Cary Fagan, *The Fred Victor Mission Story: From Charity to Social Justice* (Winfield, BC: Wood Lake Books, 1993), 20, 47, 57, 62. Armstrong is quoted in Thompson, "Working Class Anguish," 228.

100. *Annual Report of the Chief Constable of the City of Toronto: A Record of Its Activities from 1914 to 1919* (Toronto: Cardwell Company, 1916), 20; Phillip Morris, ed., *The Canadian Patriotic Fund: A Record of its Activities from 1914 to 1919* (n.p., n.d.), 23, 271, cited in Struthers, *No Fault of Their Own*, 14; Desmond Morton and Glenn Wright, *Winning the Second Battle: Canadian Veterans and the Return to Civilian Life, 1915–1930* (Toronto: University of Toronto Press, 1987), ix, 24; Nancy Christie, *Engendering the State: Family, Work, and Welfare in Canada* (Toronto: University of Toronto Press, 2000), 46–93; Naylor, *New Democracy*, 23.

101. The above paragraphs draw on Struthers, *No Fault of Their Own*, 14–27; *Report of the Ontario Commission on Unemployment*; Sauter, "Origins of the Employment Service of Canada," 89–112; Morton and Wright, *Winning the Second Battle*, 108; Judy Fudge and Eric Tucker, *Labour Before the Law: The Regulation of Workers' Collective Action in Canada, 1900–1948* (Toronto: Oxford University Press, 2001), 97; Thompson, "Working Class Anguish," 257–308 provides an invaluable survey of the range of state relief innovations in this period and how far they fell short of adequately addressing the needs of the wageless. On the climate of this era see Gregory S. Kealey, "1919: The Canadian Labour Revolt," *Labour/Le Travail* 13 (Spring 1984): 11–44; McKay, *Reasoning Otherwise*, 417–530; Kramer and Mitchell, *When the State Trembled*; Craig Heron, ed., *The Workers' Revolt in Canada, 1917–1925* (Toronto: University of Toronto Press, 1998); and Daniel Francis, *Seeing Reds: The Red Scare of 1918–1919* (Vancouver: Arsenal Pulp Press, 2010).

102. Morton and Wright, *Winning the Second Battle*, 124–29; Struthers, *No Fault of Their Own*, 28; Ian Angus, *Canadian Bolsheviks: The Early Years of the Communist Party of Canada* (Montreal: Vanguard, 1981), 58; James Naylor, *The New Democracy: Challenging the Social Order in Industrial Ontario, 1914–1925* (Toronto: University of Toronto Press, 1991), 212. Thompson, "Working Class Anguish," 452–99 presents a wide-ranging discussion of veterans and unemployment premised on the view that, ""Unemployment was *the* central issue of veterans during demobilization" (457). There is particular discussion of the 1917–19 "back to the land" push (461) and of Flynn, the bonus, and the GAUV (466–69).

103. "Work of the Frontier College, Toronto: Proposal for Reduction of Unemployment," *Labour Gazette* XXI (1921), 1289. See also Alfred Fitzpatrick, *The University in Overalls: A Plea for Part-Time Study* (Toronto: Hunter Rose, 1920).

104. Struthers, *No Fault of Their Own*, 33; Thompson, "Working Class Anguish," 280–308.

105. G. D. Robertson to Walter Rollo, December 15, 1921, in *Labour Gazette* XXI (1921), 46; Morton and Wright, *Winning the Second Battle*, 142; Struthers, *No Fault of Their Own*, 29; Piva, *Condition of the Working Class in Toronto*, 83–84; "Emergency Relief for Unemployed in Canada," *Labour Gazette* XXI (1921), 999; *Annual Report of the Chief Constable of the City of Toronto, 1925* (Toronto: United Press Limited, 1926), 24; Marsh, *Canadians In and Out of Work*, 257–70.

106. "Can't Keep Wolf From Door with Doles from City. Families Would Starve If They Had to Depend on Civic Help Alone. Tales of Sufferers. Work of Other Institutions Hampered

by Parsimony of the City," *Toronto Daily Star*, August 27, 1921.

107. "No Man Needs to Beg on Streets Though Destitute in Toronto. Your Response to Appeal of Furtive Individuals is Likely to Be Tribute to the Professional 'Pan-Handler'," *Toronto Daily Star*, January 14, 1922.

108. The above two paragraphs draw on the excellent discussion in Thompson, "Working Class Anguish," esp. 323–33, 339–45, 349, 377, 397–99. On the unemployed harvesters' trek to Ottawa and William Leslie see as well W. J. C. Cherwinski, "A Miniature Coxey's Army: The British Harvesters' Toronto-to-Ottawa Trek of 1924," *Labour/Le Travail* 32 (Fall 1993): 139–65. On A. E. Smith and what he refers to as the Toronto Unemployed Association in this period see Rev. A. E. Smith, *All My Life: An Autobiography* (Toronto: Progress Books, 1949), esp. 71–81.

109. Again, we draw on Thompson's important research in the above paragraphs. Thompson, "Working Class Anguish," esp. 318, 323–33, 339–40. Thompson discusses the role of the Workers' Party of Canada, later renamed the Communist Party of Canada, in the unemployed movement. Thompson also points out how major Workers' Party figures, such as Florence Custance and Jack MacDonald, might disagree on the relationship of the mainstream trade unions and the unemployed agitation, with Custance adopting early positions that tended to accent the independence of the jobless struggles from the conservative officialdoms of the labour movement.

110. Thompson, "Working Class Anguish," 271–73, 356–66, 458, 464, 469–74; "Where to Get Relief, Many Still in Doubt," *Toronto Daily Star*, February 7, 1922; *Report of the Commissioner of the Ontario Provincial Police, 1922* in *Ontario Sessional Papers*, 84 (1923), 29–31, cited in Morton and Wright, *Winning the Second Battle*, 142.

111. Bryce Stewart, "The Problem of Unemployment," *Social Welfare* (March 1921), 170 quoted in Struthers, *No Fault of Their Own*, 43.

112. Struthers, *No Fault of Their Own*, 4.

113. "Too Many Single Men Expecting Civic Relief," *Toronto Daily Star*, April 2, 1924; "Says

Winnipeg Mayor Sends Her Unemployed Here. Controller Cameron Discusses Unemployed Situation at Earlscourt Meeting. Had Many Clashes," *Toronto Daily Star*, December 23, 1924.

114. On Hastings see Piva's repeated accounts of his aggressiveness as a public health official in Piva, *Condition of the Working Class in Toronto*; "Is Appointed to Study Single Man's Problem. Dr. Hastings Also Warns Non-Residents Not to Expect Aid during Winter," *Toronto Daily Star*, September 17, 1925; "Women Pledge to Help Unemployed Men," *Toronto Daily Star*, February 3, 1925.

115. Naylor, *New Democracy*, 248; William Rodney, *Soldiers of the International: A History of the Communist Party of Canada, 1919–1929* (Toronto: University of Toronto Press, 1968), 47–48.

116. Margaret Hobbs and Joan Sangster, eds., *The Woman Worker, 1926–1929* (St. John's, Newfoundland: Canadian Committee on Labour History, 1999), 27, 29–31; Thompson, "Working Class Anguish," 323–33, 431–32.

117. Naylor, *New Democracy*, 118–21; Palmer, *Working-Class Experience*, 227.

118. On early Canadian communism see also Rodney, *Soldiers of the International* and Angus, *Canadian Bolsheviks*.

PART III

1. James Struthers, *No Fault of Their Own: Unemployment and the Canadian Welfare State, 1914–1941* (Toronto: University of Toronto Press, 1983); G. M. LeFresne, "The Royal Twenty Centers: The Department of National Defence and Federal Unemployment Relief, 1932–1936" (History Thesis, Royal Military College, 1962); Victor Howard, *The On to Ottawa Trek* (Vancouver: Copp Clark, 1970); Ronald Liversedge, *Recollections of the On to Ottawa Trek* (Toronto: McClelland and Stewart, 1973); Lorne Brown, *When Freedom Was Lost: The Unemployed, the Agitator, and the State* (Montreal: Black Rose Books, 1987); Bill Waiser, *All Hell Can't Stop Us: The On to Ottawa Trek and the Regina Riot* (Calgary: Fifth House Publishing, 2003).

2. Michiel Horn, ed., *The Dirty Thirties: Canadians in the Great Depression* (Toronto: Copp Clark, 1972); L. M. Grayson and Michael Bliss, eds., *The Wretched of Canada: Letters to R. B. Bennett, 1930–1935* (Toronto: University of Toronto Press, 1971).

3. Benjamin Katz, "Idle Stands the Linotype," *Masses* (April 1932), quoted in James Doyle, *Progressive Heritage: The Evolution of a Politically Radical Literary Tradition in Canada* (Waterloo: Wilfrid Laurier University Press, 2002), 136.

4. Claudius Gregory, *Forgotten Men* (Hamilton: Davis-Lisson, 1933), quoting 7.

5. Irene Baird, *Waste Heritage* (Toronto: Macmillan, 1974 [1939]).

6. William Gray, *The Winter Years: The Depression on the Prairies* (Toronto: Macmillan, 1966); Barry Broadfoot, *Ten Lost Years, 1929–1939: Memories of Canadians Who Survived the Depression* (Markham, Ontario: Paperjacks, 1975); Pierre Berton, *The Great Depression, 1929–1939* (Toronto: McClelland and Stewart, 1990).

7. Todd McCallum, "'Still Raining, Market Still Rotten': Homeless Men and the Early Years of the Great Depression" (PhD diss., Queen's University, 2004); McCallum, "The Reverend and the Tramp, Vancouver, 1931: Andrew Roddan's 'God in the Jungles,'" *BC Studies* 147 (Autumn 2005): 51–88; McCallum, "Vancouver Through the Eyes of a Hobo: Experience, Identity, and Value in the Writing of Canada's Depression-Era Tramps," *Labour/Le Travail* 59 (Spring 2007): 43–68; Marcus Klee, "Between the Scylla and Charybdis of Anarchy and Despotism: The State, Capital, and the Working Class in the Great Depression, Toronto, 1929–1940" (PhD diss., Queen's University, 1998); Klee, "Fighting the Sweatshop in Depression Ontario: Capital, Labour, and the Industrial Standards Act," *Labour/Le Travail* 45 (Spring 2000): 13–52. Klee's work is notable in focussing on Toronto, which has received surprisingly little attention. Note that in Horn, *Dirty Thirties,* the representation of the Depression follows a classic contour of dating it from the stock market crash

of October 1929 and accents the significance of Canadian staple resource production in the west. This necessarily leaves important centres of manufacturing and urban concentrations of the working class marginalized in the study of the economic collapse and its human dimensions.

8. John Herd Thompson and Allen Seager, *Canada, 1922–1939: Decades of Discord* (Toronto: McClelland and Stewart, 1985), esp. 193–221 and Struthers, *No Fault of Their Own,* 12–103 present excellent summaries of the dimensions of the unemployment crisis in the early 1930s, but for a usefully concentrated contemporary account, on which we also draw, see A. S. Whiteley, "Workers during the Depression," in *The Canadian Economy and Its Problems,* ed. H. A. Innis and A. F. W. Plumptre (Toronto: Canadian Institute of International Affairs, 1934), 110–26. Note as well the excellent discussion and compilation of data in H. M. Cassidy, *Unemployment and Relief in Ontario, 1929–1932* (Toronto: J. M. Dent & Sons, 1932) and the national overview in Leonard C. Marsh, *Canadians In and Out of Work: A Survey of Economic Classes and Their Relation to the Labour Market* (Oxford: Oxford University Press, 1940).

9. Struthers, *No Fault of Their Own,* 215; Thompson and Seager, *Decades of Discord,* 299–300, 350.

10. Cassidy, *Unemployment and Relief in Ontario,* 274. A wide-ranging discussion of the broad social impact of unemployment is Leonard C. Marsh, A. Grant Fleming, and C. F. Blackler, *Health and Unemployment: Some Studies of Their Relationships* (Oxford: Oxford University Press, 1938). For an explicitly antisocialist discussion of unemployment that continued to stress the importance of the issue of ex-servicemen see C. P. Gilman and H. M. Sinclair, *Unemployment: Canada's Problem* (Ottawa: Army and Navy Veterans in Canada, 1935).

11. Quoted in Struthers, *No Fault of Their Own,* 42; Thompson and Seager, *Decades of Discord,* 198.

12. Bennett correspondence quoted in Grayson and Bliss, *Wretched of Canada,* xx.

13. Struthers, *No Fault of Their Own,* 52; and for similar warnings see Horn, *Dirty Thirties,* 320–22; Ivan Avakumovic, *The Communist Party in Canada: A History* (Toronto: McClelland and Stewart, 1975), 74; H. A. Logan, *Trade Unions in Canada* (Toronto: Macmillan, 1948), 340–42. For Communists and the unemployed see as well John Manley, "'Starve, Be Damned!' Communists and Canada's Urban Unemployed, 1929–1939," *Canadian Historical Review* 79 (September 1998): 466–91. For the developing social democratic perspective on national unemployment insurance and other aspects of social provisioning, including family allowances, see Research Committee of the League for Social Reconstruction, *Social Planning for Canada* (Toronto: Thomas Nelson, 1935), esp. 367–88.

14. *Toronto Mail and Empire,* November 10, 1932, quoted in Norman Penner, *Canadian Communism: The Stalin Years and Beyond* (Toronto: Methuen, 1988), 117.

15. Cassidy, *Unemployment and Relief in Ontario,* 17–51 presents a wealth of figures on the dimensions of unemployment and dependency.

16. The above paragraphs draw on Cassidy, *Unemployment and Relief in Ontario,* esp. 35–44, 65, 121–22, 129–50; Klee, "Fighting the Sweatshop in Depression Ontario"; Struthers, *No Fault of Their Own,* 221; Thompson and Seager, *Decades of Discord,* 210; James Lemon, *Toronto Since 1918: An Illustrated History* (Toronto: James Lorimer, 1985), 62; Patricia V. Schulz, *The East York Workers' Association: A Response to the Great Depression* (Toronto: New Hogtown Press, 1975), esp. 5–8; "Figures Show Plight of Canadian Workers," *Vanguard* 3 (December 17, 1935). General accounts of welfare provisioning in the 1930s include Horn, *The Dirty Thirties,* 251–304; Dennis Guest, *The Emergence of Social Security in Canada* (Vancouver: UBC Press, 2003), 83–102; James Struthers, *The Limits of Affluence: Welfare in Ontario, 1920–1970* (Toronto: University of Toronto Press, 1994), 77–116; and Struthers, *No Fault of Their Own.* But whatever the system in place, there is no discounting that it was a mix

of public/private provisioning. As late as 1933 Albert N. Laver, Commissioner of the City's Department of Public Welfare, was insisting that regarding the meals served to those on relief, "It is not generally known, but the city has not paid one cent towards meals. Of the 1,000,000 or so meals last year, the city tax payer hasn't paid one cent. They come from private sources." See "Try Not to Make Jobless Too Comfortable—Laver. 'Handle These Men So They Won't Want to Come Back,'" *Toronto Daily Star* (hereafter *Daily Star*), July 6, 1933.

17. The discussion of the Campbell Report in the above three paragraphs draws on Struthers, *Limits of Affluence,* 83–89. See also Lara Campbell, *Respectable Citizens: Gender, Family, and Unemployment in Ontario's Great Depression* (Toronto: University of Toronto Press, 2009), 33–34; and John Stapleton and Catherine LaFramboise, "The Campbell Report: The Origins of Modern Public Assistance in Ontario," *Open Policy Ontario* (2005): 1–12. For a Montreal attempt to grapple with issues associated with health and unemployment that the Campbell Report glossed over cavalierly see Marsh, *Health and Unemployment.*

18. Municipalities attempting to follow the Campbell Report would have found, in its eschewing of minimal standards, the impossibility of imposing uniform dispensation of relief. As one commentator pointed out, each municipality necessarily made decisions about relief provisioning that flew in the face of any mechanical, province-wide standardization. But throughout the 1930s the Ontario government would reference the Campbell Report and call for municipalities to set their provisioning of the poor on a fictional scale based on the Report's expenditure ceilings. Particularly under the Hepburn Liberals in the later 1930s, the Campbell Report plus a percentage to account for change over time was the foundation on which repeated reductions in relief provisioning were imposed. On problems of municipal uniformity in relief provisioning, see Dorothy King, "Unemployment Aid (Direct Relief)," in *Canada's*

Unemployment Problem, ed. Lothar Richtar (Toronto: Macmillan, 1939), 99 and Campbell, *Respectable Citizens*, 34.

19. Struthers, *Limits of Affluence,* 90–91.

20. See Paula Maurutto, *Governing Charities: Church and State in Toronto's Catholic Archdiocese, 1850–1950* (Montreal and Kingston: McGill-Queen's University Press, 2003), 90–97.

21. As early as 1929 Simpson was deploring that Draper's relentless attacks on the Communist Party actually shored up support for those whose "influence was on the wane, when they were torn by internal strife, when their disruptive policies were being strenuously resented by organized labour generally and when the fruits of their intrigues and their internal borings were rapidly slipping from their grasp." Quoted in *The Worker*, February 9, 1929, cited in Lita-Rose Betcherman, *The Little Band: The Clashes between Communists and the Canadian Establishment, 1928–1932* (Ottawa: Deneau, 1980), 26.

22. Leslie Morris, "The Unemployment Crisis and Our Party," *Toronto Worker* (hereafter *Worker*), April 19, 1930; "A Carpenter" to R. B. Bennett, June 28, 1934, in Grayson and Bliss, *The Wretched of Canada*, 70–72. Also note Leo Gadali to Bennett, no date, 185, which comments on the suicide of an unemployed bookkeeper: "I would say the Dominion government was the murderer of this young Canadian, in that it is in their power to do something for the unemployed, but have not done so."

23. On the formation of the NUWA and the Communist Party's claims about its origins, development, and purpose see Tim Buck, *Yours in the Struggle: Reminiscences of Tim Buck,* ed. William Beeching and Dr. Phyllis Clarke (Toronto: NC Press, 1977), esp. 44–45, 147–48, 154–55; Buck, *Thirty Years: The Story of the Communist Movement in Canada, 1922–1952* (Toronto: Progress, 1975), 69–75; Tom McEwen, *The Forge Glows Red: From Blacksmith to Revolutionary* (Toronto: Progress, 1975), 137–205; McEwen, *Canada's Party of Socialism: History of the Communist Party of Canada, 1921–1976* (Toronto: Progress, 1982), 83–99.

24. For Maguire's "Unemployment," originally published in *Canadian Labour Monthly* (May-June 1928), see also Richard Wright and Robin Endres, eds., *Eight Men Speak and Other Plays from the Canadian Workers' Theatre* (Toronto: New Hogtown Press, 1976), 5–14. The Progressive Arts Club's Toronto work is outlined in Toby Gordon Ryan, *Stage Left: Canadian Workers' Theatre, 1929–1940* (Toronto: Simon and Pierre, 1985), 24–48 and James Doyle, *Progressive Heritage: The Evolution of a Politically Radical Literary Tradition in Canada* (Waterloo: Wilfrid Laurier University Press, 2002), and in Oscar Ryan's fictionalized autobiographical memoir, *Soon to Be Born* (Vancouver: New Star, 1980). On Edward Cecil-Smith's role see Tyler Wentzell, "Not for King or Country: Edward Cecil-Smith, the Communist Party of Canada, and the Spanish Civil War," unpublished manuscript, forthcoming October 2016.

25. See McEwen, *The Forge Glows Red*, 137–205; Betcherman, *Little Band*, 86–115; David Bright, "The State, the Unemployed, and the Communist Party in Calgary, 1930–1935," *Canadian Historical Review* 78 (December 1997): 537–65; and in Stephen L. Endicott's *Raising the Workers' Flag: The Workers' Unity League of Canada, 1930–1936* (Toronto: University of Toronto Press, 2012), the NUWA being an affiliate of the Workers' Unity League, a position apparently criticized in the Comintern by Lozofsky. Stewart Smith, *Comrades and Komsomolkas: My Years in the Communist Party of Canada* (Toronto: Lugus, 1993), 143 claims that Lozovsky could see "numerous leftist mistakes being made in Canada, such as making the unemployed movement an affiliate of the WUL, opposing "relief work" which was very acceptable to unemployed workers, demanding lump sum cash handouts for the unemployed." *The Worker* on Unemployed Councils and drawing into struggle new sectors, is quoted in Avakumovic, *The Communist Party in Canada*, 75. The most useful single focused treatment of Communism and the unemployed is John Manley, "'Starve, Be Damned!' Communists and Canada's Urban Unemployed, 1929–1939,"

Canadian Historical Review, 79 (September 1998): 466–91. Examples of Communist propagandizing around unemployment include Leslie Morris, "The Unemployment Crisis and Our Party," *Worker,* 19 April 1930; Harvey Murphy, "The Stagger System—A Quack Remedy for Unemployment," *Worker,* 7 November 1931.

26. Reg Whitaker, Gregory S. Kealey, and Andrew Parnaby, *Secret Service: Political Policing in Canada From the Fenians to Fortress America* (Toronto: University of Toronto Press, 2012). 113.

27. Manley, "Starve, Be Damned," with quote at 490; and there is much on the arrest and conviction of Buck and his comrades, known as "The Eight," in Thompson and Seager, *Decades of Discord,* 228–29; Betcherman, *Little Band;* Merrily Weisbord, *The Strangest Dream: Canadian Communists, the Spy Trials, and the Cold War* (Toronto: Lester and Orpen Dennys, 1983), 34–40; Rev. A. E. Smith, *All My Life: An Autobiography* (Toronto: Progress, 1949), 130–39; Oscar Ryan, *Tim Buck: A Conscience for Canada* (Toronto: Progress, 1975), 147–62; Gilbert Campbell Baker, "The Spirit of 98: Attitudes Toward Freedom of Speech and Assembly in Ontario, 1919–1936" (PhD diss., Queen's University, 1977). Cohen is quoted on Section 98 in Laurel Sefton MacDowell, *Renegade Lawyer: The Life of J. L. Cohen* (Toronto: University of Toronto Press, 2001), 44. The imprisonment of Buck and his comrades led to the agitational-propaganda theatrical production, *Eight Men Speak: A Political Play in Six Acts* (Toronto: Progressive Arts Clubs of Canada, 1934). The 1931 conviction of Buck and his comrades unleashed a vicious Red Scare, evidence of which was commonplace in the newspapers. See, for instance: "Deport Foreign Reds Bar Atheist Voters Black Knight Demands," *Mail and Empire,* June 17, 1931; "Special Red Group Examining Outlook, Evidence Indicates," *Toronto Globe* (hereafter *Globe*), November 5, 1931; "Buck Denies Reds Planned Use of Force," *London Free Press* (hereafter *Free Press*), November 7, 1931; "Canadian Court Sets Empire Precedent in Declaring Communist Organization Illegal," *Mail and Empire,* November 13, 1931; "Three Schools in City Teaching 'Red' Doctrine, M. P. P. Tells Legislature," *Mail and Empire,* March 17, 1932.

28. The above paragraphs draw on Schulz, *East York Workers' Association,* 46–53, quoting *The Worker,* July 4, 1931; July 25, 1931. On Ben Spence, Jerry Flanagan, and the EYWA see also Bryan D. Palmer, *A Communist Life: Jack Scott and the Canadian Workers Movement, 1927–1985* (St. John's, Newfoundland: Committee on Canadian Labour History, 1988), 29, 39; Gregory S. Kealey and Reg Whitaker, eds., *R.C.M.P. Security Bulletins: The Depression Years, Part 3, 1936* (Toronto: Canadian Committee on Labour History, 1996), 422. For Trotskyist comment see "Unemployed Organize!," *Vanguard* 2 (December 1934), and for evidence of the use of epithets like "social fascist," "fascist," "counter-revolutionary," "fascist," "renegade," and "cess-pools of Trotskyite journalism," see William Dennison to Dear Editor, "CCF Leader Subscribes to Vanguard," *Vanguard* 2 (February 1935).

29. Manley, "Starve, Be Damned," 487–91.

30. See the Ewart Humphries-introduced pamphlet, issued from the 383 Queen Street West headquarters of the NCUC, *Building a Mass Unemployed Movement: For Full and Free Unemployment Insurance; Against Relief Cuts! Against Evictions! Against Forced Labor!* (Toronto: National Committee of Unemployed Councils, 1933).

31. See *The Communists Fight for Working Class Unity* (Montreal: Contemporary Publications, 1934).

32. John Manley, "Introduction," in *R.C.M.P. Security Bulletins: The Depression Years, Part 4, 1937,* ed. Gregory S. Kealey and Reg Whitaker (St. John's, Newfoundland: Canadian Committee on Labour History, 1997), 1–23; Palmer, *A Communist Life,* 51.

33. Debates abound about Stalinism and its meaning. It is nonetheless clear that avoiding the extent to which Stalinism compromised the revolutionary project of the 1930s is as unacceptable as failing to appreciate its

decisive influence in the overall working-class struggle of the decade. See Bryan D. Palmer, "Rethinking the Historiography of United States Communism," *American Communist History* 2 (December 2003): 139–74 and the resulting responses to this symposium piece by James. R. Barrett, John Earl Haynes, Melvyn Dubofsky, and John McIlroy, 175–214.

34. G. Pierce [Stewart Smith], *Socialism and the C. C. F.* (Montreal: Contemporary Publishing, 1934), 145–46; with Smith quoted on blood running in Toronto streets in Bryan D. Palmer, *Working-Class Experience: The Rise and Reconstitution of Canadian Labour, 1800–1980* (Toronto: Butterworth, 1983), 205; and in Stephen L. Endicott, *Raising the Workers' Flag: the Workers' Unity League of Canada, 1930–1936* (Toronto: University of Toronto Press, 2012), 24. For Smith's later, self-serving reflections see Stewart Smith, *Comrades and Komsomolkas: My Years in the Communist Party of Canada* (Toronto: Lugus, 1993), 147–66. See also "Shots Fired, Weapons Wielded as Reds Start Free-for-all to Break Up Church Lecture," *Mail and Empire*, October 29, 1931.

35. For an accessible account of these developments see Betcherman, *Little Band*, 15–28.

36. Betcherman, *Little Band,* 24–26; Andrée Lévesque, *Red Travellers: Jeanne Corbin and Her Comrades* (Montreal and Kingston: McGill-Queen's University Press, 241–42.

37. Betcherman, *Little Band*, 27–28; "The 'Victory' for the Reds," *Globe*, November 1, 1929; "Refused Use of Labor Temple—'Free Speech' Advocates Angry," unattributed newspaper clipping, dated February 15, 1929, in "Communism in Canada" scrapbook, in possession of Bryan D. Palmer. For the climate of anti-communism in the late 1920s see, for instance: "The Communist Fester," *Globe*, May 27, 1927; "The Communist Menace," *Montreal Gazette*, March 29, 1928; "Communism Here and There," *Montreal Gazette*, September 6, 1928; "Again the Communists," *Montreal Gazette*, December 19, 1928; "Red 'Citizens'," *Globe*, January 14, 1929.

38. Betcherman, *Little Band*, 133–34; Lévesque, *Red Travellers*, 42–45; "'Red Day' Propaganda Confiscated by Police. Communists On Carpet," *Daily Star*, August 1, 1929.

39. "Curb on Communism by Toronto Police Discussed in House," *Globe*, May 9, 1929. On deportations see Barbara Roberts, *Whence They Came: Deportation From Canada, 1900–1935* (Ottawa: University of Ottawa Press, 1988), 125–58.

40. Lévesque, *Red Travellers*, 187, citing *Timothy Buck v. Emerson Coatsworth, F. M. Morson, Samuel McBride*, Ontario Supreme Court, October 28, 1929, no. 2633, MG30 A94, vol. 1, file 6, J. L. Cohen Papers, Library and Archives Canada.

41. "Spectators Ill-Used When 'Reds' Silenced," *Daily Star*, August 2, 1929; "No Speeches, No Parade; Police Force Steps in, Clearing Queen's Park," *Globe*, August 2, 1929; "Reds Not Mistreated by Police Officers Says Chief Draper," *Globe*, August 3, 1929.

42. On MacDonald see Ian Angus, *Canadian Bolsheviks: The Early Years of the Communist Party of Canada* (Toronto: South Branch, 2004). MacDonald appears in fictional form as MacCraddock in Earl Birney's *Down the Long Table* (Toronto: McClelland and Stewart, 1955).

43. See "Chief Draper's Stand in Quelling Reds Here Is Upheld by Mayor. Insists, However, Policemen Responsible for Brutality Must Be Disciplined," *Daily Star*, August 14, 1929; "Mayor Insists Police Must Be Disciplined. Toronto Police Use Fists, Feet and Batons to Clear Queen's Park," *Daily Star*, August 14, 1929. See also "Communists and Curious Spectators Suffer as Draper's Men Charge Queen's Park Crowd with Horses, Motorcycles and Wooden Clubs," *Mail and Empire*, August 14, 1929; "Draper Says Reds Publicity Seekers," *Mail and Empire*, August 14, 1929. The Edward Smith quoted was likely Edward Cecil-Smith, a *Mail and Empire* journalist who reported on the August 1929 Queen's Park events, and was influenced by them to join the Communist Party. See Wentzell, "Not for King or Country," 30–33, citing Cecil-Smith, "Police Drive Communists Away from Queen's Park," *Mail and Empire*, August 2, 1929; "Batons and Feet Used Freely

as City Police Rout Reds," Mail and Empire, August 14, 1929.

44. "Chief Draper's Stand in Quelling Reds Here Is Upheld by Mayor," and "Mayor Insists Police Must Be Disciplined."

45. "Locked Doors Greet Communists Who Arrive for Memorial Meeting," *Mail and Empire*, August 23, 1929; "Communists Lay Plans for Further Meetings Despite Police Stand," *Daily Star*, August 28, 1929; "Reds Afraid to Enter When Park Is Closed by Cordon of Police," *Globe*, August 28, 1929; "Becky Buhay Arrested. Communists Disperse," *Daily Star*, September 7, 1929.

46. "Mayor Does Not Favour Permits for Meetings," *Daily Star*, October 2, 1929.

47. "Mayor Does Not Favour Permits for Meetings."

48. "Prominent Men Will Not Speak for Communists," *Daily Star*, October 8, 1929; "Cause and Effect," *Globe*, October 12, 1929; "Williams Washes Hands of Aiding Draper's Men Suppress Communists," *Daily Star*, October 12, 1929.

49. "Eight Arrests Made by Police When Communists Stage Effort to Hold Meeting at Queen's Park," *Globe*, October 14, 1929; "Police Make Eight Arrests When Reds Attempt Rally," *Daily Star*, October 14, 1929.

50. "Police Make Eight Arrests When Reds Attempt Rally"; "Eight Arrests Made by Police When Communists Stage Effort to Hold Meeting at Queen's Park"; "Communist Candidates Not Allowed to Speak," *Daily Star*, October 21, 1929; Lévesque, *Red Travellers*, 42–44.

51. "Chief Draper's Stand in Quelling Reds Here Is Upheld by Mayor"; "Mayor Insists Police Must Be Disciplined"; "Bolshevism Must Go Asserts Coatsworth in Supporting Draper," *Daily Star*, August 15, 1929. Coatsworth would be embroiled in other anticommunist controversies over the next immediate years. See "Police Commissioner's Daughter Receives Message by Telephone While Waiting Arrival of Judge," *Globe*, January 17, 1931; "Speech Bogey Bursts," *Globe*, January 24, 1931.

52. For only a sampling of evidence see Workers Educational League, *Unemployment—Wage*

Reductions—*The Open Shop* (Toronto: n.p., 1930), 2pp broadside; and for unstudied Trotskyist agitation among the unemployed, "Unemployment Crisis Does not Slacken," *Vanguard* (November–December 1932); "Unemployed Organize!" *Vanguard* (December 1934); "R. B. Bennett's New Deal to Dupe the Masses," *Vanguard* (February 1935); "Figures Show Plight of Canadian Workers: Employed and Jobless Suffer Alike," *Vanguard* (December 17, 1935); "Unemployed Strike in Toronto's Suburb," *Vanguard* (July 1936); Schulz, *East York Workers' Association*.

53. T. P. Mill, "Unemployment: The Tasks of the Vanguard," *October Youth* (August–September 1933).

54. See Manley, "Starve, Be Damned," 471.

55. Palmer, *A Communist Life*, 18, 38.

56. "'Red Thursday' in Toronto Proves a Fiasco. Police Disperse Mob as 'Red' Agitators Obey Moscow Order. Communists Whisked Into City Hall After Leaders Attempt to Spout Doctrines—Kicking Shins Chief Method of Attack. Eleven Arrested at Disturbance," *Daily Star*, March 7, 1930.

57. "Demonstrations by Jobless Encounter Stern Opposition; 38 Are Arrested in Canada," *London Advertiser*, February 26, 1931; "Red Attempts at Disorder are Blocked by Police," *Globe*, February 26, 1931. See also Minerva Davis, *The Wretched of the Earth and Me* (Toronto: Lugus, 1992), 130–36; McEwen, *The Forge Glows Red*, 167–205.

58. "May Day Marked by Riots in Number of Canadian Cities," *Free Press*, May 2, 1932; "Police Round Up 18, Foil May Day Meet," *Daily Star*, May 2, 1933; "May Day Quietly Marked in Canada," *Free Press*, May 2, 1933.

59. "Would Concede All Free-Speech Right," *Daily Star*, May 8, 1933.

60. "Bloody Riot Develops as Saskatoon Jobless Are Charged by Police," *London Advertiser*, November 8, 1932; "Unity Needed to Fight Reds," *Free Press*, December 6, 1932; "Communism Not Solution, He Declares," *Mail and Empire*, January 16, 1933; "Red Menace at the Sault," *Montreal Gazette*, February 21, 1933; "Harbord's

'Red' Students Demand Free Politics and Children's Car Fare," *Mail and Empire*, January 26, 1933; "Red Menace Is Real in Canada," *Mail and Empire*, January 27, 1933; "Alleged Communistic Trends of University Student Bodies Reported to Be Under Probe," *Mail and Empire*, March 21, 1933.

61. "Stairs Barricaded at Park Bandstand," *Daily Star*, June 22, 1933.

62. Manley, "Starve, Be Damned," 484; "For Free Speech."

63. "Police Halt Rallies of CCF and Jobless Charge Violence Used," *Daily Star*, August 4, 1933; "Baby-Carts Weapons to Fight with Police," *Daily Star*, August 10, 1933. On the issue of permits and park speaking see also "Freedom of Speech 'Within the Law' Allowed in Parks," *Globe*, August 3, 1933; "Who Gives Permit to Hold Meeting," *Daily Star*, August 19, 1933.

64. For the above two paragraphs see "Motorcycle Fumes Billow Effectively at Allan Gardens. Peaceful Scene Is Rudely Disturbed as Men Unfurl Banner and Start Speeches. No Permit for Meeting. Sign Is Torn Down in General Mix-Up," *Daily Star*, August 16, 1933; "Police Smoke Out Meeting but Crowd Won't Disperse," *Daily Star*, August 16, 1933; "Police Clear Park Using Smoke Screen," *Daily Star*, August 17, 1933; "Jobless Assert Free Speech Victory," *Daily Star*, August 18, 1933; Manley, "Starve, Be Damned." A. N. Willicombe is also referred to as W. Willecombe in newspaper reports, but we have assumed that these differently named men, regularly featured as WESL speakers, were actually the same individual. On the Left Opposition meeting see "L. O. Mass Meeting in Earlscourt Pk," *October Youth* (August–September 1933).

65. "Work for Every Man Is Objective of CCF," *Daily Star*, August 28, 1933; "Charge Police Refused Aid to Girl Trampled by Horse. Protest Alleged Neglect as Allan Gardens Meeting Broken Up," *Daily Star*, August 30, 1933; "No Police Move So 'Free Speech' Is Quiet. Policy Reversed and Officers Allow Workers to Talk in Allan Gardens. Gathering of 1,000. Big Squad of Draper's Staff on Hand but Mounted Men Absent," *Daily Star*, August 31, 1933. For another articulation of veterans' grievances see F. Deane to R. B. Bennett, 24 June 1932, in Grayson and Bliss, *The Wretched of Canada*, 27–30.

66. "Toronto Orders Free Speech," *Free Press*, April 13, 1933.

67. "Police Force Allow Free Speech Fight in Park But Ban CCF Paper," *Daily Star*, September 1, 1933; "Speaking Is Sought in Four More Parks," *Globe*, September 23, 1933; "Orders More Parks Open to Speakers," *Daily Star*, September 23, 1933. See also "Simpson Resists Orders of Police to Move Meeting," *Mail and Empire*, May 14, 1934. The future leader of Canadian Trotskyism, Ross Dowson, was involved in the York Township unemployed protests of this time, although still a teenager. He recalled helping to organize open-air meetings at Earlscourt Park and being encouraged to speak at such meetings himself, which he did. See "Ross Dowson: A Short Biography," rossdowson.com.

68. Gregory S. Kealey and Reg Whitaker, eds., *R.C.M.P. Security Bulletins: The Depression Years, Part 1, 1933–1934* (St. John's, Newfoundland: Canadian Committee on Labour History, 1993), 85, 105–6, 145, 154–55, 163, 180; Manley, "Starve, Be Damned," 479; Peter Hunter, *Which Side Are You On Boys: Canadian Life on the Left* (Toronto: Lugus, 1988), 64–65; John T. Saywell, *"Just Call Me Mitch": The Life of Mitchell Hepburn* (Toronto: University of Toronto Press, 1991), 179–81.

69. The above three paragraphs draw on Saywell, *Just Call Me Mitch*, 181, 207–8, 263–67; Struthers, *Limits of Affluence*, 90–98; Hunter, *Which Side Are You On Boys*, 21–26; McEwen, *The Forge Glows Red*, 159; Gregory S. Kealey and Reg Whitaker, eds., *R.C.M.P. Security Bulletins: The Depression Years, Part 2, 1935* (St. John's, Newfoundland: Canadian Committee on Labour History, 1995), 227–28. Collins and the CPC were not the only leftists critical of Roebuck. See, as well, "Can Codes Save Capitalism? Att.-Gen. Roebuck's New Deal to Coerce Workers," *Vanguard* 3 (October 1934); "Ontario Hunger March Gets Soft-Soap From Roebuck," *Vanguard* 3 (July 1, 1935).

70. "10,000 Radicals in May Day Parade," *Globe*, May 2, 1935.

71. Canadian, "May Day in Queen's Park," *Mail and Empire*, May 11, 1936.

72. Horn, *The Dirty Thirties*, 306; Bob Russell, *Back to Work: Labour, State, and Industrial Relations in Canada* (Scarborough: Nelson, 1990), 173.

73. "85 Per Cent Registered at 'Wayfarers' Lodge' Rode Rods to Get Here," *Daily Star*, October 30, 1930.

74. "85 Per Cent Registered at 'Wayfarers' Lodge Rode the Rods to Get Here."

75. Material in the above paragraphs from "Army of Homeless Huddle in Park, Mission, Box Car. About 1500 Were Stranded Last Night. 'Pogey' Shelters 250," *Daily Star*, October 31, 1930; "Homeless Steal Warmth From Brick Kilns," *Daily Star*, December 2, 1930; "More Beds for Homeless. House of Industry Accommodation Extended," *Daily Star*, December 18, 1930; "Two Hostels Opened Today for Homeless Men of City," *Daily Star*, December 8, 1930; "Co-operate in Relief with Central Bureau. Thousand Men Have Registered—Other Organizations Agree to Keep in Touch," *Daily Star*, December 9, 1930; Pat Schultz, *The East York Workers' Association: A Response to the Great Depression* (Toronto: New Hogtown Press, 1975); Jennifer L. Bonnell, *Reclaiming the Don: An Environmental History of Toronto's Don River Valley* (Toronto: University of Toronto Press, 2014), 99–110. Toronto's Don Valley history of squatting is paralleled by similar experiences along Hamilton's Burlington Bay. See Nancy B. Bouchier and Ken Cruikshank, "The War on the Squatters, 1920–1940: Hamilton's Boathouse Community and the Re-Creation of Recreation on Burlington Bay," *Labour/Le Travail* 51 (Spring 2003): 9–46.

76. "Two Hostels Opened Today for Homeless Men of City."

77. Struthers, *Limits of Affluence*, 85.

78. "Apathetic Acceptance Marks Club Dinners. No Anger or Resentment Shown as 500 Jobless Eat in Dead Silence," *Daily Star*, February 23, 1931.

79. Horn, *The Dirty Thirties*, 251–304.

80. Maurutto, *Governing Charities*, 72; "Co-Operate in Relief with Central Bureau"; "Apathetic Acceptance Marks Club Dinners"; "Ivy Maison Is 'Gatineau-bewitched," *Ottawa Citizen*, November 8, 1962.

81. Maurutto, *Governing Charities*, 76.

82. "Taking Care of Toronto's 100,000 Needy," *Daily Star*, February 3, 1933; "Laver Voucher Report 'Camouflage' Is Charge Sincerity Is Doubted," *Daily Star*, March 30, 1933; Margaret H. Hobbs, "Gendering Work and Welfare: Women's Relationship to Wage-Work and Social Policy in Canada during the Great Depression" (PhD diss., University of Toronto, 1995), 149.

83. "House of Industry Attack Called 'Political Intrigue'. Mrs. Laughlen Charges M. O. H. Report Linked with Plot by Laver. Collusion Denied," *Daily Star*, January 15, 1932; "Charge That Laver Threatened to End House of Industry. Began Campaign at Start of Duties, Day Asserts. Coveted Property. Ald. Beamish Assails Laver's Charge against House of Industry," *Daily Star*, August 29, 1933. Other social welfare figures of stature were also criticizing the economies of the House of Industry central depot. See, for instance, Cassidy, *Unemployment and Relief in Ontario*, 185.

84. "Veterans Complain of Relief System. Want It Taken Out of Hands of House of Industry," *Daily Star*, June 22, 1932; "Boos, Cheers, Police at Riverdale Meeting. Con. McBride Heckled Unceasingly, Particularly on Relief Issue," *Daily Star*, December 24, 1932; "Allegedly Tainted Meat Is Produced. House of Industry Supplies Challenged—Ward One Ratepayers Turbulent, Police Keep Order," *Daily Star*, December 29, 1932; "Salary-Slash Plan Gets Big Support," *Daily Star*, December 28, 1932.

85. "Relief Coupon Plan Favored by Labor," *Daily Star*, September 2, 1932; "Boos, Cheers, Police at Riverdale Meeting"; "Police Take Red Flag of Hunger Marchers," *Daily Star*, January 16, 1933; "Hunger Marchers Storm Control Board. I'll See You Get Back to Russia, Mayor Tells Woman with Marchers. Controllers in Stormy Scene, Hear Spokespersons of Hunger Marchers," *Daily Star*, January 18, 1933; "Foresee Big Change in Giving Out Relief," *Daily Star*, February 2, 1933; "Laver Voucher

Report 'Camouflage' Is Charge Sincerity Is Doubted."

86. Betcherman, *Little Band*, 143; Manley, "Starve, Be Damned," 479; "Refusing Relief, Irishman Arrested for Deportation," *Daily Star*, October 24, 1932; Maurutto, *Governing Charities*, 75, 78, 80. On the issue of judgmental moralism and relief see also Margaret Little, *"No Car, No Radio, No Liquor Permit": The Moral Regulation of Single Mothers in Ontario, 1920–1997* (Toronto: Oxford University Press, 1998), esp. 76–106; Hobbs, "Gendering Work and Welfare," 177–80.

87. "Foresee Big Change in Giving Out Relief," *Daily Star*, February 2, 1933; "Grocers Ask Right to Supply Relief. Say Many Face Extinction Unless Given Share of Business," *Daily Star*, November 9, 1932.

88. "Laver Voucher Report 'Camouflage' Is Charge Sincerity Is Doubted"; "Work Test for Relief Called Slavery," *Daily Star*, June 30, 1933.

89. "Urge House of Industry Supervise Relief Depots," *Daily Star*, July 11, 1933; "Thinks Laver's Post Requires No Salary," *Daily Star*, March 17, 1933; "Let Advisory Board Die. Volunteer Help Ignored," *Daily Star*, March 18, 1933; "City Will Never Know Cost of New System Charges C. T. Stark," *Daily Star*, March 28, 1933; "Demand Inquiry as Relief Given Liquor Buyers," *Daily Star*, March 30, 1933; "Spent $305 on Liquor Man Put Off Relief Is Restored by Laver," *Daily Star*, March 29, 1933; "Charge That Laver Threatened to End House of Industry."

90. Struthers, *Limits of Affluence*, 89. Hobbs, "Gendering Work and Welfare," 150 points out that the House of Industry was not totally done away with. During 1933–34 it continued to provide outdoor relief of food to over three thousand families, and as late as 1939, with the number of families dropping annually, there remained seven hundred domestic units drawing on House of Industry supplies. Toronto still provided a grant to the House for these indigent families, but the funds did not come out of resources earmarked for unemployment relief.

91. Foucault, of course, provides a set of shifting interpretive paradigms depending on which period of his extensive *oeuvre* is being considered. Relevant translated studies (of works first published in 1961 and 1975) with respect to the disciplinary order include *History of Madness* (New York: Routledge, 2006) and *Discipline and Punish: The Birth of the Prison* (New York: Pantheon, 1977).

92. For a Foucauldian governmentality statement indicative of this approach's disregard of resistance see Mariana Valverde, "Some Remarks on the Rise and Fall of Discourse Analysis," *Histoire Sociale/Social History* 33 (2000): 59–78.

93. This is an obvious reference to E. P. Thompson, *The Making of the English Working Class* (Harmondsworth, England: Penguin, 1968), 9: "The working class did not rise like the sun at an appointed time. It was present at its own making."

94. Betcherman, *Little Band*, 109; Endicott, *Raising the Workers' Flag*, 91.

95. "Say City's Relief Scale Is Totally Inadequate. Unemployed Ask for Increased Allowance, Declaring They Are Undernourished. Police Stand on Guard," *Daily Star*, March 12, 1930; Betcherman, *Little Band*, 109–10.

96. "Two Refuse to Work Get 30 Days in Jail. House of Industry Residents Balk at Allotted Tasks Again To-day," *Daily Star*, January 19, 1932.

97. "City Indigents Protest Quality of Hostels' Food. Controllers Consider Petition and Criticize Ald. Rogers' Address to Men," *Daily Star*, October 12, 1932.

98. "At the Hostels," *Daily Star*, October 22, 1932; "Refusing Relief, Irishman Arrested for Deportation," *Daily Star*, October 24, 1932.

99. "Men at Hostel Blame Epidemic of Illness upon Thawed-Out Beef. But Welfare Commissioner Laver Convinced Meat Was Tampered With," *Daily Star*, May 23, 1933; "100 Jobless Ill in Hospital. Unemployed Insist Roast Beef Is Cause of Stomach Trouble," *Daily Star*, October 6, 1933; "Claims Riot Incited. Charged as Vagrant," *Daily Star*, October 23, 1933; "Charged $6,100 Theft. Tried to Address Jobless," *Daily Star*, October 26, 1933. Onie Brown was the junior partner of lawyer Hugh John MacDonald in 1931, when MacDonald defended Tim Buck and

other Communists in their Section 98/seditious conspiracy trial. See Betcherman, *Little Band*, 184–85.

100. Palmer, *A Communist Life*, 20.

101. "Relief Official Says Recipient Struck Him. Complained of Food, Court Told—Only Scuffle, Accused Pleads," *Daily Star*, December 22, 1934.

102. For the above two paragraphs see "Finds Hostel Charge Merits Swift Probe. Mayor Promises Investigation If Controllers Decide It Is Available," *Daily Star*, February 22, 1935; "Labour Men Want Inquiry into Wellington House," *Daily Star*, February 22, 1935; "Brands Wellington House as 'Hell Hole' and Fire Trap. John W. Bruce Accuses City Council of 'Callousness and Inhumanity'," *Daily Star*, March 9, 1935. In 1933 Bruce, attending a Labor Temple discussion of CCFers and Trades and Labour Congress–affiliated unions, argued that the Communist Workers' Unity League had no place in the mainstream labour movement. See Peter Campbell, *Rose Henderson: A Woman for the People* (Montreal and Kingston: McGill-Queen's University Press, 2010), 183–84, 210. For a fuller account of Bruce, unemployment, and the Toronto labour/socialist movements see Donald R. Montgomery, *John Bruce, O. B. E. Journeyman Plumber* (Victoria: Trafford Publishing, 2000) and David Alexander Thompson, "Working Class Anguish and Revolutionary Indignation: The Making of Radical and Socialist Unemployment Movements in Canada, 1875–1928" (PhD diss., Queen's University, 2014), 159–61.

103. "Board Asks Survey of House of Industry. Members Will Themselves Inspect Wellington House, Seaton House Hostels," *Daily Star*, February 17, 1937; "Robbins Threatens to Clear Gallery. Mayor Objects to Boos, as Hostel Food Is Shown," *Daily Star*, February 24, 1937.

104. "Abolish Hostels Urged by Inmates. Call Conditions Deplorable. Ask Men Be Allowed $5 Weekly," *Daily Star*, February 2, 1937.

105. "Ministers See Life in Hostel as 'Deplorable', Charge 'Cruel' and Unsanitary Conditions and Insufficient Food. Probe Is Asked," *Daily Star*, December 8, 1937. Almack's sympathies with

the more militant sectors of the unemployed movement of the 1930s are discussed by Jack Scott in Palmer, *A Communist Life*, 39. On the history of non-working class investigators masquerading as the poor to provide chronicles of the "down-and-out" see Mark Pittenger, *Class Unknown: Undercover Investigations of American Work and Poverty from the Progressive Era to the Present* (New York: New York University Press, 2012).

106. "Try Not to Make Jobless Too Comfortable—Laver. 'Handle These Men So They Won't Want to Come Back'."

107. Ruth Roach Pierson, "Gender and the Unemployment Insurance Debates in Canada, 1934–1940," *Labour/Le Travail* 25 (Spring 1990): 77–78, with quotes from House of Commons statements by Macphail and others; Hobbs, "Gendering Work and Welfare," with quote at 162, and discussion of Macphail, 116–20. So commonplace was the association of single unemployed women and moral decay that it is important not to attribute outrageous views to all commentators. An example of sensationalist misrepresentation of social work commentary around single unemployed women is Nancy Christie, *Engendering the State: Family, Work, and Welfare in Canada* (Toronto: University of Toronto Press, 2000), 230, which comments on an article cited as Ruth Low, "The Unattached Woman," *Child Welfare News* 11, no. 5 (1936): 19, where Christie states that Low "contended that one of the worst effects of the Depression was that it had caused an alarming increase in female promiscuity, and worse, had made fully half of all unemployed and idle single women in the nation into homosexuals." Low is represented by Christie as a middle-class woman who classified "women's poverty as a product of 'social' rather than 'economic' dependency," thus helping to "reinforce rather than deconstruct the gendered divisions that were already well enmeshed in state relief policies." In actuality, Low's commentary, while indeed guilty of remaining trapped in certain conventional, moralistic "wisdoms" concerning "womankind," is far more complex (and less egregiously

irrational) than Christie's characterization suggests. On the issue of the crisis of the 1930s making lesbians of half of all unemployed and idle single women in Canada, Low said no such thing. What she did state (and not without a plethora of problematic assumptions) was that the insecurity of "unattached" women living through the conditions of the Great Depression extended beyond the economic into realms social/sexual. Low insisted that this process, which the crisis of the 1930s highlighted and exposed with more clarity than had been possible in the past, deserved "thought and study." She suggested, without any pretence to scientific rigour, that unattached women had been experimenting, and she offered a rough guide, composed of three classifications: "Some have sought the temporary release through sexual promiscuity. Some have learned the fine art of redirecting this force of creativity into lines of service and helpfulness to others. Then, a third group has received what pleasure and satisfaction is possible through homosexuality. From studies made in Canada concerning the prevalence of the latter, the participation in some groups has been estimated as high as 50 per cent." Whatever the problems and confusions in this way of posing issues related to single unemployed women, Christie has clearly misrepresented Low, doing so in a most peculiar way. We draw on Ruth Low, "The Unattached Woman in Canada—Who She Is and Some of Her Problems," *Child and Family Welfare,* 11, No. 5 (1936): 13–21, quoting 19.

108. These figures are usefully drawn together with much other information in Katrina Srigley, "'In Case You Hadn't Noticed': Race, Ethnicity, and Women's Wage Earning in a Depression Era City," *Labour/Le Travail* 55 (Spring 2005): 69–105, but see also Srigley, *Breadwinning Daughters: Single Working Women in a Depression-Era City, 1929–1939* (Toronto: University of Toronto Press, 2002) and Joan Sangster, *Earning Respect: The Lives of Working Women in Small Town Ontario, 1920–1960* (Toronto: University of Toronto Press, 1995). Hobbs has a lengthy and useful discussion

on how the gendering of joblessness and the effect of economic crisis on women's work in the 1930s obscures unemployment in women's historical experience. See Hobbs, "Gendering Work and Welfare," 226–300. For a thorough and convincing discussion of the reasons why official, census-developed statistics on women's unemployment present unreliable data on women, the labour market, and the problem of female joblessness, see Marjorie Cohen, "Women at Work in Canada during the Depression," Unpublished conference paper, Blue Collar Workers Conference, University of Windsor, May 1979.

109. Veronica Strong-Boag, *The New Day Recalled: Lives of Girls and Women in English Canada, 1919–1939* (Toronto: Copp Clark, 1988), 3. Whether single unemployed women have been hidden from the history of the Great Depression because of gender ideology or because of the social justice claims of the working class as a whole, in which single unemployed women appear to be caught outside some of the identities wage-earning women might have adopted as family members, mothers, wives, and even earning breadwinners, requires more research. For some of the parameters of discussion see the following exchange: Alice Kessler-Harris, "Gender Ideology in Historical Reconstruction: A Case Study from the 1930s," *Gender & History* 1 (Spring 1989): 31–49; Margaret Hobbs, "Rethinking Antifeminism in the 1930s: Gender Crisis or Workplace Justice—A Response to Alice Kessler-Harris," *Gender & History* 5 (Spring 1993): 4–15; Kessler-Harris, "Reply to Hobbs," *Gender & History* 5 (Spring 1993): 16–19. For a discussion that brings gender into play in interesting ways with respect to Toronto relief, employment, and unemployment see Klee, "Between the Scylla and Charybdis of Anarchy and Despotism"; Klee, "Fighting the Sweatshop in Depression Ontario."

110. Note Leonard Marsh, *Employment Research: An Introduction to the McGill Programme of Research in the Social Sciences* (Toronto: Oxford University Press, 1935), 55, quoted in Christie, *Engendering the State,* 196. Christie leads her

chapter on the Great Depression with the quote from Marsh but ignores the extent to which Marsh prefaced it with a statement about gendered labour market divergences and then, surprisingly, cuts the middle of the quote in which Marsh states that if home-making was a paid occupation the extreme difference in the statistics of males and females officially recognized as "working" would be significantly reduced.

111. Cohen, "Women at Work in Canada during the Depression," 17, 30.

112. Christie, *Engendering the State*, 225–29.

113. Barry Broadfoot, *Ten Lost Years, 1929–1939: Memories of Canadians Who Survived the Depression* (Don Mills, Ontario: Paperjacks, 1975), 70; Hobbs, "Gendering Work and Welfare," 54; Srigley, "In Case You Hadn't Noticed," 70–71, 73.

114. Quotes and discussion in the above two paragraphs from Hobbs, "Gendering Work and Welfare," 134–41; Maurutto, *Governing Charities*, 75. See also "Why Girls Work," *Canadian Congress Journal* 10 (August 1931), 88; Gwethalyn Graham, "Women, Are They Human?" *Canadian Forum* 16 (December 1936): 21–22; Christie, *Engendering the State*, 218.

115. Hobbs, "Gendering Work and Welfare," 163–64, 169–71; Christie, *Engendering the State*, 220; "Landlady Provides Weekly Pocket Money for Four Jobless Girls," *Daily Star*, June 8, 1935. Hobbs, "Gendering Work and Welfare," 164–69, provides comment on the rare and quite limited female hostels, such as Georgina House, and soup kitchens like the Scott Mission that were willing to provide meals to women alongside the far more numerous men.

116. "Landlady Provides Weekly Pocket Money for Four Jobless Girls"; "Unemployed Women Relate Pitiable Tales to Croll," *Daily Star*, March 15, 1935; "Jobless Girls Fight Rent Allowance Cut," *Daily Star*, February 21, 1935; "Jobless Girls on Relief Can Not Get Any in Cash," *Daily Star*, June 5, 1935; Jean Laing, "Authorities Turn Deaf Ear to Single Women's Needs," *The Worker*, December 19, 1935; Srigley, "In Case You Hadn't Noticed," 88; John T. Saywell, *Just Call Me Mitch*, 218.

117. Davis, *The Wretched of the Earth and Me*, 135–36. For a fictional critique of the lack of unity/class consciousness among workers, rooted in conventional gender relations, see Mona Weiss, "My Fellow Stenos," *Masses* (July–August 1932) and the discussion in Doyle, *Progressive Heritage*, 136. On Wilkinson see Stephen L. Endicott, *Raising the Workers' Flag: The Workers' Unity League of Canada, 1930–1936* (Toronto: University of Toronto Press, 2012), 138–40, and 167–68, quoting *The Worker*, "Woman Defies Premier," August 6, 1932. For the plea of an unemployed married woman with eight children, a proofreader whose husband was a skilled but out-of-work plasterer, see Coleen Trehern to R. B. Bennett, January 15, 1934, in Grayson and Bliss, *The Wretched of Canada*, 66.

118. "Jobless Girls Fight Rent Allowance Cut"; "Jobless Girls on Relief Cannot Get Any Cash"; "Dollar a Week Not Enough for Shelter, States Laver," *Daily Star*, February 27, 1935; "Girls on Relief Too Hungry to Seek Jobs, Says Doctor," *Daily Star*, May 30, 1935.

119. Christie, *Engendering the State*, 230–32 has an interesting discussion of Lade.

120. See Struthers, *Limits of Affluence*, 89–98; Saywell, *Just Call Me Mitch*, 263–67. John Strachey, patrician Communist from England, spoke at the Toronto Empire Club in January 1935, condemning the capitalist system and warning his audience to beware of "the ballyhoo of the New Dealers." See "Communist at Empire Club," *Free Press*, January 25, 1935. Note as well, for similar critiques, "Can Codes Save Capitalism? Att.-Gen. Roebuck's New Deal to Coerce Workers," *Vanguard* 2 (October 1934); "R. B. Bennett's New Deal to Dupe the Masses," *Vanguard* 2 (February 1935).

121. Croll is quoted in "Hon. David Croll Would Abolish All City Hostels. Would Place All Single Jobless in Private Homes, Minister Says," *Daily Star*, February 12, 1937.

122. "Girl Robbed of Pride Under Changed Rules of Receiving Relief," *Daily Star*, June 6, 1935. The Hepburn quotation and the discussion of married vs. single women in the civil service labour market are from Hobbs, "Gendering

Work and Welfare," 48–53; Struthers, *No Fault of Their Own*, 149–50, accents the firing of women and their replacement by males. Communists defended the rights of married and single women to work for wages. See Margaret Hobbs and Joan Sangster, eds., *The Woman Worker, 1926–1929* (St. John's, Newfoundland: Canadian Committee on Labour History, 1999); Stephen L. Endicott, *Raising the Workers' Flag: The Workers' Unity League of Canada, 1930–1936* (Toronto: University of Toronto Press, 2012), 166–69; Hobbs, "Gendering Work and Welfare," 116, 131; Anne Smith, "With Our Women," *Daily Clarion*, May 1, 1936; Jean Laing, "Authorities Turn Deaf Ear to Single Women's Needs," *The Worker*, December 19, 1935; Manley, "Starve, Be Damned," 485–86.

123. Cohen, "Women at Work in Canada during the Depression," 8–9; Christie, *Engendering the State*, esp. 222–24, 390; and for Communist discussion of domestic service in the late 1920s, there is much in Hobbs and Sangster, *The Woman Worker*.

124. Srigley, "In Case You Hadn't Noticed," 82–89. See also Hobbs, "Gendering Work and Welfare," 171–76.

125. For the above two paragraphs see "Want Welfare Committee to Study Girls' Problems," *Daily Star*, June 8, 1935; "Girl Robbed of Pride Under Changed Rules of Receiving Relief"; "City Failed to Pay Rent, Landlord Ejected Girl," *Daily Star*, June 7, 1935; "Jobless Girls Now Threaten to Take Trek," *Daily Star*, July 29, 1935; Srigley, "In Case You Hadn't Noticed," 82–87; Christie, *Engendering the State*, 240–48.

126. Thompson and Seager, *Decades of Discord*, 213; Whitton quoted in Catherine Mary Ulmer, "The Report on Unemployment and Relief in Western Canada, 1932: Charlotte Whitton, R. B. Bennett, and the Federal Response to Relief" (master's thesis, University of Victoria, 2009), 114.

127. Quotes from Thompson and Seager, *Decades of Discord*, 267–69.

128. Thompson and Seager, *Decades of Discord*, 269–70; Liversedge, *Recollections of the On to Ottawa Trek*, 58–84; Richard McCandless,

"Vancouver's 'Red Menace' of 1935: The Waterfront Situation," *BC Studies* 22 (1974): 56–63; "BC Relief Camp Strikers Blaze Trail," *Vanguard* 3 (June 1, 1935).

129. The On-to-Ottawa Trek and the Regina Riot are the subject of much commentary, from personal recollections to historical reflection. See, for instance, Liversedge, *Reflections of the On to Ottawa Trek;* Lorne Brown, *When Freedom Was Lost: The Unemployed, the Agitator, and the State* (Toronto: University of Toronto Press, 1987); Bill Waiser, *All Hell Can't Stop Us: The On-to-Ottawa Trek and the Regina Riot* (Calgary: Fifth House, 2003). For a militant, contemporary account see "Class Struggle Flares Over Dominion: Bennett Mobilizes Mounties and Military to Suppress Hunger March on Ottawa," *Vanguard* 3 (July 1, 1936); "Labor Stands Behind On-to-Ottawa Trek," *Vanguard* 3 (July 15, 1935).

130. "Unemployed Single Men Expelled From Toronto Hostels. Homeless Men Evicted To-Day Blame Politics," *Daily Star*, August 1, 1935; "440 Unemployed Found Farm Jobs Hepburn States," *Daily Star*, August 7, 1935; "Begged Meal's Price Though Already Fed," *Daily Star*, September 28, 1935; "Raise Meal Standard in the House of Industry," *Daily Star*, October 2, 1935; James Lemon, *Toronto since 1918: An Illustrated History* (Toronto: Lorimer, 2002), 59–60; Ryan George, "The Bruce Report and Social Welfare Leaderships in the Politics of Toronto's 'Slums', 1934–1939," *Histoire Sociale/Social History* 44 (Mai–May 2011): 90.

131. "Unemployed Single Men Expelled From Toronto Hostels"; "Raise Meal Standard in House of Industry"; "House of Industry Food Is Criticized," *Daily Star*, July 15, 1936; "Returned Men Exploit Selves Says J. Parnell," *Daily Star*, September 25, 1936.

132. "Returned Men Exploit Selves Says J. Parnell"; "Abolish Hostels Urged by Inmates"; "Change Hostel Conditions Endanger Inmates Lives. Determined to Get Change Jobless Leader Warns City Council 'Sowing the Wind'," *Daily Star*, February 8, 1937; "Close Hostels Urge of Pastor at Metropolitan. Put Inmates in

Boarding Houses at $5 a Week His Plan," *Daily Star*, February 11, 1937.

133. "Raise Meal Standard in House of Industry."

134. "Jobless Veterans Flay Work for Nothing Idea," *Daily Star*, July 3, 1933; "Relief Hostels Bad Say Camp Strikers," *Daily Star*, September 23, 1933.

135. "Chokes Officer in Council Hall as Fists Fly. Detective Doubled Over Desk Freed as Heron Fells Assailant, Jobless Shout Defiance. Finally Carried Out Bodily by Police, Shooed Away From City Hall," *Daily Star*, June 13, 1934; "Three Men Are Fined for City Hall Fracas," *Daily Star*, June 22, 1934.

136. "Out-of-town Trekkers Plan to Pitch Tents: Will Not Sanction Tag Day for Trekkers," *Daily Star*, July 13, 1935.

137. Struthers, *No Fault of Their Own*, 215–16.

138. *Building a Mass Unemployed Movement: For Full and Free Unemployment Insurance! Against Relief Cuts! Against Evictions! Against Forced Labor!* (Toronto: National Committee of Unemployed Councils, 1933). This unemployed program was not dissimilar to other left organizations' views on how to alleviate the crisis of joblessness. Trotskyists, for instance, put forward a four-point program in November–December 1932: 1. Immediate adequate cash relief; 2. Non-contributory unemployment insurance; 3. The six-hour working day, and the five-day week, with no reduction in pay; 4. Extension of long-term credits to the Soviet Union and the removal of the trade embargo on Soviet products. See "Unemployment Crisis Does Not Slacken," *Vanguard*, November–December 1932.

139. "Not a Hunger Marcher Going to Get Through Police Head Declares," *Daily Star*, July 16, 1935; "Truckers Carrying Ottawa Marchers May Lose Permits," *Globe*, July 15, 1935; "Marchers Continue after Scarboro Halt," *Daily Star*, July 18, 1935; "1,000 Trekkers Now Moving On Ottawa," *Globe*, July 18, 1935; "Seven City Trekkers Ill, Rest Ready to Carry On," *Daily Star*, July 20, 1935; Kealey and Whitaker, *R.C.M.P. Security Bulletins, The Depression Years, Part 2, 1935,* 408.

140. "Will Not Allow Public Appeal for Funds Here," *Daily Star*, July 13, 1935; "Trekkers

Revolutionaries If Order Defied, Says Mayor," *Daily Star*, July 15, 1935; "Eight Trekkers Fined $50, Five Others Assessed $10," *Daily Star*, July 18, 1935. Royal Canadian Mounted Police reports on the preparations for the 1935 Hunger March indicate that local authorities in Toronto did all they could to suppress the initiative. See Kealey and Whitaker, *RCMP Security Bulletins, The Depression Years, Part 2, 1935,* 285, 344, 402.

141. The above paragraphs draw on Palmer, *A Communist Life*, 28–31; "1,000 Trekkers Now Moving On Ottawa"; "Marchers Continue after Scarboro Halt"; "Seven City Trekkers Ill, Rest Ready to Carry On"; "Ottawa Mayor Ask Hepburn to Stop Trek," *Globe*, July 13, 1935; Joan Sangster, *Dreams of Equality: Women on the Canadian Left, 1920–1950* (Toronto: McClelland and Stewart, 1989), 141–42.

142. "Hatred Taught Boys as They March Says Ex-Trekkers," *Daily Star*, August 8, 1935; "Chaos, Unrest Red's Sole Aim, Says Bennett," *Globe*, August 12, 1935.

143. "Trekkers Leader Threatens Hepburn," *Daily Star*, August 26, 1935; Kealey and Whitaker, *RCMP Security Bulletins: The Depression Years, Part 2, 1935,* 471, 532–24.

144. "Board Asks Survey of House of Industry. Members Will Themselves Inspect Wellington House, Seaton House Hostels," *Daily Star*, February 17, 1937; "House of Industry Welcomes Inquiries. President of Institution Declares Complaints Unfounded—Explains 'Floor Sleepers'," *Daily Star*, February 17, 1937; "Labor Club Reports Food Is Insufficient. Protest of Conditions at House of Industry," *Daily Star*, February 20, 1937; "Hostel Conditions," *Daily Star*, February 19, 1937; "Robbins Threatens to Clear Gallery"; "Stronger Steps Forecast Makes 500 Jobless Cheer. Rogue Agreement as Leader Discusses Hostel Abolition," *Daily Star*, February 25, 1937; "Health Board Finds Hostel Doughnuts Are Delicious. Members Favorably Impressed with Visit to Wellington House. Sanitation Is OK," *Daily Star*, February 26, 1937; "Laver Asks Province for Higher Allowance to Make Up Increase," *Daily Star*, May 26, 1937;

"Jobs Available for All Single Men, Hepburn Says. Will Cut Them Off Relief June 1—Farmers Need Men," *Daily Star*, May 27, 1937; "Single Jobless Back in Wellington House. Doors of Hostel Temporarily Reopened Pending Future Civic Policy," *Daily Star*, May 29, 1937; "City Will Ask Hepburn to Continue Single Relief," *Daily Star*, June 10, 1937; Struthers, *No Fault of Their Own*, 169; "Won't Cut Single Men From Relief, Mayor Says. Will Keep Hostels Open, He Adds—Orders Report on Cost," *Daily Star*, November 24, 1937; "Hepburn Taking Easy Way Out, 'Tis Claim. Adviser Gave Premier 'False Picture' of Unemployment Pastor Says. Called 'A Bluff'," *Daily Star*, November 25, 1937; "Over 200 Sleep in City Sheds Go From School to Hostels," *Daily Star*, February 18, 1938. Ross Dowson recalled that in York Township the homeless took over Coronation Park at Keele-Eglington, burrowing into the ground and erecting makeshift lean-tos in order to secure some shelter from the elements. The police eventually drove those occupying and living in the park away and dismantled their crude quarters. See "Ross Dowson: A Short Biography."

145. The above two paragraphs draw on "Stronger Steps Forecast Makes 500 Jobless Cheer. Rogue Agreement as Leader Discusses Hostel Abolition," *Daily Star*, February 25, 1937; "370 Inmates of Hostels Declared Unfit to Work. City Shelters. 165 Men Put on the Street by Hepburn," *Daily Star*, June 5, 1937; "City Will Ask Hepburn to Continue Single Relief"; "Keep Hostel Open Agreeable to City," *Daily Star*, June 22, 1937; "Discourage Able Bodied Using Hostels in Summer. Mayor Declares That Has Been Policy of Welfare Department for Several Years—Men Sleep in Parks," *Daily Star*, May 25, 1938; "Sky Is a Roof for Many Toronto Jobless at Night. 500 Men and Two Women with 'Bo Beds 'Sleep Out', All Tell the Same Story. 'No Work and No Relief'," *Daily Star*, July 21, 1938; "483 Face Eviction Tonight Single Unemployed State. Offer to Take Over and Run Wellington House. Board to Consider," *Daily Star*, October 1, 1938; "Suggest Homeless Sleep in CNE Annex, Not Parks. If Men Stage Violent Demonstration

Who Can Blame Asks Quinn," *Daily Star*, October 4, 1938; "Declares Men in Hostels Have to Live Like Brutes. Church and Social Workers Urge Substitution of Direct Relief. Conditions Rapped," *Daily Star*, April 2, 1937; "'Let Us Run Our Own Home' Say Wellington Inmates. 500 Sleeping at Berkeley Street—Nearly On Top of One Another, 'Grave Emergency'," *Daily Star*, October 4, 1938; "Queen's Park Seeking Assistance, Mayor Ralph Day Hears," *Globe and Mail*, October 6, 1938; "Shelter for Single Men Ends Monday, When Aid of Government Stops," *Globe and Mail*, March 27, 1939; Gregory S. Kealey and Reg Whitaker, *R.C.M.P. Security Bulletins: The Depression Years, Part 5, 1938–1939* (St. John's, Newfoundland: Canadian Committee on Labour History, 1997), 317–18. See also the letter from George Harris and Harvey Murphy, "Hostel Conditions," *Daily Star*, February 19, 1937, in which they argue for changes to the hostel system by stating that "We are convinced that if citizens of Toronto really knew the conditions under which the men, for the most part established citizens of our city, are living to-day in the hostels, they would be compelled to abolish them." The letter then closed: "Our suggestion that the hostels should be abolished and that the men provided with an allowance that will enable them to live in homes should be supported by every socially minded person and organization." This was the tone of the Popular Front. In less than a year, it would translate into a substantive shift in the actual policies of the CPC organizers as they proposed to take over hostels such as Wellington House.

146. "Hostels Ruin Youth Mrs. J. Laing Asserts. Ald Quinn Would Inquire If $5 Weekly Enough for Unemployed," *Daily Star*, March 5, 1937; Advertisement, Relief Reform Association, *Daily Star*, April 1, 1937; "Declares Men in Hostels Have to Live Like Brutes."

147. "To Pay 70 P.C. for Single Jobless Cost $18,000 Last Winter, Welfare Commissioner Laver Tells Cross," *Daily Star*, October 7, 1938.

148. "Jobless Waterfront Work 'Slavery Return'—Labor. 900 single Men to Toil Two Days Weekly

for Relief. May Start Nov 1," *Daily Star*, October 28, 1938; "Pay Us or We Won't Work Single Jobless Tell City," *Daily Star*, November 2, 1938; "Police Seize Pickets' Signs Chase Single Unemployed," *Daily Star*, November 8, 1938; "Board Sticks to Work Edict," *Globe and Mail*, November 10, 1938.

149. "Jobless Work for Shelter Then City Says 'No Beds'. 'We're at Our Wits' Ends,' Says Welfare Official. Many Are Refused," *Daily Star*, December 1, 1938.

150. Sixth Annual Convention, Ontario Federation on Unemployment, "Reports, Proceedings, and Constitution: For Jobs & Security," Toronto, April 20–21, 1939, 8–9.

151. The above two paragraphs draw on "Idle Single Men Describe Vain Searching for Work. Wonder What Will Happen When Relief Ends On Tuesday," *Daily Star*, May 29, 1937; "Single Jobless Back in Wellington House. Doors of Hostel Temporarily Reopened Pending Future Civic Policy," *Daily Star*, June 7, 1937; "Won't Cut Off Single Men From Relief, Mayor Says. Will Keep Hostels Open, He Adds—Orders Report on Cost," *Daily Star*, November 24, 1937; "Hepburn Taking Easy Way Out, 'Tis Claim"; "Queen's Park Seeking Assistance, Mayor Ralph Day Hears," *Daily Star*, October 6, 1938; "Jobless Waterfront Work 'Slavery' Return—Labor"; "Pay Us or We Won't Work Single Jobless Tell City"; "Police Seize Pickets' Signs Chase Single Unemployed"; "Single to Work or Starve Hepburn Warns Toronto," *Daily Star*, November 8, 1938; "Board Sticks to Work Edict"; "Shelter for Single Men Ends Monday, When Aid of Government Stops," *Globe and Mail*, April 28, 1939.

152. "Ignoring Plight Is Pagan Domm Tells Transients," *Daily Star*, March 27, 1939; Sixth Annual Convention of the Ontario Federation of Unemployment, "Reports, Proceedings, and Constitution: For Jobs & Security"; "Queen's Park Seeking Assistance, Mayor Ralph Day Hears," *Globe and Mail*, October 6, 1938.

153. See Kealey and Whitaker, *R.C.M.P. Security Bulletins: The Depression Years, Part 5, 1938–1939*, 59, 242, 255, 268, 278, 308, 329, 240–341, 369; Manley, "Starve, Be Damned," 488; "Police

Seize Pickets' Signs Chase Single Unemployed." For a sustained discussion of the way in which the adoption of the Popular Front on the part of the CPC in 1935 ultimately curtailed the mobilization of the unemployed, see Martin Schoots-McAlpine, "Class Struggle, The Communist Party, and the Popular Front in Canada, 1935–1939" (master's thesis, Trent University, 2016). The SUWA would remain in existence in June 1940, with the RCMP reporting a meeting of five hundred addressed by Dorise Neilson. See Gregory S. Kealey and Reg Whitaker, eds., *R.C.M.P. Security Bulletins: The War Series, 1939–1941* (St. John's, Newfoundland: Canadian Committee on Labour History, 1989), 272–74.

154. Earle Birney, "Canadian Capitalism and the Strategy of the Revolutionary Movement—Thesis Adopted by the Executive Committee of the Canadian Bolshevik-Leninists for a Fourth International: National Political Perspective," May 1938, Box 155, folder 4–6, Earle Birney Collection, Thomas Fisher Rare Book Library, University of Toronto.

155. "Shelter for Single Men Ends Monday, When Aid of Government Stops"; "Closing of City Hostels Remains Official Secret," *Globe and Mail*, May 1, 1939; "Jobless Work for Shelter Then City Says 'No Beds'"; "Give Us Begging Permits or Will Starve Say Group," *Daily Star*, April 18, 1939.

156. For an excellent discussion of Toronto's blue-collar suburbs see Richard Harris, *Unplanned Suburbs: Toronto's American Tragedy, 1900 to 1950* (Baltimore: Johns Hopkins University Press, 1996), quote from 50.

157. Adapted from Harris, *Unplanned Suburbs*, 42–43.

158. "Landlords Refuse to Rent Property to 'Relief Tenants'," *Globe*, April 17, 1934; "Landlord with Axe Smashes Down Door," *Daily Star*, May 29, 1934.

159. For the iconic fictional representation of Cabbagetown and unemployment in the Great Depression see Hugh Garner, *Cabbagetown* (1950, reprinted Toronto: McGraw-Hill Ryerson, 1968).

160. The above paragraphs draw on a wide array of sources, including Dr. Herbert A. Bruce, *Report of the Lieutenant-Governor's Committee on Housing Conditions in Toronto* (Toronto: Toronto Board of Control, 1934). It was somewhat ironic that, in spite of the poor conditions in the two wards addressed by the Bruce Report, the call for industrial suburban development outside the Toronto downtown core that Bruce and his collaborators recommended had in fact already happened in the blue-collar outlying districts studied later by Richard Harris in *Unplanned Suburbs*. For comment on this Bruce Report and other similar developments elsewhere in Canada see Ryan George, "The Bruce Report and Social Welfare Leadership in the Politics of Toronto's 'Slums', 1934–1939," *Histoire Sociale/Social History* 44 (Mai–May 2011): 83–114; John Bacher, "One Unit Was Too Many: The Failure to Develop a Canadian Social Housing Policy in the Great Depression," *Journal of Canadian Studies* 22 (1987): 50–61; Bacher, *Keeping to the Market Place: The Evolution of Canadian Housing Policy* (Montreal and Kingston: McGill-Queen's University Press, 1993), 66–74. Cassidy's published statements on unemployment included: Harry M. Cassidy, "Unemployment Insurance for Canada," *Queen's Quarterly* 38 (1931): 306–34; *Unemployment and Relief in Ontario* (Toronto: J.M. Dent & Sons, 1932); and the subsequent *Social Security and Reconstruction* (Toronto: Ryerson Press, 1943). Cassidy is commented on in most of the scholarly writing on unemployment relief and social security. See, for instance, Struthers, *No Fault of Their Own;* Christie, *Engendering the State*, 236–42; Dennis Guest, *The Emergence of Social Security in Canada* (Vancouver: UBC Press, 2003), 80–87; Campbell, *Respectable Citizens*, 118, 142. A full-scale discussion of Cassidy remains unpublished: John Allan Irving, "A Canadian Fabian: The Life and Work of Harry Cassidy" (PhD diss., University of Toronto, 1983). Cassidy would move away from the CCF to become a prominent figure in the Ontario Liberal Party. On the future development of low-income housing in Toronto see Albert Rose, *Regent Park: A Study in Slum Clearance* (Toronto: University of Toronto Press, 1958); Sean Purdy, "Ripped Off by the System: Housing Policy, Poverty, and Territorial Stigmatization in Regent Park Housing Project, 1951–1991," *Labour/Le Travail* 52 (Fall 2003): 45–108; Kevin T. Brushett, "Blots on the Face of the City: The Politics of Slum Housing and Urban Renewal in Toronto, 1940–1970" (PhD diss., Queen's University, 2000). For comment on The Ward see W. E. Mann, "The Lower Ward," in Mann, ed., *The Underside of Toronto* (Toronto: McClelland and Stewart, 1970), 33–64; Stephen A. Speisman, "St. John's Shtetl: The Ward in 1911," in *Gathering Places: Peoples and Neighbourhoods of Toronto, 1834–1945*, ed. Robert F. Harney (Toronto: Multicultural History Society of Ontario, 1985), 107–20.

161. See *Report of the Lieutenant-Governor's Committee on Housing Conditions in Toronto*, 35; Daniel Hiebert, "The Social Geography of Toronto in 1931: A Study of Residential Differentiation and Social Structure," *Journal of Historical Geography* 21 (1995): 62; Lemon, *Toronto Since 1918*, 65–67; Richard Harris, "The End Justifies the Means: Boarding and Rooming in a City of Homes, 1890–1951," *Journal of Social History* 26 (1992): 342–43; Harris, *Unplanned Suburbs*, 248. For a left-wing critique of the Bruce report, suggesting that it was offering little more than "pie-in-the-sky," see "Neglect of Slums Scored by Bruce: Toronto Ignores Lieut-Governor's Year-Old Report," *Vanguard* 3 (December 17, 1935); S. Jourard, "Death Rate Soars in Slums: Government Report Shelved as Stricken Areas Fester," *Vanguard* 3 (February 1, 1936).

162. "See Lights through Cracks in Houses of the Unemployed," *Daily Star*, July 26, 1934. On Williams and the EYWA see Patricia V. Schultz, *The East York Workers Association: A Response to the Great Depression* (Toronto: New Hogtown Press, 1975), 20, 38–39; Struthers, *Limits of Affluence*, 92–97; Hunter, *Which Side Are You On Boys*, 25; Manley, "Starve, Be Damned," 481.

163. *Report of the Lieutenant-Governor's Committee on Housing Conditions in Toronto*, 115–16; Labour Gazette 34 (November 1934): 1008–10.

164. Buck, *Yours in the Struggle*, 154–55; Rick
Salutin, *Kent Rowley: The Organizer—A
Canadian Union Life* (Toronto: James Lorimer,
1980), 11; Peter Hunter, *Which Side Are You On
Boys*, 21–22; "Attempting Evictions, Bailiffs are
Balked," *Globe*, April 10, 1933; George H. Rust-
D'Eye, *Cabbagetown Remembered* (Toronto:
Stoddart, 1984), 39; Cy Gonick, *A Very Red Life:
The Story of Bill Walsh* (St. John's, Newfound-
land: Canadian Committee on Labour History,
2001), 86–87. For a discussion of resistance
to evictions in the United States see Randi
Storch, *Red Chicago: American Communism at
its Grassroots, 1928–1935* (Urbana: University of
Illinois Press, 2007), 111–15.

165. On the Trach eviction, see "Jobless Fight as
Bailiffs Evict Bed-Ridden Mother," *Daily Star*,
March 1, 1935; "Bailiffs, Police, Alleged Brutal to
Sick Woman," *Daily Star*, March 6, 1935; "Bru-
tality Charge Refuted by Police," *Globe*, March
7, 1935; "Detectives Get 8-Hour Day. Other
Changes Left in the Air," *Daily Star*, March 17,
1935. On Simpson and his 1933 charges against
Communists using evictions to embarrass him,
see Manley, "Starve, Be Damned," 476, quoting
The Worker, April 29, 1933.

166. "Evicted From Their Home They Slept in Mil-
itia Tent," *Daily Star*, June 11, 1932; "Over 100
Homeless Sheltered in Tents," *Daily Star*, June
25, 1932; "To Move Tent Colony to Warmer
Quarters," *Daily Star*, September 9, 1932;
"Tent Colony Vanishes," *Daily Star*, September
13, 1932.

167. "Seeking Legislation to Stop Evictions," *Daily
Star*, July 5, 1932; "Bailiffs Are Warned to Avoid
East York," *Daily Star*, August 3, 1932; "Bailiffs
Foiled by Unemployed," *Daily Star*, August 6,
1932; "'Outraged' Says Benefactor of Evicted
'Old Original'," *Daily Star*, August 11, 1932;
"Motorcycle Police Save Two Bailiffs," *Daily
Star*, August 11, 1932; "Workers Picket Home to
Keep Bailiff Out," *Daily Star*, January 26, 1933;
"Attempting Evictions, Bailiffs are Balked";
"Army of 2,000 Watch Bailiffs," *Daily Star*,
April 10, 1933; Campbell, *Respectable Citizens*,
126–28; Schultz, *East York Workers' Association*,
15, 33–35.

168. Manley, "Starve, Be Damned," 476–77. Schultz,
East York Workers' Association, 17–20 discusses
an East York Women's Study Group that read
Marxist works, organized a library, sold CCF
literature and the publications of the Chicago
socialist publishing house of Charles H. Kerr,
and arranged babysitting and social events.
Ross Dowson was recruited to the politics of
revolutionary Trotskyism during the 1930s,
these views consolidating out of his experiences in "the hungry thirties." He then played
a role in building and attending the Mount
Dennis Spartacus Club classes on scientific
socialism at the age of seventeen. Dowson also
recalls the formative influence of resistance to
evictions, and his participation in such protests. See "Ross Dowson: A Short Biography";
"Ross Dowson: Life's Work Was 'Labour of
Love'," *Globe and Mail*, March 18, 2002. Hunter,
Which Side Are You On Boys, 29–32, 50 discusses a Marxian Youth Group that arranged
lectures, reading lists, and social/sporting
events.

169. "Bailiffs Throw Out Two More Families," *Daily
Star*, January 20, 1933; "Bailiff and Police Sweep
Family Out," *Daily Star*, February 1, 1933.

170. "Women Oust Two Officers. Third Takes to His
Heels," *Daily Star*, June 2, 1933.

171. See Palmer, *A Communist Life*, 36; Ian Angus,
*Canadian Bolsheviks: The Early Years of the
Communist Party of Canada* (Toronto: Trafford,
2004), 76–77.

172. On the Patterson eviction, see "'Amazing,
Stupid, Cruel' Says Paterson Minister," *Daily
Star*, July 8, 1936; "Die Rather Than Fail Eviction Officer States," *Daily Star*, July 8, 1936;
"Howling Mob Battles Police as Eviction Order
Executed, Twelve Citizens Arrested," *Globe*,
July 8, 1936; Palmer, *A Communist Life*, 36–37;
Campbell, *Respectable Citizens*, 127–28, which
also has a discussion of how understandings
of British citizenship rights were utilized by
the unemployed, 174–83. More on patriot-
ism of this kind and the unemployed can be
gleaned from Manley, "Starve, Be Damned,"
480–81; Betcherman, *The Little Band*, 31–32,
96, 118–19.

173. For the plight of a Toronto woman similar in her circumstances to Mrs. Patterson, save for the existence of a prominent Communist brother, see Laura Bates to R. B. Bennett, September 3, 1933, in Grayson and Bliss, *The Wretched of Canada*, 49–50.

174. "Landlord Planning to Evict Tenant Gets Sample of His Own Medicine," *Daily Star*, July 4, 1933; "Workers' Pickets Still Guard House," *Daily Star*, July 8, 1933 and "Jobless Prevent Entry by Bailiff; Police on Hand," *Globe*, July 15, 1933; "Sale and Eviction Do Not Take Place," *Globe*, July 23, 1933.

175. Other successful thwarting of evictions and sales in July 1933, including those involving the house and belongings of a black man, Wilfred Foster, are discussed in "Jobless Prevent Entry by Bailiff; Police on Hand" and "Eviction Is Halted for Foster Family," *Daily Star*, July 20, 1933. Issues of racial and ethnic prejudice in evictions are difficult to discern in the evidence we have seen, but there is suggestion that landlords and their agents sometimes refused to rent to Jews and used evictions to enforce this discrimination. See Benson Orenstein, "Memoir of Beach Hebrew Institute in the 1930s," www.beachhebrewinstitute.ca.

176. "Jobless Prevent Entry by Bailiff; Police on Hand"; "Sale and Eviction Do Not Take Place"; "Detectives Get 8-Hour Day. Other Changes Left in the Air," *Daily Star*, March 17, 1935; "Hang Effigy of Eviction Officer," *Daily Star*, April 26, 1934; Campbell, *Respectable Citizens*, 127. Manley, "Starve, Be Damned" criticizes effigy hangings of Liberal Minister of Welfare David A. Croll as personalizing the politics of unemployment protest, but we think he is unappreciative of this expression of popular antagonism, which constitutes a long tradition.

177. "Hangings Don't Bother Sheriff, but Evictions Do, Council Told," *Daily Star*, June 18, 1936.

178. The above two paragraphs draw on "Tenants to Resist Effort of Bailiff," *Daily Star*, April 14, 1934; "Landlords Refuse to Rent Property to 'Relief Tenants'"; "Plan Housing Evicted Family in Tent at War Memorial," *Daily Star*, April 28,
1934; "Still Hold Threat Over Council Heads," *Daily Star*, April 30, 1934; "Jobless On Guard to Halt Eviction," *Daily Star*, April 26, 1934; "Hang Effigy of Eviction Officer," *Daily Star*, April 26, 1934; "Attempt to Cut Power Is Foiled," *Daily Star*, April 26, 1934; "Evicted Family Brings Bed Bugs to Council to Show Conditions," *Daily Star*, March 12, 1935; "Lakeshore Unemployed Make Two Mass Efforts to Gain Demands," *Daily Star*, March 15, 1935.

179. "Tenants to Resist Effort of Bailiff"; "200 Guard House to Stop Eviction," *Daily Star*, March 16, 1935.

180. "Evictions Feared as Fund Augmented Rent Runs Out," *Daily Star*, March 16, 1935; "List Influx From Toronto Among Eviction Causes," *Daily Star*, December 6, 1935; Campbell, *Respectable Citizens*, 126.

181. Schulz, *East York Workers' Association*, 33–35.

182. "Five Hundred Families Are Expecting Eviction," *Daily Star*, February 14, 1936; "Family Evicted Into Snow. Police Scorned for Aiding," *Daily Star*, April 2, 1936; "Says 100 Evictions Might Be Fought," *Daily Star*, April 29, 1936; "Reeve Asks Veterans' Rally to Prevent Five Evictions," *Daily Star*, June 8, 1936; "Hangings Don't Bother Sheriff, but Evictions Do, Council Told."

183. "Family Evicted into Snow. Police Scorned for Aiding."

184. "Shall Not Pass, Bailiffs Told," *Globe*, 6 June 1936; "Reeve Asks Veterans' Rally to Prevent Five Evictions"; "Evictions Situation Grave in East York Sheriff Says," *Daily Star*, June 17, 1936. They shall not pass/On ne passe pas/No pasaran was a slogan of determination to defend a position against an enemy. It was apparently first proclaimed during the First World War at the Battle of Verdun, and it would gain popular currency in the summer of 1936 (after the evictions discussed above) as the slogan of Republicans in the Spanish Civil War, where the term was used in relation to the Battle of Madrid.

185. "Jobless Won't Run Like Dog Tail between Legs, Warning," *Daily Star*, July 24, 1936.

186. "Plan Relief Strike if Tenants Evicted," *Daily Star*, July 30, 1935.

187. Stephen L. Endicott, *Bienfait: The Saskatch-ewan Miners' Struggle of 1931* (Toronto: University of Toronto Press, 2002); Endicott, *Raising the Workers' Flag: The Workers' Unity League of Canada, 1930–1936* (Toronto: University of Toronto Press, 2012); John Manley, "Canadian Communists, Revolutionary Unionism, and the 'Third Period': The Workers' Unity League, 1929–1935," *Journal of the Canadian Historical Association* 5 (1994): 167–94; McEwen, *The Forge Glows Red.*

188. Endicott, *Raising the Workers' Flag,* 200–1, presents figures on strikes drawn from a 1933 report by Charles Sims, National Secretary of the WUL, that are undoubtedly exaggerated, but that convey some sense of the organization's importance in leading strikes in this period.

189. "Will Not Accept Tickets Workless Say," *Daily Star,* July 4, 1932; "York Plant Is Barricaded. Jobless Talk Legal Ouster," *Daily Star,* July 6, 1932; "Continued to Work. President Deposed," *Daily Star,* July 7, 1932.

190. "'Go Home to Your Dishes' Woman Strike Picket Told," *Daily Star,* July 22, 1932; "All Police On Duty during York Strike," *Daily Star,* July 23, 1932; "Say Strike-Breakers Ineligible for Relief," *Daily Star,* July 25, 1932; "Extra Police Guard Workers in Strike," *Daily Star,* July 28, 1932; "Striking Unemployed Go Back to Old Jobs," *Daily Star,* July 29, 1932.

191. The above account of the development of the Lakeview relief protests and strike of May–June 1933 draws on "Huge Signs Protest Lakeview Wage-Cut," *Daily Star,* May 6, 1933; "Warns Trouble Likely If Students Are Withdrawn," *Daily Star,* June 3, 1933; "Jobless Hold Official Force Aid From Ontario," *Daily Star,* June 8, 1933; "Unemployed Express Feelings with Sticks and Stones," *Daily Star,* June 17, 1933; "Workless Men Cheer for New Relief Plan," *Daily Star,* June 22, 1933.

192. The account of the Etobicoke relief strike draws on "Children Will Quit School If Jobless Plea Unheard," *Daily Star,* October 26, 1933; "Monday Will Provide Test of Relief School Strike," *Daily Star,* October 27, 1933; "Strikers

Meet. Face Police. Force Relief Fuel Issue," *Daily Star,* October 30, 1933; "Strikers Modify Demands Avoid Dangerous Deadlock," *Daily Star,* October 31, 1933; "New Concessions Offered Etobicoke Relief Strikers," *Daily Star,* November 1, 1933; "Compromise Ends Strike of Township Unemployed," *Daily Star,* November 2, 1933. Campbell, *Respectable Citizens,* 174.

193. "Convention Refuses to Admit Communists," *Daily Star,* July 13, 1932; "We're Not Communist Is Workers' Protest," *Daily Star,* July 20, 1932; "Holds Workers' Body Is a Rudderless Ship," *Daily Star,* March 3, 1933.

194. For a general discussion of the Ontario relief camps see Laurel Sefton MacDowell, "Relief Camp Workers in Ontario during the Great Depression of the 1930s," *Canadian Historical Review* 76 (June 1995): 205–28, which mentions the Long Branch events discussed in detail below only in passing (221).

195. The above paragraphs draw on "Mobile Police for Relief Camp Strike," *Daily Star,* September 18, 1933; "Armed Police Reserve Maintain Lonely Vigil in Camp of Strikers," *Daily Star,* September 20, 1933; "Relief Hostels Bad Say Camp Strikers," *Daily Star,* September 23, 1933; "Mass Gathering Holds No Status," *Mail and Empire,* October 2, 1933.

196. "Will Restore Water to Relief Families," *Daily Star,* February 6, 1934; "Workers Expel Men Who Didn't Strike," *Daily Star,* February 8, 1934; "We Don't Want Beer and Wine, We Want Water," *Daily Star,* May 6, 1934; "May Quit All Relief Work Unless Family Given Water," *Daily Star,* May 10, 1934; "Workers to Keep On Fighting for Water," *Daily Star,* May 12, 1934; "Court Is Thronged as Workers Charged," *Daily Star,* May 16, 1934" "Magistrate Hints Conviction Likely," *Daily Star,* June 7, 1934; "Water Issue Keeping Relief Workers Idle," *Daily Star,* May 14, 1934.

197. "Inspector Is Prisoner Until Demands Are Met Says East York Crowd," *Daily Star,* October 25, 1934; "Provincial Relief Officer Released as Demands Met," *Daily Star,* October 26, 1934; "Crowd Ends Siege as Relief Demands Are Met," *Globe,* October 26, 1934; "Croll Will Ignore

'Riotous Assemblies', *Daily Star*, October 26, 1934.

198. The Long Branch events of November 1934 are detailed in "Siege Will Continue Until Croll Gives in Threat of Unemployed," *Daily Star*, November 2, 1934; "Demands Denied, Long Branch Siege Ends," *Globe*, November 3, 1934; "Cannot Allow Violence to Rule Crown Declares," *Daily Star*, November 3, 1934; "Council Turns Down Request of Workers," *Daily Star*, November 5, 1934; "Requests Denied Besiegers Depart," *Daily Star*, November 8, 1934; "Workers Demand Cases Be Dropped," *Daily Star*, November 7, 1934; "Quash Six Charges at Long Branch in Relief Siege," *Daily Star*, November 21, 1934; "Launch Charity Drive to Secure Mattresses," *Daily Star*, November 23, 1934; Campbell, *Respectable Citizens*, 157.

199. "'Lilliputian Lenins' Abated by Council, Croll Charges," *Daily Star*, April 5, 1935; "Plan Relief Strike If Tenants Evicted," *Daily Star*, July 30, 1935.

200. On the New Toronto strike/occupations see "Assert Children Starving Threaten Ghandi Campaign," *Daily Star*, March 14, 1935; "Milk and Children Basis of 'Strike'," *Globe*, March 15, 1935; "Won't Yield Say Jobless Until Demands Are Met," *Daily Star*, March 16, 1935; "Police Recapture Station Arrest Eleven Jobless," *Globe*, March 18, 1935.

201. "Call Strike in East York on Relief Work Projects," *Daily Star*, November 5, 1935; "Relief Strikers to Protest Again," *Globe*, November 6, 1935; "Will Keep 5000 Children From School Strikers Say," *Daily Star*, November 8, 1935; "East York Jobless Demands Granted," *Daily Star*, November 13, 1935." Standing by Demands Say Striking Jobless," *Daily Star*, November 21, 1935.

202. "Standing by Demands Say Striking Jobless"; "Four Men Injured in Relief Strikers' Clash with Police," *Globe*, November 23, 1935.

203. "Relief Strike Is Answered by Cancelling All Jobs," *Daily Star*, November 28, 1935; "Relief Workers Vote to Remain on Strike," *Daily Star*, November 29, 1935; "To Break East York Strike with Big Force of Police," *Daily Star*, December

5, 1935; "Neighbouring Police Give Aid in Strike," *Daily Star*, December 7, 1935; "Leader of Strike Wants More Strikes," *Daily Star*, December 7, 1935; "Plan 'United Action' by Those on Relief," *Daily Star*, December 7, 1935.

204. "Jobless Threaten Strike Unless Demands Granted," *Daily Star*, November 28, 1935; "Strikers Jeer Men On Job. Police Call Outside Help," *Daily Star*, December 2, 1935.

205. The East York–Long Branch relief strikes detailed in the above paragraphs are addressed in "Strikers Go Back to Relief Works," *Daily Star*, December 18, 1935; "Five More Arrested in East York Relief Strike," *Daily Star*, December 6, 1935; "Arrest 2 Relief Strikers as 65 Jeer Nine Workers," *Daily Star*, December 9, 1935; "Strikers May Vote to Return to Work," *Daily Star*, December 18, 1935; "Took Work to Stir Strike Laurie Tells Jobless," *Daily Star*, December 13, 1935; "'No Interference' Is Nixon's Reply to Relief Strikers," *Globe*, December 17, 1935; "Work Under Protest Is Strikers' Decision," *Daily Star*, December 21, 1935; "Relief Recipients to Work for Food," *Daily Star*, December 23, 1935; Kealey and Whitaker, *RCMP Security Bulletins: The Depression Years, Part 2, 1935*, 652. There is an account of the East York strike in Schultz, *East York Workers' Association*, 26–32.

206. "13 Arrested Following Row with Police," *Globe*, March 28, 1935; Kealey and Whitaker, *R.C.M.P. Security Bulletins: The Depression Years, Part 2, 1935*, 214.

207. "Batons Stones Bottles Used When Jobless Riot," *Daily Star*, March 28, 1935.

208. "Moscow Blamed by Police for Riot at Relief Office," *Daily Star*, March 29, 1935; "Chief Charges Conspiracy to Stir Trouble Among Idle," *Daily Star*, April 6, 1935.

209. "Batons Stones Bottles Used When Jobless Riot."

210. "Moscow Blamed by Police for Riot at Relief Office."

211. The above paragraphs draw on "Suburban Jobless March On Queen's Park," *Daily Star*, April 4, 1935; "Hepburn and Ministers to Accompany Jobless to See How They Live," *Daily Star*, April 5, 1935; Kealey and Whitaker, *RCMP Security*

Bulletins, *The Depression Years, Part 2, 1935*, 227–28.

212. "'Lilliputian Lenins' Abetted by Councils, Croll Charges."

213. This discussion of Crowland and its Toronto ramifications draws on a number of sources, both secondary and primary. The major account of the Crowland relief strike is Carmela Patrias, *Relief Strike: Immigrant Workers and the Great Depression in Crowland, Ontario, 1930–1935* (Toronto: New Hogtown Press, 1990). See also Fern A. Sayles, *Welland Workers Make History* (Welland, Ontario: Winnifred Sayles, 1963), 124–33; Saywell, *Just Call Me Mitch*, 217–18. The struggle was covered extensively in the *Daily Star* in April–May 1935. See particularly, "Rout Strikers with Tear Gas Jail for Four," *Daily Star*, April 10, 1935; "Cannot Let Children, Women Go Hungary," *Daily Star*, April 12, 1935; "Relief Strikers Fight Off Police Despite Tear Gas," *Daily Star*, April 17, 1935; "Crowland Strikers to Send 40 Little Ones to Toronto," *Daily Star*, April 23, 1935; "Strikers' Children Go Home in Government Buses," *Daily Star*, April 27, 1935; "Niagara Falls Mob Threatens Relief Head," *Daily Star*, April 27, 1935; "Relief Strikers Won't Interfere Is Promise as Work Is Re-opened," *Daily Star*, April 25, 1935; "If Bloodshed We Are Not the Only Ones, Strikers Warn," *Daily Star*, May 10, 1935; "Crowland Strike Seen Crumbling, 30 Resume Work," *Daily Star*, May 11, 1935; "Two Crowland Men Get Year in Prison," *Daily Star*, June 14, 1935.

214. "Knock Constable Senseless in Mimico Town Hall Row," *Daily Star*, April 25, 1935; "Refused Increase in Food 150 Relief Workers Strike," *Daily Star*, April 29, 1935; "More Than 3000 Expected to Stage Strike," *Daily Star*, May 4, 1935; "Hepburn Hints More Arrests in Relief Riots," *Daily Star*, July 10, 1936; "Women Plan to Protest 'Brutal Axe of Economy'," *Daily Star*, August 27, 1935; "'Mickey Mouse' Sweaters Evoke Workers' Protest," *Daily Star*, September 12, 1935.

215. "Cash Relief New Ruling Starts Jan. 1," *Daily Star*, August 29, 1935; "Hepburn Reveals True Colors Prepares to Slash Relief," *Vanguard* 3 (August 17, 1935); Saywell, *Just Call Me Mitch*, 218–20.

216. See Saywell, *Just Call Me Mitch*, 264–65; "Keep Vigil Til Tots Fed Say Women after 40 Hours," *Daily Star*, April 18, 1936.

217. "Relief Men Picket Dump Site against Food Cut," *Daily Star*, June 2, 1936. For indications of the Communist Party's intention to step up unemployed agitation see Kealey and Whitaker, *R.C.M.P. Security Bulletins: The Depression Years, Part 3, 1936*, 124–25, 143, 381, 405, 421–22. On the Trotskyist Workers Party involvement see "Unemployed Strike in Toronto's Suburb," *Vanguard* 3 (July 1936); "Relief Prisoners Committed for Jury Trial," *Vanguard* 3 (August 1935).

218. "1000 York Relief Workers Call Strike to the Finish," *Daily Star*, June 3, 1936; "Strikers Hear Suggestion for Two-Cent Meal Tax," *Daily Star*, June 5, 1936; "Single Men Denied More Relief Money," *Globe*, June 6, 1936; "Single Workless Youths Founding Summer Village," *Daily Star*, June 9, 1936; "Sympathetic Strike Will Be Discussed," *Daily Star*, June 9, 1936; "York Strikers Annoy Workers by 'Scab' List," *Daily Star*, June 9, 1936; "Pastor Back Strike of York Relief Men," *Daily Star*, June 10, 1936; Kealey and Whitaker, *R.C.M.P. Security Bulletins: The Depression Years, Part 3, 1936*, 243.

219. "Will Advise Strike for Relief Increase," *Daily Star*, June 13, 1936; "500 Join Relief Strikes, Seven Municipalities Involved," *Daily Star*, June 30, 1936; "Croll Declines to Accept 25 Percent Relief Cut," *Daily Star*, June 30, 1936; Kealey and Whitaker, *R.C.M.P. Security Bulletins: The Depression Years, Part 3, 1936*, 287.

220. "Women to 'Storm Relief Office' Today," *Daily Star*, June 24, 1936; "Reeve Made Truce with York Women," *Daily Star*, June 25, 1936; "Lakeshore Jobless Strike Women Held Relief Office," *Daily Star*, July 2, 1936.

221. "Lakeshore Jobless Strike Women Held Relief Office"; "Says Children of Jobless Go to Picnics to Beg Food," *Daily Star*, July 4, 1936; Campbell, *Respectable Citizens*. 157.

222. "Hope They Get Action, We Can't, Strikers Hear," *Daily Star*, July 3, 1936.

223. "Police Stoned. Women Hurt Them. Relief Cut Restored," *Daily Star*, July 7, 1936; "2 Officers are Injured by Jobless," *Globe*, July 7, 1936; Kealey and Whitaker, *RCMP Security Bulletins: The Depression Years, Part 3, 1936*, 290–91; Hepburn, *Just Call Me Mitch*, 265–66.

224. "Reeve and Relief Officer Are Freed by Compromise," *Daily Star*, July 9, 1936; Kealey and Whitaker, *RCMP Security Bulletins: The Depression Years, Part 3, 1936*, 290–91; Hepburn, *Just Call Me Mitch*, 266.

225. "To Apprehend Those Guilty of 'Overt Act'," *Globe*, July 10, 1936; "Hepburn Hints More Arrests in Relief Riots," *Daily Star*, July 10, 1936; "Police Round Up 17 More on Hepburn's Instructions," *Daily Star*, July 11, 1936; Saywell, *Just Call Me Mitch*, 266–67.

226. "Communists Plotted Riot Cabinet Is Told," *Daily Star*, July 10, 1936; Saywell, *Just Call Me Mitch*, 266–67. On two Trotskyists arrested— Comrades Smith and Butterworth—and the subsequent attempt to mobilize a defence campaign, see "Relief Prisoners Committed for Jury Trial," *Vanguard* 3 (August 1936).

227. "Provincial Police Rescue Officials," *Daily Star*, October 7, 1936.

228. On the election of Communists in the Toronto area in this period, which included successful candidates in York, Long Branch, and Wards 4, 5, and 6 see Hunter, *Which Side Are You On Boys*, 25. Also note "Provincial Police Rescue Officials," *Daily Star*, October 7, 1936; "Charges against 29 Are Finally Dropped," *Daily Star*, December 15, 1936; Manley, "Starve, Be Damned," 476; MacDowell, *Renegade Lawyer*, 55–56; Saywell, *Just Call Me Mitch*, 266–67.

229. Saywell, *Just Call Me Mitch*, 264–65, 378–79.

230. Schulz, *East York Workers' Association*, 38–41.

231. "Relief Offense Was Political Roebuck Holds," *Daily Star*, May 16, 1938.

232. "Recipients Refuse to Work as Relief Allowances Cut," *Daily Star*, April 21, 1938; "Maguire Refuses to Join Deputation of Unemployed," *Daily Star*, April 23, 1938; "Got $7.10 Week to Feed Eight Reliefee Says," *Daily Star*, June 10, 1938; "Accused Driver Who Aided Relief Strikers on Trek," *Daily Star*, April 30, 1938;

"Hepburn's Arrest Order Spectacular Insult— Rowe," *Toronto Daily Strike*, April 30, 1938; "No Mother Will Stand By and See Children Hungry," *Daily Star*, June 11, 1938.

233. "Maguire Refuses to Join Deputation of Unemployed."

234. "3 Police Autos Rescue Official From 4 Women," *Daily Star*, April 27, 1938; "No Mother Will Stand By and See Children Go Hungry"; "Mothers, Babes, Sleep by Road in Relief Fight," *Daily Star*, April 28, 1938.

235. "Accused Driver Who Aided Relief Strikers on Trek"; "4 Arrests Ends Relief Strikers' Hearing," *Globe*, April 30, 1938. For a conceptual discussion of "weapons of the weak" see James C. Scott, *Weapons of the Weak: Everyday Forms of Peasant Resistance* (New Haven: Yale University Press, 1985); and Scott, *Domination and the Arts of Resistance: Hidden Transcripts* (New Haven: Yale University Press, 1990).

236. "4 Arrests Ends Relief Strikers' Hearing"; "Accused Driver Who Aided Relief Strikers on Trek"; "Hepburn's Arrest Order Spectacular Insult—Rowe."

237. "Accused Driver Who Aided Relief Strikers on Trek"; "Hepburn's Arrest Order Spectacular Insult—Rowe"; "Padlock Law Is Cited as Menace to Liberty. Fear for Democracy," *Daily Star*, June 4, 1938; "'No Work, No Food' Is Ruling of Reeve in Lakeview Row," *Daily Star*, May 3, 1938. Hepburn opposed the organization of the automobile workers in Oshawa and demanded of all Cabinet Ministers that they support the government's resistance to "John L. Lewis and communism, which are now marching hand in hand." He wanted the federal government to send the RCMP into Oshawa to crush workers' initiatives, and when Ottawa declined to do so, Hepburn organized his own constabulary, known as "Hepburn's Hussars" or "Sons of Mitches." The Lewis-led Congress of Industrial Organizations (CIO) sustained the United Automobile Workers organizational drive in Oshawa, and both Roebuck and Croll, while declaring their opposition to Communism, insisted on workers' rights to organize, defended the CIO as a legitimate

organizational centre of industrial unionism, and denied any formal alliance between Lewis and the Communist Party. Croll, whose ties were to organized labour in Windsor, declared in a letter to Hepburn that, given the Liberal Premier's extremism, his place was "marching with the workers rather than riding with General Motors." Hepburn thus forced Croll's and Roebuck's resignations, although, as we have seen above, Roebuck had for some time been reluctant to pursue Hepburn's course. Roebuck's response to Hepburn was less rhetorical than Croll's and exhibited a standoffish coolness. He wrote of his opposition to "massing force prior to the absolute necessity arising" and replied to his dismissal coyly, if curtly: "this relief from responsibility is received with equanimity." See Saywell, *Just Call Me Mitch,* 314–19; Thompson and Seager, *Decades of Discord,* 288–90; Eric A. Havelock, "Forty-Five Years Ago: The Oshawa Strike," *Labour/Le Travailleur* 11 (Spring 1983): 119–24; Irving M. Abella, "Oshawa, 1937," in *On Strike: Six Key Labour Struggles in Canada, 1919–1949,* ed. Irving Abella (Toronto: James Lorimer, 1975), 93–128.

238. "Recipients Refuse to Work as Relief Allowance Cut"; "No Mother Will Stand By and See Children Hungry"; "Hepburn's Arrest Order Spectacular Insult—Rowe"; "'No Work, No Food' Is Ruling of Reeve in Lakeview Row."

239. "Relief Report Is Introduced in Strike Trial," *Daily Star,* June 9, 1938; "Roebuck and Common Clash When Striker Held for Trial," *Globe,* May 12, 1938; "Lakeview Men Sent to Trial at Brampton," *Globe,* May 17, 1938; "Scene in Hepburn's Office Barred at Trial," *Daily Star,* June 10, 1938; "Hepburn's Arrest Order Spectacular Insult—Rowe"; "Got $7.10 Week to Feed Eight Reliefee Says"; "No Mother Will Stand By and See Children Hungry"; "Relief Offence Was 'Political' Roebuck Holds," *Daily Star,* May 16, 1938.

240. On these proceedings see "Judge Dismisses Assault Charge at Relief Trial," *Daily Star,* June 11, 1938; "Verdict Given against Seven Lakeview Folk," *Globe,* June 13, 1938; "Lakeshore Strikers

Guilty—Remanded," *Daily Star,* June 13, 1938; "Judge Concurs When Leniency Recommended," *Daily Star,* June 18, 1938; "Lakeview Relief Strikers Rejoice Over Court Ruling," *Globe,* January 17, 1939; "Four Are Dismissed on Hepburn Charges," *Daily Star,* July 4, 1938.

241. Struthers, *No Fault of Their Own,* 215, 218.

242. Struthers, *Limits of Affluence,* 107–8.

243. Struthers, *Limits of Affluence,* 107.

244. "Refuse Plea of Reliefees after Parade," *Globe,* April 25, 1939; "York Relief Scale Is Cut after Grant Drop Threat," *Daily Star,* April 3, 1939; "Work Depots Are Picketed as Relief Strike Continues," *Daily Star,* April 5, 1939; "'Stop Hepburn' Drive Urged by Reliefee, Protests Cuts," *Daily Star,* April 4, 1939.

245. "York Jobless Plan Protest of Relief Office," *Globe,* April 5, 1939; "Scarboro Reliefees Vote to Strike on Grant Cuts," *Daily Star,* April 6, 1939; "Insists Reliefees Must Do Some Work," *Daily Star,* April 8, 1939; "Jobless Army Plan Protest Walk April 19," *Globe,* April 7, 1939; "Scarboro Relief Cut on Government Orders," *Globe,* March 30, 1939; "Ballot Boxes Seized, Jobless Vote Blocked," *Globe,* March 17, 1939; "Most Strikers Defy No-Work-No-Relief," *Daily Star,* April 26, 1939; "Will Prosecute Strikers Collecting Relief Cards," *Daily Star,* April 18, 1939; "Wait in Vain for Vouchers," *Globe,* May 2, 1939.

246. Stapleton and LaFramboise, "The Campbell Report," 9, 12.

247. "Need Women to Help Frame Relief Scale, Says Reeve," *Daily Star,* April 8, 1939; "East York Riots May Follow Relief Cut," *Globe,* April 8, 1939; "May Restore Relief Cuts From Township Treasury," *Daily Star,* April 12, 1939; "No Work Means No Relief Says Queen's Park Dictum," *Daily Star,* April 15, 1939; "'Trouble' Seen in 'Strike' If Reliefees Go to Work," *Daily Star,* April 18, 1939; "'Waste Basket' Motion Is Passed for Strikers," *Globe,* April 19, 1939.

248. "Relief Strike Cost $350 Per Week," *Daily Star,* April 21, 1939; "Threatened Relief Strike to Protest New System," *Daily Star,* April 24, 1935; Kealey and Whitaker, *R.C.M.P. Security Bulletins: The Depression Years, Part 4, 1937,* 475.

249. "Reliefees Picketing Mayor Waites' Home,"
Daily Star, April 20, 1939; "Thwart Strikers'
Attempt to Picket Home of Mayor," *Globe*,
April 20, 1939; "Cut Strikers From Relief
Council Blames Agitators," *Daily Star*, April
24, 1939; "Would Go to Jail to Get Food for
Wife, Seven Children," *Daily Star*, May 13,
1939; "Council Refuses to Lift Relief Strikers'
Penalty," *Daily Star*, May 5, 1939; "Strikers Stay
on Relief Mimico's Council Decide," *Daily Star*,
April 29, 1939.

250. "Relief Cuts Must Stand," *Daily Star*, April 25,
1939; "Refuse Plea of Reliefees after Parade."

251. "Mother Promises to Steal If Denied Relief,"
Daily Star, April 28, 1939; "Relief Riots Feared If
Vouchers Refused," *Daily Star*, May 2, 1939.

252. "Strikers Stay on Relief Mimico's Council
Decides"; "Relief Riots Feared If Vouchers
Refused"; "Seizing Office Said Averted by
Leaders," *Daily Star*, May 2, 1939; "Must Work,
York Decides," *Globe*, May 4, 1939; "Families
Face Starvation Relief Strike Called Off," *Daily
Star*, May 5, 1939; "Wait in Vain for Vouchers";
"Would Go to Jail to Get Food for Wife, Seven
Children"; "Council Refuses to Lift Relief Strik-
ers' Penalty."

253. As indicated in Sixth Annual Convention,
Ontario Federation on Unemployment,
"Reports, Proceedings, and Constitution: For
Jobs & Security," Toronto, 20–21 April 1939,
esp. 7–8, which placed the critical accent on
assigning to the Ontario Hepburn government
the bulk of the blame for inadequate relief
provisioning and holding back the development of social policy on a national scale, while
sidling up to the Mackenzie King-led Liberal
federal leadership of the country. "The point
of departure of Hepburn from the liberal fold
and from liberal policies into the circles and
councils of the financial overlords came with
the struggle of the steel and auto workers
under the banner of the CIO. It was then plain
to be seen that Hepburn was out to protect the
privileges of the few against the interests of the
many. Because the King government did not
subscribe willy nilly to the policy of Hepburn
the break came and today progress is being

obstructed and essential necessities being
denied the people."

PART IV

1. For a classic statement on the welfare state's
regulation of the poor see Frances Fox Piven
and Richard A. Cloward, *Regulating the Poor:
The Functions of Public Welfare* (New York: Pantheon, 1971).

2. For outlines of progressive thinking on postwar
reconstruction and social security see Leonard
Marsh, *Report on Social Security for Canada*
(1943, reprinted Toronto: University of Toronto
Press, 1975); Harry M. Cassidy, *Social Secur-
ity and Reconstruction in Canada* (Toronto:
Ryerson Press, 1943); Cassidy, *Public Health and
Welfare Reorganization: The Postwar Problem
in the Canadian Provinces* (Toronto: Ryerson
Press, 1945).

3. Bryan D. Palmer, *Working-Class Experience:
Rethinking the History of Canadian Labour,.
1800–1991* (Toronto: McClelland and Stewart,
1992), 276; James Struthers, *The Limits of Affluence: Welfare in Ontario, 1920–1970* (Toronto:
University of Toronto Press, 1994), 4–5, 190–91;
R. Marvyn Novick, "Social Policy: The Search
for a Provincial Framework," in *The Government and Politics of Ontario*, ed. Donald C.
MacDonald (Toronto: Van Nostrand Reinhold,
1980), 382.

4. Social Planning Council of Metro Toronto,
"Social Allowances in Ontario: An Historical Analysis of General Welfare Assistance
and Family Benefits (with special focus on
adequacy of allowances), 1961–1976" (July
1977), 75. For a useful discussion of women,
children, and poverty in this period see Wendy
McKeen, *Money in their Own Name: The
Feminist Voice in Poverty Debate in Canada,
1970–1995* (Toronto: University of Toronto
Press, 2004).

5. K. J. Rea, *The Prosperous Years: The Economic
History of Ontario, 1939–1975* (Toronto: University of Toronto Press, 1985), 3–4.

6. Alvin Finkel, "Origins of the Welfare State
in Canada," in *The Canadian State: Political
Economy and Political Power*, ed. Leo Panitch

(Toronto: University of Toronto Press, 1977), 362; Doug Owram, *The Government Genera-tion: Canadian Intellectuals and the State, 1900–1945* (Toronto: University of Toronto Press, 1986).

7. Cassidy, *Social Security and Reconstruction*, 5–6.

8. John Kenneth Galbraith, "How Keynes Came to America," in *Essays on John Maynard Keynes*, ed. Milo Keynes (Cambridge, UK: Cambridge University Press, 1975), 137; Scott, quoted in Robert Bothwell, Ian Drummond, and John English, *Canada Since 1945: Power, Politics, and Provincialism* (Toronto: University of Toronto Press, 1989), 55.

9. One expression of this was the break-up of the 1946 Conference on Reconstruction, which saw Ontario's provincial government, more wedded to fiscal conservatism than Ottawa's federal government, refuse to concede the taxing authority necessary to fund a national program of social security. Fiscal centralization trauma-tized Ontario's Conservative government in the immediate postwar period, while the cen-tralization of a social security apparatus con-trolled by Ottawa was something it was willing to concede. A fully effective welfare state was thus always constrained by provincial-federal differences. See Marc Gotlieb, "George Drew and the Dominion-Provincial Conference on Reconstruction of 1945–46," *Canadian Histor-ical Review* 66 (March 1985): 27–47.

10. See, among many possible discussions, David A. Wolfe, "The Rise and Demise of the Keynes-ian Era in Canada: Economic Policy, 1930–1982," in *Modern Canada, 1930–1980s: Readings in Canadian Social History*, vol. 5, ed. Michael S. Cross and Gregory S. Kealey (Toronto: McClelland and Stewart, 1984), 46–78; Robert Campbell, *The Politics of the Keynesian Experi-ence in Canada, 1945–1975* (Peterborough: Broadview, 1987). For quotes on the 1943–45 period see Palmer, *Working-Class Experience*, 276; Jack Granatstein, *Canada's War: The Politics of the Mackenzie King Government, 1939–1945* (Toronto: University of Toronto Press, 1975), 276–78; Cassidy, *Social Security*

and Reconstruction in Canada*, 3; Marsh, *Report on Social Security for Canada*, 273–74.

11. Wayne Roberts and John Bullen, "Heritage of Hope and Struggle: Workers, Unions, and Politics in Canada, 1930–1982," in Cross and Kealey, *Modern Canada*, 112.

12. Struthers, *Limits of Affluence*, 115, 111, 150; with national unemployment rates in Wolfe, "The Rise and Demise of the Keynesian Era in Canada," 50–51; and regional rates calcu-lated from a table presented in Rea, *Prosper-ous Years*, 34, where the comment on mass unemployment is on 241.

13. The above paragraphs draw on Cassidy, *Public Health and Welfare Reorganization*, 347; Struth-ers, *Limits of Affluence*, 108–16.

14. Struthers, *Limits of Affluence*, 108–16.

15. Struthers, *Limits of Affluence*, 100–23; Margaret Jane Hillyard Little, *"No Car, No Radio, No Liquor Permit": The Moral Regulation of Single Mothers in Ontario, 1920–1997* (Toronto: Oxford University Press, 1998), 109–17.

16. Struthers, *Limits of Affluence*, 129–38.

17. Jacqueline Gale Wills, "Efficiency, Feminism, and Cooperative Democracy: Origins of the Toronto Social Planning Council, 1918–1957" (PhD diss., University of Toronto, 1989), 231, quoted in Struthers, *Limits of Affluence*, 141. For a broad discussion of the Community Chest and its role in fundraising, private charity, and the development of the welfare state see Shirley Tillotson, *Contributing Citizens: Modern Charitable Fundraising and the Making of the Welfare State, 1920–1966* (Vancouver: UBC Press, 2008).

18. "Seaton House. Addition to House of Industry Mooted," *Globe,* December 2, 1941; Cary Fagan, *The Fred Victor Mission Story: From Charity to Social Justice* (Winfield, BC: Wood Lake Books, 1993), 83–92; John Bacher, *Keeping to the Marketplace: The Evolution of Canadian Housing Policy* (Montreal and Kingston: McGill-Queen's University Press, 1993), 174–75; Richard Harris and Tricia Shulist, "Canada's Reluctant Housing Program: The Veterans' Land Act, 1942–1975," *Canadian Historical Review* 82 (June 2001): 252–83; Jill Wade,

Houses for All: The Struggle for Social Housing in Vancouver, 1919–1950 (Vancouver: UBC Press, 1994); Marc Choko, *Crises de logement à Montréal* (Montréal: Editions cooperatives albert Saint-Martin, 1980); "Keep Out of Toronto House-Hunters Told," *Toronto Daily Star*, August 29, 1947; Kevin Brushett, "'Blots on the Face of the City': The Politics of Slum Housing and Urban Renewal in Toronto, 1940–1970" (PhD diss., Queen's University, 2001), 51; Sean Purdy, "'Ripped Off' by the System: Housing Policy, Poverty, and Territorial Stigmatization in Regent Park Housing Project, 1951–1991," *Labour/Le Travail* 52 (Fall 2003): 45–108; Albert Rose, *Regent Park: A Study in Slum Clearance* (Toronto: University of Toronto Press, 1958); Humphrey Carver, *Houses for Canadians: A Study of Housing Problems in the Toronto Area* (Toronto: University of Toronto Press, 1948).

19. The above paragraphs draw on Struthers, *Limits of Affluence*, 142–49, 192–93, and for a general statement on private charity and the welfare state, Tillotson, *Contributing Citizens*. A local study of community welfare accents the combination of public services and private charity that provided social security in the 1950s. See D. V. Donnison, *Welfare Services in a Canadian Community: A Study of Brockville, Ontario* (Toronto: University of Toronto Press, 1958).

20. James Struthers, *No Fault of Their Own: Unemployment and the Canadian Welfare State, 1914–1941* (Toronto: University of Toronto Press, 1983), 202; Ann Porter, *Gendered States: Women, Unemployment Insurance, and the Political Economy of the Welfare State in Canada, 1945–1997* (Toronto: University of Toronto Press, 2003), 42–43; Robert Bothwell, Ian Drummond, and John English, *Canada Since 1945: Power, Politics, Provincialism* (Toronto: University of Toronto Press, 1989), 199; F. H. Leacy, ed., *Historical Statistics of Canada*, 2nd ed. (Ottawa: Statistics Canada, 1983), E166–71.

21. The above paragraphs rely on accounts in a number of treatments of the period. See Struthers, *Limits of Affluence*, 150–81, esp. 169–70; Little, *No Car, No Radio, No Liquor Permit*, 107–38. Note also Tillotson, *Contributing*

Citizens, 177–78; Franca Iacovetta, *Gatekeepers: Reshaping Immigrant Lives in Cold War Canada* (Toronto: Between the Lines, 2006).

22. For the gendered limitations of the Unemployment Insurance regime, see Ann Porter, *Gendered States*. Donnison's study of welfare in Brockville, Ontario, while ordered by liberal premises, captures something of the limitations of the welfare state, even as it is envisioned from a generous and progressive viewpoint: "No one starves but some fare little better. When work is scarce in winter and early spring, the uninsured and those who have exhausted their rights to unemployment benefit have nowhere to turn. The sick, the elderly, and the infirm draw cash allowances, but they may be as sorely in need of companionship, encouragement, and practical help in their homes. The municipal Welfare Department, the courts and the Health Unit find that poverty, delinquency, and ill health are often related to personal maladjustment and family breakdown, but they do not have the resources or the trained workers needed to help people deal with such problems." Donnison, *Welfare Services in a Canadian Community*, 161.

23. Dan Azoulay, "'A Desperate Holding Action': The Survival of the Ontario CCF/NDP," *Ontario History* 85 (March 1993): 19, quoted in Struthers, *Limits of Affluence*, 141.

24. As brief introductions only, see Cy Gonick, Paul Phillips, and Jesse Vorst, eds., *Labour Gains, Labour Pains: 50 Years of PC 1003* (Winnipeg: Fernwood, 1995); Roberts and Bullen, "A Heritage of Hope and Struggle," 112–23; Palmer, *Working-Class Experience*, 278–90; Peter S. McInnis, *Harnessing Labour Confrontation: Shaping the Postwar Settlement in Canada, 1943–1950* (Toronto: University of Toronto Press, 2002); Stuart Marshall Jamieson, *Times of Trouble: Labour Unrest and Industrial Conflict in Canada, 1900–1966* (Ottawa: Information Canada, 1972), 214–343.

25. Magda Fahrni, *Household Politics: Montreal Families and Postwar Reconstruction* (Toronto: University of Toronto Press, 2005), 128–34; Wade, *Houses for All*, 140–46; Jill Wade, "'A

Palace for the Public': Housing Reform and the 1946 Occupation of the Old Hotel Vancouver," *BC Studies* 25 (March 1997): 19–29; Roberts and Bullen, "A Heritage of Hope and Struggle," 120.

26. Roberts and Bullen, "A Heritage of Hope and Struggle," 120.

27. Ernest Tate, *Revolutionary Activism in the 1950s and 1950s: A Memoir*, vol. 1, *Canada, 1955–1965* (London: Resistance Books, 2014), 41; "23,777 Vote for R. W. P. Candidate: Dowson Makes Big Gains as LPP and CCF Drop," and "Radio Speech Heard by Toronto Workers," *Labor Challenge* (January 1949), 1, 3.

28. David Alexander Thompson, "Direct Action, Subsidiarity and the Counterhegemonic: Three Case Studies of Antipoverty Activism in Twentieth Century Canada" (master's thesis, University of Victoria, 2006), 59–88.

29. See, for instance, Little, *No Car, No Radio, No Liquor Permit*, 146; and Margaret Hillyard Little, "Militant Mothers Fight Poverty: The Just Society Movement, 1968–1971," *Labour/Le Travail* 59 (Spring 2007): 183–84.

30. Henry Mayhew, *London Labour and the London Poor: The London Street Folk*, vol. 1 (New York: Dover, 1968), 20.

31. Bothwell, Drummond, and English, *Canada Since 1945*, 199; R. M. Fowler, *Unemployment in Canada* (Montreal: Canadian Pulp and Paper Association, 1960), 3.

32. The above paragraphs draw on Bob Russell, "Social Wages in a Period of Economic Crisis," in *Working People and Hard Times: Canadian Perspectives*, ed. Robert Argue, Charlene Gannagé, and D. W. Livingstone (Toronto: Garamond, 1987), 116; Bothwell, Drummond, and English, *Canada Since 1945*, 199; and the excellent discussion of "work for relief" in this period, from which we quote liberally, in Struthers, *Limits of Affluence*, 182–91.

33. The history of these 1950s and 1960s protests of the jobless, at national, provincial, and local levels, remains to be written. We have gained insight into these episodic movements, concentrated around 1952–54 and 1960–61, through looking at the massive photographic collection, Toronto *Telegram*

fonds, "Unemployment," File 1974-001, 491-3230, Clara Thomas Archives and Special Collections, York University, Toronto (Hereafter Thomas Archives). Some of the quotes in the above paragraphs appear as part of newspaper descriptions taped to the back of loose photographs of unemployed activities. See also Bryan D. Palmer, *Canada's 1960s: The Ironies of Identity in a Rebellious Era* (Toronto: University of Toronto Press, 2009), 32–43, 217; and for background on the economic and social context, Bothwell, Drummond, and English, *Canada Since 1945*, 169–70, 198–210; Struthers, *Limits of Affluence*, 142–210; Walter Stewart, *The Charity Game: Greed, Waste and Fraud in Canada's $86-Billion-a-Year Compassion Industry* (Toronto: Douglas and McIntyre, 1996, 62–63.

34. Struthers, *Limits of Affluence*, 142–210; Porter, *Gendered States*; Christie, *Engendering the State*, 249–309; Little, *No Car, No Radio, No Liquor Permit*, 107–38.

35. In the Toronto *Telegram* fonds, Thomas Archives, File 3230, there is a photograph from February 7, 1961, with women holding signs such as "Women to Work" (reproduced in text above), but such a representation is a rarity. On the forces pressuring conservatism within the mainstream labour leadership see Palmer, *Working-Class Experience*, 290–305, 333–39. The defeat of Communists within the Cold War in the unions contributed mightily to this end. For the major statement on this history, albeit one that does not question rigorously the costs of "cleansing" the Communists, see Irving Martin Abella, *Nationalism, Communism, and Canadian Labour: The CIO, the Communist Party, and the Canadian Congress of Labour, 1935–1956* (Toronto: University of Toronto Press, 1973). Thompson, "Direct Action," 59–88 contains a suggestive discussion of a conservative Canadian Congress of Labour (CCL) initiative to organize the unemployed in the downturns of the 1950s, steering the jobless away from the leadership of left-led forces. Thompson sees the actions of CCL President A. R. Mosher as motivated by

a conscious recognition of mainstream trade union officials to provide a direct counter to Communists organizing among the out-of-work. One measure of the labour leadership's growing conservatism was the vehemence with which it was attacked by militant workers in a 1965–66 "wildcat strike" wave. See Palmer, *Canada's 1960s*, 211–41; Peter McInnis, "'Hothead Troubles': Sixties-Era Wildcat Strikes in Canada," in *Debating Dissent: Canada and the Sixties*, ed. Lara Campbell, Dominique Clément, and Gregory S. Kealey (Toronto: University of Toronto Press, 2012), 155–70.

36. See as an introduction Jenny R. Podoluk, "Low Income and Poverty," in *Poverty in Canada*, ed. John Harp and John R. Hofley (Scarborough: Prentice-Hall, 1971), 119–35. Discussion of inequality was commonplace in this era because of the wide reading and generous reception accorded a major 1965 study, John Porter, *The Vertical Mosaic: An Analysis of Social Class and Power in Canada* (Toronto: University of Toronto Press, 1965).

37. Struthers, *Limits of Affluence*, 211–18.

38. Struthers, *Limits of Affluence*, 211–60; Little, *No Car, No Radio, No Liquor Permit*, 139–63.

39. David A. Croll et al., *Poverty in Canada: Report of the Special Senate Committee on Poverty* (Ottawa: Information Canada, 1971), esp. vii–xiii. See as well the comments on the Croll Report and other studies in Rea, *Prosperous Years*, 132, 248.

40. Comment on Trudeau's conception of the Just Society runs through John English, *Just Watch Me: The Life of Pierre Elliott Trudeau, 1968–2000* (Toronto: Knopf Canada, 2009); Struthers, *Limits of Affluence*, 248.

41. On the United Citizens see Struthers, *Limits of Affluence*, 247, 376. For background on 1930s unemployed activism in Peterborough and on the UE, a site of contentious conflicts between Communist Party and Co-operative Commonwealth Federation supporters in the Cold War climate reaching from the late 1940s into the 1960s, see Joan Sangster, *Earning Respect: The Lives of Working Women in Small-Town Ontario, 1920–1960* (Toronto: University

of Toronto Press, 1995), 126–27; Doug Smith, *Cold Warrior: C. S. Jackson and the United Electrical Workers* (St. John's, Newfoundland: Canadian Committee on Labour History, 1997). On corporate welfare bums see David Lewis, *Louder Voices: The Corporate Welfare Bums* (Toronto: James, Lewis and Samuel, 1972), and on Peters and the UC in the 1990s, Legislative Assembly of Ontario, Committee Transcripts, 1996, August 29, United Citizens Organization, www.ontla.on.ca. For the ongoing relevance of the term "corporate welfare bums," see Stewart, *Charity Game*, 69–75.

42. On the Kingston Community Project see Palmer, *Canada's 1960s*, 26–64; Cyril Levitt, *Children of Privilege: Student Revolt in the Sixties—A Study of Student Movements in Canada, the United States, and West Germany* (Toronto: University of Toronto Press, 1984), 162–64; Myrna Kostash, *Long Way from Home: The Story of the Sixties Generation in Canada* (Toronto: Lorimer, 1980), 17–20; Richard Harris, *Democracy in Kingston: A Social Movement in Urban Politics, 1965–1970* (Montreal and Kingston: McGill-Queen's University Press, 1988); Peggy Morton, "Kingston Community Project," *SUPA Newsletter* 1, no. 4, June 23, 1965.

43. Margaret Daly, *The Revolution Game: The Short, Unhappy Life of the Company of Young Canadians* (Toronto: New Press, 1970); Ian Hamilton, *The Children's Crusade: The Story of the Company of Young Canadians* (Toronto: Peter Martin, 1970); John Loxley, "A Political Economy of Citizen Participation," in Panitch, *The Canadian State*, 446–72; Kevin Brushett, "Making Shit Disturbers: The Selection and Training of the Company of Young Canadian Volunteers, 1965–1970," in *The Sixties in Canada: A Turbulent and Creative Decade*, ed. M. Athena Palaeologu (Montreal: Black Rose, 2009), 246–69; Dal Brodhead, Stewart Goodings, and Mary Brodhead, "The Company of Young Canadians," in *Community Organizing: Canadian Experiences*, ed. Brian Wharf and Michael Clague (Toronto: Oxford University Press, 1997), 113–36.

44. See Keith Whitney, "Skid Row," in *The Underside of Toronto*, ed. W. E. Mann (Toronto: McClelland

and Stewart, 1970), 65–74; Rose, *Regent Park*, 101–2, 181–86; City of Toronto Planning Board, Research and Overall Planning Division, "Report on Skid Row," A Report Presented to the Committee on Neighbourhoods, Housing, Fire, and Legislation, November 7, 1977, 6; John Sewell, *The Shape of the City: Toronto Struggles with Modern Planning* (Toronto: University of Toronto Press, 1993), 105–6, 150–63; Graham Fraser, *Fighting Back: Urban Renewal in Trefann Court* (Toronto: Hakkert, 1972); Social Planning Council of Metropolitan Toronto, "The Don District Study: A Study of the Impact of Urban Redevelopment Planning and Activities Upon the Residents and Organization of the Don Planning District of the City of Toronto," March 1970; James Lorimer and Myfanway Phillips, *Working People: Life in a Downtown City Neighbourhood* (Toronto: James, Lewis and Samuel, 1971). The working poor of this period are discussed extensively in Canada Council on Social Development, *Income Supplements for the Working Poor: Proceedings of a Conference on Income Supplementation, 8–9 April 1974, Toronto* (Ottawa: Canada Council on Social Development, 1974). For a sense of the differences that divided New Leftists and community activists see Marjaleena Repo, "Organizing the Poor— Against the Working Class," *Transformation* 1 (March–April 1971).

45. Alice Sparberg Alexiou, *Jane Jacobs: Urban Visionary* (Toronto: Harper Collins, 2006), 164–65; Opportunities for Youth, "Free Bleecker Street—1974," vimeo.com/100057091.

46. On the JSM see Howard Buchbinder, "The Just Society Movement," in *Community Work in Canada*, ed. Brian Wharf (Toronto: McClelland and Stewart, 1979), 129–52, esp. 134, 136, 139–40; Struthers, *Limits of Affluence*, 247, 249; Little, *No Car, No Radio, No Liquor Permit*, 147–49; Little, "Militant Mothers," 179–97; "Just Society Movement: Toronto's Poor Organize," *Canadian Dimension* 7 (June–July 1970): 19–22; Howard Buchbinder, "Guaranteed Annual Income: The Answer to Poverty for All but the Poor," *Canadian Dimension* 7 (October–November 1970): 27–32. On the JSM and feminism

see Wendy McKeen, *Money in their Own Name: The Feminist Voice in Poverty Debate in Canada, 1970–1995* (Toronto: University of Toronto Press, 2004), 38, 42–43.

47. Ian Adams, William Cameron, Brian Hill, and Peter Penz, *The Real Poverty Report* (Edmonton: Hurtig, 1971), esp. v–vi, 245–46. See, as well, Ian Adams, *The Poverty Wall* (Toronto: McClelland and Stewart, 1970).

48. Little, "Militant Mothers," 194–97 and Buchbinder, "The Just Society Movement," 129–52 offer different perspectives on the demise of the JSM. On NAPO, discussed in Stewart, *Charity Game*, 66–69, see also McKeen, *Money in their Own Name*, which accents the visibility of women's/children's poverty.

49. The war on organized labour that we allude to below could be commented on far more extensively. See Leo Panitch and Donald A. Swartz, *From Consent to Coercion: The Assault on Trade Union Freedoms* (Toronto: Garamond, 2003); Roberts and Bullen, "Heritage of Hope and Struggle," 131–38; Robert Argue, Charlene Gannagé, and D. W. Livingstone, eds., *Working People and Hard Times: Canadian Perspectives* (Toronto: Garamond, 1987); Thom Workman, *If You're in My Way, I'm Walking: The Assault on Working People Since 1970* (Halifax: Fernwood, 2009); Yonatan Reshef and Sandra Rastin, *Unions in the Time of Revolution: Government Restructuring in Alberta and Ontario* (Toronto: University of Toronto Press, 2003).

50. M. J. Webber and D. L. Rigby, "The Rate of Profit in Canadian Manufacturing, 1950–1981," *Review of Radical Political Economics* 18, nos. 1 & 2 (1986): 33–55; Workman, *If You're in My Way*, 17; Murray E. G. Smith, *Global Capitalism in Crisis: Karl Marx & the Decay of the Profit System* (Halifax: Fernwood, 2010), 162; Palmer, *Working-Class Experience*, 272, quoting Lower.

51. Leo Panitch, *Workers, Wages, and Controls: The Anti-Inflation Program and Its Implications for Workers* (Toronto: New Hogtown press, 1976), 1, 18; Leo Panitch and Donald Swartz, *The Assault on Trade Union Freedoms: From Wage Controls to Social Contract* (Toronto: Garamond, 1993), 19–28; Jean-Claude Parrot, *My Union, My Life:*

Jean-Claude Parrot and the Canadian Union *of Postal Workers* (Halifax: Fernwood, 2005), 86–134; Desmond Morton, *Working People: An Illustrated History of the Canadian Trade Union Movement* (Toronto: Summerhill, 1990), 305.

52. Palmer, *Working-Class Experience*, 345–47; Wolfe, "Rise and Demise of the Keynesian Era," 51; Cy Gonick, *Out of Work: Why There's So Much Unemployment, and Why It's Getting Worse* (Toronto: Lorimer, 1978), esp. 10–11.

53. Leo Panitch and Sam Gindin, *The Making of Global Capitalism: The Political Economy of the American Empire* (London: Verso, 2012).

54. Allan Fotheringham, "For This Is the Law—and the Profits," *Maclean's*, April 7, 1980; Panitch and Swartz, *Assault on Trade Union Freedoms*.

55. Palmer, *Working-Class Experience*, 347–50; Workman, *If You're in My Way*, 60–78. In the United States, where shifts in the social climate inevitably affect Canada, the decline in labour militancy as registered in strike data was even more pronounced. The number of workdays lost to strikes has toppled from a post–Second World War high of 60 million to 180,000 in 2010. Micah Uetricht comments that "it might be an exaggeration to state that today the strike is nearly extinct, but not by much." See Doug Henwood, "Strike Wave!" *Left Business Observer*, August 18, 2010; Micah Uetricht, *Strike for America: Chicago Teachers against Austerity* (London: Verso, 2014), 114.

56. For material and quotes in the above four paragraphs see Russell, "Social Wages in a Period of Economic Crisis," 117–19; Social Planning Council of Metro Toronto, "Social Allowances in Ontario," 76; Rea, *Prosperous Years*, 237–38; Patrick Burman, *Poverty's Bonds: Power and Agency in the Social Relations of Welfare* (Toronto: Thompson Educational, 1996), 12, 44; Ontario Welfare Council and the Social Planning Council of Metropolitan Toronto, "… And the Poor Get Poorer: A Study of Social Welfare Programs in Ontario" (February 1981), esp. 84–86; Little, *No Car, No Radio, No Liquor Permit*, 149–53.

57. Canadian Council on Social Development, *Income Supplements for the Working Poor: Proceedings of a Conference on Income Supplementation, April 8–9 1974*, Toronto (Ottawa: Canadian Council on Social Development, 1974), 20, 128; Pat Armstrong and Hugh Armstrong, "Women and Economic Crisis," in *Working People and Hard Times*, ed. Robert Argue, Charlene Gannagé, and D. W. Livingstone (Toronto: Garamond, 1987), 232; Leon Muszynski, "A New Social Welfare Agenda for Canada," in *Getting on Track: Social Democratic Strategies for Ontario*, ed. Daniel Drache (Montreal and Kingston: McGill-Queen's University Press, 1992), 182; Thom, *If You're in My Way*, 72–74, 85.

58. See Greg Albo, Sam Gindin, and Leo Panitch, *In and Out of Crisis: The Global Financial Meltdown and Left Alternatives* (Oakland: PM Press, 2010).

59. Burman, *Poverty's Bonds*, 42–45; Armine Yalnizyan, "Securing Society: Creating Canadian Social Policy," in *Shifting Time: Social Policy and the Future of Work*, ed. Armine Yalnizyan, T. Ran Ide, and Arthur Cordell (Toronto: Between the Lines, 1994), 45.

60. Robert J. Brym, "Affluence, Power, and Strikes in Canada, 1973–2000," in *Inequality in Canada: Patterns, Problems, Policies*, ed. James Curtis, Edward Grabb, and Neil Guppy (Scarborough, Ontario: Prentice-Hall, 2003), 55. For a broad discussion of the attack on organized labour and "unprotected workers," see Workman, *If You're in My Way*, 55–120.

61. Roberts and Bullen, "Workers, Unions, and Politics," 137.

62. See, for instance, Bryan D. Palmer, *Solidarity: The Rise and Fall of an Opposition in British Columbia* (Vancouver: New Star, 1987); Palmer, *Working-Class Experience*, 361–416. And, from the horse's mouth, so to speak, Jack Munro, *Union Jack: Labour Leader Jack Munro* (Vancouver: Douglas and McIntyre, 1988).

PART V

1. Sylvia Bashevkin, *Welfare Hot Buttons: Women, Work, and Social Policy Reform* (Toronto: University of Toronto Press, 2002), 28–32.

2. Patrick Burman, *Poverty's Bonds: Power and Agency in the Social Relations of Welfare* (Toronto: Thompson Educational, 1996), 48.

3. Bashevkin, *Welfare Hot Buttons,* 31; Murray Dobbin, *The Politics of Kim Campbell* (Toronto: Lorimer, 1993), 158–59.

4. Bashevkin, *Welfare Hot Buttons,* 31–32.

5. Margaret Jane Hillyard Little, *"No Car, No Radio, No Liquor Permit": The Moral Regulation of Single Mothers in Ontario, 1920–1997* (Toronto: Oxford University Press, 1998), 153–55; Ruth Morris and Colleen Hoffren, *Street People Speak* (Oakville, Ontario: Mosaic Press, 1988), 11; George Ehring and Wayne Roberts, *Giving Away a Miracle: Lost Dreams, Broken Promises, and the Ontario NDP* (Oakville, Ontario: Mosaic Press, 1993), 210–14; Thomas Walkom, *Rae Days: The Rise and Follies of the NDP* (Toronto: Key Porter Books, 1994), 195–97; Brian Wharf, *Communities and Social Policies in Canada* (Toronto: McClelland and Stewart, 1992), 72–77; Jonathan Sydney Greene, "Visibility, Urgency, and Protest: Anti-Poverty Activism in Neo-Liberal Times" (PhD diss., Queen's University, 2006), 82–83. Two commentators suggest that this liberal climate of advance in the late 1980s actually kept new social movements that had emerged and that were focusing on poverty and housing somewhat marginalized in Toronto's urban reform politics. See Stefan Kipner and Roger Keil, "Toronto, Inc? Planning the Competitive City in the New Toronto," *Antipode* 34 (2002): 239–40.

6. The above paragraphs draw on Leonard Shifrin, "Budget Batters the Poor," *Toronto Star* (hereafter *Star*), February 26, 1990; Ronald Melchers, "The Cap on CAP: Ottawa Plans to Put a Lid on Its Money for Social Assistance Services," *Perception* 14 (Fall 1990): 19–23; Bashevkin, *Welfare Hot Buttons,* 33; John Clarke, "Ontario's Social Movements: The Struggle Intensifies," in *Culture and Social Change: Social Movements in Québec and Ontario,* ed. Colin Leys and Marguerite Mendell (Montreal: Black Rose Books, 1992), 214; Thomas Walkom, *Rae Days,* 201–3; Walter Stewart, *The Charity Game: Greed, Waste and Fraud in Canada's $86-Billion-A-Year Compassion Industry* (Vancouver: Douglas and McIntyre, 1996), 80–81.

7. Brooke Jeffrey, *Breaking Faith: The Mulroney Legacy of Deceit, Destruction, Disunity* (Toronto: Key Porter Books, 1992), 141–43; Burman, *Poverty's Bonds,* 48; David P. Ross, E. Richard Shillington, and Clarence Lochhead, *The Canadian Fact Book on Poverty* (Ottawa: Canadian Council on Social Development, 1994), 47. The C. D. Howe Institute was especially concerned with unemployment insurance payments and the system of provisioning for the jobless. It lobbied to put a cap on the number of weeks anyone could draw benefits over the course of a five-year period, advocating as well other measures that would curb federal outlays. See Christopher Green, Fred Lazar, Miles Corak, and Dominique M. Gross, *Unemployment Insurance: How to Make It Work* (Ottawa: C. D. Howe Institute, 1994).

8. Bashevkin, *Welfare Hot Buttons,* 33; Little, *No Car, No Radio, No Liquor Permit,* 162; Janet Conway, *Identity, Place, Knowledge: Social Movements Contesting Globalization* (Halifax: Fernwood, 2004), 79–90; Walkom, *Rae Days,* 107, 199–200; Greene, "Visibility, Urgency, and Protest," 84–85; Ron M. Sheldrick, "Welfare Reform Under Ontario's NDP: Social Democracy and Social Group Representation," *Studies in Political Economy* 55 (Spring 1998): 37–63; Kelly Toughill, "Welfare Cuts an 'Option' if Federal Funding Frozen," *Star,* December 17, 1993; William Walker, "Welfare Cuts May Come Swiftly," *Star,* March 22, 1994; "Province to Target Welfare Fraud Cases," *Star,* March 28, 1994.

9. The above paragraphs draw on *Common Sense Revolution* (1995), 9–11, quoted in Maeve Quaid, *Workfare: Why Good Social Policy Ideas Go Bad* (Toronto: University of Toronto Press, 2002), 174–75; Little, *No Car, No Radio, No Liquor Permit,* 186–90; James Struthers, "Can Workfare Work? Reflections from History," Keynote address, "Getting People to Work and Off Welfare" Conference, Kitchener, Ontario, December 7–8, 1995 (Ottawa: Caledon Institute of Social Policy, February 1996); and for more on workfare the essays in Eric Shragge, ed., *Workfare: Ideology for a New Underclass* (Toronto: Garamond, 1997); Jean Swanson, *Poor-Bashing:*

The Politics of Exclusion (Toronto: Between the Lines, 2001), 122–26; Bashevkin, *Welfare Hot Buttons*, esp. 84–86; Jamie Peck, *Workfare States* (New York: Guilford, 2001), esp. 240–43. Note as well, on other issues raised in the above paragraphs, including the climate of suspicion around "welfare fraud," Barbara Murphy, *On the Street: How We Created the Homeless* (Winnipeg: J. Gordon Shillingford, 2000), 119–23; Jack Layton, *Homelessness: The Making and Unmaking of a Crisis* (Toronto: Penguin, 2000), 15, 22, 81–84; Greene, "Visibility, Urgency, and Protest," 88–91, 106–7; and, with respect to the complexity of the circumstances through which women were written out of the poverty discourse in these years at the same time as the number of women on social assistance multiplied, Wendy McKeen, *Money in their Own Name: The Feminist Voice in Poverty Debate in Canada, 1970–1995* (Toronto: University of Toronto Press, 2004), 89–107.

10. For a broad statement about poverty and inequality in 1990s Toronto see Andrew Jackson, Sylvain Schetagne, and Peter Smith, *A Community Growing Apart: Income Gaps and Changing Needs in the City of Toronto in the 1990s* (Toronto: United Way of Greater Toronto, 2001). Greene, "Visibility, Urgency, and Protest" is premised on the critical importance of homelessness, which he suggests brings poverty into the streets in provocative and visible ways that demand active engagement in the struggle to alleviate obvious human distress.

11. Ruth Morris and Colleen Heffren, *Street People Speak* (Oakville, Ontario: Mosaic Press, 1988), 14.

12. Layton, *Homelessness*, esp. 80, 99; Alex Murray, "Homelessness: The People," Ramesh Mishra, "The Collapse of the Welfare Consensus? The Welfare State in the 1980s," and Tom Carter and Ann McAfee, "The Municipal Role in Housing the Homeless and the Poor," in *Housing the Homeless and the Poor: New Partnerships among the Private, the Public, and Third Sectors*, ed. George Fallis and Alex Murray (Toronto: University of Toronto Press, 1990), 16–48, 82–114, 227–62; Anne Golden et al., *Taking*

Responsibility for Homelessness: An Action Plan for Toronto (Toronto: City of Toronto, Report of the Mayor's Homeless Action Task Force, 1999), v; Barbara Murphy, *On the Street*, 13. For a useful overall account of the conditions leading to homeless in this period see Greene, "Visibility, Urgency, and Protest," 74–110.

13. The above paragraphs draw on Thomas O'Reilly Fleming, *Down and Out in Canada: Homeless Canadians* (Toronto: Scholar's Publishing, 1993); Layton, *Homelessness*, 53; John Sewell, *Houses and Homes: Housing for Canadians* (Toronto: James Lorimer, 1984); Jon Caulfield, *City Forms and Everyday Life: Toronto's Gentrification and Critical Social Practice* (Toronto: University of Toronto Press, 1993); Greene, "Visibility, Urgency, and Protest," esp. 77–80; Little, *No Car, No Radio, No Liquor Permit*, 150; Murray, "Homelessness: The People"; Mishra, "The Collapse of the Welfare Consensus?"; Carter and McAfee, "The Municipal Role in Housing the Homeless and Poor."

14. Jean Swanson, *Poor-Bashing: The Politics of Exclusion* (Toronto: Between the Lines, 2001), 67–70; Stewart, *Charity Game*, 69.

15. Sheila Baxter, *No Way to Live: Poor Women Speak Out* (Vancouver: New Star, 1988); Pat Capponi, *The War at Home: An Intimate Portrait of Canada's Poor* (Toronto: Viking, 1999), 129.

16. The above two paragraphs quote and refer to James Rinehart, "Foreword," in Patrick Burman, *Killing Time, Losing Ground: Experiences of Unemployment* (Toronto: Wall and Thompson, 1988), xi–xv; Clarke, "Ontario's Social Movements," 216; Swanson, *Poor-Bashing*; Capponi, *War at Home*, 129.

17. On DERA see Shlomo Hasson and David Ley, *Neighbourhood Organizations and the Welfare State* (Toronto: University of Toronto Press, 1994), esp. 34, 172–204.

18. Howard Buchbinder, "Inequality and the Social Services," in *Inequality: Essays on the Political Economy of Social Welfare*, ed. Allan Moscovitch and Gleen Drover (Toronto: University of Toronto Press, 1981), 366.

19. Clarke, "Ontario's Social Movements," 216–17, 223.

20. The above two paragraphs draw on Clarke, "Ontario's Social Movements," 215, 217, 222; Burman, *Killing Time*, 97–121, 207, 232, a study that also reveals the extent to which Clarke's radicalism was a minority position within the unemployed and that addresses the London Union of Unemployed Workers and the attitudes of the unemployed toward trade unions; and David Alexander Thompson, "Direct Action, Subsidiarity and the Counterhegemonic: Three Case Studies of Antipoverty Activism in Twentieth-Century Canada" (master's thesis, University of Victoria, 2006), 89.

21. Robin Harvey, "Last Resort Hostel Banned Bag Lady, Inquest Jury Told," *Star*, February 18, 1986; Paul Taylor, "Woman Too Difficult for Hostel to Control, Director Tells Inquest," *Globe and Mail*, February 18, 1986; Robin Harvey, "From Budding Starlet to Bag Lady: Drina Joubert's Tragic Life and Death," *Star*, February 13, 1986; Cathy Dunphy, "How a Frozen Women Forced a City to Wake Up," *Star*, January 10, 1999; Paul Taylor, "Homeless Face Frigid Death: Lack of Rooms Forced Bag Lady to Sleep in Truck," *Globe and Mail*, December 19, 1985; Jim Wilkes, "Bag Lady, 64, Dies in Parking Garage," *Star*, January 29, 1986; Paul Taylor, "Frozen Body of Bag Lady Is Found in Outside Stairwell," *Globe and Mail*, January 29, 1986; "Dead Man Identified," *Globe and Mail*, February 8, 1986.

22. Taylor, "Woman Too Difficult for Hostel to Control, Director Tells Inquest"; June Callwood, "Friends of Homeless Mobilize to Get Results from Inquest," *Globe and Mail*, February 12, 1986; Ryan Scott, "Living—and Dying—on the Street: How the Social Service Industry Failed Drina Joubert," *Pheonix Rising: The Voice of the Psychiatrized* 6 (June 1987); Rosie DiManno, "Women's Death Spurs Toronto Homeless to Demand Housing," *Star*, February 12, 1986; Dana Flavelle, "Homeless Women Forced to Sleep on Street as Hostel Turning Away Dozens Each Night," *Star*, December 19, 1985; John Wilkes, "Truck Was 'Home' for Bag Lady Who Froze to Death," *Star*, December 19, 1985; Robin Harvey, "Nearly 200 Women Trapped in Hostel Life, Inquest Told,"
Star, February 19, 1986; Paul Taylor, "Inquest Is Told of Need for Affordable Housing," *Globe and Mail*, February 20, 1986; "Housing for the Homeless," *Star*, December 20, 1985; Harvey, "From Budding Starlet to Bag Lady"; Paul Taylor, "Probation Officer Couldn't Persuade Woman to Leave Truck," *Globe and Mail*, February 15, 1986; Paul Taylor, "Lifestyle Choice Cited in Death," *Globe and Mail*, February 13, 1986; "Joubert Faced Alcoholism, Grief Alone," *Globe and Mail*, February 26, 1986; Robin Harvey, "Female Tenants Seen as Trouble," February 20, 1986; Verdict of Coroner's Jury, "Inquest into the Death of Drina Joubert, 1986," Coroner M. Naiberg, MD, February 25, 1986.

23. Dunphy, "How a Frozen Woman Forced a City to Wake Up," *Star*, January 10, 1999; Drew Fagan, "31.5 Million Package to Aid Homeless," *Globe and Mail*, December 18, 1987; Helen Armstrong, "Help from Church: Renovated Theatre to House Women," *Globe and Mail*, April 21, 1987; Cathy Crowe, *Dying for a Home: Homeless Activists Speak Out* (Toronto: Between the Lines, 2007), 13.

24. Clarke, "Ontario's Social Movements," 218; Little, *No Car, No Radio, No Liquor Permit*, 154–55

25. Little, *No Car, No Radio, No Liquor Permit*, 155; Clarke, "Ontario's Social Movements," 218; Ehring and Roberts, *Giving Away a Miracle*, 210–14, 246–47; Thompson, "Direct Action Subsidiarity and the Counterhegemonic," 89; Shelley Page, "3,000 Rally to Demand Queen's Park Fight Poverty," *Star*, April 9, 1989.

26. Clarke, "Ontario's Social Movements," 219; Ehring and Roberts, *Giving Away a Miracle*, 269.

27. Clarke, "Ontario's Social Movements," 218–19; Thompson, "Direct Action, Subsidiarity and the Counterhegemonic," 90, citing Susan Reid, "Put Yourself in Our Shoes, Peterson Told," *Star*, April 12, 1990.

28. John Clarke, "OCAP Marks Its First 20 Years," *rabble.ca: news for the rest of us*, rabble.ca; and Clarke quoted in Greene, "Visibility, Urgency, and Protest," 93.

29. The above paragraphs draw on Clarke, "OCAP Marks Its First 20 Years"; John Clarke, "Anticapital/antipoverty," *They Call It Struggle for*

a *Reason* 4 (June 2001): 12; John Clarke, "Is 'Fighting to Win' a Criminal Act?" *Dominion*, March 16, 2004, www.dominionpaper.ca. For a 1998 listing of immigration/deportation casework and an account of challenging the state's claims about cheating on welfare see "Report on the Successes of OCAP 'Team Immigration',", and "Who's Cheating Who?", *OCAP Newsletter* 2 (April 27, 1998), hpn.asu.edu. See also Norman Feltes, "The New Prince in a New Principality: OCAP and the Toronto Poor," *Labour/Le Travail* 48 (Fall 2001): 125–57; Thompson, "Direct Action, Subsidiarity and the Counterhegemonic," 92–94; Jeff Shantz, "Fighting to Win: The Ontario Coalition Against Poverty," *Capital & Class* 26 (Autumn 2002): 1–8; Jonathan Greene, "'Whatever It Takes': Poor People's Organizing, OCAP, and Social Struggle," *Studies in Political Economy* 75 (Spring 2005): 5–28.

30. The above paragraphs draw on Feltes, "New Prince in a New Principality," 146; Greene, "Visibility, Urgency, and Protest," 95–96; Thompson, "Direct Action, Subsidiarity and the Counterhegemonic," 105–6, 122, quoting Brian Dominick, "Reinventing Antipoverty: The Ontario Coalition Against Poverty Employs Fresh, Winning Tactics," *ZMag* (January 1999), www.zmag.org, and "Two Victories: OCAP's Daily Victories for, and by, the Poor," *ZNet* (May 23, 2002), www.ZMag.org; Shantz, "Fighting to Win," 3–4; "Direct Action Casework Victories," *They Call It Struggle for a Reason* 5 (Summer 2002): 8; OCAP, "Direct Action Casework Manual," ocap.ca/node/322.

31. John Clarke to Gaétan Héroux, March 27, 2015.

32. Quotes from Clarke, "OCAP Marks Its First 20 Years" and Layton, *Homelessness*, 10. Trade union funding of OCAP in the 1990s included contributions of $10,000 annually from the Canadian Automobile Workers' Union and $4,000–$6,000 yearly from the Canadian Union of Public Employees, such funds being supplemented by other donations from labour organizations, other bodies, and individual contributions. In this period OCAP operated on $50,000 annually, which covered the costs of two full-time organizers, one part-time organizer, rent, legal fees, and clerical expenses. OCAP has never taken money from government agencies. Funding from unions has always been precarious, subject to withdrawal. On such matters and budget issues see Thompson, "Direct Action, Subsidiarity, and the Counterhegemonic," 99; Greene, "Visibility, Urgency, and Protest," 92–93. We were asked by one peer reviewer of this manuscript to address the make-up of the OCAP activist constituency. "What sorts of people got involved? Were they motivated by analysis, anger, what? Did they come from other activist groups?" This is a legitimate inquiry, but the kind of sociological profile of OCAP that it asks for is beyond what this study can provide, and could only be established through detailed interviews with hundreds of people drawn to OCAP over twenty-five years. OCAP does not keep records of membership that would answer such questions. Even if evidence were available, responding to these questions with definitive kinds of identification would perhaps not ultimately tell us that much. For all sorts of people came to OCAP over the years, among them scholars and sex trade workers; union members and the unemployed; social workers, students, and psych survivors; professionals (such as lawyers, nurse practitioners, paralegals, and doctors); and, of course, the homeless. Their motivations? Anger, analysis, and a commitment to right wrongs and stand up to social injustice would all factor into what prompted people to join OCAP. Did they come from other activist groups? Yes, to some extent, and OCAP's activist core did, at times, include figures drawn from other anti-poverty mobilizations, trade unions, the organized, extra-parliamentary left, anarchist collectives, anti-racist organizations, and indigenous peoples' campaigns. Coming from these political spaces, many worked with OCAP as well as with other groups, and some passed through OCAP and went back or on to other places of protest. We are reminded of E. P. Thompson's admonition that class is not neatly measured because it is not a structure or a category, but

a fluid historical relationship. OCAP, similarly, has a "fluency which evades analysis if we attempt to stop it dead at any given moment and anatomize its structure." Thompson insisted that "The finest meshed sociological net cannot give us a pure specimen of class any more than it can give us one of deference or of love." (E. P. Thompson, *The Making of the English Working Class* (1963; repr., Harmondsworth: Penguin, 1977), 9.) OCAP, similarly, cannot be anatomized because its membership was eclectic and diverse and changed over the course of differing periods of its history. Transgender people and struggles to defend them and secure their safety as they lived on the streets of Toronto, for instance, were perhaps less significant in the earliest years of OCAP and more central to the organization and its work in subsequent periods. Other groups could be similarly, if differentially, situated, among them various immigrant communities, such as Somalis or Filipinos. That said, a continuous thread runs through this history, and that is OCAP's anti-capitalist embrace of militant struggle and direct action casework, both of which were guided by the "fight to win" orientation articulated at the organization's founding. It is this accent on resistance that we chart in our study, situating it within the long, rebellious history of Toronto's poor.

33. The above paragraphs draw on Robert MacLeod, "Anti-Poverty Group to Set Up Tent City," *Globe and Mail*, July 10, 1991; Jane Armstrong, "Tent City Folding Up Amid Cheers and Boos," *Star*, August 10, 1991; Paul Jackson, "Secrets Behind Mulroneyville," *Calgary Sun*, August 25, 1991.

34. Clarke, "Ontario's Social Movements," 221.

35. On the Social Contract attack on the public sector see Leo Panitch and Donald Swartz, *The Assault on Trade Union Freedoms: From Wage Controls to Social Contract* (Toronto: Garamond, 1993), 159–88; Walkom, *Rae Days*, 130–46, and for the discussions inside the NDP on welfare reduction, with claims of ultimate reluctance to go all in on an attack on the poor, 199–203.

36. William Walker, "'Welfare Dependency' Must End," *Star*, March 7, 1994; Editorial, "Why Is NDP Hitting Those on Welfare?" *Star*, March 22, 1994; "Fingerprint or Photo ID Urged for All Canadians," *Star*, February 17, 1994; "Province to Target Welfare Fraud Cases," *Star*, March 28, 1994; "'Crackdown on Welfare Cheats Expected to Save $50 Million," *Globe and Mail*, March 28, 1994; William Walker, "NDP Set to Root Out Welfare Cheats," *Star*, March 28, 1994; Peter Small, "Crackdown on Welfare Fraud Called a Pre-Election Gimmick," *Star*, March 29, 1994; Peter Edwards and Rebecca Bragg, "Silipo Booed at Meeting Over Welfare Crackdown," *Star*, April 20, 1994.

37. Derek Ferguson, "Axworthy to Target Social Aid 'Dependency'," *Star*, February 1, 1994; "Tight Time-Table Set for Social Reform Talks," *Globe and Mail*, February 21, 1994; Edison Stewart, "Protesters Lash Chrétien for UI Cuts," *Star*, March 18, 1984; Edward Greenspoon, "Chrétien Shaken by UI Protest," *Globe and Mail*, March 19, 1994; Edison Stewart, "PM Sorry for Offending the Jobless," *Star*, April 22, 1994; Allan Thompson, "Minister Unveils Steps to Curb Welfare Abuse," *Star*, March 10, 1994; Edison Stewart, "Worst Cuts Yet to Come, Martin Says," *Star*, April 19, 1994.

38. The above paragraphs draw on Gaétan Héroux, interview with Richard St. Pierre, Montreal, June 26, 2006.

39. Laurie Monsebraaten, "Protesters Storm Hearing," *Star*, November 30, 1994; Rosie DiManno, "Who Is Speaking in Our Name," *Star*, November 30, 1994.

40. Héroux, interview with St. Pierre; "Dehors Axworthy!" *Le Devoir*, December 6, 1994.

41. Héroux, interview with St. Pierre; Maxime Ruvinsky, "Stunned MPs Forced to Flee as Protesters Thrash Hearing," *Star*, December 7, 1994; Graham Hamilton and David Johnson, "Mob Crashes Hearing On Axworthy Reforms," *Montreal Gazette*, December 7, 1994. On Madeleine Parent see Andrée Lévesque, ed., *Madeleine Parent: Activist* (Toronto: Sumach Press, 2005).

42. Bashevkin, *Welfare Hot Buttons*, 33–34, 82–83, 88; Derek Ferguson, "Social Reform Price Tag:

$7 Billion," *Star*, October 5, 1994; Scott Feschuk, "Klein to Forge Ahead with Major Cuts," *Globe and Mail*, January 12, 1994.

43. William Walker, "Welfare Cuts May Come Swiftly," *Star*, March 22, 1994.

44. For the general contours of the dismantling of the welfare regime in Ontario under the 1990s Tories see Bashevkin, *Welfare Hot Buttons*, 83–85; Little, *No Car, No Radio, No Liquor Permit*, 186–90; Greene, "Visibility, Urgency, and Protest," 88–91; Scott Magnish, "Poor Vow War on Tories," *Sun*, July 30, 1995.

45. Magnish, "Poor Vow War on Tories," *Toronto Sun*, 30 July 1995; John Clarke, "Fighting to Win," in *Open for Business, Closed to People: Mike Harris's Ontario*, ed. Diana S. Ralph, André Régimbold, and Nérée St-Amand (Halifax: Fernwood, 1997), 159; Clarke, "OCAP Marks Its First 20 Years"; Greene, "Visibility, Urgency, and Protest," 100.

46. Jane Gadd, "Police Push Back Demonstrators," *Globe and Mail*, September 28, 1995.

47. Tanya Talaga, "Protesters Face 14 Years," *Star*, February 9, 1996; Virginia Galt, "Student Leaders Condemn Raucous Demonstration," *Globe and Mail*, February 9, 1996; "Public Probe Set on Strike Violence," *Star*, March 21, 1996; Phillip Mascoll and Jim Rankin, "OPP Defends Riot Squad Called 'Animals' by Pickets," *Star*, March 19, 1996; Daniel Gerard, "MPP's Demand Public Inquiry into OPP Acts," *Star*, March 20, 1996; John Duncanson, "Labour Plans Big Protest at Queen's Park Today," *Star*, March 25, 1996; "Thousands March to Protest Harris," *Sunday Star*, October 27, 1996. On the OPSEU strike and the Days of Action an immense number of sources could be cited. As examples see David Rapaport, *No Justice, No Peace: The 1996 OPSEU Strike against the Harris Government in Ontario* (Kingston: McGill-Queen's University Press, 1999); Vincenzo Pietropolo, *Celebration of Resistance: Ontario's Days of Action* (Toronto: Between the Lines, 1999); David Camfield, "Assessing Resistance in Harris's Ontario, 1995–1999," in *Canadian Public Policy in an Age of Global Capitalism*, ed. Mike Burke, Colin Mooers, and John Shields (Halifax: Fernwood,

2000), 306–17; Bryan D. Palmer, "Showdown in Ontario: Build the General Strike," *Canadian Dimension* 30 (May–June 1996): 21–26; "Halloween in Harrisland: Teachers, Bureaucrats, and Betrayal," *Canadian Dimension* 32 (January–February 1998): 29–32; "Where Ya At, General Strike?!," *Canadian Dimension* 32 (September–October 1998): 20–24; Shantz, "Fighting to Win," 2–3.

48. Tresh Tervit, "Finger Salutes Scheme," *Toronto Sun*, June 20, 1996; Peter Small, "Dozen Rap Plan to Put the Finger on Cheats," *Star*, May 14, 1996; Dick Chapman, "The Prints and the Paupers," *Toronto Sun*, May 14, 1996; Peter Small, "Metro Set to 'Scan' Welfare Recipients," *Star*, June 20, 1996; Commissioner of Community and Neighbourhood Services, City of Toronto, "Client Identification and Benefits System Update," May 14, 1999.

49. "Tsubouchi Flayed over Tuna Remarks," *Globe and Mail*, October 4, 1995; Greene, "Visibility, Urgency, and Protest," 100–1.

50. Much of this paragraph relies on Gaétan Héroux, but on Rosenthal's defence strategy see also Sylvia Fraser, "The Agitator," *Toronto Life*, January 1, 2008.

51. "Tsubouchi Not Home When Protesters Call," *Markham Economist and Sun*, May 29, 1996.

52. For the crisis of homelessness in Toronto in 1995–96 see Layton, *Homelessness*, 1–16; Greene, "Visibility, Urgency, and Protest," 102–3; Henry Stancu and Bruce DeMara, "Homeless Fear Rejection at Doors of Metro Hostels," *Star*, October 22, 1995; "More Deaths among Homeless Expected," *Star*, October 24, 1995; Peter Small, "919 Beds to Be Added for Metro's Homeless," *Star*, October 27, 1995; Paul Moloney, "216,500 Plan Backed to Help Homeless," *Star*, November 16, 1995; Joe Warmington, "Mom Mourns Son Who Lost His Way," *Star*, January 4, 1996; Moira Welsh, "Death on Our Streets," *Star*, February 2, 1996. The OCAP action at Seaton House is detailed in Theresa Boyle, "Seaton House Stormed in Angry Protest by Homeless," *Star*, February 9, 1996, and discussed briefly in Greene, "Visibility, Urgency, and Protest,"

103–4. On Crowe see Cathy Crowe, *Dying for a Home: Homeless Activists Speak Out* (Toronto: Between the Lines, 2007), esp. 3–31. Rosenthal is profiled in Sylvia Fraser, "The Agitator," *Toronto Life*, January 1, 2008.

53. Michael Valpy, "One Is Too Many," *Globe and Mail*, June 1, 1996; Toronto Coalition Against Homelessness, "One Is Too Many: Findings and Recommendations of the Panel of the Public Inquiry into Homelessness and Street Deaths in Toronto" (May 25, 1996), 2.

54. Rebecca Bragg, "Hostel Beds Empty as Men Froze to Death," *Star*, July 6, 1996; Christie Blatchford, "They Had the Right to Freeze to Death," *Star*, July 10, 1996; Mark Gollom, "Protest Slams Hostel Policies," *Toronto Sun*, February 9, 1996; Rebecca Bragg, "Freezing Victim Died 'For Nothing' Brother Says," *Star*, December 3, 1996; Welsh, "Death on Our Streets." On Melvin Tipping as an expert witness see Crowe, *Dying for a Home*, 32–44; Rebecca Bragg, "'Victim Could Have Been Me', Frozen Man's Pal Tells Inquest," *Star*, July 19, 1996. Kompani's family found out about his death only through a friend telling them that their brother had died months earlier, one of the men frozen to death while living on the street during the last winter. Kompani's body remained unclaimed at the morgue for six months, but as soon as his brother and sister knew of his death they immediately took steps to secure his remains and belongings, which included four binders filled with his writing.

55. The above paragraphs draw on Jane Gadd, "Housing Not Issue in Deaths, Coroner Tells Toronto Jury," *Globe and Mail*, July 27, 1996; Crowe, *Dying for a Home*, 12–13.

56. Layton, *Homelessness*, 16–18; Coroner's Report and Jury's Findings, Eugene Upper, Mirsalah-Aldin Kompani, Irwin Anderson, July 30, 1996; Gay Abbate, "Homelessness Helped Kill Men, Jury Finds," *Globe and Mail*, July 31, 1996; Editorial, "'Wet Hostels' Wrong Approach," *Star*, August 8, 1996.

57. Abbate, "Homelessness Helped Kill Men, Jury Finds"; Jack Lakey, "More Homeless Facing Killer Winter," *Star*, September 14, 1996;

Patricia Orwen, "Need for Hostels Soaring," *Star*, November 17, 1996; Laurie Monsebraaten, "Cafeteria to Become Hostels," *Star*, September 24, 1997; Margaret Philip, "Public Buildings to Be Considered for Homeless Shelters," *Globe and Mail*, September 20, 1997; Gail Swanson, "Care for Homeless, Government Urged," *Star*, October 8, 1997; Dick Chapman, "Homelessness at 30-Year High," *Toronto Sun*, October 9, 1997; Jack Lakey, "Hostels Bulge with Homeless," *Star*, October 9, 1997; Lakey, "Homeless to Get Extra $600,000," *Star*, December 11, 1997; Henry Stancu, "Bag Lady Dies Alone in Public Washroom," *Star*, October 1, 1997; Bruce DeMara and Jack Lakey, "Lastman Says No Homeless in North York," *Star*, October 1, 1997.

58. Layton, *Homeless*, 35, 47; Jan Wong, "A Tale of Two Solitudes in the Heart of Rosedale," *Globe and Mail*, October 11, 1997. Throughout this book we treat the displacement of all poor people from urban neighbourhoods without addressing the extent to which racialized groups have become especially vulnerable to the displacement of gentrification and the so-called clearing of the slums. Native peoples, who suffered an original dispossession from the land through North American colonization by European powers and settlers, are now subject to invigorated waves of urban dispossession, forced into homelessness of the kind that eventually led to Mary Louise Sharrow's death. For a discussion of this urban displacement as it relates to Aboriginal and Métis men and women see Glen Sean Coulthard, *Red Skin, White Masks: Rejecting the Colonial Politics of Recognition* (Minneapolis: University of Minnesota Press, 2014), 175–76, which argues that just as colonizers justified their seizure and settlement of Native lands through the rationalization that such Aboriginal settlement was a "waste" of resources because it did not utilize the land sufficiently productively, contemporary gentrification is also driven by an ideology of improvement. Coulthard thus suggests that urban "frontiers" of dispossession are an ongoing expression of colonization, "central to the accumulation of capital. Through

gentrification, Native spaces in the city are now being treated as *urbs nullius*—urban space void of Indigenous sovereign presence." See also Jean Barman, "Erasing Indigenous Indigeneity in Vancouver," *BC Studies* 155 (2007): 3–30; Bonita Lawrence, *"Real" Indians and Others: Mixed Blood Urban Native Peoples and Indigenous Nationalism* (Vancouver: UBC Press, 2004).

59. Michelle Warren, "Protests over Homeless Deaths," *Star*, November 22, 1997; Scott Magnish, "Body Found in Ravine," *Toronto Sun*, December 31, 1997.

60. Layton, *Homelessness*, 38; Murray, "Homelessness: The People," in Fallis and Murray, *Housing the Homeless and the Poor*, 16–48; Jack Lakey, "Hostels Bulge with Homeless"; Anne Golden et al., *Taking Responsibility for Homelessness*, 14. For an account of youth living on Canadian streets in this period see Marlene Webber, *Street Kids: The Tragedy of Canada's Runaways* (Toronto: University of Toronto Press, 1991).

61. Laurie Monsebraaten, "Squatters May Hurt City's Image," *Star*, May 12, 1996.

62. "Toronto Man Guilty of First-Degree Murder for Killing Prostitutes," Canada-CBC News, www.cbc.ca/news.

63. Phinjo Gombu, "Squatters Vow to Fight Back as Police Evict 20," *Star*, March 6, 1997; Rosie DiManno, "Inside Boarded Up Buildings, Profits May Be Lurking," *Star*, March 14, 1997. The "Use It Or Lose It" bylaw OCAP proposed was not dissimilar to legislation in countries such as Brazil, where urban and rural land occupation movements have won court and other battles to utilize land and buildings that have been abandoned as owners speculate that soaring prices will reward them eventually.

64. Jason Cumming, "Protesters Fight for Vacant Building," *Toronto Sun*, April 20, 1997; Thomas Claridge, "Housing Activists Spared Jail for Break-In," *Globe and Mail*, December 15, 1998; Don Weitz, "Why I Joined OCAP," *OCAP Newsletter* 2 (April 27, 1998), hpn.asu.edu/archives/Apr98/0397.html.

65. All Saints Church figures importantly in the East Downtown, serving as a refuge for the poor. Established in the nineteenth century, All Saints was, for many decades, "as solid a church as Victorian, middle class protestant piety could make it." But as the once affluent East Downtown was transformed into a neighbourhood of boarding houses and "flops" catering to transients, the church's upper- and middle-class parishioners were no longer living in the area. With a dying congregation and a largely empty church, All Saints faced tough decisions, including whether to sell and/or demolish the building. In September 1964 the Reverend Norman Ellis arrived at All Saints or, as he was later fond of saying, "I crash landed in skid row." As he entered the Church, Ellis read the notice board, which was headed by the "jolly slogan," "THE WAGES OF SIN IS DEATH, EVERYONE WELCOME." Ellis determined to put things at All Saints on a different footing, laying "to rest" long established orientations. In 1971, All Saints Church was disestablished and began to function officially as a community centre. In Ellis's words, "it was only when we opened the church doors each weekday and let the crowds of the poor, unemployed, and transient people come into the church, sit around and drink coffee, that Christ really came into the church." Convinced that, "If the church is of no use in the slums, what real use is it anywhere?" Ellis helped transform All Saints from a flagging religious institution into a place of broad social assistance, with as many as forty people working in the various programs and clinics offered through the auspices of the church. See Norman Ellis, *My Parish Is Revolting* (Don Mills, Ontario: Paperjacks, 1974), 2, 16, 29, 70, 73; Ellis, *The Church Is Dead! Long Live the Church! (A Study of the Church in the City)* (Toronto: All Saints Church Community Centre, 1981), 89.

66. The above paragraph and much of what follows below relies on Héroux's first-hand knowledge, but the opposition to services in poor downtown districts was longstanding, crystallizing in the 1970s, and had been commented on in the 1980s by Patricia J. O'Connor, *The Story of Central Neighbourhood House*,

1911–1986 (Toronto: Toronto Association of Neighbourhood Services, 1986), 47. O'Connor noted that Central Neighbourhood House worked with a group known as the South of Carleton Working Committee, a community worker sitting on the Committee for a several years. But CNH ended its involvement as the Working Committee became dominated by "the interests of the newer more affluent residents." One of the more vocal early antagonists of the East Downtown poor was a self-described working-class resident, Pat Shipley, who insisted that services for the poor were a blight on the district, would not be accepted in other Toronto residential neighbourhoods, and were lowering the value of housing. Shipley attacked "the way of living of the poor": "Lining up for their meals, getting drunk on cheap wine or at the local tavern, sleeping in flop houses, getting into fights, landing in jail. Out of jail back to the tavern ... more lining up for meals ... the people want to be rid of those winos and drunks and anyone who thinks this problem is going to just disappear without any drastic action are just wasting their time." Quoted in City of Toronto Planning Board, Research and Overall Planning Division, South Carlton Working Committee, "Skid Row Subcommittee Report of the South Carlton Working Committee" (March 26, 1974), 14–15.

67. The full poster can be found in "Yuppies Back Off," Ontario Coalition Against Poverty Archives, ocap.ca/node/108.

68. Seaton Ontaro Berkeley Residents Association, Inc. (SOBRA) to Pam McConnell, July 24, 1997, in possession of Gaétan Héroux.

69. Executive Director, CNH, Memo: To All Staff Re: CNH Opposition to OCAP Demo of Augsut 5/97, July 30, 1997, in possession of Gaétan Héroux.

70. Greene, "Visibility, Urgency, and Protest," 113–14, quoting Andrew Cash, "Backlash in Cabbagetown," *Now Magazine* 17, March 26—April 1, 1998; Robin Benger, "East Side Show Down," www.youtube.com; Margaret Philp, "Poverty Crusade Gets Personal," *Globe and Mail,* September 20, 1997; "Coming Soon to a Street

Near You!" *OCAP Newsletter* 2 (April 1998), hpn.asu.edu. After the 1997 OCAP confrontation with residents' associations calling for the closure of the CNH drop-in centre in their East Downtown neighbourhood, OCAP protested businesses that lobbied to shut down hostels or to make sure that proposed shelters did not open. In 1998, OCAP picketed Toronto's oldest restaurant, the Senator, and continued the daily demonstrations until the owner of the well-known eatery formally requested that the city reopen the homeless refuge. In 1999, a gas station was picketed by OCAP when it became known that its manager prevented a shelter from opening next to his business. See John Clarke, "The Meek Shall Inherit Diddley-Squat," *Briarpatch* 30 (April 2001), 11; Thompson, "Direct Action, Subsidiarity, and the Counterhegemonic," 11.

71. Philp, "Poverty Crusade Gets Personal"; Susan Kastner, "Taking Fight to the Streets," *Star,* September 13, 1997. See also Greene, "Visibility, Urgency, and Protest," 112–14.

72. Lakey, "More Homeless Facing Killer Winter"; Orwen, "Need for Hostels Soaring"; Margaret Philp, "Public Buildings Considered for Homeless Shelters," *Globe and Mail,* September 20, 1997; Swanson, "Care for Homeless, Government Urged"; Chapman, "Homelessness at 30-Year High"; Lakey, "Hostels Bulge with Homeless"; "Cafeterias to Become Hostels," *Star,* September 27, 1997; Lakey, "Homeless to Get Extra $600,000."

73. Patricia Star, "Squeezing Out the Poor," *Star,* May 11, 1998; Jane Gadd, "Homeless Numbers May Double," *Globe and Mail,* May 9, 1998; Margaret Philp, "Least Needy of Homeless Won't Find Shelter," *Globe and Mail,* August 25, 1998; Mark McKinnon, "Bed Shortages Worsens Plight of Homeless," *Globe and Mail,* October 5, 1998; Peter Edwards, "Home Is a Cardboard Box—And Woman Facing Eviction," *Star,* October 23, 1998.

74. The above paragraphs draw on Cathy Crowe, "In the Calculation of Real Disasters Homelessness Has Easily Won its Place," *Star,* October 30, 1998; Crowe, *Dying for a Home,*

22–25; Capponi, *The War at Home*, 111, 115; Layton, *Homelessness*, 8–18; Murphy, *On the Street*, 129–32; Lila Sarick, "Homeless Problem Declared Emergency," *Globe and Mail*, October 9, 1998; Nicholas Kueng, "The People of the Street," *Star*, October 28, 1998; Laurie Monsebraaten, "Plight of Homeless a 'National Disaster'," *Star*, October 8, 1998; Bruce DeMara, "Relief for Homeless Pledged," *Star*, October 29, 1998. There is a useful discussion of TDRC, another housing advocacy group, Homes Not Bombs, and the Anne Golden–led Mayor's Task Force on Homelessness in Greene, "Visibility, Urgency, and Protest," 115–28.

75. Greene, "Visibility, Urgency, and Protest," 123–24; "Armories May Be Open Tonight," *Star*, January 14, 1999.

76. Jonathan Culp, "RECAP: Video Images of the Ontario Coalition Against Poverty—OCAP Strikes Back" (Vineland Station, Ontario: Satan Macnuggit Collection/Culture from Below, 2000), 21:57.

77. "Armory Stays Open for Homeless," *Star*, May 31, 1999; Cathy Dunphy, "City Turns Metro Hall into Emergency Shelter," *Star*, June 5, 1999; Dunphy, "The Bureaucrat Who Led Homeless to Metro Hall," *Star*, June 8, 1999; Tonda MacCharles, "Anne Golden Hits Inaction on Homelessness," *Star*, May 29, 1999; Jack Lakey, "Armory Deal Eases Hostel Crisis: Facility Will Open to Homeless for Half Year," June 24, 1999; Susan Bousette, "City Rents Armory, but Homeless Problem Grows," *Globe and Mail*, June 24, 1999.

78. Golden, *Taking Responsibility for Homelessness*, 14, 40; Catherine Dunphy, "Its 'Too Little Too Late' for the Homeless," *Star*, June 15, 1999; Dunphy, "Mayor Urged to Act as Hostels Fill Up," *Star*, September 23, 1999; MacCharles, "Anne Golden Hits Inaction on Homelessness"; James Rusk, "City Considers Building Shelter for the Homeless," *Globe and Mail*, September 24, 1999; Bruce DeMara, "Province Offers Shelter Site," *Star*, December 7, 1999.

79. On squeegeeing see Jim Rankin, "Squeegee Life, Toronto Style," *Star*, August 8, 1996; Rankin, "Squeegee Kids Get Squeezed," *Star*, May 31,

1998; Robert Case and Jim Tester, "Can I Wash Your Windshield? Squeezing Canadian Youth in the 1990s," *Canadian Review of Social Policy* 45/46 (Spring/Fall 2000): 207–17.

80. Cal Miller, "Chief Aims to Hit Robbers," *Star*, December 27, 1996; "Toronto's Beggar Problem 'Going to Explode'," *Toronto Sun*, August 25, 1996; "A Squeegee Solution: $50,000 Plan Would Help Only," *Star*, June 17, 1997; Rankin, "Squeegee Kids Get Squeezed"; "Bossoms' Bylaw," *Star*, July 16, 1998. On social cleansing see Greene, "Visibility, Urgency, and Protest," 132; John Clarke, "Unemployed Movements of the 1930s: Lessons for Today (Ontario Coalition Against Poverty)," mouv4x8.perso.neuf.fr/R9990120a.htm.

81. "Mel to Squeegee Kids: Out," *Toronto Sun*, July 23, 1998; "New Law Targets Squeegee Kids, Begging," *Star*, November 3, 1999; "Squeegees Soon to Be Outlawed," *Star*, December 9, 1999; Greene, "Visibility, Urgency, and Protest," 131–32, quoting Collis and pointing out how successful OCAP was in beating back the ticketing of squeegees; Shantz, "Fighting to Win," 3, 5; Clarke, "The Meek Shall Inherit Diddley-Squat"; Thompson, "Direct Action, Subsidiarity and the Counterhegemonic," 109–10. For a discussion of anti-panhandling/anti-vagrancy laws in Canada in this period, including the Safe Streets Act, see Todd Gordon, *Cops, Crime, and Capitalism: The Law-and-Order Agenda in Canada* (Winnepeg: Fernwood, 2006), esp. 82–93.

82. "Panhandlers Threaten Mass Action," *Star*, June 17, 1998; "Hands Off Street Youth!," Ontario Coalition Against Poverty Archives, ocap.ca; Greene, "Visibility, Urgency, and Protest," 114; Royson James, "Helping the Poor to Be Heard," *Star*, June 5, 1998.

83. "New Law Targets Squeegee Kids, Begging."

84. Gaétan Héroux, "Pigs in Poor Neighbourhoods," *They Call it Struggle for a Reason* 4 (June 2001): 19.

85. "Park Takeover Could Be Lengthy Activists Predict," *Toronto Sun*, August 5, 1999; "Sue-Ann Levy, Antipoverty Protest or Political Stunt," *Toronto Sun*, August 6, 1999; "We're Ready to

Rumble, Homeless Advocates Say," *Toronto Sun,* August 11, 1999.

86. For a brief account of the Safe Park see Greene, "Visibility, Urgency, and Protest," 132–35.

87. The above paragraphs draw on Gaétan Héroux's recollections and "Bracing for Trouble," *Toronto Sun,* August 10, 1999.

88. "An Early Morning Raid Ends Protesters' 'Safe Park' Sit-In," *National Post,* August 11, 1999; Bruce DeMara and Cal Miller, "Park Protest Misdirected, Councillor Tells Homeless," *Star,* August 11, 1999. For a visual depiction of the Safe Park see Rebecca Garrett, "Safe Park" (2001), www.youtube.com.

89. Stefan Pilipa to Mayor Lastman and Toronto City Council, on behalf of OCAP, August 18, 1999, quoted in Greene, "Visibility, Urgency, and Protest," 135.

90. Greene, "Visibility, Urgency, and Protest," 136–37; Catherine Dunphy, "Homeless Protest Dulls Glitter of Egoyan's Movie Premiere," *Star,* September 10, 1999; "Toronto Film Festival 'Madder Than Cannes'," CNN.com, www.cnn.com. Aside from bringing the homeless to the Word on the Street festival in this period, OCAP also conducted a snake-march of poor people and supporters through the Yonge-Dundas tourist redevelopment zone.

91. On Clarke and a sense of history as it related to Ottawa protests see Clarke, "Unemployed Movements of the 1930s: Lessons for Today"; Clarke, "Ontario's Social Movements," 215; Thompson, "Direct Action, Subsidiarity and the Counterhegemonic," 94; Greene, "Visibility, Urgency, and Protest," 129–30 and 137.

92. "Joe Clark Shoved as Protesters Get Nasty," *Globe and Mail,* February 11, 1999; "Police, Protesters Clash," *Ottawa Sun,* February 11, 1999; "Joe Clark Jostled during Unruly Protest," *Ottawa Citizen,* February 11, 1999; Thompson, "Direct Action, Subsidiarity and the Counter-hegemonic," 113–14. For OCAP's response to the media frenzy around Joe Clark see Erik Anderson, "Clark Invited Mishap, Antipoverty Group Says," *Globe and Mail,* February 13, 1999.

93. "RCMP in Riot Gear Halt Ottawa Poverty Protest," *Edmonton Journal,* November 18, 1999;

Shawn McCarthy, "RCMP Officers Pepper-Spray Demonstrators," *Globe and Mail,* November 18, 1999; William Walker, "$750 Million Pledged to Aid Homeless," *Star,* December 17, 1999; Greene, "Visibility, Urgency, and Protest," 130–31; Thompson, "Direct Action, Subsidiarity and the Counterhegemonic," 114. On the rise of food banks in Canada in the 1980s and 1990s, a direct consequence of social assistance cutbacks and the erosion of the purchasing power of such assistance through inflation, see Stewart, *Charity Game,* 78–80; Graham Riches, *Food Banks and the Welfare Crisis* (Toronto: James Lorimer, 1986).

94. Layton, *Homelessness,* 35, 98; Colin Perkel, "Number of Homeless People Dying Show Tories Don't Care, Advocates Say," *Globe and Mail,* May 5, 2000; "Homeless Man Charged in Killing," *Globe and Mail,* April 6, 2000; Patti-Ann Finlay, "Homeless Man Injured by Axe-Wielding Assailant," *Globe and Mail,* April 26, 2000; "Activists Accuse City Council of Putting Homeless at Risk," *Globe and Mail,* April 27, 2000; Caroline Alphonso, "Witness Sought in Death of Vagrant," *Globe and Mail,* May 24, 2000; Margaret Philp, "Advocates Fear Wave of Homeless Murders," *Globe and Mail,* June 6, 2000; Colin Freeze, "Homeless Man Charged on Death of Street Person," *Globe and Mail,* June 10, 2000.

95. Peter Small, "Poverty Activists Demand a Hearing: Labour Chiefs Join Call to Address the Legislature," *Star,* June 13, 2000; "Protesters' Open Letter to Harris," *Star,* June 16, 2000; Greene, "Visibility, Urgency, and Protest," 137–40; Shantz, "Fighting to Win," 5.

96. This outline relies on a first-hand account as well as standard press descriptions, which embellished the violence and armed nature of the protesters. John Clarke's views are presented in Clarke, "Is 'Fighting to Win' a Criminal Act?"; "Fight to Win—June 15, 2000, Part I and Part II," TV Adotca, www.youtube.com. See also Bryan Palmer, "The Riot Act: Reviving Protest in Ontario," *Canadian Dimension* 34 (September–October 2000): 28–32; "Antipoverty March Erupts in Violence," *Star,* June 16,

2000; "Anti-Poverty Protest: 18 Arrested, 29 Police Officers Injured in the Melee," *National Post*, June 16, 2000; Richard Brennan, "Facing a Cloud of Pepper Spray," *Globe and Mail*, June 16, 2000; "Riots at Queen's Park: Violence Explodes at Legislature Protest," *Globe and Mail*, June 16, 2000; Harold Levy, "Professor Saw Police Beat Protester," *Star*, April 23, 2003.

97. Palmer, "Riot Act," 28; "Anti-Poverty Protest: 18 Arrested, 29 Police Officers Injured in the Melee"; "Antipoverty March Erupts in Violence"; "Media Lose Fight over Riot Images," *Star*, November 2, 2000; Editorial, "The Right to Associate," *Globe and Mail*, July 26, 2000; "Police Had to Seize Pictures of Queen's Park Riot: Fantino," *Star*, July 13, 2000; Thompson, "Direct Action, Subsidiarity and the Counterhegemonic," 123–25.

98. Rick Salutin, "The Press Riot," *Globe and Mail*, June 23, 2000; Palmer, "Riot Act": "Anti-Poverty Protest: 18 Arrested, 29 Police Officers Injured in the Melee"; Brennan, "Facing a Cloud of Pepper Spray"; "Antipoverty March Erupts in Violence"; Richard Mackie, "Queen's Park Rioter Says Violence Works," *Globe and Mail*, July 15, 2000; John Barber, "Rioters Helped Mike Harris," *Globe and Mail*, June 16, 2000; Naomi Klein, "Would You Invite John Clarke to Your Riot?" *Globe and Mail*, June 21, 2000; Dalton Camp, "Sometimes the Mob Should Be Heard," *Star*, June 23, 2000; Greene, "Visibility, Urgency, and Protest," 137–40, quoting Clarke.

99. Sayesteh Mohammadian, "Statement of the Accused," in Queen's Park Riot Defendants, *June 13½* (Toronto: OCAP, 2002), 22–23.

100. The above paragraphs draw on "Media Lose Fight over Riot Images"; "Police Had to Seize Pictures of Queen's Park Riot: Fantino"; R. vs. Clarke, Between Her Majesty the Queen and John Clarke, Gaétan Héroux, and Stefan Pilipa, accused, 2003, O.J. No. 3883, Ontario Supreme Court of Justice, Toronto Region, Toronto, Ontario, Ferrier, L., January 29, 2003; "Lawyers Ask for Mistrial as Jury Anxiety Mounts," *Star*, May 11, 2002; "Letter to Judge Reflects a Jury Mired with Crisis," *Globe and Mail*, May 22, 2003; Thompson, "Direct Action, Subsidiarity,

and the Counterhegemonic," 127–28; James Semple, "Expect the Worst; Fight for Better," in Queen's Park Riot Defendants, *June 13 1/2*, 17; Bryan Palmer, "Repression and Dissent: The OCAP Trials," *Canadian Dimension* 37 (May–June 2003): 12–15. One of Clarke's excellent responses to the state's suppression of the Queen's Park demonstration is Clarke, "Is 'Fighting to Win' a Criminal Act?" See also "Fight to Win—June 15, 2000, Part I and Part II," TV Adotca, www.youtube.com.

101. The above paragraphs draw on Clarke, "Ontario's Social Movements," 215; Palmer, "Riot Act," 32; Palmer, "Repression and Dissent," 12–15.

102. Gay Abbate, "Homeless Man Found Slain in Sleeping Bag," *Globe and Mail*, September 7, 2000; Jane Gadd, "Tuberculosis Makes Comeback Among the Homeless and Poor," *Globe and Mail*, March 7, 1996; Dr. David McKeown, Medical Officer of Health, "Update on the 2004–2005 Tuberculosis Outbreak Investigation in the Homeless and Underhoused Population," Toronto Board of Health Staff Report, March 7, 2005; Andrew Chung, "City's Homeless Succumb to 'American-Style' Deaths," *Star*, December 28, 2001; Linda Priest, "Street Deaths Spark Calls for Shelters," *Globe and Mail*, December 28, 2001.

103. Kerry Gillespie, "Secret Video Exposes Plight of Homeless," *Star*, May 21, 2002; *The Shelter Inspection Report: A Report of Conditions in Toronto's Shelter System* (Toronto: TDRC, May 2003); Kerry Gillespie and Philip Mascoll, "Shelter Gets One Week More," *Star*, February 5, 2004.

104. "Police Wary as Activists Plan Anti-Tory Action," *Star*, June 14, 2001; "Poverty Activists Vow to Increase Civil Disobedience," *National Post*, June 13, 2001; personal information of Gaétan Héroux.

105. Greene, "Visibility, Urgency, and Protest," 93; OCAP, "Help OCAP Survive Buzz Hargrove's Funding Cut!" An Urgent Appeal to All Trade Unionists, Community Activists, and Those Fighting the Harris Government, July 31, 2001, www.ainfos.ca. See also Jeff Goodall,

"Squishing the Truth," *Canadian Free Press,*
May 26, 2003; Stefan Christoff, "Interview: John
Clarke from OCAP on Jim Flaherty," *The Media
Co-op: Local Independent News,* April 16, 2014.

106. "Riot Police Bracing for Bay Street Protest,"
Star, October 16, 2001; "Police Security Cordon
Keeps Demonstrators Moving," *Star,* October
16, 2001.

107. The above paragraphs draw on Clarke, "Is
'Fighting to Win' a Criminal Act"; "Police Secur-
ity Cordon Keeps Demonstrators Moving";
"Property Protest Snarls Traffic," *Star,* October
17, 2014; Shantz, "Fighting to Win," 6; Greene,
"Visibility, Urgency, and Protest," 136–37.

108. Thompson, "Direct Action, Subsidiarity, and
the Counterhegemonic," 129; "Poverty Protest
Snarls Traffic."

109. "Poverty Protest Snarls Traffic"; Thompson,
"Direct Action, Subsidiarity, and the Counter-
hegemonic," 129–30; Greene, "Visibility,
Urgency, and Protest," 140; Shantz, "Fighting to
Win," 6; Tim Groves, "Disruptive Tactics," *They
Call It Struggle for a Reason* 4 (June 2001): 26.

110. The above paragraph and what follows in the
next paragraphs draw on the recollections of
Gaétan Héroux as well as "Protesters Occupy
Building," *Star,* March 23, 2002.

111. For these developments see Shantz, "Fighting to Win," 6–7. In Peterborough evidence
of PCAP's orientation is in Sarah Lamble,
"Peterborough Coalition Against Poverty
GUIDE FOR SQUATTERS: Legal, Practical &
Historical Information for Anyone Considering
Squatting" (Unpublished essay prepared for
the Peterborough Coalition Against Poverty
as part of a Trent University Centre for Community Based Education Project, April 2002).
Our thanks to James Struthers for providing us
with this paper.

112. There is an excellent collection of Pope Squat-
related material online at Squat!net. The above
paragraph draws on OCAP, "The Pope Squat,"
July 22, 2002, and OCAP, "Pope Squat Establishes New Social Housing in Toronto!" July 27,
2002, en.squat.net.

113. Thompson, "Direct Action, Subsidiarity, and
the Counterhegemonic," 117; Thomas Walkhom,

114. OCAP, "Pope Squat Establishes New Social
Housing in Toronto" and "Radical Garage Sale,"
both in Squat!net, en.squat.net.

115. The above paragraphs on the Pope Squat
draw on Walkhom, "We Need Leaders Who
Give a Squat"; "Squatters Renew Call for
Housing," *Star,* August 1, 2002; "Pope Squat
Friday Report, August 2, 2002, "Pope Squat
Radical Street Festival!" "Michele Landsberg
on the Squat," *Star,* September 28, 2002, all in
Squat!net, en.squat.net.

116. Toronto City Council, Motion J (40), August 1,
2002, Request for Transferal of Ownership of
1510 King Street West; "Squatters Clean, Repair
Building. Poverty Activists Won't End Protest
Until City Takes Over," *Star,* August 8, 2002.

117. Edward Keenan, "Housing Activists Won't
Give Up On Squat," *Eye News,* November 2,
2002; OCAP, "Pope Squat Update: What Happened and Why Squat More," October 21, 2003,
ocap.ca; Thompson, "Direct Action, Subsidiarity, and the Counterhegemonic," 119.

118. Andrew Chong, "Tent City Slated for Forced
Eviction," *Star,* November 26, 2000; Catherine
Dunphy, "Squatters Refuse to Leave," Novem-
ber 29, 2000; Michael Clement, "Fighting for a
Home," *Toronto Sun,* December 3, 2000.

119. Clifford Kraus, "Amid Prosperity, Toronto
Shows Signs of Fraying," *New York Times* (International), June 16, 2002. Shaughnessy Bishop-
Stall, *Down to This: Squalor and Splendor in a
Big-City Shantytown* (Toronto: Vintage Canada,
2004), 450 notes the hostile press coverage of
Tent City. There are ethical and political considerations in reading Bishop-Stall's book. Our
sense is that he was anything but forthright in
explaining to Tent City's residents what he was
writing when he lived among them. Throughout the book, there is a dismissive tone toward
those who are critical of power and have an
analysis of the structures of domination. This

critique is generally levelled at groups like TDRC, about which Bishop-Stall writes: "The more I get to know the members of the TDRC the more baffled I become. Sometimes it seems that in trying to open people's eyes to their cause they blind themselves to what's going on down here. In order to make their struggle a valiant one, they tend to turn people here into victims—not of their lives, but of politics and the status quo. They are sure it's about housing, but I'm just not convinced. Tent City is a place of drug addicts, alcoholics and criminals." (338–39) Protest is dismissed condescendingly: "The TDRC is here, and they've got a team of professional protesters with them, like rented mourners at a funeral" (458, see also 88–89). Because Bishop-Stall lived homeless for a year, he presents himself as of Tent City, in a way that no one working to improve the lives of the homeless ever could be, yet he, of course, always knew he was able to depart Tent City for improved circumstances at any time, and that he would be leaving living on the street eventually, once his book was completed. He manages to have it all ways, being of the poor while also judging the poor and those supporting them harshly. This is evident in his dismissal of Beric German, Cathy Crowe and TDRC for trying to mobilize the dispossessed of Tent City to fight back, a dismissal that instinctually comes to the defence of the police. "I don't believe in whining. Beric assures everyone here that hydro is our right, as is running water, sanitary toilets and a daily life free of police harassment. But who says? And really, … it may be that Tent City's salvation is actually in the hands of the cops, as long as they bust the right people.... Meanwhile, if things go according to Beric's plan, we will all come out together a hundred strong. We will join hands, smile for the cameras, then break into song like the Whos down in Whoville" (410–11). Bishop-Stall declares, after attending one TDRC event, "It was surreal, sitting there among all these well-off, well-meaning professionals listening to speeches and badly-written poems about how we should all be nicer to bums and beggars" (169). Yet Bishop-Stall is himself now a relatively well-off, well-meaning professional, whose book on Tent City also concludes that we should all be nicer to beggars and the like. If Bishop-Stall's bashing is definitely directed at the left, it can also surface against the poor, all in the name of an individualism of the street that is highly useful to those whose commitment to individualism pays lucrative material dividends. Even as it is apparent that affordable housing has allowed 50 percent of those Tent City residents with whom Bishop-Stall lived for a year to do better than they were doing when they were living on the street (which for Bishop-Stall means, apparently, "cleaning up their act"), his conclusion is still that this is about pulling oneself up by one's own bootstraps. "It was a circus in there, and we were all swept up in it. When the show was strong we all laughed along and kept on raging. And when it fell apart we all fell apart with it, raging even more. But once we left, the circus was gone. And then it came down to each one of us, and what we could accomplish on our own" (474–75). So hostile are many anti-poverty activists to the Bishop-Stall book that most such people to whom we showed preliminary drafts of this chapter insisted that we eliminate reference to it entirely. We have resisted such a course precisely because the book is published, widely read (often sympathetically), and there has been virtually no substantive criticism of its voyeuristic nature, ethical irresponsibility, and political prejudices. For another particularly egregious case of literary slumming among the Toronto dispossessed in this period see John Stackhouse, "My Life Without a Home," *Globe and Mail,* December 18, 1999, reprinted and responded to forcefully in Layton, *Homelessness,* 55–61.

120. Bishop-Stall, *Down to This,* 455–69. It is typical of Bishop-Stall that he considers the end of Tent City in individual terms, rather than as one part of a wider experience of poverty and homelessness that of course continued to exist and to be resisted. "The blemish on Toronto's

face had been dug out clean; the land had been razed, the people housed and the public outcry had died. And for the most part, we, of the disappeared shantytown, were still alive." (470) For another representation of Tent City see Michael Connelly, "Shelter From the Storm," hotdocslibrary.ca.

121. Raise the Rates, "Yorkville Feast Takes It to the Tory Trough," August 25, 2003, ocap.ca.

122. The above paragraphs draw on "Cash to Build 900 Affordable Houses a Sure Thing," *Star,* February 26, 2004; Paul Maloney, "Housing Approvals Signal a City Trend," *Star,* August 3, 2004; Carol Goar, "Welcome Truce on Housing Front," *Star,* April 28, 2004; Jennifer Lewington, "Eyeing Winter, Miller Pushes Warm-Up Plan for Homeless," *Globe and Mail,* November 4, 2004; Catherine Porter, "City Shelter to Help Find Homes," *Star,* December 2, 2004; Jennifer Lewington, "West Don Lands Gets the Nod," *Globe and Mail,* May 6, 2005; Jeff Gray and Jennifer Lewington, "Council Approves Affordable Housing Changes," *Globe and Mail,* July 20, 2005; Neil Hetherington, "Mayor's Successor Should Build On Miller's Commitment to Affordable Housing," *Star,* April 15, 2010; Michael Peeling, "Regent Park Bricks Begin to Tumble," *National Post,* February 14, 2006; CBC News, "First Families Return to Renewed Regent Park," www.cbc.ca/news.

123. Dave Trafford, "Build Toronto Fails to hit Affordable Housing Targets," March 19, 2015, globalnews.ca/news; Jane Lytvynenko, "Build Toronto Fails to Meet Affordable Housing Targets," *Torontoist,* March 10, 2015, torontoist.com.

124. For a rare critical assessment of Toronto's Streets to Homes program see Beric German, "Toronto Adopts Bush Homeless Czar's Plan: Another View of Streets to Homes Programs," *Cathy Crowe Newsletter* 48 (Summer 2008), 2–6.

125. The above paragraphs draw on Catherine Porter, "Homeless Face Icy Reception," *Star,* January 20, 2005; Porter, "From the Street to Their Own Homes," *Star,* January 31, 2005; Jeff Gray, "Hundreds of Homeless Off Streets," *Globe and Mail,* December 30, 2005; Royston James,

"Spectacle Only Helps Miller's Plan," *Star,* February 2, 2005; Jenny Yuen, "Building 'Living Hell', MP Says," *Toronto Sun,* January 26, 2011; Lisa Schofield, "Taking It Back: The Campaign for Housing and Services in Toronto's Downtown East," *rabble.ca: news for the rest of us,* September 17, 2013.

126. The above paragraphs draw on "'A Useless Waste of Skin' Offers Chilling Testimony—And a Civic Lesson," *Globe and Mail,* April 3, 2008; Christie Blatchford, "Tearful Soldiers Admit They Acted Like Wolves," *Globe and Mail,* April 18, 2008; Rosie DiMano, "Reservists Irate Before Slaying, Trial Told," *Star,* March 27, 2008; Kate Hammer, "Two Reservists Get 11 Years in Death of Homeless Man," *Globe and Mail,* May 2, 2008; Sam Pazzano, "Deadly 'Savagery' Nets Reservists 11 Years," *Toronto Sun,* May 8, 2008; Emily Mathieu, "Pair Jailed 10 Years in Homeless Beating Death," *Star,* May 2, 2008.

127. See "Charges against Women's Housing Takeover Organizers Withdrawn," July 27, 2007, womenagainstpoverty.blogspot.ca.

128. The above paragraphs draw on "Charges against Women's Housing Takeover Organizers Withdrawn"; The A-Info Radio Project, 2984-1-20070603_wapc_takeover.

129. Clarke, "OCAP Marks Its First 20 Years."

130. The above paragraphs draw on Ontario Coalition Against Poverty Archives (hereafter OCAP Archives), which are available online, "Report from May 12 Raise the Rates Demonstration," May 21, 2005,; "Activists Trying to Take a Bite Out of Hunger," *Star,* July 20, 2005; "City Nurses Okay Diet Benefits," *Star,* July 26, 2005; Rob Ferguso and Robert Benzie, "Activists Protest 'Diet' Cut OCAP Says Poor Need Food Assistance," *Star,* October 4, 2005; "Dietary Allowance Comes with a Snag," *Canadian Press,* October 4, 2005.

131. Ferguson and Benzie, "Activists Protest 'Diet' Cut OCAP Says Poor Need Food Assistance"; "Serving Up a Rebellion," *Now Magazine,* October 6, 2005; "Increase Rates Now," *Star,* October 7, 2005; OCAP Archives, "MD Launches Privacy Complaint over New Special Diet Applications," November 23, 2005.

132. OCAP Archives, "Special Diet Fightback Taken to Pupatello's Doorstep," November 29, 2005; "Violence against Women Activists Call On Government to Reinstate Special Diet Allowance," December 1, 2005; "Women Confront Sandra Pupatello at Domestic Violence Conference," December 1, 2005.

133. OCAP Archives, "Two More Housing Tribunals Disrupted," March 9, 2006; "Peterborough Housing Tribunal Shut Down," March 21, 2006; "MPP's Office in Permanent 'Lock-Down over Special Diet Cuts," March 1, 2006; "Tenant Action Group (Belleville) Update," January 20, 2007.

134. OCAP Archives, "Hunger March, Wednesday 15 March," March 15, 2006; "Night March on Rosedale," April 13, 2006; "OCAP Crashes Liberal Fundraising Dinner, Confronts McGuinty," October 26, 2006; "City to Probe Abuse of Special Diets," *Toronto Sun,* March 9, 2009.

135. "MDs Welfare Prescription Probed," *Star,* December 10, 2009; Catherine Porter, "Robin Hood Doctor Gave to the Poor but Earned Big Money," *Star,* October 3, 2011; Ontario Council of Hospital Unions, press release, October 3, 2011; Wendy Gillis, "'Robin Hood Doctor' Roland Wong Has Licence Suspended," *Star,* January 22, 2014; Jane Gerster, "'Dr. Robin Hood' Has No Regrets about Helping Welfare Patients Get Extra Money," *Star,* July 30, 2013. On November 28, 2015, Dr. Wong, once again working as a physician, attended a 25th anniversary OCAP celebration. He spoke with pride about how he had helped poor patients access the special diet supplement and received a standing ovation from OCAP members and supporters.

136. OCAP Archives, "Powerful Demonstration at Metro Hall: More Than 250 People Occupy Municipal Welfare Office," December 9, 2009; Left Streamed, "OCAP Metro Hall Occupation," (December 8, 2009), www.youtube.com; "A Call to Action against the Cuts to Come: Submission on the Ontario Provincial Pre-Budget 'Consultations'," February 3, 2010; "Poor People Crash Lavish Dinner Party," March 5, 2010.

137. OCAP Archives, "Anti-Poverty Activists Shut Down Office of Minister of Community and Social Services," March 18, 2010; "OCAP Confronts Duncan for Killing the Special Diet," March 26, 2010.

138. The above paragraphs draw on OCAP Archives, "Report-Back: May 20 Day of Action for the Special Diet at MPP's Offices," May 26, 2010; "Liberal MPP Reads Letter of Condemnation in Ontario Legislature," November 11, 2010; "Eleven People Arrested at OCAP Rally Released on Bail; Fight against Cut to Special Diet Continues," July 22, 2010; "Criminal Charges against OCAP and Allies at Liberal Party HQ Go Out the Window," November 11, 2010; "Special Diet," 2011, but mistakenly dated October 16, 2008.

139. The discussion of the special diet struggle and its ramifications in the above paragraphs draws on Michelle Mandel, "City to Probe Abuse of Special Diet Allowance," *Toronto Sun,* March 9, 2009; Laura Eggertson, "Ontario Minister Says Doctors Among Those to Blame For Cut in Special Diet Allowance," *Canadian Medical Association Journal* 182 (May 18, 2010): E329–E330, www.ncbi.nlm.nih.gov; OCAP Archives, "Reverse the Policy Slashing the Special Dietary Supplement," OCAP Press Release, 2005; Clarke, "OCAP Marks Its First 20 Years."

140. Carol-Anne Hudson and Peter Graefe, "The Toronto Origins of Ontario's 2008 Poverty Reduction Strategy: Mobilizing Multiple Channels of Influence for Progressive Social Policy Change," *Canadian Review of Social Policy* 65–66 (2011): 10.

141. Developments discussed in the above paragraphs are detailed in Hudson and Graefe, "The Toronto Origins of Ontario's 2008 Poverty Reduction Strategy," 9–10, 25; Beric German, "Recession and Ontario's 'Poverty Reduction'," *RABBLE,* September 24, 2008.

142. Theresa Boyle, "Anti-Poverty Protesters Make an Election Pitch," *Star,* September 27, 2007, www.the star.com.

143. "School House Shelter Saved?" *Now Magazine,* November 9, 2012; Daniel Dale, "Homelessness: Ontario $21 Million Cut Likely to Leave More People Without a Roof," *Star,* October 18, 2012.

144. OCAP Archives, "Women and Trans Day of Action: Stop the Cut to Community Start-Up,"

November 15, 2012; "Confront the Liberals: Stop the Cut to Community Start-Up, Raise the Rates Now!" December 12, 2012.

145. OCAP Archives, "Cross-Ontario Events: Fighting the Cuts to Community Start-Up," September 24, 2012; "Week of Action on Community Start Up Takes the Fight to a New Level," December 21, 2012.

146. OCAP Archives, "Province Earmarks $42 Million to Offset Cuts to Anti-Poverty Programs," *CBC News,* December 27, 2012.

147. "Province Earmarks $42 Million to Offset Cuts to Anti-Poverty Programs."

148. Phil Brown, General Manager, Shelter Support and Housing Administration, "City of Toronto Staff Report Information Only: Update on School House Shelter," 349 George Street, Ward 27, May 8, 2012.

149. OCAP Archives, OCAP to Ms. Ann Longair, Director, Hostel Services, City of Toronto, "Letter to Hostel Services on School House," March 12, 2012.

150. Wendy Gillis, "Protesters Decry Looming Closure of Toronto Men's-Only Shelter, School House," *Star,* March 7, 2012; "Homeless Shelter Allows Alcohol to Close," *CBC News,* March 8, 2012; Don Peat, "OCP Disrupts City Meeting over Shelter," *Star,* May 23, 2012; OCAP Archives, "Letter to Hostel Services on School House"; "Letter to Kristyn Wong-Tam," March 12, 2012; "Councillor Kristyn Wong-Tam Response to OCAP Letter March 12th," March 13, 2012.

151. "Protest Unlikely to Save Unique Schoolhouse Shelter," *Globe and Mail,* May 23, 2012; Sue-Ann Levy, "Schoolhouse Shelter Should Be Slam Dunk for Closure," *Star,* May 22, 2012; OCAP Archives, "An Open Letter to Kristyn Wong-Tam On the School House Shelter," June 5, 2012; "'Left' City Councillor Votes to Close School House Shelter," July 4, 2012; "Update from August 23 Action to Stop the Closing of the School House Shelter, Plus FAQ," August 25, 2012.

152. Brown, "City of Toronto Staff Report, Information Only: Update on School House Shelter"; Philip Abrahams, General Manager, Acting, Shelter, Support and Housing Administration,

"City of Toronto Staff Report Action Required: Update on the School House Shelter," October 31, 2012; OCAP Archives, "Save the School House Shelter, FAQ," June 25, 2013.

153. OCAP Archives, "Come to City Hall—Eviction at 9:30 PM—OCAP Turns City Hall Into Emergency Shelter," February 16, 2013; Samuel Greenfield, "Anti-Poverty Activists, Homeless People Camp Out in Front of Rob Ford's Office to Demand More Shelter Beds," *National Post,* February 15, 2013; Don Peat, "Mayor Rob Ford Says Toronto Has 'More Than Enough Shelter Beds'," *Toronto Sun,* February 19, 2013.

154. Natalie Alcoba, "OCAP Threatens to Take Over Metro Hall If City Does Not Address Shelter Bed 'Crisis'," *National Post,* February 20, 2013; Don Peat, "OCAP Denied Council Emergency Shelter-Bed Debate," *Toronto Sun,* February 20, 2013; OCAP Archives, "Come to City Hall Now," February 16, 2013; "No More Homeless Deaths," February 21, 2013.

155. OCAP Archives, "City Must Open Shelter for the Homeless Now!" March 21, 2013; "Shelter Crisis at a Breaking Point: Important Update On Toronto Homeless Shelters & Call to Action!" September 4, 2013.

156. OCAP Archives, "City of Toronto Moves to Redevelop Largest Men's Shelter in Canada," July 15, 2013; "Support Expropriation of 230 Sherbourne—'Drina House'," September 22, 2013; "Fight for 'Drina House' at 230 Sherbourne Kicks Off with OCAP Takeover," September 26, 2013.

157. The above two paragraphs draw on OCAP Archives, "OCAP Women's Delegates Visit Shelter Administration," October 10, 2013; "Downtown East Emergency Women's Night Watch: This Saturday Eve," October 10, 2013; "Women's Organizations and Community Members Have Rallied and Released an Open Letter to the City of Toronto," November 25, 2013; "Crisis in the Shelter System: Report in the Lead-Up to December 4," November 29, 2013; "The Fight for Shelter for the Homeless Is Being Won!" December 6, 2013.

158. OCAP Archives, "Creating Spaces for Street-Involved Women in Toronto," June 27, 2014; Ben

Spur, "Five Women Arrested at Homelessness Protest," *Now Magazine,* November 25, 2014.

159. The above paragraphs draw on OCAP Archives, "Open Letter to Mayor John Tory on the Toronto Homeless Shelter Crisis," December 5, 2014; Patricia D'Cunha, "Additional Warming Centres, Shelters to Be Opened after Homeless Deaths," *City News,* January 6, 2015; "Man Dies after Being Found Unconscious in Bus Shelter," *CBC News,* January 6, 2015; Sam Colbert, "Homeless Man Dies at Toronto Shelter during Extreme Cold," *Star,* January 13, 2015; Terry Davison, "Homeless Man Killed in Fire Once Had Normal Life," *Star,* January 26, 2015; Betsy Powell, "Mayor John Tory Orders Warming Shelters to Open Amid Deep-Freeze," *Star,* January 6, 2015; Jill Mahoney and Tu Thank Ha, "Toronto's 'Cold Weather Plan' under Scrutiny after Two Men Die," *Globe and Mail,* January 6, 2015; Canadian Press, "John Tory: Toronto Will Rent Motel Rooms for the Homeless," *Huffington Post,* January 16, 2015.

160. Elizabeth Church, "Mayor Tory Steps Up Efforts to Open Beds for Toronto's Homeless," *Globe and Mail,* January 13, 2015.

161. Michael Laxer, "John Tory, Toronto City Council and the Austerity Consensus," *rabble.ca,* March 16, 2015, rabble.ca.

162. The above paragraphs draw on John Clarke, "Toronto's Plan to Push Out the Homeless," *The Bullet,* Socialist Project E-Bulletin No. 1094, March 24, 2015, www.socialistproject.ca.

PART VI

1. A. J. Peacock, *Bread or Blood: The Agrarian Riots in East Anglia: 1816* (London: Victor Gollancz, 1965), 63, 116.

Index

Canadian Pacific Railroad, 51

Canadian Patriotic Fund, 76

Canadian Seamen's Union, 263

Canadian Socialist League, 63

Canadian Union of Postal Workers (CUPW), 283, 359, 362

Canadian Union of Public Employees (CUPE), 362, 387, 410, 417, 487n32

Canadian Welfare Council, 146

Can We Avoid a Post Armament Depression? 249

capital: accumulation of, 18, 287; challenge to, 304; march against, 53; private, 61; retrenchment of, 284

capitalism, 5–6, 53, 106, 124, 247, 249, 281, 430–31; attitude toward poor, 373; consolidation of, 63–76; contradictions of, 251; and crisis and class, 6–10; as crisis, 9, 12, 14, 16, 21, 46, 52, 63, 65, 74–75, 77, 86, 89, 96–98, 104, 281–90, 306, 431; cycles of, 6–7; industrial, 93, 444n41; monopoly, 280; productive, 250; regime of accumulation of, 55; repressive essence of, 107; as socioeconomic political order, 6; socioeconomic trajectory of, 19; and state formation, 35–40

Capponi, Pat: *The War at Home*, 302–3

Careless, J. M. S., 28

Carey, Albert, 232, 236

Carlton Street squat, 337–40

Carter, Jim, 406, 408

Cash, Andrew, 343

Cashman, C. J., 214

Cassidy, H. M., 90, 178–79, 181, 250–51

Catholic Women's League Hostel, 147

C. D. Howe Institute, 296

Cecile, Louis, 267

Central Bureau of Unemployment/Relief, 129, 140, 146

Central Cabbagetown Residents Association, 342–43

Central Neighbourhood House (CNH), 318, 339–40, 342–44

Chalkof, Edith, 114

charity, 69, 128, 139, 147–48; private, 97, 129, 257; public, 11, 27; voluntary vs. legal, 43; women's, 147. *See also* Toronto: Associated Charities

Chicago: Haymarket Square riots, 63

children: as members of working class, 99; and welfare state, 252, 297–98, 325, 477n4. *See also* youth

China, 16

cholera, 31

Chong, Gordon, 328–29

Chow, Olivia, 331, 388

Chrétien, Jean, 320–22, 324, 359–61, 425

Christie, Rev. D. Wallace, 187

Churley, Marilyn, 319

Citizens' Defence Committee, 173

citizenship, 90, 247; British, rights of, 470n172

Citizen's Housing and Planning Association (CHPA), 258

Citizens' Rehabilitation Council of Greater Vancouver (CRCGV), 263–64

Civic Employees' Union, 238

Civic Employment Bureau, 66, 73

Civic Unemployment Relief Committee, 128–29

civil libertarians, 109

Civil Liberties Union, 173

Clark, Joe, 360

Clarke, Claire, 147

Clarke, Edward, 55

Clarke, John, 29, 295, 304, 309–13, 315–16, 359–61, 363–67, 412, 425, 427; activism of, 305–6, 325, 327, 339, 349, 355–57; and Axworthy Commission, 322; and London Union of Unemployed Workers, 309, 312; red-baiting of, 319; on trial, 5, 339, 360, 366, 370–73, 376, 422

class: antagonisms of, 29; and capitalism and crisis, 6–10; against class, 99, 105; coherence, 17; collectivity of, 52; consciousness, 17, 80, 464n117; formation, 9, 10, 20; and homelessness, 398; inequalities, 75, 251; and means of production, 8; politics of, 20–23; and poverty, 398; resentment, 55

class relations: capitalist, 40; Fordist, 281–82; Marxist analysis, 10

class struggle, 7, 14, 18–20, 102–3, 106, 282–84, 288–89; periods of, 97; single unemployed as vanguard of, 156; Third Period, 96–106, 107, 117, 124, 156, 167, 175, 196, 236, 243; as waged, 20

Client Identification and Benefits System (CIBS), 328–29

Cloward, Richard A., 436n9

Clutterbuck, Burton, 238

Coalition pour la survie des programmes sociaux, 321

Coatsworth, Judge Emerson, 115, 140

Cohen, J. L., 100, 110, 227

Curry, James, 47
Custance, Florence, 85–86, 452n109

Daigle, Edith, 230, 234
Daley, Charles, 268
d'Aquino, Tom, 296
Darlington, William, 60–61
Davey, Martin, 213
Davies, Libby, 304, 360
Davis, A. L., 267
Davis, Mike, 16, 17
Davis, Minera, 149
Dawson, William, 433–34
Day, Ralph C., 134, 170
Deganis, Brian, 397–99
democracy, 251, 367–68. *See also* participatory
    democracy; social democracy
Demographia International Housing Affordability
    Survey, 3
Denning, Michael, 11–12, 16
Denton, John, 214
Department of National Defence, 164, 202, 203,
    263, 350
Department of Public Welfare, 129, 131, 133–36,
    140, 146, 148, 151, 163, 167, 169, 171, 178, 180,
    182–83, 187
Department of Veterans' Affairs, 262
depressions, 79, 250; in 1873–77, 41, 50; in
    1907–8, 65–66; in 1911–15, 65, 72–73. *See also*
    Great Depression
deprivation, 6, 271, 432
deregulation, 276, 292
"deserving poor," 51, 294
destitution, 4, 6, 30, 54, 66, 80, 91, 170, 247, 292, 431–
    32; absolute/abject, 233, 273; of women, 147
Diefenbaker, John, 267, 269–70
DiManno, Rosie, 322
Direct Action Casework, 312–16
disabilities/disabled, 248, 261; and poverty, 273, 294;
    and welfare state, 252
Disability Action Movement Now (DAMN), 414–15
discipline, 32, 82, 136; capitalist, 29; of labour, 14, 27,
    34, 47, 69, 74, 137, 283
discrimination: against immigrants, 162; against
    Jews, 74; of Ontario Housing Corporation, 279;
    against poor, 328; against unemployed, 162;
    against women, 308; against youth, 162

displacement, 27, 336; of Indigenous peoples, 27,
    490n58; of poor, 277, 395, 490n58
dispossessed/dispossession, 3–7, 14, 18–20, 312–13,
    431–32; agency and initiative of, 6; attacks on,
    328; class politics of, 20–23; class struggles of,
    103; colonial, 336; commonality of, 17; criminal-
    ization of, 72; demoralization of, 304; disappear-
    ance of, 273; division in, 52; fallout from, 31; as
    human subjects, 247; immiseration of, 15; of
    Indigenous peoples, 26–28; left-wing advocacy
    of, 265; making of working class as act of, 26; as
    nursery of class struggle, 10–12; organization and
    mobilization of, 304; origins of, 25–86; powerless-
    ness of, 303; radical leadership of, 272; rebellion
    of, 70; remaking subject of, 136; return/revenge of,
    344; state assault on, 281–90; union of, 53; upris-
    ing of, 263; vagrant, 77; war against, 49, 54
dissent, 90; labour discourse of, 51; role of state in
    mediating and incorporating, 282
dissidence, 63, 100, 139, 208, 227, 242–43, 377; and
    destitution, 59; and pepper spray, 360; terror
    against, 379; in unemployed movement, 59
Dixon Hall, 418–21
Doctor's Hospital shelter, 348–50
Don Jail, 38
Don Mount, 277
Don Vale, 277
Dorchester, Lord (Guy Carleton), 28
Doucet, Michael J., 40
Douglas, William, 217
Downtown Fight Back Campaign, 405
Dowson, Murray, 186
Dowson, Ross, 186, 264–65, 459n67, 467n144
Draper, Dennis Colborne, 92, 97, 107–15, 118, 120–21,
    131, 163, 184, 191
Drew, George, 256
Drina House, 423
Drury, Ernest, 67–68, 70, 141
Duncan, Dwight, 409
Dundas House, 127
Dunlop, William, 61
Dunphy, Cathy, 350
Durant, George, 194
Dyer, P., 208, 210

Earlscourt Park, 118–21
Earlscourt Unemployed Council, 117, 118

Fred Victor Mission, 75–76, 127, 129, 139, 204, 258

freedom of assembly, 108

freedom of association, 113–14

freedom of speech, 108–16, 118, 120–21

Free Employment Bureau, 66

Free Speech Conference, 108

Free Trade Agreement, 317–18

freezing deaths inquest, 330–36

Friendship Centre, 340

Friends of the Soviet Union, 102

Frontier College, 78

Frost, Leslie, 256, 265, 268

Fung, Dr. Richard, 348

Gagnon, Henri, 263

Galbraith, John Kenneth, 250

Garner, Hugh: *Cabbagetown*, 468n159

Geary, G. Reginald, 109–10

Gee, Marcus, 2

Geggie, R. B., 212, 220–22, 224

gender, 21, 90, 438n35; bias in government relief policies, 146; ideology of, 151; norms of, 145; poverty and, 273; and work and welfare, 144

General Welfare Assistance Act (GWA), 248, 402

gentrification, 300, 340, 427

George Street Redevelopment, 427

Georgina House, 464n115

German, Beric, 307, 331, 346, 389, 391, 414–15, 497n119

German Workingmen's Club of Brussels, 10

Germany, 102; Revolution (1923), 97

Gershman, Joshua, *124*

Gibson, W. O., 189

Gill, James, 114

Gindin, Sam, 283

Goderich, Lord (Frederick John Robinson), 30

Godfrey, Byron, 330

Golden, Anne, 300, 345, 348, 350

Golden, Sherrie, 347

Gompers, Samuel, 65

Goodfellow, William, 256

Goodhead, Norman, 267–68, *269*

Good Shepherd Mission, 332

Gorofsky, Louis, 74

Gorrie, A. M., 191, 194

Graefe, Peter, 414

Graham, J. J., 69

Granatstein, Jack, 251

Grand Army of United Veterans (GAUV), 78

Grasett, Lt.-Col. H. J., 46

Gray, A. J., 196, 221

Gray, William, 89

Great Depression, 5, 8, 12, 22, 88–90, 92, 115, 124–25, 195, 197, 243, 248, 254, 256, 262, 270, 318, 330, 411, 416; Communism and unemployed in, 96–106; as crisis of unemployment, 89; winding down of struggles from, 167–78

Great Upheaval, 13; underside of, 40–48

Green, Jim, 304–5

Greene, Barbara, 293

Greene, Jonathan, 314, 331

Greenfield, W. J., 147

Gribble, Wilfrid, 67, 70

G-20 Summit, 114

guaranteed annual income, 274–75

Guelph Housing Tribunal, 404

A Guide to Family Spending in Toronto, 257

Haig, George, 140–41

half-employed, 53

Hall, Barbara, 337, 341, 344

Hall, Jeffery, 397–99

Halperin (Halpern), Philip, 108

Halton, Rev. Nobel, 168

Hamilton, George, 84

"Hammer-the-Mug," 182

Hands Off Street Youth, *351*, *353*, 354

Harbour Commission, 170–71

Harcourt, Mike, 324

Hardill, Kathy, 400, 402

Hargrove, Buzz, 372, 376–77, 387

Harkness, David B., 93, 198–200, 207

Harrington, Michael: *The Other America*, 273

Harris, George, 160, 166, 167–69, 172, 222, 231, 233, 242

Harris, James, *247*

Harris, Mike, 15, 320, 327–28, 349, 361, 364, 402; and Common Front, 373; and Common Sense Revolution, 287, 297, 324, 409; protests against, 328, 362, 368, 375, 377, 380; resignation of, 380; and squeegeeing, 352; and welfare, 299, 324

Harris, Richard, 176, 180

Haslam, Frank, 217

Hastings, Dr. Charles, 84

ideological initiative, 281–90

immigration: antagonism to, 83; from Australia, 64; from Britain, 64, 66; from Bulgaria, 127; and bureaucracy, 262; as cause of unemployment, 267–68; from Finland, 127; from Ireland, 19, 28, 30, 33–34, 36; from Newfoundland, 64; from New Zealand, 64; pauper, 51; and poverty, 273; and resistance, 373; Roma, 127; from Somalia, 321; from South Africa, 64; unemployment and, 92, 450n89; from United States, 64; and welfare fraud, 320–21

Improving Social Security in Canada, 301, 321

incarceration, of indigent, 35, 66, 77, 137

income: guaranteed, 274–75; household, 3, 277, 284, 301; social, 396

income security, 246, 413

Income Security Advocacy Centre, 413

Income Security for Canadians, 301

Independent Labour Party, 141

Indigenous peoples, 13, 327, 373, 440n3; activism of, 317; dispossession of, 26–28; expropriation of, 26–27; original presence of, 28; and poverty, 273, 294; racialization of, 336

individualism, 17; acquisitive, 52, 59, 178, 274, 313, 431

Industrial Banner, 74

industrial farms, 35

Industrial Workers of the World (IWW), 73, 86

inequality, 26, 236, 390, 430–31, 433, 481n36, 485n10; class, 75; social, 313; systemic, 249, 431

inflation, 13, 281, 282, 284, 300

Ingrosso-Cox, Maria, 328

institutionalization: and poor relief, 34, 39; of wageless, 32

International Labor Organization (ILO), 15

International Monetary Fund (IMF), 15

Ireland: immigrant labour from, 19, 30; immigration from, 28, 30, 33–34, 36

Irwin, Steve, 377

isolation, 271, 304, 306

Jackman, Hal, 326

Jackson, Dr. Gordon, 130

Jackson, Harvey, 136–37, 141

Jacobs, Jane, 393

Jagt, John, 337, 346, 350, 356, 422

James, Royson, 354

Japan, unemployment benefits in, 285

Jarvis, Sheriff William Botsford, 32, 34

Jews, discrimination against, 74, 471n175

joblessness. *See* unemployment

Johnson, J. T., 131

Johnson, Lyndon, 273

Johnson, Richard, 309

Johnston, Patrick, 309, 311

Joliffe, E. B., 233

Jonna, R. Jamil, 15

Jouard, Sadie, 186

Joubert, Drina, 307–9, 332–35, 346, 423

Jury, Alfred, 60

"Just Society," 14, 275–76

Just Society Movement, 278–81; *Community Concern*, 279, 304

Kashtan, William, 114

Kastner, Susan, 344

Katz, Michael B., 40

Kealey, Gregory S., 28

Keegan, Sean, 338

Kellerman, Bob, 370

Kellett, George, 230, 232–33, 236

Kelly, Norm, 329

Kenealey, Ellen, 85–86

Kennedy, Gerard, 367

Kennedy, L. O. R., 146

Kennedy, Warring, 56–58

Keynes, John Maynard, 248–49

Keynesianism, 12, 248–51, 284

Keyssar, Alexander, 7

Khun, Sam, 405

Kidd, David, 318–19

King, Tom, 160

King, William Lyon Mackenzie, 81, 90–91, 157, 174, 228, 251, 253, 477n253

Kingston Community Project, 276

Kingston Penitentiary, 31

Kitchener: Mothers and Others Making Change, 305

Klee, Marcus, 89

Klein, Naomi, 367, 387

Klein, Ralph, 324, *373*

Klig, Meyer, 113

Knights of Labor, 13, 40, 52, 60, 447n63

Kocsis, Lisa, 386

Kompani, Mirsalah, 330, 332–35

Macdonald, Sir John A., 54

Mackenzie, William Lyon, 31

Macphail, Agnes, 109, 144

Maguire, Charles A., 83

Maguire, E. D., *211*, 229–30, *231*, 233

Maguire, Trevor, 98–99; *Unemployment*, 99

Mahar, Aiden, *364*

Maison, Ivy, 129

Maison Club, 127, 129

The Making of Global Capitalism, 283

Malcolm, James, 205

Mammoliti, Giorgio, 420

Mance, A. W., 70

Mandel, Ernest, 6–7

Mandeville, Bernard de, 11

Mangano, Philip, 395

Manley, John, 104, 117, 186

Mann, Daniel, 107

manufacturing, 17, 40, 64–65, 152, 282

March Against Poverty Committee, 309

Marchi, Sergio, 320–21

marginalization: by capitalism, 306; of dispossessed, 304; of ethnic minorities, 74; of Indigenous peoples, 26; of single unemployed women, 144–54; of women, 74

Markis, Bly, 400

Marks, Joseph T., 74

Marriott, George, 242

Marsh, Leonard, 145–46; *Report on Social Security for Canada*, 251

Martin, Charles, 185

Martin, Fred, 332

Martin, Paul, 321

Marx, Karl, 15, 20, 27, 30, 248, 306, 439n47, 470n168; *Capital*, 8, 11, 18–19; *Grundrisse*, 9; *Wage-Labour and Capital*, 9–10

Masaryk Cowan Park, 383–84

Mashery, Clifford, 139–41

Matheson, Fitz, 330

Mathieu, Jean-Philip, 50

Matthews, Deborah, 413, 414

Maurutto, Paula, 128, 148

Maxwell Meighen Centre, 374

May Day, 98, 101, 116–17, 123, *124*, 156, 233, 243

Mayhew, Henry, 265, 437n19

McBride, Sam, 112–14, 131–32, 138

McCallum, Todd, 89

McChesney, Robert W., 15

McConnell, Pam, 339–41, 349

McDonald, A. M., 200–201

McDonough, Alexa, 355, 360

McDowell, Jim, 414

McEwen, Bob, 263

McEwen, Tom, 99, 101, 109, 116

McGeer, Gerry, 156

McGuinty, Dalton, 394, 402, 406, 409, 412–16

McHenry, Dr. E. W., 253–54, 257

McKay, Colin, 64

McKay, Ian, 63, 73

McKiernan, Charles, 41–42

McKnight, William M., 137–39, 141

McLean, Peter, 141–42

McMaster, C. J., 194, 238

McMaster, Sam, 112

McNaughton, General Andrew, 155

McVicar, Heather, 329

mechanization, 36, 64

Meeker, Elizabeth, 230, 232, 234, 236

Meeker, Elmer, 232, 236

Meilleur, Madelaine, 409

Melasel, Nick, 75

Melinzer, Dr. Patricia, 403

men: married vs. single, 56–57, 92; sense of entitlement of, 146; single unemployed, 69, 92, 101, 103, 106–28, 132, 135, 136–43, 146, 155–59, 167–78, 204, 221–22, 224, 237, 257, 271

Meridian Property Management, 277–78

Métis, 27–28; racialization of, 336

Metro Association for Unemployed Workers, 267–68, *269*, *272*

Metro Hostel Services, 345–46, 350, 422

Metro Neighbourhood Services Commission, 318

Metro Network for Social Justice, 362, 387

Metro Toronto Commissioner of Community Services, 299–300

Michel, Louise, 54

middle class, 3, 431

Middleton, Jesse Edgar, 38, 59

Mielen, Vincent, 192

migrant labourers, 42

Mihevc, Joe, 422

militancy, 103, 105, 115, 120, 156, 168, 191, 196, 199, 275, 314, 327, 344, 371, 382; of Communist Party, 173, 243; disappearance of, 196; in

O'Brien, Buck, 200–201

O'Connor, Brian, 368

October Youth, 115, 117–18

Old Age Security, 274

Old Ontario: land and labour in, 28–31

O'Leary, Arthur, 86

Oliver, Farquhar, 254

Oliver, Joseph, 68, 70

One Big Unionism (OBU), 80, 82, 86; *One Big Union Bulletin*, 82

Ontario: Advisory Committee on Debt Relief, 93; Charity Aid Act (1874), 39; College of Physicians and Surgeons, 407; Commission on Unemployment, 73; Common Sense Revolution, 15, 287, 298–99, 324, 328, 332, 367, 375, 409; Community Start Up and Maintenance Benefit, 416–18; Crime Control Commission, 352; Days of Action, 328, 489n47; Family Benefits Act (FBA), 325; Highway Traffic Act, 352; Liberal-NDP coalition, 293, 309–11; Liberal Party, 295, 408–9; NDP government in, 14, 295–97, 319–20; Poverty Reduction Act (2008), 413, 415; Queen's Park protests, 22, 67, 78, 98, *104*, 109–16, 121–23, *143*, *144*, 154, *161*, 164, 166, *167*, 168, 173, 176, 214–15, 221–22, 225–26, 229–33, 241, 268, *271*, 309–11, 319, 325–27, 336, 361–73, 376, 382, *401*, 403, *405*, 415; Safe Streets Act (1999), 352–54, 358, 362, 396; Social Assistance Review Committee (SARC), 293–97, 309–10; Social Contract, 319; and special diet allowance, 401–12, 416; Tenant Protection Act, 298, 362; and Unemployment Assistance Act, 266

Ontario Association of Food Banks, 413

Ontario Coalition Against Poverty (OCAP), 4–5, 15, 289, 331–32, 335, 347–50, 352, 354–58, 396, 400; Direct Action Casework, 312–16; escalation of struggle, 336–45; June Days, 362; lack of bureaucracy, 315; "Long Retreat Is Over," 373–82; origins of, 311–17, 370–71; Ottawa cavalcade, 359–61; and papal visit, 382–93; Queen's Park riot, 362–73; Raise the Rates campaign, 402, 404, 410, 417; Save the School House Campaign, 420–22; "Shut Down Bay Street," 377–80; trade union funding of, 487n32

Ontario Coalition for Abortion Clinics, 309

Ontario Coalition for Better Child Care, 309

Ontario Coalition for Social Justice (OCSJ), 311–12

Ontario Common Front, 373, 375, *376*, 377, 404–5

Ontario Council of Hospital Unions (OCHU), 407

Ontario Court of Appeal, 236

Ontario Federation of Labour (OFL), 273, 381

Ontario Federation of Unemployment (OFU), 158, 160, 167–68, 171–73

Ontario Housing Corporation, 279

Ontario Hunger March, 121, *122*, *161*, 164, 166

Ontario Medical Association, 94, 238, 311

Ontario Municipalities Association, 219

Ontario Provincial Police (OPP), 328

Ontario Public Service Employees Union (OPSEU), 327–28

Ontario Supreme Court, 110

Ontario Welfare Council, 278, 285; "And the Poor Get Poorer," 285–86

Ontario Welfare Officers Association, 267

Ontario Workers' Federation, 163

Ontario Workman, 40

Ontario Works, 325

On-to-Ottawa motorcade: (1933), 132; (1954), 267, *268*, *270*; (1999), 359–61

On-to-Ottawa Trek (1935), 88, 103, *104*, 125, 154, 155–67, 202, 359

On-to-Toronto trek (1989), 310

Operation Desert Gypsy, 321

Opportunities for Youth, 276, 278

Orange Order, 117

Organization of the Petroleum Exporting Countries (OPEC), 282

O'Rourke, Eva, 241–42

Orphans' Home, 38

Oshawa (Ontario): auto workers' strike, 233

O'Shea, John, 119

O'Sullivan, Kelly, 329

Ottawa: protests in, 22, 50, 54, 80–81, 83, 288, 310, 382. *See also* On-to-Ottawa Trek

Ottawa Under Pressure Collective, 409

Out of the Cold program, 330, 338, 350, 423

Palladium of Labor, 40, 42

Palmer, Bryan D., 5, *373*

panhandling, 94, 351–53, 358

Panitch, Leo, 283

Parent, Madeleine, 323

Paris, Vincent, 366, 369

radicalism, 14, 23, 74; bohemian, 63; youth, 276

Rae, Bob, 14, 295, 297, 310, 319–20, 324, 342

Rae, Kyle, 351

Reagan, Ronald, 13

The Real Poverty Report, 280–81

Rebick, Judy, 367

recession, 40, 250, 286, 305

red-baiting, 86, 220, 319

Red Cross, 262

Red International, 100

Red Scare, 63, 77, 100, 456n27

"Red Spadina," *96, 107*, 109, 176

Red Squad, 92, 97, 99, 108–10, 116, 120, 160

Redwood Shelter, 424

Reform insurrection (1837), 35

refugees, 313–14, 321, 373; camps, 374–75, 383

Regent Park, 180, *182*, 258, 276, 326, 394, 402; Community Health Centre, 424

Regina Riot, 88, 157, 159, 162, 167

Retail Merchants' Association, 133

relief, 38, 67; broadened approach to, 103; budget system, 222; call to abolish relief work, 237–44; cash wages for, 219, 221, 224; cuts to, 220, 222, 228–29, 237; disciplining power of, 48, 49; diversity of, 95; government responsible for, 128; and illegitimacy, 132; indoor, 33, 43, 69; inspectors, 237; labour, abolition of, 172; and "low intelligence," 132; outdoor, 33, 45–46, 66, 69, 79, 134; payments for food, 254–55; rates of, 93, 237, 240, 262; reforms in, 219–20; riots over, 212–20; slowing of, 158; standards of, 253; strikes, 103, 196–244; unemployment, 66, 68, 73, 74, 79, 91, 116, 123, 125; and vouchers, 130–36, 148–49, 151–52, 196–97, 199–200, 207–8, 221–22, 224, 242; women and, 148–49

relief camps, 79, 155–56, 159

Relief Camp Workers' Union, 156

Relief Reform Association, 169

religion, 9, 34, 43; crimes against, 398

rent: controls, 264, 276, 287, 298, 362, 383, 387; relief, 83, 135, 148–50, 193, 215, 258–59, 392; strikes, 264, 278

rentier socioeconomic stratum, 178

resistance, 6, 20, 21, 61, 246; broadened approach to, 103; against joblessness, 96; by unemployed, 140

Revolutionary Workers Party (RWP), 264

Rheinische Zeitung, 19

Rhind, Alex, 134

Rhomer, Aprille, 353

Rinehart, James, 303–4

Rivers, John, 63

Roaring Twenties, 106

Robarts, John, 267, 273–74, 324

Robbins, William D., 159, 187

Roberts, Helen, 150

Roberts, Wayne, 294

Robertson, Gideon, 91

Robillard, Daniel, 342

Roblin, Duff, 266

Roebuck, Arthur, 121, 214–15, 227, 233–36

Rogers, Alderman, 138

Rose, Fred, 114

Rosedale, 326

Rosenthal, Peter, 330, 332–34, 347, 370, *371, 373*, 407

Ross, Finlay, 54

Ross, J. Allan, 127–28

Royal Canadian Mounted Police (RCMP), 99, 156–57, 162, 164, 173–74, 203, 360, 466n140

Royal Commission on Prisons and the Reformatory System, 44

Royal Commission on the Relations of Labor and Capital, 53

rural migration, 15, 29

Ruskin, John, 64

Russell, Frank, 233

Russian Revolution. *See under* Soviet Union

Ryan, Oscar, 99, 109

Ryan, Sid, 372

Ryerson, Stanley, 99

Salutin, Rick, 367

Salvation Army, 66, 112, 127, 153, 157, 170, 262, 337

Sandler, Louise, 164

Saunders, Robert Hood, 258

scapegoating, 4, 184; of Communists, 172, 217; of foreign agitators, 100; of immigrants, 267; of poor, 136; post 9/11, 379; of single unemployed women, 146; of unemployed, 62, 71, 73, 159

Scarborough, 226, 238–39, 241, 306; Poverty Eliminators, 307

Scarborough Relief Union, 238

Scarlett, Sam, 166, 222

school dropouts, and poverty, 273

School House Shelter (SHS), 418–21

Splane, Richard B., 34

squats, 336–45, 381; papal, 382–93; women's, 399–401

squeegeeing, 351–53, 358

Srigley, Katrina, 153

stagflation, 13, 282, 300

Stagg, George, 171

Stalin, Josef, 105–6

Stalinism, 102, 105, 456n33

Stapleton, John, 413

Stark, C. T., 134

Starr, Michael, 270

state: as agency of capitalist exploitation and oppression, 312; formation of, 19, 35–40; insolvency, 296; regulatory, 77; as servant of property, 20

St. Catharines Labour Council, 362

St. Christopher House, 413

Steele, Dick, 182

Sterling, Norm, 370

Stern, Mark J., 40

Stewart, Bryce, 83

Stewart, William, 121–22, 132, 138–39, 160

stigmatization: of poor, 328; of single people, 309; of unemployed, 160, 243

St. James Town, 277–78

St. Lawrence Hall, 257

stock market crash (1929), 92, 106, 196

Stockwell, Chris, 376

Stoki, Dr. Stephen, 333

stone-breaking, 43, 47, 49–50, 56, 62–63, 70, 72, 74–76, 79, 244

Stop Community Food Centre, 413

Stowe, Dr. Emily H., 61

St. Pierre, Richard, 321–23

Strachan, Bishop John, 39

Street Health, 398, 423–24

Street Patrol, 395

Street People's Association, 396

Street People Speak, 299

Streets to Homes initiative, 393, 395–97, 426

strikes, 36, 40, 79, 106, 175, 233, 257, 283–84, 327–2/8; General Strike (1919), 77–78; relief, 103, 196–244; rent, 264, 278; wildcat, 13, 481n35; Winnipeg General Strike, 86, 100, 187

Strong-Boag, Veronica, 145

Struthers, James, 79, 96, 252, 257, 260, 298

Student Christian Movement, 387

student radicalism, 276, 327

Student Union for Peace Action (SUPA), 276

subprime mortgage crisis, 13, 287

Supreme Court of Canada, 236

surveillance, 71, 82, 95, 132, 135–36, 282, 284, 324, 411

Sutherton, Jim, 101

Swanson, Gail, 344

Swanson, Jean, 301, 303, 304

Sweeny, John, 310

Tabuns, Peter, 332

tailors, 31, 36

Tassew, Sam, 388

Tenant Action Group (TAG), 405

Tent City, 389–92

tent colonies, 185, 337–38, 355–57

Teskey, Dr. Luke, 213

Thatcher, Margaret, 13

Third Period. *See under* class struggle

Thompson, Bill, 159

Thompson, David, 50, 60, 68, 70–71, 80, 83, 265, 437n25

Thompson, E. P., 487n32

Thompson, Phillips, 52–53, 59, 69–70, 72, 136, 448n76; *The Politics of Labor*, 53

Thomson, George, 310

Thomson, Lillian, 258–59

Tiffin, J. S., 205

Tipping, Melvin, 333

Tisdale, Dr. F. F., 253

Tolmie, S. F., 91

Tonner, John, 180

Toronto: Act of Incorporation (1846), 35; annexation by, 65; Associated Charities, 43, 64, 68–70; Black Flag demonstration, 54; City of Toronto Act, 413; City Services Committee, 406; Community Development and Recreation Committee (CDRC), 413; and crash of 1857, 37, 40; 1830s as turning point for evolution of, 29; gaols in, 31, 42, 47; indigent population of, 262; industrial-capitalist revolution in, 40; influx of wageless into, 84; as locale within global, 15–17; Old (Muddy York), 28; origins of, 28; Poor House: *see* House of Industry; population of, 28, 36, 40, 65, 93, 130, *177*; real estate bubble, 54; suburbs, *177*; transformation of (1900–25), 64; ward boundaries, *176*

Toronto Against Poverty (TAP), 412–16

of, 115; shift in activities of, 50; supervision and monitoring of, 123

Unemployed Association, 70–71, 85, 159, 184

Unemployed Councils, 99, 117–20

unemployed movement, 57–86, 87–244, 265

Unemployed Review, 80–81

Unemployed Single Girls' Association (USGA), 149–50

unemployment, 3–4, 8, 27, 36–37, 48, 50, 55, 251, 270, 432; broadened approach to, 103; as *cause célèbre* among left agitators, 115; chronic, 64; crisis of, 72, 74, 88–90, 92, 125, 128, 147–48, 151, 155, 175, 178–82, 184, 195, 248, 276, 285; as crucial working-class issue, 102; definition of, 261; and dependency, 454n15; fear of, 91; federal assistance for, 248; and gender, 271–72, 463n108; human costs of, 89; institutional response to, 246; left perspective on, 65; men and, 42, 272; and moral collapse, 144; periodic, 154; as personal pathology, 132; rates of, 73–74, 77, 79, 83, 89–90, 92, 128, 137, 180, 237, 249, 252–53, 261, 265–66, 269, 272, 281–84, 286, 294, 296–97, 300; responses to, 36, 63–86; seasonal nature of, 92; as state industry, 260; and suicide, 283; urban landscape of, 93; vs. employment, 7; and wartime production, 76

Unemployment Assistance Act (1956), 265–66

unemployment insurance (UI), 4, 77, 80, 91, 121, 153–54, 162, 172, 202, 247, 259–61, 272, 274, 284–85, 296, 302, 306, 310, 320–22

Unemployment Insurance Act (UIA; 1940), 256, 259–61, 271, 284–85, 287

Unemployment Insurance Commission, *255*, 260, *269, 272*

Unemployment Insurance Fund, 266

Unemployment Relief Committee of Ontario, 90

unions. *See* trade unions/unionism

United Citizens (UC), 275–76

United Electrical Workers (UE), 276, 481n41

United Empire Loyalists, 187

United Nations, 17, 374

United States: craft unions in, 97; decline in labour militancy in, 483n55; economic stimulus in, 90; FTA with, 317; immigration from, 64; resistance to evictions in, 470n164; unemployment benefits in, 285; union organization and density in, 14

United Tenants of Ontario, 309

universality, principle of, 287

universal programs, 247

Upper, Eugene, 330, 332–35

vagrancy, 31, 33, 45–48, 77, 352, 395; arrests for, 47, 66, 71, 74–75, 80, 109, 137, 139–40, 162, 218. *See also* tramps

Valen, Valerie, 397–99

Valpy, Michael, 332, 367

Vancouver: Downtown East Side Residents Association (DERA), 304–5; Unemployed Action Committee, 265

Vaughan, Adam, 421–22

veterans: of First World War, 78–80, 82, 118, 120, 194; and low-income housing, 257–58; of Second World War, 263–64

Victoria, Queen, 44

voluntarism/volunteerism, 34, 128–29, 136, 178, 247, 315–16, 331, 403, 424

Vosko, Leah F., 438n35

vouchers, 128–36, 148–49, 151–52, 196–97, 199–200, 207–8, 221–22, 224, 242

Wage and Price Control initiatives, 282

waged employment: class jurisdictions of, 21; and dispossession, 27; economy of, 15; and wageless-ness, 33, 40, 51, 53, 62, 63, 74, 77, 82, 89, 286, 288

wage-labour market, uncertainties of, 30

wage-labour society, 28

wagelessness, 7–8, 12, 16, 20, 37, 41, 50, 56, 60, 64–65, 125, 302; coercion against, 35; and criminaliza-tion and institutionalization, 32, 37; crisis of, 44, 78, 85; improvidence and dissipation as elements of, 41; problems of, 90; proliferation of, 40; and waged employment, 33, 40, 51, 53, 62, 63, 74, 77, 82, 89, 286, 288

wage rates, 59, 90, 198, 238, 283, 286; declining, 30, 300; disparity between male and female, 294; trade union, 137

Waites, Amos, 241

Wakefield, Edward Gibbon, 30

Walker, Talbot, 174

Walker, William, 202

Walkom, Thomas, 387

Wallace, Rick, 375

Walsh, Bill, 182

Walters, Ann, 164, 166

Walton, N. P., 170

Workers' International Relief Association, 203

Workers' Party of Canada (WP), 81, 85, 102, 220, 452n109

Workers' Unity League (WUL), 91, 103, 149, 160, 196, 455n25, 462n102

workfare programs, *325*, 337

"work for relief" programs, 267

work-for-welfare schemes, 293

workhouses, 34

working class: attack on, 282; and class struggle, 283; co-operation among, 53; despoliation of, 52; emergence of, 8, 28; expansion of, 65; fighting ranks of, 99; formation of, 27; global informal, 16; home-owning, 181; immiseration of, 304; lack of unity among, 464n117; making of as act of dispossession, 26; militancy, 77, 97, 106, 196, 289; mobilization of, 13; power of, 287; and precariousness, 41; protests by, 40–41; solidarity of, 21, 27, 53, 80; in South, 17; suburbs, 66; united, 289; validation of, 16; war against, 13; worsening circumstances of, 288

working hours, reduction in, 79, 137, 202–3

"working poor," 275, 286–87, 294, 300–301; income supplements for, 287; raising social income of, 296

Workman, Thom, 284

work tests. *See* labour tests

Yakabuski, Konrad, 3

York Township, 220–24, 226, 228, 238–43

York Township Unemployed Association, 184

York Township United Workers' Association, 117, 195, 196, 205, 208, 214–15

York University Faculty Association, 362

Young, Benjamin, 307

Young, Dave, 388

Young Communist League (YCL), 118, 149, 166, 202, 204

Young Men's Christian Association (YMCA), *325*

"Young Pioneers," *135*

Young Women's Christian Association (YWCA), 148

youth: and homelessness, 336–38, 351; as members of working class, 99; radicalism, 276; revolt by, 13; unemployment rates for, 269, 283

Yu, Edmund, 396

Bryan D. Palmer was the Trent University Canada Research Chair in Canadian Studies (2001–2015), and has been an editor or co-editor of *Labour/Le Travail* since 1997.

Gaétan Héroux is a long time anti-poverty activist with the Ontario Coalition Against Poverty.